MW00335950

THE ART OF PEACEMAKING

WORLD THOUGHT IN TRANSLATION

A joint project of Yale University Press and the MacMillan Center for
International and Area Studies at Yale University, World Thought in
Translation makes important works of classical and contemporary political,
philosophical, legal, and social thought from outside the Western tradition
available to English-speaking scholars, students, and general readers. The
translations are annotated and accompanied by critical introductions that
orient readers to the background in which these texts were written, their
initial reception, and their enduring influence within and beyond their own
cultures. World Thought in Translation contributes to the study of religious
and secular intellectual traditions across cultures and civilizations.

Series editors

Steven Angle
Karuna Mantena
Andrew March
Paulina Ochoa
Ian Shapiro

THE ART
OF PEACEMAKING

Political Essays by István Bibó

István Bibó
Translated by Péter Pásztor
Edited and with an Introduction
by Iván Zoltán Dénes
With a Foreword by Adam Michnik

Yale
UNIVERSITY
PRESS
New Haven & London

Published with assistance from the foundation established in memory of
Philip Hamilton McMillan of the Class of 1894, Yale College.

Original Hungarian essays owned by István Bibó and Borbála Bibó and
translated from the following editions: *Bibó István Válogatott tanulmányok*, vols. 1–4
(Budapest: Magvető, 1986–1990); *Bibó István munkái: Centenáriumi sorozat*, vols. 1–12
(Budapest: Argumentum and Bibó István Szellemi Műhely, 2011–2012).

Yale University Press books may be purchased in quantity for educational, business,
or promotional use. For information, please e-mail sales.press@yale.edu (U.S. office)
or sales@yaleup.co.uk (U.K. office).

Set in Postscript Electra and Trajan type by Newgen North America.
Printed in the United States of America.

Library of Congress Cataloging-in-Publication Data
Bibó, István.
[Essays. Selections. English]
The art of peacemaking : political essays by István Bibó / István Bibó ;
translated by Péter Pásztor ; edited and with an introduction
by Iván Zoltán Dénes ; with a foreword by Adam Michnik.
pages cm. — (World thought in translation)
Includes bibliographical references and index.
ISBN 978-0-300-20378-3 (hardback)
1. Europe, Eastern—Politics and government—1945–1989.   2. Hungary—
Politics and government—1945–1989.   3. Anti-Semitism—Hungary—History—
20th century.   4. Political science—Philosophy—History—20th century.
I. Dénes, Iván Zoltán, editor.   II. Title.
DJK50.B53 2015
303.6′6—dc23
2014014290

A catalogue record for this book is available from the British Library.

This paper meets the requirements of ANSI/NISO Z39.48-1992 (Permanence of Paper).
10 9 8 7 6 5 4 3 2 1

Contents

FOREWORD: ISTVÁN BIBÓ:
A SAGE IN THE WORLD OF HISTORY

István Bibó (1911–1979) was a great sage of a small nation living in an epoch of hysteria. He therefore had a remarkable biography: in an era of totalitarian regimes and ideologies, he was a persistent advocate of democratic values. Before the war he was affiliated with the non-communist anti-fascist movement. After the Nazi invasion of Hungary in 1944 he protected Jews against deportation. That same year he was arrested by agents of the Hungarian Nazi regime (the Arrow-cross Party), and once he was freed, he went into hiding until the arrival of the Soviet Army. After the war, he published articles in which he defended democratic values and undertook a harsh examination of Hungarian politics in the preceding decades. He was criticized for these writings by both the traditionally minded émigrés and Communist Party ideologues (including György Lukács). For his part, Bibó criticized nationalist politics and the principle of collective responsibility (the expulsion of Hungarian Germans, among other things). Then, during the 1956 Hungarian Revolution, he joined Imre Nagy's government. Upon hearing about the Soviet intervention, he went to the parliament building, where for three days he was the only minister to remain in the government's official seat. During this time he prepared proposals for compromise solutions in dealing with the Soviet authorities. Once he left the parliament, he wrote proclamations and memoranda about the situation in Hungary. In 1958, he was sentenced to life in prison, but he was freed after five years when a general amnesty went into effect. He died in May 1979. His funeral became the first public rally of the nascent Hungarian democratic opposition. A small nation spoke with its own voice. What a pity that things are different today.

István Bibó's central concern was the question of the genesis and form of political hysteria in Central Europe; he analyzed this question by examining the specificity of the historical development of Hungary, Poland, and Bohemia. Each of these small nations had a tragic history of long years of existing under foreign domination, without having its own state; each was entangled in ethnic and territorial conflicts. This kind of past gives rise to frustration, especially when historical memory suggests that one once belonged to a nation that ruled over other nations. Such frustrations lead to collective hysteria. And fascism tends to be a product of national hysteria.

Thus a great man of a small nation is someone who has the courage to fight against foreign aggression directed against his nation but who is also not afraid of entering into conflict with the dictatorship in his own country and the imprudence of his own people.

From a global perspective, these conflicts among small nations can seem like some sort of exotic Lilliputian spectacle, but it is worth remembering that the two great wars of the twentieth century that changed the fate of the world erupted precisely in Central Europe.

In 1956, the whole world was looking at Hungary. The Hungarian anti-totalitarian revolution—and Bibó was one of its quiet heroes—exposed the true nature of Soviet imperialism and led to a new, illusion-free way of thinking about the Soviet Union and the Communist system. Today, Hungary is once again attracting attention. At that time—in 1956—it was a symbol of glory and tragedy; today it is a symbol of apprehension and disillusionment. The policies of Viktor Orbán's right-wing government, a strong-arm government with an anachronistic vision of sovereignty, Euro-skeptic policies that treat the state as the property of the ruling-party nomenklatura—all of these necessarily cause anxiety among Hungary's friends. The rule of the Hungarian right wing seems to be more and more like Vladimir Putin's model of "sovereign democracy." Why is this happening? István Bibó's essays from a long time ago help us understand.

István Bibó's fundamental experience—and the experience of all the intellectuals of his generation—was a confrontation with two totalitarianisms: the brown and the red.

The Bolshevik Revolution—Bibó wrote—must be analyzed through the prism of the French Revolution. The French Revolution, in turn, "is at the same the most successful and the most unsuccessful revolution in Europe's history." It is the most successful because it transformed France into a country of "freedom and equality; it changed the social structure in the state." But it is also the most unsuccessful because it "unleashed great anxiety that paralyzes Europe with the fear of revolutionary terror to this day." According to Bibó, this terror called into existence "two previously unknown and completely unproductive human types, which hopelessly constrained European thought:

the professional reactionary and the professional revolutionary. . . . The former clutchingly guards everything; the latter thoughtlessly attacks everything." Both are fanatics who multiply brutality and violence; both "find fulfillment in exposing eternal plots."

By sowing ubiquitous fear, the revolutionary terror and "the limitless cult of violence" triggered a reaction that resulted in fascism. In this sense—Bibó wrote—"fascism is one of the most terrifying side effects of the French Revolution." The second—no less terrifying—was Stalinism. The Stalinist and the fascist still cast their shadows over the world.

The accuracy of Bibó's analyses was confirmed further in later years in the synthesis of fascism and Stalinism, when communism appealed to chauvinistic slogans and reactionary policies. And later still, anti-communism with a Bolshevik face appeared in Central Europe—but that's an altogether different story.

Among this Hungarian humanist's works, the long essay entitled "The Jewish Predicament in Post-1944 Hungary" deserves special attention; it is a penetrating study of Hungarian-Jewish relations, anti-Semitism in Hungary, and the Hungarian society's attitudes toward the Holocaust. This essay, published in 1948, gave rise to brief polemics, but it was later veiled in silence for many years. In a certain sense, that silence prevails to this day because the author's diagnoses have not lost their relevance.

Bibó's analysis is multifaceted, exploring issues that range from susceptibility to "soft anti-Semitism" or economic discrimination all the way to attitudes toward the Holocaust, which was perpetrated by the Germans but with partial Hungarian participation. In such a situation—Bibó wrote—"you can do only one thing: take upon yourselves a small piece of the responsibility that applies directly to us. Acknowledge, for example, that everything that the author of these words did about helping Jews—whether as a result of the whispers of his conscience or in response to the requests of those in need—was so terribly insufficient. . . . How we've run short of anything going beyond the desire to display good will, how we've run short of being moved by somebody else's misfortune. It is essential that everyone carry out an examination of conscience." Bibó's essays are his examination of conscience.

Bibó was a rather uncommon witness to history—a witness who understood the tragic nature of his times, who readily reached for sarcasm and mockery, but who simultaneously looked around him with a gaze full of brutal realism. How great is our need today for a witness with that kind of gaze, that kind of pen, and that kind of courage.

Adam Michnik

ACKNOWLEDGMENTS

We acknowledge the generous financial support of the István Bibó Center for Advanced Studies and the Hungarian Academy of Sciences, which sponsored the translation of this book from Hungarian into English.

The translator also owes thanks to Jaya Chatterjee and Bojana Ristich, members of Yale's staff, and Hugh Brogan in particular, whose blue-pencil work greatly helped shape the tone of Bibó in English.

INTRODUCTION:
ATTEMPTS TO RESOLVE POLITICAL HYSTERIA

Iván Zoltán Dénes

I. POLITICAL HYSTERIA

Those who experienced the government paranoia and the closing down of public discourse in the wake of the destruction of the Twin Towers will find familiar the analyses of political hysteria in Central Europe included in this volume of writings by István Bibó. Those who experienced the consequences of African American segregation will find Bibó's discussion of anti-Semitism similarly familiar. All those who have been through serious conflicts or crises will know what it means to assume a mediator's role. This was the role the political thinker István Bibó (1911–1979) assumed.

Hysteria, Bibó maintained, is based on fear. As a young student of the philosophy of law, he pointed out in his doctoral thesis that he who is forced and afraid comes into conflict with himself. As he feels he is a victim, he begins to shun responsibility, even the solution to his problems. The result is a misperception of reality and a series of bad decisions, which create a vicious cycle. Though abstract, these were the original recognitions he began to work out in concrete and historical contexts when he encountered the works of Guglielmo Ferrero in the second half of the 1930s, where the Italian historian argued that if a revolution was unable to establish a new and stable legitimacy, great fear would be engendered, which would lead to the fall of democracy. An acquaintance with the insights of Adlerian psychoanalysis enabled Bibó to describe, with great empathy, vicious cycle-like political-psychological processes and hysteria-accompanied political schizophrenia in concrete situations of conflict.

According to Bibó, the starting point of political hysteria is the traumatic experience of a community. By way of response, the community seeks guarantees that the historical shock will never occur again. This pursuit of guarantees of course cripples the thinking of the community. Perfectly matter-of-fact or trivial issues that need to be resolved, if somehow connected to the trauma, become increasingly insurmountable. A false situation develops where the community does not face up to the crisis its political strategy and system face. The situation in turn is covered up by a pseudo-solution, a formula to reconcile that which cannot be reconciled, or a compromise, to which the community clings obstinately. This step necessarily distorts self-assessment. Hysteria is increasingly grafted onto identity, resulting in excesses of power and a sense of inferiority, a will to live off entitlements, a depreciation of genuine performance, and a compulsive protection of the false reality.

Elaborating on this interpretative framework, Bibó made seminal analyses of the mental heritages of the *ancien régimes* of the German, Habsburg, and Russian empires and the mental states of their successor states (Germany, Poland, Czechoslovakia, and Hungary), and he also looked further afield, to Northern Ireland and the Middle East. His groundbreaking analysis was "The German Hysteria," written for his massive *On the Balance of Power and Peace in Europe: A Handbook for Peacemakers* during World War II (see below). In this essay he interpreted Nazism in terms of political hysteria, not as gangster or mob rule, or as the rule of the most reactionary elements of haute finance, or as the fundamental aggressiveness of Germans since Arminius, and not even as a mere response to the Treaty of Versailles. Instead, he saw it as a distortion of democratic mass emotion due to a hysterical lack of realistic self-knowledge and an inability of the community to act. The conclusions he arrived at through his careful, historically grounded analysis would be confirmed indirectly by German historians writing thirty years later.[1]

His other case studies of political hysterias elsewhere attest to an exceptional interdisciplinary knowledge and empathy, and they apply a critical stance and therapeutic approach. He examined various states of affairs in which democratic mass emotions were overwhelming but democratic political culture was weak and challenged by national grievances and the uncertainties involved in nation-building processes.

According to Bibó, a traumatic event or process engenders a discourse of grievance (transmitted through the media, literature, popular culture, etc.). Representatives of such discourse are seen or see themselves as victims. This was the phenomenon Bibó defined as *political hysteria* and on which he focused much of his investigations. He coined the concept, borrowing the term "hysteria" from psychology in a metaphorical sense and reflecting the crisis literature of the interwar period.[2]

István Bibó focused on political hysteria when he analyzed the situation in Germany and the Jewish predicament in Hungary; when he revealed the historical reasons for the distortion of the political cultures of the small nations of Central and Eastern Europe; when he made his careful and emphatic deconstruction of the psychological, linguistic, and political *circuli vitiosi* of the ethno-protectionist responses to territorial loss by hurt national pride; when he rejected the suppression of the 1956 Hungarian uprising and pictured Hungary as both the scandal and the hope of the world; when he dwelled on the anthropological role of the fear of death in tyranny; and also when he outlined his vision of the humanization of power leading from personal power to impersonal service as the meaning and opportunity of European political development.

Coming from psychology, the concept of *trauma* has been successfully applied in social psychology as well as in the sociology of law.[3] Recently, the social sciences and historical literature have explored similar phenomena. Wolfgang Schivelbusch has examined the culture of those vanquished in the American Civil War, the Franco-Prussian War, and World War I in terms of national trauma, mourning, and healing.[4] The examination of the memory regimes of the Spanish Civil War provides food for thought outside Spain as well.[5]

Why should we read Bibó today? What has Bibó to say to people working for a stable world order based on freedom and lasting international security? If we want to have a world with more and more countries turning and remaining democratic in it, it is worth reading Bibó, for he is an expert of failed democracies. He called it political hysteria when a country tried to introduce democracy but made a mess of it and so fell out with the values and institutions of democracy and became a hotbed of dictatorship and terror. Bibó himself lived through such predicaments, and not only was he an outstanding witness and diagnostician of them, but he also offered well-wrought therapies. The forces of tyranny happened to hold sway in his lifetime, and thus his concepts could not materialize.

In 1989, it seemed that democracy would achieve glorious victory throughout the world; all it required was the introduction of the institutions of democracy, and the rest would take care of itself. However, the turn of the century brought about serious dangers; several waves of terror swept over the world, and in the wake of an economic downturn, the influence of the opponents of democracy increased. There was a threat to democracy. It is therefore time to turn to Bibó, the expert on democracy in crisis and trauma.

This volume thus concentrates on Bibó's analyses of political hysteria; case studies of Germany, Eastern Europe, and Hungary written in the 1940s; and two documents in which Bibó attempted actual crisis management—a declaration to the Hungarian people at the moment of the Soviet occupation in 1956 and a political memorandum after the suppression of the revolution addressed to the international community in 1957. Also included in this volume is his seminal study of the Jewish question, an astonishing tour de force in social criticism, a guidebook for the intellectually honest written on the eve of total Communist takeover, in the last moments of relative free speech. In order to provide a broader perspective on Bibó's views, the volume also includes "The Meaning of European Social Development," a kind of philosophical testament recorded in 1971 and 1972. This, the best of his prolific oeuvre, includes highly important essays and book-length studies. Other writings of his have been translated and are ready for publication too.

II. BIBÓ'S PREDICAMENTS

István Bibó was born in Budapest on August 7, 1911. This region of Europe provided the battleground among four empires: the Holy Roman Empire, the Habsburg Empire (which was the Austro-Hungarian Monarchy from 1867), the Russian Empire, and the Ottoman Empire. It was a region where two world wars broke out in a century, at the beginning of which the majority of European countries belonged to increasingly anachronistic dynastic empires and at the end of which most of them were politically independent democratic republics.

Bibó was the offspring, on the father's side, of a Reformed gentry-professional family of many generations (presumably coming from Transylvania and settling in Kiskunhalas, Hungary) and, on the mother's side, a Roman Catholic family (perhaps coming from Alsace or Germany). His father, István Bibó Sr., was a civil servant at the Ministry of Culture and later director of a university library, an amateur philosopher and ethnographer. His mother, Irén Graul, was an erudite lover of literature and an amateur painter, as well as a Tolstoyan humanist who believed that the world could be made a better place. Both parents generated intellectual circles around themselves in Budapest and later in Szeged.[6] They had two children, István and Irén.

István attended school in Budapest and Szeged. He studied law at the University of Szeged (1929–1933). He wrote his doctoral theses in international law and the philosophy of law (1933–1934) at his alma mater. He pursued further studies at the University of Vienna (1933–1934) and the famous Graduate Institute of International and Development Studies of the League of Nations in Geneva (1934–1935), where he was a student of Hans Kelsen, Alfred Verdross, and Guglielmo Ferrero, and took part in the debates on the theory of law. He took up civil service at the Ministry of Justice (1938), where he worked until the fall of 1944. He qualified to teach the philosophy of law in Szeged (1940). In 1941, his post was moved to Kolozsvár (Cluj), where he taught until 1944. He married in 1940. His wife was Boriska Ravasz, a secondary school teacher of Latin and history and the daughter of Reformed bishop László Ravasz. They had one son, István, and two daughters, Anna and Boriska. Anna died at the age of eight.[7]

1. THE TRAUMA OF THE DISSOLUTION OF HISTORICAL HUNGARY

István Bibó wanted to try and influence the great powers victorious in World War II not to commit the same mistakes they had committed after World War I. His first and defining historical experience was the dissolution of historical Hungary when he was between the ages of eight and ten, when two-thirds of the area of Hungary and over 60 percent of its population was ceded to Romania, Czechoslovakia, what would later be Yugoslavia, and even Austria. The territory of Hungary was decreased from 282,000 square kilometers to 93,000 square kilometers and its population from 18.2 million to 7.6 million.[8]

Decision makers drew the borderlines incongruously and often in arbitrary ways, and they subjected the principle of self-determination to the fleeting needs of power politics. In their application of the principle of self-determination, they gave way to all kinds of strategic, waterway, transport, and military points of view—the momentary interests and unrestrained greed of the successor states of the Austro-Hungarian Monarchy. They thus forced Hungary to accept a treaty that cut off not only non-Hungarian majority areas but also areas with mixed (Hungarian and non-Hungarian) populations and large Hungarian majority areas.

In 1918–1919, the leaders of the new, independent Hungarian republic had not accepted the terms set by the victors, but as a result of four years of war and their hopes of eliciting benevolence from the Entente, they would not counter the occupying French, Czech, Romanian, and Serb armies. This strategy proved untenable, the revolutionary government resigned, and the Communists took over, declaring the dictatorship of the proletariat. In the spring of 1919, the Communists opposed the invading Czech Army and then in the summer, the invading Romanian troops, yet they fell. As a result, the country was occupied by Romanian forces and a counterrevolutionary government put in place by the Entente. In exchange for the withdrawal of the Romanian Army, the counterrevolutionary government accepted in the fall of 1919 and signed on June 4, 1920, a treaty that the democratic republic had first refused to sign.[9] The victorious great powers and their allies forced not only Hungary to accept an unjust and, in the long term, unacceptable peace treaty, that of Trianon, which obstructed the growth and consolidation of democracy, but they also forced Germany (among others) to accept the Treaty of Versailles, which thwarted the consolidation of the Weimar Republic, primarily because of its humiliating and unacceptable conditions.

The separation of non-Hungarian areas meant an assertion of the principle of self-determination, which could have been stomached and accepted sooner or later. In areas with a mixed population, consensus or agreement should have been sought and plebiscites arranged wherever and whenever possible. In the vast majority of cases, this was not the course taken. The separation of all-Hungarian areas was a blatant breach of the principle of self-determination. From the perspective of Hungary and the all-Hungarian areas ceded, this injustice glossed over the separation of the non-Hungarian and mixed areas, which would have required a case-by-case plebiscite. Thus the acceptable and unacceptable were mixed up, making unacceptable what was just in the Treaty of Trianon. In this way Hungarian foreign and internal policies were forced onto a course of revisionism, which in turn hindered democracy.

In 1938 and 1940, when it had the opportunity, the Hungarian state recovered northern and southeastern parts of its historical territories (a part of Upper Hungary and Northern Transylvania) on the basis of awards by Nazi Germany and fascist Italy. Before the recovery, it had referred to Transylvanian Jews as Hungarians. As soon as it moved into the regained territories, it treated them as enemies. Moreover, it would not stop at non-Hungarian areas. In 1939 and 1941, the Hungarian Army occupied areas mostly populated by non-Hungarians in the northeast (Carpatho-Ukraine) and the south (Vojvodina). It moved Yugoslavia into these latter areas as a military occupier in 1941.

In order to regain Southern Transylvania, mostly populated by Romanians, Hungary declared war. It did so not against Romania, an ally of Germany, but against the Soviet Union in order to ensure the recovery of all of Transylvania after the war, taking German victory for granted. In the recovered areas, it applied not the federative minority-protection policy it had promised but one of ethnic homogenization. Its conduct was that of an occupier. True, it had little time in comparison with the brutal and aggressive ethnic homogenization policies of its neighbors previously and subsequently.[10]

2. YET ANOTHER PEACE

Bibó wrote about the causes of the disruption of the balance of power in Europe resulting from the closure of World War I and contributing to the outbreak of World War II in a massive manuscript, *On the Balance of Power and Peace in Europe: A Handbook for Peacemakers*, which he committed to writing in 1942–1944 but never had the opportunity to finalize and could thus never share with its intended readers. The manuscript discussed the nation-building processes, national traumas, distortions of political culture, and connections among political hysterias. In it, he analyzed the inability to consolidate the achievements of the French Revolution for well over a century and its consequences for all of Europe, the causes and history of the German hysteria, the French dread, the lack of Italian confidence, and the distortions of the political culture of small East European states. He tried to lay out the foundations of a good peace settlement by helping to understand and identify the situation and to recognize the root causes, fears, and experiences—in other words, by way of a political diagnosis and therapy with appropriate historical and psychological foundations, which markedly differed from the schematic interpretations of the period—as well as outlining the techniques of concluding a good peace.[11]

The manuscript never reached the experts of the peace talks, even though István Bibó sought the help of Karl Mannheim, professor at the London School of Economics and Political Science. In 1946, he wanted to at least have parts of his work find their way to the addressees. His efforts came to naught. Translation had begun, but there was no time left for finalizing and printing the text, and it remained in manuscript form. Finally, he published a part of it in a serial version for the Hungarian public and later as a pamphlet entitled *The Miseries of East European Small States*, included in this book. Apart from his two doctoral theses, this was his only book to appear in his country in his lifetime.[12]

The mistake made in the Treaty of Trianon was repeated by the victorious powers in 1947 in the Treaty of Paris closing World War II; in fact, it was somewhat aggravated due to the conquering policies of the Soviet Union. The Communist dictatorship established by the Soviet occupiers put a taboo on the peace treaty, including the questions of the cross-border Hungarian communities, the Holocaust, world war losses, and the suffering at the hands of occupying Soviet troops. As a result, the pain, defenselessness, offense, fear, and loss that continue to plague Hungarian individuals and communities within and outside the country were left untouched. The grievances, fear, pain, and loss, in turn hinder the creation of positive socialization patterns of democratic community identity and foster the seeking of amends, victim roles, parallel and contrary memory regimes, and symbolic civil war—indeed, political hysteria.

The primary problem was that the peace was dictated. Moreover, it was done without a proper knowledge of the situation precipitating the war. Partly because of this proper knowledge the principle of self-determination was applied inconsistently and equivocally and partly also because democracy lacked the

elaborate procedures of peace negotiation that rulers and aristocrats had developed in the eighteenth and nineteenth centuries. Thus the vanquished had
to be divided instead of addressing and resolving the problems that had originally caused the war, a path that would have rendered acceptable the society-
building duties of the vanquished in the long run in the interest of restoring the
balance of power in Europe, which had been disrupted.

Bibó's attempts to influence the peace talks were thus thwarted, yet he did
try to help make sense of the peace process in an essay entitled "The Peace
and Hungarian Democracy" in 1946. The questions of settling international
conflicts and good peacemaking had occupied István Bibó for a long time. As
a university student, he had written up case studies of the attempts at territorial dispute resolution in Alsace-Lorraine, the Vistula Corridor, Macedonia,
Thrace, and South Tyrol.[13] Bibó would later elaborate on his notions of the
cooperation of the international community of states and its role in resolving
local conflicts in *The Paralysis of International Institutions and the Remedies:
A Study of Self-Determination, Concord among the Major Powers, and Political
Arbitration*, which he published in Britain in 1976, eliciting disapproval from
the Hungarian authorities.[14] The case studies on Cyprus and the Middle East
he drafted were left out of this volume for lack of space.

3. RADICAL AGRARIAN POPULISM

István Bibó was an unrelenting critic of the social conditions of his native land.
The defining experience of the talented and promising young philosopher of
law and lawyer was the anachronistic social structure of Hungary, which, like in
the Baltic republics, Poland, Spain, and Portugal, he maintained, was governed
autocratically, and the exploited and underclass condition of the Hungarian
peasantry in particular. The majority of peasants were deprived of the opportunities of civilized and urbane life. Exploited by the landlords above them, they
desperately revolted against their own condition, demanding the achievements
of urbanized civilization and a dignified existence. Bibó and the radical agrarian movement of the so-called populist writers of the 1930s believed that this
state of affairs could be overcome by the elimination of the large-estate system;
the promotion of the good practices and organizational patterns of the peasants of Western and Northern Europe, and particularly those of the peasants in
the Hungarian areas of Nagykőrös, Kecskemét, and Cegléd, who had risen to
middle-class status; and the national development of agrarian urbanization.[15]

The ruling elite, however, regarded the master-servant relation as self-evident.
Among those revolting against this relationship, not in the least because of the

indigestibility of the dissolution of historical Hungary, an ethno-protectionist and a national egotist public discourse arose, with its fundamental thesis the ethnicization and mythicization of the peasantry. The most effective formulation of this ethnicist interpretation was by Dezső Szabó in the 1920s. In his opinion, due to the fact that the Habsburgs had ruled Hungary for four hundred years from their seat in Vienna, the center of the country had been moved out of Buda, outside the country, with catastrophic consequences for both the Hungarian state and society.[16] The aristocrats were the creatures of the Habsburgs, and the middle class was primarily made up of Jews, Germans, and Slavs. By contrast, the Hungarian characteristics were preserved primarily by the peasantry. The antidote to Habsburg rule and Jewish, German, and Slav influence was that all renewal was to come from the peasantry.[17]

The peasantry, however, was a social class that could not only not offer any solution to the civilization problems of modernizing societies, but it was also crippled by deep crisis and seeking to break out from its oppressed condition. This condition was what the Communist dictatorship, establishing itself from 1945, sought to adjust to its own ideological schemes, and it did so, although not in the direction of greater freedom but rather in that of greater defenselessness, servitude, land-boundness, a state-owned great-estate system, and the making of a new serfdom and proletarianization.

4. THE BIBÓ FAMILY POLITICAL HERITAGE: LIBERAL NATIONALISM

National characteristics and national history were old topoi of European public discourse. In Central, Eastern, and Southern Europe, including Hungary, the stereotypes of harmonizing the protection of local tradition with the import of Western institutions were developed. Hungarian historical tradition was identified with constitutionalism, the Hungarian nation with a brave, warlike, politically conscious people that deliberated and decided on its problems and, having originated in the East, mediated between East and West. As a result of its own constitutional traditions, it was ready to adapt Western institutions. The import and promulgation of Western institutions and rights-extending assimilation were seen as the mission and raison d'être of historical Hungary.[18]

The proto-liberal and liberal concepts of the nation and nation-building strategy were formulated by liberal nationalists such as József Hajnóczy and Lajos Kossuth from the 1780s to the middle of the nineteenth century in terms of the ancient constitution, enlightened government, advancement, and the republicanism of the nobility.[19] Their addressees were the only pluralist estate within the Habsburg Empire, the political public of the Hungarian nobility.[20]

The most important achievement of the program was the regime and social change enshrined in the Acts of 1848: the abolishment of serfdom, the introduction of equality before the law, general and proportionate tax sharing, popular representation based on the sovereignty of the people, a government responsible to the legislature, and the separation of powers. In order to guard against the conquering threats of the Russian Empire and to promote a constitutional unification of Germany, the responsible government proposed a political and economic alliance between Hungary and the Austrian Empire. It was upon and not for this initiative that the alliance materialized.

From the summer of 1849, after more than a year of warfare, civil wars fought by nationalities, and the campaigns of the two largest armies of Europe, the Austrian and the Russian, Austrian absolutism began to establish itself in Hungary. In no more than eighteen years' time, Hungary tied up with the Austrian Empire as an associate member.

The Austro-Hungarian Monarchy and the multinational historical Hungary within it existed for fifty-one years. As it became increasingly clear that the masses of Croats, Serbs, Slovaks, and Romanians would not be assimilated by way of the rights-extension assimilating strategy, so the policies of rights extension and assimilation separated and ran contrary to each other, leading to the exhaustion of liberal nationalism and the rise of conservative nationalism and right-wing radicalism.[21]

5. UNDOING THE DISCOURSE OF NATIONAL CHARACTEROLOGY

Incongruously and shoddily realized, the dissolution of historical Hungary in the wake of World War I was a tremendous shock that enhanced a cyclical interpretation of history rather than the linear scheme, the protection of national features rather than the adoption of Western modernization, an anti-modernity modernization rather than the affirmation of modernization, deprivation rather than an extension of civil rights, dissimilation rather than assimilation, and ethno-protectionism rather than a catching up with the West. The discourse on national characterology increasingly dominated, within which national ontologies, the timeless schemes of national features, became widespread alongside reinterpreted national historicism. All this was expressed in the collectivist political languages of national egotism, ethno-protectionism, and the homogenous nation-state—the fallout of social Darwinism.

The Hungarian debates over national character simultaneously meant the decline-history reinterpretation of national history, the formulation of stereotypes of national character and national ontologies, and programs of collective identity. The enemy image of foreign invasion and influence was countered by the mythicization of the peasantry, the branding of those successfully assimilated—primarily the Jews, due to the separation of the non-Hungarian nationalities—and the definition of some kind of national character.[22]

It was this ethno-protectionist tradition Bibó broke with and unmade. It was a political language, genre, theme, and mode of argument he had learned from his father, Dezső Szabó, and László Németh, a major influence on Bibó for a while, so much so that it had been his "father's tongue" in his youth.[23]

This was the first interpretation whereby Bibó broke with the ethno-protectionist tradition. The next one was his doing away with the various forms of community mythicization, the notion that communities could be regarded as subjects; subjects capable of action can only be individuals.[24] He also rejected all kinds of peasant romanticism, including the idea that the peasantry could and should be the source of national renewal.[25] He rejected the public belief that national character could be created and established in a programmatic fashion. It can develop only through the successful solution of concrete tasks.[26]

In writing *On the Balance of Power and Peace in Europe: A Handbook for Peacemakers*, Bibó went even further, revealing the superiority and inferiority complexes behind the mythicization of national features, amends-seeking, and victimhood; the political hysterias deriving from the historical fears of a community and the traumatic experiences behind them; and the mechanisms and methods of allaying the hysterias.[27]

Bibó related his assessments to the mechanism of contra-selection László Németh had been so very precise in describing but had placed in the wrong context—the fact that the opportunistic members of the national elite had been successful while the valuable ones had been marginalized in the period between 1860 and 1944. In Bibó's view, such an outcome was truly contra-selection. But he believed it had nothing to do with the national or non-national characteristics of those setting the patterns but with the political constructions that were bound to political hysterias and community fears, primarily the fear of the dissolution of historical Hungary.[28] In "The Warped Hungarian Self: A History of Impasse," which is included in this edition, we get a depiction not of what a healthy and intact Hungarian self would be like, but the uncovering of the causes and history of Hungarian political hysteria. As he elaborated the new theme, he also invalidated national characterology; national ontology; national historicism; the subject matter, presuppositions, and arguments of the history of national decline; and the political language of national egotism. He deconstructed the discourse on national character and reinterpreted its thesis on the contra-selection of the national elite in the context of the causes and history of

Hungarian political hysteria. The combination of the process of deconstruction
and the analysis of hysteria it prompts explains the tension between the title and
the subject matter.[29]

6. THE JEWISH QUESTION

Bibó's third defining experience closely tied to the dissolution of historical Hungary and the situation of the peasantry was the Jewish question. According to the topos of ethno-protectionist and the national egotist version
of political discourse, the root problem of all Hungarian ills was Jewish and
German economic and cultural expansion at the expense of ethnic Hungarians in the second half of the nineteenth century and the interwar period. On
this view, to cite Dezső Szabó, among the "minority majoritarians"—Jews
and Germans achieving majority status in Hungary—Jews with increasing
exclusivity had forced Hungarians into a minority status in their own country, a condition that could and should be set aright by relegating Jews to the
background and regulating and decreasing their numbers in economic and
cultural life.[30]

With the rise of ethno-protectionist anti-Semitism, redistributive statist conservatism and extreme-right radicalism led to the restriction of the number of
Jews admitted to universities (Numerus Clausus) in 1920 and to business and
cultural careers in 1938. Anti-Semitic legislation initiated by the conservative
government in trying to adapt to Nazi expansion, to ward off extreme right-wing
radicalism, and to embark on a revisionist foreign policy devolved from the state
regulation of proportions of Jews entering these fields into racist law.[31]

After the German occupation of Hungary (March 19, 1944), the executive
power subservient to the Germans divested Jews of their remaining civil rights,
sequestered and robbed them, and then with the help of its power-enforcement
organs transferred its former citizens to the German occupiers, who deported
them. Thus the Hungarian state became an accomplice in the industrialized
genocide aiming to annihilate the third largest Jewish community in Europe in
the spring and summer of 1944, when World War II was coming to a close and
German defeat was already a certainty. As a result, the Jews of the countryside
were deported and killed, while a part of the Budapest Jewry was murdered in
the autumn and winter of 1944. All together some half a million people perished, a figure that amounted to two-thirds of Hungary's war losses.[32]

István Bibó traversed a long path with respect to the Jewish question. We note
his spontaneous anti-discriminatory and philo-Semitic gestures in his childhood
in his *Recollections* and the television interview that served as its basis: he had

torn away anti-Semitic posters and posted others saying "Long live the Jews!," for which he got smacked. He had also rebuked a playmate for not wanting to marry a little girl because she was Jewish.[33] However, some twenty years later, he did not protest against the First Jewish Act in 1938; moreover, as a political adviser, he would suggest ethno-protectionist additions to the draft program of the March Front.[34] In 1942, however, the murder of his former classmate, university colleague, and best friend, Béla Reitzer, a Jew on forced-labor service in the Ukraine, must have affected him to the point that he finally and irrevocably turned against the anti-Semitic logic of ethno-protectionism.[35] In 1944, he initiated a middle- and working-class alliance against the German occupation.[36] He refused to partake of any, even indirect, collaboration.[37] As a civil servant in the Ministry of Justice, he produced false papers for Jews, whereby he saved the lives of many—several hundred according to certain sources.[38]

The aesthetician Péter György recently recalled how his mother survived the anti-Jewish persecution: "In her meek, fleeting, and objective manner, my mother told her story with István Bibó, who, as a civil servant in the internal ministry, gave her papers without hesitation when she, as a sixteen-year-old, introduced herself as a refugee from Transylvania. It was thus that, without actually knowing him, I considered him a personal acquaintance, just as my mother kept track of his career mindfully, fearfully, and with love. She read pieces of news related to him as though it all happened to a distant relative who we numbered among the family but could not trouble."[39]

When the national socialist Arrow-cross Party took over, Bibó was arrested, handed over to the SS but released after a few days "until further action." Disciplinary action was initiated against him for "his conduct in issuing written notifications for certain Jewish persons."[40] He was to have been interrogated on November 30, 1944.[41] Instead, he went underground, also sabotaging under the burden of death the call-up order of the Arrow-cross government. He hid in the cellars of the Reformed Theological Academy, the offices of his father-in-law, but continued his life-saving activities.

After several years of research, Bibó published "The Jewish Predicament in Post-1944 Hungary" in 1948, which is included in this edition. In this book-length essay, he distinguished three phenomena: medieval Christian anti-Judaism, the "development disorders" of an assimilating society, and the mutual experiences of the dehumanized association of non-Jews and Jews. He faced up to his own responsibility, with which he set an example to all non-Jewish Hungarians. He called on both Jews and non-Jews to refrain from sermonizing to one another but rather to find humane ways of relating to one another and possible levels and modes of communication.[42]

Several of its implementers being of Jewish background, the Communist dictatorship prompted a new anti-Semitism and banned all free expressions of opinion. István Bibó refuted the claim reflecting the anti-Communist and anti-Semitic scheme that Communist dictatorship was identical to Jewish rule. He accepted and sought to have others accept that there were several justifiable and understandable Jewish responses to the Holocaust: the patterns of conduct of assimilation, Jewish minority consciousness, and Zionism.[43] He nevertheless dared analyze the encounters, the "misleading experience" at the heart of anti-Semitic attitudes, and discuss the responsibility of the victims, and, as one who had been influenced by ethno-protectionism, he refuted anti-Semitism.

Later, Bibó would often return to the subject. For example, he wrote a highly inventive study of the situation in the Middle East, stating that it was the consequence of European anti-Semitism, for which, in the final analysis, Europe was to be held responsible. With profound insight, he analyzed the fundamentally different processes of the making of the Israeli and Arab nations and their delimitations, and he elaborated on a consolidation plan to resolve the permanent tension under international guarantees.[44] For saving many lives and in recognition of his entire oeuvre, he should have been awarded the title Righteous among the Nations.

7. UNDER THE SHADOW OF TOTALITARIANISM

In 1944–1945, Hungary became a battleground in which the Red Army beat out the German and Hungarian troops. Soviet victory simultaneously meant liberation from German and Soviet occupation and the establishment of a Communist dictatorship. This was the case at the end of 1945 and the beginning of 1946. At the free elections held on November 4, 1945, six parties competed, and the Smallholder, Agrarian Laborer, and Civic Party won an absolute majority. Yet it did not form a government alone or together with its wartime allies, the Social Democratic Party and the National Peasant Party. Upon Soviet demand, a four-party coalition was set up, wherein the Communists obtained the most important positions, including the Ministry of the Interior, which controlled the police forces.[45] The Communists had no scruples about taking advantage of their position, and they did all they could to destroy the biggest party of the coalition, blackmail the prime minister and force him to resign, undermine the parties of the coalition, and then establish one-party rule. They did so in the name of fighting reaction between 1945 and 1948—in the way that Bibó had already cautioned against in 1945. In 1949, a Stalinist constitution was introduced, and thus the political system of Hungary became a single-party proletarian dictatorship, a totalitarian system—a tyranny, as Bibó put it. It had no room for any analyses of hysteria, mediation, political examination, independent opinion, or socialization based on cooperation.

However, not all regarded a Communist dictatorship as a historical inevitability, and they did what they could to avert it, as did István Bibó, so that democracy could be established and consolidated. For this reason in the summer of 1945, he wrote his seminal essay, "Hungarian Democracy in Crisis."[46]

As the head of the Public Administration Department of the Ministry of the Interior between 1945 and 1946, Bibó devised acts related to elections and administrative reform that the dictatorship being set up would not allow to be implemented. Unable to obstruct the expulsion of Germans from Hungary on the basis of collective responsibility, Bibó resigned from his position as departmental head in the ministry.[47] Then in 1946, he was appointed professor and chair of the political science department at the University of Szeged and to a corresponding membership in the Hungarian Academy of Sciences.[48]

Bibó delivered his inaugural lecture at the academy, entitled "The Separation of Powers Then and Now," on January 13, 1947. He took stock of the old and new forms of power concentration, including, among the new ones, the rise of the organization aristocracy in economic, cultural, and information areas referring to efficiency. Human aspirations to freedom would have to find new forms of disrupting and counterbalancing these concentrations of power.[49] Half a year later he announced a seminar entitled "Democracy and Socialism," where, according to the notes taken by one of his students, he discussed the concentration of political power and the new aristocratic social organization harming human equality. Let me cite from the notes:

> The genuine question is: How is the subjective experience of freedom of the individual to become social method? . . . Freedom becomes objective when, beside the subjective experience of freedom of the individual, two persons are associated *without one being made a means of the other*. The means relationship reacts upon the user of the means: a state oppressing others cannot be free because it calls its own freedom into doubt, and it thus becomes uncertain. Personal freedom is thus likewise endangered. . . . Unrestrained power relations bring about mutual relations: all tyrannizing gives rise to the dread of backlash. . . . The majority decision is valid, but it is not made use of in a tyrannical way, because freedom would then be endangered. The will of the minority must also be asserted. The possibility of opposing must not be excluded. . . . In a democracy, all people rule themselves. In theory, everyone partakes of government. Quality can also have a role. Birthright quality has disappeared, or loses its strength (property), but the role of quality in culture

is retained. In socialism, workers' quality is narrower than all others, and thus new quality can arise out of it. A new aristocracy is being put in place to fill this; see ideological single-party system. The Communist Party is consistently attempting to introduce a new type of aristocratic order.[50]

It was only for a single year, in 1946–1947, that Bibó offered a lecture at the university. In the following academic year, 1947–1948, he did not announce a major course.[51] As he could not teach politics in the way his convictions would have it due to the dictatorship establishing itself at the university, he accepted the position of ministerial commissioner of the Pál Teleki Research Institute. His duty was to mediate between institute president Loránd Dabasi-Schweng, whom the Communists wanted to sack, and his deputy, Domokos Kosáry, who wanted to realize his ambitious goals at all costs. He assumed the mediator's role and succeeded.[52] Having reorganized the institute as the East European Research Institute, he became its vice president and initiated various research projects in the social sciences, but the dictatorship first placed restrictions on and then closed the institute. Bibó was deprived of his membership in the academy in 1949, then of his university professorship. Between 1951 and 1957, he worked at the Eötvös Loránd University Library as a classifier.[53]

8. "THE MEANING OF EUROPEAN SOCIAL DEVELOPMENT"

In his essay on European social and political development, which he drafted between 1953 and 1956, Bibó discussed the Bolshevik Revolution as one of the failures of the European belief in progress in the twentieth century:

This revolution shocked the world from the outset by the amount of blood spilled and violence applied, surpassing anything hitherto. . . . The Marxist-Leninist revolution did not assume any solidarity with the moral pathos of former revolutions, but, on the basis of the related theses of Marxism-Leninism, regarded all political ideologies and movements, thus all revolutions, its own included, as a war of class interests and deemed all justifications of this war or indeed any noble rule binding it as mere hypocrisy. The most shocking practical consequence of this was not the greater bloodshed and violence used — the French Revolution had already presented plenty of that — but its utter intentional and programmatic nature. That the Russian Revolution or any milder version of it that was nonetheless successful in establishing socialism meant a step forward in progress was categorically doubted. This open and admitted doubt appears as the public opinion wherever the political ideology of Marxism-Leninism is not in power. But more important, this doubt is implicitly and unadmittedly, but frighteningly, present in all those on either side of the Iron Curtain who profess and proclaim the ideology of Marxism or Marxism-Leninism as the European social program based on the fundamental principles of justice, freedom, and human dignity. This doubt is nonexistent only for those who regard these matters merely in terms of expedience in rising to power and holding on to it.[54]

Bibó would go on to develop the conclusion that the Bolshevik Revolution and Bolshevism did not belong in the European program of progress, freedom, justice, and human dignity. By way of introduction, he pointed out, "Following the glorious revolution of Hungarians arming themselves and the last, desperate attempt of tyranny to cling to power, the truths of social and state theory, which those obsessed with ideological omniscience would not understand in all the hopeless and hair-splitting debates of yesterday, can now be stated as self-evident, without our having to engage in protracted argumentation."[55]

Stalinism is a consequence of Leninism, and Leninism that of Marxism. The programmatic use of unrestrained violence is a consequence of the unrestrained power and omnipotence of the party, while the unrestrained power and omnipotence of the party is a consequence of revolution for its own sake, the cult of violence, class war, and proletarian dictatorship. Bolshevism is not the bad realization of a good theory, a theory-distorting consequence of Russian backwardness, but a bad and inhuman theory being forced onto the human world. Marxism-Leninism is the worst kind of idealism, a theory founded on metaphors; it is against liberty and leads to tyranny.[56]

Nominated by the former National Peasant Party, now called the Petőfi Party, Bibó became a minister of state in the last Imre Nagy cabinet on November 3, 1956. Hearing the news of the Soviet intervention, he went to the Parliament early the next morning, and finding there no cabinet members who would assume political responsibility, he worked in his office as the only member of the legitimate cabinet holding out at his post and working in the building occupied by Soviet troops for three days, between November 4 and 6.[57] He rewrote a draft foreign-policy declaration he had prepared previously for the cabinet meeting as a letter to the president of the United States, took it across to the nearby building of the U. S. Embassy, and there reworded it as a cable, which the embassy then sent to President Eisenhower. He requested that the president initiate the withdrawal of British and French troops from Egypt and Soviet troops from Hungary.[58] He then returned to the Parliament and typed a declaration refuting the slander against the Hungarian revolution, which was referred to as the justification for the Soviet intervention. He called on the Hungarian people to resist passively and the great powers of the world to demonstrate the power of the principles of the Founding Charter of the United Nations and the freedom loving peoples, and he asked God to safeguard Hungary.[59] On November 6, he wrote a letter and an exposition, and he drew up a compromise draft for settling the Hungarian situation that he as a minister of state handed over to the British, French, and Indian embassies.[60] After three days, he no longer saw any reason for staying in the Parliament, and so, avoiding the Soviet patrols, he walked home. At home and at his office in the university library, he continued to work on his draft compromise and composed declarations for Soviet troops to be withdrawn from Hungary in exchange for international and Hungarian guarantees that Hungary would not pursue anti-Soviet policies. He also wrote a memorandum on the Hungarian and the world situations (also included in this edition), and he sent it abroad for publication. Its import and timeliness is self-evident.[61]

The government and its authorities, which the occupiers had put in place, deemed Bibó's patriotic activities to be treason and arrested him on May 23, 1957. On August 2, 1958, a month and a half after the execution of Imre Nagy and his associates, Bibó was spared the death sentence at his trial by the intercession of Indian ambassador Kumara Padmanahba Sivasankara Menon, whom he and Árpád Göncz (the future, post-1990 president of Hungary) had met and given a declaration in December 1956. He was thus sentenced to life imprisonment. He was held in the harshest prisons: Vác, Márianosztra, and the Budapest Transit Prison (a place of execution). He was released under an amnesty on March 27, 1963. He worked as a librarian in the Library of the National Statistical Office between 1963 and 1971.[62]

Between 1971 and 1979, the pensioner Bibó wrote extensively. In these years he elaborated on the principles and outlook of his *Memorandum* in the Hungarian original of *The Paralysis of International Institutions and the Remedies* and the case studies. At the behest of his son and daughter-in-law, he recorded on tape his views on the meaning of European social development. His recollections were recorded in a television interview and on tape, as well as in extensive, study-like comments to and reflections on a book. His intellectual testament was preserved on tape recordings and in a few pages of notes. Like Béla Bartók, he left with "a full satchel." His wife, Boriska, died of lung cancer on April 14, 1979, and, after a heart attack, Bibó followed her on May 10. He was not quite 68.[63]

III. AFTERLIFE

1. INTELLECTUAL HERITAGE

The mass experience of human defenselessness, humiliation, and suffering caused by two world wars, revolutions, counterrevolutions, civil wars, genocides and population exchanges, and totalitarian dictatorships that threatened the entire world and globalized the ruthlessness of the religious wars through modern technology have prompted many to conclude that the claim to human adulthood and a social organization based on the principles of freedom and democracy replacing personal dominion and a social hierarchy of masters and servants was the cause of all evils. Not so István Bibó. He believed that political development from personal rule to impersonal service and a social organization based on the principles of freedom and democracy belonged among the greatest enterprises and achievements of mankind. This enterprise is far from over, yet it does not assert itself with self-evident automatism and has in many ways run aground. So the possibilities of moving out of the impasse, of a breakthrough, need to be found.[64]

No final explanation of the world, no saving scheme, no philosophical system, no surrogate religion, no concept of a single and final solution to a puzzle, no indoctrination will undo but will only gloss over or intensify the fears engendered by individual and collective forlornness,[65] the fears related to those politically dim situations that personal rule no longer defines and impersonal service still does not determine and where political culture and socialization and the patterns of community assessment and conduct foster the rebirth of personal rule due to the spread of fear. The gradual establishment of a legitimate status and the foundation of a democratic system presuppose that we understand and awaken others to how conditions of fear came into being. If we come this far, we can start finding a solution. All this calls for individual and collective efforts to understand the situation and to decrease the amount of fear.[66] In other words, it insists and presupposes that we find the mistake in the equation "Democratic freedom equals self-determination, which equals the nation-state, which equals nationalism, which equals fascism and war."[67]

In Bibó's view, nationalism (meaning both national feeling—i.e., patriotism, the program and process of nation building—and the notion that a given nation stands above and is superior to others—i.e., nationalism in the pejorative sense) is not a self-reliant ideology; it has no independent principle. Self-contained ideologies are conservatism, liberalism, and socialism. Conservatism based on the authoritarian-aristocratic principle has by now become anachronistic, selection by birth having lost its validity. The principle of liberalism is freedom. Socialism is a development of liberalism that takes the principle of freedom further, developing the techniques of freedom and the freedom of enterprise in the name of equality and social justice. Birthright selection and the inequality of human qualities have lost their validity, as has inherited and mammoth property following inherited rank.

Nationalisms (in the pejorative sense) mutually destroy one another's validity. The successes of nationalism have the fact of the nation behind it. The elements of dominion and aggression are related to the confusions of nation making, the deformations of political culture, the abuse or equivocal application of the principle of self-determination,[68] to what has led the power-humanizing political enterprise that turns personal rule into impersonal service, the great experiment of social organization based on the principles of freedom and democracy, into a rut, from which a way out needs to be found.

Bibó was no system-creating or analytical political philosopher. Averse to all kinds of indoctrination, he was anti-speculative, an empiricist, eclectic, and an empathic rationalist, a problem-solving political thinker. Whenever he could, he dictated his trains of thought formulated in long sentences. Many of his texts can be classified as in the genre of lecture rather than essay. His style and language often reflect the metaphoric formulations of the essayist tradition of the interwar period. His approach and method were interdisciplinary. He was far from the instrumentalism so widespread in current political theory, though he was well aware of their versions of his time. He applied the aspects of political theory, moral philosophy, personal and social psychology, history, sociology, the philosophy of law, and international law in his original analyses. His investigations related historical traumas and processes of nation building and pointed to mediation in situations of conflict and crisis. Essentially, his role transpiring from his works was that of the mediator.

2. INFLUENCES, PARALLELS, AND UNIQUENESS

István Bibó was inspired by the synoptic method of the philosopher of law Barna Horváth; the interpretation of legitimacy and the narration of the French Revolution of the historian Guglielmo Ferrero; the social regeneration plan of the philosopher Karl Mannheim; the concept of Eastern Europe and contraselection of the Hungarian elite of the novelist and thinker László Németh; the social concept of mutual services of the historian István Hajnal; and the concept of embourgeoisement and agrarian urbanization plans of the sociologist Ferenc Erdei. He was influenced by ancient and modern political theorists and the interpretations of "nation" of Johan Huizinga and José Ortega y Gasset from the crisis literature of the interwar period. At the beginning of his career, he shared many of the observations of the crisis literature of the period, but he reinterpreted them under the principle of freedom. Another defining socialization and interpretation framework for Bibó was East European agrarian populism, a highly complex phenomenon, encompassing Russian Narodnikism to

Zionism. From among the interpretations of power, society, and history, he embraced Robert MacIver's concept of the humanization of power and drew a great deal also on the investigations of Bertrand Russell, Raymond Aron, Dankwart A. Rustow, Hugh Seton-Watson, and Arnold Toynbee. In the debate between the positivist concept of the law and natural law theory as hallmarked by Hans Kelsen and Alfred Verdross, he tended to side with the views of the latter.

Róbert Berki has already taken stock of the many influences on and parallels to Bibó. Since then, many of these connections have been developed (to Wilhelm Röpke, Karl Raymund Popper, John Rawls, Félicité Lamennais, Dietrich Bonhoeffer, László Németh, István Hajnal, Ferenc Erdei, Guglielmo Ferrero, Isaiah Berlin, Hannah Arendt, and János Kis); others, however, still need to be explored (to George Orwell, Martin Buber, Hubert Butler, Robert MacIver, and Walter Wink).

In many ways, Bibó recalls the work of Isaiah Berlin, Hannah Arendt, and John Rawls, though the differences cannot be overstressed. In his characteristic way, Berlin defended personal liberty against the new tyranny of political freedom and thought of political freedom as a means of personal liberty, as classical liberals tend to do. Arendt extolled political freedom and underestimated the importance of personal liberty. John Rawls focused on the cohesive role of the rules and procedures in a pluralist democracy on the basis of common socialization. They had no answer to the question of what was to be done if this foundation was lacking. How could the non-free citizens of a non-free state become free, and how could they make their political community free? The establishment of a free political community is principally based on the everyday experience of people taking possession of their community. However, the building of a free political community presupposes free individuals, whereas people become free if they live in a free political community. How can one break out of this vicious circle? István Bibó had timely, important, and challenging answers.

Research into effects and influences is helpful when the oeuvre is already known and we wish to relate it to others. But Bibó's thought cannot be reduced to the influences upon him and dissolved in any parallels—neither individually nor collectively. His approach cannot be pigeonholed; he cannot be identified solely with liberalism, radicalism, socialism, Christianity, or conservatism. From all these tendencies, we find something in his work in various contexts and in different measures. The most important characteristic of his thought is its autonomy and originality. His analyses of political hysteria, his investigations in international conflict resolution, his diagnoses and therapies aiming to establish the conditions of democracy are hardly precepts with universal validity and applicability, yet his mediatory approach, his seeking to understand the often perplexing mentality of a region in conflict over self-determination, enabled him to make critical observations and recognitions that are not only edifying and highly productive, but also provide reliable guidelines for conflict resolution. Of course Bibó remains the most reliable guide for anyone wanting to grasp the vicissitudes of Central-East European and Hungarian politics.

3. RECEPTION

Bibó's funeral was a dignified demonstration by those revolutionaries of 1956 who were still alive and the Democratic Opposition that was beginning to organize itself—under the watchful eyes and cameras of plainclothesmen. In less than six months, dissidents of different persuasions honored his memory with a memorial volume, which was distributed as a samizdat until changes were made.[69] His name became the symbol of resistance to the Kádár regime, a democratic and independent Hungary. At the time of the political changes, the late 1980s, he was the most often-quoted Hungarian thinker. Since then, his work has gained currency, particularly in the last fifteen years.[70]

Bibó lived his entire life under authoritarian or totalitarian systems. Alien to the oligarchic characteristics of the post-Communist period, encapsulated in a language and culture almost unreachable for the greater part of the world, his oeuvre is not part of any canon. Though unsystematically, he was nevertheless known to many thinkers: Hannah Arendt learned of him via Károly Kerényi in Ancona in the early sixties; Isaiah Berlin, who had been among the British scholars to petition the authorities in Hungary to release Bibó in 1961–1962, learned of him through the conversations I was honored to have with him between 1981 and 1994; Bronislaw Geremek and Václav Havel knew him as a fellow dissident; and Richard Holbrooke, the eminent statesman, was also drawn to him.

Bernard Crick wrote an introduction to Bibó's *The Paralysis of International Institutions and the Remedies: A Study of Self-Determination, Concord among the Major Powers, and Political Arbitration* in 1976.[71] The British political scientist with Hungarian roots, Róbert Berki, planned to write a monograph on Bibó and suggested that his essays be published by Cambridge University Press in the late eighties.[72] Alas, he died in 1991, and no one carried his efforts further in Britain. In the United States, East European Monographs published *Democracy, Revolution, Self-Determination* in 1991, but the volume, for all its merits, failed to capture either an academic or a general readership.[73]

Bibó's reception in France, Germany, Italy, Poland, and other East European countries is far more extensive, his books have reached a much wider readership, and his ideas have exerted an influence; his concept of political hysteria has, for example, inspired a number of scholarly conferences on trauma management in Europe, under the aegis of the Academia Europaea (London).[74]

Obviously, an English-language edition of Bibó requires the full-blown infrastructure of a major publisher. Though some of Bibó's writings have appeared in various translations, this edition makes eight of his most important essays available in a new English translation. The translation of his texts is an act of interpretation, complex from the point of view of thought, language, genre, and speech. The texts have been ably translated by Péter Pásztor of Szentendre, Hungary. The financing of the translation was arranged by the István Bibó Center for Advanced Studies in the Humanities and Social Sciences. For several years, we relentlessly submitted applications for the funding of translations worthy of the author and by a translator up to the task. The necessary funds were magnanimously provided by the Hungarian Academy of Sciences and Szerencsejáték Zrt (Hungarian lottery).

It was through the kind offices of Jan-Werner Müller of Princeton University that my learned friend and colleague Balázs Trencsényi of the Central European University found his way to Yale University Press, an excellent custodian of the texts. István Bibó Jr. and Mrs László Tegzes, née Boriska Bibó, granted the rights to publish this edition, which features Bibó's texts in the order in which they were written.

Yale's two anonymous readers delivered thoughtful and poignant opinions, and I am grateful for their remarks and observations, which were highly useful in preparing this edition. I must also thank Iván Balog, István Bibó Jr., András Csepregi, Péter Cserne, and Balázs Trencsényi, my fellow members of the István Bibó Center for Advanced Studies in the Humanities and Social Sciences, for their advice and comments when I was writing this introduction. I also appreciate the dedication of Jaya Aninda Chatterjee and Bojana Ristich, the editor and copy editor of this book, at Yale University Press.

CODA

It is a safe prediction that, especially now with cultural contacts freely flowing between East and West in both directions, the Hungarian thinker István Bibó will soon be given full accolade as one of the most outstanding political

theorists of this century, in stature equal to the "greats" in the entire European tradition of political thought. Bibó's significance far exceeds local, pa-
rochial interests. While profoundly original and organically stemming from
Hungarian culture, Bibó belongs also to the "West." If his political thought
is to be epitomized in one succinct phrase, it is "the realism of moralism," or
the almost flawless synthesis of a deeply radical, morally infused *vision* and
value-system with the hard-nosed, unsentimental realist's *insight* into enduring problems of politics and society.[75]

As a result of much effort, the prediction of British political scientist Róbert
Berki may now, after many years, come true.[76]

ON THE BALANCE OF POWER AND PEACE IN EUROPE

All writings have an obligation to render a more or less detailed account of the influences that have enriched it. This work has relatively few such references; if it were to acknowledge all its debts, it would have to list, beyond books, not all of them scholarly, all the inspiration it gained through lectures and friendly conversations. At this time, it would not be appropriate to list them.

The author must not forget his indebtedness to one person; it is this obligation he fulfills by dedicating this book to the memory of Guglielmo Ferrero.

BOOK I: THE CAUSES OF THE WORLD WAR AND THE CURRENT CRISIS

CHAPTER I: EUROPEAN POLITICAL DEVELOPMENT

1. ON THE NATURE OF THE CURRENT CRISIS

A) LIMITING THE PROBLEM TO EUROPE AND POLITICS

Written as part of a "Handbook for Peacemakers," this work is about the causes of the world war and the current crisis. For all the grand claims of this introduction, it might seem odd that it is mostly about Europe—the miseries of Eastern Europe in particular and primarily political phenomena. In view of the scale of the current world war, it might be deemed unjustified to limit the discussion to Europe, especially the matters of Central-East Europe. Current thought is guided by a phony worldwide approach, whereby the problems of Central Europe (i.e., Germany and Italy) and Eastern Europe (i.e., the region between Germany and Russia) are treated as one complex among those many of the Middle East, the Far East, and the Western Hemisphere. This attitude is mistaken, however. Even if Europe will no longer fulfill the role it used to have, it will continue to be in the focus of the political forces of the world, and the political order of the world cannot be set aright without restoring the balance of power in Europe. The critical point of the balance of power in Europe is the anarchy and the collapse of political authority in Central-East Europe. The "minor" difference between this region and the Middle East, the Far East, and the Western Hemisphere is that the lack of consolidation of this region has sparked two world wars within a short period of time, and a third one, should it break out, will undoubtedly start out from here. Now, this is enough reason to give it "disproportionate" attention.

Our discussion consciously opposes any interpretation that sees primarily *economic forces and interests* behind wars and that regards wars as the spinoff of economic development. Economic factors can of course influence the objectives, turns, means, course, and outcomes of war. In the final count, however, these are accessory causes and interests rather than primary causes. The political fears, feelings of insecurity, and passions that overturn political balance are far beyond the measure of warlike passions that can be "incited," movements that can be "funded," and political intrigue that can be "plotted"; moreover, they are beyond the point where long-term economic trends or economic crises and slumps are enough to cause political developments. The commonplace that wars are caused by conflicting interests is worth no more than saying that this war or wars in general are the fruit of *sin*; it is true enough but will not do if one wants to understand and help. It is time to try and explore—as Karl Marx discovered the economic factors hidden behind politics—politics and its effects on mass psychology behind the economic factors made overly much of nowadays, the painful and confused process of establishing modern nations in particular, which has been a chronic cause of confusion in Central-East Europe and thereby the disruption of the balance of power in Europe as a whole.

Obviously, many will not be convinced by our attributing decisive import to politics and will regard political and economic factors only as superficial reasons, seeking "deeper" reasons in race, society, and ideology. I am convinced that however much race, society, and ideology have contributed to the turns of the crisis, they cannot account for final causes and decisive motives. It will be likewise surprising that we attribute to politics effects that distort the mental makeup of entire peoples when it is common knowledge that the majority of the people are apolitical, even anti-political. However, the politics we have in mind is not what people usually associate with politicians and what certainly elicits indifference or enmity from many, but "polis," the cause of the community, its conditions and relation to individuals.

Now this is what many have a passionate concern for. This concern has been with us since the turn of the eighteenth century—that is, from the rise of the modern sense of community, where the relation to the community of the state, the functioning, nature, and prestige of the community of the state, has in theory become the shared and personal concern of everyone. Not necessarily entailing democracy, this theoretical and emotional democratization of relating to the community swept all over Europe. Hence the situation of most recent times that the concerns of national communities have resulted in various community hysterias, which in turn have disrupted the European balance of power.

In passing, we must take our stance on the rather unfruitful debate between *anti-rational emotionalism* and *anti-instinctual rationalism*. The rule of reason over passion is a requirement humankind must not relinquish for the sake of irrational impulses if it does not want to give up the advances it has achieved. The primacy of reason, however, does not mean that it is possible to establish a rational setup in community and generally in human affairs without regard to impulses as though they did not exist. This naive rationalism must be countered by a higher rationalism that concentrates all the capacities of reason on finding bearings in the thicket of impulses. Recognizing this, we must first clarify two concepts that loom large in the following discussion.

B) BALANCE OF POWER

It is fashionable these days to say that the concept of the balance of power has become passé. Let us not be mistaken that, because certain forms of balance have proved insufficient, a community can exist without balance. Balance is not the sum of quantifiable relations or small-minded political deals, swapping peoples and territories. All this is but the local or historical manifestation of a higher principle without regard for which material, intellectual, or community creation is impossible. The precondition of all creation, community creation in particular, is that the fundamental power relations and principles of the creative community that define the entire setup are neither too rigid nor too supple. An overly rigid setup puts up too much resistance against the changes of reality and development and can only change through catastrophe, while an excessively tractable setup cannot resist the pressure of the external world and thus lacks even the minimum sense of identity and security required by any creative individual or community life. *Balance*, however, is the proportionate existence of mobility and stability; in other words, it is the condition of community life in which the power relations and guiding principles of the community are capable of maintaining an optimal level of flexibility and stability between the excesses of rigidity and tractability.

Establishing balance in a community means disabling unrestrained power concentration, which corrupts both those exercising it and those subject to it; it means juxtaposing organizations of power and scopes so that, should destructive forces arise in one or the other, they are countered not only by principles and precepts but also by the power of the rest; it means providing power organizations with moral substance and a sense of calling in order to increase their stability and decrease their brutality; it means increasing the sense of security of both those exercising and subject to power by clearly and objectively defining scopes of authority; it means thinking up methods and procedures for the continuous changes of life so that a breakdown of a fossilized regime does not destroy the entire system; it means creating patterns of courageous and magnanimous action and thereby freeing individuals and communities of the fear of the other or the rest taking advantage; it means shaping a type of man who preserves the conventions and traditions of the system in order to ensure that the intellectual sloppiness of people will not take it for granted that moral effort is needed for upholding the system; it means instilling in people a sense of security in the face of the chimeras of fear; objective courage against actual danger; binding the forces of destruction, confusion, and barbarism; and enabling the rich profusion of creativity.

In this light, we will be able to appreciate the classical system of the balance of power in Europe quite differently and guard against rashly declaring it outdated. The question is not whether it is possible to ensure the security and peace of a community through new, superior organizations replacing the policy of the balance of power, but what new, more enduring, deeper, and morally better grounded forms the *eternal* policy of the balance of power is to assume in the new organizations that are necessary.

Two extreme views can dishevel the common life of states, these relatively independent units; one extreme cannot accept or imagine any law, regulation, or principle ruling the relationship among states and sees and wants to see the entire relationship as a power game; the other extreme attributes the laws, regulations, and principles applicable as a result of the momentarily prevailing balance of power to a nonexistent supra-state authority. Not that this cannot ever come into being; it can of course be brought into being, but what matters is that *at this time* it does not exist, and any interpretation that looks to it as though it did exist is going to have a false relation with reality and can thus end up in catastrophe.

If we recognize that the fundamental problem of international organization is to avoid these two extremes, we will also have to realize the singular import of the fact that the system of the balance of power in Europe was a conscious realization that the relationship among states could and should be some sort of balance.

No less significant is the parallel realization that the balance of power in Europe must primarily rest on territorial balance. Though in the final count balance is a social-psychological phenomenon, this does not lessen its objective, territorial nature. All situations of social balance have objective conditions, embodying the very essence of balance, trust, and security. In an internal social and legal order, these objective conditions are the trust and security attached to means of evidence, "sacred" and "authentic" places, regulated procedures, and possession. The objective condition on which international balance rests is *state territory*, or, to be more precise, the notion of relative exclusivity associated with it. This is the point on which the permanent fear or relative security of the international community hinges; the value of an international organization depends on its ability to ensure the stability of borders and to resolve territorial disputes. For the time being, no close international cooperation has altered the decisive significance of borders. Indeed, all international cooperation, whether loose or close, means, in the final count, the provision of some sort of guarantees for territorial stability, or it fails or succeeds in stabilizing territory, frontiers. This is why it is difficult to bring into international political organizations states that feel they have no territories to lose, and thus nothing to protect, nothing for which to be concerned. Conversely, this is why it is difficult to bring states into international political organizations that are based on the significant modifiability of territorial stock. Hence the insurmountable resistance to subjecting "political" disputes to international arbitration; much ink has been wasted on the definition of "political" dispute, and the notion is only beginning to be broached that "political" dispute is rooted in territorial stock.

This is why the peacemaking efforts of the League of Nations have been so futile; these have turned the complex into an issue of international law and failed to separate critical territorial disputes from the general group of "disputes." Without doing so, however neatly and laudably it has developed international law, the League could not recognize the fundamental problem of international organization and the prevention of war—that it has to provide some guarantee of territorial security for its members, yet that it simultaneously has to be flexible enough to be able to resolve territorial disputes without alarm, anarchy, and war. The way Guglielmo Ferrero put this is that the duty of any conclusion of peace is to draw the consequences of victory and, at the same time, to create a situation in which the loser can loyally acquiesce; this duty is contradictory and unfulfillable if fear has sway but is logical and accomplishable if fear is dispersed. This is the point where territorial compensation becomes meaningful;

it does not mean that population and territorial exchange should be renewed but that any change in the territorial stock of Europe is the shared concern of its entire community and that it must be implemented under joint control, unified principles, after thorough reasoning, in coherent order, and with the preferable omission of threats and fear, with all applicable principles and problems being consciously considered. This notion was first put forward by William III of Orange and England in his negotiations to prevent the war of Spanish succession. Its perfect examples were the Vienna Congress and the Treaty of Paris in 1814, while it was bankrupted in Versailles and Munich.

Being aware of the fact that the balance of power among states is a mental balance in the final count, we must not fall into the fallacy of holding that territorial balance prescribes some sort of quantitative territorial equality or predetermined quantitative proportion for states. Territorial balance means not mere territorial relations, but also the interaction among territory, power relations, and mental states. That two states are quantitatively the same size and equally powerful becomes important if they are afraid of each other for some reason. This is why the *feared* growth of certain nations and the *feared* fall into anarchy of certain countries have been recurrent themes in the concert of Europe. This is why the excessive power of Habsburg Spain and Austria, of France, and of Prussian Germany has recurrently grown into a European problem, while the excessive yet unfeared power of Britain is unlikely to become a difficulty. On the other hand, a fall into anarchy became a Europe-wide problem with the disintegration of the Holy Roman Empire, the Spanish Empire, the Polish Rzeczpospolita, the loss of authority in early nineteenth-century Italy, the decline of the Ottoman Empire, and most recently the Danubian anarchy left after the dissolution of the Habsburg Empire. We will not be able to grasp the neuralgic points of the balance of power in Europe unless we study the combined effects of geopolitical givens or shifts in power relations and politico-psychological changes; even in our day, the critical points in the balance of power in Europe are made up of countries that are marked by a critical geographical situation as well as some sort of deformation in their politico-psychological state.

C) SUMMARY

In what follows, we wish to describe in general the jerks and shocks that have accompanied the progress of the greatest enterprise of Western mankind, democracy. We will then go on to discuss the establishment of modern nation-states, a process that jumbled up the territorial status of Central-East Europe and thus contributed to the grave befuddlement of the political culture, the proliferation and exacerbation of territorial disputes, and the rise of political hysterias in the region. We will dwell on the details of the German hysteria, which has disrupted the balance of power in Europe since 1914, and then discuss the hysterias of the countries around Germany (France, Italy, Poland, Hungary, and Bohemia), which rendered the localization of the German hysteria impossible. Finally, we will examine the concrete factors of how the interaction of these hysterias brought about the collapse of the European balance of power and the outbreak of the current crisis.

2. THE SHOCK OF THE FRENCH REVOLUTION AND THE DISTURBANCES OF EUROPEAN POLITICAL DEVELOPMENT

The crisis tormenting Europe goes back to the fearful jerks of the development from a society of personal rule and birthright privilege to a democratic and classless society. Democracy is the great enterprise of Western civilization. Apart from a few isolated and stalled experiments, the majority of humankind has lived for millennia under social and political systems based on the rule of man over man and the notion that this power could be, and as a rule was, attained by birthright. Western civilization first tamed and supplemented birth-order social structure and then dared go on to draw the secularized consequences of the Christian concept of the inalienable dignity of the human soul—the dignity, freedom, and equality of all people—and to attempt to put into practice the spiritualization of power, self-government, and personality-based selection.

The long-standing institutions of this development meant a preschool for this practice. First among them was the spiritualization of monarchy and aristocracy through the practical school of the chivalric ideal taming domination by calling and sublimating it into service; second came the school of monastic self-discipline and self-government, the ecclesiastic order somewhat independent of sheer domination; and then followed the practical and professional traditions of the order of the intelligentsia, the ability of the Western-style feudal system based on personal relationships, contracts, privileges, and liberties to teach how to live with liberty; the school of parliament turning against monarchy, of the liberties of estates and local autonomy; the arrangements between city and citizens inherited from antiquity; the Christian self-discipline and freedoms of civil life; the autonomy of guilds; the free-peasant lifestyle that survived from archaic times in certain areas of Europe; the schools of Presbyterianism and the Protestant sects; and, finally, the most modern development, trade unions.

These factors came into play in varying degrees in different European countries. The Christian ideal of monarchy spread throughout Europe; chivalry and the relatively independent ecclesiastic order flowered primarily in Catholic

Western Europe; with a focus in France, the independent intellectual class was again widespread throughout the Catholic West; Western-style feudalism was characteristic in France, the Western parts of Germany, and England; atomized by feudalism, a French-German Europe was surrounded by medieval constitutionalism: Aragon, the British Isles, Scandinavia, Poland, Bohemia, and Hungary; city life spread throughout Europe, though at a decreasing rate in an eastern direction; a free peasantry existed throughout Northern Europe and Switzerland and in patches in Central-East Europe and the Balkans; Presbyterianism and sectarian communities spread in the Calvinist countries, England and America; and trade unions spread throughout the continent. Preschooling for democracy had varying degrees of intensity in the different parts of Europe, but there was no corner of the continent where it did not carry weight.

The most daring move of the democratic enterprise was when the French Revolution rejected the deal the medieval church had concluded by putting forward the ideals of a Christian monarch and knight with birthright domination and social organization. In terms of intellectual power, the French Revolution surpassed all other revolutionary phases in European social and political development. By striking down on monarchy and aristocracy, which had been tamed yet sanctified by Christianity, it *ad oculos* showed that the world would not end with the dethroning of the old idols that no longer had any authority and thus freed European political and social development from many deadweights—hence the vast outpouring of creativity in the nineteenth century. As opposed to the English and Russian revolutions, the French Revolution was uncontrolled; not only its leaders but also those taking over from them let the reins slip through their fingers, and thus, instead of leading through a coherent scheme of political education, it pushed both its active participants and its passive sufferers into a vortex of insecurity and hapless frenzy. The hysterical fear to which this gave rise was what European mankind has not been able overcome ever since; apart from England, Europe has not been able to embark on a policy of reform in a calm spirit of unbiased courage. This state of fear and shock unleashed the rampant and romantic political mentalities responsible for the imbalances of European politics.

The French Revolution inflicted a mortal wound on European monarchy and aristocracy, which had been not only putrefied institutions, but also living and practical institutions of community leadership, responsibility, assessment, development, and inter-community relationships. In the void suddenly left behind them, the community mind developed new, fearful, and rampant formations.

The internal collapse of the prestige and authority of monarchy confused the established habits of political leadership. As it stood at the breakout of the French Revolution, monarchy had been the result of a two-thousand-year-old process of civilization with powerful roots in the political traditions of Roman republican emperorship and with mediaeval Christianity transforming the sheer power wielding of adventurers and despots into a regular human vocation undergirded by rights and obligations, roles and duties, professional ethics and convention. In varying degrees, this meant that European monarchy was not the exercise of plain and raw personal rule but a more or less spiritualized and depersonalized version of it. There is a direct line of development leading from the Christian prince, the enlightened ruler, and the constitutional monarch to the non-personal head of state. This development was radically broken in two by the French Revolution and other countries following its lead, and the internal democratic forces of the new republics established overnight did not have the time and opportunity to shape new institutions of political leadership. Innate human humbleness before birthright privilege and personal authority does not cease overnight; a society dropped into the joys of democracy will soon be overcome by topsy-turvy and a lack of leadership. This is what gave rise to the most dubious traditions of the French Revolution, the romanticism of the great man, the political genius; it established the pseudo-image of the monarch or the image of the *pseudo-monarch* in the person of Napoleon, for whom wielding power was not a vocation and a series of roles but a romantic, heroic, and spectacular individual enterprise. Now, beyond not squaring with the ideal of democracy, it was a major backslide from monarchy because it subjected the community not to spiritualized but to raw personal rule. Luckily for Europe, European dynasties did not take cognizance of this until the end of the nineteenth century but more or less continued to live up to the standards of rulerly correctness that had been established for a thousand years. It was only at the end of the nineteenth century that the most grotesque phenomenon of political development occurred: the born-to-the-throne pseudo-monarch Wilhelm II, who had a romantic concept of himself in spite of his royal lineage. We will come to see what fateful consequences this would have in European political development.

Another consequence of the French Revolution was the intensification and democratization of community feeling, the birth of *modern nationalism*. This is where the otherwise superficial observation that European nationalism was born with the French Revolution has some point. Neither the concept of nation as such nor the emotion it elicits was born in 1789; indeed, it had been born much earlier, even a millennium earlier. The difference is that, prior to 1789, it had been the aristocracy that was the conscious vehicle of this community formation, bearing the related emotions and responsibility with the composedness of possessing and exercising power for several centuries. From the end of the Middle Ages, the intellectual and middle classes, the third estate, had been making their way into the national framework. This penetration, however, took a triumphant form, an overnight taking of possession, during the French Revolution. This experience was what brought about modern national feeling.

Through declaring the freedom of all men, revolutionary democracy—indeed any democracy—puts that freedom into practice in a given community, and this experience rather than lulling in fact enhances and strengthens feelings of attachment to the community even in cases where the revolution was anti-nationalistic, like the Russian Revolution. Two ingredients lend keenness and expansive force to democratic community feeling: first, the third estate, the people, all take possession of what had been the property of kings and nobles, the nation, with all its historical and political prestige and representative and challenging consciousness, but, second, they attribute to it all the warmth and attachment they had for their immediate surroundings. In this union, commoner feelings were more powerful, necessarily due to the essence of democracy; in the final count, democracy is the victory of the lifestyle of the commoner, one who creates with craft, over aristocratic man, who indulges in wielding power and representation. This connection between democracy and nationalism continues to be a living reality in Northern and Western Europe, where no major disturbances and deformations of political consciousness have evolved.

It is a gross misunderstanding of the shaping forces of history to hold that the nation, national feeling, and nationalism are in an *organic* relationship with the interests of the capitalist grande bourgeoisie. People or groups with statically vested interests can never hammer out or become imbued by ideologies or mass emotions; all they do is use them for their own ends—this was how the capitalist grande bourgeoisie became the beneficiary of modern democracy and nationalism. The decisive ideas and emotions of history precede and survive all such interest relations.

Modern national feeling means that the life and conditions, glory or shame, power and decline of the nation, which had in principle been the causes of the king, nobility, or royal administrators, become the personal causes of everyone and thus constitute a mass feeling. This was what brought about the romantic ideal of the *patriot,* a man who is qualified not by his birth, rank, or office but by the keenness and purity of his emotions to be fully alive to the glory of the nation and to care for all its troubles. One grave consequence of this was that patriots lacking political culture and experience put themselves forward for political roles, referring to nothing but the keenness of their emotions, while the political emotions and opinions, for which crowds became the vehicles, for all their unbridledness, subjectivity, and irrationality, had to be reckoned with by all politics.

Another range of ideas related to the intensification of community feeling in the French Revolution was the *romanticism of the people*. The fundamental recognition of European political development was that a mature community governs itself; to put it more precisely, it efficiently controls its leaders. This idea was what led to the romanticism of the perfect, sovereign people; in the wake of the shock of the revolution and the void it created, it turned out that the natural virtuosity that monarchic feeling had attributed to monarchy could be transposed to the new sovereign, the people. It is particularly oppressed people, those who have risen up under oppression, who possess the miraculous ability to settle the problems of the community well and justly. It is a psychological commonplace that the exact opposite of this is true: rebellion against oppression elicits an emotional disposition that obstructs an unbiased condition of virtuosity from being conceived; a people is able to govern itself insofar as it has acquired political culture. However, the romantic belief in the virtuosity of the people could become a means of political morals becoming more earnest and the spread of political culture, where acquiring political culture had clear prospects and where major shocks did not derail it.

A further alarming heritage of the shock of the French Revolution was the romanticism of *revolutionary* social change. The beneficial effects of the vast purifying tempest of the French Revolution are inextricably interwoven in the historical memory of European mankind with barricade fights, plots, the guillotine, the Committee of Public Safety, and the people flocking in the streets who now terrified the former mighty. These accidents of the chaos of the French Revolution turned into romantic patterns and norms, and these were what the front-line men of the revolutions of the following century regarded the most important. This empty romanticism and its contrary, excessive fear, prompted people to be concerned not for the conditions of society, the changes needed and the vision of their future society, but how to take their stance on the romanticist historical opportunity of "revolution." This gave rise to two types of man, the revolutionary and the reactionary, for whom the most important question is not what changes are needed in social order but that, whatever happens, revolution or *no* revolution must take place. Both types are *ab ovo* unproductive; a reasonable and courageous mind would find it equally possible to safeguard tradition in the face of a barbarian and visionless revolution or, footing the bill, to take sides with liberating revolution against a rigid organization of power that has entangled itself in lies and is unable to develop. Radical socialism and communism then went on to rationalize revolutionary romanticism and built up a system of revolutionary tactics and underground organizational techniques. Thus, apart from Russia, where the total failure and ineptitude of the czarist government drove the best minds to the side of the revolution, the Communist parties in Europe became the collecting stations of unproductive minds interested in change and revolution for its own sake.

The loosening of the political and moral forces of monarchy and aristocracy had the gravest consequences in the relations among nations. The actual organs of international relations had been monarchy and aristocracy until 1789 and between 1814 and 1914. Rooted in the Christian theory of state and modern natural law, their political culture established the refined forms and customs of European diplomacy, as well as the system of the balance of power in Europe as a means of maintaining peace in Europe, which Guglielmo Ferrero so masterfully described in *The Gamble: Bonaparte in Italy* and *Reconstruction of Europe*. The eighteenth-century concept of war without passion also belonged here, a concept that regarded war not as a leap into catastrophe but as an apt means of resolving disputes, as something to be fought with as little passion as possible and only until one opponent is ready to yield to the other, who is not to increase his original demands as the fortunes of war favor him. The system of territorial compensation also belongs here; though seen as cynical dealings among peoples and nations today, it was, in fact, a profoundly civilized and successful method of avoiding war. Its fundamental principle, which holds true today as ever, was that all changes in the stock of European territories must be consciously recorded, reviewed, and implemented in a coherent system. Parallel to these, we had the life- and material-sparing type of war of the eighteenth century that sought to limit war to armies, military stores, and battlefields—so much so that cultural and scholarly relations were uninterrupted between countries at war.

This culture of international relations started to fall apart the moment the forces of democratic nationalism had their say in foreign policy. Not that community feelings made more intense by democracy were any more aggressive toward neighboring communities. Quite to the contrary, democratic nationalism, the enthusiastic taking possession of the nation by its community, tended to stop on the border with neighboring nations, dynastic conquest being alien to it. Precisely because it was the victory of the commoner over the aristocrat, democracy could not accept the sending of thousands to war to "settle a dispute" but regarded it as wholly evil, and its culprits had to be found out and punished. It could imagine only a just war of defense against a conqueror or an uprising of the people against a tyrant. In characteristic democratic fashion, this then put war into the arsenal of highly tense community moral feelings. This in turn had a beneficial effect on matters of war being taken more seriously but also the adverse effect of whipping up emotions it could not control. War remained a necessary means in an unorganized system of European states. From this time on, to start a war, intense fears of threat and attack had to be aroused where there had been none such. Now, this had a particular reality in one of the direst consequences of the French Revolution, born out of fear: general conscription.

The French Revolution, Napoleonic warfare and its later development, today's total warfare, conceived of war as the effort of entire nations, radically changing the social effects of war. As Edward Jenner's cow had carried smallpox, so had Europe waged war for a thousand years; it adapted to it, only soldiers and people living in the theaters of war being afflicted, and the day-to-day life of the majority was left unaffected. It was in 1792 that Europe first experienced the kind of war in which peasants, artisans, and tradesmen were dragged away from their otherwise peaceable labors, put in uniforms, and marched into bloody battle and which, like a raging epidemic, attacked the entire body of society, turned its customary life inside out, and shook its very foundations.

In these surges of suffering and fear, hatred and justice seeking, with which such wars fill souls, the traditional dispassionate peacemaking methods of monarchy and aristocracy were relegated to the background. For all our trust that democracy has more and better to say on matters of war and peace than monarchy and aristocracy, we must concede: the situation today is that a democratic makeup is expressly adverse from the point of view of overcoming the psychological aftereffects of war. To no avail is democracy more keen on condemning war than monarchy and aristocracy; to no avail does it ground itself in world peace if it cannot finish a war without the conflict leading to another one. The statesmen leading victorious democracies seldom have the authority to be fearlessly open, courageous, magnanimous, and trustful in advance, qualities that are required by any good peacemaking. Instead, peacemaking has come to mean that the statesman at the level of domestic politics obtains satisfaction for the justice-seeking passion accumulated in the people of the victorious nation. This necessarily precludes the foreign-policy aim of peacemaking, that of "settling" a dispute. The democratic makeup of the losing side, by virtue of the fickleness of public opinion, cannot be trusted for its word without guarantees providing means of control. Now, this control is precisely what renders the final closing of the conflict impossible.

After Napoleon, the Treaty of Frankfurt was the first European peace whereby the European tradition of dispassionate peacemaking was disregarded in the spirit and name of "national" requirements. With the Treaty of Versailles, even the trappings of peacemaking were cast aside, and small-mindedness ran riot. What we are now going to have is an open question; it is often said the mistakes of the past are not to be repeated. The lessons of the past have a double edge; apart from objective and reasonable lessons, lessons can be drawn at will — lessons conceived in passion.

Born of democratic revolution, the romanticism of the great man, the patriot, the people, the revolution, and the war of the people have led all the countries of Europe to the brink of disaster, from where only those can hark back whose democratic political culture and training have matched the advance of democratic mass feeling. Why this did not develop in Central-East Europe is what we will seek to answer in what follows.

CHAPTER II: THE GERMAN HYSTERIA[1]

THE CRUX OF PEACE

The most burning political issue of our day is what is to be done with Germany. The officials concerned behave as though they were perfectly knowledgeable about their task; however, the world public is justified in suspecting that the plans are unfounded and misconceived. To the best of my knowledge, two elements of the official plans have been disclosed to date: an independent Austria and compensation for Poland by eastern German territories. Neither of the schemes reveals any understanding of the heart of the German matter. Yet two-thirds of the success or failure of a future peace depends on solving the German problem and one-third on solving those of the small countries between Germany and Russia. Its crux, whether the English-speaking nations and Soviet Russia can come to an agreement or clash, turns not on the socialization of capitalism, not on Soviet embourgeoisement, not on the Dardanelles, not on oil in the Middle East, not on India, not on Manchuria, but on whether or not Germany and the small countries east of it become territories of anarchy and failed political authority. This assertion might sound oddly unequivocal. However, current political thought is misguided by certain false global scales deeming that the problems of Central-East Europe are just one of the complex issues beside the equally thorny matters of the Middle East, the Far East, and the Western Hemisphere. But if we consider the fact that the problems of Central and Eastern Europe differ from all the other quagmires of world politics only in that it is now the second world war that has broken out for a lack of stability in this region within a matter of but thirty years, we will certainly give credence to the statement that a third world war, if it should occur, would undoubtedly break out from nowhere else but here.

What is to be done with Germany hinges wholly on what we deem to be the reason for all the troubles that have surged out of Germany onto the world.

THE MYTH OF A GOOD AND AN EVIL GERMANY

Two mutually exclusive commonplaces have crystallized in the current public mind. According to one, the Germans are by nature or at least very old conditioning an aggressive, barbarian, power-worshipping, herd-minded lot; being slaves of a hazy metaphysic, they took up neither the Roman nor the Christian civilization; and their history, from Arminius through Barbarossa, Frederick the Great, Bismarck, Wilhelm II, and all the way to Hitler has been but a constant war on the rest of Europe. In their political and social organization, they have been unable to implement the European forms of democracy and socialist progress; they are as a rule unable to rid themselves of the rule of tyrannical princes, feudal landlords, and military cliques. From Medieval German mystics through Luther, Hegel, Nietzsche, Wagner, and Treitschke to Rosenberg, their thought has been a protracted rebellion against Latin lucidity and Christian humanism. Their scholarship is but punctiliousness lacking all genius; moreover, nothing stops them from putting their learning in the service of even the most vicious intent. From time to time, they broadcast pernicious monstrosities around the world, such as the Lutheran Reformation, Prussian militarism, the Wilhelmine power cult, and the Hitlerite myth of race and violence.

Whatever reasons their inherent vice is traced back to—their racial characteristics, the feudal structure of German society, the violence of the German propertied classes, the reactionary and nationalist German educational system—it is regarded as obviously most perilous to give them freedom as it would further aggravate their evils and facilitate their organizing of newer and newer attacks. All plans based on the supposition of a deep-seated German wickedness seek to lay down stringent terms for peace and fetter German independence. We hear voices calling for long-term occupation, efficient control, and interference with matters of education. Even the most moderate approach deems it natural that Germany be allowed greater freedom in its own affairs only if it is able to *guarantee* that it will improve and change.

The contrary opinion holds that the Germans are fundamentally good and sophisticated. They are a people of poets and thinkers and a pillar, together with the French, the British, and the Italians, of the thousand-year-old European civilization. Their country has been a stronghold of European scholarship; it gave Bach, Handel, Beethoven, Leibniz, Kant, Goethe, and Humboldt to the world. Seminal minds of liberalism and socialism came from among its ranks. The German socialist revolution unfolding at the turn of the century would have set an example to the whole of Europe had the Great War not thwarted its development and the Treaty of Versailles not driven it into an impasse. It was only the foolishness and callousness of the treaty that deformed the political mentality of Germans and made them passively accept and tolerate the terror of the Hitlerite armed minority. If this is the case, all that is needed is a peace with mild conditions and that the country be put under the authority of progressive and democratic-minded Germans.

As in the case of most such either-or schemes, the issue is hopelessly misapprehended, and the resulting concepts are gravely mistaken.

IS THE GERMAN HYSTERIA A MATTER OF TEMPERAMENT OR HISTORY?

The idea of the intrinsic corruption of Germans is naively unhistorical. The organic and uninterrupted line purportedly extending between Arminius and Hitler and the German mystics and Rosenberg is neither organic nor continuous. Arminius was not a whit more or less against civilization than any other Germanic, Celtic, Slavic, Hun, or Arab tribal chief ruling in the neighborhood of the Roman limes. German haziness is not any greater than the Norse; nevertheless, the Norse have not the slightest intention of revolting cut-and-thrust against Europe. It would be difficult to argue that the Lutheran Reformation—hardly "hazy" indeed—was a revolt against Europe, Latin order, and lucidity while the far more radical Calvinist one was not. It would be reasonable to say that the Calvinist Reformation had more Latin elements than the Lutheran one, but it would be hard to understand how the Lutheran Reformation could have reinforced individualism and thus prepared the way for democracy in Scandinavia (much like Calvinism in Western Europe) while it was the precursor of the revolt of barbarism, paganism, slavery, and power worship in Germany. Hitlerish utterances can be quoted from any German medieval thinker or Luther himself, as they probably can be from the past literature of all other peoples; a future German dissertationist will no doubt track them down. Funnily enough, the Nazis themselves have gone out of their way to espouse this whole philosophy of history spanning Arminius, Luther, and Hitler, merely reversing the signs; in their opinion, German history is the everlasting struggle of the superior, culture-creating northern race against Mediterranean anarchy, Latin rationalism, oriental Judaism, and unwarlike Christianity. The only blemish on this philosophy of history is that the more purely northerly Scandinavians and English want to have nothing do with it.

The intrinsic trouble with such historical perspectives is that they are subsequently contrived or sought out for the purposes of interpretation of a given historical situation. Imagine someone expounding in 1750 the theory of everlasting German revolt against Europe—the whole idea would seem mere balderdash. Think of saying in 1792, 1830, or 1848 that the Germans were disposed to political hysteria more than the French—it would be pointless even arguing how untruthful this would have been. As all national temperaments, the German one also has its own recurrent keynotes. This is not to say that the inclination to brutality, fury, dogmatism, and metaphysical speculation was not part of the German character. No doubt German political development and the current deformation of German values have their roots in both the German past and the German temperament; surely, no *similar* historical fate would have given rise to *such* reactions in other peoples. But this holds for all the good and bad turns in the histories of all nations. The question is not whether the inclination to violence, savagery, dogmatism, and hazy metaphysics is a constant German trait because Germans are not the only violent, savage, herd-minded, stiff-necked, and murky people in the world; rather the question is whether the will to not partake of European development, to not accept the fundamental principles of European community life and the aggressive defiance of European ideals are constant factors in them or not. In other words, are they constantly marked by a hysterical attitude to the community of Europe? For now they certainly are, but that this has been one of their characteristic features can be credibly said only of the period after 1871.

On the other hand, it would be utterly naive to surmise that if the present rage of the Germans is the consequence not of any of their temperamental givens but of historically traceable factors, then, as from a magic top hat, the dove of a "good" Germany can be conjured up from "oppressed" groups in German society or certain German territories. It is a gross misunderstanding of community hysterias to believe that Hitlerism is something founded on the "Hitlerite"—that particularly corrupt type of man. It would be perfectly futile to calculate the proportion of Junker, petty bourgeois, northern or Alpine Germans among Hitlerites and try to draw far-reaching conclusions from such an exercise. The ascendance of Hitlerism was caused not by the totality of Hitlerites but, to at least an equal degree, the ineptness of the anti-Hitlerites and all the many falsities and impasses that enabled Hitlerism to be a cause and symbol for all Germans. It would be pointless therefore to even think of what percentage of the Germans are Hitlerites and how the good can be separated and differentiated from the bad. The question is whence this pathological development of German community life originates and from which point it started out.

It is therefore wholly mistaken to attribute the deformation of German political mentality wholly to the Treaty of Versailles. No doubt, the treaty was traumatic for the political development of the German nation, and without it Hitlerism as we know it could hardly have taken shape. But it is likewise indubitable that it came into being not *merely* as a result of the treaty and that Prussian militarism and the Wilhelmine power cult are both precursors of National Socialism.

The question is immediately sidetracked when the way it is put is whether the Germans' going berserk derives from Versailles as a *historical* factor or is a feature of their *temperament*, inherent to them from the beginning. We have little doubt as to the historical origin of the deformation of German political mentality, but its historical antecedents date back much earlier than Versailles. Most of those disputing the historical rootedness of the German befuddlement tend to stop at Versailles. In reaction, those who still remember the aggression and power worship of Wilhelmine Germany will go beyond Versailles and not stop until poor old Arminius. The likes of Robert Vansittart had their direct experiences of eternal German violence in Wilhelmine Germany. It was the same personal experience that led William Brown to argue that the power frenzy of Hitler's Germany was an outcome not of any inferiority complex but a paranoid psychic condition, an excessive feel for real power, for it had been present in a powerful Wilhelmine Germany no Versailles had ever humiliated. Consequently, the German power craze is going to reappear whenever Germany attains a certain degree of power. It must therefore be prevented from doing so.

The correct answer to the question is that the distortion of the German political psyche has *historical* roots; it derives from concrete factors, unfortunate historical antecedents, and it can be cured through fortuitous changes. Those unfortunate antecedents, however, were shaped not in Versailles but several centuries earlier. Our purpose is therefore to show the historical precursors of the unhinging of the German political mind from the moment they took a decisively harmful and dangerous turn at the beginning of the nineteenth century.

THE PRIMACY OF POLITICS

In what follows, we shall consciously counter the approach that sees economic forces and interests behind this war and wars in general and presents them as by-products of the processes of economic development.

Economic factors no doubt influence the purport, the turns, the means and the course, and even the outcomes of wars. In the final count, however, these are but accessory reasons and interests, not primary causes. The political fears, perceptions of instability, and emotions that lead to the loss of political balance are beyond the point where it is possible for economic interests to "stir up" belligerence, "fund" movements, or "plot" war; moreover, they overstep the limits within which long-term economic tendencies or economic crises and depressions in themselves can cause political developments. The commonplace that conflicts of economic interest cause wars to break out is worth as much as saying that a war in particular or wars generally are the fruit of *sin;* it is true but hardly enough for those who seek to understand and help. Like Karl Marx, who exposed the economic factors behind politics, it would be timely to expose politics and its mass-psychological effects behind the now overemphasized economic factors and particularly to uncover the racking and chaotic process of establishing modern nations, which has been the chronic cause of Central-East European disarray and thereby the overturn of the European balance of power since 1789.

Our attribution to politics of effects that deform the mental habits of whole peoples might seem surprising, especially when it is widely believed that people throughout the world are apolitical, even anti-political. But the politics we have in mind has little to do with what men usually associate with the term "politician" and what they are usually indifferent or hostile to, but with the matters and situation of the "polis," the community, and how they relate to individuals. And the vast majority of people are keenly interested in these matters. They have been particularly interested in them since the turn of the eighteenth and nineteenth centuries—that is, since the emergence of the modern sense of community, when the attitude to the body politic and the nature, functioning, and prestige of the state itself became, in principle, a shared and personal affair for everyone. This fundamental and emotional democratization of the relationship to the community, not necessarily implying democracy, swept over all Europe. Hence the situation in modern times, when the affairs of national communities gave rise to various community hysterias, which had a definitive role in the fateful overturn of the balance of European power and among which that of the German nation stands out for its severity.

We therefore have to be clear about the nature of political hysteria. The platitudes used to describe the feverish phenomena of our times waver between two extremes, starting out from either a naive rationalism doggedly wanting to discover soundly calculating interests behind even the wildest of political movements or a naive emotionalism that attributes political changes to the unpredictable waves of crowd emotion and that sees any attempt at rationally understanding them as a futile exercise. This is another of those fruitless alternatives we need to surpass. The rule of reason over passions is a requirement humankind cannot waive for the sake of any irrational impulse if it does not want to renounce the results of its development. But the primacy of reason does not imply that we see rational interest where passion is decisive, that we act as though there were no passions involved, and that we assume that passions should have no role in a properly organized community. The great rationalists of the world were great in that they never gave up tracing effects back to their own causes even in the thorny world of human emotions and affections. It is in this respect that we seek to follow in their footsteps.

THE NATURE OF POLITICAL HYSTERIA

A decisive and fateful change took place in the transformations of the political psyche in Europe at the end of the eighteenth century. From that moment in time the slow pace of European development shifted to a fast, eruptive, and feverish mode that has, at certain points, gone dangerously awry. The vehicles of European political culture up to this time—the monarchy and aristocracy—partly unexpectedly, partly gradually lost their authority, parallel to which community feelings greatly intensified and seized the masses. The most significant manifestation of this is the rise of modern nationalism. This introduced a new, fearful phenomenon among the factors of European political development: states of mind much like individual neuroses and hysteria have appeared in the lives of whole nations and have acquired decisive political significance.

In the following, we shall use the expressions "political hysteria" and "community hysteria."[2] In psychology, the word "hysteria" stands for a variety of disputed phenomena, each of which can be called and discussed separately as "hysteria." It would be meaningless, however, to dub all political emotions and affections more vehement or heated than average that accompany the democratization of community feeling (not necessarily democracy itself!) community hysterias. We would be more justified in deeming as hysterical Guglielmo Ferrero's protracted conditions of fear that occur in the wake of major historical shocks to communities, such as the demise of political authority, revolution, foreign invasion, military defeat, and that are manifest in the constant dread of conspiracies, revolts, attacks, alliances, and the raging persecution of presumed or actual political enemies. Real community hysteria occurs when all its characteristic symptoms are present together: an entire community's loss of touch with reality, an inability to resolve the problems life creates, an insecure yet overblown self-assessment, and an unrealistic and disproportionate response to the impacts of the outer world.

It would be a mistake, I believe, to infer the "mental disturbances" of a community from individual psychic disturbances and simply identify them with the sum of individual psychic disturbances and with the effects of certain mentally disturbed individuals and the various types of mass hysteria. And, however captivating it might seem, the analysis of hysterical members or leaders of a community would not seem to me to be fruitful when we want to know more about community hysteria. On the other hand, we should steer clear of all community metaphysics that ascribe certain "mindsets" or "mental disturbances" to a given community.

Community hysteria is made up of the combined effects of *individual* psychic states, but alone, these individual states are not necessarily hysterical, as community hysterias often run their course through several generations; the difference is the people who go through the initial experiences, shape the false depiction of the state of the community, and manifest the hysterical responses of the community. For those who shape the hysterical manifestations of their community, whether by direct political action, approval, or mere acquiescence, taking a common political stand often engages only one area of their mental world; moreover, they themselves may personally be of sound mind and spirit, very appealing even; and whatever they do, profess, or think in the name of their community may seem perfectly reasonable, practical, or inevitable under the given conditions. The sum of these manifestations, non-hysterical in themselves, nevertheless results in a community relation to reality, to its interests, tasks, and environment, that is analogous to the situation and responses of a hysterical person. This is why it is vain and pointless to attribute community hysterias to certain mentally damaged individuals or groups, social classes, and followers of political creeds; to try to figure out what proportion they represent in the entire community; and to consider ways of debarring them from the community.

Naturally, community hysterias generate their blind, furious, and obtuse type of man, primarily prone to falling for and ranting their characteristic self-deceiving follies; their beneficiaries, who swim with the hysteric tide and profit by it; as well as their gangsters and henchmen. A variety of reasons may dispose members of certain groups, natives of certain areas, and so on to number proportionately higher among them. Plans seeking to cure hysteria by destroying, isolating, or casting out its carriers, grouped on whatever basis, will not help at all. Community hysteria is the condition of the community as a whole, and there is no use in eliminating the visible carriers of hysteria when its conditions and grounds remain untouched, its initial traumas are unrelieved, and the make-believe situation on which it is actually founded is unresolved. There is no use in eliminating all "evil" men; the delusions and false responses of hysteria will live on in peaceful patresfamilias; in mothers of six; in clear-headed persons who would not hurt a fly; in noble, lofty, exalted minds; and the community will bring forth the madmen, the beneficiaries and thugs of hysteria, in a generation.

Political hysteria always starts out from a *traumatic historical experience* in the life a community, particularly one the members of the community believe to be intolerable and think the solution to the problems to which it gave rise is beyond the abilities of their community. Much like a healthy individual, a community capable of putting its abilities to good and safe use, however great or small, is strengthened when encountering catastrophe because it makes a reasonable assessment of the causes of its troubles, draws lessons from them, bears what it deems elemental calamity, assumes the moral responsibility it recognizes as its own fault, finds redress for the injustices committed against it, resigns itself to what cannot be undone, renounces dreams impossible to attain, and defines and performs its duties. For all its vehement or feverish reactions, a balanced community will thus finally solve its problems; in other words, it will not fall into hysteria because hysteria per se means shunning the problem. This is why the French and the Russian revolutions cannot fully be regarded as hysterias, however vehement the traumas they involved, however severe the excesses of political development they might have fired up, and however much they demonstrate elements of hysteria. The community problems at the heart of both the French and the Russian revolutions (the establishment of community life based not on personal rule and on that of a classless society respectively) were after all *resolved* by those communities. The French Revolution, which essentially lasted from 1789 to the Dreyfus affair, bore the marks of hysteria especially in its first period (1789–1814); and the French Revolution especially, but also the Russian, acquired hysterical symptoms in foreign relations. However, the classical area in which almost chronic hysterias have defined the entirety of political life is Central-East Europe.

There are many reasons why a trauma might surpass the ability of a community to endure: the trauma might be unexpected and enormous; the sufferings it causes might feel undeserved, unjust, and disproportionate; the problems it engenders might be too severe; the community might have an uncomprehending, adolescent mentality and have prior, misleading experiences that breed high hopes and unfounded optimism; and so on. As a result of such an exceedingly great trauma, the political thinking, emotions, and intentions of a community become obdurate and paralyzed; the memory of the trauma, the lessons drawn from it for good or ill, and the desire that the community be fully guaranteed that the catastrophe will not be repeated predominate. Thought, feeling, and activity are thus morbidly *attached* to one interpretation of a single experience. In this petrified and lame state, pressing problems become irresolvable if in some way they have a bearing on the critical issue. The community, like an individual, will not be able or have the courage to admit this. So it escapes into a make-believe solution, the illusion of solution, and hatches a formula or compromise to reconcile the irreconcilable, carefully skirting the forces impeding solution, the forces it would have to face up to in order to solve the problem. These are the situations when a nation behaves as though it were unified while it is not, as though it were independent while it is not, as though it were democratic while it is not, and as though it were involved in revolution while it is only languishing.

A community living in such a false situation develops an increasingly crooked relation to reality; when turning to new problems as they arise, it starts out not from the givens and the potentials but from what it imagines itself to be or wants to be. It thus gradually loses its ability to find the causes of its troubles and failures in the normal chain of cause and effect, and it concocts explanations for all its problems, which are obviously false in the eye of common sense and in fact, but which enable the community to perpetuate the falsity of the situation in which it lives.

That a community living in falsity does not "face up to" something does not mean that the issue in question was not noticed or spoken about by many. It means that the public mind or governing opinion of the community fosters a rhetoric whereby embarrassing observations can be brushed aside or rebuffed. The worldview of hysteria is closed and perfect: it can explain and justify everything; whatever it describes and prescribes perfectly squares with everything else. Everything tallies with everything in it. There is only one thing amiss. Everything concurs in it not because it corresponds to genuine values and actual facts but because it systematizes the requirements of the false situation and says precisely what the one living in falsity wants to hear. In the life of communities, this false situation and false worldview slowly engender a long-lasting contra-selection: it pushes to prominence men of false compromise; masters of formulas reconciling the irreconcilable; phony realists behind whose realism there is but aggression, cunning, or pigheadedness; as well as those whose individual hysteria is echoed by that of the community, while, on the other hand, it renders those with a clear view and judgment of the situation unproductive because their alarm signals have fallen on the deaf ears of the closed and smug worldview of hysteria.

Hysterical communities foment the inclination to false self-assessment: with never admitted reverence, they sneer at the performance of vigorous communities capable of facing up to the tasks before them, while they rejoice in hearing exaltations of themselves—preferably at the expense of reality. The well-known symptoms of the discrepancies between desires and reality also show up: the abuse of power and inferiority complexes, wanting to live off entitlements and the diminution of genuine accomplishment, the excessive reverence of mere success, the pursuit of great amends, and the belief in the magic power of speaking of nonexistent things—that is, propaganda. The more failures the community meets in this way, the less it will be able to make good use of the lessons drawn from them; this is the point where the *false and disproportionate response* to the influence of the outer world comes in. The hysteric will always find someone or something on which to cast the blame and exonerate himself from responsibility; he populates the world around him with bogies—much in the way primitive man endows the natural calamities that befall him with intention and attributes the events he cannot explain by his experience to magic forces and wicked spirits. The senselessness of the magic explanation is glaringly obvious for those who see the genuine causes and who have no part in the fear behind the magic explanation, but sound arguments leave the sufferer cold. In this respect, the hysterical individual and community behave like the primitive, except that the latter is *unable* to understand the genuine causes, while the hysteric has no *intention* of doing so.

In due course, the hysteric concentrates all his efforts on overwhelming the magic forces that are threatening through some sort of counter-magic, and he will gradually make the resolution of all the pending issues of his life hinge on the amends he intends to achieve through the counter-magic. Sooner or later, he will apply the unreal worldview he constructed in his relation to the world around him, localize his bogies somewhere in the real world, and attack his environment so fervently in his exasperation and cruelty, conceived in fear, that he will arouse the very harmful and destructive impulses and intents that he suspected. Should that environment decide to make amends, the hysteric will regard it as a justification of his own worldview, and he will lose restraint the moment the longed-for amends are offered. He will no longer be satisfied by any compensation, and his exceeding moral complacency and bullying will challenge his environment to fight. Irrespective of the strength, the number of soldiers, and the amount of supplies either party may have, the outcome of the clash is never in doubt: the damaged person or community will fail not because of being weaker than his or its environment but because of his or its false relation to reality. As the pursuer of amends runs amok, the factors that helped him until his cause had some genuine basis and justification or that he forced or imagined to side with him fall away. In the final count, the individual or community that goes berserk runs his or its head against a wall of facts harder than any magic, spell, or illusion. After the catastrophe comes awakening or recovery or, in a worse case, a newer, more severe bout of hysteria.

THE ROOTS OF THE GERMAN HYSTERIA:
THE FIVE GREAT IMPASSES OF GERMAN HISTORY

A series of such hysterias have been at the heart of the overturn of the European balance of power in modern times. It was the *foreign-policy hysteria of the French Revolution* that set off the series. It had begun with the great shock of the fall of the French monarchy; then it conjured up the satanic image of the anti-revolutionary coalition of emigrants and European monarchies and plunged into the monstrosities of the Terror; to defend itself it hatched, squaring the circle, the Napoleonic revolutionary dictatorship; it attained its great success and justification in the treaties of Amiens and Lunéville; by its aggressive policy between 1801 and 1804, it lost restraint; on this basis, it hammered out its phantasmagoria of a European empire; with the Spanish campaign, it started on the downward path and met with catastrophe in 1812.

As an offshoot, the *Prussian hysteria* came into being. This had commenced with the defeat at Jena; it thought up the satanic, hereditary foe, the French *Erbfeind*; to defend itself, it established Prussian militarism; it obtained amends at Königgrätz and Sedan, lost restraint with the Treaty of Frankfurt, engrossed itself in a foolish self-adulation and sham romanticism in Wilhelmine Germany, and begat catastrophe in 1914. As its counterpart, the *dread hysteria of the French* evolved. Not linked to any internal disturbance, it ran its course at the of level foreign policy only. This had originated in the defeat of 1870–1871; it drew up the satanic image of Prussianism; to defend itself, it brought together the Entente alliance, obtained amends in 1918, lost restraint in Versailles, escaped into the illusion of French hegemony after 1919, and ended up in catastrophe in 1940.

The *hysteria of post-Versailles Germany* reached a gravity in both depth and rapidity far greater than any in the series. It suffered its great damage in the Treaty of Versailles; it drew a satanic image of democracy and the Jews pulling all the strings of capitalism and communism; out of pathological self-defense, it molded the Hitlerite worldview and revolution, obtained its magnificent amends with the *Anschluss* and Munich, lost restraint when occupying Prague, and was already on the downward path when starting World War II; its doom is taking place before our very eyes.

In this series, the Wilhelmine and the Hitlerite hysterias make up an organic whole: the catastrophe of 1918–1919 was the conclusion of the one and the beginning of the other. We shall therefore have to begin our discussion of the German hysteria at the cradle of Prussian Wilhelminism—that is, the dissolution of the Holy Roman Empire in 1806 and the disaster this unleashed on Prussia. Hysterias usually have two phases: the first one is a deadlocking crisis that the community concerned cannot overcome and thus opts for a pseudo-solution; the second is the impasse of the pseudo-solution, bringing catastrophe. As the German series of hysterias was started off by a catastrophe, a political impasse, though not a hysterical situation that resulted from the anarchy of the Holy Roman Empire, German history in the modern era can be described as a sequence of five political impasses—namely, the Holy Roman Empire, the German Confederation, the Wilhelmine German Empire, the Weimar Republic, and the Hitlerite Third Reich. That the Holy Roman Empire, the German Confederation, and the Weimar Republic were impasses is a commonplace. That Hitler's Third Reich, appearing in the guise of dynamism and political upturn, bore the germs of disaster from the outset is now professed, in hindsight, by people who failed to anticipate it. That the Wilhelmine German Empire, purportedly born of German national unity and a rise in power, was characterized by political paralysis and torpor has been recognized by only a few. This is the recognition I wish to enlarge upon in the following because I believe this is where we can dig to the root of the current calamity, and, starting out from this point, we can dispel the legend of both the evil and the good Germany.

THE IMPASSE OF THE HOLY ROMAN EMPIRE

The Great Deadweight of German History:
The Territorial Principalities

The German state has been a reality of European political structure since the middle of the ninth century. This was when, following the Treaty of Verdun, the area of the German tribes was established as the Kingdom of the Eastern Franks under Louis the German. In a century's time, after the Carolingian dynasty died out, the German nation was already a lively entity as the nobility of the four tribes (the Franks, Swabians, Saxons, and Bavarians), which the iron hand of Charlemagne had drawn together, now assembled of their own accord to elect a "German" king. In the ensuing centuries, Germany, like the other countries of Western Europe, lived in the organized anarchy of feudalism, where unity, as in France, was maintained by a dynasty surviving in the female line and the prestige of royal rule. However, while the French monarchy gradually broke down the power of the great lieges and thus set out on the road to modern statehood, the German kings, hankering after the chimera of the imperial crown, let the great landlords become increasingly all-powerful rulers of their own territories and seek to develop their estates into "states" from the beginning of the modern age.

This system of territorial principalities was the gravest drawback in German political development because it meant that an alliance of the monarchy and the commoners, so significant in French political progress, if it could be forged at all, would not carry weight. From the outset, birthright selection acquired much greater importance in Germany than in the Western and Mediterranean territories of Europe that had been atomized and rationalized by the Roman Empire, and the principality system bound the whole nation in the fetters of a hyper-aristocratic social order. Nowhere in Europe did the overbearing power of the aristocracy weigh down on the confidence and consciousness of the average man, nowhere was it so constant, keen, and die-hard as in Germany. The principality system also drastically curtailed the concept and personal scope of freedom. Even in the less developed countries east of Germany, the compass of liberty was relatively wider and extended to greater numbers (even though granted through privileges only). In contrast, the increasingly exclusionary Libertas Germanica meant the liberty and absolute power of the princes, and not even the boldest of abstractions could bring it into a common denominator with the freedom of the people.

The Anarchy of the Holy Roman Empire and the
Continuity of the German Nation

For all the anarchy of the Holy Roman Empire and increasing independence of the territorial princes, the German nation did not cease to exist. Though it is widely believed that there had been no nation to speak of under the Holy Roman Empire because it was the French Revolution that would create the national idea, the French Revolution in fact was not the begetter of the nation; what it did was to turn national feeling into crowd emotion. The nation as a characteristic unit of Europe can actually look back to a much longer history. Its rudiments had unfolded as early as the fifth and sixth centuries; most of its elements were in place at the turn of the tenth and eleventh centuries; and a few, though major, nations joined the existing ones in the turmoil of the fifteenth and sixteenth centuries and then the nineteenth and twentieth centuries. Some hold, usually in order to justify unprincipled border changes, that European state boundaries and the related national frameworks have been in a state of continuous flux for the past millennium and a half, and no regularity can be observed in them apart from the effects of power relations. However, in spite of major or minor shifts in state borders, the national framework of Europe has displayed a surprising steadiness. Only it is not effective state power in the current sense that should be meant when using the term "political framework."

The nation had meant a political framework, the kingdom, the land, from the earliest times. In contrast to the effective power of the thousand-handed and thousand-headed feudalism, this was signified by cobweb-thin symbolic relations and titles that could prove to be fearfully powerful and remarkably tenacious forces. Though a royal title was but a title, it did express political unity, and the framework to which it referred was already a unit of shared law, mutual exchange, and intensive and continuous cultural and political interplay, knit together by the strong bonds of an elected dynasty, a nobility with a sense of calling, and a budding sense of community among the commoners and the intelligentsia. By about the fifteenth century, all the ideas had been conceived that have ever since been used to turn national feeling into consciousness: the welfare of the nation as the most important community concern; the tracing and assessment of national characteristics; the rejection of foreign rule; and even esteem for the national language.

By the witness of European history, these nations, once they came into being, never fell apart as a result of the weakness of central authority and the independence of local power; a local unit that increased its independence became a nation only if powerful or enduring political experiences supported its self-esteem and provided a basis for its breaking away from the original unit. In this respect, the territory of the original German nation was affected by the coming into being of three new nations: the Dutch, the Belgian, and the Swiss. Otherwise, the growing independence of the territorial principalities, lacking other political experiences, never led to the breaking up of the German people into several nations. To a certain extent Prussia followed a breakaway course, but for various reasons, the development of the Prussian state tied in with general German development. Much less did such development occur in Austria, for centuries the land of German emperors, who symbolized German unity. Though the German emperor gradually lost of much of his effective power, this did not alter the fact that the German Empire had its own borders, head of state, common institutions, shared law, a consciousness, and a language that Germans shared. Not to mention the fact that the people of the royal free boroughs, the church principalities, and the countless small dukedoms regarded their belonging to the German Empire and their being subjects of the emperor as a living political reality that gave them rank and a name throughout Europe. For a long time, the fragmentation of the German state implied no more than the fact that the power of the great liege lords could not be overcome to the extent that it had been in France. In the eyes of both the world and the Germans, an Austria, Bavaria, Brandenburg, or Palatinate were but provinces of the German kingdom, as the Île-de-France, Normandy, Anjou, or Gascony were parts of France.

It was only with the Peace of Westphalia that the institutionalized political reality of the German Empire became finally nominal; however, the nominal borders of the empire were retained, and, more important, the German nation as a political-psychological reality persisted. We have grown used to reading European history from the maps and attaching import to the colors (red, yellow, etc.) showing the lands of the Habsburgs, the Hohenzollerns, and the Wittelsbachs, and we regard the black line representing the borders of the German Empire as the trace of an antiquity hardly worth our respect, one that actually would deservedly and finally disappear from the maps in 1806. There is hardly anything more foolish than to underestimate the psychological reality of the continued existence of the German nation from the beginning of medieval times only because it had no unified political power behind it. If the Roman Empire as an effective political factor could survive the fall of its actual power structure by a millennium and a half, we have no reason to be surprised that the idea of the German nation, the German monarchy, and the German Empire weathered without impairment the 150 years between the Westphalian settlement and the rise of modern national emotions. If we recognize that feudal bonds, now regarded merely symbolic, had an enormous significance until the French Revolution, we will not belittle the importance of the fact that the Habsburg emperors continued to be crowned heads of the German kingdom.

The Great Shock of 1806

The Holy Roman Empire would have enabled the German nation to live on peaceably for a long time, as its fragmentation never obstructed it from reaching a level of intellectual advance and performance at the end of the eighteenth and the middle of the nineteenth centuries, whereby no contemporary ever doubted its being a great nation. However, its deadlocking and benumbing political situation, the German body politic's utter lack of support, and its total feebleness were made glaringly clear by the monstrous experience of the Napoleonic invasion. The two major German powers, Austria and Prussia, had worked up the beast of a revolutionary France in 1792, but when they met with the frenzy of a people who had risen up and the hell-bent determination of the Napoleonic adventure, they began to confront a new, fearful factor; first they ceded the Rhineland and then had to come to terms with the Rhine Confederation, yielding the small dukedoms of Central and Southern Germany to France. The loss of the Rhine area did not yet fire up any elemental kickback; Schiller peacefully and resignedly broached the matter of two nations, the French and the British, struggling for world dominion, not even bothering to mention that there was another great nation in Europe—one that happened to be his own.

In the wake of the Battle of Austerlitz, the setting up of the Rhine Confederation, the winding up of the Holy Roman Empire, the fall of Prussia, and the coming of half of Germany under direct or indirect French rule meant that a Germany that had been in a state of dormant greatness now fell into palpable smallness and vulnerability. With the power of experience, this fall drove it home to all mindful Germans that it was not enough to be a great nation in mere numbers and culture and that the most impressive manifestation of a great nation was a unified and powerful state authority, *like the one the French had.*

The Strain on the Birth of German Nationalism

This lesson drawn from the catastrophe of 1806 came to be a strain on the German national idea from the outset. Modern national feeling was born of the democratization of emotions concerning the nation. Until 1789, the nobility was the bearer of the nation as a form of community, assuming the related responsibilities and opportunities with the serenity of having possessed and exercised them for hundreds of years. From the end of the Middle Ages, the incorporation into the national framework of the intelligentsia and the commoners, the third estate, had been continually on the agenda. In the French Revolution, however, this incorporation took the shape of a triumphant and immediate taking possession, and this experience forged modern national feeling. Revolutionary democracy, democracy in general, however much it proclaims the liberty of *man,* has always realized this liberty within a community and by taking possession of it. The experience has meant not the abatement but the augmentation of the emotions related to the given community, even when, as in the Russian instance, the revolution was consciously anti-nationalist. This is what makes the extraordinary heat and expansive force of modern national feeling, two kinds of emotion adding up in it: the third estate, the people, take possession of the nation of the kings and nobles, with all its historical and political prestige, its representative and challenging self-assurance; and they endow the country with all those warm and genial affections with which burghers were wont to grace their immediate communities. The feelings of the commoner, the burgher, the bourgeois, were and had to be more powerful because the essence of democracy is the victory of the way of life of the industrious and creative burgher over that of the aristocratic man indulging in power and representation. To our day, this twining of democracy and nationalism has been a vibrant and living reality in Western and Northern Europe, where political consciousness has not undergone disorders and chronic deformations.

For the German nation, like the Italian, the democratization of national feeling brought up not only the issues of taking possession of the nation of kings and nobles. The national framework could not be taken possession of because it first had to be established. The concurrence of the national framework and state power, self-evident in Western Europe, was lacking in Central Europe. Neither the lesser or major German and Italian principalities nor the conglomerate Habsburg Empire proved to be fit for a framework of new nations; it was not Austrian, Bavarian, Prussian, or Sardinian national feeling that enflamed the masses, but German, Italian, Polish, and so on. What was missing in this region was what was so obviously, clearly, definitely, and palpably present in Western Europe: the reality of the nation's own state borders, public administration, unified political culture, developed and habitual economic administration, capital city and intellectual elite, etc. The creation of a modern national framework in these countries called not only for internal political movements and democratization, but also territorial reorganization, changes that would affect the entire system of European states. It is at this point that the democratic content of the nationalisms of Central Europe began to wane. It was not dropped all together—there is no nationalism without it!—but the issues of creating a national framework pushed themselves ahead of it. Now, this gave significance to elements that otherwise had little to do with democratic development. The dynasties—worse, the aristocracies and armies—had a role in establishing the longed-for national unity and thereby obtained the opportunity and right to assert their own concerns and ideals, perhaps even at the expense of democratic ideals.

As a result, from among the two components of national feeling, the noble-military, the aggressive and representative emotions related to power, prevailed over the commoner-civic or civilized, intimate, and peace-loving emotions. It is thus superficial and useless to attribute special significance to the interests of the grande bourgeoisie in the shaping of nationalism and to the interests of the landed aristocracy and the intrigues of military circles in deforming it. People and groups statically steeped in interest will never be able to create and live by any serious ideology; all they can do is take advantage of it. The moneyed upper-middle class was but the first to take advantage of the democratic transformation; the feudal landowners and the military caste then availed themselves of the dire situation of nation-states and national unity in Central Europe, Germany in particular.

The great shock of 1806 exacerbated this fateful line of development. Even without corrupting democratic ideas, the trials of that year would have been enough to inflame widespread nationalist and anti-foreign movements; however, the French example spread the conviction in all walks of life that the best medicine for avoiding such ills would be a strong and powerful nation-state. This is why the schoolbook commonplace, that it was to the credit of the revolutionary and Napoleonic wars that democratic ideas gained currency, is totally amiss. On the contrary, it was particularly damaging for European democracy that the spread of democracy was associated with historical memories of foreign invasion in three major countries of the continent: Germany, Italy, and Spain; and the birth of the national ideal was linked to resistance to it. It was as a result that democracy and nationalism, however interrelated they were, could be played out against each other.

The Beginnings of the German Unification Movement
and the Chances of the Habsburg Dynasty

The example of France and the shock of 1806 aroused the desire for democratic transformation and a unified German state throughout Germany. The two tendencies remained parallel and linked almost flawlessly until the middle of the nineteenth century, though the memory of the great humiliation of 1806 exerted such influence as to put greater emotional emphasis on national union than on democratic change. As mentioned, it was due to the great obstacles to German unification, the vested interest in the institution of the territorial principalities dividing the country, that the German unification movement sought support from non-democratic forces. Its first support-seeking move was encouraging and hopeful: it turned to the most powerful and prestigious German dynasty to fulfill the great task of national unification through its own military and administrative resources and European authority.

At the time of the inception of the German national movement, there was little doubt that the House of Habsburg was entitled to this role. As Ernst Moritz Arndt, the poet of the anti-Napoleonic German war of liberation, put it: "'Liberty and Austria!' shall be our battle cry; long live the House of Habsburg."

The Habsburgs had all the necessary qualifications. First and foremost, they possessed both constitutional and dynastic legitimacy, which was particularly important at the time of the Vienna Congress. In 1815, the last Holy Roman Emperor, who was also the head of the House of Habsburg, Francis II, was still alive. Over five centuries earlier the first Habsburg had ascended the German throne by virtue of succession in the female line from the Carolingians and the Hohenstaufens, and apart from minor interruptions, his descendants held the

throne from then on. Their Holy Roman emperorship was the only legitimate
and palpable symbol of the historical unity of the Germans because the other
legitimate institution of German constitutional law was the territorial principality—the greatest obstacle in the way of German unification.

Moreover, the Habsburgs also had the moral qualifications for this role. Their
empire was one of the most serious and responsible monarchies of Europe;
their somewhat patronizing yet humane governing and administrative traditions
had been put in place in the most productive and lofty period of feudal Europe,
the eighteenth century, and had earned a distinguished place among the great
German accomplishments of the time. It should not be forgotten that the best
German and European civil code was the Austrian one of 1811. It should also
be borne in mind that none of the members of the dynasty seated on the German throne was ever frivolous or irresponsible, as Maria Theresa claimed: "All
are good and graceful rulers, good Christians, good husbands, good fathers,
friends of their friends." Even the proverbial Habsburg ingratitude has more
to do with royal depersonalization than actual moral defect. Perhaps no other
European dynasty manifested such an uninterrupted effort toward the ideal of
"Christian prince" and, as time passed, "enlightened prince" as did the House
of Habsburg, giving rise even to the modern type of "constitutional monarch"
in the figure of Leopold II.

The Habsburgs have often been said to have had mediocre abilities, but this
perception probably goes back to the fact that two important periods in the
history of the dynasty were hallmarked by the long reigns of two certainly run-
of-the-mill rulers, Leopold I and Francis II. But at least three-quarters of the
twenty-two monarchs who sat on the royal and imperial thrones of Germany,
the Holy Roman Empire, and Austria can be said to have been intellectually
and morally fit to rule. They were never as spectacular as, for instance, some of
the Capetians, but not for nothing were they Germans and not French. That
the House of Habsburg was a non-Teutonic, Latin hue amid the Germans is
pure nonsense. Naturally, they represented European and Catholic colors, and,
like all dynasties, they too had their international sort of members (such as
Charles V, Ferdinand I, Charles VI, and Francis II). On the whole, the family
and its most representative members—Rudolph of Habsburg, Maximilian I,
Ferdinand II, Maria Theresa, and Franz Joseph—were all out-and-out German
in the good and bad sense too: they were all marked by a strong sense of duty,
their sense of dignity easing up only in the closest circles; there was single-
mindedness; a lack of flamboyant emotions; a practical, commonsense way of
thinking; and an utter lack of wit, though plenty of cheerfulness. Even God
made them to be the emperors of the Germans.

It would have been particularly advantageous for all Europe if German unification, ripe as it was, had been conducted under Habsburg rule. The most
alarming though ineluctable development in the modern balance of European
power, a unified Germany, would have gained the continuity, the traditions,
and the sense of European responsibility of one of the most revered dynasties
of the continent.

The idea of reestablishing the German Empire under Habsburg rule was
widely professed and popular among those concerned with German union at
the time of the Vienna Congress in 1815. Had Emperor Francis II declared
that his abdication had been made under duress in 1806 and was thus void in
1815, the great moment of restoring legitimacies, no one would or could have
disputed his being the legitimate Holy Roman Emperor and the symbol of all
German unification efforts. Emperor Francis, however, was unwilling to re-
claim his German emperorship. His unwillingness and whatever was behind
it had repercussions on all world history, and, we must add, they were fateful
repercussions because it was from this moment that German political development foundered.

The Faux Pas of 1804: The Assumption of Austrian Emperorship

The encouraging possibility of German unification under the leadership of
the Habsburgs traditionally qualified for the task was hindered by an unfortunate historical process: Habsburg land holdings had largely been squeezed out
of Germany, and the unfortunate assumption of the title of Emperor of Austria
finalized this process.

As a result of the reformation, too, the lands of the Austrian Empire had been
pressed into Southern Germany, and the Habsburgs established lasting relations with non-German countries. The political framework of the individual
nations, however, had clearly separated in medieval times, and the Austrian,
Hungarian, Czech, and Moravian lands of the Habsburgs constituted a purely
incidental inter-"national" dynastic union, like the relationships between Aragon and Sicily, England and Hannover, and so on. When first established, the
core of the Habsburgs' empire had been nothing near what it is nowadays believed to have been: a "Danubian" state. One of its constituent elements, the
Austrian principality, wearing the German imperial crown, had brought along
all its Italian and West European holdings; the Czech kingdom had not really
been a Danubian country, and the Hungarian kingdom, which had shrunk due
to Ottoman advances, came to be but a military foreground for the German
Empire toward the east. For a long time, there had been no efforts to actually
unify this "union." Until the middle of the eighteenth century, no one had

ever doubted that the House of Habsburg, being the emperors of the Romans, represented the full political weight of German royal authority. The Habsburg ruler appeared simply as "the Emperor" in Europe; his power rested on his German and Italian positions, and he also happened to be the Hungarian and Czech king.

However, in the eighteenth century, the Habsburgs' German positions were again weakened through the loss of Silesia, and during the War of the Austrian Succession, the absurdity of the situation came out with glaring clarity that the Empress Maria Theresa had no country to call by a single name but a conglomerate of the Austrian, Hungarian, Czech, Lombard, Belgian, and Croatian nations or nation fragments, each of which had its own law, language, administration, and mindset. At the other, hardly less grotesque side of the coin, Maria Theresa's French-duke-turned-Italian-prince husband bore the title of emperor, to which he had been elected by her express wish, but he owned not a foot of land in Germany, demonstrating the hollowness of the title of Holy Roman Emperor to all the world.

In consequence, there were various attempts from the middle of the eighteenth century to establish a state with a continuous area out of the Danubian lands of the Habsburgs and to instill some sort of "Austrian" consciousness in it. However, this aim was closely related to strengthening the German positions of the Habsburgs and emphasizing the German nature of their empire, even in the case of Joseph II. This tendency took a fateful turn only under Francis II, through an unfortunate historical act without parallel, the assumption of the title of Emperor of Austria in 1804. As Guglielmo Ferrero pointed out, this act belonged in the series of arbitrary and coercive state foundations that the French Revolution initiated by setting up the Cisalpine, Helvetian, Batavian, Etrurian, and Westphalian states, and how absurd it was that the oldest and most conservative monarchy of Europe should follow suit because taking up the title of Emperor of Austria implied that the Holy Roman Emperor had rebelled against himself.

Ferrero believed that the key to the internal policies of Francis II was to be found in his Italian upbringing; in what follows, I wish to discuss also the long-term consequences of these policies, so unresponsive to German unification. The logical conclusion of the assumption of the title of Emperor of Austria was to give up the title of Holy Roman Emperor two years later. What this meant was that the head of the House of Habsburg was simply degraded from the position of Holy Roman Emperor, symbolizing German unity, to the rank of a territorial prince: he became one among the many. While it would have been most opportune for both the Holy Roman Emperor and the German nation to wind up or at least hold back the institution of territorial principality, the Austrian emperor now became as much interested in maintaining it as all the other princes, from the Prussian king to the Landgrave of Hesse-Homburg. This drove the House of Habsburg onto a downward path; a century was enough for it to run its full course; the Habsburg pretender now living in Austria no longer refers to himself as the Emperor of Austria—an empire of 7 million would be pathetic!—but as a *Landesfürst*, a territorial prince.

Anticipating the Fall of the Habsburgs

Francis II and his advisers obviously believed they were but naming what had already come into being, replacing the old façade inscription of Holy Roman Emperor, which did not square with reality any more and made a laughing stock of its bearer. As a matter of fact, the change in title inflicted a mortal wound on this old-standing European monarchy. By doing away with the "German" title, the House of Habsburg rid itself of a banner that could have acquired a new and hitherto unmatched significance in the coming centuries and could have rallied all Germans behind it. Apart from this enormous opportunity, as a spinoff, the problem of breaking away for the non-German lands of the Habsburgs could also have been achieved relatively smoothly. The title "Emperor of Austria" brought the illusion that the Habsburgs ruled a territorially contiguous, compact state that could perhaps be instilled with an "Austrian" consciousness in due course. In the light of this vain hope, the job of ensuring hegemony in Germany seemed tedious and illusory, and, moreover, it would pit the Habsburgs against other princes. Austrian emperorship seemed a less "waivable," more "secure" and "stable" position to take, and Francis II did not want to renew a claim for superiority he believed he could not fill with substance.

In truth, however, this decision, which might have at first glance seemed to have been informed by realpolitik, set the House of Habsburg on the path of decline. In vain did the territories of its empire become contiguous under the resolutions of the Vienna Congress; in vain did its army command respect and just pride in its glory; in vain was its political weight greater than ever before; its internal balance had been tilted, and it was as though the spirit had fled from it. Its German policies turned completely static, unable to step beyond the makeshift and increasingly detested arrangement, the so-called German Confederation, which we shall discuss in the following. On the other hand, it haplessly tolerated being an alien power held in contempt in Italy while it was no longer really the German state.

The German, Italian, and Hungarian events of 1848 made it glaringly clear that state and national borders did not correspond in Central Europe and that

no national movement identified with the fate of Austria. It was this terror of annihilation that prompted Austria to crack down so ruthlessly on the Italian and
Hungarian revolutions in 1849—a blemish on an Austria making so much of its
placidity today. (Fear tuning into cockiness would manifest itself in the life of
the Austrian house on the threshold of destruction again in 1914.) Between 1849
and 1866, Franz Joseph tried the impossible: to retain his position as both head
of the Germans and his many-peopled "Austrian" empire. But he too fulfilled
the biblical dictum: "Whosoever will save his life shall lose it." The Habsburg
Empire was driven out of Germany and Italy at the same time, out of the sphere
of power of the thousand-year-old Holy Roman Empire; and the moment it
ceased to be both *German* and *Roman* and had no choice but to be *Austrian*,
it was forced to give in to the secessionist endeavors of the Hungarian state,
and thus the one Austria was dismembered into *Austria-Hungary* in 1867. It is
enough to glance at the maps of 1792, 1815, and 1867 to see the rapid shrinkage
of power that the House of Habsburg went through because of giving up the
Holy Roman emperorship and assuming the Austrian emperorship. The tragic
consequences of this shrinkage can be fully grasped when one considers today's
aspirations to revive a Danubian monarchy. The heir of the Holy Roman Emperors, the successor of Rudolf the Habsburg, Emperor Maximilian, Empress
Maria Theresa, and Emperor Joseph II, is singled out to counter any design to
unite Germany and Austria and build a protective wall from the east against
the German Empire. In order to fulfill this role, he aspires to be the emperor
of 6–7 million in Austria and the king of about twice as many in Hungary. He
would love to include the Czech and Slovak areas in his empire, but there is no
one to offer them to him. He has not waived his rights concerning Croatia and
Slovenia, but it would be unwise to mention them. In order to carry out these
aspirations, he is forced to turn in three directions—the Austrian, the Hungarian, and the Czech—simultaneously striking up their local and patriotic tunes.
The writer of these lines is little moved by these attempts, but they are exceedingly humiliating in Habsburg eyes. There is little likelihood of the Habsburgs
ever assuming any European role, but of all the roles that could be dreamed up,
heading such a Danubian monarchy would be the most pathetic.

Digression on European Monarchy

It might seem odd to dwell so long on and shed so many tears over the long-
past and now immaterial fact that the unity of Germany was headed not by the
House of Habsburg but by the Hohenzollerns. Where, it may be asked, are the
Houses of Habsburg and Hohenzollern now, and what has the outcome of their
rivalry to do with the fate of the modern world? Alas, a lot. We must first make

it plain that European monarchy is the most significant institution of our political past, and one dynasty or another had always had a decisive role in shaping European nations, developing their political character. Second, we must be aware that the central issue of today's European crisis is that the authority of monarchy was turned into a shambles and nothing has come to replace it, at least not in Central and Eastern Europe. The most audacious move of European democratic revolution was to declare war on monarchy, but, it must be pointed out, it has not yet fully prevailed. Our prospects and hopes of eliminating monarchism are indeed auspicious, yet in order to bring them to fruition, we must be clear about its historical role and function and the gap it has left behind.

When the French Revolution erupted, European monarchy had been the achievement of an over two-thousand-year-old process of civilization. As Guglielmo Ferrero pointed out, this institution had strong roots in the political tradition of the Augustinian Roman emperorship, in which the old republican idea lived on. It was this tradition and medieval Christianity that turned the rule of Germanic tribal chiefs from the power they wielded as wild marauders and ruthless despots into a vocation regulated and girded by rights and duties, roles and tasks, a professional ethic and convention. This was what made European monarchy mean by the end of the Middles Ages and the beginning of modern times not sheer and raw personal rule but a form of power whose personal aspect was more or less and could be further spiritualized. Whenever we see West Europeans in key positions—presidents or monarchs—managing their offices with a fair degree of rigor and trustworthiness without the idea ever crossing their minds that they could exploit their opportunities with a view to personal power, we must never forget that the only reason this is possible is that we have a centuries-old form of authority in Europe where unrestricted power has become a conventionalized role, the wielding of raw power has been tamed into dignified representation, and power over life and death has been humanized, holding together various functions and capacities in key positions. To perform this role, a particular type of man was bred who, from early childhood, grew into holding representative honors as impersonally as possible. There is a direct line leading from the "Christian prince" through the "constitutional monarch" and "enlightened ruler" to the impersonal head of state of our time. The status, scope, and professional ethic of the French president goes back not to Robespierre, the Directoire, or Napoleon but to Louis XVIII and Louis-Philippe, and it is no mere coincidence that the French constitution of 1875, which brought about the first stable political settlement for the country after the revolution, was drafted by monarchists.

Where this advantage was lacking, the impersonal type of head of state could not evolve (e.g., in America). However strange it may sound, it is the diffusion of the European monarchic ideal that can be sensed in the fact that the American head of government, who has enormous personal power, is strictly constrained by a sophisticated democratic apparatus and that the essence of the even greater personal power of the president of Russia is to implement a defined program of social reform. Naturally, this is not to say that an impersonal head of state is a sine qua non of a working democracy, but it certainly is one of the best regulators of a democratic apparatus; and, whether monarchical or republican, nothing is better suited for leading a society more or less accustomed to personal power toward the final democratic ideal, where it is not persons exercising political power that rule others, but it is law, principle, and plan themselves that govern the administrators of the political power apparatus.

With such an approach, we are better equipped to assess and judge the falsification of the monarchic ideal that goes back to the most dubious tradition of the French Revolution, the romanticism of the leader as political genius. Through the person of Napoleon, this phony romanticism created the phony image of the European monarch or, alternatively, the image of the *phony monarch*, for whom ruling is not a profession and a system of roles but a romantic, heroic, spectacular, and individual enterprise. Not only was this no development, but it was also a regression from the divine-right, "hereditarily inept," and degenerate kings of old because it again subjected the community to total and raw personal power instead of the spiritualized personal power of the traditional monarch. To the good fortune of all Europe, European dynasties took no notice of all this but by and large fulfilled the thousand-year-old roles of royal correctness throughout the nineteenth century. It was only at the end of that century that a most grotesque and fateful phenomenon of political development occurred—the throne-born phony monarch Wilhelm II, who, though king by birth, entertained a romantic notion of his role. He was a phenomenon not at all coincidental for a second-rate, upstart, German territorial princely dynasty but would have been inconceivable in the House of Habsburg, the family of Holy Roman Emperors.

It will now be less incomprehensible why it was fateful for German political development that the most decisive event in European political history, German unity, was established not under the House of Habsburg, best qualified for the task, but the Hohenzollerns—a family not particularly illustrious even among the German territorial princely families. The House of Habsburg was the perfect example of royal impersonality, not only in the German but even in the European context, holding for over five hundred years without interruption the symbolically most pregnant dignity in the European system of states: the Holy Roman emperorship, a rank whose historical weight and prestige, opportunities, and symbolic significance one had to be worthy of even when it meant little actual power. In contrast, the German territorial princes, being as feudal and seignorial as they were, wielded a far more personal power than did European monarchs in general. It was fateful for German internal political development that when the elimination of the system of personal power was the most important task before all the peoples of Europe, Germany, the country in the greatest need of terminating it, backslid into personal power.

THE IMPASSE OF THE GERMAN CONFEDERATION

Inborn Defects

As the Holy Roman Empire could not be revived in 1815, the only legitimate political institution of the German nation was the territorial principality. In vain had Baron vom Stein written: "I have but one homeland, and it is called Germany; and, in this moment of enormous advance, dynasties are inconsequential for me." The dynasties had commanded the loyalties of the army, the bureaucracy, and the peoples, and Stein himself had had to serve them and spur them to war to be able to finally defeat Napoleon. It was thus the dynasties that went about settling the fate of Germany at the Vienna Congress, and it was up to them to decide what kind and how much unity to implement. And they were above all interested in upholding, even reinforcing, the institution of territorial principality. They were also aware that after the great year of 1813, they had to provide some sort of political form to Germany as a whole. It was bickering on this that gave rise to the German Confederation of 1815.

Ferrero regarded this as an imperfect political formation but one that was not the worst option and acceptable from the point of view of the European balance of power. No doubt the German Confederation mopped up anarchy in the land, ended its being a no man's land, and eliminated hundreds of Southern and Central German dukedoms, and as an organization it had a more stable footing, was more visible, and was better framed than the Holy Roman Empire. For all these benefits, it was a far cry from what the German unification movement would have minimally wanted and was much too flawed from the outset to be capable of continuing.

We have already hinted at its first major defect: the German Confederation had no visible head. The Holy "Roman" Emperor might have been a laughing stock for his deflated power—that was why he had also been the German king, a role that could have been a symbol carrying significant content in given situations. In a society so much used to personal power, the lack of a visible head proved to be a crucial shortcoming.

The second major fault was an upshot of the first one. That the Holy Roman emperorship was not renewed meant that the German Confederation said amen to Napoleon's work, the breaking up of the Holy Roman Empire in 1806; in particular, the princes and dukes officially ceased to be subjects of a higher state entity, became fully "sovereign" in their lands, and, at best, it was a voluntary alliance among themselves they entered into. The electors and landgraves became kings and grand dukes. It is pointless to say that these were but nominal changes and that the actual situation had already been one of full independence under the Holy Roman Empire. The change in titles and full sovereignty meant that the territorial princes, who had been all-powerful landlords rather than genuine dynasts, put on airs and made the claims of the great European dynasties, often overdoing it because, apart from the Habsburgs and one or two other reigning families, they had little prestige. One cannot overemphasize the regrettable aspect of German political development that it was not the central ruler who put down the feudal lords but the feudal lords who became sovereign in their lands, as a result of which the features of feudal lords that the major European dynasties had long before sublimated into the professional ethic of the Christian monarch persisted in them inextinguishably to the very end.

The third great defect of the German settlement of 1815 was that the countless princely families of the Holy Roman Empire, the so-called mediatized princes, were endowed with a special legal status, the most conspicuous attribute of which was their equality with royals for marriage purposes, but their socially most momentous privilege was that they retained and were guaranteed seignorial power and jurisdiction in a given area. This meant not only that Germany now got more or less feudally minded families *as dynasties,* but also that the word of the dynasties and the constitution of the German Confederation guaranteed for *other families* seignorial-like privileges, which, being the greatest obstacles to social development, were being eliminated throughout Europe.

Though it did put an end to the anarchy of the Holy Roman Empire, the German Confederation was an impasse of German unification all the same because it reinforced and brought under the protective umbrella of universal European monarchic legitimacy the greatest obstacle to German unity: the system of the territorial principality. At the same time, it was a provisional arrangement that fortified the desire that had been aroused by the great shock of 1806—the desire for a strong and unified Germany. It was no mere coincidence that Hegel developed his philosophy of state, elevating it to a metaphysical plane, at this time. Though propounding his theory in defense of the Prussian state—that is, the territorial principality already on the defensive—the reaction he prompted gave shape to the desire for an unrealized, imaginary, unified *German state*, existing only as a postulate, as a metaphysical entity.

The Great Debacle of 1848

The recognition that the German Confederation was not a viable or sound political arrangement for German unity became ripe to drive political events and movements in 1848. This was a year of revolutions for Germany too, the liberal bourgeoisie and intelligentsia taking the lead and achieving appealing and promising results. However, when, following the local revolutions of the individual "states," the issues of the whole German body politic were mooted; a national assembly was elected and the popular Archduke John of Austria was chosen as the regent of the German realm, but the nation ran into the stumbling block of German territorial-political distribution: the unfortunate fact that three-quarters of the Austrian state, the one historically and legally destined to assume leadership, was made up of non-German peoples. The dilemma was that the political development of the German people was not ready for putting an end to the dynasties, yet while upholding a concord with them, an Austrian leadership would not do in a unified German Empire. This predicament gave rise to the sham resolve that would prove fatal for German political development, the so-called "lesser German solution" that was contented with a Prussian-led, partial German unity without the Austrians, as opposed to the requirement of a "greater German solution" that included Austrian Germans too.

The Frankfurt Assembly sought to deliberate on and resolve this issue. As it tried to do so, it became obviously and desperately clear that Germany had no center of gravity: the government that the national assembly and the regent had appointed wanted to go about its business of running the empire without soldiers, bureaucrats, and subjects from a city that was the capital of no country. Small wonder no one obeyed the government, and in the spirit of the "lesser German solution," the Prussian king elected to be the emperor rejected the imperial crown, calling it a name that was blasphemous to both the German title and the idea of popular sovereignty. Finally, the German National Assembly was forced to wander from town to town and ended up being plainly quashed by the government of a second-rate German state. The year 1848 came to be seen as foolish in the memory of the German nation and the year of shame in the memories of the devotees of German unity. Though many a constitution concluded in this year proved to last, this year was disastrous in the history of the German nation. It was disastrous because the lessons drawn from this year meant an experimental proof of the dismal German misconception that the *problem of German unity could never be resolved.* The truth was that the problem of German unity could not be resolved *as long as the territorial principality was retained.* As there was no other traditional institution from the time the Holy Roman Empire had ceased to exist, full German unity came to be identified with the idea of revolutionary chaos. Thus the inclination of the forces of tradition to yield to democracy, which manifested itself throughout Europe in the nineteenth century, did not come into play in Germany—or only ostensibly. It seemed that the task the best Germans had set their nation, a unified democratic nation-state, the course on which most European nations, after initial hitches, had managed to start out, would encounter insurmountable difficulties, and overcoming the forces in the way was next to impossible.

The Rise of the German Myth

It was at this point that the German nation began to think in terms not of genuine objectives and achievements but of delusive solutions, false political formulas, symbols, and phantasmagorias. As it was no coincidence that the Hegelian metaphysic of the state had responded to the experience of the desperate lack of a German state in 1806, so were Wagner and Nietzsche hardly accidental phenomena in German intellectual life. Not that their art and philosophy would have been fundamentally different without the events of 1848—indeed, Wagner himself was a full-fledged man at the time—but neither would have ever warranted the roles they assumed in shaping German values without the great debacle of 1848. Unable to cope with the task with which history had confronted it and lacking the courage to fight the forces in the way of solution, this community needed a worldview that populated life with otherworldly powers that only mythical-miraculous beings and supermen could match. History, however, provides communities only with *men* for resolving current problems, and thus the past had to be filled with the miraculous beings of German myth and the future with *Übermenschen.*

In this mental state, wherein the whole nation was inclined to favor makebelieve solutions rather than genuine ones, a force came into prominence that was not powerful enough to resolve the problem of German unity but was powerful enough to be the carrier of a false solution: Prussian militarism. It was in these circumstances that the greatest sham realist of European history excelled: *Bismarck.*

Prussian Militarism

A myth and a horror story have gained currency about the Prussians. The best-known proponent of the Prussian *myth,* Oswald Spengler, made the Prussians out to be the types of a superior, invincibly aristocratic, creative European man and spiritualized the Prussian principle so much that he believed all Europe needed an abundance of "Prussians" to be born. Even humbler glorifiers of Prussianism regard the full execution of one's duties as a characteristic feature of the Prussian mindset and speak of Prussian officials as though all other civil services in Europe were mired in corruption.

The *horror story* about the Prussians was shaped by the French. On this view, the German craze of recent times goes back solely to the Prussian contagion, and the recent German worship of power and violence derives from the mentality of Prussian feudal and military cliques.

It would nevertheless be futile to look for the essence of Prussian militarism in the mind of the Prussian Army, aristocracy, or people. It is indeed gross and foolish to seek the root of any militarism in the naturally given brutality or military coterie of one people or another. It is difficult to tell the difference between the innate brutality of the Germans and the Swedes, the militarist outlook of a Hindenburg or a Lord Kitchener. Militarism is a *social* phenomenon, and a society becomes militaristic not because of the way its soldiers think of war and themselves but because of how society thinks of the army. Today, there is no structurally militaristic society in Europe—militaristic in the sense that the Spartan and Cossack societies were, societies that would have collapsed even economically without warfare and their resulting dominion. German society is not militaristic, or at least no attempt at making it fully so has been successful.

If the officer corps of the Prussian Army was concerned only with and disposed to war, little did it differ from the military of any other European continental power. That the Prussian Army loved stiff maneuvers and rigid drills might have been a racial characteristic, historical tradition, or the fallout of a rigid social structure, but such practices have occurred elsewhere as well and have led to neither modern militarism nor war. That the Prussian aristocracy used rigid and harsh methods of rule might have been a serious obstruction to the democratic development of Eastern Germany, but such factors have come into play elsewhere too and have not prompted any militarism. For an industrious European society to regard the army not as a necessary evil and a costly burden but, regardless of whether it is needed or not, an entity to make its greatness and fearfulness be a question of honor and a source of constant enthusiasm, it requires the historical experience of being deprived of arms, defenseless, and without military force. This was what Prussia had experienced in the period between 1806 and 1813, and Guglielmo Ferrero was perfectly right in looking for the birth of Prussian militarism in this period. It leads nowhere to point out the army worship of the soldier-king or the ravaging wars of Wilhelm the Great;

these had been but postures, not the hysteria that would fill Prussian souls following 1806. The German people remembered only the havoc the armies of
Frederick William I and Frederick the Great had wreaked, not any greatness of
theirs. It was only in the delirious year of 1813 that the newly organized Prussian
Army, marching through the streets, became the central symbol of liberation,
German freedom, and unity. The expectation of both great rises and falls was
what spurred the Prussian political elite to formulate its virtues and values in
overblown categories, and the memory of 1813 inclined the Germans to turn
Prussian qualities into a myth and set themselves this myth as an example.

The Role of Prussia in Germany and the *Erbfeind* Complex

This role of Prussianism came to be fully established in the German system
of values only at the end of the nineteenth century. Before it developed this
role, the Prussian Army cult and militarism had already had their say in actual German political development. As a consequence of the fear, uncertainty,
and pursuit of amends that had been instilled into the minds of the Prussian
elite, the Prussian state—alone in all Europe—retained general national service even after 1815, and thus the Prussian state acquired a political weight and
power substantially more than its population would have justified. This was
further reinforced by the fact that Prussia, which had had almost as many Polish as German subjects, left the Vienna Congress—thanks to the indifference
of Francis I to his role in Germany!—as the largest German state, having received the Rhineland in return for ceding its Polish territories to Russia. It was
the combination of these two factors that the idea that the Prussian state would
assume German leadership could occur at all in the face of all the factors that
would have qualified the House of Habsburg for such a role. Not all the soldiers
and Prussian advances in Germany would have been enough to turn this idea
into reality without the great letdown of 1848.

In the first half of his political career, before willy-nilly becoming the author
of German unification, Bismarck's central effort was to represent and demonstrate the fateful and misleading historical lesson drawn from 1848: that the
problem of full German unity was insurmountable because the institution of
territorial principality could not be overcome. This was the moral he deployed
to safeguard German territorial principalities, notably the Prussian royal house,
against all dangers threatening it from the side of German unification, primarily
under the House of Habsburg. It was to counter this possibility that he gathered
together all the resources of Prussia, and this was what he fended off in 1866.
Still, this would not have been enough for Prussia to embody national unity
in the eyes of Germans without a factor of social psychology; Prussia had felt

the great shock of 1806, the great experience of German humiliation, more intensely than had Austria and could more fully identify with the urge to find amends stirred up in the Germans. It was in 1806 that the *Erbfeind* complex came to life in Prussia and some lesser German states: the idea that France was the hereditary foe of Germans and that its sole aim for centuries had been to obstruct German unity and greatness. Oddly enough, the peoples concerned had scarcely been aware of this centuries-old, predestined conflict before 1806; they had known far more about the traditional "predestined" English-French conflict. Austria, the traditional and more powerful representative of Germans, had no grasp of the problem, nor had France, the other party concerned; nevertheless, Prussia and the "lesser" Germany made much of it.

It is a historical fact that the European balance of power had for centuries been based on the distribution of power between the French and the Germans, and this had been the cause of several wars between them, between the Bourbons and the Habsburgs, but neither did the two peoples, nor the two dynasties, harbor any axiomatic, predestined hatred between themselves. During the Napoleonic Wars, Austria, whose power Napoleon was never able to break, hated the French only to the extent a self-confident great power hates its momentary enemies, and this impulse gradually abated after the Napoleonic era.

Similarly, the French had not entertained any notion of an *Erbfeind*; naturally, French politics had been delighted to see the shift of the German Empire to the southeast and sought to thwart the development of a strong German realm on French borders. The French intellectual elite of 1806 had a good deal of sympathy for Germany, and there was no anti-German or anti-Prussian sentiment among the French public of the time. This was born in 1870–1871. I do not know what the Germans did in France at the time and in what ways this differed from what had happened in wars and on battlefields in the period, but whether making war or peace, they did it in the spirit of avenging the *Erbfeind*, and there is nothing more terrifying than being defeated by such an enemy, not only physically, but mentally too. This gave rise to the terrible shock and Prussophobia of the French, which was to find its own, none the less fateful counter-vindictiveness.

As both the Prussians and the Germans concerned regarded 1871 as the great amends for the humiliation of 1806, it became possible for the Prussian state and military power to embody the cause of German unity.

The Real Prussian Policy

It should be borne in mind that this result went beyond the original Prussian objective. The main aim of the policy of Prussia and Bismarck himself had been to establish a Protestant-type power complex out of Northern Germany, irrespective of German unification, and thereby join its territorially separated western and eastern parts. Before 1866, Prussian policymakers had repeatedly suggested dividing Germany in two: a northern part under Prussian leadership and a southern part under Austrian leadership; however, it was the House of Habsburg, still the embodiment of German unity, that could and would not see eye to eye with such a proposal. The Prussian-Austrian onslaught of 1866 meant such a loss of face for the Austrian Empire that not only did Northern Germany come under the dominance of Prussia, but also a power vacuum developed even in Southern Germany, which Prussia, partly in its terror of the French and partly under the sway of the German unification movement, quickly took advantage of and drew the territories into its sphere. Then, following the victory of 1870–1871, it could no longer decline founding a new German Empire.

From the point of view of Prussian policy, however, all this amounted to not a unified Germany but a Prussia extended far beyond any expectation. Bismarck was perfectly cognizant of the fact that Prussia had attained not 100 but 150 percent of its aims and that it has nothing to conquer and nowhere to expand; it only had to safeguard what it had acquired. No serious person would have brought up the idea that a Hohenzollern policy could attempt a German unity beyond this—that is, an annexation of the German territories of Austria. From a dynastic point of view it would have been absurd to suppose this, as it would have meant that the Austrian emperor would join the German Empire as a subject or that the Prussian dynasty would drive the Catholic Austrian dynasty out of its ancient, Catholic, and Austrian lands. That the focus had not been German unity from the point of view of the Prussian royal clout would be made glaringly clear by the last appearance of the House of Hohenzollern on the stage of German politics: Wilhelm II tried to give up his title of German emperor while retaining his Prussian kingship. This has usually been seen as an example of the Kaiser's feeblemindedness, though it actually sheds light on the deeper interrelation that, from the point of view of Prussian politics, the German emperorship had been but an incidental and decorative gain that could be abandoned in case of danger, like a ballast from a balloon.

The year 1871 was thus a success of not a democratic and nationalist German unification movement but of Prussian politics. The generation that still remembered the great blunder of 1848 went back on rapidly eliminating German territorial principality and acquiesced in 1871 as a *partial* success of the aspirations of German unification. In what follows we shall try to find out how this partial success became full-blown catastrophe.

THE IMPASSE OF THE WILHELMINE GERMAN EMPIRE

The Grave Misunderstanding of 1871

We have all learned the schoolbook lesson that the German democratic forces were unable to establish German unity, while the Prussian royal house was able to do so in 1871 and that the rise of German power marked the history of continental Europe until 1914; this was what the contemporaries believed and what continues to be believed. It was this vast misunderstanding that brought ruin to both Germany and Europe. What had happened in 1871 was quite different. All the events concerning German unity in 1866, 1871, and 1879 had essentially been a series of dynastic compromises set *against* German national unity and German democratic development. In 1866, the lesser Northern German principalities submitted themselves to Prussian military and political leadership; in 1871, the larger Southern German lands acceded to this league; and in 1879, by concluding the Double Alliance, the House of Habsburg, the last forum that could have represented all-out German unity had it not been disabled from doing so since 1804, surrendered to this series of compromises.

That it was a compromise was not a secret to the contemporaries. It was less clear whom it was *between* and whom it was *against*. In the public eye, the establishment of the German Empire was a deal between monarchy and national democracy, as it had been in all European states in recent times. This was the greatest of misunderstandings. The deal was actually struck not by the forces of monarchy and democracy but primarily by dynastic and aristocratic ones among themselves, and they made a few democratic concessions to eke out their otherwise finalized agreement. The political structure of the "new" and "unified" Germany of 1871 followed the very pattern that the German Confederation, this graveyard of German unity and democratic development, had drawn in 1815, the only difference being that what had been provisional in the earlier setup was final in the later one. Showing unity outward, the new German Empire meant internally that an emperor-augmented Prussia and the German Empire would guarantee that the institution of territorial principality, the greatest obstacle to German unity and democratic growth, would remain intact and inviolable; moreover, its most characteristic and crudest representative, the die-hard echelon of its privileges, the Prussian dynasty, took the credit for creating the new "unity," and thus the entire structure was built into the new Germany.

As compared to 1815, there were, however, three novelties: the title of emperor, the German Army, and the Reichstag (Imperial Diet), the organ of public opinion. The emperor as emperor and not as Prussian king had a rather limited power, but the Reichstag had even less, tottering without a sound base between verily powerful dynastic and military forces. This situation fostered the cult of the German Army based on the reminiscences of the 1813 Prussian Army—it being the only novelty of the three that was not an empty title but a genuine force. In terms of both law and reality, the sovereignty of the empire was vested neither in the emperor nor in the people but in the collectivity of princes in the Imperial Council (Bundesrat). Though little seen from without, this was the real sovereign, which the subjects of (for instance) the king of Württemberg or the prince of Schaumburg-Lippe sensed and experienced far more than any power of the Kaiser or the Reichstag.

German politics therefore continued along its fateful course, running contrary to European development, buttressing the institution of territorial principality further, and foreshadowing doom. This fact, however, could hardly be noticed in the jubilation over the renewal of the title of emperor, the institutionalization of German popular representation, and the victory of the German Army. To come forward in such circumstances and declare that this was no German unity and that German democratic development had fewer prospects now than during the German Confederation would have amounted to disavowing the martyrs of two bloody wars and questioning the rights of not only the Kaiser, but another twenty-five princes as well.

It would be futile to look for any cunning intrigue by this or that interested party in this vast misunderstanding. Though always in the interest of some, great historical misunderstandings have far deeper causes and cannot be hatched at will. The overwhelming prestige of the birthright principle and the system of territorial principality forced German society into the fetters of an overly aristocratic social structure, which the German democratic movement could far less cope with than could the Italian one, with its principalities sprung up from rootless Renaissance tyrants. In this situation, the German princes and people, Bismarck and the democrats, were more than delighted by German unification, an aim for which they all strove in their own ways and that they had attained without having to go for one another's throats, so they would leave the trouble of improvement to the following generation. They had not the faintest idea what burdensome heritage they were passing down to their grandchildren. The new German unity was one of those false solutions that seek to find a way out of an impasse by trying to square things that are incompatible, ruling out the possibility of development by healthy compromise, and lead to an even more disastrous impasse.

The Instability of German Territorial Status

What unity should have achieved was to provide the German nation with a stable territorial framework instead of the wholly incidental setup the

German dynasts—better said, the lieges-turned-rulers—achieved by their wrangling and haggling. Apart from Bohemia and Eastern Prussia, with their separate problems, the territories of the German Confederation had more or less been identical with the historical power base and linguistic boundaries of the Germans. Instead of this, the new, unified Germany had to do with the territorial framework of the Wilhelmine German Empire, which, internally, retained the absurd territorial maze of the small German states; but what was far worse is that externally, it was wholly incidental: its boundaries were marked out by the affair of partitioning Poland to the east, the casual wrangling with Austria to the south, and the excessive defeat of France to the west. At essential points, these borders were neither historical nor linguistic. From a German point of view it was certainly difficult to explain why Posen belonged to Germany and why Innsbruck did not—or, conversely, from an Austrian-German point of view, why Tarnopol belonged to Austria while Cologne, Hamburg, or Passau belonged to another country. Germany remained what it had been: a community lacking a settled territorial framework.

The Delusion of the House of Hohenzollern

The impasse of political development was exacerbated by the uncertainty of the European status and position of the Hohenzollern dynasty. We have alluded to the nation-shaping role of reigning families. To our day, France is where the Bourbons had always been. Germany, however, embodied not the solid and continuous position of the Habsburgs but the unstable and novel one of the Hohenzollerns. Certainly this was one of the good, old, puritan German families with a serious moral tradition behind it, but it lacked the form and dimension the role it dropped into in 1871 would have required. It should not be forgotten that the Hohenzollerns had been living the lives of provincial absolute monarchs at the beginning of eighteenth century, and, but a century and a half later, they were supposed to have filled the European position of the Holy Roman Emperors out of Berlin, a position that was qualified for the role neither by its genius loci nor its social environment. It is enough to read Emil Ludwig's *Bismarck* for a description of the preparations for and the formalities of the proclamation of the German Empire in Versailles and see how utterly the forms and traditions needed for such a role were wanting in the "simple" and "puritan" Prussian house.

It would not have been inevitable, but it was certainly not coincidental that the Napoleonic falsification of European monarchy was echoed by the Prussian governmental system and that it was in the person of Wilhelm II that the figure of the *phony monarch* appeared for the first time after Napoleon—the romantic notion of the ruler, one prone to histrionic and inordinate posturing, to putting on airs of grandiosity. Both traditional monarchies and democracies sooner or later get rid of such unbalanced personalities, as did the Family Council of the House of Habsburg, which pushed the neurotic and extravagant Rudolph II out of the way, or British democracy, which forced the abdication of Edward VIII, who had tried to express himself through original and personal gestures. However, Germany was neither a long-established monarchy nor a full-fledged democracy. Nevertheless, the German people might have decided not to put up with the imperatorial gestures of Wilhelm II and unseat him. However, prior to such an outcome, he managed to send off various telegrams, make statements, go on boating trips and white-horse marches in and out of certain places, and thereby ensure that the external crisis broke out before the internal one did.

The Exhaustion of the House of Habsburg

The pit the Habsburgs had maneuvered themselves into was perhaps deeper and more devastating than all the delusions of the Hohenzollerns; an entire state organization, military and bureaucratic apparatus, had lost its raison d'être and bearings. What was left of Austria after the Austro-Hungarian compromise of 1867 was but a grotesque, crescent-shaped state formation that lacked a genuine center but included Dalmatians, Italians, Slovenes, Austrians, Bohemian Germans, Czechs, Poles, Galician Ruthenians, and Bukovina Romanians and thus attempted to patch together an unprecedented political, historical, and linguistic incoherence with which no community could identify. The main party to the Austro-Hungarian construction, the eponymous Austrian Germans, found themselves in a most ridiculous situation because, apart from the Italians and Serbs, all the rest of the ten constituent peoples of the dual monarchy could have satisfied or hoped to satisfy their interests by maintaining the framework of the empire. But what had the Austrian Germans to look for in an empire four-fifths of whose population was not German and half of which detested even the name Austrian?

To make this situation bearable, the German press concocted the notion that the monarchy represented German leadership toward the small peoples of Eastern Europe. This was an entirely false interpretation because the Habsburgs could represent German hegemony only as long as the German emperorship had any reality. Since this opportunity had been lost, the common army and civil service gradually lost its roots, and the Hungarians in Hungary or the Poles in Galicia held the reins of power in their lands so much so that they could deem all complaints on behalf of the 2-million-strong German minority as intervention in their internal affairs.

Actual German hegemony within the Dual Monarchy lacking, a place for it had to be found, and this was how the mission of the Habsburgs on the Balkans was hatched. On this view, the Habsburg Empire had foolishly and pointlessly sought power bases in the German and Italian areas far from its Danubian center and should have realized such aims on the Balkans. This, however, is based on a gross misunderstanding of the historical roots and the Holy Roman aspect of the House of Habsburg. Where should the Holy Roman Emperor of the German nation have sought power bases if not in Germany and Italy? The concept of Balkan hegemony was but a shoddy ersatz thought up for an illustrious ideal; it was not good enough to breathe new life into the Dual Monarchy but good enough to unleash deadly disaster on it and so on all Europe. Enmeshed in grave internal troubles, the Austro-Hungarian Monarchy was neither of a mind to nor did it have the energy to venture on an expansive foreign policy. The further the monarchy was crippled by the baffling conflicts of its internal political life, the more its aristocratic official and military strata, which were steeped in a venerable moral tradition and were the only ones to regard the rotting body politic as their own, were overtaken by a sense of aimlessness, rootlessness, and uselessness; but due precisely to the power and venerability of their moral tradition, they could not silently give into decay but succumbed to psychotic fear. This was how insisting on the past turned into blindness to fact, dignity into prestige politics, and moral courage into impudent mortal fear. That the ultimatum sent to the Serbs in 1914 laid down unprecedentedly brutal conditions is certainly an exaggeration. But in the fact that it had been worded so that it would preferably not be accepted and that the diplomacy of the monarchy went out of its way to interpret its 90 percent acceptance as all-out rejection, those knowledgeable in the workings of the human mind will recognize the characteristic conduct of a soul terrified of its own annihilation, seeking to prove its own existence, and thereby provoking its very destruction. As Count Ottokar Czernin, adviser to Franz Ferdinand and later common foreign minister of the monarchy, was to poignantly remark, "We were bound to die. We were at liberty to choose the manner of our death, and we chose the most terrible one."

The Foreign-Policy Impasse of the Central Powers

The complete loss of the internal balance of the two main German dynasties and the impasse created by German unification led the entire foreign policy of the Central Powers into disaster. Above all, this was what bound together the two rival dynasties, the Houses of Habsburg and Hohenzollern. The essence of the dynastic compromises of 1866 and 1871—that German unity had been mutilated, Austrian Germans being artificially excluded—had to be made bearable and even glossed over. The Dual Alliance of 1879 was a surrogate meant to remedy the tormenting unsettledness of German unification. The negotiations and correspondence preceding its conclusion make it abundantly clear that both parties were driven by a desire to provide some "national achievement" to their respective national publics. This was how the German nation got, instead of the unassuming and solid fact of full German unification, the fiction that what was lacking from actual German unification was to be made up for fully and finally by this act of diplomacy. This is why it would be childish to debate what would have happened had Austria-Hungary implemented a pro-French foreign policy, and it would be equally childish to want to reestablish this state formation; the monarchy of the Habsburgs could not have followed a Francophile line in face of Germany because of its own Austrian-German subjects.

The fiction of the Dual Alliance "diplomatically" realizing full German unity was complemented by the fiction of the Danubian and Balkan mission of the monarchy, which was amplified by Germany if only to make amends to Austria for being squeezed out of Germany. In a Germany greatly puffed up through these false situations and catchphrases, a rather murky journalism arose: in proportion to its being unable to speak with any serious hope of the German national question, the union with Austrian Germans, and the liquidation of the territorial principality, it began to rant about German Mitteleuropa, the German world vocation, the hegemony of the German people here or elsewhere, their overseas expansion, and so on. It was thus that the two Central Powers, neither of them having any area they could realistically or urgently needed to conquer, were compelled to give way to realizing "national aspirations" at least "externally" and to embark on a cavalier foreign policy that actually vacillated without compass between a dynastic and a national course of action.

The system of dynastic correctness allowed for war over certain well-defined and restricted disputes but certainly not for a systematic arousal of national passion to conquer. International democratic correctness, just undergoing institution, allowed for war against tyranny and aggression. The foreign policy of the Central Powers, however, could not be squared with standards of dynastic or national-democratic correctness and reliability. From a dynastic point of view, both German monarchies renounced their time-honored principles of foreign policy; by harping on their world role, the Hohenzollerns alienated Britain and abandoned traditionally good Prusso-English relations, while the Habsburgs, by insisting on their role in the Balkans and campaigning around Bosnia, turned the traditionally even rivalry with the Russians—which had been based on the tacit principle that both parties would oversee the dissolution of Turkey but that neither of them would make any direct conquests in the Balkans—into a life-and-death struggle.

Due to the impasse of German unification, the Central Powers bound themselves together for life and death, severing the traditionally excellent Anglo-Austrian and Russo-Prussian relations, and their alliance, contrary to Bismarck's belief, led not to both benefiting by the other's friendship but to turning the tensions of one into the destiny of both. This was how they were embroiled in a war that had no justification from a dynastic point of view and that was useless in realizing any popular national objective because the only genuine national aim, the inclusion of Austrian Germans into the German union, had been rendered impossible by the Habsburg-Hohenzollern compromise.

Seen thus, it becomes obviously clear that the German-English naval and industrial rivalry had but a secondary role in the outbreak of World War I. It was only in the gloom of Central Europe that the legend of "Merchant Albion" could be taken seriously—that getting rid of German competition on world markets was worth a European war for Britain. The realistic object of Anglo-German antagonism over marine, colonial, and oriental expansion was definitely slighter than the object of Anglo-French rivalry in the Middle East, and Anglo-German industrial competition fell far behind the scale of Anglo-American competition, which has never led and is not likely to lead to war. The various gestures of Wilhelm II had embarrassed British politics far more than any industrial or commercial rivalry had. Moreover, the Kaiser's personality was deeply and organically bound to the impasse of German political life and the hazy political journalism to which it gave rise to, a journalism that suggested that Germany's ambition was world hegemony by military means or power politics—a suggestion that was not true *at the time*. Bold ambition was only the externalization of internal tension. It is a superfluous notion, which has gained wide currency in Central Europe, that the Central Powers were "inept" in their foreign policy and that the Germans were unrefined and had no sense of diplomacy. (Oddly, no one ever noticed this in the age of Frederick the Great, Kaunitz, Metternich, and Bismarck!) The truth is that everyone is "inept" in both his internal and external policies—however cunning he might be—if he stands in a false relation to fact.

In view of the above, World War I was born of the troubles of the German nation and of the unrealistic and unbalanced foreign policy that both German powers followed as a result of the impasse of German unification. This is not meant to underpin a thesis of responsibility for World War I. It is merely a statement of fact.

The Beginnings of German Anti-Democratic Nationalism

The impasse of German unification came to be the source of major disruptions in internal political development. The inexorable compromise of the dynastic state administration, aristocratic organization, and democratic national feeling became a mortal embrace in time for all three factors, suffocating each. Their exhaustion reached finality in 1933, when it turned out that the dynastic, the aristocratic, and the democratic forces were equally incapable of standing up against the terrifying revolt of barbarism. What had happened after 1871 was no more than the dynastic principle switching over into demagoguery, the aristocratic principle picking up the gibberish of aggressive jingoism, and the democratic principle being muddled up, having justly believed that the letdown of 1848 was only temporary. After 1871, the cause of full German unity and full democracy had to be represented in the face of a deadlocked, sham, yet existing and visible unity and democracy, as a result of which realism and idealism ceased to run in the same direction—the precondition of the vigor of any progressive movement. Realists therefore took up with the devotees of a unified Germany, arguing that the existing one had to be "improved," while idealists fell into dogmatism and stargazing; but, far worse, the two components of nineteenth-century libertarianism, democracy and nationalism, in this initial vulnerability of German unification, as in all like conditions, came to be pitted against one another. Those obsessed with full German unification hated the petty dukedoms and the Habsburgs as much as they could not deny their admiration from the massive edifice of Wilhelmine Germany (see Hitler's *Mein Kampf*) and looked to it to bring about full union. Had anyone told them that the entire Wilhelmine compromise had to be discarded, he would have committed sacrilege in their eyes because of attacking the only visible reality of German unity. Austrian-German nationalists would particularly have regarded it as blasphemy, for they had not lived in or experienced the inner delusions of Wilhelmine Germany, shut out from, as it were, and longing for the paradise of German unity.

It was in this situation and it is in such situations that the most terrifying monstrosity of political development in modern times, anti-democratic nationalism, was and is born. The Great German Unification Movement in Austria had been resolutely liberal until 1866, the year of the exclusion from union, when it shifted and began to toe an anti-democratic line. It would require a deeper immersion into the history of ideas to find out what made this movement become anti-Semitic; suffice it to say that it became a movement whose way of thinking eluded the normal chain of cause and effect because it suffered from a malaise the actual causes of which were covered up by delusive historical experiences.

Power Cult and Political Metaphysics

The German power cult of modern times arose from the cul-de-sac of the lesser German unification and had a decisive role in shaping the anti-democratic surge mentioned above. How could this come to pass? The grave misunderstanding of 1871 was that German unity *had come into being,* and this was eked out by the fateful lesson that what the rallying of all the democratic forces in 1848 had been unable to manage, the military forces of the most powerful German state had achieved "by blood and iron," as Bismarck himself put it. Alien to all myths, the myth of power included, the great realist had coined this catchphrase to snub the democrats and nationalists in the way of his Prussian agenda. Nevertheless, his success would beguile the following generation, which, at the same time, was utterly vexed by what it could not become fully conscious of, the fact that unity had come into being neither by blood and iron nor anything else. This tension was what gave rise to the mythology of power, which, like the mythology of revolution, endowed the means of violence with a conceptual or mystical efficacy, an all-time precedence over peaceful, gentle, humane, and tractable methods.

What would have been unimaginable in the time of Prussians like Frederick the Great, Kant, Humboldt, and even Bismarck, became, with the ascendance of this delusion, not only possible but also usual: historians, journalists, and politicians disapproved of gentle and humane means on principle and doctrine, as ends in themselves, and judged historical situations and persons by the use or non-use of the tools of power. The delusive lesson drawn from 1871 led people into believing that completion required a similar wielding of power and military force. However, this was impossible because it would have undermined territorial principality and the Hohenzollern-Habsburg compromise, the foundations of the Bismarckian edifice. To top this absurdity, there was the debilitating contrast, which every German who took the cause of national community to heart had a sense of, that a German was purportedly, to the outside world, a member of the most powerful nation of Europe, while, at home, he was bullied by puffed-up and petty princelings and their officious servants.

This internal weakness of Wilhelmine Germany should never be lost sight of when one is trying to grasp the roots of the German hysteria. Up to now, those of the opinion that the German hysteria came into being as a result of a series of *historical* shocks have not gone any further than the Versailles peace treaty because they had taken a powerful and strong Germany for granted. They believed that Wilhelmine Germany, which had experienced no Versailles-like humiliation, had indeed been in the prime of its glory and had taken to imperialism, power worship, and aggression because these must have been some temperamental, "archaic" German traits. It is following this concept that, for instance, Robert Vansittart goes back all the way to Arminius to explain German violence and aggression, but as a matter of fact, he too had acquired the experiences needed for this conviction in Wilhelmine Germany. Based on similar personal experiences, William Brown argues that power frenzy was already part and parcel of Wilhelmine Germany and had nothing to do with any inferiority complex but was a paranoid psychic condition, an excessive feel for actual power, and consequently this power craze was going to reappear whenever Germany attained a certain degree of power. This whole concept is based on the fundamental mistake both observers and contemporary Germans made in not realizing that Wilhelmine Germany was *not* at all a powerful but a lame and hapless political community, or if anyone did notice, his misgivings were pooh-poohed as they did not square with the delusion that the world and the Germans framed on the meaning of 1871.

Power worship and aggression were the other side of this haplessness and lameness. Germans may still be temperamentally aggressive, but there are nevertheless many other aggressive peoples apart from them, and some are even more aggressive than the Germans. Being naturally aggressive, however, is not the same as turning aggression into a program and a value principle—always a sign of weakness. A young German once made the point to me that "Great Britain is the greatest power in the world because it can breach international law whenever it wants to." In vain did I explain to him that Britain took no pleasure in breaching international law if it happened to do so and that it was not by this that it measured its power. This is where the imperialism of healthy peoples, notably the British, differs from that of the Germans. A healthy people, *when* imperialist, wants to simply make as much of its power as it can, to deploy it fully and efficiently; this also means that it takes particular care of what can and cannot be done by sheer power. By contrast, German imperialism and sense of power are typically what psychology dubs overcompensation. In proportion to their increasing malaise at not having the *power* to resolve the burning issue of their national life, the Germans entertained a magic worship of power and were increasingly bent on demonstrating their power. The proverbial German conceit, the unending protestations of the excellence of all things German (*bei uns*), is the same phenomenon. Unable to be masters in their own country, they declared their mission to lead others; unable to make sense of their own national predicament, they wanted to teach everyone else; unable to redress their own troubles, they asserted that the recovery of the world depended on them. (Am deutschen Wesen soll die ganze Welt genesen.)[3]

This tied in with the spread of a rather hazy metaphysical manner of speaking in German political life and journalism. That the Germans have a propensity to metaphysical speculation may be a racial or temperamental feature, but a murky and misplaced metaphysical speculation is the result of concrete confusion, a false relationship with facts. The more they racked their brains and theorized on these matters, the more they got ensnared by the nonentities disguised as wonders and the powers disguised as nonentities that determined their political and social life. In so doing, they got into the habit of mythicizing their existence and giving overblown and fake names to the simplest facts of life. In all the world, politics is wont to beating about the bush, to euphemizing the odious, and to not calling a spade a spade, but to do so in terms of science, even metaphysics—this will forever remain a German characteristic. Baptizing things has an odd rule: weighty facts cannot be allayed by finer names, but insignificant matters can certainly be inflated by the names they are given. No war will become less significant if the enemy is called *Artfremd* (racially alien), but the Berlin-Bagdad railway line would have caused far less trouble had it not been called Drang nach Osten (Drive toward the East) but something simpler.

Though seemingly trifling, it is characteristic that the truth that Wilhelmine Germany was essentially doomed to torpor was most poignantly manifest in the German national anthem. According to the "Deutschlandlied," Germany is "above all," and the song repeats this three times. Imagine how an enthused German sings it: his sense of identity surely surges, he is exalted into even more solemn and sublime spheres—thanks to the genius of Haydn, as well—but having had his fill of singing, he will not have the faintest idea of what it means for him, what his duty is in the world. Imagine the same with "The Marseillaise," and the difference will be plain as day.

The Aborted Chances of German Democratic Revolution

There had been a chance of egress from the political and social impasse before 1914—one chance: broad-based, all-German democratic revolution that would do away with the major and the many petty dynasties in the way of full German unity and establish a democratic, unified Germany. This could have opened the way to free development for not only Germans, but also the smaller peoples of Eastern Europe. A revolution of this kind would have had to face major obstacles, but it did have promising prospects. However precarious its footing was among the real powers of German politics and society, the Reichstag did develop into a considerable mouthpiece of public opinion. Nevertheless, the success of Wilhelmine Germany having primarily dumbfounded liberal circles (Bismarck's whole policy was founded on this confusion), the role the liberal German bourgeoisie and political science had fulfilled in the middle of the nineteenth century was now waiting to be assumed by German social democratic labor and sociology. It took some time before the recognition that the way of achieving German national aims led through the far left because those who had been branded anti-nationalist but had in fact been impressed by Wilhelmine Germany were initially forced to the far left.

By the turn of the century, though, a broadly based democratic movement had developed, the earnestness, radicalism, honesty, and prospects of which should not be underrated. It is now fashionable to blame the dogmatism and bureaucracy of the Social Democratic Party and other immaterial issues for the failure of democracy and labor in 1933. These arguments carry no weight: Weimar democracy was benumbed by wholly other factors that had played no or only a minor role before 1918. Pre-1918 social democracy had been an audacious and energetic movement consciously facing up to its national, democratic, and social tasks and ready for struggle. That it was somewhat bureaucratic and doctrinaire? What else should it have been if it was German? At the turn of the century, there was a very strong likelihood that an imminent German socialist revolution in the new century would be as important a stage in European democratic development as the Dutch and English Puritan revolutions of the sixteenth and seventeenth centuries and the French libertarian revolutions of the eighteenth and nineteenth centuries had been. Sooner or later, the German revolutionary movement would have obviously clashed with the blustering Kaiser, whose entire mental makeup would have disposed him to play—in a modified mise-en-scène, perhaps with no tragic, only a tragicomic end—the role of a Charles I or a Louis XVI, that a people who have risen up experience their own strength and take possession of their land in opposition to and through the fall of their king.

This never came to pass. Before any such internal political dénouement, foreign-policy catastrophe set in, and the peace that followed it terminally thwarted the hopes of German democracy.

THE FOURTH IMPASSE: THE GERMAN REPUBLICS

1) Weimar
The Chances of German Internal Development in 1918

The fall of the Wilhelmine empire in the wake of World War I in 1918 opened up both a new perspective and an enormous rift for the future development of all Europe and European politics. Europe, however, turned a blind eye to and shut out that perspective and, with deadly assurance, plunged into the rift.

The perspective that had opened up for European internal development was the final demise of the territorial principality, which had grown out of the power of lieges and landlords, the institution that had come to replace monarchy in Germany without, however, endorsing all the spiritual traditions of European monarchy. The most astonishing change in 1918 was not the fall of the German emperor but the vanishing of all the petty monarchs of Prussia, Bavaria, Saxony, etc., down to the princelings of Schwarzburg-Sondershausen. This meant good riddance to the great dead weight of German political development, a situation that had not only been the greatest obstacle in the way of German democratic development and unity, but also the cause of German internal and external political befuddlement, ultimately of World War I. This therefore opened up the possibility of making up for the disadvantage that had encumbered Germany in democratic development compared to the rest of Europe, particularly Western Europe, from the beginning of the nineteenth century.

This perspective, however, included a terrifying risk as well. The year 1918 brought about the fall of all kinds of monarchy east of the Rhine, the ancient central monarchy of Russia, the territorial principalities of Germany, and the transitional formation of Austria-Hungary in between. In other words, the political authority on which the entire political structure of the whole region and indeed European coexistence had been built collapsed overnight. This frightening void was rendered all the more fateful by the fact that the decisive blow to the fall of monarchy was delivered not by democratic, revolutionary movements, apart from Russia, but by military defeat. In vain did the political vacuum lay success at the feet of democratic movements; the success proved to be unproductive because the democratic forces did not have the opportunity to crystallize into a new political authority through the achievement of overthrowing the old. As a result, the lack of political authority has been characteristic of all these countries ever since 1918.

This was the encumbrance of the democratic turn in Germany in spite of the fact that its socialist and democratic movement was the largest and most distinguished in the region. This movement could not boast that it had been due to its efforts that monarchy collapsed in 1918. The only chance German republican democracy had of establishing its political authority through a major achievement was by carrying out a full German unification that included Austria. This did not materialize.

The Chances of a European Balance of Power in 1918

The collapse of 1918 opened up new possibilities for Central-East European settlement. Defeat swept away both German dynasties, as well as the Russian one. In this unprecedentedly fortuitous situation, German unification could have been finally resolved, and the overturned and confused territorial status of Central-East Europe could have regained its sound framework. The peacemakers had a reasonable basis available for settling unresolved questions in the principle of self-determination, and the correct recognition that disputed borders should be settled on an ethnographic basis had been clearly outlined to them.

In respect to Germany, this would have obviously meant ceding territories to France and Poland but also hands down winning German Austria, which, after the fall of the Habsburgs, no longer had any reason to exist. Germany would have increased territorially but would have been far less dangerous because of the cessation of the Habsburg monarchy, the only factor that had kept the Danube region in the German sphere of interest. Without further ado, freed Poles, Czechs, Hungarians, and South Slavs could have been organized into a power group that could counter any German attempt at eastern expansion—which would hardly have been imminent in the event of German unity with Austria.

Such a peace could have been an excellent cure for Prussian militarism and German power worship, as it would have clearly demonstrated that the cause of German unification was *not* a matter of power politics and military effort. This would have given an incomparably favorable send-off to German democratic development and engendered the opinion throughout Germany that only sarcastic minds were to come out with in the Weimar period: "Thank God we didn't win the war."

This was not what came to pass. It would have required a reasonable deal between Germany and the other Western democracies. For the first time in its history, democracy, with its particular means and methods, came to determine the overall political structure and territorial status of Europe, and it failed this first trial. This was the abyss into which the peoples of Europe fell in 1918.

The Art of Peacemaking

Recently, it has become fashionable to assert not only that the peace was not harsh enough, but also that it was far too lenient and that, not being able to arrest German power fury, it helped Hitler grab power and unleash German aggressive instincts upon the world.

This gives the matter a grossly false slant. The only moment of truth in it is that the Treaty of Versailles was neither ruthless nor cynical, as the Germans were wont to say. The treaty was bad not because it was far too harsh or far too lenient but because it did not settle the issue that brought about the world war in the first place: the final establishment of the German territorial framework. Not only did it not settle it, but it did not address it either, not even suggesting

what issue it should have attempted to resolve. It indeed lacked the ambition—
one dominating all former treaties—to put an end to something.

Democratic Europe forgot something in which feudal Europe had been
well-versed—the art of peacemaking. Indeed, monarchy and aristocracy had
been organs of intercourse among nations until 1789 and between 1814 and
1918. Their political culture, rooted as it was in the Christian theory of the state
and the natural law of modern times, created the delicate forms and traditions
of European diplomacy and the peace-organizing technique of the balance of
European powers—masterfully described by Guglielmo Ferrero in *The Gamble*
and *The Reconstruction of Europe*. This was eked out by the eighteenth-century
concept of war without passion, which regarded war not as a leap into catastrophe but an appropriate means of resolving political disputes. With as little
passion as possible, the process was to be carried only to the point that one party
was, to a certain degree, ready to yield to the other, who, at the same time, was
not meant to step up his original demands by the fortunes of war. This attitude
also gave rise to territorial compensation as a means of settlement ; regarded
today as a cynical swapping of peoples and countries, it was one of the most
efficient means of averting war. Its fundamental thesis, however, holds true to
our day: all changes in the territorial stock of Europe were to be consciously ac-
counted for, kept track of, and carried out in a consistent system. Indeed, wars
in the eighteenth century were conducted in a way that would systematically
spare life and material, follow clear-cut rules, and limit conflict to armies, ord-
nance stores, and battlefields—so much so that social and scholarly intercourse
was not rendered impossible between enemy countries.

This culture of international relations seemed to fall apart the moment
new democratic nationalism began to have its say in foreign policy. Not that
democracy-heightened community feeling was more aggressive toward neighboring communities. On the contrary, democratic nationalism, being an enthusiastic taking possession of one's own community, was inclined to stop at
neighboring territories and was alien to dynastic conquest. Democracy, the victory of the lifestyle of the commoner over that of the noble, was incapable of
regarding war, the sending of thousands to death, as a means of settling disputes;
instead, it necessarily saw it as evil, the perpetrators of which had to be discovered. It could imagine a war to be just only if it were fought in defense against
an aggressor or in a popular uprising against a tyrant. Thus war also came to
be included in the arsenal of heightened, morally loaded community feelings
characteristic of democracy. On the one hand, this meant a turn toward high
seriousness on issues of war, but on the other hand, it inflamed spirits whereby

war could no longer be fought or peace made without passion in the manner of the eighteenth century.

Waging a war dispassionately was rendered impossible primarily by the fact that as a result of various factors, not only did emotional judgment in matters of war come to be a concern and right of the masses, but, alas, so did participation in the war effort. Conceived in terror, general conscription, the fateful heritage of the French Revolution, carried into very direct effect for everyone the romantic notion that war was against aggressors or tyrants and fought by the people who had risen up. This radically changed the social consequences of war.

Even this might have been of little account had the war of the peoples who had risen up remained one against a tyrant or an aggressor. Even after the ascendancy of general conscription, democracy did not become inherently aggressive—only its fears made it that. The European political system, lacking any central power as it did, sometimes gave rise to mutual fears leading to wars, and a sense of being threatened and attacked had to be instilled in the people if they were to rise up and wage war against them. In other words, the more or less just concerns of politicians had to be turned into mass emotion on both sides. This led to the obnoxious concept that the democratization of war simply meant that war between rulers had been replaced by war *between peoples*. The first genuine experience, the breeding ground of this awesome idea, had been the havoc the revolutionary and Napoleonic armies had worked upon Germany—being, among other things, the source of the Germans' *Erbfeind* complex. Yet to a certain degree, the tyrant Napoleon could be blamed for this destruction.

The first war to be fought with national and democratic emotions on both sides was the war between Germany and France in 1870–1871. After the *levée en masse* was ordered, the people of France fought thinking that they were protecting their national territory from the invasion of the Hohenzollern tyrant, while the Germans, fired by national unity, went to war against Napoleon III and the French people *representing him* who were hell bent on thwarting German unification. The idea that an entire neighboring people could be put into the position of a tyrant was the root of the horrendous thought of a *war of extermination between peoples*, a notion that Europe had forgotten long centuries earlier.

Parallel to this, warfare grew desperately ruthless. At this point the blemish is not only Central European; the English-speaking world is also at fault. Regulated, moderate combat and a military moral tradition had been the achievements of the European continent in the eighteenth century. Britain and America had never had standing armies and were thus inclined to think of war as between peoples. A combination of the Anglo-American concept of war, the

French romanticism of general conscription, and the decline of Central-East European manners have contributed to the ferocity of war in our day. Based on mutual mistrust, a most narrow-minded military materialism came to rule World War I and even more so World War II. This is not to say that ruthlessness at war had no further opportunities; rules of war hitherto more or less respected could be overstepped further—toward sheer extermination.

The waves of suffering and terror, hatred, and vindictiveness with which war of this kind fills souls swept away the traditionally dispassionate peacemaking techniques of monarchy and aristocracy. We are obliged to trust that democracy has more and greater things to say to the world in matters of war and peace than did monarchy or aristocracy. It must be acknowledged, however, that to-day the democratic system of the countries concerned is not at all helpful in finding a way out of the mental quagmire into which war has thrust people. In vain does democracy denounce war more vehemently than did monarchy and aristocracy; in vain does it base itself on the principle of world peace if it is incapable of ending an *actual* war in a way that does not necessarily lead to another one. For it is more than difficult to instill a mood of trust, agreement, and acquiescence in partners who were drilled by all the means of mass propaganda into believing that the enemy started the war of aggression against them due to that enemy's inherent destructive intent. This is the very reason why the statesmen of victorious democracies seldom have the flair for unflinching openness, courage, generosity, and anticipatory trust required by any successful peacemaking. In fact, they tend to understand by peacemaking the duty of satisfying the vindictive passions built up in their populations, with which they necessarily jeopardize the very aim of peacemaking, the settlement of the issue. By reference to the erratic nature of public opinion, the only use they can make of the democracy of the losing party is not to accept any of its promises without palpable and controllable guarantees. And controlling guarantees make actual settlement impossible. Following Napoleon, the first treaty that did not take the European tradition of dispassionate peacemaking into consideration in the spirit and the name of "national" requirements was the Treaty of Frankfurt. With the Treaty of Versailles, even the trappings of peacemaking were cast aside, and small-mindedness ran riot.

French Fears and the Mood at Versailles

To top this, fear had ruled France ever since it had become the victim of the vindictive passion of a similarly anxiety-tormented German nation in 1870–1871. Now the time was ripe for the French nation to even the score! With Germany's marked population growth in the meantime, France could no longer be sure that the terrifying experience of being left alone in the face of overwhelming German power would not be repeated. In 1870–1871, Germany, on its own, had been able to defeat France, and, for all the glorious victories on which the French could pride themselves in 1914–1918, for all their efforts and loss of blood, all they had been able to achieve with the British on their side was to stay the Germans fighting on two fronts. This fear then strengthened the drive to find fault and take revenge, and with such a drive the West European democracies set to their peacemaking business in 1919.

The world was still staggering from the shock of the four-year-long war of mass armies and attrition that had surpassed all human expectation and had utterly confounded people in their judgment of causes and effects. The troubles that swept the world were so immense that people wanted to see a wickedness and obduracy of equal proportion; the teachings of the earthly powers of Satan were borne out by reality in an age of disbelief as they had never been in the two-thousand-year-old history of Christianity. The idea of a satanic conspiracy gripped the minds of many even through vulgar Marxism. The satanic phantoms of cannon manufacturers, bribed politicians, dictators and marshals wallowing in blood, money-grubbing speculators, Masonic lodges plotting to murder, Jews striving for world dominion, sadistic reactionaries, and revolutionists delighting in destruction have filled the political imagination of white mankind ever since the Great War. Amid the satanic accounts, few noticed that these were but episodic figures in the real drift of history and that fear, insolence, false romanticism and rampant justice seeking, a craving for the limelight, and a disregard of convention can bring more misery to the world than all *wickedness joined together.*

In this mood of terror, incomprehension, and quixotism, everything was debated except the European tradition of clear-headed peacemaking and how the tilted balance of power ought to be restored. Nothing would have seemed more absurd than a militarist Germany, the vanquished "cause of war," emerging from the peace with territorial gains and retaining its army without being "punished."

To aggravate this, democracy's total lack of experience in the technique of peacemaking led the Paris Peace Conference into many awkward acts: a fearful inundation of paper; the grotesque role of sometimes starry-eyed, sometimes slavish experts and lawyers; the disconcerting effect of the high-sounding yet wholly impracticable avowals of open diplomacy; the scores of self-righteous formulas the participants ground out by the sweat of their brows to bridge over the gap between genuine interests and naive catchphrases. It was in this situation that three old men who had no grasp of either one another or the task that lay before them were meant to make peace, all the while nervously on the lookout for erratic changes in public opinion, itself ruling out any open-handed peacemaking. Small wonder that the Versailles peace treaty, as Guglielmo Ferrero succinctly put it, "was the beginning of the greatest fear that ever anguished the world," sowing the dragon's teeth from which sprang the most horrifying, fear-inspired monstrosity European mankind had ever seen: Hitlerism.

Diktat

The first dragon's tooth the Versailles peace treaty sowed was that the primary condition of any peacemaking was not to be observed—that it should be a *pact* among parties and not a *diktat*. The Germans were excluded from the negotiations not the least because the contradiction between lofty principles and foolish slogans, chimerical fears and genuine interests, could hardly be ironed out even in their absence. The Germans, however, have been convinced ever since that they were debarred only to satisfy the sadism of the victors and to humble the Germans, a belief in which they were confirmed by a series of histrionically peevish scenes born of the spirit of vindictiveness and the many petty-minded pinpricks that they regarded as most cunning acts of disgrace. In addition, negotiations, when they were held at all, were conducted exclusively in writing. To make matters worse, not only was the blockade upheld all the while, but also negotiations went on for almost a year, during which even the meager spirit of reconciliation that had sprung up at the close of the war was wasted. But thanks to democracy, all pettifoggers had the opportunity to come forward with their ideas; even the French champagne manufacturers were given the chance to put their conditions of making peace with the Germans in the grand edifice of the treaty.

Declaration of War Guilt

The second dragon's tooth was the declaration of Germany's guilt. At first, the fault-finding urge had not been directed against the German people as a whole, only the sabre-rattling Kaiser, the feudal Junkers, and the top-brass military. The more absurd were the burdens that war-waging democracies had to put up with—that is, the masses, peasants, laborers, tradesmen, and civil servants dragged away from their bread-winning toil and their families at home—the more they were carried away by fault-finding fervor. The bill of the guilty was far too overcharged with reparations; guarantees; and all kinds of emotional, political, and moral deposits for a fallen, empty-handed imperial regime to honor, so it all had to be put down to the German people, who had just happened to turn to democracy. This could only be construed through the democratic formula that the German people, though it had not really wanted the war, had nonetheless been guilty of tolerating a regime that had driven it and Europe into the war.

The dreadful psychological shock of this thesis, its application to the German people, and its effect on democratic development in that country has still to be properly assessed. The Germans would most probably have had no difficulties in accepting that the pugnacious regime of Wilhelm II had been responsible for the war. But that this responsibility would *devolve* on them because they had tolerated that regime was as absurd for them as a *not yet* democratic people as it was evident for the masses that had grown up in democracies.

To forestall war and depose leaders for sowing the seeds of war can strictly be expected only of people that have learned and experienced what it means to rid themselves of a ruler by divine right. For a conservative-aristocratic society subject to personal rule, the decision on war, even if kings and ministers are known to make it, is an elemental calamity, like a flood or a hailstorm. In 1918–1919, the Germans were as dumbfounded by a world demanding their punishment as would have been a Rip Van Winkle who had gone to sleep while having a cup of coffee in a Biedermeier lounge chair and awoken as a black in the midst of a crowd preparing to lynch him.

The Germans expended a lot of effort and paper on trying to prove that a Poincaré or an Izvolsky was as much or even more to blame for the war than Kaiser Wilhelm or Count Berchtold. The deeper psychological truth was that the whole issue of war guilt struck them as absurd, and along with it, the whole democratic ideology, in the name of which they had been declared guilty, also became absurd. In hindsight, though I believe clear-minded contemporaries did sense it, the declaration of German guilt was a great weakness—by no means a strength—of the peace. As the passions the war had aroused began to abate and the reasons for the war began to be seen in all their complexity, even the victors became less and less convinced that the war had been "caused" by Germany and that it had been "responsible" for it. Alongside this, the legal system established by the treaty, many provisions of which had been founded on the declaration of war guilt, began to lose its binding force. The defeated no longer saw the treaty as a closed historical fact, as any reasonable peace should be, but as a lost lawsuit that could be reopened on new evidence.

Reparations

The clause on reparations was the third dragon's tooth the treaty sowed—particularly the fact that the total sum was not defined for several years. I doubt whether the payment of reparations had a direct role in the German hyperinflation and economic crash. Had the sum been defined and realistic, reparations would have elicited from Germans efforts to discharge them as soon as possible, but as they were exorbitantly high and undetermined, people felt they would be working not for themselves but for the victors, and this mood led to a self-defeating policy whereby inflation and reparations were inextricably bound together. No West European can imagine a hyperinflation like the one that struck Germany or the deviation from normal economic experience it brought about. The existence, wealth, savings, and incomes of millions dwindled to nothing, and from then on, a hideous fault-finding urge overcame them. They looked for those who had ripped off their money and found them in those who had actually, seemingly or in their imaginations, profited by the peace treaty or the inflation: the victors without, the speculators—the Jews—within.

Unilateral Disarmament

Again, an industrious society like the German will fall into the perverted mental state of worshipping its great, powerful, and fearful army for its own sake, as an end in itself, only under extraordinary and gruesome experiences, the sense of being deprived of arms, defenseless, and without military force. German militarism does not exist because the average German likes to fight more than the average Englishman but because his sense of identity is buttressed by seeing the army march along the street, and he is of the belief that the parties that do not vote for increasing military spending are traitors to their country. This occurs only in communities in whose historical memories the lack of an army is associated with unforgettable miseries. It arises from a mental disposition that regards military defeat as the greatest possible evil a nation can undergo; hence also the German historical attitude of disputing the fact of military defeat and attributing defeat to subversive internal forces, the undermining of military morale.

This is why it is foolish to trace today's German militarism back simply to Prussianism. In form and language, it may have inherited something from it, but the political backsliding and intellectual confusion in the wake of the disarmament would in themselves have been enough to elicit some sort of militarism. Moreover, the Prussians, who had earlier undergone a milder form of militarism, did not fall into Hitlerism and Hitlerite militarism as much as others. The Prussians may be far more boorish than the Austrians are, and the *Anschluss* may have given them ample opportunity to be boorish to the Austrians. However, if we are asking whether the disjointing of moral outlook that Hitlerism has meant is to be found among the Prussians more than any other group, the answer must be in the negative, as there is no evidence to support it. Hitlerite militarism has been a cause embraced by not only feudal Prussians, crude Pomeranians, and peremptory Brandenburgians, but also industrialized Saxons, idyllic-minded

Thuringians, Hanseatic conservatives, democratic Württembergians, Catholic Bavarians, freedom-loving Tyroleans, and, *horribile dictu,* jovial Austrians—in other words, all those who were struck by the sense and experience of the disarmament and humiliation of Germany in 1918–1919.

The Ban on Anschluss

The territorial provisions of the Treaty of Versailles—the fifth dragon's tooth —were by far the most fateful ones. They wrought trouble not so much by taking areas away from Germany but by failing to give it any. In contrast to the other treaties prepared by the Paris Peace Conference, the territorial changes the Treaty of Versailles brought about were a result of thorough and conscientious work, which I will discuss in greater detail when examining border issues.[4] For twenty years, Danzig and the Corridor were said to be the most critical points of the treaty, points that would inevitably lead to a new world war, and 1939 seemed to have proved this prediction. However, if we consider that the Corridor meant an area with a Polish majority, where the dominance of the Teutonic order had been based on a not particularly thorough-going conquest, and if we also take into account that the Corridor, an even larger area in fact, had belonged to Poland for over 350 years and had been ceded to the Prussian kingdom upon its partition, we will begin to doubt whether this was a major factor in unleashing World War II. The truth is that the annexation of the Corridor, and particularly Posen, was not so much a German but a Prussian grievance.

This brings us to the gravest mistake that the Treaty of Versailles made— the prohibition of annexing Austria. The peacemakers, like most of Europe, had been exceedingly under the influence of the Bismarckian edifice; they had mistakenly identified modern Germany with Bismarck's enlarged Prussia and had believed that Austria was a separate nation. The ban on union with Austria meant that Germany would retain the incidental territorial framework of Wilhelmine Germany, which had no meaning after the fall of the Houses of Hohenzollern and Habsburg. The incidental territorial framework of Germany had given rise to a murky theory attempting to attribute metaphysical depth to the unfortunate fact that the Germans "are a people without borders." Greater calamity can befall neither community nor individual than being without borders because it paralyses creativity in both the concrete and the figurative senses of the word.

What Germany needed most in 1918–1919 was to find its way back to its clear, historically and linguistically outlined borders. A full-fledged Germany would no doubt have lost interest in the extra-German territories that former German states had acquired—Posen and the Corridor Prussians, Bukovinan and Dalmatian Austrians. Versailles, however, meant that Germany retained its desire for full unity and its claims to Polish areas based on memories of Wilhelmine Germany and Prussia. In vain were there predictions that a new world war would break out as a result of German-Polish disputes; the root cause of the catastrophe was that the *Anschluss* and the self-determination of the Sudeten-land took place not back in 1918, as the closing accord of the self-determination process and the beginning of a new period of peace, but twenty years later, as a consequence of a destructive and maniacal effort in power politics by the German nation, which was bound to swing beyond the point where realistic political action would have naturally applied brakes.

Versailles and the German Inferiority Complex

We have already pointed out that the Germans had undergone a sort of political hysteria before 1914 too. This hysteria had been rooted in the unbearable contrast between externally ostensible power and internally experienced impotence. This brought about a sense of uncertainty in Germans, and it had to be compensated. What actually happened at the time of the Treaty of Versailles was that material and moral defeat laid German weakness bare to all the world, which then drove them into seesawing between the two extremes of inferiority complex and power frenzy. The Versailles-elicited inferiority feeling looms through even a most intense effort in power politics. What else are we to make of the lines of "Das Englandlied," which states that Germans will not put up with the English making a *laughing stock* of their power! I doubt there is any English-language song with a similar message, and I cannot forget the remark by a *knowledgeable* German: "It must be dreadful to be the member of a small nation like Switzerland." It is worth taking a closer look at this comment. We will be none the wiser by observing its nonsense. It certainly is nonsense! The question really is what makes a knowledgeable German utter such claptrap. At heart, the person who said this actually meant: "It would be horrible to realize that the nation I belong to is not great." Now, this is not at all nonsense; if it were to turn out that the German people, who had been great for a thousand years, were not great, that would certainly be dreadful for a German.

Nothing worse can be done to a hysterical state of mind than to subject it to moral stricture and vilification. The hysterical psyche finds satisfaction only in itself; it lives in a closed world, in the name of which it will always be able to justify itself, and thus moral judgment will only make its worldview even more closed. Moral judgment will never crush a hysterical worldview, only crude and simple fact, just as no shake of the head or moral disapproval or punishment will ever bring a hysterical woman under control, only a bucket of cold water. The Germans should have simply been left alone with the crude and simple fact of their defeat and of the however harsh yet fixed-sum reparations, as well as the wide-ranging political possibilities opened up by the disappearance of the German dynasties.

Unfortunately, the irresistible itch in the victorious democracies for moralizing would not have this. Instead of the simple truth of defeat at war and fixed reparations came the clause on war guilt, which had to be proved and could be refuted; came disarmament, which had to be supervised and could be dodged; came unspecified reparations, which could be jacked up and haggled down; and came the ban on *Anschluss*, which had to be justified and was unjustifiable. The very concept of a peace treaty defining moral responsibility would have fueled German hysteria even if it had been 100 percent objective and incontestable, but having been self-righteous and small-minded, it exacerbated its reception even further.

Though the fresh awareness of the horrors of Buchenwald and Mauthausen might seem to overrule this, it still must be made unmistakably clear that it was Versailles that turned German hysteria into a conscious break with the European system of values as a whole. It was Versailles that ingrained in Germans— most Germans, not only Hitlerites—the conviction that all moral judgment in international life needed was a victorious war, and, consequently, if the Germans wanted to rid themselves of the terrible burden embodied in the Treaty of Versailles, all they needed was to win a war next time.

The most direct effect of Versailles was that the Germans could not make use of two tremendous opportunities: full German unification and unqualified democratization. Both causes were thwarted, but, even worse, they were pitted against each other.

Stresemann's Narrow Way

After the collapse in 1918, the only possible aim a sound and moderate German foreign policy could have set was to establish full German political unity through an accurate application of the principles of ethnicity and self-determination and thereby settle the territorial status of Germany in Europe for good. The Treaty of Versailles forbade this. And so it turned this rather straightforward and utterly unaggressive ambition into an unattainable wish-dream and branded its mere mention as aggressive intent. This situation made a straight and balanced foreign policy without internal ruptures impossible for the Germans. Their own dignity, weight, and place in Europe having been questioned, German politics as a whole became characteristically extroverted, being defined not by internal objectives and programs but by the relationship with Europe, foreign countries, *others*. Every German political act was driven by either self-justification or self-assertion; either emphatic willingness to cooperate or spiteful pigheadedness not to; either conformity to European consensus at all cost or defiance at all cost.

The mental state of the Germans and the crushing burden of Versailles inevitably exacted a German foreign policy seeking to redress military and territorial grievances in a Europe where any such German quibble would be regarded as a fresh example of German war guilt and warlikeness. Gustav Stresemann found the only possible, narrow route out of this quagmire: first, restore German self-confidence and outsiders' trust in the German people, and then begin to wind up whatever was left to wind up in the Treaty of Versailles. Experts on German monstrosity have since discovered that Stresemann was no better than Hitler or better only in disguising the cannibal German hidden in him; after all it has turned out from his letters, published after his death, that the maker of the Treaty of Locarno had also set himself the long-term aim of annulling disarmament, unification with Austria, and changing the borders with Czechoslovakia and Poland. This is sheer narrow-mindedness, informed by a total ignorance of the reasons for the German and European crises. Read the core of the Treaty of Locarno, the Rhineland Pact, with common sense. Won't we find that it meant on the part of the Germans that they regarded the Treaty of Versailles as a *diktat* but that they would accept the finality of some of its provisions, their western borders, and the demilitarization of the Rhineland? Their ambition had *therefore* been to change the rest! There was little point in waiting for Stresemann's death and the posthumous publication of his letters: the Rhineland Pact made it abundantly clear that its German signatory had been aspiring to undo the demilitarization, to unite with Austria, and to modify the borders with the Czechs and the Poles. Whoever seriously affirms that, just like Hitler, Stresemann would have marched into the Rhineland, conquered the Czechs and the Poles, attempted to bring about the dominion of the German race over others, disregarded the moral and legal principles of European coexistence, and equally brought ruin to the continent certainly deserves to live in a Hitlerite Europe.

The narrow path Stresemann had marked out was blocked after his death, and a European confidence crisis broke out over the issue of demilitarization. Military equality was seen as indispensable for regaining German self-confidence, and whichever German government was to obtain it would hold the winning trump in home politics. It would have been elementary wisdom to put this trump into the hands of a German government with a European mind-set. Such wisdom was not to be found, and whatever novelty is unearthed about Hitler's road to power, I am convinced that had the disarmament conference not miscarried, Hitler would never have risen to power because this was what finally justified his slogan that restoring the *face* of Germany was impossible through European methods.

The Arrest of Democratic Development in Germany

It was the European status of the German nation that arrested its democratic development. The great hopes of Germany's moving toward democratic and socialist transformation were ruthlessly dashed after 1918. With its history and prestige, German social democracy achieved no less than the abdication of all dynasties and the proclamation of the republic. However, following the collapse of the old political authority, democratic factors could not shape a new one. The long-discredited institution of territorial principality could no longer lay its former claims—for all its tenacity, it had long been living on borrowed time; no one seriously gave a thought to reviving it. It did, however, have one feature that could be revived in the power vacuum, one that would make it most dangerous—personal power. Serious democratic efforts and experiences lacking, Germany had not had the opportunity to learn the most important lesson of democracy: the art of government and obedience without personal power and rule. At heart, post-1918 Germany felt no one was ruling, governing, or leading it. This was why it preferred Hindenburg the moment it had the opportunity instead of all other democratic politicians, and this was why it went so easily into the romantic madness of expecting to be cured from all its ailments by a leader flaunted as a political genius.

It is no wonder therefore that, in such circumstances, Weimar democracy was lame, poor, and hapless. Internal political transformation had actually come into being with no major social-political setback, but Versailles delivered a debilitating shock: Western democracies had no sense of solidarity with the new German democracy, and this immediately imprinted the image that Germany had lost its European authority and position the very moment it had started out on the way toward democracy. This was the root cause of the terrifying helplessness of German socialism between 1918 and 1930. It was in this atmosphere following 1918 that it broke in two, both of its parts becoming barren. Throughout the world, there have always been more and less radical socialists, but in Germany, the Communists meant catastrophe socialism and the Social Democrats, a lame socialism. Throughout the period between 1918 and 1930, the Social Democratic Party was either the governing party or in a governing alliance, but apart from bloodlessly obtaining certain institutions, it could establish nothing in either democratizing German society or socialist construction because it continuously had to prove itself in responding to national grievances and claims to a public opinion that was mentally unhinged. This was how it maneuvered itself into the absurd situation where, though it kept bringing up national grievances, it became the bête noire of German national movements and was branded as an accomplice of an international democratic plot against Germany.

It had been no coincidence that the little that could be exacted from the Germans and the Entente to mitigate Versailles had been exacted not by social democracy but a right-wing politician, Gustav Stresemann. But no sooner had Hitlerism brought up the issues of German redress, hegemony, and polyvalence with all its might in 1930, the situation of those parties that had intended to handle these matters with certain European restraint became impossible. The center parties dared no longer govern in an alliance with the Social Democrats, leading first to the chancellorship of Heinrich Brüning, then to the anti-socialist schemes of Hindenburg, and ultimately to the paralysis of democratic forces and the total collapse of the democratic political machinery. As a grotesque apogee of this collapse, Social Democrats cast their votes for Hindenburg, and what was even more grotesque was that they were able to do no better—even that would have helped Hitler's rise to power. It would be a wasted effort to look for the reasons for the fall of the Weimar democracy in the dogmatism of democrats, the overcentralization of the Social Democratic Party, the academic-me-chanical election system, the German herd instinct, or any such childishness. Obviously, none of these were causes, only effects. German democracy started out without powerful democratic experiences but with massive emotional and historical dead weights and thus could hardly have been anything but dogmatic, mechanical, and soulless.

The Beginnings of Pathological German Anti-Semitism

Again, it was in the cul-de-sac of Weimar democracy that pathological German anti-Semitism was born. There had always been anti-Semitism in Germany, and it had even been somewhat more powerful than elsewhere. The German and the Jewish minds have certain complementary characteristics (both being "either-or-nothing" and amends-pursuing people) and disparate features (German naivety and irrationalism versus Jewish speculative ability and rationalism), both turning their possible opposition into conflicts sharper than in other nations. As anywhere in the world, it was only in the heads of a particularly ill-tempered and specter-haunted minority in Germany that Jews became the cause of all possible troubles and the central figures of a pathological worldview. However, the horror stories this minority told found a particular response in the German state of mind after 1918.

I feel the most important cause of this particular response was the different reaction German Jews had to the factors that paralyzed and possessed German political life and mentality—primarily democracy, international relations, and the Depression. There is no doubt that German Jews were of the same opinion about the Treaty of Versailles as all the rest of the Germans, and their livelihoods suffered from the economic crisis in essentially the same way as did those of all other Germans. (The fortunes made by speculators, among whom Jews in the eyes of the public were disproportionately highly represented, are the most fickle and fleeting phenomena of business life.) It was the psychic reaction of the Jews that was different. As a result of their whole historical situation, the majority of Jews regarded democracy and more intensive international relations as the only hopeful possibilities, and not even the most foolish of treaties could have caused any fundamental psychological crisis in their relationship to democracy and internationalism. In vain did they therefore have the same *opinion* on the Treaty of Versailles; they felt perfectly at home in the atmosphere of democracy and intensive international relations after 1919 and did not share the psychological debilitation Germans felt in contrast to them.

Similarly, the majority of Jews, for all their suffering and losses in the economic crisis, had a historically attained mental flexibility and did not see it as the doom of an entire world, as millions of lower- and upper-middle-class Germans did. If we add to this the inclination of Jews to be impervious to and contemptuous of emotional attachments of other people that they do not share and to explain and reassess everything rationally and in modern terms, we begin to grasp the irritation they elicited in the German middle classes and petite bourgeoisie, who felt deadlocked in every way and had been seeking with a pigheaded imperviousness for twenty years to find the culprits who had "stolen" their money in the inflation and deprived them of their national dignity in the treaty.

The participation of some Jews in the socialist movement allowed them to be associated with the bête noire of Marxism, and the part of Jewry that had a role in capitalism discredited socialism and turned the socialist feeling of the masses against *Jewish* capitalism. That all this together was contradictory was of no import for a state of mind that looked not for truth but for the culprit. In this psychological situation, a whole people became inclined to derive the mad complexities and chaos the world had fallen into from a satanic plot—vulgar Marxism having accustomed them to the idea of a satanic plot—and so the pathological phantasms of an anti-Semitism that had been an isolated phenomenon earlier on now came in very handy, exactly fitting their Satan-seeking appetite and irritating experiences. Satan found, only a Messiah was wanting, and he did not keep them waiting for long.

2) The Austrian Republic
Is Austria an Independent Nation, or
Is It Fundamental to the German Crisis?

The Allied climate of opinion currently seems to be that Austria and Austrians belong in the line of small nations Hitlerite Germany has conquered — the Czechs, Poles, Norwegians, Dutch, Belgians, Yugoslavs, Greeks, etc. It is thought to be self-evident that after the fall of Hitlerism, Austria will also regain its independence. The formula seems quite simple: there has been an independent Austrian state, so there is and there wants to be an independent Austrian nation.

This approach is in marked contrast with the fact that Austria had to be held back from voluntarily uniting with Germany through a variety of international treaties, regulations, and political and economic advantages between 1918 and 1934. And now not only those living at home in Austria, but also émigrés cannot agree on whether they want an independent Austria or not.

In the light of what we have said on the historical roots of the German crisis, there is nothing to be wondered at in this. Austria is not an independent nation; it is but one of the many German territorial principalities, which, with their varying degrees of independence, never ceased to be constitutive parts of the German nation. Only the Dutch, the Belgians, and the Swiss had acquired separate and powerful historical experiences that finally cut them away from Germany and established them as independent nations. In the others, it was but an awareness of locality that developed, most powerfully in Prussia and Bavaria, but never so strongly as to undo their sense of belonging to the German nation. And the Austrians, for all their local sense of belonging, had always been more German than the Prussians or the Bavarians. For all the inglorious political record of a Vienna-centered Austrian dukedom and later emperorship, the greatest glory of Austria was that it was the home country of the German Empire, its Île-de-France — in other words, the political center of Germany.

Austria has not only been a central part of the German body politic, but it has also had a central role in the political fever of the Germans. In the critical, birth-pang period of German unification, between 1806 and 1866, the waves of German national feeling rose high in Austria, much higher than in many German countries. Then, the policy of blood and iron after 1866, having excluded Austria from German unification, thrust the political life of Austrian Germans in a profound torpor, it being increasingly difficult for them to grasp what business they had in the Austrian Empire when there was a united Germany.

One of the outcomes of this political torpor was the half-hearted, unconvincing, humdrum, day-in-day-out sort of political practice called *fortwursteln* (to wangle), which Austria developed between 1866 and 1918. Today, this is often described as a political manifestation of the characteristic Austrian joviality, though it was obviously a symptom and had nothing to do with any Austrian national feature.

An Austria that had been the center of German politics from the fifteenth century until 1866 looked quite different. Hardly fitting in with the common image of Austrian national characteristics, the post-1866 "joviality" had its seamy side: the appearance of unruly and hysterical political formations. It might sound odd in Western Europe, but everyone in Central Europe knows perfectly well that Hitlerism was born not in "aggressive," "feudal," and "militarist" Prussia but in meek, mild, and Latinate Austria. It is not a mere coincidence that Hitler is himself an Austrian, and it was not accidental that the anti-Semitic Great German Movement became rife in Austria, providing decisive impulses to Hitler and Hitlerism.

This sickly, extreme, one could say schizophrenic state of Austrian political life continued after 1918. Though the empire of the Hapsburgs had been dissolved, the "obligatory" independence that both the peace and the Austrian economic treaties had laid down was as aimless and pointless for Austrian Germans as the Austro-Hungarian Monarchy had been; both meant that they were excluded without any apparent reason from the German body politic to which they had belonged until 1866. So the humdrum, wangling political practice was reborn, together with its latent political tension and hysteria. What is the explanation for the fact—which is likewise unknown in Western Europe but is common knowledge in Central Europe—that the Nazi hysteria captivated the Austrians far more than, for instance, the Bavarians?! It would be difficult to say that Bavaria is more Catholic and European than Austria and has a larger store of antitoxins against barbarism and nihilism. The explanation is quite simple: Hitlerism managed to identify itself with the cause of German unification, and belonging to a unified Germany was self-evident, something relatively uninteresting for Bavaria, while it was a central, burning issue in Austria. This would have been impossible had Austria been an independent nation!

However, Austria is not only not a separate nation, but also *the central issue of the German crisis*. German political development had taken its fateful turn toward impasse when the *Austrian* ruler first had not wanted to and later had been unable to take the lead in German unification. The German unification of 1871 became the cause of so much internal and then external tension because *Austria* had been barred from it. The grave mistake of the 1918 European settlement was that it forbade the unification of Austria with Germany even when German internal development no longer put any obstacle in its way.

This was why final unification in 1938 came into being through a burst-out of the cankered and festering German forces that shook and are still shaking the whole world.

Austrian Resistance between 1934 and 1938

Austria had therefore been legally, politically, and emotionally an organic part of Germany up until 1866 and underwent no experiences between 1866 and 1918 and 1918 and 1934 that would have brought it any closer to becoming an independent nation. That there was an Austrian nation at all, and that it was ready to fight for its independence in the face of Germany, occurred at most in the brief period between 1934 and 1938, the assassination of Dollfuss and the *Anschluss* by force. This is a rather short period for the making of a nation. It remains to be answered whether it as a *nation* at all resisted Hitlerite Germany. Apparently, it was not one.

The most important force behind resistance was the Christian Socialist Party, backed by the Catholic Church. Never urging union with a Protestant-majority Germany, it never took a stance against the *Anschluss*. It displayed resistance only from the moment *Anschluss* meant joining up with a Germany that availed itself of pagan mythology and persecuting the church. This was the very resistance the German Zentrumspartei attempted, albeit with less success. The Austrian resistance, however, had the means of an independent state and the added security that a centuries-old established Catholic Church provided.

Another force behind resistance was *legitimism*, which had no mass bases apart from aristocrats, former officers, and reminiscing old men. It gathered some strength when the resistance movement began to feel that holding out against a Germany beating the drum for German unity needed something more authoritative and spectacular than a Christian Socialist republic.

The third force behind Austrian resistance was the *Heimwehr*, an odd mix of border-guard squad, a fascist front-line soldiers' league, and the private army of an ambitious aristocrat (Prince Starhemberg, a former associate of Hitler). It had been in the prime of its life when Hitlerism was establishing itself in Germany and was regarded as its Austrian pendant. In proportion to Hitlerism becoming the movement embodying German unity, the internal cementing force of the Heimwehr dwindled away. A jovial Austrian joke of the time was very much to the point: A soldier marching in a Heimwehr column says to his neighbor, "Do all these Nazis we are hoofing it with know we are both Commies?"

The last force, which I should have mentioned first had it participated in resistance to Hitlerism, is *Austrian Socialist Labor*, which had sided with the

Anschluss up until Hitlerism and has gone back on its position only for the time being, until Hitlerism is defeated.

It was thus not a *separate nation* that showed resistance between 1934 and 1938. The assassination of Dollfuss was not an event that could have prompted the making of a nation because neither the Grossdeutsche nor labor, the two movements making up the Austrian majority, saw in him a national hero or martyr. It has been much debated what would have come to pass had Dollfuss tried to negotiate a policy with Austrian labor and given a broader base to resistance. In his position, he could surely have been smarter and more humane to the socialists, but this will not change the fact that even if he had wanted to, he could never have agreed on a policy with them. The moment that the German hysteria finally painted the image of Social Democrats as a gang of international traitors, the same image began to apply in Austria too; and Dollfuss could not strike a deal with labor, just as Heinrich Brüning had not been able to in Germany, because Austria was not an independent nation, and so it verily had its share of the German hysteria.

Even at the peak point of resistance, no Austrian politician would have had the courage to set the Austrian *nation* against the German *nation*, and even if he had had the courage, he would have been immediately ousted from government. There was mention of only the particular German mission of the Austrian people, and independence was needed to fulfill this. Many sought to make this Austrian mission more tangible through the idea that an independent Austrian state would preserve European-minded German forces until Germany overcame the Hitlerite fever. In other words, this was also a temporary and conditional independence. That Austria should wage war on Germany, and, to obtain support, enter into alliances with alien powers, would have been unthinkable. Had Western powers started a war to prevent the *Anschluss* in 1938, they would have been able to find many allies for this endeavor, but the Austrians would not have been among them.

Whether the events taking place after 1938 are enough to start the making of a separate Austrian nation is now difficult to tell. That union with Germany came into being by force and aggression; that jovial Austria suffered a lot from the insolence of the schoolmasters of Hitlerism; that Austria, after a brief year and a half in the German world, got involved in the most catastrophic adventures of German history; that Austria now receives some degree of particular attention from the Allies and can hope to be afforded further discernment—all this may lead Austrians and Germans to drift apart. This perhaps is enough for a future referendum, where the other option would be sharing in the terrible liabilities of a defeated Germany, to result—a result that would, I believe, be highly unlikely—in a majority for an independent Austria. But these are only negative statements, based as they are on urges not wholly noble. If it has not yet been able to do so until now, none of this will ever foster the making of a nation. Whether political hysteria or regeneration is the question, it is highly unlikely that Austria will develop, as it has never developed, independently of German political development. And by all likelihood the verve of Austrian youth is going to be directed at union with Germany and so exert its influence in Austria, as it has always done.

THE FIFTH IMPASSE: THE HITLERITE THIRD REICH

What Is Fascism?

In our discussions above, our understanding of Hitlerism has been that it is a one-time phenomenon: it is a final consequence of concrete antecedents and concrete shocks in German political development. However, it also belongs to the type of social-political development usually termed *fascism* today. Is it to no avail to speak of the *psychological* antecedents of Hitlerism and *shocks* when fascism has its generally known social and economic preconditions and necessarily comes into being when those are given? Indeed, fascism does have its *typical* preconditions, but the most decisive of these are the psychological ones. All explanations attempting to keep these out are hopelessly empty.

The most general explanation of fascism is that it is the defense organization of the feudal, capitalist, and militarist groups—briefly and simply, the reactionary upper classes—against progress and socialist revolution in particular. What is undoubtedly true in this statement is that in all kinds of fascism, these elements offered some sort of approval, or if not unconditional then certainly perceptible assent, manifest even in deed. But this is far from anything that could have been a cause of fascism. There is no greater naivety than to suppose that a major mass movement can be founded on the funds, instigation, or intrigue of anyone. Money, incitement, and schemes may help organize a mass movement and assist it in overcoming critical or dangerous moments, but a mass movement comes into being irrespective of these, and once it has come about, no group activity will be able to arrest it.

Feudal, capitalist, and militarist groups helped tyranny into power in several periods of history—for instance, in the First and Second French Empires—without, however, attempting or being able to set up fascist organizations. For them, it is not the *movement* but the readiness of the masses to *obey* that is important. That this takes the form of mass movement is a nuisance rather than an aim. The alliance of feudal, capitalist, and militarist forces with fascism has always and everywhere been a compromise in the strictest sense of the word, where both sides, reactionary and fascist, have attempted to use the other as a means to their own never forgone and often contradictory ends. For this very reason, the compromise between reaction and fascism usually breaks up in due course. It is therefore insufficient to explain fascism as a means or a manifestation of reaction.

It is even more useless to apply the opposite formula, that it is a revolution of the petite bourgeoisie. This is a spinoff of vulgar Marxism, according to which no revolution can be explained without first designating a social class as the primary beneficiary and vehicle of the revolution. However, many members of the petite bourgeoisie appeared as followers of fascism; their representation as the main bearers of fascism was obviously conceived in pain, an explanation concocted subsequently. For a hundred years everyone in Europe believed it natural that the revolution of the bourgeoisie would be followed by that of the proletariat, and to no one did it occur to have to insert an interim revolutionary phase in honor of the petite bourgeoisie until the 1930s. Moreover, it would be difficult to explain how world power, success in wars of conquest, and the subjugation of other peoples relate to the interests of the petite bourgeoisie as a class, not to mention the fact that the British and the French petite bourgeoisies, which have disproportionately much greater social influence, never stood forward to be the vehicles of this interim revolutionary phase.

As opposed to the social or social-class explanations of fascism, we have the no more productive accounts that view it as the crisis of the moral system or as a singular world of values, totally different from the one European mankind had developed formerly. No doubt evaluation is far more a feature of fascism than its basing itself on various social classes. However, it would be an unintended overestimation to describe it as a debatable yet independent value system that cannot be brought under—and whose fundamental principles cannot be derived from—any common denominator.

Fascism is often said to be some sort of primitive, tribal, warlike, heroic system of values opposed to the Christian, humanist, and socialist one based on humanity, love, and freedom. It would, however, be a gross mistake to imagine that, though latently, the former existed independent of the latter. The only core of truth in this is that a warlike, tribal, and primarily birth-based value system had prevailed among the newer barbarian peoples of the European continent. The two-thousand-year achievement of Christianity, however, was to sublimate the tribal virtues of the new peoples of Europe and seek to turn blind obedience into responsible self-discipline, blind allegiance into conscious self-sacrifice, and racial feeling into a sense of community. True enough, this tribal and birth-based value system lived on longest in Germany and had been both a cause and effect of the unhappy hyper-aristocratic structure that had shaped the territorial principality, resulting in the falling apart of the German body politic, the difficulties and ambiguous resolution of unification, and ultimately the current crisis of the German nation. It is also unquestionable that Hitlerism consciously drew on reminiscences of this tribal-birth value system.

Nevertheless, it must be made emphatically clear that fascism has no central moral principle. Its conceptions of value are not based on an independent, war-like, heroic moral value system but are mere derivatives of Christian, national, and democratic values, and their essential meaning is that they seek to resolve certain current social and moral issues of Western man, reviving moral heroism, social authority, and community spirit, by way of distorted and disproportionate chimeras (the myth of force, *Führerprinzip*, racial theory).

It is a very idle exercise to blame philosophical systems for the distortions of thought that may have drawn on them. No doubt in order to have the daring to utter, formulate, and systematize the warped human thought fascism would pile up, there was a need for the contribution of the cult of the hero, force, power, will, action, the irresistible energy of life, etc., conceived in the name of a false romanticism; these surfaced as constitutive parts of serious and significant philosophical systems at the end of the nineteenth century and were debased into the misconceptions of vulgar philosophizing by the beginning of the twentieth. But we must not, in German fashion, avail ourselves of a false history of ideas and attribute effects to philosophical notions or ideological whims that they are unable to achieve. Catastrophes arise not from ideas themselves but from the impulses that can find their way into the schemes made up of ideas. However great the importance of notional formulas is, the fact that a person or a community chooses a moral formula from among those offering themselves cannot be deduced from the formula itself.

We will likewise not get far with the simple explanation of fascism as the revolt of the gangster or outlaw type of man. True enough, gangsters have been extremely highly represented in fascist activities, but this only means that they would not miss the excellent opportunities fascism affords them. It is, however, out of the question that the association of outlaws was a significant factor in the formation of fascism. The main point of fascism was to confuse the value system of law-abiding and honest citizens. For the outlaw to be cast in a role, first something was needed to muddy the waters of law itself, and not even the most well-organized plot of criminals is capable of achieving this. The greatest enemy of the rule of law is not the outlaw but the shady and spurious situations that make the law ill, meaningless, and self-righteous.

The difficulties of finding the place of fascism become obvious when observing the odd ballgame that has been going on between European conservatism and radicalism over fascism from the moment of its inception and which can be noticed in the tensions between the English-speaking world and the Soviets. The upholders of the European tradition simply regard it as a version of value-destroying revolution and emphasize its common features with communism. In contrast, the followers of European progressivism deem it "mercenary pseudo-revolution" backed by the darkest anti-progressive, feudal, and reactionary elements. In other words, the right points the finger at the far left, while the left points at the far right because of fascism.

Now this is hardly accidental; it ties in organically with the essence of fascism. Certainly fascism refers to traditional emotions, but it simultaneously brushes off the European tradition. It calls for the support of reactionary forces, but at the same time, it shatters their social prestige. It mobilizes democratic mass emotion but drives it into an impasse. It conjures up revolution but resolves nothing. Naturally, it is difficult to pinpoint the central concept of fascism because all its thoughts are negative. Fascism is far from being a self-contained scale of values; it is not even antithetical; it is but the product of a crisis brought about by the European democratic revolution. This is why it includes, in a distorted form, all the elements of democratic revolution and of the reaction it has elicited. What holds them together is that they were precipitated by the same historical hysteria from the chaos that the Christian and humanist value system fell into in certain parts of Europe in recent times. The one feature that surely distinguishes fascism from the other major currents that have defined European social and political development is that it is *distorted*.

Wherefore this distortion? Even political development in a modern European community requires that the cause of the community and the individual be one cause. In other words, what is needed is that when a revolutionary moment does ensue and revolutionary shocks liberate the individual from the psychological pressure of social forces tyrannizing him by the grace of God, it is glaringly clear and self-evident that the liberation of the individual implies the liberation, expansion, and inner and outer enrichment of the whole community. This was not the course events took in the life of a number of nations in certain parts of Europe, Central and Eastern Europe in particular. On the contrary, these nations went through historical situations where the collapse of the oppressive social and political powers of the past meant the catastrophe of the national community as a whole. Fascism is always rooted in situations where, for whatever reason, shock or misconception, the cause of the nation and the cause of liberty, are pitted against each other, where a historical crash infuses the convulsive fear that the progress of liberty will jeopardize the cause of the nation.

Over and above these, however, a full-blown fascism requires one more thing—that the social and political development of the country concerned reach a stage where the full and mass democratization of community feeling and democratic revolution are imminent. It is in a political community at such a stage of development that a convulsive fear can engender the absurd idea that all the forces that would take sides with the power of democratic revolution, with the cause of the nation and liberty in countries with a harmonic development, should, with all their might, side with *only the cause of the nation* but *not the cause of liberty*. However paradoxical it may sound, we must say that fascism can exist only where there are democratic mass emotions. Without some sort of precursor, example, debacle of, or experiment in democracy, fascism cannot come into being. The way fascism relates to democracy is not simple negation or opposition but that certain phenomena in a crisis of democratic development are deformed in it: fascism is a deformed product of democratic development.

It now becomes clear why we have said that fascism cannot be represented simply as the instrument of reaction. Fascism and reaction organically belong together. But they do not love one another. The fear at the root of fascism favors the political and social powers of the past, saying that their total elimination brings about catastrophe. This thesis enables and encourages the historical aristocracy and military groups to join the mass movements fascism diverted because they are no longer directed against them but against some external enemy. Nevertheless, the aristocracy keeps away from fascism, in the same way that it keeps away from democratic revolution, and, in the final count, fascism ruins the social prestige of historical forces as does democratic revolution. Aristocrats and soldiers indeed merely assist in the great process of fascism, but they can neither help it progress nor obstruct it. The social and class background of fascism is an all-inclusive muddle of all social forces brought together by shared convulsive fears and the resulting, often contradictory delusions: aristocrats and officers preferring the authority of power to everything else, groups of intellectuals entangling themselves in rabid fears for their nation, upper- and lower-middle-class groups giving up liberty for the sake of order, as well as labor, ready to swap freedom for social benefits and indivisible human dignity for a preposterous exultation of national quality.

All the characteristically distorted contradictions of fascism arise from its paradoxical objective of mobilizing *only* for the cause of the nation, *not* for liberty: the contradiction of the absolute despot supported by a mass movement, the nonsense of a populism derisive of the crowds, the circle-squaring anti-democratic nationalism, the absurdity of anti-libertarian revolution, and the monstrosity of peoples waging wars of extermination against one another.

However common these features of the various fascisms are, none of them can be understood without a grasp of the particular shocks and the resulting fears in which a given fascism is rooted. It is not without reason that we have sought to draw up a historical sequence of events going all the way back to the Napoleonic Wars in order to comprehend German fascism, Hitlerism.

Hitlerism and Versailles

The defining shock for German National Socialism was undoubtedly the Treaty of Versailles. Most regrettably, we have to refute again and again the now common opinion that the treaty was, instead of being bad, actually far too mild because the Germans have proved that fathomless and ineradicable urges of aggression and power have been at work in them long before and irrespective of Versailles. We have pointed out how the legend of the ancient German power cult should be looked upon; it certainly goes back beyond Hitler—not as far back as the sinister Germanic predecessors but only to the crisis that unfolded around German unification in the middle of the nineteenth century.

Nowhere was it written, however, that after being defeated in the Great War, the Wilhelmine power cult had to necessarily and naturally develop further. Quite to the contrary, military defeat could have been an excellent cure for the German power cult, for it had achieved what no military had ever before managed: to move the dynasties out of the way, to get rid of their dead weight, obstructing German political union and democratic development. That defeat in 1918 would not cure but aggravate the German power cult was undoubtedly caused by Versailles. Not because of its being far too strict but because of its taking the form of moral judgment instead of making peace; worse, it ruled in the name of moral principles that the German political community was not mature enough to accept, and, to top it all, it itself did not apply them in earnest. As a reaction, the entire value system on the basis of which the charge had been based plunged into a crisis within the German political community.

It is at this point that the internal contradiction of the hysterical mind becomes sharply visible. On the one hand, it vilifies, with hysterical exasperation, the entire value system in the name of which it was condemned; on the other, it binds itself more than ever before to this order of values as it seeks redress before the very tribunal in which it suffered its injury. All the destructive dog-mas of Hitlerism stem from the desire to gainsay the whole world in this am-bivalent and contradictory manner; while it wants to obtain moral justification and exemption from the charges, it also shakes off all responsibility, assuming as virtues all just and unjust accusations against it. As the German nation was not treated as an equal party at Versailles, so Hitlerism has ceaselessly demanded the restoration of the equality and honor of the German people while elevating it above all others; as the German people had been held responsible for the outbreak of the war and to have criminally wanted it, so Hitlerism has end-lessly claimed and sought to prove that the other side had in fact wanted and instigated it, and, simultaneously, it has proclaimed war as the rule and fulfill-ment of national life. As the German people were forced to pay reparations, so Hitlerism has not desisted from asserting and protesting that the reparations reduced Europe and Germany to beggary and, at the same time, has laid it down as law that all peoples proving to be weaker than the Germans are but a means to their prosperity and enrichment. As the German people were dis-armed by Versailles because it was feared that they would use their military power for wars of conquest, so Hitlerism has not ceased from pronouncing the German people's desire for peace and that it only needs the army for honor's sake, no other, while it has followed a policy justifying the wildest fears about the German Army. As the victors at Versailles did not allow the German people to exercise the right of self-determination they themselves had proclaimed and to establish a Great German Empire, so Hitlerism has unremittingly demanded the self-determination of all German persons and lands, and it has simulta-neously denied the self-determination of all nations except the German. As Western public opinion has called into question German achievements in their own right, political performance in particular, so Hitlerism has incessantly pre-sented German achievements as unique, and, at the same time, it has declared the superiority of the German people, shirking the possibility of any, perhaps disadvantageous, comparison. As the Western climate of opinion has cast doubt on the European spirit of the German people, so Hitlerism has desperately tried to pass itself off as the representative of the European cause, and it has simulta-neously nullified all the heretofore effective rules of coexistence between men and states, replacing them with the single law of power and racial supremacy.

With this in mind—the response of Hitlerism to all the burning and unre-solved issues that tormented the entire German community and to which a lame Weimar democracy had had no answer—calculations of what percent-age of Germans are Hitlerites are obviously beside the point. For all Germans who took the fate of Germany after 1918 to heart in the slightest degree, Hitlerism has necessarily meant something. Even if one was never a Hitlerite at all, the subtlest of highbrows, perhaps even a Jew, there has been "something to" what Hitlerism has said. Hence the terrible paralysis of democratic, European-minded Germans in the face of Hitlerite agitation: Hitlerism appealed to emotions from which they could not be aloof. The question is not how many Germans are Hitlerites but how Hitlerism was able to raise issues with the effect of Aqua fortis on German political life, prompting a positive answer from those to whom the outlook of Hitlerism was entirely alien. It could be put it in this way: where Hitlerism sought to find redress for Germans before the world, 90 percent of Germans are Hitlerites. However, where Hitlerism wanted to radically break with the European order of values, 90 percent of Germans have not been Hitlerites even to this very day. The vast majority of Germans were Hitlerites when issues of the military provisions of the Treaty of Versailles and the Austrian and the Sudeten *Anschluss* were raised, and, except for an insignificant minority, they are not Hitlerite when the massacring of Jewish women and children is concerned. The only trouble is that a political constellation arose where a political party and ideology bent on mass murder appeared to be the only formation that could handle the unresolved internal and external matters of the nation.

The internal contradictions of Hitlerism, its simultaneous reference to and denial of the moral values of Europe, have brought about its internal rupture and external fall. This rupture and fall can be observed in how the three critical issues over which Hitlerism attacked the value system of European social, political, and international coexistence—namely, *international cooperation, democracy,* and *socialism*—have finally ensnared it.

THE SNARE OF IDEAS

1) Self-Determination and the Power Cult

Hitlerism unbound itself from the so far effective principles of *European coexistence,* the freedom and equality of nations, and the right of self-determination because the German people had the one-time bitter historical experience of a very scanty, one-sided, and self-righteous application of these principles. Thus Hitlerism set out on a course of foreign policy based on fully exploiting situations of domination, the uniform brushing aside of dictated or voluntary agreements, and the vindication of unlimited force. In so doing, it achieved incredible successes. It turned out that it could without consequences take no notice of the obligations stipulated by the Treaty of Versailles, of which the Weimar Republic had in vain requested mitigations. It also turned out that it could provoke territorial changes the Weimar Republic would never even have dreamed of. Why? I have heard people say, "The Germans have learned the business of politics and diplomacy." Others have been keen on discovering the "accomplices" of the Germans in the enemy camp, the fifth column, Chamberlainism, the anti-Bolshevik intrigues of the capitalists, etc. Many, even his deadliest enemies, have called Hitler a "political genius." Others have pointed out the belated military preparations of the Western powers and attributed all German successes to this time advantage.

These observations may grasp elements of truth, but all in all, they childishly blur the issue. The deeper reason for the initial success of Hitlerite foreign policy was fair and simple: up to a point, it squared sufficiently with facts and the fundamental principles of the European value system. When Hitler referred to the desire of all Germans to join Germany, he referred to *actual* fact, and the fulfillment of this desire followed from the freedom, equality, and right of self-determination of nations. In spite of all superficial and accidental causes, the actual reason why German foreign-policy campaigns met with surprising successes between 1935 and 1938 was that *indeed* no war could be started on the grounds that Germany had arbitrarily achieved the military equality that everyone had known would be implemented in time. Indeed no war could be started because 7 million Austrian and 3 million Czech Germans, the vast majority of whom, by all signs, had felt and professed to be Germans, had joined Germany not through proper referenda but through an aggressive power policy.

This is why it is meaningless to say that Hitler's aggressive steps should already have been beaten back by military force in 1935, 1936, or at least in the spring of 1938. No democratic country can be pulled into a war without appropriate moral justification, and war could only have been justified on moral grounds had the Western powers clearly laid it down that they were not ready to make military and territorial concessions to Hitler's Germany but they would do so to a European-minded Germany through appropriate forms (referenda, etc.). Such a declaration, however, would have lacked conviction in view of how the pre-Hitlerite, European-minded Germany had been treated. Nevertheless, such a statement would not have been late even in 1938. Without it, the moral position of the Western powers would have had a much weaker footing than Germany in a war started in 1938. The way Munich took place was of course disastrous, but it does not change the fact that it was what gave the Allies the moral advantage over the Germans. What the *Anschluss* and Munich proved to the wide world was that the Western powers would not stand in the way of the unification of the German nation.

It was at this point that the drama of the monstrous hysteria embodied in Hitlerism came to a head, and Germany began to lose its European standing.

The vast majority of Germans had expected Hitler to gain redress before the value system of Europe for all the injuries that the German nation had suffered and that had also been injuries to that value system, and they had hoped that Hitler would obtain it without war. But all his statements to the contrary, *he did not believe and failed to notice—after all, he has never believed in the European value system*—that all his successes had been based on the overwhelming power of the international principles of freedom, equality, and the right of self-determination. Instead, he was convinced that he owed his successes to his aggressive power policies and his disregard of the forms of European coexistence and that he had acquired the German territories of Austria and the Czech lands because he had applied force rather than proceeding through referenda.

Munich should have been followed by a break according to the expectations of the German nation, by the measure of reality and the true requirements of the European value system; however, German policy, the negation of all European values embodied in Hitlerism, continued to pursue success through power policies in keeping with the everlasting laws of hysteria. So Hitlerism went beyond the limits of moderation with its repeated territorial demands upon the Czechs in the months following Munich, the limits of all decency with the march on Prague in March 1939, and the limits of all other possibilities by starting the war in September 1939. The occupation of Prague immediately brought to naught the entire moral position that Germany had had, and the outbreak of the war damped the hopes most Germans had put in Hitler. The very movement and leader that had promised to obtain moral redress for Germany contributed more than anyone or anything to losing Germany's moral stature and to the subsequent justification of all that Germany had suffered undeservedly.

2) Democracy and the *Führerprinzip*

Another point where Hitlerism set itself against the European scale of values was the question of *democracy* and *personal rule*. The millennium-and-a-half-long progress of European political development has meant the elimination of personal rule and the spiritualization of power and has pointed to the establishment of democracy and self-government. The desire not to be ruled in the traditional, dynastic, and personal way but according to the needs and expectations of the people has gradually become a mass emotion. This essentially and fundamentally democratic desire, however, can backslide where the breakdown of traditional personal rule takes place far too suddenly, without appropriate groundwork. Feeling derelict and masterless, the community might choose to raise dictatorial personal rule above itself. This was what happened in Germany.

The Hitlerian *Führerprinzip* resolved the tension between the desire for democratic leadership and the oppressive sense of being unled, providing seemingly satisfactory answers in all directions; dynastic personal rule has indeed waned, but in its stead, we now have a modern, appropriate rule rooted in the people and a leader who is the embodiment of the innermost desires of the people, who is a more genuine expression of the will of the people than the unknown and abjectly tolerated heads of the Weimar democracy, and who is the only worthy expression of the political organization of a great and ambitious nation. Again, we face the characteristic contradiction in the hysterical worldview between reality and phantasmagoria. The realistic basis of Hitler's rise to power was that his person was a perfect embodiment of the hysteria of the German people and that he offered to resolve the great grievances of the Germans.

What the Germans wanted was not dictatorship but a leadership that would voice and realize the desires of the whole community, and they would even tolerate dictatorship from such. In other words, they desired what they should desire according to the fundamental principle of democracy; however, the impasse into which their political thought had been led made them believe the nonsense that they could obtain this from a dictator. It is paradoxical but nevertheless true that the dictator who in his every utterance has bitingly ridiculed democracy and democracies has contributed more than anyone else to the involvement in the political process of a politically indifferent and unconscious people, an indifference that had weighed frightfully down on the Weimar democracy. Mournful as this debut was, democracy began as this crowd started to move. The German people accepted the Führer but received whatever this entailed with profound and increasing abhorrence—the ever brutal fettering of the freedom of speech and movement, even of grumbling; the gradual elimination of private life, eavesdropping and reporting; the myriads of miniature Führers that swamped all aspects of life in the name of the Party, the SA, or SS.

Paradoxically, yet truly, it was Hitlerism that gave the experiential proof to the German people that unlimited personal rule and the non-spiritualization of power are intolerable. Whatever havoc Hitlerism unleashed among the democratic forces of Germany, it is the lesson of Hitlerism that a people hitherto far too loyal to personal rule first satisfied the precondition of democracy that society abhor personal rule with the might of mass emotion.

3) Equality and Racial Theory

While European social development has long sought to put an end to the belief in the magic power of selection by birth and all birthright privilege, Hitlerism, with its racial theory, brought about a boom in birth mysticism, tracing noble and peasant forebears that not even the flowering periods of feudal nobility had ever seen. Again paradoxically, there is an aspect of Hitlerism that has affirmed European development in point of fact and in the long run. Nowhere in Europe has selection by birth burdened social development as it had done in Germany.

This is the one point in the deformation of German political thought that can be traced back to hazy Germanic ancestors and the period of the great migration, when the Germanic tribes established a rather strident birthright society on the ruins of an atomized Roman society. Through being moralized by Christianity, this form of social organization had become an important and even worthy factor in European social development, yet it was rendered obsolete in recent times. In Germany, however, it held out with unique doggedness. Now, Hitlerism actually relieved German society of its awful burden insofar as it radically denied the significance of any differences in birth or social standing within the nation, extolled to the skies and mystically glorified German birth, and dimmed all birthright privilege by attributing various far-reaching personal advantages to the privilege of being born German.

If Hitler has ever said that it is better to be a German chimney sweep than a count in any another nation, do not let us be deluded that this is mere cant. This was exactly the encouragement German chimney sweeps were in need of, lacking as they did—in contrast to their British or French brethren—the assurance of their full human dignity. We should not belittle the significance of the fact that Hitlerism radically merged German classes in the "melting pot" of the labor camps. Nowhere is the narrow-mindedness of the doctrinaire opinion that Hitlerism is but the disguised defense organization of the ruling classes more conspicuous than in this respect: were I a ruling class, I would scarcely be thankful that countesses were having their hands and feet frostbitten in compulsory labor service.

Nevertheless, this is the third critical point where Hitlerism undoubtedly had its internal fissures. What was really important for German chimney sweeps was not quite what was important for Hitler: that they were *better* than British earls but that they be the *equals* of German counts and factory owners. It has painfully dawned on the German masses that what they had gained by obligatory nation-brotherly beer-drinking sprees with office heads, they lost in the tightening discipline and right to command. Labor also had to awaken to the fact that its conditions were little improved by being called *Gefolgsmann* in Old High German, while the capitalist gained a lot by being called *Betreibsführer*—that is, a small Führer.

It is not true that Hitlerism is the disguised defense organization of the German ruling classes, but it is true that due to its inherent crowd-scorning and power-worshipping tendencies, it has realized only the disciplinary and organizational aspect of socialism and that it has necessarily suppressed its egalitarian and social liberation part—that is, it has nothing to do with socialism in the European sense of the word. Nevertheless, it is what has removed the greatest obstacle in the way of socialism—the prestige of birthright (social and property) privilege. The glorification of the German race has been consumed in the historical conflagration into which Hitlerism has dragged the German people, and so has the oppressive burden of birthright privilege, which it had dissolved in its racism.

Hitlerism on Balance

We now see the final shattering of the hysterical worldview of Hitlerism, its internal collapse parallel to its external demise. It has furiously attempted to defy the three definitive tendencies of European social development: international cooperation based on the system of self-determination, democracy replacing personal rule, and socialism dissolving birthright social organization. As these principles had once been defectively, contradictorily, and self-righteously applied to Germany, Hitlerism wanted to create a world where these principles were not valid. The final principles of European development, however, cannot be replaced by "new" ideas, camouflaged or misinterpreted.

The reference to "true" self-determination, democracy, and socialism that the Hitlerite leadership added onto the myth of power and race for tactical purposes proved to be a fatal snare: Hitlerism was powerful and successful inasmuch as it *truly* represented the right of self-determination, democracy, and socialism; as soon as it tried to drop them as time-expired tactical means from its arsenal, it turned out that it had no ideological weapons. The only lasting value it has left behind is what is truly self-determination, democracy, and socialism: it was the first to clearly delineate the borders of the German nation, it demonstrated to the German nation that personal rule is intolerable with the overwhelming power of experience, and it rendered the obsolescence of birthright privilege obvious.

This is not to say that Hitlerism is to be credited for all this or that it is a possible and suitable stage in democratic development. No credit can be due to a regime that has instilled a spurious romanticism in a whole nation, that has set forth pseudo-values to its youth, and that has overwhelmed a whole continent with terror and shocks of unforeseeable consequence. The havoc Hitlerism has wrought in the development of Europe is unfathomable. This, however, does not mean that through it, profound and irresistible social and psychological processes more powerful than ideology, infectious thought, and propaganda cannot assert themselves.

Summary

In the above we have tried to make our initial recognition more perceptible that the monstrous political hysteria of the Germans is not a matter of character but of history. We have demonstrated how two persistent historical factors, the territorial principality and selection by birth, have prevailed and have rendered the resolution of the German problem preterhumanly difficult. We have shown how the unhappy assumption of the Austrian emperorship in 1804 divested German development of a very useful consolidating tool, the legitimate Habsburg emperor. We have also pointed out how the three historical shocks of 1806, 1848, and 1918 infused fear and a sense of uncertainty in German political consciousness and how these have inclined it to escape into incomplete and make-believe solutions. We have explained that Germany went through five political systems in a short two-hundred-year period that fixed situations unviable in the long run, unable to establish political and social equilibrium. An attempt was made to correct internal instability by making sacrosanct the absurd compromise or precondition on which the system was built. The line of progress from the Holy Roman Empire through the German Confederation, Wilhelmine Germany, and the Weimar democracy to the Third Reich leads from impasse to impasse, from nothing to nothing. The dormant anarchy of the Holy Roman Empire, as Ferrero called it; the reactionary haplessness of the German Confederation; and the paralyzed democracy of the Weimar Republic are common knowledge. What I have primarily tried to demonstrate is that both the Wilhelmine and the Hitlerite Reichs, though putting on the guise of dynamism and movement, perfectly belong in the series of impasses based on unreasonable compromise and preposterous presupposition that have made up modern German history.

Though the political hysteria of the German nation goes back to historical reasons and is not based on character, the series of impasses and shocks has by now resulted in a certain degree of *deformation* in the German character. In the world wars, hundreds of thousands of Germans have now had the most direct experience of their being Germans: at once powerful and weak, victorious and lacking authority, justice-seeking and hated for their injustices, eminent in everything and unrespected, wonderfully organized and fickle. These experiences attracted even the average Germans to the ambivalent tendencies of raw power worship, the seeking of moral redress, and the sense that they were carrying a psychological dead weight of which they must some time relieve themselves.

The way out is not blocked; the German character has not been fully and finally changed. The original reasons for the German political impasse have virtually been obliterated. Political disintegration, the territorial principality system, and the hyper-aristocratic organization of society have been smashed, consumed in the terrible inferno in which the German hysteria has ended. But the internal factors capable of advancing German political development have also been consumed or paralyzed. Today, German political regeneration depends wholly on the clear-sightedness, unafraid calm, and humane wisdom of the surrounding world. The German trouble is not an incurable organic disease; it is a terrible community cramp, and allaying it is the most important task facing Europe.

CHAPTER III

1. THE FRENCH DREAD

It is not our task now to analyze all the hysterical moments of French political development; what we need to examine is the ways in which French hysteria has contributed to the current crisis. The great hysteria of French history was the Great Revolution, the effects of which on the balance of power in Europe were relatively fortuitously settled in 1814, but they continued to be felt in the German and Italian hysterias. The political-mental state of France has, however, had its role in the current disruption of the European order, which began in 1914. Since 1870–1871, the hysterical fear of Germany has, if not exclusively, defined French foreign policy.

The period 1870–1871 was one of the most shocking turning points in French history because, as 1941 would do so again, it questioned the great-power rank of France. The starting point of this was a simple material fact: the fall in the French birthrate. We have no remit to discuss the causes of this. Yet we should be advised against being taken in by the naive materialism that the French people had been biologically exhausted or the sermonizing dictum that France had fallen into moral decadence. Biological exhaustion does exist, and I am not aware of any comparative examination of the French population in this respect. As moral decadence is concerned, however, the final cause of a falling birthrate may be the crisis and change of social morality; this decadence can hardly be limited to France, and, moreover, there are greater problems with social morality in other continental countries. The only realistic formulation of the fall in the French birthrate is that the Europe-wide process of falling birthrates had begun in France a hundred years earlier than elsewhere. This might have been caused by French social advance, refined savoir-vivre, the mental exhaustion due to the human loss of the Great Revolution and the Napoleonic Wars, and other factors of social psychology. What counts, however, is that as a result, the proportion of inhabitants in France and the neighboring major countries has shifted by almost 100 percent. This was aggravated by the fact that the political power relations of a country hinged much on the number of its inhabitants because of national service. Now, this took place at the very moment German unity was established after a long period of gestation. The shift in the power proportion between Germany and France was particularly radical and sudden.

Now this explains why 1870–1871 was a major shock, but it does not explain why it led to a hysteria of fear. The loss of power and prestige by a country is not easy to stomach, but a fundamentally democratic society, like the French one was, would have the moral resources for the country to face up to these facts. In the final count, if the adventurer second emperor jumped into the war with Germany, it would hardly have been likely for a democratically minded French public to support in the long run a policy seeking to thwart German unification or its non-acknowledgment. In 1870–1871, however, the meaning of the war, due to several unfortunate events, proved to be more than and different from the recognition of German unity. The period 1870–1871 was not only a great turning point in the history of France, but also the great vengeance by Germany for 1806, as well the beginning of the great and tragic political dead end into which Germany steered itself. What was genuinely tragic was that this fateful moment bound all the fundamental problems of either nation to the aggressive intervention of the *other*. For in 1870–1871, it was not a self-confident Germany, aware of its power and embedded in the European political tradition, that taught the French adventurer-dictator the lesson of respecting Germany's self-determination; perturbed by internal insecurities, confused by make-believe successes, and unable to get its bearings on its problems, indeed an upstart Germany avenged itself on the country and nation to which it had attributed all its troubles and miseries since the terrible memory of Germany's humiliation in 1806.

The French had been caught unawares by this; they had had no direct experience of the *Erbfeind* complex of Little Germany, run by Prussians since 1806, or of its thirst for settling scores for that humiliation. For both individuals and nations, there is nothing worse than to fall into the hands of an enemy pursuing amends. It is beside the point what atrocities the Germans committed or did not commit; obviously, they were hardly any better than the victors of 1814, for whom the French had developed no phobia. The point is that the Germans did whatever they did with a mind toward avenging their *Erbfeind*. This was how the French became the victims of the Treaty of Frankfurt in 1871, the first instance of a break with the European tradition of sane and dispassionate peacemaking since Napoleon. To crown this, it carved off Alsace-Lorraine, with the wholly French area around Metz, whose population could under no guise be expected to have a sense of belonging to Germany. Apart from divided Poland, there had been few such cases in the Europe of the period. True as it is that Alsace-Lorraine and revenge did not come to define French politics, as territorial issues would later determine Central-East European policy, the French came out of the war with a definite Prussophobia, and thus fear and the pursuit of amends became mutual for both nations.

The period 1870–1871 thus came to be not what it should have been in the historical experience and memory of the French nation; instead of an occasion to face waning French power, it was a shocking and fear-raising catastrophe at the hands of a brutal, inveterate, and barbarian enemy attacking unexpectedly. This is how the specter of Prussianism was born. We say "specter" not because we believe in the no less fanciful image of an idyllic and harmless Germany of poets and philosophers. We are aware how Germans, in their ever-increasing hysteria, sought to live up to the spectral image that first the French and then the world had made up of them in the period after 1871. We call it a "specter" because as it entered French political consciousness, it lost touch with reality; moreover, it became the means of avoiding facing reality in accordance with the eternal rule of hysteria.

As a democratic and grown-up nation, the French political public tried to respond to the great historical experience of defeat by regarding it as a starting point of national and moral regeneration, as outlined by the best minds and writers of the country. This national soul-searching contrasted the moral exhaustion of the adventurer dictatorship of the Second Empire with the moral uprightness of the French tradition and the moral glow of revolutionary democracy. As a result, France started out on a road of political and social development leading to its final and full democratization. However important such national soul-searching might be, the overmoralization of causes and factors can become the source of misunderstanding. What would have been decisive was avoided in 1871: the entire public facing the material loss of French power. Not that no perceptive Frenchmen knew, saw, and spoke out loud that France's positions had changed. The problem was that this recognition failed to be acknowledged by the wider public, the German specter brushing it aside.

The shift in power between Germany and France could be glossed over all the more so because France could uphold its equality, even an advantage over Germany, in wealth and in economic, cultural, and intellectual performance — that is, in peace — since France was establishing the second biggest colonial empire in the world and undergoing one of the greatest periods of cultural flowering, while the confusion of values, political values in particular, increasingly transpired in the oversized and overemphasized German achievements. French public opinion saw the new and unified Germany not as a stable and unavoidable historical fact but as a monstrous specter with no human face.

The decisive effect of this on the European state of affairs was that French foreign policy was increasingly defined by anxiety, the fear of the recreation of a European constellation where France had to fight it out with Germany alone. This together with Germany's contrary policy of fear brought about the opposing alliances and ultimately World War I.

Not only did victory in the Great War not mellow the dread complex of French political thinking, but it also aggravated it. The year 1918 was the great moment for France to settle scores, but it could not obtain full revenge, as full a one as Germany had obtained in 1870–1871, because it could not alter the shift in power. For all its glorious victories in the war, there was the disquieting experience that, together with its allies, it could hardly hold the front line with Germany battling on two fronts. This is what prompted Clemenceau to say, "There are 20 million Germans too many!" Germans hear only the sadistic anti-German hatred in the exclamation, the pleasure at 20 million Germans perishing. Its true meaning, however, emerges if we turn it around: the trouble with France and Europe alongside it is that there are 20 million Frenchmen fewer.

Had French foreign policy faced this fact at the end of World War I, it would have had two options. First, it could have put an end to rivalry with Germany, limited its European great-power politics, and built its security on the hope that Germany would see no point in attacking a France not involved in great-power politics aside from obtaining an Alsace-Lorraine whose German identity was only questionable. Second, it could have tried to create a broad-based alliance capable of maintaining balance in the face of German military might. The first option was precluded for two reasons: dread and victory. It would have been impossible to believe that fiendish Germany would not seize upon the advantage and attack France, either subjugating it or carving it up, and it would have been equally impossible to disavow the preterhuman efforts of the victor by not obtaining unconditional guarantees against the threat of increasing German power. So the second option was left, broader cooperation against Germany, which, in the form of a permanent British-American-French alliance, the French outlined already at the Paris Peace Conference. The plan foundered on the withdrawal of America and the disinterest of the British. As no defense system based on Eastern Europe was seriously considered, this failure steered all French foreign-policy efforts into a dead end that could not be faced in the double clutch of dread and victory. Being caught in a dead end and not wanting to face reality determined the atmosphere of Versailles, where the peace treaty was drawn up not to settle the political dispute but to set the peacemakers the impossible task of rendering the momentary, but only momentary, advantage of France over Germany permanent through institutional provisions. It was at this point that French politics no longer stood on the firm ground under its feet.

In this atmosphere of rampant unrealism, the security of France was based on the phantasm (which would have a major role in eliciting the Hitlerite hysteria) that Germany, at the moment of its defeat, was to undertake to maintain a small army and not unite with Austria—two undertakings that could hardly have been forced on Germany without an awareness of their makeshift nature. This same mood of unrealism was also responsible for the grotesque relationship between French politics and the League of Nations, which meant that France, which had disdained the charitable catchwords and plans of Wilson in 1919, tried to redress, a better solution wanting, its lack of security through the League. This was doomed to fail from the outset; the League was not meant to establish a new security but to shape the one that had already been established.

At each turn and move between 1919 and 1938, French policy was but a permanent thrashing about between the concrete aim of securing France against Germany and the League of Nations policy of postulating universal principles of peace. The opposition to the idea of collective security was itself grounded in misunderstanding; French policy wanted assurances of collective security against the central factor of European insecurity, Germany; the League of Nations ideology had all aggressors in mind.

Apart from this unrealistic line, France also followed a realistic policy line and tried to establish cooperation schemes among Britain, France, and Italy and between France and Eastern Europe, an effort that was the only possible way of counterbalancing the power shift to Germany. The Treaty of Locarno and the Franco-Polish, Franco-Czechoslovak, Franco-Yugoslav, and Franco-Russian treaties were milestones of this policy. Yet the aspiration could not rid itself of the destructive effects of fear—all the more so because the defense line to be built around Germany had had holes in it at several fatal points or was contradictory (Italy, Hungary, later Czechoslovakia, the Polish-Russian enmity).

Time and ensuing events clearly proved the French plans for both alliances and collective security right. Those reproaching France for its unrealistic rigidity against Germany should note that given the mental state of fear, the rigidity of French policy and the lack of French security were mutually interrelated: the less French foreign policy was able to obtain a realistic stabilization of peace, the less was it in a mental condition to follow a rational policy in the face of Germany. It was easy for the British and the Americans, who had no inkling of fear, to be understanding and conciliatory; it was indeed due to their remaining aloof to French plans that France could not give up on its rigidity. Had either a French-British-American alliance or a ring made up of Italy, Yugoslavia, Hungary, Czechoslovakia, Poland, and Russia or perhaps some kind of collective security been established, magnanimous concessions could have been given to Germany. Since none of these was realized, French foreign policy continued to be determined by its anxiety. Much philosophical ink has been spilled on security's being a narrow, petit bourgeois, lifeless, and defensive aim. There might be a pinch of truth in this, but most of it is gibberish; French foreign policy was cramped and rigid not because it strove for security; all policy, except for adventurism, strives for security. The trouble was that to no avail did it strive for security; moreover, simultaneously, it was forced into assuming a level of moral and political responsibility it could not meet alone. The enemy took advantage of the dread and the internal insecurity this enhanced.

Whatever is said about the shrewd reactionary-capitalist intrigue preparing the way for Munich, it was obviously clear without presuming any ploy that if both security systems—the close political alliance of the countries around Germany and the League of Nations policy—failed simultaneously, there was nothing else that could follow other than a sort of Munich.

In the dispute of the advocates and opponents of Munich, the dilemma of French policy manifested itself under the guise of the left-right conflict: opponents of Munich were justified by the truth that European peace could be defended against Hitlerism only by a united European effort, while advocates of Munich were justified by the truth that in the lack of a solid West and East European ring of defense, such an undertaking must necessarily lead to the collapse of France. That France entered into the war against Germany a year after Munich and under more severe and disadvantageous political constellations can be attributed to the great shift in European moral positions after the march into Prague; up to that point, Germany had had serious moral trumps but now forwent all moral support of its policies.

In this situation, the French policy of dread underwent an odd process of sublimation. Do not let us think now of the greatness or pettiness of certain persons, the wrangling between leftists and rightists; advocates and opponents of Munich; the struggles determined by interest, influence and intrigue, but of the change in atmosphere that characterized French politics after the march on Prague. The element of dread was either relegated to the background or ennobled. After Munich, it had become likely and probable that Germany would not attack a France that did not exercise great-power politics on the continent, in Eastern Europe in particular; it had become believable and probable that

France, if it had wanted to, could, without taking major risks, keep out of the world conflagration into which Hitlerism was about to thrust Europe and the world.

The cause of the French dread did not cease, only lessen. When moral positions radically shifted following Hitler's Prague perfidy in March 1939, a sublimated or ennobled "dread" made France take its stance under the most disadvantageous conditions—the dread of being unable to live up to itself. In contrast to the great undertakings between 1919 and 1938, which had ostensibly been driven by anxiety, the new ones clearly lived up to upholding Europe and the timeless historical role of France and had nothing to do with population numbers and military force. French foreign policy, which had been foolish and petty-minded hair-splitting over the Treaty of Versailles for twenty years, now showed itself at its best without any public storm or change of persons; it had not had a magnanimous, courageous, clairvoyant period since 1919, as it now had after Hitler's march on Prague to its collapse in 1940. However monstrous the collapse was, it also crowned this ennoblement: France stood its ground for Europe and the world alone even though it had not been forced to, as it could have avoided it. Many deem it a major breach that Pétain and Vichy followed the promising first impetus. There will be acts to be ashamed of by the Vichy government, particularly in the occupied territories and during the full occupation. There is, however, nothing to be ashamed of that the Vichy mood was born of the recognition following the terrible collapse that France could have "avoided" it.

I cannot tell what the psychological residue of the 1940 collapse will be in France—perhaps a new anxiety. The lesson that had been the deeper reason behind advocating Munich and the Vichy mentality will continue to hold after victorious liberation; it exceeds the power of France to withstand Germany alone, without major continental support.

This is why it is useless and dangerous to overmoralize the causes of the collapse in 1940. At this point, we have to observe the fundamental differences in political self between the collapse of France and Italy. That France collapsed, all sermonizing to the contrary, had material reasons. Anyone seeing how France overcame the domestic political crisis of 1936 and the crisis in foreign policy in 1938; anyone noting the undaunted humanity, serenity, and moderation manifest in the background of the wave of strikes and apparent chaos in 1936; anyone watching how conscriptions took place with an unflaunted taking up of fate in 1938 and 1939 will not believe that it was a rotten community without moral uprightness that collapsed in 1940. Given enough time, France, just as Britain did, could have overcome the first confusion resulting from the outbreak of the war. But time was not given, and this turned on material factors: the shift in power to Germany and the vulnerability of France. The collapse of France was fundamentally caused by material reasons, and only its aggravating concomitants had a moral nature, while the Italian collapse was a fundamentally moral one, the fall of a policy based on phony assumptions, and only its concomitants had a material nature.

2. SICKLY ITALIAN CONFIDENCE

The Italian political hysteria was a no less decisive factor in the collapse of Europe. The biggest breach in the defense line against German prevalence was Italy. Following France's fall in population, a solid cooperation among Britain, France, and Italy or just France and Italy could have effectively countered any disruption of the balance of power in Europe. The final disruption of the balance of power in Europe occurred when Italy harked back from the Stresa Front.

The world does not appreciate Italian military prowess much these days, and perhaps many think that an Italian stance would hardly have changed the balance of forces significantly. This is a mistaken approach. The military efficiency of a modern nation does not hinge on the fighting bent or physical daring of its members. The masses of a modern nation obey the command to kill with the same mix of nausea, resignation, and moral courage, and I do not believe the nerves of Italians are worse due to degeneration or any other cause than those of any other nation. However, the military prowess of a modern nation is, as it were, in proportion to how it understands and senses the aim, necessity, and meaning of the war it is to fight. The bad soldiery of the Italians had not been the current of opinion before the twentieth century, just as it had not been that the Germans were the enemies of Christian civilization or that the French were degenerate. What was lacking in Italian military performance was the community's sense of identification with the political and military objectives of the nation. The causes of this are to be found in Italian political development.

Italy had ceased to exist as an independent European political factor after the sixteenth century, but in spite of breaking apart into several minor states, it enjoyed a degree of autonomy, being the master of its own household in the shade of the great powers. It was the Napoleonic Wars that brought to light the internal withering and exhaustion of Italian political and social structure, as masterfully portrayed by Ferrero in *The Gamble: Bonaparte in Italy*. As a result, Italy partially came under immediate and visible foreign rule in the beginning of the nineteenth century, but irrespective of this, it became a country of lost political authority and constituted a vacuum in the middle of the continent. However strange it might sound, the cause of Italian unity was not the irresistible Italian national consciousness but the need to fill this void. That this happened to take the shape of a united Italy was certainly assisted by enthused Italian patriots and the shrewd policies of the House of Savoy, and that this house led the unification owed as much to clever politics as to the fact that it was the only serious dynasty of Italian origin, the rest, apart from the special case of the popes, being either Renaissance-tyrants-turned-princelings or rootless rulers apportioned pieces in the deals and exchanges of the European concert. As a joint effect of all these factors, Italian unity was established under the leadership of the Savoy dynasty, but it never became the universal enthralling experience of the Italian nation, as the birth of the modern French state had, or not even as German unification had become the single concern of all Germans.

Naturally, the Italians were well pleased about unity, that Italy had regained its position among the great nations of Europe. But they did not acquire the historical experience that a nation can only be established and kept great by the joint effort of the entire nation. Quite to the contrary, the lesson they mistakenly drew was that the greatest success of Italian national politics was not the revolutionary movement of 1848 but the shrewd politics of Cavour, the clever intrigues of a person or persons. As a power policy became the single salutary means in the eyes of Germans due to the successes of Bismarck, and thus their misleading political perception, so did shrewd diplomatic maneuvering, a program of promptly siding with the winner, become the misleading political perception of the Italian nation. And as the words of the realist Bismarck, "blood and iron," became myth and magic spell, so did the honestly passionate "sacred egotism" of D'Annunzio become the slogan of political unprincipledness. If the French people acquired a bent for overmoralizing issues in the course of their political development, to look for moral causes even where material causes dominated, Italian political thinking meant an undermoralization, the rejection of morals even where those alone were what counted.

More than Italian poverty, the emptiness of Italian political thinking was what cast a shadow of doubt over the greatness of Italy among the great nations of Europe. This doubt, which was that of both the European public and the Italian nation itself, was the reason Italians swayed between the extremes of unrealistic oversensitivity and excessive submissiveness in matters of national pride.

It was in this context that Italy entered the Great War, scrupulously mindful of the program of *sacro egoismo*. The decisive symptom of this was not backing out of the Triple Alliance, for that had been a purely dynastic alliance that had had no root or elicited no response from the Italian public. As Ferrero pointed out, it was much more the fact that it was the only country to join the war without actually having been attacked, having felt or declared that it had been attacked, and without establishing some higher aim for itself. It joined the war because it found it timely to achieve certain territorial aims. It is quite dangerous to start a modern war by striking such a note. Its dissonance can be outblared only by a major victory. The lack of such a military or diplomatic victory led to a crisis in Italian political development. The Italian Army had stood its ground, even had an important role in the collapse of the Austro-Hungarian Monarchy, but its contribution to the outcome was not at all appreciated, and, to top it all, Italian territorial claims suffered a major blow because the London Treaty finally gave Dalmatia not to Italy but to Yugoslavia.

Lacking a significant Italian population, Dalmatia could not have been a serious and decisive territorial aspiration for Italy. Yet it was what gave Italian territorial hopes and aspirations during the war an air of grandiosity and imperialism (through Venetian reminiscences of a rule over the Adriatic). In 1915, when Italy joined the war and the London Treaty was concluded, Dalmatia was, all in all, a realistic and conceivable aspiration. The dismemberment of the Austro-Hungarian Monarchy had not been raised yet, only a few of its provinces were to have been carved off it, and it seemed only natural that Italy had a greater entitlement to Dalmatia in view of the historical claims of Venice than did the Austrian half of the Austro-Hungarian Monarchy, which had had no serious link with it. The country that had had a serious historical and linguistic claim on it, Croatia, was lost in the constitutional quagmire of the Austro-Hungarian Monarchy, and the future state, a unified Yugoslavia, was still unborn in the womb of time. In three years' time, in 1918, however, Yugoslavia was a political reality in the making that was to be reckoned with, and it would have been a blatant breach of the principles of self-determination and ethnicity to not grant Dalmatia to Yugoslavia (an ally).

This was a major letdown for Italian prestige, and a serious consequence of the disrespect Italy earned with *sacro egoismo*. The lesson was not irresistible and allowed for misinterpretation: Italy lost the war, which had been won militarily, at the level of diplomacy because its allies defrauded it. It was the lack of a deep-rooted political authority within and the shame on diplomatic prestige that led to the disruption of political balance and subjected Italy to the rule of fascism and the political deformation inherent in it.

The first attempt fascism made to attain prestige and success in foreign policy was the Corfu case, but it proved to be a blunder. From this time until 1935, the fascist regime had recourse to the proven tradition of political cunning. For a time, it even distanced itself from Hitlerism; Mussolini could present himself not only as a clear-headed realist, but also a statesman assuming the responsibility for all Europe, being promoted to the rank of an *honoris causa* democrat. The fascist regime used this growth in political weight to return to the type of power and prestige politics it had never really left behind, only suspended. The Ethiopian venture meant a decisive point in Italian political development in two respects. On the one hand, it brought about a major increase in political prestige and a respectable colonial empire, making amends for the glorious victory it had missed in 1918. In this respect, it meant the same as Munich did for the Germans. On the other hand, that the League of Nations attempted to sanction Italy and declare it a war criminal meant that it got into radical conflict with European values; this was what instilled the idea in the minds of Italians that a policy of peace and cooperation was only a hypocritical defense of the advantages the more powerful had gained by force earlier, so the sanctioning attempt had roughly the same effect on the Italians as Versailles had on the Germans. Then came the slaps to Europe in the Spanish case; these proved to Italian policymakers, as did the successes of Germany foreign policy between 1935 and 1938, that bluff and aggression can overwhelm a policy of reason and tradition. By 1937, the embankment that was meant to have protected Europe against the German flood was hopelessly broken at the Brenner Pass. The only inklings of the possible directions of a European policy loomed in the actions of Mussolini (the Stresa Front; the Italian, Yugoslav, and Hungarian attempts; the Italian-Polish cooperation, etc.) between 1933 and 1940, but what was lacking from them, what would have given them continuity and coherence, was a sense of responsibility for all Europe. In spite of the shared interest, it was impossible to put into practice a joint European policy, with one side standing for principles and responsibility and the other for adventure and irresponsibility.

When World War II broke out, Italy based itself more completely and more dogmatically on the *sacro egoismo* than it had done in 1914. Precisely following it, it jumped headlong into the war in 1940, and with the fortunes of war turning, it backed out of it in 1943. Yet, parallel, the Italian national catastrophe came to pass between 1940 and 1943, which meant the failure of the policy of *sacro egoismo* and its being taken *ad absurdum*. It had already been clear in 1919 that joining the winners in time does not necessarily increase the political prestige of a country, and now 1940–1943 demonstrated irrefutably and unequivocally that this policy had debased the prestige of Italy more than ever before. The ease with which the Italian nation, from its top leaders down to average Italians, allied itself overnight with the other side and wanted to see itself as a winner astonished the world, and this astonishment was not meant to flatter the

Italian nation. According to a benevolent explanation, at heart the Italians have always hated the Germans and only followed their truest emotions when pulling out of the alliance they had entered into in spite of their taste and will. The less benevolent explanation is that the Italians are politically dishonest. Both interpretations are erroneous. True, the Italians have never liked the Germans, perhaps even less so than the British or the French, but we all know that the current of opinion even among those who could never sympathize with fascism before 1940 had been the program of siding with the winner in time. Now this is not an organic or inherent dishonesty. Tracing *sacro egoismo* back to Machiavelli and the Italian Renaissance is as false as tracing German aggression back to Arminius. The thinking of a country has its characteristic formulas and recurrent partial truths, and the false doctrines its political thinking falls into are no mere coincidence. The current corruption of Italian politics, as any other hysteria in Europe, is a deformation that can be traced back to concrete and misleading causes and exposable historical experiences and can be cured and undone. Italian political thought was carried away by the shock of the French Revolution; foreign invasion and the fall of internal authorities elicited a sense of weakness and haplessness; the failure of 1848 prompted the false lesson that the Italian nation was not powerful enough to unite and grow of itself; and the success of Cavour' s policies bound Italian political thinking to the idea of siding with the winner in time, to the delusion that a shrewd choice of allies was omnipotent.[5]

(1942–1944)

THE MISERIES OF EAST
EUROPEAN SMALL STATES

1. EUROPEAN NATIONS AND THE MAKING
OF MODERN NATIONALISM

Nation-building was one of the most important processes Europe as a political community went through. Within this process, the birth of *modern nations* has had a momentous significance. Essentially, this meant that new, very powerful mass movements took possession of the frameworks of existing or newly established nations, and the emotions nations had always engendered now turned into highly charged mass feelings. It is not true that the nation and nationalism as such were born along with the French Revolution or, generally, the bourgeois revolution. The only novelty in this was that the political processes of nations took the form of *mass movements*, and the emotions they had always commanded now became *mass feelings*. This transformation took place relatively smoothly in some nations, but like a blast in others, and it ran or is running its course in major social catastrophes. Some nations have increased in terms of both wealth and morality, some have incurred material losses and were debased morally, and others' entire development has ended up in deadlock. It is the process of the making of modern nations that we wish to examine in what follows.

The nation as a characteristic entity of Europe is the result of fifteen centuries of development. It is a widespread folly to hold that state and national boundaries have been in a state of constant flux for the past fifteen hundred years and that the only constancy or internal law that governed them was power. This view fails to take notice that for all the changes in state borders and the confusion of feudal relations, the national boundaries of Europe have shown a remarkable constancy and extraordinary persistence except for the critical periods of establishing, locally changing, and partitioning national borders (the fifth through sixth, tenth, fifteenth through sixteenth, and nineteenth and twentieth centuries AD). By the witness of history, nations once established never fell apart due to the weakening of central authority and the growing independence of local power; independent local units became separate nations only when undergirded by powerful or lasting political experiences that grounded their internal self-consciousness and external authority.

It was between the fifth and sixth centuries that European nations started to emerge from the Germanic kingdoms that, under the leadership of powerful dynasties, split the legacy of the Roman Empire among themselves and that, starting out from wayward conquests, took on the shapes of the various territorial units of the Roman Empire after some adjustments and alignments: the Franks fit themselves into Gallia, the Western Goths into Hispania, the Anglo-Saxons into Britannia, and the Lombards into Italy. The Carolingian empire having united the west and later fallen apart, the Italian and the Western Frankish, the French, kingdoms reestablished themselves only to witness the creation of the German kingdom in the ninth century. These were joined by the three Norse states and the three East European Catholic states, Poland, Hungary, and Bohemia. Europe began the zenith period of the Middle Ages with this fixed number of nations. National boundaries looked more diffuse in the areas of eastern Christendom. The House of Rurik united Russia between the ninth and tenth centuries. The Byzantine Empire continued the Greco-Roman tradition; in the Balkans, however, newer peoples—the Bulgarians, the Serbs, and the Croats—established kingdoms on Western models between the eighth and eleventh centuries, the Romanian and Lithuanian principalities being founded somewhat later.

At the Council of Constance in 1414, the five leading nations of Europe—the Italian, French, English, German, and Spanish—appeared as *units* with established characteristics and were consciously recognized as belonging together. It was also at this time that the features of the West and Central European national frameworks began to be distinguished; the French, English, and Spanish kingdoms became increasingly solid and efficient realities, while the German and Italian kingdoms began to lose their substance, turning more and more invisible and symbolic. It was at this point that certain smaller European nations came into being. In the midway area between Germany and France, the Dutch and Belgian nations arose from the political experiences of the Kingdom of Burgundy (subtly spelled out by Huizinga) and the great uniting and splitting experiences of the Dutch Revolt. Though begun earlier, the secession of Switzerland from the German Empire became final at this time. As the Italian kingdom fell apart, the Glorious Venetian Republic and the Sicilian kingdom showed signs of separate nationhood. The Iberian Peninsula was also reunited at this time but came to be divided into separate Spanish and Portuguese nations, in which the great experience of overseas conquests had no doubt had a role. The first popular nationalist, Jean d'Arc, made the scene at this time; moreover, all the ideas we associate with national consciousness were formulated in this period—the welfare of the nation as the most important community concern; recording and appraising national characteristics; rejecting foreign rule; and even the appreciation of the national vernacular. Linguistic unity, however, was not regarded as a factor in building a nation at this time. Ortega y Gasset poignantly remarked that the states in modern Europe were monolingual not because the people of one language flocked together and established their nation but because the political, cultural, and numerical superiority of a people *made* the existing state and national frameworks be monolingual. To our day, several European linguistic borders have preserved the memory of long-fallen political borders—the French-Walloon and the French-Catalonian linguistic borders, the Danish-Norwegian and Swedish-Norwegian dialect borders, etc.

The national borders established in medieval times, though shifting a little here and there, did not alter significantly. Based merely on feudal or familial relations, political structures that ran across these national borders usually proved fickle, and even if they did survive in some places for longer periods, they finally disappeared without leaving as much as a mark on the borders between the major states. Thus were the English-Norman and later English-French, the Aragonese-Sicilian, the Spanish-Neapolitan, the Spanish-Milanese, the later Austrian-Milanese, the Spanish-Low Countries, the English-Hanoverian, and the almost thousand-year-old Savoy-Piedmont ties unbound, and above all, the Italian-German bond embodied in the Holy Roman Empire. Each of these left mementos behind, but never did they cause any major shift in the national borders concerned.

The modern state system was gradually established in Western Europe between the fifteenth and seventeenth centuries. Central authority, which had been but symbolic, began to hold sway over the political processes of nations, and the intelligentsia in charge of state administration and the middles classes acquired an increasingly prominent role in the national consciousness. Royal seats soon came to be possessed by whole countries, as they became characteristic units in terms not only of politics and law, but also administration and the economy. It was in this context that the French Revolution broke out, one of the main consequences of which was the intensification and democratization of community emotion, the birth of modern patriotism. This is where the rather perfunctory notion that European nationalism was born alongside the French Revolution springs from. As already pointed out, neither was the nation as a fact nor the related emotion born in 1789; they had come into being centuries, even a millennium, earlier. The difference lies in the fact that the conscious bearer of the nation had been the nobility. The incursion into the nation by the intelligentsia and commoners, the third estate, had been in progress from the end of the Middle Ages, but it now turned into an overnight victorious taking of possession, and this was the experience that gave rise to modern national feeling. Revolutionary democracy, indeed all democracy, however it proclaims the freedom of every man, always puts this freedom into practice within a *given* community, and this experience, far from dampening it, heightens and braces emotions toward that community. The enormous heat and vigor of democratic community feeling derives from its combining of two emotions: the taking possession of the nation by the third estate, the people, everybody, whereas royals and nobles had exclusively owned it with all its historical and political prestige and representative and challenging consciousness, as well as the endowment of the nation with the warm and intimate feelings with which the middle classes surrounded their immediate environments. Middle-class feelings were of course more powerful in this merger, and by the principle of democracy, they very well should be; democracy brought about the victory of the lifestyle of the hard-working and dexterous man over that of the aristocratic man gratifying himself by wielding power and representation. This link between democracy and nationalism is very much a living reality in Western and Northern Europe, where political consciousness did not decline into disturbance or pathological deformation.

2. THE DISRUPTION OF THE TERRITORIAL STATUS OF CENTRAL-EAST EUROPE AND THE RISE OF LINGUISTIC NATIONALISM

When modern democratic nationalism arose in Western Europe at the end of the eighteenth century, there was no doubt as to what framework or country the people intended to take possession of—the *existing state system* of France, Great Britain, Spain, Portugal, Belgium, the Netherlands, etc. Not so in Central-East Europe. The Holy Roman Empire had muddled up the political development of both Germany and Italy, and the conquests of the Ottoman Empire had disrupted previous national frameworks without creating new ones with any degree of constancy or stability. Both factors contributed to the establishment of a disastrous state formation that terminally confounded national development in Central and Eastern Europe. This was the empire of the Habsburgs.

At the time of its inception, the Habsburg Empire was just another incidental, "inter"-national dynastic state association, like the Aragonese-Sicilian or the English-Hanoverian ties, etc. When it came into being, it had nothing to do with what it is now fancied to have been—a "Danubian state." One of its constituent parts, the German Empire, which had been forced back into Southern Germany due to the Reformation, brought along all its Italian and West European interests; Bohemia had little to do with the Danube, and the Hungarian kingdom, which had withered due to the Ottoman conquest, became a mere military front zone to the east for the German Empire. No genuine intent of unification arose in this union for a long time. Until the middle of the eighteenth century no one doubted that the House of Habsburg represented the political weight of German royalty as attached to the title of Roman emperorship in Europe. He was "the Emperor" who ruled much of Germany and Italy and also happened to be the king of Bohemia and Hungary. In the wake of the religious wars, however, the German emperor was gradually forced out of German territories, and as the House of Habsburg cemented its positions in Italy, it began to gain ground also, not at all primarily in the Danube region, managing to conquer the old territories of Hungary from the Turks. In the eighteenth century, it incurred further losses in Germany. For a time, the War of the Austrian Succession displayed the grotesqueness of the situation; without the title of empress, Maria Theresa ruled a country without a single name, a conglomerate of the Austrian, Hungarian, Czech, Lombard, Belgian, and Croat nations or fragments of nations, with their different laws, languages, administrations, and self-consciousnesses.

It was only as late as the second half of the eighteenth century that serious attempts were made to forge some kind of "Austrian" consciousness in all the Danubian lands of the Habsburgs. However, before this Austrian consciousness could assert itself, modern democratic nationalism spread with elemental force throughout the region as a result of the French Revolution and created a wholly new situation.

THE RESURRECTION OF OLD NATIONS

The primary question that the democratic movements springing up in this region had to answer was of *which* framework they sought to take possession in the name of the people. Modern democratic nationalism was unable and justly unwilling to fill power structures (the Habsburg Empire, the petty states of Germany and Italy, the Ottoman Empire) with their mighty emotions and their displays of force but turned toward frameworks that existed only in their vestiges, partly in institutions and partly in symbols and memories (the German Empire, a unified Italy, the kingdoms of Poland, Hungary, and Bohemia, etc.), which, for all their falling into provincialism or anarchy, meant more potent political experiences than the existing, not particularly old or deep-rooted, frameworks. The Ottoman Empire could not advance any national structure among the peoples of the Balkans partly because of the merely military and conquering nature of its organization and partly because of its cultural strangeness to the peoples concerned. The Habsburg Empire, as already noted, had been an occasional union and was capable of weakening the nations that happened to be included in it but could not melt them away. The Austrian consciousness that arose at the turn of the nineteenth century did not lack human and warm feelings, but it had deeper community roots only in the German hereditary lands and matched not so much European national feeling as the provincial emotions of the small German states. This Austrian local patriotism could hardly have engendered a new nation, all the more so because the glory of the German-speaking Austrian hereditary lands arose from the fact that they had for five and half centuries been given to the emperors and rulers of the *German* Empire and were regarded as the land, the Île-de-France, of the German ruling house. Unifying experiences and external prestige wanting, the rest of the small German states never came anywhere near establishing themselves as independent nations in the way the Dutch, the Belgians, and the Swiss did. The small states of Italy had reached a nadir of political impotence and exhaustion by the nineteenth century, and they could no longer counter the idea of national union with any form of separatism. In every direction, the old national frameworks gained ground; it was not Austrian, Bavarian, Sardinian, or Neapolitan feelings but German, Italian, Polish, Hungarian, and Czech national feelings that flared up.

THE PANGS OF REBIRTH AND THE FOLKISH IDEA

This victory, however, proved to be a Pyrrhic victory for each one of them. The new national movements had expended most of their energies on demolishing the existing frameworks and rebuilding their own, and in doing so, they had to face the fact that no one had established a modern state and national organization for them, a process that had taken place elsewhere in Europe in the seventeenth and eighteenth centuries. They had no capitals of their own in the modern sense of the word; they had only partially organized state administrations; they had no economic organization that could stand on its own, no unified national culture, no savvy national elites. The Habsburg Empire and the other frameworks of state power had an adequate supply of these but could give rise only to dull dynastic feelings and limp local patriotism. Thus these new national movements had to prove that they were entities with deeper roots and more vitality in the face of the bankrupt state organizations that were nevertheless endowed with all the means of wielding power. In order to do so, they had to dig deeper than the superficial relations of power to the factor of the "folk." This was how the "people" or *peuple,* implying as it did the dynamic of upward mobility in Western Europe, came to be the bearer of distinct national characteristics *(Volk)* and be seen as upholding the criteria of national belonging, language, custom, etc. more purely than the mixed ruling elite. This is at the heart of the untranslatable emotional difference between the otherwise logically identical words *populaire* and *völkisch.* This was what gave rise to a factor that made the territorial status of this region even more fluid than it had been: linguistic nationalism.

Linguistic nationalism is a Central-East European specialty. Basing themselves on theories of nationalism formulated in this region, we now even have West European proponents of the idea that a nation is born as a people of the same language "combine" and establish themselves as a nation. Now, nowhere on earth has this ever come to pass in this way. The modern concept of nation is preeminently political: at the start, there is a state that the people, through the power of democratized mass emotion, seek to take possession of and own. At the beginning of the nineteenth century, such movements mostly aligned themselves with historical state frameworks and attempted to shake off only rootless state organizations (the Habsburg and Ottoman Empires, etc.); however, with the rise of linguistic nationalism, all the nations in this regions took stock of their situation in terms of the balance of language forces; nations on whose historical borders linguistically related peoples lived or who no longer had historical borders set themselves the aim of uniting their linguistic kin, while nations who had other language speakers within their historical borders started programs to make single-language nation-states. Both programs were driven by the effort to buttress unstable political frameworks with ethnic factors.

This does not mean that linguistic factors create nations and that a nation can be conjured out of a dialect. As everywhere else, nations were brought into existence even here by political factors. Most nations in the region—the Poles, Hungarians, Czechs, Greeks, Romanians, Bulgarians, Serbs, Croats, and Lithuanians—have had their state or semi-state organizations and characteristic political consciousnesses. The few nations that might at first sight seem to have been established on a linguistic basis, through the combination of those speaking the same language (the Slovaks, Latvians, Esthonians, Albanians, etc.), actually came into existence through historical experience and process. For instance, Slovak national consciousness developed in a series of historical experiences starting with the political and cultural resistance to Hungarian linguistic nationalism, the secession from Hungary and a joining with the Czechoslovak state, the establishment of the independent Slovak state, and the restoration of Czechoslovakia. It is worth noting that a tumbling hither and thither among state communities can be observed in the establishment or reestablishment of some West European smaller nations as well—for example, the Finnish and the Norwegian. It is the series of such experiences that shapes nations. What the advocates of the historical entities of Eastern Europe repeatedly proclaim is therefore true: language is not a nation-constituting factor; only history is. What they want to infer from this, however, does not follow from it; conversely, it is also true that linguistic belonging has become a historical and political factor in the conditions of Central-East Europe, in the territorial separation of existing frameworks, and occasionally in the establishment of new nations.

The ascendance of linguistic nationalism brought about a fluidity in the borders between the nations of Central-East Europe. While historical status quo retained its nation-separating significance in Western and Northern Europe, the borders between the nations of Central-East Europe were either completely lost in the vicissitudes of history (in the Balkans), or if they did survive, they lost their cohesive power (Poland, Hungary, the Czech lands). The gravest problem with this was not that linguistic borders were far too meandering or that they did not conform to geographic and economic expectations but that the historical emotions of these nations, most of them having historical memories, were attached to other and, as a rule, larger areas than the one occupied by the population speaking the appropriate language. Here too, as everywhere else in the world, national feeling not only brings together the members of a group, but also connects them to localities, holy cities, and the historical memories of a territorial entity. These emotions were particularly powerful when the locality concerned was inhabited by a group of speakers of the national language who constituted a minority or were territorially enclosed. The popular movements opposed to historical frameworks had a likewise powerful desire to take possession of city centers. The newly reborn nations were thus soon embroiled in ferocious border disputes with most of their neighbors, sparking several wars and disasters that brought about further destabilizations of territorial statuses. This was the major source of the political hysterias of Central-East European nations.

3. THE DISSOLUTION OF THE THREE HISTORICAL
STATES OF EASTERN EUROPE

It is worth dwelling on the disaster that befell the three historical countries of Eastern Europe—Poland, Bohemia, and Hungary. We need to do so because, on the one hand, their fall had a much greater role in the catastrophe of the European state system than we would assume at first sight, and on the other hand, the imbalances in the political consciousness of these nations characteristically demonstrate the causes and nature of the Central-East European quagmire.

It is misleading to focus on the fall of the Habsburg Empire in discussing the confusions of Central-East Europe. It was rather the *existence* of this monarchy that wreaked the turmoil. It is no use enlarging on its collapse because the Habsburg conglomerate of states was an incidental hybrid that had no internal cohesive force and could not have contributed to the stabilization of the region even in more fortunate circumstances. In contrast, there were the three historical states, Poland, Bohemia, and Hungary, which were roughly concealed by the Habsburg monarchy and which came to light after its fall. That they were genuine and living nations they managed to prove, yet they were unable to assume the roles they had fulfilled before the rise of the Habsburgs. It was the internal imbalances of these three states that had a crucial role in the collapse of the European system of states: Hungary represented a gap in the French anti-German defenses after 1918; Czechoslovakia was the point where these defenses collapsed before being put in use in 1938; and Poland was the Archimedean point where German expansionism was able to temporarily undo the solidarity between the west and the east resisting it, and it was through this breach that it could unleash the horrors of World War II on to the entire world.

The troubles of all three states began at the end of the eighteenth century and have been, in the final count, related to the obstacles to the establishment and stabilization of nations in the region.

THE POLISH WOE

The trouble with Poland was that historical Poland had a *Polish half*—Polish homogeneously in the strict sense of the word—and another, *Lithuanian* half attached to it through personal union, the ruling elite of which became almost completely Polishized, but the majority of its population was partly Lithuanian and mostly Russian and Greek Orthodox. In the modern era, this population was increasingly drawn to a rising Russia. Concurrently, there were German expansionist claims on Western Prussia belonging to Poland, but they were far less well founded either historically or ethnically than the Russians ones. As Poland fell into anarchy and both Russia and Prussia sought to carve parts of it off, there appeared another claimant for the spoils, the hybrid Austria, which had never had any serious claim on Polish territories. Following the first partitioning of Poland, a vastly powerful democratic movement arose, Polish patriots hoping to achieve both an internal and external renewal of their country. The movement brought about significant educational and political reforms, culminating in the 1791 constitution, which created quite a stir throughout Europe. However, the French Revolution drew European political attention away from it. Thus Polish anarchy, certain repercussions of the general European situation and Austrian intervention, created the steps to truncate Poland into full dismemberment.

In Poland's third partitioning, Russia obtained in full the Russian-Lithuanian territories, while Prussia and Austria shared the entirely Polish areas between themselves. The historical lesson Poles should have drawn from this was that they should have behind their backs a Russia that had not put its teeth into strictly Polish areas and so try to reestablish their national existence. However, the Poles were utterly dumbfounded by their dismemberment, which they attributed solely to brutal aggression, and were unable to distinguish between what was historically necessary and what was sheer aggression. Thus they did not relinquish the chimera of a historical Greater Poland, and this was why they grouped around Napoleon. That they were after dreams was demonstrated in 1812, when Napoleon, marching into the Lithuanian Grand Duchy, was nowhere received by the Polish uprising his Polish associates had promised him. The only use of the venture was to arouse the feeling in Russia that *it continued to be threatened by the intact parts of Poland*.

This was what prompted the fourth partitioning of Poland in 1815; it was all the more severe insofar as it ceded major, strictly Polish areas to Russia and thus meant that all three great powers now had an interest in the nonexistence of Poland even in the strictly Polish territories. There was thus no major power in Europe that would or could have supported the restoration of Poland. A full century had to pass, tsarist Russia had to fall, and the Central Powers had to simultaneously collapse before Poland could be reestablished.

The same historical lesson should have been drawn: base national life on *Polish* territories and be able to forfeit regions where there still were many-acred Polish landowners but no Polish masses. The Curzon Line drew the consequences from this situation. Not so Poland. It could not withstand the temptation to take advantage of the embattled situation of Soviet Russia and to cross the Curzon Line in 1920. The Treaty of Riga subjected a 6-million-strong *Russian and Ukrainian minority* to it, a significant factor in Poland's drifting away from democracy; not being sure of the national emotions of these groups and with the painful memory of the historical catastrophes, it did not have the courage to bind these territories to itself through open-handed and democratic concessions.

Celebrating the Treaty of Riga for attaining the borders of historical Greater Poland, it did not realize that this had been carried out in the most threatening moment for the new Soviet state and thereby only instilled in Soviet minds that it was the symbolic incursion of ill-willed aggression that threatened the new socialist empire from the capitalist world. Twenty years later, in 1939, when German attack threatened its existence again, Poland failed the same historical test for the third time—*the test of confidence with Russia.*

By the end of World War II, Poland found itself in the same mental condition, that "Europe was indebted to it." And when Russia decided to claim the Curzon Line, it did not respond to it as the lesson drawn from the repeated disasters of 150 years, as the only possible solution, but as a *grave* offense that entitled it to major redress. It so happened that the powers in charge of Europe felt that they owed it this remedy. They paid their debt in the form of Silesia and half of Pomerania, with the rider that all the Germans in these areas could be expelled. What rebounds this is going to have cannot yet be assessed; it is to be feared, however, that it is going to become a critical issue of conscience for all Europe, and one day it will dawn on Poland that less of a remedy would have been more.

THE DELUSION OF HISTORICAL HUNGARY

Initially the problem with Hungary was the same as with Poland. A historical state framework was once given that, however, was not entirely Hungarian-speaking, several nationalities sharing it. These nationalities fell into two groups: the nationalities of the *northern areas* had lived through the entire fate of historical Hungary and demonstrated a willingness to participate in maintaining a multilingual Hungarian state with a shared historical consciousness. To the *nationalities of Southern Hungary,* however, the significance of the Hungarian state was lost during the long Turkish occupation, their having expected protection and obtaining liberation not from the Hungarian state but from the Habsburg Empire, and they rejoined Hungary in a closer or weaker relationship under its historical claim over their territories as the Turks were driven out, but this relationship no longer meant anything to them. As the linguistically kin states were established in the Balkans, they immediately drew to them with full force. The members of the Hungarian democratic and nationalist movement believed that democratic freedom would bring about national unity within the boundaries of historical Hungary. This hope proved to be an illusion. When a spirited Hungarian nation started out on the road to freeing itself from the Habsburg fetters in 1848, it found itself facing the non-Hungarian-speaking nationalities of the country—the Croats, Serbs, and Romanians—whose separatist aspirations it would not recognize. Thus Hungary, fighting for its freedom, had to face the opposition of both the reactionary powers of Europe and its own disaffected nationalities, the end of which was the disaster of 1849.

The political consciousness of the Hungarian nation fixed on two lessons drawn from this disaster: first, Europe left freedom-fighting Hungary in the lurch, and second, the nationalities would use democratic freedom to secede. The first lesson prompted the Compromise of 1867 between Austria and Hungary, the meaning of which was that Hungary forfeited part of its independence in exchange for territorial intactness. The second lesson made Hungary drift away from democratic ideals because the 1849 disaster instilled the anxiety in Hungarian minds that undertaking all the consequences of democracy would inevitably lead to the breakaway of nationality-dominated areas. The lesson that the proponents of historical Hungary should have drawn was that they should try and hold onto the northern parts of historical Hungary and take cognizance of the fact that alienated peoples lived in the south. Instead, a rather small-minded policy came into being that believed it could secure the continued existence of historical Hungary by way of constitutionally limiting the use of the various non-Hungarian languages in the country. The outcome of this was that following the southern nationalities, which had long before awoken to separate national consciousness, the Slovak and Russian[1] populations also gave up the idea of belonging to historical Hungary.

This was the situation in which Hungary was stuck by the collapse of 1918, when it turned out that historical Hungary could no longer be maintained. It was dismembered, however, in such a slapdash manner that not only nationality areas, but also major, wholly Hungarian areas were carved off the county. One consequence of this was a series of domestic political crises that finally brought to power the most blatant reactionary forces, and another was that Hungarian public opinion saw only brutal aggression and hypocrisy on the part of the victors in the entire dissolution of Hungary and was unable to distinguish between the detaching of non-Hungarian areas ripe for separation and the unreasonable and unjust wrenching off of wholly Hungarian territories. As a result, it could not rid itself of the delusion of a historical Greater Hungary and fell into the mental state that Europe was deeply indebted to it for the injustice. Thus, after 1938, it felt it was exempt from all its European obligations, and given the opportunity of changing the territorial status of the country, it did not stop short of going beyond strictly Hungarian territories but went on pursuing the delusion of a Greater Hungary in proportion to such chances opening up and forged straight ahead toward disaster in 1944. The delusion of a historical Greater Hungary was thus finally ruined, but not even this was enough; Hungary has to face a prospectively final peace that will likewise not ensure ethnic boundaries. Whether it is going to have the internal resolve to suffer this will be the crucial matter of its future democratic development.

HISTORICAL BOHEMIA AND CZECHOSLOVAKIA

The problem of the third East European country, historical Bohemia, likewise arose from the divergence of historical and linguistic borders. In the geographically confined historical Bohemia of medieval times, two-thirds of the population lived in the center, and the rest, Germans, were settled along the borders. The German population had its own Bohemian-German consciousness, just as the Czechs had their Czech-Bohemian identity. The tensions between the two people sometimes came to a head—for example, the Hussite Wars—and sometimes abated. The Germans tended to tie up with the German Empire, while the Czechs pursued an East European policy, but this was lost in the characteristic clashes of petty medieval interest. With the Habsburgs' rise to power, the German orientation also gained ground, and the independent statehood of Bohemia was obscured by the Thirty Years' War. Nevertheless, the historical framework of the Bohemian state survived, as did the separate German-Bohemian and the separate Czech-Bohemian identity. By the turn of the nineteenth century, the two identities evolved their mass followings and stood pitted against one another, yet each owned and claimed for itself the Bohemian state framework. The language struggles growing ever sharper, both parties departed from the Bohemian state idea, the Czechs seeking a rear-guard action in Pan Slavism and the Germans in the *grossdeutsche Idee*. It was in the name of the Slavic Idea that the Czechs began to turn culturally and politically toward the Slovaks of Northern Hungary, who were increasingly alienated from Hungary and linked up with the Czechs. During World War I, independent Czechoslovak legions were set up, and the autonomous Czechoslovak state was established as the war ended.

Germany collapsing, the new state managed not only to retain historical Bohemia with its mixed population, but also to attach, on the east, the territories of historical Hungary with a Slovak population, as well as significant purely Hungarian areas in the name of territorial rounding off. Its founding principles were contradictory: it included the Czech areas by virtue of historical and ethnic continuity, the German areas by virtue of historical but not ethnic connections, the Slovak areas through ethnic but not historical relations, and the Hungarian areas by way of neither ethnic nor historical connections.

In this situation the advocates of the Czechoslovak nation sought to base the existence of their state on the ideas of *democracy* and the *territorial integrity of the Versailles settlement in 1919*. What made the Czechoslovak state better qualified for democracy than its East European neighbors was that Czech society was much more advanced, industrialized, and middle-class than the Polish or Hungarian ones, but it was also far more optimistic. The Poles had had to struggle with their disasters since the eighteenth century and the Hungarians since the middle of the nineteenth century, and they had lost their optimism toward democracy at roughly this time. The Czechs, on the other hand, had lived through the century in the shadow of the Habsburg Empire, amid powerful political struggles but with unfaltering hopes, and it was on this confidence that they could base the establishment of democracy between 1918 and 1938 — a genuine oasis among all the fascisms and absolutisms.

The Czechs are justified in claiming that it was not at all unbearable to have to live as Germans or Hungarians in the Czechoslovak state. However, the ethnic principle being focal not only at the foundation of the new body politic, but also in the way it was structured, the German population of the historical area found the new state increasingly alien, not to mention the Hungarians, whose inclusion was utterly incidental. Not that they were badly off, but what had they to do in a country of Czechs and Slovaks now tying up with each other in the name of Slavic brotherhood?

The other idea that served as a basis for the Czechoslovak state was the integrity of the Versailles territorial settlement in 1919. As the Czechs began to feel that the idea of democracy could not save their state from centrifugal forces, so they insisted all the more on this settlement, more vehemently and obdurately than even the French, and this die-hardness of theirs also had a role in the catastrophic turn of European politics.

In 1938, as the Hitlerite aggression started toward the German areas of Bohemia, it soon turned out that not only the Germans and Hungarians, but also significant portions of the Slovaks had no sense of solidarity with the Czechoslovak state. The grievances were unserious or puffed up, but estrangement was pervasive. This visible lack of solidarity had its part in the Western powers' acceptance of the principle that in the application of the ethnicity principle, historical Bohemia was also to be divided in two. The way Munich carved up the country also put it at the mercy of Hitler's Germany, which annexed it within half a year's time. What happened to Czechoslovakia was what had happened to Poland and Hungary: a historical process long in the making now came to pass in the form of most brutal aggression. This made the Czechs blind to the process that had been long under way behind the aggression and in line with East European development. They simply and justly felt that *Europe had forsaken them, the nationalities had stabbed them in the back,* and Europe owed them the restoration of their free state.

At the end of World War II, this debt was duly honored. The Czechoslovak state lifting up its head after the catastrophe, however, wears the indelible mark of catastrophe on its face, as do the mental countenances of the Polish and Hungarian nations. Czechoslovakia likewise no longer expects democracy to forge a united nation out of its multilingual country, just as Poland and Hungary have lost that hope. However, while the disillusionment prompted the latter to implement anti-democratic measures, the small-minded linguistic oppression and denationalization of nationalities, today's Czechoslovakia outdoes these, having opted for a program of expelling all non-Slavic nationalities from within its borders. It is madness but not without logic; the Czechs want democracy, not to be perturbed by nationalities, and an intact territorial stock—in other words, everything at once. This will to have everything, however, is driven not by a sense of power but the fear of the disaster they have been through. This is the point where Czech development and Yugoslav development, which have had many similarities, part ways; in 1938–1939, Czechoslovakia underwent a want of internal cohesion to the extent that even the relationship between state-founding Czechs and Slovaks was shattered; in contrast, Yugoslavia felt its fearful power in 1941–1944, and this experience is going to have a fundamental role in forging a nation out of Serbs and Croats, both originally sharply opposed to each other. The Yugoslavs want much because they feel they are powerful enough. The Czechs want everything because they feel no security is enough and know that up to now Europe still remembers its historical debt toward the Czechs. Indeed, the powers in charge of Europe's fate have succumbed to the Czech claim of expelling nationalities from their territories—at least in respect to the Germans. What we noted concerning Poland, however, holds equally here as well: the issue is showing signs of becoming a severe European crisis, and it is questionable whether insisting on 100 percent territorial integrity is finally worth being part of this moral crisis for Czechoslovakia.

COMMON FEATURES IN THE FATES
OF THE THREE HISTORICAL STATES

It is not difficult to outline the common features of the three historical East European nations. All three were served the lesson of becoming nations—to

be more precise, the transformation back into nations. In its own time, each—
Poland in 1772–1794, Hungary in 1825–1848, and Bohemia in 1918–1938—responded to the European democratic and patriotic movement with such vigor
that it elicited the highest hopes in West European contemporaries. All three
nations had to face the fact that their inherited historical territories, to which
they were deeply devoted, could not be drawn into a single national consciousness due to their several languages. For a while, all three believed that the cohesive power of *democracy* and *freedom* would bind their populations, which
were gravitating centrifugally. This hope was fostered for all three by the great
example of French development, where the tremendous experience of the
revolution engrafted other-language minorities into the single French national
consciousness. However, the French example had two thousand years of cultural development, fifteen hundred years of national boundaries, a thousand
years of central authority, five hundred years of national consciousness, and the
prestige of the French Revolution behind it. This was the example these East
European states resurrected from their long period of apparent nonexistence
and struggle with the difficulties of merely sustaining themselves. Thus their
hope of democracy welding together different peoples was naturally dashed and
proved unfeasible; *Poland was totally partitioned, the Hungarian War of Independence was crushed in 1849, and Czechoslovakia came to a disastrous fall in
1938–1939.* To top the catastrophe in all three cases, the nations battling with
European powers found themselves face to face with their nationalities. All
three nations justly felt that Europe had shamefully left them in the lurch. The
fall of all three nations—precisely the fivefold partitioning of Poland, the crushing of Hungary in 1849 and its dismemberment in 1919, and Czechoslovakia's
tragedy in 1938–1939—occurred amid brutal violence and blatant injustice, and
none of them were in a mental state to realize the part historical logic had had
behind the brutal aggression at the hands of the powers that be.

Moreover, as a rebound of the violence and injustice, the dogged delusion
arose that the historical frameworks as a whole had been dismantled merely as a
result of contingencies, factors of power, and brutal aggression and had nothing
necessary or undoable about them, and they could be restored without obstruction when the dominion of aggression and injustice collapsed. Attested to by
the suffering and woes of oppressed Poles, Hungarians, and Czechs, the images
of a bleeding Poland, a bleeding Hungary, and a bleeding Bohemia seemed
genuine, but they were actually associated with the dismembered *historical*
countries; it was the maps of the historical territories that were bleeding away in
people's imaginations, not the actual immediate communities made up of real
Poles, Hungarians, or Czechs. The greatest good for these three nations would

have been to carve them up strictly under the principles of self-determination and ethnicity. The dissection would still have hurt for a good while, but the sufferings of their oppressed compatriots would not have troubled them, and it would have been highly sobering for them to note that no serious woes or desires to rejoin their historical frameworks were arising. In this way, the public mood would have had to accept the unavoidability of partial dismemberment and would have sooner or later gotten accustomed to the new borders underpinned by the power of fact.

But this was not how it came to pass, and all three countries insisted on their historical borders, Czechoslovakia continuing to insist on them to our day. In the wake of its own particular catastrophe, each one of them was disillusioned by the power of democracy to bind together, and when faced with the alternative to be either faithful to the ideals of democracy or insist on their territorial claims, none of them had qualms about choosing the latter, flouting the fact that each one of them had, in its own time, been the pride of European democracy. In order to uphold their historical state territories, the Poles and Hungarians experimented with the useless means of minority oppression and denationalization, and, most recently, Poland and Czechoslovakia have taken the wholly radical road of fully expelling their minorities, not even keeping up democratic appearances. Each one of them fell short of the perfect example of democratic wisdom Denmark had set in 1919, declaring that it would have historically Danish territories back only if sanctioned by referenda. Under the shocks befalling them, all three nations fell into a mental state wherein they felt they had only claims on the *world* and no obligations or responsibilities toward it. This was manifest primarily in the lack of inhibitions in the way they all attempted to restore the "status quo" they deemed valid. No less irresponsible were they, having been disillusioned by democratic methods and insisting on their historical status quo, in trying to ensure the use of their single language either by denationalization or expulsion.

To a certain extent, Europe, which had forsaken these three nations in critical situations, did feel it was under obligation for the debt the three brought up ceaselessly. From among the three, Hungary put in its moral bill in the wrong way and at the wrong time—first, during the hopeless period of post-1849 reaction; second, in the form of querulous revisionism under the reign of a rigid status quo between 1918 and 1938; and third, as an ally of fascism between 1938 and 1941. In contrast, Poland and Czechoslovakia submitted their bills in 1918 and 1945, moments when Europe sensed and could honor its liabilities.

The fates of the three nations have parted at this point; while Hungary cannot expect to have even its ethnically based boundaries, Bohemia is having its historical areas purged of minorities with international assistance, and Poland is receiving territories with which it is compensated for the loss of its historical areas, likewise cleansed of minorities. In Hungary, we can therefore expect to encounter a serious mental crisis touching even the future of democracy, while Czechoslovakia and Poland can become participants in a major European crisis of conscience through the expulsion of masses of minorities. The conditions for all three nations to mentally reconcile themselves to their now customary and undisputed borders have thus been relegated to the distant future.

4. THE DEFORMATION OF POLITICAL CULTURE IN CENTRAL-EAST EUROPE

It is common today to hold that the political culture of Central and East Europe—that is, the area east of France, between the Rhine and Russia—suffers from an *original backwardness*. And observers refer to the underdeveloped and anti-democratic social relations; the coarse political methods; and the narrow, small-minded and aggressive nationalisms of the area; to the fact that political power is in the hands of aristocratic estate owners, tycoons, and military cliques, of whom these countries cannot rid themselves on their own; and to the belief that this area is the hotbed of various befuddled, foggy, and deceptive political philosophies.

This way of looking at the matter does have factual grounds, but its final conclusions are gravely misconceived. It nonetheless serves very well in supporting the offhanded avoidance of having to take up the tiring and inconvenient task of consolidating the area and the endorsement of the most contradictory proposals of solution that tally only in being half-baked and dangerous.

These countries are undoubtedly a far cry from the full-fledged and mature democracies of Western and Northern Europe. There is likewise no question that much of this has to do with the givens of their social structure. The institutions that were a preschool for democracy in Western Europe did not work on the society of this area as intensely. Feudalism in the Western sense of the word—that is, a personal, contractual-like system of relations—spread only as far as the Elbe, and beyond that, unvarying serfdom dominated. A middle-class lifestyle and the social methods and intercourse tamed by Christianity and humanism trickled down to the working classes less and less from west to east. Accordingly, the city-dwelling middle classes, the bearers of the revolutionary movements of the modern era, and labor striving upward in their wake had a less organic development in these countries, their numbers were smaller, and they were more isolated than their Western counterparts.

There are numerous advantages to counterbalance these. First, though to a lesser extent, the Christian, humanist, middle-class, and labor-movement precursors of modern social development did exist here as well. In terms of social, political, and economic development, it was differences in degree, not in kind, that distinguished the peoples of Central-East Europe from those of Western Europe; not only are they nearest geographically, but in character also. There were quite noteworthy precursors of the lifestyle of free peasants and political liberty in Eastern Europe, and the great hope of nineteenth-century Europe was the enormous response the idea of liberty elicited in Eastern Europe. This hope was finally not fulfilled apart from Russia, but the fact that this region fell behind Western Europe more than previously cannot be explained away by mere social factors. No doubt there were keen West European observers fifty years ago who noticed the stagnation and lifelessness of Italian political culture; who recognized that for all its cultural and scholarly achievements, Germany had a backward social structure; and who recognized that the idea of liberty was not as profound and deeply rooted in the "freedom-loving" small nations of Eastern Europe as it might have seemed from afar. No one, however, would ever have foreseen on grounds of character that Russia and even Turkey would take a straighter road to social development by the middle of the twentieth century than, for example, Poland or Hungary. This can hardly be explained by other than social development having been halted by historical shock.

Aristocratic estate owners, tycoons, and military cliques wield so much clout and influence in this region that no free-minded country with a healthy development would tolerate it. However, the common opinion that it is the interests of aristocratic magnates, industrialists, and military circles in power that have held their peoples in slavish obedience and distracted from social concerns is gravely shallow and barren. These interests do lurk somewhere in the background and are happy if a political movement turns up to deliver obedient masses. Should this be a decisive factor, we would have no aggressive nationalism, only servitude and bestial backwardness. National feeling, even when mean and small-minded, is a mass feeling closely akin to democracy, and people or groups with vested interests cannot elicit or feel serious crowd feelings. At most, they might try to take advantage of or beef up the misleading or deadlocking effects of the shocks and anxieties the development of their countries undergoes.

It is also true that this region has seen the burgeoning of the murkiest political philosophies and blandest political deceptions, which a society with any healthy development would not only not take in, but also would not think up. It is, however, childish to imagine that muddled philosophies or malevolent instigation can distort the development of political culture. Serious crowd emotion can only arise out of passion, and passion only out of actual experience. Messy philosophies and the deceptions of propaganda can only influence individuals or communities if intense experiences of fear or shock incline them to believe in lies and connivances because they can thereby justify their self-delusions, entertain vain hopes, fix on false notions, and satisfy passions. Half-truths and the lies of propaganda bounce off a balanced mind. The question is what has thrown the Central-East European mind off balance?

All factors point in the direction of some sort of *political hysteria.* Now any attempt to undo these political hysterias will first have to unearth the historical shocks that disrupted the development and balance of these countries. The shocks stem from the pangs and adversities of *nation-building* in Central-East Europe. We have described how state and national borders diverged due to the fragmentation of Germany and Italy and the establishment of the Habsburg and Ottoman Empires and how this brought into being *linguistic nationalism* and the confusion of national frameworks in the region. This meant that the nations in this region lacked what was self-evidently, clearly, circumscribably, and graspably present in both the reality and the consciousnesses of West European communities—the reality of their own national and state frameworks, their capital cities, their being politically and economically accustomed to one another, a single social elite, etc. The political rise and decline of a country in Western and Northern Europe—its acquiring or losing a role as a major power or its establishing or losing a colonial empire—could remain episodic, distant adventures, pleasant or sad memories, and could be suffered without major shocks because there was something that could not be taken away or questioned. In Eastern Europe, in contrast, the national frameworks were something *to be fashioned, restored, fought for, and be anxious about* not only because of the overpower of the state framework of existing dynasties, but also because of the indifference of certain quarters of its population and the fickleness of national consciousness.

This is the situation that gave rise to a characteristic feature of the unbalanced Central-East European political mentality: *existential anxiety for the community.* East European nations were always overshadowed by alien, rootless state powers either bearing European forms or wielding unbearable pressure, whether they were called emperor, tsar, or sultan, who deprived them of their sons either by offering the most talented ones a career or sending the most upright ones to the gallows or jails. The mismatches between historical and ethnic borders soon brought bad blood among the peoples themselves, and given the opportunity, they tried out on one another what they had learned from the emperors, tsars, or sultans. They all got to know the feeling when alien powers endangered, seized, or ruled their sacred places of national history and suppressed or governed their people in whole or in part. They all had territories for which they were justified in being anxious or in claiming, and all have been close to partial or full destruction. "The death of the nation" or "the annihilation of the nation" rings empty in West European ears; Westerners can imagine extermination, subjection, or slowly going native, but political "annihilation" overnight is sheer bombast to them, yet it is a *palpable reality* for the nations of Eastern Europe. Here there is no need to exterminate or expel a nation to make it feel endangered; it is enough to *call its existence into doubt* with a sufficiently aggressive rhetoric. This could be done in the hope of success because these nations had vacillating crowds behind them that *had to be won over to* the national idea, or, as it is put in this part of the world, *awoken to national consciousness.*

What meaning could this have in, for example, France or Britain? There the vast majority of people are not consciously British or French, just as they are not consciously *fathers, husbands, middle class, working class, or human*; it is at critical moments that they become sharply conscious of their belonging and their duty in the world. In a French or British context, there is no point in continuously keeping national consciousness awake as it will necessarily awaken when needed, and when it awakens, there will be no doubt that it is British or French consciousness, for what else could be awakened? In Central-East Europe, however, everything was disputed; first dynastic, then national frameworks fought their battles for every single soul. As prompted by passion, interest, or prejudice, the local landlord, district administrator, priest, teacher, judge, newspaper reader, and craftsman had their say in the matter, often each saying something quite different. Final riddles of community existence have confronted Hungarian or Slovak peasants day after day—ones their French counterparts would need to answer once a century at most.

When contrasting the quivering consciousness of the East European masses with the ranting of nationalists, the national idea that was made so much of might have seemed grotesquely limited to a very small circle in this region. Hence the quite different appeal of the denial of the national idea by vulgar Marxism in Central-East and Western Europe. In the West, where the national framework meant a long-standing genuine reality, the Marxist position could be seen as one possible, somewhat doctrinaire, nevertheless informative theory. In the East, however, the idea that the *national idea was merely an ideology concealing the interests of a narrow circle of capitalists* could be seen as a deadly danger to national existence because there was something to it in the region. Not that the capitalist middle classes of the area were the prime beneficiaries and movers of the national idea; that was chiefly the so-called national intelligentsia, which had not grown together with, indeed had few links with, the bourgeoisie. What was certainly true was that the great masses of people in whose eyes the national framework did not square with the historically known reality of the dynastic state were initially little moved by the national idea, and the national intelligentsia made immense efforts to *teach the national lesson* to the people. It goes without saying that it was only history that could teach this lesson, but until then, the vulgar Marxist notion that the national idea had narrow group interests behind it was a deadly threat to this "teaching" effort by the national intelligentsia. This was why a veritably psychotic fear of Marxist socialism could be instilled in the minds of even those quarters of the intelligentsia that had no interest relations with the capitalist system whatsoever.

ANTI-DEMOCRATIC NATIONALISM

Existential anxiety for the community has been the decisive factor in making democracy and democratic development waver in these countries. There is one essential requirement for the modern political development of a European community to be harmonious and even—that the cause of the community and the cause of liberty be one cause. In other words, in the revolutionary moment, when great revolutionary shock frees the individual from the psychic pressure of the social forces ruling over him by the grace of God, it should be obviously clear that the liberation of the individual means also the liberation, unfolding, and inner and outer enrichment of the *entire community*.

Democracy and nationalism are movements with the same root, profoundly related, and their imbalance can be the cause of grave confusions. And grave confusions did arise in Central-East Europe. A taking possession of the national community and the liberation of the people did not intertwine; quite to the contrary, these nations experienced historical moments that seemed to prove that the collapse of the oppressive political and social powers of the past and the carrying of democracy unrelentingly to its logical conclusion jeopardized, even brought disaster to the national community. These shocks brought into being the greatest monstrosity of modern European political development: *anti-democratic nationalism*. Sadly, we have become so much used to it that we do not take notice what a squaring of the circle it is to expect and develop the characteristic features of free men, the spontaneous enthusiasm, conscious self-sacrifice, and responsible activism for a community while that community fails to guarantee the elemental conditions for the growth of free men.

In a state of convulsive fear and the belief that the advance of freedom endangers the cause of the nation, the benefits of democracy cannot be made use of.

To be a democrat is first and foremost not to be afraid—not to be afraid of those who have a different opinion, speak a different language, and are of another race; not to be afraid of revolution, conspiracies, the unknown evil intentions of the enemy, hostile propaganda, disdain, and generally all those imaginary dangers that become real because we are afraid of them. The countries of Central-East Europe have been afraid because they are not full-fledged and mature democracies, and being afraid, they were unable to become democracies. The unfolding of an undisturbed, free, and unfearful political life would have run straight against the very anxiety complexes of these nations; it would have upset a war effort, disabled the pursuit of an aggressive foreign policy born of fear, unmasked the sham political construct the national anxiety erects, or provided too great an opportunity for national minorities threatening national unity and feeling alien in or unconcerned or inimical about the national framework, and so on.

Thus what genuine democracies know only in the actual hour of danger became the rule in the permanent anxiety and sense of danger—the curbing of public freedoms; censorship; a search for the "hirelings" of the enemy, the "traitors," excessively forcing order or its veneer at the expense of liberty. An infinite variety of ways of falsifying and abusing democracy came into being, from the most subtle and even unconscious to the most brutal: playing off general suffrage against democratic development; striking coalitions and compromises on unsound and unclear bases; election systems obstructing or falsifying the healthy articulation of community will; rigging elections; coups d'état; and transitory dictatorships.

This course of Central-East European political life brought about a characteristic type of politician: the *phony realist*. Descending from aristocratic heights or ascending on the wings of democratic representation, these politicians, beside their undoubted talents, had cunning and a bent for aggression that made them perfectly suited for running and epitomizing anti-democratic governments and aggressive political pseudo-constructs in the midst of democratic trappings. They thus came to be renowned as "great realists" and could relegate their Western counterparts as "doctrinarians" or "idealists" to the background. Bismarck was the prime example of this type, and the Tiszas, Brătianus, Pašićes, Bethlens, Venizeloses, etc. were its great representatives. Interestingly, though quite logically, all this came to reinforce the power of the heads of state in these countries, which democratic advances had begun to overshadow. Governments had weight insofar as they managed to balance between the two factors of power, but by having systematically corrupted one factor, popular representation, they strengthened the other. Moreover, it was by the authority of the head of state that faithful subjects expected to be protected against the ravages of government power. This pulverized existing democratic forces and meant a fallback into the pre-democracy condition, when society had expected to be saved from troubles not through law, the efficient control of government, and the political reasonableness of citizens but the graceful goodwill and wise determination of the head of state exercising his personal authority.

The difficulties of nation building in Central-East Europe also contributed to forces, gaining or regaining *social leadership*, who, in turn, diverted sound and democratic political development. In the West, the elite leading democratic and national development consisted primarily of lawyers, civil servants, political authors, leaders in business life, professionals, and trade union leaders. In contrast, Central-East Europe saw a shift in two directions: in opposition to the spirit of democracy, the *ruler*, the *noble*, and the *soldier* again acquired a definitive role, while the so-called *national intelligentsia* assumed a unique function.

The *ruler*, the *noble*, and the *soldier* acquired a central role in Central-East Europe because the shaping of national frameworks required not only an internal political movement, but also a territorial reorganization, changing the European system of states. The dynasty, aristocracy, and military that assumed a role in national unity or independence *temporarily* avoided the preordained fate of the monarchic, aristocratic, and military spirit—gradual or abrupt decadence—and secured a *noli me tangere* status in the struggle of democracy against all wielding of personal power. It was on such a national basis that the public desisted from criticizing certain dynasties (e.g., the Houses of Hohenzollern, Savoy, and Karađorđević) and some aristocracies (e.g., the Prussian, Polish, and Transylvanian) and all national armies. As a result, the *noble-military* component of national feeling—the feelings of dominance, aggression, and representation—prevailed over the other component, the *middle-class* civilized, intimate, and peaceable feelings.

The *national intelligentsias* could not boast the social prestige and past, tradition, and political culture of their Western counterparts but had a much greater importance and responsibility in national existence. The intellectual professions that had to do with defining and cultivating the distinctive features of the national community had a prominent role—writers, linguists, historians, priests, teachers, and ethnographers. This was why "culture" acquired an added political significance in these countries, and it brought about not so much a flourishing but a *politicization* of culture. Because these countries did not "exist" in the West European sense of unbroken continuity, it fell to the national intelligentsias to uncover and cultivate the distinctive and separate linguistic and popular-folkish individuality of these new or reborn nations, to prove that these popular-folkish frameworks, for all the wants of national life, had deeper roots and were more vigorous than the prevailing dynastic state frameworks — which was indeed true. This was, however, what gave rise to the ideology of linguistic nationalism. In itself, this would not have jeopardized democratic development; in fact, these intellectual layers were often much more democratic than the politically influential capitalist bourgeoisie and lawyers of Western Europe.

This development became the starting point of a fateful deviation because it gave rise to murky political theories and philosophies that would later engulf the political life of these fear-stricken communities. This does not in the least mean that the dynastic, aristocratic, and military-chivalric world in the classical sense lived on in this region. It was only the power and sway over society that the dynastic, aristocratic, and military forces retained; otherwise they adopted the values, aims, anxieties, and desires of the national intelligentsia. Insofar as the mental state of anxiety required certain monarchic, aristocratic, and military dispositions, their sole contribution was the assertion of unity, discipline, order, anti-revolutionism, and respect for authority.

THE DEFORMATION OF THE POLITICAL SELF

The deformation of social structure was followed by the warping of the political self and a hysterical mental condition when there was no healthy balance among things real, possible, and desirable. The characteristically contrary psychic symptoms of the maladjustment between desires and realities can readily be observed among all these peoples: an excess of self-documentation and self-doubt, overblown national vanity and abrupt submissiveness, endless protestations of achievements and a striking devaluation of genuine achievements, moral claims, and moral irresponsibility. The majority of these nations give themselves over to ruminating on former or possible great-power statuses, while they can so heart-sickeningly apply to themselves the term "small nation," which would be utterly meaningless to a Dutchman or a Dane. Should any have managed to achieve their wish-dreams of territory, power, and prestige for a while, pointing out the fickleness and deficiency of the enterprise would immediately incur yelled charges of treason, but depriving them of their unrealized pipe dreams would not be had.

In such a state of mind, political sensibility is confounded; it is a common feature of the primitive states of mind dominated by the struggle for life to relegate values to the background, when the everlasting uncertainties of life and ways out lacking baffle the system of values. This is why it is a very dangerous vulgar wisdom of existentialism to believe that the condition of danger is fertile and that it is only facing annihilation that awakens the individual and the community to the real meaning of life and that enables them to marshal creative energies ("Stirb und werde!"; "Vivere pericolosamente!") This holds only for mature, balanced, and grown-up minds; the uncertainties of existence will only elicit uncertainties of value from an immature and adolescent individual or community.

This is how these countries came to develop a sort of *national materialism*, a distant deformation of the Marxist social materialism. As labor in the fever of class war had little feel for the subtle values the propertied classes developed in the serenity their property afforded them, so the nations in the fever of establishing themselves did not realize that the greatness of Western nations lay in living their national lives with a self-evident serenity, not wanting to flaunt their achievement as a nation at all cost. While, however, the value system of labor fighting the class war proved to become deeper and richer in proportion as it increased its political weight, as political opportunities opened before them and their hopes were realized, the national mindset of most of the peoples of Central-East Europe, due to a whole series of historical disasters, became increasingly narrow and gave itself over to serious community hysterias. In this way, their national materialism itself proved to be a destroyer of values. All manifestations of national life were subjected to the most furious national teleology; all their genuine or imaginary achievements, from Nobel prizes to Olympic records, lost their spontaneous purpose in themselves and were put in the service of national self-documentation. From forgery to assassination, everything was sacrosanct and inviolable if done in the "name" or "interest" of the nation. Befitting proper materialists, no one was bothered that this would exhaust the basic moral reserves of the nation. One of the greatest deeds of Tomáš Masaryk was to reveal—decades before becoming president—that a document that romantic national self-indulgence had venerated was a forgery. Alas, there were few to follow in his footsteps in the rest of the East European countries.

Throughout the region, including Germany and Italy and the rest of the East European countries, this precipitated a massive body of journalism using hazy and phony categories and turning all the ordinary concepts of European political thought into weapons in this arsenal of self-documentation and self-justification. Simple ideas and more or less correct generalizations became manifestations of the Absolute Good and the Absolute Evil raised to metaphysical rank, mystic essences, and spells, the main duty of which was to buttress pipe dreams and blur facts the community was not ready to face. Scholars of the "national" sciences set out to establish the historical—or, such lacking, the prehistorical—entitlements of national existence, the "scientific" grounds for territorial disputes, the fundamental principle of national existence, the separate national mission justifying independence, and, moreover, *horribile dictu*, the concept of foreign policy, which, being scientifically established, the nation was to follow.

This use of science, pursued not for itself, not only corrupted the scientific quality of these countries, but also put the elites of these nations in a radically sham relationship with reality; it accustomed them to build not on *reality* but *claims*, not on *achievements* but wants, and to think outside the simple chain of *causes* and *effects*.

If it was to be reckoned that one nation could not get on with another within one state body, *geopolitical givens* would be pointed out that prescribed co-existence and indirectly even who was to take the leading role in it. If asked why they wanted to rule people who wanted none of it and to be superior to those who were not inferior, they would answer by referring to *archaeological finds, folk songs, folk-art motifs, loan words, winged altars, and the effects of their books and institutions*, all of which proved that the people concerned would still be languishing in the darkest barbarism. If they were called to account for their internal disorders, dictatorship and oppression, they would point out the wounds they had suffered from Attila and the Turks in defending European liberty and democracy. If they were reproached for their thoughtless and vain foreign policy, they would invoke the centuries-old, moreover metaphysical, "meaning" of their history, which fatefully defined this or that policy of theirs. Do not let us think that these have remained mere extravagances; in less crude form, they continue to weave through and falsify the most expert, most objective, and most modern trains of thought.

As a joint effect of all these factors, the social and political development of these countries came to a standstill, and if it did continue, it did not demonstrate the evenness and internal authenticity that characterizes the development of both Western Europe and the Soviet Union.

5. THE MISERIES OF TERRITORIAL DISPUTES

The direst consequences of the confusions in the territorial statuses and the deformations of political culture in Central-East Europe were in the relations among the nations. For the distant Western observer, the political life of this region is awash with small-minded and inscrutable territorial differences, with every nation in the region in a constant state of discord with the others. The first among these rather repugnant conflicts is the incomprehensible and meaningless *language war*. Western Europe also knows disputes over language, but we must be aware of the difference between a Western dispute over language use and an East European language war. The Flemish-Walloon and the Finnish-Swedish disputes over language use are radically different from Czech-German, Hungarian-Romanian, or Polish-Ukrainian language wars. For the participants of Western disputes, democracy is an existing and palpable possession, while the language dispute itself is not a matter of life and death. West and North European language disputes are not really between two peoples but between the two wings of the intelligentsia of one people, and the object of the agitation is that a group of people who have broken off from their vernacular—the Finns speaking Swedish, the Flemish or Bretons speaking French, the Irish speaking English—should return to the original language of their people. The Swedish people in Finland or the Walloons of Belgium might sympathize with the struggle in which one participant happens to be the language they speak but are generally quite aloof from it, and it seldom occurs to them that they should provide a means of suppressing the other language. For most West and North Europeans, persecution for and suppression of language use seems rather strange, and so is the propaganda to revive a vernacular that has been losing out (Irish, Gaelic, Welsh, Breton, Basque, Friesian, Lapp, etc.) when people decide to change their ancient language for one they believe will open up new opportunities for them.

In contrast, the Central-East European language wars are fought by peoples who have lived in the uncertainties of state and national existence and the ensuing anxiety for generations. These peoples want to base their state life on a community of people speaking the same language, and the outcome of the language war will decide on existing or desired state borders, language statistics being believed to determine the fate of their borders or territorial claims. In such a state of mind, it would be meaningless to point out that linguistic proportions cannot be changed in an area or that it is not worth it, that winning over some would result in losing many, and that subduing some would have to be dearly paid for in acquiring many enemies. Of course, a clear-sighted, brave, and democratic public and politics have but one course of action: provide a maximum of opportunities to minorities within the existing framework and, on their own initiative, satisfy the boldest demands those minorities might have— even running the risk of their breakaway; put differently, they would follow a British dominion policy. What this requires of course is that they should not be afraid and not believe that the secession of non-national-language or minority areas would result in the death of the nation. If they continue to believe this and that the outcome of the language wars is an existential matter, then this implies actual war, the winning of which requires all the furious and final means all nations know as *exceptional* concomitants of a *real* war.

MINORITY OPPRESSION AND GRIEVANCES

It is at this point that the repression and the grievances of minorities begin. The constant debate over who started the conflict, the majority with the oppression or the minority with the seditious agitation, is utterly hopeless. The state of mind of existential anxiety, the fear for life, sifts people with common sense out of the debate, and the situation occurs when the agitation to have minority children learn majority-language folk songs is seen as a cunning and aggressive policy of language expansionism and the contrary agitation, against having children learn and have them sing in their own songs, is deemed an act of sedition. The grievances of minorities have an infinite cornucopia of terms for describing the techniques of oppression, while the majority peoples have a likewise infinite cornucopia of "grievances" for describing an upright and meek people being stirred up by fiendish agitators trained to undermine the state at foreign universities. Grotesquely, all these pseudo-reasonings and delusions turn into their diametric opposites whenever a change in territorial status turns a majority into a minority and vice versa.

One is moved to tears on hearing Hungarians going into raptures about the goodness and meekness of Slovak peasants or the Czechs extolling the noble gravity and civic virtues of Hungarian peasants and can only wonder why living under such good-willed governments and among such gracefully good peasant folk is so unbearable and why so many evil pan-Slavic agitators and no less evil revisionist agitators traverse the land ceaselessly inciting people against their lawful government. Of course, it is difficult to use the terms "lawful government" and "seditious agitator" in their Western sense where yesterday's agitators become today's lawful governments and vice versa. In this muddle of charges and countercharges, it is quite perplexing that reality, instead of gradually deviating from the picture drawn up by the charges themselves, increasingly approaches it. Though born of the imagination, community specters have the horrible characteristic of materializing in the proportion to which they are believed. In the world of good-willed governments and meek and industrious peasants, we first have prophets proclaiming the dangers to the nation or the people and enthusiastic cultural movements; then follows the suspicious watchfulness of minority cultural movements; then comes the buttressing of majority cultural movements with the police, whereby the seditious mood is established; this then is topped by the authorities' fault-finding in everything; seditious movements gradually arise, only to be followed by incarcerations and gendarme bayonets; conspiracies; the systematic routing of minorities; and finally killings, revolts, and wars of extermination.

Where the situation does not deteriorate as far as this, *minority life* gradually becomes an impossible state of being. Unless basing itself expressly on racial supremacy, the state continually embraces its other-language citizens with a rhetoric of enthusiasm, but should a minority person show any sign of insisting on his language and identity, he will be suspect and treated as such. This will make the situation of a minority person ambiguous and strange even if he belongs to a *historical* minority, but all the more so if the minority was freshly annexed. This strangeness does not really hinge on the civilized or brutal methods of state power. Until 1939, the methods of Czechoslovakia stood high above those of all the rest of Central-East Europe; still it could not count on its minorities any more than other countries on theirs. For if the Czechoslovak Army has a confidential instruction to prefer Czechoslovak to minority firms in its procurements—a perfectly logical measure for a state that considers the speakers of the state language as its basis—then minority businessmen will no less logically conclude that civil equality is but an empty slogan even if no hands have been laid on them. Even under such conditions, but all the more so under more forceful persecution, minority life ceases to be a full human life; it is marginalized and held in constant check and seeks compensation in more or less realistic hopes of reuniting with kindred people. This state of living off hope, if it is not fulfilled soon, results in an endless swinging between vain phantasmagoria and woebegone lethargy.

Existential uncertainty and the corrupting effect of territorial disputes have together brought into being a characteristic Central-East European territorial—*territoriocentric*, so to speak—notion of what the power, strength, and flourishing of a nation consist. This attitude is characteristic primarily of nations with irredentist and territorial claims and reduces them to cultural and political barrenness, but it does not leave the "possessors," the adherents of the status quo, untouched either. When the greatest concern and anxiety of a nation is what territories it is afraid of losing and what territories it claims, national prosperity is sooner or later bound to be associated with territorial status; people begin to represent the fullness of their national pride and desires by drawing maps of their *real condition and their condition-to-be* and stick them up everywhere to be always seen. This is a deeply anti-democratic attitude—deeply because in itself it means neither oppression nor oligarchy, but as an attitude it is wholly incompatible with democracy. Democracy is the victory of creativity and crafts-manship over conquering and possessing, and its most important teaching is that a nation can multiply and increase in depth and height, much more than any such effort at the expense of other nations. This is not to say that a democracy might not have just territorial claims; obviously, a claim for territory by inhabitants who want to belong politically where their desires and wills lead them cannot be objected to on democratic grounds. However, it is also certain that when a territorial dispute becomes the dominant cause in the life of a nation, it can block a not-yet-democratic community in its democratic development and can even dampen democratic spirit in a community already democratic.

"LEADERSHIP" CLAIMS

Again, it is usually unwarranted territorial claims that are behind the gritty and mutual assertions of Central-East European nations that they are superior to or that they have a mission toward other peoples, primarily those whom or whose areas they want to rule. These include the various theories of the "leader" roles of various nations, their missions in defending or propagating Christianity, culture, or democracy. These are not quite the counterparts of the German *Herrenvolk* concept, which was supposed to be applied against *all* nations. The various entitlements that East European nations allege refer only to limited areas they possess or claim, and their sole aim is to counter the secessionist or separatist aspirations of the minorities, the speakers of other languages. This type of aspiration to "leadership" is a formula bred by constraints and torments; the nations concerned are grieved to see that the territory they possess or claim is not monolingual; were it that, they would be happy to forgo "leadership" or "the spreading of democracy" and would much rather live an "unpretentious" national life in the areas to which their national feelings attach them.

The mental disposition of Central-East European peoples to approach all political matters with a view not to reality and possibility but to grievance and redress has given rise to a characteristically *querulous* notion of territorial matters—a notion basing itself on historical entitlements and the status quo, nevertheless inextricably bound to claims justifiable on the democratic grounds of self-determination. Advocates of this notion essentially declare a territorial status—one naturally more favorable—as valid at a given historical moment. Ostensibly, they claim nothing belonging to anyone else, only what they are entitled to; the unsuspecting observer will be dumbstruck only when he sees what their demands actually include. Two different methods have been used to justify such claims; we can safely call them the *Hungarian* and the *Czechoslovak* methods after their pioneers.

The Hungarian method bases itself on historical antiquity, the thousand years of possession. To ground the historical claim, all the exalted or exaltable events of those thousand years are enlisted—particularly the thesis that had the Hungarians not shed so much blood protecting Europe against the Turkish peril, they would not have grown scarce in their own land, and Europe commits an unforgivable ingratitude in now dismembering it because of its resulting multilingualism. The justification sometimes falls victim to historicizing, medieval saints and kings being marshaled to justify a historical Hungary.

The Czechoslovak justification is radically different and modern, referring to its thousand-year past only insofar as it implies democratic or humane achievement. Nevertheless, it regards the time of the establishment of the international security organization, 1918–1919, as a reference date governing all territorial claims, and since the security organization broke down due to the insistence on various territorial claims in 1938, it holds that the only way to discourage countries bent on aggression is to restore the status quo at the time of the establishment of the security organization. The rest of the East European countries interchange or combine the two arguments, adding to it a third argument, a simple ethnic claim.

For all their differences, the Hungarian and the Czechoslovak arguments are essentially the same. Both believe they are asserting rights in the face of raw aggression, while both are in fact involved in the quixotic struggle of wish against fact. The Hungarian reasoning is gravely unrealistic because it does not take account of the fundamental fact of Central-East European national development: the collapse of historical state boundaries. The Czechoslovak version is likewise gravely unrealistic because it wants to restore the very elements of the security organization that brought about its collapse. Both arguments have an element of conjuring up spirits in them: Hungarians invoke the spirit of St Stephen, the Czechs the spirit of Geneva, and they want them to do wonders they cannot. Should they happen to attain their aims through any occasional support from the great powers, they will not acknowledge this none too glorious fact but will celebrate the "victory of justice" and make thanks offerings at the altar of their protective spirits.

Political consciousness burdened with existential fears was likewise responsible for the fact that the foreign policies of the peoples of Central-East Europe were defined ultimately not by principles, mental dispositions, or even objective interests but their positions vis-à-vis territorial disputes. It was due to territorial issues that Poland, for all its interests to the contrary, fell in line with Germany in 1938; it was territorial issues that made Romania join the German camp in 1941; and it was likewise territorial concerns that led Bulgaria and Hungary, however resolutely they had decided never to join the wrong side again, to slide into the war of the Germans at the critical moment. The case of Bulgaria is particularly characteristic. Indeed, it would be difficult to claim that imperialism drove the Bulgarians to side with the Germans or that democracy prompted the Serbs to side with the Entente; having like social structures, both peasant countries of the Balkans assumed foreign-policy positions determined by territorial issues. This was how a Bulgaria that had accepted the carving off of its territories with the least racket and uproar among the "revisionist" countries, and even had Russia to back it, at the decisive point moved in the direction wherefrom it hoped to have its territorial claims honored.

No nation in the region could have been able to pursue a foreign policy rising above its territorial interests; not one of them was democratic or fascist of itself, choosing one or the other for the territorial security or gain it might provide.

One of the most disheartening chapters in the deformation of the political culture of Central-East Europe is the spirit of political irresponsibility the countries manifested in their European policies determined by their territorial disputes. Perturbed by anxiety and insecurity, misshapen by historical shocks and grievances, the disturbed mind tends to want to live off not its own being but the claims it has on life, history, and others. In this state, it loses its sense of duty and responsibility toward the community, and the only use he has of moral principles is for them to undergird his claims. The post-1918 overmoralization of European international affairs provided Central-East European nations with a vast arsenal of moralizations for disputes; the side in possession insisted on peace, and the claimant side was adamant on justice. However, this was mere pretense on both sides because they used these categories not in their authentic meaning but in how they could be used in their territorial disputes.

The lack of political maturity was nowhere more blatant than in their dividing nations into goodies and baddies, darlings and rascals. That their desire for peace or justice was insufficiently grounded became evident as soon as a fair peace or mutual justice was brought up. In response, the status quo countries' catchphrase was "Revision means war," which actually meant that "We are ready to go to war if we are expected to surrender what we unjustly possess." The revisionist punch line was, "Justice precedes peace," which amounted in reality to saying, "We are ready to set the whole world ablaze if we do not get what we claim." We might indeed ask with the biblical turn of phrase: if so ye confess, what do ye more than others, and what is the use of the reference to peace or justice? Do not the aggressive and unjust nations conduct themselves in the same way?

Nothing harmed the European prestige of the League of Nations more than the endless and pointless debates, which, disguised as matters of principle, were only about the chronic lack of permanence in the territorial statuses among Central and East European nations. In the hands of these nations, the entire ideology of Geneva became a hatchet in their disputes against each other. This was how they became increasingly indifferent to the fundamental interests of the European community and irresponsible in the face of its fundamental moral maxims. Everyone knows the depths of the irresponsibility with which National Socialism and fascism thrust Europe down the road of catastrophe. Yet it is no less significant that many attempts at Franco-German rapprochement foundered on the veto of the Petite Entente between 1918 and 1933, a foundering that also meant the perversion of the regional idea proclaimed with ardent hopes, or how a Poland and a Hungary—threatened by the same danger in 1938—could not as much as make a gesture of solidarity in the catastrophe of the Czechoslovak state.

If we look at the politics of the countries between the Rhine and Russia since 1918 in summary, it is difficult not to pass harsh judgment on them. Two reasons caution us nonetheless. One is that these countries have suffered unbearably much. The other is that should we leave them adrift, we will gain nothing because it will only exacerbate the situation of Europe and the world. It seems wiser to ask whether there is a feasible way of consolidating the region and whether there is a possibility of directing the political development of these countries back onto the even road from which they have deviated.

6. RESOLVING TERRITORIAL DISPUTES AND THE CONSOLIDATION OF EASTERN EUROPE

We have described the political miseries of the East European countries that elicit mistrust and exasperation in Western observers: their many territorial disputes; the small-mindedness and aggression of their nationalisms; their willingness to forgo decent political means; their lack of democratic spirit; their bent to political unrealism, to live off not so much their achievements but entitlements and claims, to mutually hate one another, to make gains at the expense of their neighbors, and to be irresponsible in matters of all-European concern; and their political decisions, which are informed not by deep-rooted ideals or serious long-term political concepts, nor their rational self-interest, but their territorial disputes with their neighbors. On these grounds, they draw the conclusion that this region with all its bragging, denunciations, complaints, quarrels, and border issues should be left to its fate because its inherent barbarism is going to stand in the way of its consolidation anyway.

We have painted this region's turn to barbarism with rather strident colors. Nevertheless, the attitude that brushes the problems of this region off the table because they are irresolvable is based not so much on a thorough knowledge of the region but on convenience and a bad conscience. This area is unable to consolidate not because it is inherently barbaric but because unfortunate historical events have pushed it off the road of European consolidation, and it has not found its way back.

THE POSSIBILITIES OF CONSOLIDATION

What is the final cause of all the contention in Central-East Europe? The fact that the historical states and the borders of the historical nations of the region have been blown up and the borders among its various nations have become subject to dispute. I know no basis for the opinion that the resulting confusion cannot be resolved. For has anyone ever tried to actually consolidate this region? A chance of consolidating the region occurred only in 1912 and 1918, when the two supra-national state formations, the Ottoman and the Habsburg Empires, which had been in the way of the final establishment of nation-states in this region, fell apart. Had the peacemakers of 1918 been a little more circumspect and cautious, they could have laid the foundations of consolidating the region by the end of 1919. We know this did not come to pass. Since then immeasurable difficulties, suffering, and barbarism have swamped the region, yet it is still only thirty years ago that there was anything to be consolidated. This is not particularly long. Did Western Europe acquire its final borders in a matter of only thirty years? Obviously not. And if this is the case, we ought not to raise the standard malevolently high for the peoples of this region, who themselves hardly deny that they departed from the straight, unobstructed, and promising road of European democratic development. Even less should we forgo consolidating the region; in the wake of thirty years of terrifying confusion, the way of consolidation clearly transpires. Mutual hatreds, occupations, civil wars, and wars of extermination having receded, and the borders among stabilizing national frameworks are beginning to show up quite plainly. What must be avoided is slapdash and aggressive action that will cause this filthy deluge to return to the region. Apparently, consolidation can be obstructed, for it is not an elemental force that takes possession of an area and overwhelms everything, but it is a delicate, circumspect, and easily wreckable human effort against the forces of fear, folly, and hatred. The emphasis falls on the *possibility* of consolidation in the region.

We base this possibility on the fact that the borders among these nations have begun to take a final shape in the region. All right, one could ask, but who is going to guarantee that the new border system will not fall apart and give way to the establishment of new nations in this area that lack all permanence in a few decades? The question shows a fundamental obtuseness about the political development of Eastern Europe.

As in Western Europe, the number of nations has little changed in the past one thousand years. In the Eastern Europe of the fourteenth century, the nations that existed were the Polish, Hungarian, Czech, Lithuanian, Romanian, Bulgarian, and Greek. Between 1400 and 1800, two military ventures, the Ottoman and the Habsburg Empires, attempted to create a non-national state in the region. They managed to overwhelm these nations and obstruct their political development, but they were unable to eliminate any one of them or start out on the way toward uniting them and forging them into a new one. Both ventures failed when modern national movements came into being, and the nations of the region, though having suffered major losses, reemerged. If we look around today, we see roughly those same nations in the region as six hundred years ago. There is some degree of change in that the Serbs and Croats have established a single entity, the Yugoslav community drawing to it some Slavic peoples whose national status had been unclear, notably the Slovenes. The Romanian nation became a closer unit than it had been, and the Greek one broke with the continuity of Byzantium. Only four new nations or the like were created in the region. The Slovaks of former Northern Hungary have developed their own national consciousness, and instead of the Hungarians, they have affiliated with the Czechs; the only question any longer is how sharp the dividing line between the Czech and Slovak nations is going to be. Further, the Estonian, Latvian, and Albanian nations were established in various buffers zones; they had their medieval roots as well, though they had the opportunity of founding their own states only at the beginning of the twentieth century. Finally, the Lithuanian, Latvian, and Estonian nations recently joined the supra-national state of the Soviet Union. There is no objective likelihood of any other nation being established in the region. These are rather modest changes, no greater than the changes that took place in the closed number of West European nations since the fourteenth century: the Swiss, Portuguese, Belgian, and Dutch nations were founded, and the English and Scottish have united since then, etc. The change in Eastern Europe was greater in that these nations came to be divided not by historically established but ethnic borders; or, putting it more simply, East European nations are made up of the totality of people speaking the same language. It goes without saying that this does not imply that there can be no language minorities or islands in this region; it only means that the stability of the dividing lines among the nations of the region is to be found not in historical borders, as in Western Europe, but along linguistic boundaries. All attempts to follow the West European pattern and instill a unified national consciousness into several nations on the basis of a single historical structure—primarily by the Poles, Hungarians, and Czechs—were bound to fail, and they are largely aware of that. Interestingly, there is only one current prospectively successful attempt at a single nation formation that is attractive beyond language borders, but this is based not on historical grounds but on the unifying power of the struggle for democratic liberation: the Yugoslav experiment. The core of na-tionhood is language here as well, but the role the Yugoslav nation has assumed in the cause of European liberation is an attraction that points beyond language borders today. It is natural that the success of this experiment can be assessed only from a historical perspective; nevertheless, if we contrast the success of this experiment with the failure of the three historical states, we have to agree with Ortega y Gasset, who, contrasting the rise of the British Empire and the decline of the Spanish one, argues that nations are bound together by not only a shared past, but also a future, the perspective giving prestige, optimism, and momentum to the shared aims and ventures of a community.

HISTORICAL STATUS QUO AND ETHNIC BORDERS

Having taken note of these, we now need to find a way of consolidating the region, the principles and methods whereby consolidation can begin and whereby state and nation can again become notions with the same scope. Any-one dealing with the consolidation of this region will sooner or later feel on the verge of madness, lost in the maze of principles and arguments brought to buttress one side or the other. This, however, is only an optical illusion. If we once perceive the decisive political process in this region, we will immediately realize that all genuine border issues in Central-East Europe revolve around the opposition of two approaches: claims based on some historical condition, status quo, or historical sentiment, on the one hand, and on ethnic or language belonging, on the other. The problem arises from the fact that where linguistic nationalism calls into question a given situation, the state borders have to be shifted to the language borders, but this has to be carried out with due consid-eration for the resistance that historical attachments, emotions, and current situations might bring to bear. Having so reduced the question to its essence, we can exclude the damaging and menacing superstitions with which border issues are befogged.

The first and most widespread superstition in this respect is that no just bor-der can be established in the region because there are so many possible contra-dictory criteria that some will be bound to be breached. However, there is only one criterion that needs to be considered: a good border is one that conforms to national belonging, which, in Europe, means either historical status quo or language boundaries. All other criteria are merely alleged; geographic, economic, strategic, rounding-off, transport, and all God-knows-what criteria that are fashionable to bring up in a most irrational swirl are actually quite meaningless, and their vast application is bound to become the source of grave troubles. We must be very careful with these criteria, which seem "practical," "rational," and "objective" at first sight. The absurdities of redefining borders have always been illustrated by new borders cutting through houses and gardens, forcing local villagers to obtain passports to go to the nearest market town. It was the favorite procedure of Hungarian irredentists to take compassionate foreigners to a border and show them how it ran through the kitchen of a house, to which the unsuspecting visitors would immediately say it could not remain like that, and that statement would be presented the next day as a major victory of the Hungarian historical concept of state.

We must not forget that these necessarily occur where a border is established not on the basis of old situations to which life had been accustomed but by drawing the consequences of changed realities. The situation that recurs throughout Central-East Europe is that there is a town on the border of a given language area with a majority speaking that language; its immediate vicinity, however, has come to be dominated by another language group. So a desperate race ensues to tear the town away from its language community in the interest of its surroundings or to tear away those surroundings in the interest of the town. However odd it may sound, the wisest solution is a third option: follow the linguistic boundary and, if necessary, cut the town and its surroundings apart. But even the first two options are better than the neither-fish-nor-fowl concoctions based on squaring ethnic, economic, or other considerations, as in the case of the free town of Danzig. The task is to separate nations; any arrangement, therefore, that does not clearly cede a territory immediately or in the near future to one or the other nation will but present the opportunity for dispute. Rapprochement, which will ensue following the reassuring demarcation of nations, will manage to find the solution to the problem of peasants wanting to go to the nearest marketplace. An excellent West European example to refer to is the city of Geneva, which is surrounded in every direction by French territories, and even God created it to be the capital of Savoy. History, however, ceded it to Switzerland, a situation that has caused a whole gamut of economic and transportation problems, even international legal disputes, but it is not a bone of contention between France and Switzerland. A similar Central European example is Sopron in Hungary, which a plebiscite ceded to Hungary, while the surrounding German-speaking area, Burgenland, went to Austria. Hungarians acquiesced in the ceding of the German villages because the town, replete with Hungarian historical mementos, remained in Hungary. The result was that though Sopron would be the "natural" capital of Burgenland by all economic and rational criteria, the Austrian-Hungarian border came to be one of the few borders in the 1918–1919 arrangement that were seen as mentally reassuring and balanced. Whether the nations concerned will be appeased or go into desperate disputes with each other will be decided not by the inhabitants of Dustfield having to obtain passports to visit the market of Gloriton but by politicians, history teachers, and pupils in the capital and schools of one country who have no reason to lament the loss of the national monument in the main square of Gloriton, whose population speaks their language, and who in the other country have no reason to bemoan that the children of the ceded villages are forced to learn alien folk songs at school.

This is not meant to be mockery; these sentiments are just as venerable as the emotions of the French attaching them to the cathedral of Chartres or the folksongs of the Auvergne. Our entire train of thought has sought to demonstrate that these are the most important factors that nourish the strifes of Central-East Europe. We have no intention of calling into doubt the truth of the thesis set up by many an eminent and learned author that it is landlords, tycoons, and militarists that generate these strifes ; we only want to add to this deep truth that these ploys can run their course only if history teachers and folksong collectors side with them, without whom monopoly capitalists are but lame ducks. One of the finest examples of this is the Habsburg Empire, the Eldorado of landlords, the joy of monopoly capitalists, and the paradise of the military, which nevertheless fell because history teachers and folksong collectors stood up against it. The "reasonableness" and "practicality" of considering the economic, transport, and similar criteria so often referred to are a mere illusion. In their current size, these countries are far too small to be self-sufficient geographical, economic, strategic, and transportation entities. Beside the enormity of World War II, what military import would shifting the border between two small East European countries from Small Hill to Big Mound have? The likelihood of this acquiring military significance might be, let us say, 10 percent, and that it may be beneficial for the future of mankind cannot be more than 5 percent. But that the grievances of a minority ceded to another country for military purposes will be inflammatory, sowing the seeds of war, is absolutely certain. No want of timber or oil imports is hardly worth not reconciling with one's neighbor. This holds true for any drawing of borders that cedes foreign minority areas to other countries on any practical or rational grounds. A border is important insofar as it contributes to stability, and, if stabilization does come about, it will not be disastrous if it is due to non-rational geographically or economically absurd factors.

Another superstition, often stated out of conscious bamboozling, is that no just borders can be drawn in this part of Europe because the population is so mixed. In fact, an ethnographic mixture of the populations does not necessarily imply problems. Linguistic islands, particularly those that have come into being due to settlement policies, do not constitute a problem of themselves; problems arise when the linguistic island has some historical possession or claim in its background. In other words, mixture becomes a problem only when the dispute over its belonging brings about the clash or intertwining of the two main criteria, the historical (status quo) and the ethnic principles, and renders the transition from the historical border to the linguistic one or orientation among the historical and linguistic claims difficult. Now, there are but two or three such cases in all Central-East Europe. Such was the Danzig Corridor, and such is primarily the case of Transylvania and the Greek-Bulgarian dispute over the northern shore of the Aegean Sea. In contrast to these, the Serbs and the Romanians established the demarcation between themselves relatively easily. Mixture did not cause any particular problem in the other highly mixed territory of the region, Bessarabia, where the territorial dispute was hardly related to the population mix resulting from the various settlement policies.

No less dangerous a superstition is the thesis that there is no point in undertaking the complexities of drawing new border lines because the answer to the problem is not the resolution of border disputes but the creation of a supranational confederacy where the borders between the nations will ultimately lose their significance. This is a very dangerous concept because the region has been subject to a supra-national confederacy, the empire of the Habsburgs, and it burst apart and thrust the region into instability because it could not draw satisfactory dividing lines between the nations of which it was made up. Like a marriage, confederacy must not be entered into with unresolved problems because it is essentially meant to open up new perspectives (and so creates scores of new problems) and not to avoid having to resolve pending issues. Any future confederacy will be viable only if borders acquire a minimal stability, which is the mental condition of joining the confederacy. Nations join a confederacy only if they all have something to lose that the confederacy can protect.

The example of the Soviet Union is not as straightforward as it might seem at first. It is well worth learning how to tolerate nationalities and set up institutions, but this does not mean that the problem of Central-East Europe is the same as that of the Soviet Union. In Central-East Europe, historically established nations face one another, and it is in modern times that their borders have become fluid. As nations, they have a long-standing and established historical existence, and for all the similarities in their fate and character, no uniting experience or situation has developed among them. What took place in the Soviet Union is all together different. The historical Russian Empire was a given fact; it had not melted its national minorities into one nation, but state fusion had had significant precedents until 1917. This historically existing empire was blended into a single nation by the shocking historical experiences of the socialist revolution and the Great Patriotic War. After these, this single nation had no qualms about providing linguistic and political autonomy, even the right to secede, to the nations and nation parts it united. It did so with no fear of such an eventuality, like the British Empire did with its dominions. Should such a unifying experience or development take place in Central-East Europe, it would have to face, in spite of the smallness of the region and some exceptions, much more powerful historical realities than the Russian Empire had in the various national minorities and tribal communities.

Political catchphrases are even more damaging than the various misleading theories and principles. The status quo slogan that no border is a good border, and that therefore the existing ones should be stabilized and mental rapprochement should be sought instead, is a damaging superstition; so is the revisionist slogan that life is an unending movement and change, and borders can never be fixed finally. Europe has become fully mature to have its territorial stock stabilized, if not for "ever," then for at least a long period, and this is also the condition of its becoming more unified and for its future peace. In this sense, we must be unrelenting in upholding the "status quo." However, it is only possible to stabilize—moreover quickly stabilize—borders that are reasonable and mentally acceptable, to which people can get accustomed, and that are adjusted to the psychologically and sociologically palpable borders of national entities. It is hopeless to preach appeasement while borders are no good, while "good borders" must be protected from the dynamic of "unceasing change."

Giving territorial disputes a moralizing twist is likewise harmful. If we recognize that the way to consolidate this region is to adjust state borders to shifted national borders, we will also realize that it is not moral justice to be administered but an objective situation to be grasped. The most pressing duty in the territorial disputes of the region is to rule out all moralizing interpretations the peoples of the region have kept expounding to international fora. The moral arsenal of the politically hamstrung peoples, war losers, is made up of pleading justice, appealing to the sublime and customary sense of justice of this or that great power and its magnanimity toward the oppressed and downtrodden, and requesting that no power policy interests be enforced in concluding the peace. Countries that are better off politically, war winners, or that at least think of themselves as winners, refer to their merits and submit their bills in the form of territorial claims. Both claims to justice and merit are in fact war axes wielded maliciously to obtain an advantage in the disputes between the parties, which are usually but territorial.

The duty of consolidation has to do with neither sublime justice nor imperishable merit. It is an objective task that has to do with recognizing objective political and social facts and with drawing consequences. No doubt justice, moral principles, and merit have their role in deciding border disputes but only insofar as they contribute to the conditions of stabilization. To be more precise: on the one hand, there is a minimal degree of justice without which no stabilization or mental satisfaction can be expected, and it thus cannot be left out of account; on the other hand, there are merits to be considered in the momentary historical and political circumstances that to *a certain extent* all parties recognize as a basis for settlement.

THE SELF-DETERMINATION OF PEOPLES

It is with this in mind that the right of self-determination of peoples should be assessed. The question is not from what we derive it or with what moral arguments we justify it but whether it is capable of tidying up Central-East Europe.

Even at first glance, it is clear that this principle looks for the solution to the confusions of Central-East Europe in the right place. We have already pointed out that nations have become the sum of those speaking one language in the region. Whoever wants to separate these nations well will have to follow not historical but language borders. The right of self-determination in this region is recognition that the characteristic Central-East European situation is that a good number of people have come to belong to historical communities that are not identical with their national belonging. The right of self-determination would have worked to allow the expression of the changes in peoples' national belonging. Unfortunately, the peacemakers of 1919 were unable to consistently apply the principle they had accepted and thereby fix the map of Central-East Europe for centuries. This was due to their weakness, to the simple inability of Western Europe to grasp the characteristic problem of Central-East Europe, the shift from historical borders to linguistic borders. They did understand, however, the right of self-determination of *nations*, which was meaningful for them in respect not to border disputes but to the right of nations to secede or become independent, such as the establishment of the United States or the secession of Belgium from the Netherlands. On this basis, they were happy to see and approve that Central European nations, such as Poland, Czechoslovakia, and Yugoslavia, which had theretofore not had or lost their independent statehood, established themselves as states. When, however, endless territorial disputes began over these areas, everyone wanting a plebiscite everywhere indiscriminately, West European peacemakers began to get muddled. They had essentially asserted the self-determination of peoples so that entire nations could be liberated and not so that every village or town, if it so wished, could ask for a plebiscite to shift from one nation to another. From a West European perspective, based as it was on the stable establishment of historical state borders, endless plebiscites and the hubbub to which they would give rise were not seen as desirable methods from the point of view of peace. This was the point where the principle of self-determination of nations was not adjusted to the concrete needs for which it ought to have been used in Central-East Europe. The consequent application of the right of self-determination in every respect being burdensome and beyond their powers, the peacemakers of 1919 were glad to forgo it. Violating these principles would have its role in bringing about the German policy of venting grievances and thereby Hitlerism too. The latter referred to self-determination merely as a pretext for a maniacal power policy, and it discredited the entire concept. Its mere mention is not advisable, the ready retort being, "We have heard it all too often from Hitler."

It should be laid down that the self-determination of peoples means not Munich but plebiscites. True, even these are viewed with considerable mistrust. Indeed, if the self-determination of peoples means that plebiscites are a permanent institution of international law that can be invoked at will, then we certainly have no need of it. Consolidation begins when some basic issues cease to be disputed. In international relations, this is primarily the question of borders. It is not at all desirable to be able to dispute them anywhere at any time. This would not be needed even when genuine disputes arise; ethnic or linguistic borders can be established in Central-East Europe on the basis of statistics or comparative statistics without major difficulty. It would be definitely harmful to hold plebiscites in areas where landlords speaking another language and few in number have the clout to influence the voting of their—often backward— majority populations, for the process of becoming a nation undoubtedly hinges on linguistic belonging in Central-East Europe as well. In this regard, the results of plebiscites in Silesia and Eastern Prussia were doubtful, demonstrating overwhelmingly German consciousness in obviously Polish areas under the pressure of German landlords and industrialists, where, in all probability, only a minority was actually German and the majority were Polish speakers, yet emotionally still unconscious. The real ground for plebiscites is not large, linguistically homogeneous areas but towns on the fringes of linguistic regions whose belonging has come to be disputed. This is all the more important because it is the historical attachment to certain areas, mostly cities, their populations, monuments, and stones, that is most difficult to undo in the transition from historical borders to linguistic borders. In such cases, if the people of a city decide on their belonging in a referendum, whether for or against historical attachments, it will surely help the process of acquiescence and relinquishment.

If we thus think of using plebiscites for stabilizing Europe, we have to be careful about two things; first, plebiscites should be arranged not where linguistic borders are clear but where they are critical; second, plebiscites, it should be remembered, are a means of stabilization, not of causing trouble, and thus should not be used for bringing into dispute stabilized borders and should never be repeated in the same place. If we yield in this, plebiscites will cease to be the means of consolidation and will lose all their advantages.

The recognition that linguistic borders have become the dividing lines between nations in Central-East Europe has brought up a novel and effectively monstrous solution: the exchanges and expulsions of populations. This method was first applied to the Greek-Turkish problem, and it was carried out amid major disorder, tumult, and inhumanity, but its results were surprising and have tempted copying; in a matter of only a decade, it ended Greco-Turkish animosity, which had had a centuries-long past and prospect. During World War II, Hitler used this means to resettle German populations living far off on the German linguistic boundary for the sake of expanding German political boundaries while ejecting the original inhabitants. He brought back Germans from areas where they had caused no minority problem. By settling them on the fringes of the German linguistic area and removing or exterminating the original population, he sowed the seeds of terrible enmity. This kind of resettlement became the source not of stabilization but insecurity.

The consequences of the United Nations' using this Hitler-devised method would be fateful for the future development of Europe. It would mean the end of the last certainty that could be taken for granted in stabilizing European borders—the permanence of the population. Nations would be expecting not to gain certain territories but such advantageous historical moments when they could expel whole populations from the territories they claimed. Population exchange need not be ruled out completely, but if we do not want to turn Europe into a highway of displaced peoples, we must lay down definite principles for using it, drawing lessons from the Greco-Turkish example and the recent instances of population exchange. The baseline is that population exchange can be justified only when ethnographic borders cannot be physically followed but the historical condition or the status quo cannot be maintained because of heightened tensions. Furthermore, it should be most definitely stipulated that population exchange must be mutual, carried out by way of a resolution and under the supervision of the community of nations, and that it cannot be undone. If these are not clearly provided, the double-edged sword of population exchange will cut its own authors too, the means of consolidating Europe becoming the starting point of the wildest anarchy.

Is it not mere theorizing and utopia, we would be justified in asking, to formulate principles for international consolidation when peacemaking and the establishment of borders is taking place "naturally," according to the interests and balance of forces of power politics? This question leads to the most important issue of international relations: *the ways of making a good peace.*

HOW TO MAKE A GOOD PEACE?

The awesomely difficult and contradictory task of making peace was put most succinctly by the great Italian historian Guglielmo Ferrero: "Any peace implies forcing the vanquished. But the most elemental requirement of conscience is that obligation can arise only out of free assent. . . . A genuine peace . . . can only be made possible through the contradiction that the act of enforcement by nature is blended with enough freedom and the required sacrifice with enough advantage to make the treaty be a moral obligation and be in the interest of the vanquished to keep rather than try and breach." This is what is needed for the vanquished to add the binding power of approval to the sheer condition of being overwhelmed by defeat. Let us not believe that it is easy for the victor to force the vanquished to sign a treaty. We have become far too accustomed to peace dictates and realize neither the odd atavism that we insist on in the contractual forms of concluding a peace treaty even under the conditions of a dictate nor the fact that the dictating victor has to forgo a good many things to force his opponent into accepting the treaty in a contractual way. Indeed, this is an atavism, one belonging to an age that had a more developed culture of foreign relations and diplomacy—the eighteenth century.

Following Ferrero and others, the recognition has gained ground that a type of warfare systematically restricting fighting to professionals and limited areas, sparing life and supplies, became general late in the seventeenth and eighteenth centuries—a level of humanizing war never reached since. Characteristically, as the British-French wars were raging overseas in the eighteenth century, travel and scholarly and social exchange between Paris and London went on undisturbed. It might seem scandalous that while soldiers were fighting bloody battles in mud and mire, elegant gentlemen and ladies, refined literati, kept up their conversations amid sophisticated formalities. Yet only a society that has totally eliminated war as such from its life will be revolted by such events. As long as we are unable to do so, we cannot deny that a warfare strictly regulated and restricted to limited theaters of war and fought in the manner of a duel is better than nuclear war. Dueling is a dull-witted medieval residue, but it is a high-minded advance in civilization compared to the law of fists. This dueling, play-the-game and humanized style of war had its counterpart in a system of dispassionate peacemaking that relegated force into the background in the international law and political mentality of the eighteenth century. This was part and parcel of the homogeneous political culture of European monarchy and aristocracy.

This dispassionate warfare and unavenging peacemaking was overturned by the Napoleonic system of reckless and risk-all warfare, which lived off and destroyed operation areas and made terroristic peace dictates. Napoleon's armies ravaged Europe for twenty years, and it took twenty years for legitimate European monarchies to put an end to the confusion. When peace had to be concluded in the wake of the devastations in Paris in 1814 and at the Vienna Congress in 1815, the same mood vibrated in the air that would be so fatal in 1919 and could likewise be grave now in 1946; there was and is far too much anger and exasperation built up against the vanquished monster to avoid the temptation of making the defeated nation pay for all the understandable grievance, regardless of the fact that this would make the peace physically impossible and delusive. Simultaneously, continuing the Napoleonic confusion, the wildest imperialist plans were hatched mostly by second- and third-rate powers jostling behind the victors. The conditions of concluding a peace dispassionately were thus no longer available; there had been too much aggression, pillaging, and dictates in the triumphant march of Napoleon for the idea of revenge not to seem self-evident. As brilliantly portrayed by Ferrero in *The Reconstruction of Europe*, Talleyrand was the one who recognized that it was not enough to build on the common, now declining, aristocratic political culture and that peacemaking should be based on deeper basic *principles*. "To establish something lasting that will be accepted without resistance, we must proceed on the basis of principles. If we have principles, we will be strong and will not meet with resistance, or we will at least be able to promptly tackle it," said Talleyrand, as quoted by Ferrero. Talleyrand found this principle in the concept of legitimacy and managed to get it accepted by the Vienna Congress.

Today, public opinion tends to think of legitimacy as a reactionary concoction, associating it with the Holy Alliance. This is but an optical illusion, however. Legitimacy was the invention of the diplomat and liberal Talleyrand; the Holy Alliance was the making of the fantast Tsar Alexander and the instrument of the reactionary Metternich. As it was conceived, legitimacy was not at all meant to repress liberal ideas but to help stabilize European states fallen into disarray and restore their territorial status. By repeatedly saying in the foregoing that a good border is the historical border for Western Europe, we have said no more than that settling the territorial status of Western Europe needs no more than Talleyrand's principle of historical legitimacy.

Thanks to this principle, Europe swiftly recuperated after the Treaty of Paris and the Vienna Congress, and an accused and defeated France could soon reassume its normal place in the concert of Europe. In domestic politics, the liberal idea was kept at bay for a while, but when it reemerged in 1830 and made stable achievements, it had the lastingness of the international system created in 1815 in its invisible background. This system survived the crises of 1848 and 1871 and lasted until 1914, providing Europe a hundred years in which peace was the regular and war the irregular condition.

The aristocratic Europe that had created the peace of 1814–1815 had rotted away by 1914, fell into the anarchy of World War I, and collapsed in 1918. Total war had stirred up mass emotions, and thus the peace conference commenced in the name of making amends and passing judgment over the criminals. More so than in 1814, the harmful effect of this could only have been counterbalanced by a solid and common basic principle for making peace. It was particularly the territorial issues of Central-East Europe that needed putting right in a way that would ensure stability and ward off another war—the Habsburg Empire, the Ottoman Empire, tsarist Russia, and Hohenzollern Germany having simultaneously fallen into ruins. The principle that would have met the needs of the age was given—the self-determination of people, which might be reasonably called the democratic formulation of legitimacy. It was with this in his baggage that President Wilson sailed to Europe to make peace. Its practicalities—that is, that Austria-Hungary had to be dismantled and divided up into nation-states along linguistic borders—were also conceived of correctly. Many have studied, and we ourselves have pointed out above, why this voyage, which took place at a turning point of a new era with an unprecedentedly auspicious start and most unfortunate continuation, ended in failure. Suffice it now to say that 1919 differed from 1815 inasmuch as the peacemakers likewise proclaimed a principle but did not have the power to apply it. They did not give way to obvious unification movements, did not liquidate all historical entities ripe for liquidation, and did not take into account historical emotions attached to the territories, while they meticulously considered the so-called geographical, strategic, transporta-tion, and rounding-off criteria; to be more precise, they let the parties bring up purported principles in order to satisfy desires born of anxiety—for example, pushing borders forward to some "natural" protective line far beyond language borders. These gave rise to the most pernicious and pointless border disputes; the peoples of certain territories had neither any living historical contact nor any ethnic contact with their new nation, and no allegiance could be expected or supposed of them. Prior to 1914, there were only a very few instances of this: the Lorrainese French in Germany and the Poles in Prussia and Russia. After 1918, instead of a decrease in the number of such situations, they were multi-plied; *this* was why the 1918 settlement was bad, not because its principles were wrong. Its consequences were an immeasurable confusion in thought and disil-lusionment. This confusion gave rise to, among other things, the monstrous grandchild of Napoleonic nihilism, the maniacal nihilism of Hitlerism.

We went through World War II, the forms of warfare dwarfing all previous experiments in total war. Human savageness outdid all scare news, and the pas-sions it has fostered now threaten to demolish everything wanting to be stable and reasonable. It is under such circumstances that we are waiting on the mak-ing of the new peace; the victors and the vanquished have sat down to close the war. The form they have adopted is the agreement-based treaty preserved intact from the eighteenth century. But after hell has been unleashed on the world, what can we do to make the peace revive the eighteenth-century type of peace set on a smoothing out, balance, and loyal performance?

THE DANGERS OF BEING UNPRINCIPLED AND THE PRINCIPLES SHOWING THE WAY OUT OF TODAY'S CONFUSION

The passions stirred up by World War II can be allayed only by an agree-ment on principles and their application; unprincipled, opportunistic power policy has never before been as threatening as today. If 1919, which had a basic principle, led to a catastrophe because of a failure to draw its practical conse-quences and implement it consistently, what are we to expect of the current peace conference, which is morbidly afraid of adopting any principle that is plain and binding? In vain are general statements proclaimed on final, hu-man, and democratic aims when there is no practicable principle for resolving the central problem of the peace: territorial dispute. All peace treaties revolve around disputes over territories because that is where they will have a lasting influence, and they must therefore be made so that they cannot be disputed afterward.

There are two questions that arise at this point. First, where are the principles that could be applied in the current situation? Second, how can those principles be implemented at all in the face of the facts and forces of current power politics?

As far as the first question is concerned, I believe the foregoing discussion have clearly pointed out the basic principles that count and have also shown that these principles are informed not by dogmatism but by practical recognitions ostensibly and unavoidably presenting themselves. The fundamental principle is the democratic form of historical legitimacy, the right of self-determination. In Western Europe, this is roughly identical with historical legitimacy and historically established borders, which it would not be wise to upset on ethnic grounds. In Central-East Europe, however, if we want to establish borders that can be regarded as democratically "legitimate," we must insist on the principle of separating nations from one another on the grounds that actually divide them—linguistic and ethnic borders. We note these are not declarations or new principles but a system of principles that developed historically and organically from one another; 1815, 1919, and 1945 make up a system, each completing and growing out of the earlier one.

It is the questions of plebiscites and population exchange that require an agreement on principles. In respect to both, we have already pointed out that neither should be applied in a way that would create more problems than solve them. In regard to plebiscites, the following should be declared: first, plebiscites are needed only where an ethnic situation is unclear; second, plebiscites are to be held only where a population is politically conscious; third, no plebiscite is to be held on an issue already decided on by a plebiscite. In regard to population exchange, the following should be laid down: first, it is a last resort, when no other solution is available; second, it is to be mutual, not one-sided or disproportionate; third, it shall be carried out only under a resolution of and with the supervision of the community of nations; fourth, if executed, it shall never be undone or repeated.

The second question is apparently more difficult; what are we to do with our beautiful principles in the midst of power politics, or, as it is widely put, how do we think a treaty is going to consider not the forces of power but principles? The answer is quite plain: *no way*. The problem is not that power politics should not assert itself—as it was not the case in 1815 or 1919, so it is not now either. Obviously, a peace can be concluded only if the power concerns at the heart of war and peacemaking are asserted somehow. What happened in 1815 was not that power politics was disregarded but that it was affirmed *within the limits set out by principles*. If a power ran counter to a principle with a claim, it was satisfied elsewhere where no principle was in its way. It is a misconception to believe that principles hinder concluding a peace; in fact, they enable it. Not that it is easy to adjust motives of power to principles. But it is still much easier than trying to conclude a peace without any principles to follow; that would indeed be a preterhuman and impossible task. In the lack of principles, the parties would come to the verge of madness because every claim could be countered by another claim. "Why not?" would be the slogan of the peace talks. The claims, counterclaims, and solutions will then result in the most unreasonable and strained solutions, monstrosities violating common sense, fact, and international propriety. Nevertheless, they will be convulsively insisted on because even the minutest agreement in an atmosphere defined by anxiety will be reached amid such great pangs that it will seem better to hold on to it for all its absurdity. A solid grounding of principles would help avoid such monstrous "solutions."

We cannot yet tell what the peace treaty being concluded in front of our eyes is going to be finally like. That it has little good to promise is rather obvious. If we ask, "What are the hopes of not immediate but gradual consolidation in such circumstances?" we must again make it quite clear that consolidation cannot be conceived of in Europe, Central-East Europe in particular, without the clearing up of territorial issues on a solid, principled basis. Any talk blurring this central truth is but a catchword, displays an ignorance of the real problems of the region and their causes, or consciously puts up a smokescreen to conceal them. This is not to imply that free reign should be given to the grievance language of irredentism and revisionism—this would only bring further misery to this unfortunate region. The peoples of Central-East Europe must be prevented from continually harassing Europe with their territorial disputes. Europe definitely needs stability; thus irredentist agitation by truncated states must be stopped by the force of arms, just as minority oppression by possessor states must also be stopped by the force of arms.

We must not forget that only good borders to which people can get *accustomed* can be stabilized. This must be asserted with all possible forcefulness in issues where agreement still seems possible within the framework of the treaty—territorial disputes can spark terrible dangers. Nonetheless, should unsatisfactory borders to which people cannot get accustomed and for which they cannot find justification find their way into the treaty, the public opinion of the great powers in charge of the fate of the world must be made aware of the good, less good, and bad borders and their possible solutions and that these should be considered and studied because, as ever, the political history of the world is going to be made up of the alternations of stable, less stable, and fluid periods even if, as we hope, fluid situations will not end up in war. Again, the nations of this region must be stopped from creating such fluid situations. But should such fluid situations come into being, the public opinion of the world with a clearer grasp of the problem should take advantage of them and establish final consolidation in this most critical area of the world, Central-East Europe.

Though we have limited our forgoing discussion to Central-East Europe and only touched on general political truths, we believe we have treated a central and singularly important question of consolidating the world. This might seem odd at first sight; we have been accustomed to thinking in false universal terms and believing that the matters of a territorially small Central-East Europe are but one among the many major or lesser issues of the Far East, the Middle East, or the West. This is actually the gravest mistake we can fall into. There is but one trifle in which the Central-East European matters differ from the great issues of the Far East, the Middle East, or the West: they sparked off two world wars within but one generation; and, should a third world war break out, God forbid, it is highly unlikely to do so over the issues of Manchuria, the Dardanelles, or Spain; the cause will then again, as before, be the anarchy of Germany and the nations to its east. There is no effort more ludicrous and useless than to extirpate the spirit of aggression alone while escalating anarchy, insecurity, and discontent. This area can also be the cause of war not only insofar as military attack might start out from it but might *conquer* it. Central-East Europe—or, to be more precise, Germany and the countries to its east—however small, remains the greatest threat to world peace as long as it remains the region of the greatest anarchy, insecurity, and discontent.

1946

THE PEACE AND HUNGARIAN DEMOCRACY

The peace with Hungary is going to be concluded in a matter of days or weeks. It will elicit from Hungarians, we now all know, neither outbursts of joy nor the silent sigh of relief that follows the end of uncertainty and temporariness even when a none-too-beneficial agreement is signed. The only question that remains open now is how powerful the strike-down is going to be. In the worst case, if two hundred thousand Hungarians are to be deported, we will have to reckon with the fateful psychological and economic effects the en-masse influx of refugees will have on a country that is as overcrowded, run down, and pauperized as Hungary is with its industry and agriculture in shambles, its confidence and optimism ruined. If it is "only" the five villages in Moson County that are ceded, we will have to face the mental repercussions of the fact that the victors of a war fought in the name of mostly moral and democratic goals are going to burden Hungarian democracy, struggling with the difficulties of a beginning, by worsening a border, whose blatant badness and ill effect on the political situation and European standing of Hungarians are widely known throughout the world, even further, to the extent of an additional five villages. And should both dangers be averted—an outcome apparently quite unlikely at the moment—the country is going to acquiesce resignedly to the restoration of the Trianon borders with no change whatsoever—the borders whose injustice, as already noted, is a commonplace. Moreover, we have reason to expect that a Czechoslovakia that has failed to obtain international recognition for deportations will make renewed efforts—either in a roundabout or a direct manner, in the guise of fighting fascism—at de-Hungarianizing the territories it acquired under the Treaty of Trianon. The results of this will sooner or later be tantamount to "legal" deportations, though the psychological consequences will be worse.

We will have to bear this burden—bear it not only emotionally, physically, and economically, but also politically. Beyond the pure physical survival of Hungarians as a people, Hungarian democracy and the perspective of a free and dignified Hungary must also be upheld. Obviously, the most severe backlash to this new act of peacemaking will be its being bound up with the cause of democracy and that the public mind will again blame democracy for it and draw the conclusion from its injustice that democracy is as a rule false. This was the association that crippled the democrats of both Hungary and Weimar Germany and that spurred the fascists and made them be cocksure.

The danger of this atmosphere is that to hold Horthy and his system of government responsible for our collapse and new ruin will seem a powerless and pathetic effort at diversion. To sharply highlight the cynicism and self-righteousness of the victors will be all the more welcome, and sure facts will be known about the treacheries and failures of democratic Hungarian politicians. All warnings about the insufficiencies of our democracy and the need to deepen and finalize people's freedom will be rendered ineffective. It will be more rewarding to scathingly mock the Czechs and even more so the Slovaks for their doings under the mask of democracy. Calls for the country to face its own abominable responsibility and wrongs will be reduced to mere catchword status. And how simple it will be, in contrast, to point at those more fortunate nations that are not punished but praised for the same wrongdoings and are helped in continuing with them.

In vain would it be to say that all these sham reasonings are but the brainchildren of the upper and middle classes and those intellectuals who steered themselves and the nation into the impasse of irredentism and revisionism and that, to counterbalance them, there is no need but to rally the impeccable forces of labor and the peasantry. The situation is not that simple. As grave a mistake as it is to overestimate the effective political power of the upper and middle classes—a mistake often committed these days—so grave, even graver, is it to underrate their power to influence public opinion. With the massive and amorphous growth of the lower middle class, absorptive as it has been both upward and downward in the past fifteen years, this power has become particularly great and has successfully channeled the gentry manner of thinking into the working classes.

No doubt, one has to speak in the tongue of angels to be able to voice the frustration and grief of all undeserved individual suffering and all the rancor this peacemaking has wrought, to simultaneously not lapse into foolish ranting or droning complaint and damp down the forces that come into their own in democracy and lead toward a free and dignified Hungary.

Let us try and find this tone of voice.

WHO IS THEN TO BLAME?

To do so, we have to be able to answer a number of questions. The first one is who is to take the responsibility for what the peace is going to be like. Then we have to clarify what kind of justifiable relation there is between the level of democratic zeal of individual peoples and the peace treaties. We have to answer the questions of whether the Hungarian nation has deserved these outcomes or not and whether it has to and from whom it has to accept censures. Finally, we have to point out the direction we can and must take in the situation created by the peace treaties.

Who is responsible for the conclusion of a peace with Hungary that severely damages not only the fundamental interests of the Hungarian nation, but also the appeasement of the peoples of the Danube basin and the consolidation of Central-East Europe?

A calling to account is as difficult in history as it is in criminal law. Events take place as a result of an infinite number of antecedents or causes, and, if human activities, they are so diffuse, mostly so unconscious and unintentional, that the question of responsibility has no meaning in such broad terms. The question should be raised in respect to the intense moments of human authority and history when a series of events layering on one another in a continuity with no particular regularity is suddenly confronted by sharply diverging alternatives, takes a new course depending on an individual's or a well-defined circle of individuals' failures or decisions made in the name free will, and thus turns into a new series of events, the details of which become uninteresting again.

If we ask who is to blame for the Hungarian peace bearing this in mind and go back in time, we will find that the Hungarian peace was determined—or could have been significantly changed—in the fateful moments of, first, the abortive attempt to back out of the war and the Arrow-cross putsch on October 15, 1944, and then, second, the German occupation between March 19 and 22, 1944. Until March 22 and to a certain degree even until October 15, no one disputed that the Allies advancing to victory regarded Hungary as a country whose actions would have a bearing on future outcomes in spite of its responsibility, criminal shortcomings, monstrous failures, and foolish faults. So was it equally undisputed that Hungary, for all its burden of being a satellite, could, in the event that it took appropriate steps, request and hope for certain encouragements in regard to those very territorial issues that have made the peace treaty so appalling today. The Allies had declared the two Vienna Awards null and void as a matter of principle, but until March 22, 1944, this had not in the least implied the restoration of the Trianon status quo, only the need for new negotiations and a new legal basis. Actually, the possibilities had been rather close to the territorial conditions of the Vienna Awards. Now, these opportunities were partly squandered by Horthy's own personal loss of nerve and lack of judgment in the days between March 19 and 22, 1944, and they were finally lost by the letdown of an already demoralized Hungarian Army in October that year. This is what makes a clear establishment of responsibility easier today than twenty-five years ago, when Tisza's political system, insisting on the alliance with Austria and Germany, was under purview. The point now, however, is not only establishing the long-term responsibility of a regime and its policies, but also that of not being able to hold out in concentrated moments. We have comparisons near at hand—the Italian and the Romanian examples—that clearly show what kind of conduct a head of state and his army can and ought to exercise in a situation where Miklós Horthy and his army disgraced themselves. Should it be argued that the Hungarian political temperament lacks the cunning such a full turnabout needs, we still have March 19, 1944, to answer for, and it required neither artfulness nor any stabbing in the back, "only" self-respect and courage.

It can now be established with, as it were, historical validity that Horthy and his government are primarily to blame for the way the peace treaty has evolved. We can safely say and should emphasize again and again that we owe this peace to Miklós Horthy and his system. The leaders of Hungarian democracy have not failed to clearly expound and voice this. However, we have to admit, these statements create less and less stir in our public. Even those with no reactionary interest in glossing the responsibility of the Horthy regime seem to be keener on the question of whom to blame for the unfavorable turn at the peace talks in the past half a year. However true it may be that the events of 1944 precipitated our adverse situation and our want of political weight, it is also true that the final decisions on some issues were reached only weeks or months ago. That certain questions had been open until quite recently is borne out by the hopes to which the Moscow visit of our statesmen first gave rise and then dashed; obviously, our government leaders were briefed there on the questions still open and that might turn for the better. These included the Hungarian-Romanian border, the Czechoslovak deportations, and the legal status of minority Hungarians. Since then, decisions have been reached in the majority of these matters, particularly our border with the Romanians—in every way to our detriment. The Hungarian public is now riveted to the recent responsibility for this outcome. To blow this accountability up and disregard that of the Horthy regime by hushing it up is undoubtedly in the interest of factors striving to discredit democracy. But even the part of the public free from this bent, though not calling into doubt the guilt of Horthy and his acolytes, has grown weary of harping on their exclusive responsibility—understandably so to some extent.

That their onus has lost to us great opportunities has been apparent for the last two years. That the few opportunities still open until recently have also been lost to us is a new upshot, the particular causes of which can be asked under a different heading. Naturally, it may turn out that this was also mostly a consequence of the 1944 antecedents—for example, if it emerges that the powers deciding it simply contrasted the Romanian and the Hungarian war effort on their side. But even so, it remains an open question of who or what is to blame for their having only considered this factor when they could have taken into account others as well.

In regard to this latter responsibility, which, though having a lesser compass, prompts all the more heated a debate, we observe the kinds of theses that, first, appeared in the Christmas article of József Révai, which underscored the responsibility of Hungary in the war to such an extent that it could be brought up against us at the Czechoslovak peace talks and that we could hardly expect to achieve a decision more favorable to us in such circumstances; second, that no appropriate memorandum by the Hungarian government had been tabled before the four foreign ministers issued their declaration upholding the Hungarian-Romanian border defined at Trianon; or, third, that the matter of the Hungarian-Romanian border was dropped from the agenda of the Hungarian committee of the peace talks simply because no Hungarian proposal had been submitted.

The infantility of these suggestions and explications—if not manifestations of sheer antagonism—cannot be emphasized enough. The circumstances to which they accord decisive significance were but drab and gray incidents in a situation that overturned the Hungarian cause irrespective of them. József Révai's article may have been referred to at the peace conference or its press. It is indeed difficult to observe the border between unsparing self-criticism, which is indispensable, and the unwanted gestures of *Hinaus mit uns* at international fora. But the fact that Révai was "referred to" had no bearing on our chances at the peace talks. That someone refers to something while maneuvering is wholly immaterial in comparison with his ability or inability to maneuver in a given situation. There was a point at the peace talks when we "referred to" the fact that the Second Vienna Award had been requested not by us but Romania; this reference of ours seemed to bid fair prospects, all the more so as the representative of one great power went for it. Yet little did it change the positions and possible moves on the chessboard. The submission of a memorandum is of course an important factor in judging the personal aptitude and conscientiousness of people because those entrusted with the affairs of the nation must not, whether intentionally or carelessly, fail to do their uttermost best even in the most hopeless of situations. However, this will not alter the fact that no memorandum on Transylvania, the Upper Hungarian deportations, or any other important Hungarian issue will be able to come up with a decisive factor of which international decision makers are unaware or call attention to any consequences they do not foresee insofar as their own consciences or foresight allow them to. Any steps or failures by a democratic Hungary are doomed to be weightless due to the country's significance having been wasted, which is why it has not been able to put any force behind its requests and wishes. There is little point in dwelling on the accidental blunders and omissions of a country that has lost all its political weight. Again, we must state that establishing the responsibility of the Horthy regime fully answers the question of blame in respect to Hungary—but only in respect to Hungary.

The Hungarian public is justified in feeling that the question of concrete and direct responsibility can be raised in regard to the actual decisions made in recent weeks and months, and this is different from the Horthyan onus—that is, that Hungary has fallen and carries no weight at the peace talks. What it is mistaken in—or occasionally *mala fide* about—is that it wants to establish the responsibility of *Hungarian* statesmen when this has been rendered meaningless by Hungary's loss of political weight. Quite to the contrary, it is the historical responsibility of the peacemakers in concluding a good and durable peace that should be raised. Their responsibility arises not because their decisions are unfavorable to us; in itself, it would be pointless to hold alien statesmen "responsible"—alien to us. It arises because their decisions have a bearing on East European consolidation and because, as it is commonly known, they have come to ill-advised and harmful verdicts irrespective of us. We might dare raise the issue because the decision makers, even if it did not depend solely on them, had the opportunity of choosing among good, tolerable, and bad arrangements. The political weight of countries necessarily has a decisive role at peace talks, and even the most reasonable and appropriate concrete proposal remains ineffectual without political weight. However, beyond mere power relations, there is quite a wide range remaining open where the balance among the peacemakers themselves; their sober impartiality, foresightful sense of responsibility, and loyalty to themselves and their principles; and their humanity come into play and determine the goodness and durability of the peace they make. This responsibility can be established and can be localized to the historical moments of the decision making. The question is where the responsibility lies in respect to the decisions brought in matters Hungarian.

What was it that—indeed in the very last months—determined all the decisions and changes in respect to all pending Hungarian issues, the future of

Hungarians, and the general consolidation of Eastern Europe? The single fact that the Allied powers and the other states have split into two rival camps and that a crisis of confidence has broken out between them. As their relations freeze or thaw, concrete issues are thrust hither and thither. Since the Potsdam Conference, the tension between the two camps has allowed for no principled groundwork for the peace, the conference, and the conclusion of the treaty. The range that remains open beyond the givens of power relations at all peace talks has now been filled not by any shared principle or procedure, any composed and foresightful stance, but petty wrangling, irresponsible rumor, vexation of the other, sham agreements, and the disarray of all fear-laden and poisoned political situations. For over a year, these are what have decided issues not predetermined by the givens of power relations. Though obviously detrimental to the future, monstrous arrangements have been presented as major achievements simply because the big ones managed to cut a deal on them. The matter of the Hungarian-Romanian border was fixed at a meeting of the foreign ministers in less than a few minutes, the main problem being how to cover up the fundamental breakdown of the talks with an agreement on some side issue. Now, the only way to agree on this in five minutes was to take the Trianon borders as a basis; drawing a more considered borderline would have required forty or forty-five minutes.

The Hungarian public keeps recoiling on the matter of responsibility for the events of the past weeks and months simply because it cannot come to terms with the extraordinary disillusionment and frustration the peace talks have caused, the unprecedented sloppiness—far greater than that of Trianon—the formalism and whimsicalness with which the unresolved issues of the Hungarian peace treaty have been finally settled. The only reason why mentioning the responsibility of Révai and Gyöngyösi can create a stir is that they can be presented—hardly in a favorable light—as impersonators of the same democracy that appears as an international organization at the Paris Peace Conference. It is the same as back in 1919. However clear it was at the level of causes that István Tisza and the entire political establishment, which had doggedly stuck by the Habsburg Empire and the German alliance at whatever cost and in spite of the clear national interest, were to be held primarily responsible for the Treaty of Trianon, it seemed much more convenient to lay the blame of the bafflingly superficial and irresponsible peacemaking the *democratic* world powers allowed themselves on a *democratic* Mihály Károlyi.

The same association is threatening today. If we do not want the justly bitter feelings the peace talks have elicited in Hungarians to be repressed and so turn against the vital roots of Hungarian democracy, we must express our emotions about the peace talks in the name of our democracy — not by finding Hungarian scapegoats, but by reproving the victors themselves. As a party concerned and experienced in the matter, we must not shrink from formulating this historical judgment; the less hope we seem to have, the more calmly and courageously we should speak our minds — even though offense is taken. In the long-term interests of maintaining our democracy, we are required to plead; we must not allow any future whispering campaign to infer a bad conscience of "complicity" from the silence of the statesmen of Hungarian democracy. Appeasement with our neighbors also requires us to do so because we cannot declare any honest willingness to fulfill the peace treaty in its entirety when bottling up our concerns about it. Honesty must be full.

We can dare and must deliver this judgment. For if we formulate it fittingly, it will not be the complaint of a biased party but will conform to the general historical judgment conscientious minds will soon pass on the methods of negotiating and concluding the peace at the end of World War II. Irrespective of the Hungarian treaty, this judgment is going to be devastating, the world powers having maneuvered themselves into a situation in respect to the most important issues of the peace from which it will be most difficult to clamber out. The way in which they have recognized the Hitlerite ploy of unilaterally relocating the populations of entire regions under the notion that in so doing otherwise unjustifiable borders would become just and the wholly unprincipled or befuddled way of referring to principles and the outright political opportunism with which they have made their verdicts — these will have vital consequences for decades, even centuries, to come, while some of the issues could have been settled reasonably well, will prompt a crushing historical judgment by the entire world public, and will bring about a deep moral crisis. This is the judgment to which we have to give expression in the way the Hungarian peace treaty makes us shape it. Such a Hungarian statement should be made once only and formulated with dignity, without its casting doubt on our intention to comply with the treaty and becoming the starting point of any querulous and complaining revisionism, but as a final word, it should articulate our profound disappointment.

DEMOCRATIC MERIT AND DEMERIT

The second question we have to address is the relationship between the democratic or undemocratic nature of Hungary and the goodness or badness of the peace. To be more precise, do we have to accept the charge that we were given this treaty because we are less democratic than this or that neighbor of ours? Conversely, how are we to respond to the view that there is no use in striving for democracy when a democratic Hungary has been unable to negotiate a better treaty and has in fact obtained one much worse than the one a feudal Hungary managed to acquire?

We can accept the observation that the difficulties of, the obstacles to, and the deadweight on democratization are the greatest in Hungary in all Eastern Europe from anyone who does not use it as a bludgeon against us. No doubt, at a par with Poland, Hungary is in the most difficult situation as far as the conditions of democratic development are concerned. In countries west of us, the growth of the middle class and industry has provided the social and economic conditions for democratization, while in the countries east of us, the scarcity of the upper classes, their lack of an oppressive force, and the almost wholly popular background of the intelligentsia are more reassuring and convenient for democratization. In Hungary, the situation is more difficult in both respects. Whoever observes this as a sociological fact is right. But he who wants to jump to moral conclusions from this, and thereby justify otherwise inexcusable provisions of the peace, is playing foul. But not only does he play foul, so also does he intentionally and consciously impede democratic development in Hungary. The badness of the peace and the willingness to democratize are indeed related but the other way around: the wants of Hungarian democracy do not justify a bad peace treaty, but the earlier bad treaty has considerably thwarted the development of democracy in Hungary. We tend to forget these days, and it would do good to remember, that the democratic republic of Mihály Károlyi fell because the Entente issued its conditions of peace, and the only hope he had left was that the country could muster the forces of the proletariat against the absurdities of those terms. Then an about-face occurred. Horthy and his acolytes came forward as the scourges of the peace treaty because they had to compensate for having subscribed to what Károlyi had refused to sign. On the other hand, Károlyi came to proclaim that irredentism fueled by reaction was a greater danger than all the evils of the territorial provisions of the peace. Little does this recognition change the fact that the democratic republic of 1919 would have had a quite different future had it been given better terms than those of Trianon.

We are now to face the same threat of the association of democracy and peace as we had to in 1919. All the advantages in respect to territories or deportations a Czechoslovakia manages to *mala fide* extort by virtue of its unwavering democracy are but stumbling blocks in the way of Hungarian democracy. The entire procedure resembles stories of unwed mothers who murder their infants and are judged by the very person who ravished them. If we do not want Hungary to be ensnared by these, we must resolutely and clearly reject all attempts at representing democracy, in contrast to ourselves or others, as a merit that can be continually referred to and deserves a reward, something that can be wrangled or claimed.

For our own sakes, we must clearly and plainly pronounce that we need to be democrats not for the sakes of the Anglo-Americans, the Russians, or the Czechs, not for the sake of settling our territorial problems, but, irrespective of these, for our own sake, the sake of our people. Angered and frustrated, we must never again fall into the madness of depriving ourselves of all the advantages and opportunities democracy has on account of the injustices committed against us, the unfair or inhumane treatment of our brethren by countries happening to call themselves democratic. This would be like the child who denies himself his favorite toy out of a compulsive misconception that he thereby punishes his environment. It does not follow from the fact that injustice can be committed in the name of democracy that it is humbug, fraud, or a mere disguise of oppression, national prejudice, or imperialism. All these may hide behind it but are not identical with it. We must not forget that the foreign policy and internal life of democracies are likewise not identical. As great a perspective as democratic thinking opens up for the inner lives of states, it is far from being able to similarly humanize the relations among nations. Moreover, the democratization of international relations—in fact, their inundation with unorganized crowd emotions—has jeopardized international relations and has thrust particularly the craft of good peacemaking into a deep crisis. Alas, we have fallen victim to the inability of democracies to conclude feasible peace treaties—now a second time over.

On the other hand, we can calmly and firmly defy efforts by our neighbors to justify various, otherwise indefensible, advantages in the peace and power relations on account of democratic merits. In territorial issues, democracy has but one directive to follow—the right to self-determination. It is possible not to refer to this right, but it is frivolous to invoke democracy to justify not allowing the population of a territory not to belong where it wants to. It is far more respectable to openly take on plain and simple power-political motives. We will comply with the peace anyway—why instill hatred in Hungarians for democracy by unnecessary references to democracy? The truth is, as far as the armor of democracy is concerned, the small peoples of Eastern Europe, including ourselves of course, are a far cry from the ideals of impartiality, moderation, and sense of justice some of the northern nations have been able to put into action. In 1919, Denmark, for example, refused to take over from Germany areas that had historically and linguistically always been Danish without a plebiscite; or there is Sweden, which was capable of courteously splitting up with Norway. At no time have any of our miserable East European states afforded an example of likewise drawing the final conclusions of democracy in the great issues of national pride and power. Their enthusiasm for democracy and their zeal in adapting to fascism were both closely bound to either the territorial loot they were afraid of losing or the territorial sop they hoped would be hurled at them. However much reason we have to be aggrieved by our pathetic siding with democracies and however much reason we have to feel abashed by the insufficiency of the resistance we put up against the Nazi reign of terror, we must also note that there was not one nation in this entire region that was capable of taking up the good cause of democracy for itself *in spite* of its territorial interests.

If we consider the situation of Hungary and the forlorn martyrdom of the likes of Endre Bajcsy-Zsilinzsky from this perspective, these maverick, unruly, and cheerless Hungarians are magnified and prove a *qualitative* match for all the partisan gangs of countries more fortunate and less problematic than we are. In him, we have a man who was predestined by class, upbringing, and past record to hem himself up in the impasse of ruminating on Hungarian grievances, yet he had the courage to stand up for democracy in a Hungary with no crowd emotion to back it and to speak up against irredentism with all the trappings of mass feeling. It is not at all straightforward to be a democrat in such circumstances—in contrast to those where democracy means international support for wholly undemocratic national aims.

Instead of our making hollow references to democracy, it would be more truthful to notice that the small peoples of Eastern Europe have been staggering along the same downward path of political morality. It is only once in a while, in fortunate moments, that one or two stand out—the Poles at the beginning of the nineteenth century, we Hungarians with our War of Independence, the Czechs with their Masarykian democracy, and the Yugoslavs with the Great War of Liberation against fascism. High-mindedness proves to be fleeting and reverts to narrow-mindedness; the sad examples of feudal Poland, compromising Hungary, and a Czechoslovakia emulating Hitlerite concentration camps demonstrate a fallback to the usual East European spite. In the final count, these peoples are much the same whether they are fighting one another with the bludgeon of democratic or fascist merit. Though the European meanings of the words "democratic" and "fascist" are retained here as well, they are never independent of what or who they are being deployed against. True democracy and true appeasement among these peoples will begin when they come to a shared dismay over their shared debasement.

We must also be aware that by having become the most misfortunate, we have not become better than our companions; and we have reason to be afraid that had we the opportunity to extort unjust advantages at the expense of others in the name of democracy, we would not hesitate to do so. As there is little likelihood of such an opportunity arising, we might draw some hope from our otherwise quite desperate predicament: the greatness of the obstacles in our way, the absence of advantages and sops to be had, might afford the chance of a difficulty-seasoned and a deeper-founded democracy in Eastern Europe. This opportunity might of course easily be lost. It depends on us.

THE PEACE AS PUNISHMENT

It is roughly in this state of mind that we have to make our stance in respect to the question of whether Hungary has deserved its historical fate and the peace treaty in which it is manifested. Those outside observers who have a more refined moral judgment and are less formalist will obviously not focus on the problems of democratic development discussed above and which, finally, are not a matter of only merit or wrong but of the totality of a nation's deeds in history. Peace talks being in question, the stress falls on our deeds in the recent past—a foreign policy selling the country bit by bit to fascism; a breaking of the Yugoslav-Hungarian Friendship Pact; the Novi Sad [Újvidék] bloodbath; the self-implemented anti-Jewish persecutions that were, it is true, limited in scope but were witness to deep moral corruption in their small-mindedness; the more or less passive assistance to the monstrous mass deportations the Germans carried out; and the torpor into which the nation sank when the danger of going along with Germans belatedly dawned on it and the haplessness with which it submitted to its depredation and trampling under foot in the last phase of the fighting.

If we raise the question of whether Hungary has deserved what it got and is getting in view of the moral score of these deeds and its resulting responsibility, then we can conscientiously say it has. The entire moral profile this series of events has drawn is so stunning that one is prompted to ask the schizophrenic question of whether and how far the nation is identical with the nation whose moral problems were elucidated and their solutions handled by the likes of Széchenyi, Wesselényi, Kölcsey, Eötvös, Kossuth, Kemény, and Deák a hundred years earlier. No offense, no ill-treatment should be allowed to blur our most personal sense of responsibility for what we have and ought to have done. No word is powerful enough to lay down this responsibility, and it would be loathsome evil against the moral future of Hungarians to encourage any mellowing of the intensity of shame by pointing out the current or prior doings of others. All those with a sense of this responsibility and shame have a duty to keep it continually alive in others and the entire nation until the serious signs of moral regeneration manifest themselves, and these are quite far from now.

Our problem with this sense of guilt arises when we hear Hungarian responsibility being established by people for whom this is but political ammunition and a means to justify their own crimes. A public mood has already evolved in the country that regards excessive emphasis on national responsibility and the arousal of national guilt as foolishness and malevolent denunciation detrimental to our position at the peace talks, as well as unneeded and overzealous self-depreciation. For one part, these opinions are voiced most loudly by people who have a bad conscience due to their share in the historical responsibility of the nation. However, these views are far from being driven only by a bad conscience. The most mind-blowing instance of this is when convinced democrats and courageous, progressive-minded Hungarians are the ones who defy the permanent insistence on Hungary's crimes and who speak up against the crimes now committed against the Hungarian nation in the name of its crimes. In the hope of a future democracy, several of them have been persecuted in the name of fascism, and now they are persecuted in the name of democracy (apparently acts of national hatred disguised as democracy), usually ending up in a deep depression, schizophrenia, or persecution mania, depending on their individual constitutions. There are a good many examples among left-wing Hungarians who have been persecuted in or banished from Slovakia.

If we want to clamber out of this vicious circle, we must fearlessly fight the malevolent attempts of either side to justify the atrocities of one nation by those of the other. Humanness is one and indivisible, and it is worth discussing these topics only with people who are equally revolted at atrocities against their own kind and by their own kind. It is bad faith to try to extenuate wrongs Hungarians have committed by wrongs now being committed against Hungarians. But it is equally bad faith to extenuate the wrongs now being committed against Hungarians by those they had once committed. And if Hungarians are the ones going into this, it is not only bad faith on their part but folly as well. Every atrocity has a preceding atrocity by which those in the belief that atrocities can be *justified* justify their own. The banishment of Hungarians from Upper Hungary can be justified by Horthy's march into it; his march in by the injustices of the Trianon borders; the Trianon borders by the Hungarian oppression of national minorities; Hungarian anti-minority policies by the fact that Hungarians fighting reaction in 1848 were stabbed in the back by the minorities taking sides with reaction; this by previous grievances, and so on. If one wants to break free from the vicious circle of these both true and untrue theses, he must, as far as he is humanly capable, take a single stance against all offenses against human dignity.

Our equal judgment of all offenses against humanity, human dignity, and freedom will in no way imply that we regard all ideologies equal in the name of which those offenses are committed. The fact that one can equally be wretchedly slaughtered, crippled, or driven mad in a Czechoslovak or a Hitlerite concentration camp does not imply that democracy and national socialism have become equivalent or that the intentions of Beneš and Hitler are identical. Yet however great the difference between democracy and Nazism remains, there is no difference in value between the pain of the mother whose child was killed in a German death factory, a Czechoslovak concentration camp, or on the roadside of hunger and buried wrapped in a newspaper. If we are going to have too many such mothers in Central Europe, there will not be anyone to whom we can explain the difference between democracy and Nazism.

In respect to our own harsh self-criticism, it will do good to remind those who want to justify their wrongdoings with the wrongdoings of Hungarians that men commit their most gruesome and hair-raising acts not when they give free reign to their natural beastly savagery. Savagery is quick to spend its fury, even the wildest bloodbath ending up in physical nausea, and men have tame, not only wild, instincts. Men are most wicked when they believe they are threatened, morally justified, and exonerated, and particularly when they feel they are entitled and obliged to punish others. This is when they are capable of throwing off all vestiges of their sense of shame, of overcoming their physical nausea and becoming massacrers, of being inveterate even when stones soften—not to mention men who give free reign to beastly savagery.

The mental condition in which certain nations regard themselves victims of some grave offense, believe their actions to be exempt from all moral judgment, and believe their procedures as rightful judgment and punishment should be known to us Hungarians, who got from our Trianon grievances to the massacre in Novi Sad. We have every right to offer serious warnings to others in this state of mind that they have set out on the downward path. I am willing to believe that their mental disposition will not lead them to another Novi Sad, but by nature, democracy applies stricter measures, and the question now seems to be whether or not, by this measure, things have not already gotten beyond repair.

When this is going to be admitted on either side of our borders we cannot tell. Our problem, however, is how to maintain the full intensity of the spirit of national guilt and contrition while simultaneously rejecting bad-faith presentations that seek to capitalize and to base their otherwise indefensible deeds on our admission. Quite simply, by clearly and unequivocally stating that our guilt and contrition are addressed not to them. We are not seeking forgiveness from the Czechs, the Slovaks, and the Romanians because the very same emotions drive them that drove us to where we now are. It is perhaps only in respect to the Yugoslavs that we should be ashamed of ourselves. Our emphasis should, however, be on being ashamed of ourselves with a view to our grandfathers, who were better, and our grandchildren, who will hopefully be better.[1]

OUR STANCE ON THE PEACE

We have tried to answer to the questions of responsibility and merit in view of the peace in a way that might guide us away from certain misjudgments leading us into impasses and fixing us in brooding over bygones. The same questions, however, have a bearing on the future as well. What stance are we to take in respect to the future, valid content, the obligatory effect, the durability, and the changeability of the peace?

The program for taking this stance can be put quite briefly and plainly; this peace has to be accepted as binding and fulfilled in its entirety, and all political ideologies, agitations, and beliefs with a view to changing it in the near or distant future have to be dismissed. There are several reasons for this. First, any deviation from this principle could have catastrophic consequences on cross-border Hungarians. Second, this position means a realistic assessment of our actual situation; the peacemaking process, however unreassuring its conditions are, is likely to result in territorial stability for perhaps several generations of Hungarians. Third, the ideology of territorial change (revisionism) is unproductive and leads into impasses even if there is a possibility or likelihood of revision. The only productive position on the newer sanctioning of the Treaty of Trianon is one several of our leading statesmen have pointed out—follow the example of the Danes, who issued the following motto after losing Schleswig-Holstein in 1864: the territories lost were to be regained *within* the country.

On the other hand, it would be neither reasonable nor honest to try and appear as though we were more ardent supporters of the borders established by Trianon or the new peace than their beneficiaries. We cannot conscientiously say that—in the highly unlikely event that a tribunal were set up in the world to settle border disputes in trial procedures, fairly, smoothly, and with legal force—we would have nothing to say before it on the Hungarian peace. We could likewise not say that—in the similarly unlikely event that a political constellation were to evolve where border issues could be raised without the dangers back-stabbing or bad-faith maneuvering—we would not have the same opinion as today on what makes a good or a better border. However, we must be aware that an objective tribunal for settling territorial disputes is highly implausible and that the possibility of changing borders at the current stage of development of European state communities is usually linked with highly critical or war situations, and a country making use of such opportunities would have to have a very powerful moral armor not to fall into the pitfalls of body snatching, rapacity, the abuse of offenses suffered and of purported merit. We did not prove to be such a country; true, we have seen none nearby either. All our efforts should be concentrated on a future Hungary setting an example in loyalty and moderation among small peoples. If we do not want to be caught up in the vortex of mutual and endless hatred, this has to be begun by the one who has the opportunity to do so. Today, the opportunity is with others, but they do not seem to want to start; should the opportunity arise with us, it would be no less our duty and in our interest to begin.

There is, however, no point in being concerned about this issue at this time. The peace is going to be concluded within a short period of time, and it will be a *given* for us from then on; we will have to deliver our opinion on it once, but then we should close the matter for good. It would be useless for us to try and advise or prod the conscience of the world; the public of the great powers that has a say in this is quite well informed—often better then we ourselves are—about our predicament without further enlightenment; as far as their conscience is concerned, that is quite bad irrespective of our complaints and all our problems together. Let us leave the public opinion of the world to go about its own business—perhaps once it will have time for us too. Our business is to prepare ourselves both mentally and physically for the peace treaty without reservations. There is one reservation we are justified in having: we cannot remain indifferent to the fate of cross-border Hungarians. In the interwar period, the system of international minority protection required that the majority nation render accounts of its treatment of minorities to the international community; thus, the neighboring "related" country had no formal say in minority matters. Today, the times are not benevolent for the international protection of minorities; in other words, we have to do without the advantages and drawbacks of legal formalism; there is no way of making the life of minorities bearable other than through political effort, which is the duty of the "related" state, ourselves. In the light of our current political weightlessness, we must realize that such efforts on our part will be more efficient the less we drum on about it. Let no patriots or patriotic groups think that they should start banging the tables instead of the "cowardly" and "traitor" government or that international relations wind in and out of crises and come to a halt at a precipice only to carry out their delusions.

There is one more issue to broach. The disillusionment with the evolution of the peace conference has again given rise to the formula of a forlorn, desolate, and companionless Hungary even from the mouths of responsible statesmen. If this formula were to mean casting away the crutches of vain hopes, it would be a very healthy one. But it much rather seems to resurrect the forbidding and empty phraseology of "a tragic sense of life." In face of this, we have to clarify a few issues. First, our being companionless is not a cosmic, fateful, or constitutional feature of ours; it is closely related to the empty space of antipathy that has built up around us; it is only partly a result of our misfortune, much more that of our own sin. Second, we are companionless not because we are not surrounded by linguistic relatives, like our Slavic neighbors. We have had so much intercourse with the Slavs in both the past and the present that our joining the Slavic cultural and political community rests exclusively with us. There has been a place reserved for us for a long time; out of an increasingly anachronistic prejudice, we believed that it was our distinguished horse-rider Turk kinship — which, otherwise, we can safely cultivate — that did not allow us to promote the relationship with the Slavs. The fateful misconception of an anti-Slavic community of fate with the Germans, which never really captured the public mind, was particularly harmful in this respect. Concocted not by us, but Palacký, why should we have taken the likewise fateful misconception that the meaning of Hungarians' geographic situation is to divide the northern and southern Slavs seriously as our historical mission?

What follows from this is that harping on our being companionless is unnecessary and perilous even if we do so to encourage coming to terms with our fate. We ought not to stress our loneliness because this implies a head-hanging and complaining attitude, diverting the issue to an emotional plane when it is obviously a *moral* one: as in the case of any other nation, we are the only ones who can rectify our own life, and if others offer no crutches, it is not as desperate as it might seem at first sight.

It is worth summing up our train of thought in a way that might be stated in the name of the entire nation:

Hungary is aware that its own leaders are to blame for the severity of the conditions of the peace treaty. It nevertheless cannot cloak its profound consternation at the randomness, formalism, and momentary power-political considerations with which decisions were reached on the few Hungarian matters at the peace conference, decisions that no power and political condition had predetermined. This has brought about widespread disillusionment and shaken the belief in democracy in Hungary. Hungarians have been particularly appalled by the way certain countries have sought to justify democratically untenable advantages by virtue of democratic merits. This way of proceeding is far more disquieting than any open and honest reference to power because it can undermine the moral authenticity of democracy. In 1919, the development of Hungarian democracy was fatefully retarded by the lack of solidarity on the part of European democracies and the severity of the conditions of peace. Today, Hungary, disappointed as it is, does not want to deprive itself of the blessings and perspectives of democracy. For its own part, it sees the road to democracy in Eastern Europe not in securing advantages on the grounds of democratic merit but in awakening to the fateful deprivation of political morals and procedures, as well as in harsh self-criticism by every nation. Accordingly, the Hungarian nation gives expression to its deep contrition and shame at the terrible and inhuman deeds in which Hungarians participated or did not, within their scope, prevent. However, even as it does so, it must stress that no atrocity by one nation can serve as the justification of another's, and the crimes of the fascists in particular cannot be used as measures of or excuses for the ways democracies proceed. The Hungarian nation is contrite not toward those that seek to extract moral capital from this but toward its own honorable historical past and future Hungarian generations justifying better hopes.

Hungary, however severe the conditions of the peace, will fully comply with it if it has signed it. It would nevertheless be dishonest for it to act as though it were an ardent supporter of its severe provisions. But it is not going to make a program or ideology out of its revision or to speculate on international crises or disasters to find redress for its territorial grievances, and it will settle for the conditions the peace establishes without reserve. There is, however, one reservation it cannot forgo: it cannot waive its political concern for Hungarian minorities, but it will seek to assert this by the realistic assurance of their existential interests, not by strident demonstrations. Finally, Hungary declares that not even the severity of the peace treaty can be reason for it to give up its policies grounded on European humanity, democracy, understanding with its neighbors, and its integration with the political and cultural community of East European peoples.

1946

The Warped Hungarian Self:
A History of Impasse

INNATE DISCORD

Since the *fin de siècle* but for the last two decades in particular, a central concern of Hungarian community life has been what the Hungarian character is like, what makes the Hungarian self. There would be nothing surprising in this if it were merely an attempt to find the characteristic features of our people in a broad spectrum of credibility extending from momentary fancy to profound artistic insight, mindfully seeking to research, tend, and guard our people's characteristic manifestations or even attempting to buttress our difference and claim to independence by exploring our ethnic character. Yet justified as we might be in doubting the productivity of putting the question in this way and the expectation that the exploration and standardization of ethnic features would contribute to the renewal of our culture as a whole and the reinforcement of our political claims, this is far from being a particular Hungarian feature; it can be found in every nation, particularly this side of the Rhine.

In recent decades, however, seeking to find the Hungarian self and characteristics has gone beyond these and acquired an emphatically tragic feature, the notion occurring that it is our warped Hungarian self and characteristics, our innate discord, that is responsible for our centuries-long history of disaster, the unevenness of our political development, and the blatantly unhealthy features of our scale of social values and intellectual development. As László Németh succinctly put it, we must find "where the Hungarian self was lost to the Hungarian self."

In this way of putting the question, the root of troubles is to be sought in the fact that the Hungarian nation has taken a road, taken on shapes, and embraced influences that disagree with its inner characteristics; in other words, it has lost its own self to itself because of something un-Hungarian. This un-Hungarian feature could be experienced in three ways: foreign *rule*, foreign *assimilation*, and foreign *influence*. In this fashion, anyone trying to fathom the antecedents is likely to conclude that the final cause of all our ailments is, in one way or another, the four-hundred-year foreign rule. Of course, this will not and cannot satisfy him because we have not been under foreign rule since 1918; moreover, foreign dominance had manifested itself far more indirectly from 1867; yet the corruption of our community self began to precipitate in the middle of the nineteenth century and became fatal after 1918. The question of characterology thus necessarily leads to the issues of foreign assimilation and influence.

This is why a László Németh, investigating the inner breakdown of Hungarian community development and thought, feels he has to draw up the balance of the successes and failures of nineteenth-century Swabian and Jewish assimilation.[1] As a result, his whole train of thought, profoundly truthful and authentic in sensing the crisis, is hopelessly entangled in the exasperation of the former and current disputes over assimilation and will hardly ever be unraveled from them. In a similar vein, Sándor Karácsony raises the issue mostly in respect to the German-Hungarian relationship; his starting point is *foreign rule* and *colonial* dependence, but he finds the decisive symptoms of our malaise in the damaging effects of the German, moreover general Western, turn of mind.[2] The examples on which he demonstrates his thesis hit the nail on the head. Yet have not colonial-like social relations had a role in Hungarian history where the exploiters happened to be Hungarians of a similar or identical "turn of mind"? Yet both thinkers know perfectly well that a national turn of mind or self is dynamic and ramified, develops continually, and cannot be woven on the same loom. What are we then to make of the lesser investigators of Hungarian national characterology, who, alone or in groups, entertain their theses on Hungarian character and the resolution of the riddles of Hungarian fate, concurring only in so far as they regard the present condition of the Hungarian self as tragically deformed, while deeming its genuine self as particularly valuable or, at least, original and interesting?

If we want to move out of these blind alleys, yet without turning a deaf ear to the problem existing indeed, we must first spell out what we believe the problem is. On the basis of what experience can one say that this community has lost its self? We are aware of the fact that the vast majority of our youths dance international dances to international tunes, that both our spoken and written language has lost much relish and color, that we use far more subordinate clauses than our forebears did, and that the community forms of Hungarian society have been unhinged and made unsteady. These are, however,

European or world phenomena, not unique Hungarian features, even though our symptoms might be graver than those of others. What is really unique, in contrast, is that this country was unable to grasp its actual predicaments and resulting tasks in its modern history, especially since the end of the nineteenth century, primarily in the period between 1914 and 1920 and in the fateful years of 1938–1944. Apart from taking part in two wars "on the wrong side"—a mistake committed by others as well—the Hungarian nation was unable to find or raise to power leaders who could express and represent its interests and needs intellectually, socially, and politically at these critical moments. The normal instinct to recognize the interests of the community—which is no mysterious collective phenomenon but is made up of the sound power of judgment of each member of the community—was ominously lacking or befuddled in the leaders or certain members of the community, while other peoples "instinctually" acted more honorably, truthfully, and in keeping with their own community interests in similar critical situations. The point is not that these peoples live in a wonderful concord and unity and that Hungarians always pull in different ways but that the concerns of the community as a whole, the decisive issues that divide it, are continually raised in ways that have embroiled the community in unproductive and aimless striving, blinding it to its genuine tasks and real problems. The befuddlement of the Hungarian self is particularly striking in this context because our nation, right or wrong, had known itself to be gallant, courageous, easily enthused, strong in passive resistance, dignified, etc., a few years ago and had demonstrated features quite different from this image to our own eyes and those of the wide world.

All these phenomena appearing as they did in historical situations suggest that if we are seeking the causes of the crisis in the Hungarian self, we will have to look around in history first. This is why we wish to review the series of conditions and events that have defined the orientation of the Hungarian nation as a community.

HUNGARIAN DEVELOPMENT UP TO THE FREEDOM FIGHT OF 1848–1849

The malaise of Hungarian political and social development undoubtedly unfolded early in the sixteenth century. After the suppression of Dózsa's peasant revolt in 1514, Werbőczy's Tripartitum sought to perpetuate a balance of social forces in which the common nobility rigorously separated itself from the peasantry and, for all its social antagonism with magnates, was to make *noble* alliances with them at decisive junctures. This was what initiated the most damaging phenomenon of modern Hungarian history: a common nobility that hardly differed from, yet disdained, the peasantry, putting on domineering airs and enjoying noble privileges.[3]

In the wake of the terrible rout at Mohács at the hands of the Ottomans in 1526, the only power that might have countered the nobility, royalty, was cut out of the life of the nation.[4] From this moment, a more East European social structure based on a rigid feudal hierarchy and the oppression of serfs set in; moreover, Hungary as a political unit fell apart, its political focus moved out of the country—to Vienna. In spite of all these disasters, the country demonstrated a high degree of intellectual dexterity and performance in the ensuing two hundred years, joining the major European currents with greater sweep and in greater numbers than ever before. After the great political upsurge in the fourteenth and fifteenth centuries, medieval efforts at adaptation reached—or could have reached under better conditions—a level where Hungary would have counted as an independent unit of the European community capable of self-sufficient political and cultural performance.

The sixteenth and seventeenth centuries were spent on efforts at an independent Hungarian policy, a task that became increasingly difficult and illusionary to achieve. The rise to a middle class status arrested or scanty, the great intellectual currents could not present a serious threat to petrified feudal structures, yet elements of social revolution emerged for a while at the end of the period, in a great attempt at national independence in the Rákóczi revolution. With the failure of Rákóczi's freedom fight, a self-sufficient Hungarian policy was taken off the stage of European affairs; the country acquiesced at becoming a province of the Habsburg Empire and sought to recover from the loss of blood and means in a framework accordingly restrained politically and socially and intellectually provincial.

By the end of the eighteenth century, there were serious signs of a willingness to adapt to a multilingual yet German-led supra-national dynastic framework— we tend not to remember this because its documents, having no sequels, have been kept in evidence by neither the Hungarian nor the Austrian-German worlds. Efforts continued to be exerted to recover Hungarian independence, however, only within the framework of feudal privilege, the forces of social and intellectual progress not backing feudal nationalism. This became glaringly obvious under the reign of Joseph II, who belatedly sought to reshape the empire of the Habsburgs into a centralized, anti-feudal, well-administered, single-language empire subjecting the clergy to the state and supporting commoners and commerce, conditions that royal absolutism had achieved in France over the centuries. It was not feudal opposition and the death of Joseph II that terminated this policy of the House of Habsburg but a backlash from the French

Revolution a few years later, dampening the reformist spirit of the dynasty. The Francis I's, the Metternichs, and the reactionary, conservative Holy Alliance policy that compacted with feudalism were born of this backlash.

It was in the period of the Holy Alliance, in the wake of the French Revolution, that democratic community-shaping came to the forefront throughout Europe, and the entire Hungarian nation likewise took up the cause of political and social independence. The Habsburg efforts to establish a dynastic community-shaping had been far too new-fangled and rootless, its framework still incomplete, for the new democratic tendency to accept it as obligatory. Based primarily on language, all democratic aspirations upheld the frameworks of the nations that had established themselves in the area earlier and drew all social, political, and intellectual life in this direction. Democratic community-shaping bound together the cause of national independence and political-social progress in Hungary too. Hungarian energies increasing in the eighteenth century, this linking up with the great European currents created an unprecedented and yet unrepeated series of political and intellectual achievements we have come to call the Reform Era.

Political and social independence reinforced each other, each obtaining followers for the other: the program of national independence successfully broke the resistance of feudal nationalism to social reform, while the drive to social reform attracted a following outside the Hungarian community per se. It was in this period that an increasingly widespread radicalism sought to go beyond the cautious aims of reformist leaders, undo the petrified social hierarchy, and lead the nation into the great stream of European democratic and revolutionary development. Eclipsing everyone else, Petőfi and his lifework represent this radicalism to us, yet it was neither rootless nor isolated at the time; the reason we do not quite remember other figures and manifestations of this radicalism is that it was discontinued; their genuine role could have commenced only *following a successful* fight for independence.

The social, political, and intellectual development that led to 1848–1849, when closely scrutinized, undoubtedly manifests discordant tones as well. It certainly failed to distinguish feudal and power-wielding nationalism from the requirements of democratic nationalism, a failure that had fatal consequences in respect to nationalities. At its best and most productive period, the Hungarian common nobility as a class, which played the decisive role, was after all a social formation steeped in feudalism and its hierarchic social mindset and could only halfheartedly fulfill the "commoner," middle-class role into which it had been cast. For all the good efforts and promising beginnings, middle-class and intellectual development was superficial and lacked sufficient antecedents. Mass movements of craftsmen and peasants ready for political action were lacking.

The entire enterprise was not founded on well-prepared and persistently pursued performance; many a decision was made in haste, many an effort willed and forced.

László Németh reads the same lack of concert in literature, in what language reform as a problem, a program, and a method meant and the damage it wreaked in Hungarian intellectual life,[5] and he finds, primarily based on belletristic analysis, the entire development of the Reform Era as already smacking of the wishy-washiness that would become full-blown and disastrous in the second half of the century. Yet it is misleading to lump this and the ensuing period together. For all the phenomena of decay, the developments up until 1849 belonged to those highly productive dilutions that characterize communities embarking on new social and intellectual enterprises and that, in case of success, enrich and reinforce their particular characteristics.

Petőfi's optimism and rationalism certainly run counter to the Hungarian self as we know it, summing up our historical experience up until then and thenceforward. Optimism and rationalism, however, have been decisive factors in modern European development, and all nations that wanted to participate in that development have had to highlight these streaks in their self-profiles. All in all, Petőfi was a sign of the healthy development of Hungary and not a symptom of its crisis; he was sound also in the purity of his political and social conduct but even (to dabble in matters of literature) in his crystal-clear prose, readable as though he were writing today, in striking contrast to the unreadable prose of the language-reform period.

In 1848–1849, Hungarians, having so accumulated their resources, were the first to undertake to break with the Habsburg Empire, which had been in the way of all nations seeking to shape themselves democratically. This attempt proved to be beyond their capacities, partly because of the European situation, partly because of heavy odds of the forces interested in no change, and partly because Hungarians could not find a path of common action with the national movements of the minorities living in historical Hungary. The Hungarians' fight for freedom collapsed under the rallying forces of European reaction and the resistance of nationalities at home, and Austrian absolutism installed itself over the ruins.

FROM THE FREEDOM FIGHT UP TO THE COMPROMISE

Austrian absolutism between 1849 and 1860 was the last attempt by the House of Habsburg to unify its heterogeneous empire. Many have pointed out the anti-feudal, people-friendly, and modernizing aspects of the absolutist experiment, trying to picture it as more progressive than the feudalism-tincted Hungarian nationalism of the freedom fight. Indeed, it was a radical experiment because it tried to undo the historical separation of the constituent members of the monarchy; yet it was sheer anachronism because its every step was made unsure by the fear of the peoples, as all reforms removing a stone from the wall of feudalism willy-nilly advanced the cause of the people, not the dynasty. So unconfident, this absolutism was but a dreary, bureaucratic, and priestly shadow of the anti-feudal, reform, and enlightened absolutism of Joseph II; it carried out the emancipation of *serfs*[6] with no intention of continuing *social* emancipation at all; it modernized public administration and purged it of some of its feudal remains without as much as touching the feudal hierarchy of society; it reproached *national* wrangling but did not in the least acknowledge the claims to liberty of the *peoples*.

The absurdity of this experiment became glaringly clear in less than a decade: it turned out that the relatively developed lands of the Habsburg Empire could not be governed without some sort of constitution. The ruler thus issued the October Diploma in 1860, which dropped the "revolutionary" system of absolutism and introduced a cautious constitutionalism strictly maintaining the supremacy of the dynasty. This constitutionalism relied on the framework of *historical* nations—that is, nations with an aristocracy—the restoration of historical institutions and conservative social forces, the estate or limited-suffrage diets of the individual countries, and the Imperial Council with its seat in Vienna presiding over them. Thus, while offering a constitution to its peoples, the dynasty sought to make a deal with the feudal or feudal-like forces of the individual countries; in other words, it retreated at least as much as it advanced, reverting to the policies of Francis I and Metternich, updated a little.

As the whole scheme was based on reaching a compromise with the historical laws of the individual countries, the House of Habsburg began to bargain with the historical nations, especially the Hungarians. At this point, it ran into difficulty: the Hungarian feudal constitution was legally modified to be a modern parliamentary constitution, which, to top it all, was enacted by an independent nation in 1848; it was therefore difficult to pass a concession off as a constitutional achievement when it gave much less than this. Thus Hungary sent no representative to the Imperial Council, and Ferenc Deák laid it down that the condition of compromise would be the recognition of the Articles of 1848. Now, the one thing the dynasty wanted to avoid was to continue or restart the 1848 process; thus, the first attempt at compromise fell through. Yet after an interim period of conservative government, the bargaining resumed again, another lost war turning the dynasty more compliant.

What happened in Hungary in the meanwhile? The political situation in Hungary was fairly plain under absolutism. Under a tyranny that spoke an alien language and that was bureaucratic and small-minded, the nation groaned and went into passive resistance. After ten years of passive resistance, however, a fatal process ensued: the nationalist intelligentsia and the progressive common nobility balked.

This is the point from which it is indicative to study the symptoms of the befuddlement of Hungarian development. Up to then, there had been no question as to what the actual situation of the country had been; being forced into the Habsburg framework and a petrified social structure with all its narrow and provincial relations had been grave burdens, but they had been clear to all; they had been openly institutionalized and called what they were by all those concerned. Briefly put, they had been undoubtedly part and parcel of the social, political, and intellectual *reality* of the country. The confusion began in the 1860s, the time when, by László Németh's account, the breakdown of the Hungarian self began—the only moment of his analysis about which we might have doubts is whether the difficulties and impasses of the literary magazines of the 1860s are apt for exposing the symptoms of the invisible disaster of the Hungarian self that he attempts to do.[7] The trouble ought to be traced back to the changes in the conditions and orientation of the entire community.

With the indelible impression of actual experience, the great shock of the defeat of the 1848–1849 revolution fixed two—let us immediately add misleading—lessons in the political, social, and intellectual leadership of the country. The first lesson was that the empire of the Habsburgs was a European necessity from which we could never extricate ourselves; should we try destroying it, Europe would rally to piece it together again. This was not true at the time but was certainly not set in stone. The other decisive and misleading conclusion was that if the Habsburg Empire could perhaps be smashed, historical Hungary would fall apart together with it, its nationalities clearly exhibiting their intent to secede in 1848–1849. This, however, was by and large true, but not even the survival of the Habsburg Empire could have helped avoid this.

As a result of these two debilitating lessons, the patriotic Hungarian intelligentsia lost nerve and enterprise and sought to salvage whatever it could rather than bring up a new elite for a new revolution. This terminated the possibility of the common nobility, in part or in whole, which had associated with the patriotic intelligentsia, seriously and powerfully backing the cause of progress. All the more so because, the gentry had realized in the meanwhile that the emancipation of serfs brought it to the brink of ruin while it benefitted the large-estate aristocracy, which had resisted reform to the last. As both social prestige and land were slipping out of their hands, the gentry summoned up all their strength to recover their former political power through county and national offices and remold them to acquire a salary according to the rules of modern bureaucracy, which they were now getting the knack of. They thus began to be ever so keen on compromise and could hardly wait for the end of the new period of suspense after the failed parliament of 1861.[8] The pressure this impatience exerted was decisive in Deák's becoming more yielding in 1867 than he had been in 1861.

THE IMPASSE OF THE COMPROMISE

Driven by their predicaments, both the dynasty and Deák were increasingly ready to come to an agreement. It was two political forces on the defensive and petrified by fear that struck the deal in 1867, as László Németh himself rightly points out.[9] The Habsburgs yielded to the Hungarians, a nation they had known to be the most vigorous, fearful, and independence-seeking one among the peoples of their empire, and did not realize that its enterprising spirit had been gravely compromised in the meantime. And the Hungarians themselves went into the deal because they had come to believe in the ineluctable necessity of the Habsburg Empire in the European system of states and had not grasped, had not dared grasp, that the two lost wars[10] that had forced the Habsburgs to yield had proved the freedom fight and Kossuth right that their empire was actually not invulnerable. The dynasty and the Hungarian elite mutually overrated each other's power because they had both been keenly aware of their inability to maintain their positions alone—in this they were not mistaken. So they went into the settlement to preserve and protect that which was most important to them: the empire to the Habsburgs and the state to the Hungarians. Yet the two continued to be at odds—more than ever before—because of the drift of democratic community-shaping in the nineteenth century.

The principle behind the updated version of Metternichian policy, which the October Diploma had initiated but failed to carry through, was that all the historical nations, lands, and territories of the empire enjoying portioned shares of feudal self-government and imperial protection would be "knit together in loyalty to the dynasty." The 1848 policy Deák had sought to follow but failed to carry through was based on Hungarian independence and liberal constitutionalism, allowing no more than personal union with the other countries of the ruler. The only reason a common formula could finally be found was that the 1848 situation had seemed to repeat itself, though in a much mellowed and unnerved manner, harmless to all parties; in Austria, the conservatives had been pushed into the background in the wake of the "German War," and the Grossdeutsch liberals,[11] who formed a government for a short while, hoped to recover the positions of Austria in Germany through their liberal policies and acknowledged a relatively wide-ranging separation for Hungary, which was beyond the immediate German political framework.

The Compromise was thus seen as a victory of liberalism on either side of the Leitha. The government of liberal Germans in Austria was rather short-lived and replaced by an exceedingly conservative regime shortly, and the Hungarian liberals were increasingly subject to fears that inoculated them against serious reform policies. In fact, the Compromise was a full-blooded act of conservatism, and this was what made it possible in spite of all its internal contradictions; the parties had been brought together not by shared aims and plans but fears and anxieties. The liberals were needed only in order to find the formula; the structure so established could only be maintained on a conservative basis and, even so, only for the time being.

The cunning stunt with which the Compromise bridged the gap between the contradictory positions was the "common affairs." The common foreign and military affairs were to be managed by special committees composed of so-called delegations of the Imperial Council and the Hungarian Parliament, strictly organized so that they would never be thought of by anyone as some sort of common parliament. The delegations were not to debate, only to vote, ensuring that foreign and military policy would be deliberated on not by the Austrian and Hungarian parliaments but, in accordance with the original design and without any interference by any rudimentary, surrogate parliament, by the dynasty.

This arrangement of the common affairs was then incorporated in the constitutional laws of the two countries through contradictory and differently worded constructions. The Austrian Act of Compromise was drawn up merely to amend the October Diploma, the single constitution issued for the whole empire in 1860,[12] and it introduced a special privilege for the "Lands of the Holy Crown of Hungary" not to have to represent themselves in the Imperial Council. It continued to speak of the empire, which, from now on, had a part on that side of the Leitha, "kingdoms and lands represented in the Imperial Council," and one on this side of it, the Lands of the Holy Crown of Hungary.

In marked contrast, the Hungarian Act of Compromise spoke of an autonomous Hungarian state, mentioning no imperial dependence, only that it shared certain affairs with a state called Austria. This position was undergirded also by the fact that the monarchy was called Austria-Hungary from the moment the Compromise was made. In vain was it so called, and in vain did we ourselves call our part the Lands of the *Hungarian* Crown; the lands across the Leitha were never called *Austria* but "the kingdoms and lands represented in the Imperial Council" or, soon, Cisleithania, the name "Austria" being retained for the *entire* monarchy pursuant to the Austrian Act of Compromise. *There*, this produced the illusion that the old Austria was retained, while, at a closer look, it was doubtful whether it existed at all. The Hungarian nation entertained the illusion that Austria was but a neighboring country, while the truth was that neighboring country meant the international and military power of the dynasty, wielded not merely in the neighboring country, but very much in Hungary too. Legally, the entire construction seemed to buttress the Hungarian side; actually, the dynasty; but it was fundamentally *false* for either side.

The Compromise lied to the dynasty that it retained its empire by keeping its full international and military power without any serious restrictions. However, foreign and military affairs, with which the ruler only "maintained" his state, were not enough for a monarchy to be truthfully called a state; much else would have been needed for the ruler to "do good" for his people. In respect to Hungary, these were in the hands of the separate Hungarian state, which meant the establishment, in the heart of the empire, of a unit where dynastic loyalty ceased to be a community-shaping factor.

This had its repercussions on the part of the monarchy with a tongue-twister name. For Austrian Germans, the Compromise meant that they ceased to be the leading people in the *entire* monarchy, and soon, in 1871, their hopes would be dashed that Austria was going to restore its leading role in the German Empire. For the other nations, the Czechs in particular, it became increasingly difficult to justify why the Hungarians were permitted to play at being independent when they were not. This contradiction was borne out with particular poignancy in 1871, when, as a logical conclusion to the process begun by the October Diploma, the dynasty sought to strike a compromise with the historical nation next in "rank," the Czechs, over their constitution. This was thwarted by Hungarian prime minister Gyula Andrássy, who vetoed Czech constitutional aspirations in the name of an independent Hungary.

Wicked as this intervention was, spiteful of even the solidarity among "historical" nations, it can only be understood if we grasp the cunning and deceptive nature of the dualistic setup; so long as there was only one constitution apart from that of the Austrian one, the fiction that Budapest was equal to Vienna could be believed, but should the Czechs and the others lining up behind them also have had a constitution of their own, it would suddenly have become glaringly clear that the situation of Budapest was rather like that of Prague, perhaps only a little bit better. The failure to grant the Czechs a constitution meant that the dynasty, having lost the confidence of Austrians with all-German feelings, it now made enemies of the Slavic majority of its empire. No less fatal was this for the Hungarian nation because it now became a co-partner of a monarchy doomed to perish; moreover, it was *alone* in this relationship among all the peoples of the monarchy—in fact, making it a matter of prestige that it was alone.

On the Hungarian side, the Compromise lied to the Hungarians that they had their independent state except in matters foreign and military—matters where independence is decided on at critical moments. Responding to Kossuth,[13] Deák had written that the Compromise would fulfill the spirit of 1848 and settle the common matters left open by revolutionary legislation—an argument to be repeated with full arsenal by Gyula Szekfű only half a century latter. In fact, however, this was the very basis of the internal deception of the Compromise— below we will return to why it could be invoked again in 1920. But why had 1848 left foreign affairs open, and why had it spoken of *Hungarian* defense with nothing "left open"? Because, at most, it would accept personal union, and its final aim had been full-fledged independence. What was meant by the Compromise's "resolving" these partly open and partly unopen questions in favor of closer union? Why, had the question been "unresolved," had it been doubted who was meant to handle Hungarian foreign and military affairs for eighteen years? Not at all! These issues had been decided by the defeat of the freedom fight and the cooling of the revolutionary zeal of the nation.

It was a lie and self-deception for everyone to speak and argue of the constitutional issue in 1867 and ever since as though the Compromise, in the name of liberalism, had continued where 1848 had left off, as if the period up to 1867 had dropped out of Hungarian development, *as though it did not count.* The intervening period had actually not fallen out of Hungarian political development. The Compromise continued where the Austrian provisional arrangements had left off,[14] and the latter, having drawn some of the conclusions of the revolution and the intervening absolutism in the October Diploma, had continued where Metternich's system of government had left off.

The real meaning of the Compromise was that the Hungarian nation obtained, in the cunningly equivocal formulation of the common affairs, concessions whereby it would accept—the *October Diploma!* Nowhere did Hungarian constitutional law as much as mention the October Diploma or its cautious constitutionalism, based on the deal between dynastic and feudal forces, but it was actually founded on this *invisible charter*, which was much closer to it in truth and spirit than the Articles of 1848, which were vacated until only their bare bones were left. This meant that not only were foreign and military affairs to be shared, but it also rendered the most important achievement of 1848, parliamentary government, illusionary. Hungary did get a government responsible to parliament but with the strings attached that parliament would always have a majority that regarded the Compromise as binding. What would happen if there was to be no such majority? The military power of the dynasty would be wielded, as it became obviously clear in the crisis of 1905.

What was it that made such remarkable men as Ferenc Deák, Zsigmond Kemény, and József Eötvös go into this Compromise and celebrate and have the nation celebrate it as the fulfillment of its desires? We will hardly get very far by saying that they became hirelings of reaction or, put more mildly, that they surrendered to reaction. Indeed, something of the sort did happen to them, but this was not a cause but an effect—the effect of that deeper balking affecting them and their wider circles that we have already mentioned. Yet how was it possible that men renowned for their perception did not recognize these contradictions of the Compromise, which were no more hidden to reason then than they are today? To understand this we must capture how the issue presented itself in their minds.

Their first question was, as it had been back in 1848, whether they wanted an independent, constitutional, and freely governed Hungary. They answered in the affirmative, undoubtedly in full earnest and conviction in 1867 too. The next question was whether they were adherents of constitutional monarchy or republicans. Well, they all definitely stood for the former. Even if they had qualms about the Habsburgs, constitutional monarchy agreed best with their whole political and social frame of mind and temperament—as is well known, not even Kossuth was an out-and-out republican. Finally, the third question that presented itself to them was whether they wanted to maintain the territorial intactness of historical Hungary. Their answer was likewise an unconditional yes. Theoretically and in line with received opinion in a Europe that was having an extended break in revolutionary development, these latter two affirmative answers, however, were in irreconcilable contradiction with the first yes on Hungary.

As far as monarchy was concerned, the precondition of a functioning constitutional monarchy in the nineteenth century was that the monarchy be identified with *one* nation and *one* community. For Hungary, however, monarchy was given in the form of the Habsburg Empire, which was made up of *five* historical nations and a further *six* peoples that were seeking independence; these could hardly be changed into a national constitutional monarchy with any reasonable hope of success. A claim to an independent and constitutional Hungary implied a breaking up of the monarchy—a conclusion that Deák, Eötvös, and Kemény, who, together with the whole nation were suffering from the impact of a defeated revolutionary struggle and its useless bloodshed, were reluctant to draw. Only Kossuth would undertake this, identifying with the truth of the fallen Hungarian revolution with a lifetime in exile.

As to the matter of historical Hungary, the leaders of the nation ought to have faced the fact that democratic freedom implied the self-determination of its peoples, a concept that would lead to or risk lesser or greater territorial loss. Again, no one dared come to this conclusion, at least not so definitely. This was another issue that the emigrant Kossuth broached in his concept of a Danube Confederacy, the reaction to which was so meager that he never brought it up again, though he never revoked it either. The Hungarian political elite, however, could not and dared not face the irreconcilable contradiction of these three theses—an independent and free country, constitutional monarchy, and historical boundaries—because they were exceedingly fearful of the power of the Habsburgs and of the intentions of the nationalities to break away. Whoever accepted these fears as a starting point was able to deduce with unerring logic the constitutionality of the structure established by the Compromise, though it was not constitutional; its independence, though it was not independent; and the security of historical Hungary, though it was not secure. This is a classical example of fear beguiling reason.

If we are aware of this, we will know more than simply knowing the Compromise to be a reactionary edifice; we will also understand why this reactionary edifice could command the service of non-reactionary forces. The Compromise meant that the larger half of the forces that had been factors of progress in Hungary in 1848–1849 was squandered on erecting the Compromise, made up of contradictory aims, political fictions, sham formulas, and false constraints.

This point-by-point discussion has revealed the constitutional and political impasse into which the Compromise led the nation. Politics is not as material as to have to pay a heavy price for deception immediately and promptly, as, for instance, in technical innovation or production, but it is central enough for lies to wreak disaster in due course. In the face of widespread opinion, it should be laid down that *politics does not permit lies*. Or, put more exactly, lies can be *told* now and then, but they cannot be the foundations of political constructions and programs. The rest of the history of the Compromise shows with particular clarity what a heavy penalty is to be paid for deception in politics.

FROM THE COMPROMISE TO THE FALL OF THE MONARCHY

The Compromise that the dynasty and Hungary struck in 1867, based as it was on mutual deception—mutual self-deception, to be more exact—led development into an impasse primarily in the political sphere. For some fifty years, lawyers on both sides of the Leitha were entrusted with construing a shared founding document in the interests of their own country, when the first thing that ought to have been observed before all interpretation was that it was lies and contradictions at its foundation. For some fifty years, the Hungarian nation expended massive efforts on struggles to expand the national achievements of the Compromise, when the Compromise was a Byzantinely conservative settlement that could be complied with letter by letter or *could have been* overturned but could not have been developed any further. For fifty years, political wisdom in both Austria and Hungary was exhausted in thinking up political measures that could be presented to Austria and the reigning house as the strict observance of the Compromise and to Hungary as transcending the Compromise, as earth-shattering national attainments. This conduct gradually marred the political reasonableness of the elite, while the most demoralizing phenomenon Hungarian political life could come up with and maintain, election rigging, ensured that the political reasonableness of the people would be debased. Whoever accepted the Compromise and whatever it meant also had to accept the corruption of Hungarian elections and voters because the spirit of the Compromise did not allow the adherents of full independence, social revolution, or the self-determination of nationalities to attain a majority. The institutions that 1848 had conceived of as a means of political education now became the wherewithal of demagogy.

Parallel to the deadlock of politics and constitutional law, *social* development also came to a standstill. Certain disorders of social development had had their share in bringing about the Compromise, but the petrifaction of its construction also contributed to the hold-up of social development. As the Compromise continued not 1848 but 1847, so the social meaning of the Compromise was the outward acceptance of the achievements of 1848 but the abandonment of its sweep and the upholding of the centuries-old immobility of social relations. Up until 1848, it had seemed that the progressive elements of the common nobility and the bourgeoisie would develop into a European-type middle class capable of standing up against feudalism and that the gentry-and middle-class-rooted intelligentsia would become a single class of modern, free professionals advancing social transformation, but this social fluidity and movement was now utterly stranded. Social fusion continued but in the opposite direction: an intimidated intelligentsia and a middle class—isolated from the majority of the Hungarian people and mostly of German extraction—merged into the gentry class, which withdrew behind the fortifications of its old social framework. This created the Hungarian type of gentleman, the Werbőczyan noble, pretending upward and bullying downward, who could not be likened to any member of the middle class in the European sense or a reformist intelligentsia. This genteel layer was thus no longer a medium for the middle class or social mobility, but, having inherited the social status of the Werböczyan common nobility, it became a closed and immobile residue between the establishment and the lower-middle and working classes seeking advancement.

The impasse of the Compromise was most acutely manifest, however, in the area where its originating fear arose—the *nationalities policy* and their *assimilation*. The historical and intellectual elite that deployed the whole moral and ideological arsenal of democratic community-shaping to justify Hungarian independence denied Hungarian nationalities the same right on the rather meager grounds that the Hungarian state had continuous institutions—that is, it had a historical entitlement to be, while the nationalities did not. The nationalities thus had no right to political and constitutional self-determination; they had but individual and cultural rights; they were the non-Hungarian-speaking members of the single Hungarian political nation, as Ferenc Deák's well-written act and the political construction it founded had it. However, a multilingual and like-feeling Hungarian nation could have been imaginable before 1848, but after the events of 1848–1849, everyone knew that historical Hungary would be secure only if it spoke the same language.

The very fear that had prompted the Hungarian elite to enter into the Compromise and deadlocked it in the security it was hoped to provide used this transient and sham security to establish a single-language country and assimilate the nationalities—even by breaching the Act of Nationalities. This was where the lies about assimilation began. Petrified by the Compromise, Hungarian society, for all its legal institutions, remained a feudal society. Now, feudal society generally does not assimilate, or, rather, it assimilates not to society as whole but to a single caste or group. Assimilation to the entire community occurs only in a middle-class society and is carried through completely in a classless society.

This does not mean that assimilation is *merely* a social issue or that it will cease to be a problem with the resolution of social issues. What is certain, however, is that the first question of assimilation is always: what is the social medium that is doing the assimilation? The Hungarian society of the second half of the last century began to emerge from feudalism but was stranded at this stage and assimilated in a narrow and partial way. Little did assimilation take place other than in the few centers of the middle classes, urban Jews and Germans. The linguistic and emotional assimilation of these groups seemed to take place rapidly and successfully—a success that reinforced the edifice of Hungarian political illusion; the real danger in the assimilation of Germans and Jews, who were scattered and did not have a bearing on the territorial status of historical Hungary, was that it engendered the illusion that the other nationalities could be assimilated while they would not.

If there had been a serious intent to assimilate them, it could only have been tried through the sweep of a vigorous middle-class and democratic development in the competition of performances pointing to the future and progress, not shrinking back even from revolution. This would have meant both the opportunity of assimilation and the conjuring up of the danger of secession—this was a danger of which the Hungarian elite had originally been afraid and so could not bear. Thus, those who had not given up the aim of the democratic development of Hungarian society, but lived in the fear of Hungary's falling apart at the same time, sought to orient the Hungarian masses in a direction of social, human, and economic growth that would exclude nationalities. The social forces with an interest in maintaining feudal structures had nothing to do but wait for the social attempts mentioned to founder on their own contradictions. In this situation, those in power could not be cleverer than to demonstrate their nationalism and assimilating zeal in showcase police, political, and cultural-policy actions and hark back from democratizing Hungarian society— had they not already done so for their own social prejudices—because of its consequences on nationalities.

Hence the odd contradiction that this period lives in the collective memory of Hungarians as one in which nothing was done to strengthen them even within the limits that would have been defined by the purest democracy and a full acknowledgment of nationalities' rights, while in the collective memory of the nationalities it is a period in which everything was done in order to hinder their political and social advancement. Both theses are true side by side: the vast majority of Hungarians continued to live under essentially feudal and serf conditions, while the masses of nationalities, likewise living in feudal peasant immobility, did not undergo any form of assimilation; the internal linguistic boundaries of historical Hungary also remained unchanged, but the nationalities' confidence and animosity toward the Hungarian state heightened.

The internal contradictions and rottenness of the Compromise became glaringly visible in the great constitutional crisis of 1905 and afterward. The unified opposition, which had won the elections campaigning on the basis of independent Hungarian statehood, could form a cabinet only after having acknowledged the Compromise and succumbed to the ruler on major points—a ruler who had shown by illegally appointing a cabinet that the final trumps were in his hands. Taking office in this way, the only meager justice the new government could extend was to brand and eject the public men and officials serving the "infantry cabinet,"[15] which in turn demonstrated the weakness of the dynasty.

To top the confusion, *labor* demonstrated *against* the opposition coalition and *for* general suffrage, which the infantry cabinet had promised. In regard to nationalities, the coalition government first tried rapprochement with the Serbian-Croatian Alliance, which did not even cloak its secessionism, and then sparked off a great Croatian row with a far-fetched railway regulation, with which it wanted to gloss its domestic inefficiency and propagate as a great national achievement, and it is with same type of objective that it passed Apponyi's notorious Act of Elementary Schools, which finally turned the nationalities against Hungary. It was through such self-defeating national attainments that the coalition discredited itself, lost the next elections, and had to hand over power to István Tisza's strictly Compromise-based cabinet.

In the final count, the fifty years under the Compromise regime meant that for all the experiments at developing it further, not a whit of achievement was reached because it could not be overstepped, yet its moral and political credit was in shambles. By the time the world war broke out, there was no political term on either side of the Leitha that was hated more than the Compromise. The thick pillars of deceit on which it had been based decayed from within, became worm-eaten. Irrespective of the war, two clear positions came to be formulated in striking contrast to one another: first, Franz Ferdinand's concept of a dynastic empire based on the equality of peoples and, second, an utterly anti-Habsburg independence stance. This opposition of constitutional stances was far from being parallel to social and political divergences, the contrasts of reaction and radicalism, because there were pro-independence reactionaries and proponents of empire who flirted with democracy. The radical writers and journalists of the *fin de siècle* had themselves not made up their minds as to how they imagined the process of democratization, whether in an all-empire, an Austro-Hungarian, or a historical Hungarian framework or in that of completely new nations. But by raising the issues at mass-movement, social, and economic levels, not at the level of constitutional law and the interpretation of texts and history, they very much contributed to the clarification of positions. It had been perfectly clear before the outbreak of the war that the Hungarian nation would have to face the question of the continuing existence of historical Hungary, whether Franz Ferdinand acceded to the throne or the monarchy was dismantled. The first alternative, the dynasty turning against historical Hungary, was first deferred and then rendered pointless by the assassination of the archduke and the world war. The dire consequences of this matured later because this was how the legend of the dynasty, the monarchy, and the Compromise could unfold in the wake of the partitioning of Hungary.

THE IMPASSE OF COUNTERREVOLUTIONARY GOVERNMENT

The time for Hungarian independence and democratic revolution came in 1918. It seemed the victorious revolution would resolve outstanding issues and undo the mesh of deceptions in which the community life of the country had been entangled. In the twenty-five years that followed, we learned to belittle it even as a revolution, yet if we look at it from up close and compare it with the fascist pseudo-revolutions after it, we will note the liberated, spontaneous, and healthy power it manifested after breaking down the structure of lies of the preceding fifty years. In two months, however, the terrible shock of the falling apart of historical Hungary debilitated these forces. The elite was so shocked at the sight of a truncated Hungary because it was what it had been fitfully afraid of for fifty years; it was what it had tried to avoid facing by all its policies. It was this shock that prompted the leaders of the 1918 revolution, who were not of a mind to sign the prospective peace, to hand over power to proletarian socialism, which attempted military resistance. After the shock of political unpreparedness, this in turn brought about the even greater shock of social unpreparedness for the gentry class and the intelligentsia and middle class, which had melted into it and lost their independence.

By the time the Entente intervention brought about the demise of the Commune, everything was set for democracy, socialism, and indeed even independence to be not wanted by anyone but the few who had dedicated their lives to the cause of democracy and socialism—they were not wanted in particular by the intelligentsia and the middle class, which had again withdrawn behind the mask of the gentry. The inference seemed so clear and simple that drawing it could not be resisted: the democratic principle of self-determination was what had dismembered historical Hungary; it was therefore to be rejected; it was all the more easy to reject it because it was a humbug, a deception of the world; 3 million Hungarians had been brought under alien rule in its name; and because the internal democratic revolution had led directly to proletarian dictatorship wanting to do away with the intelligentsia and the middle class, it was therefore to be feared as well, and it could safely be rejected all the more so because it was but lip service, a swindle, starting in freedom and ending up in dictatorship. That, seen from further afield, this was only a mishap or transition that did not invalidate the basic principles and development tendencies could not be explained to those living them.

This interpretation of the events of 1918–1919 meant the political apotheosis and justification of the type of man that had created the Compromise and had been capable of walking the tightropes of its lies. The dynasty had fallen and the Habsburg Empire was dead in the water, yet even without them, the world of the fallen Compromise had been successfully recreated, its ideological and political construction achieving a greater esteem than ever in its lifetime, as László Németh masterfully describes.[16] This was how Gyula Szekfű could attempt to do justice to the Compromise subsequently, at a time when, looking on from without, events proved its very uselessness, even harmfulness, and fulfilled Kossuth's prophetic words that the most devastating consequence of the Compromise would be that when the peoples arose to destroy the Habsburg Empire, there would be Czech, Polish, Romanian, Serbian, and Croatian legions, but there would be no Hungarian one among them. Though the *meaning* of 1918–1919 justified Kossuth's foreboding, "experience" of those events, the *actual* dismembering of the Austro-Hungarian Monarchy, justified in the eyes of the Hungarian genteel class the very fear that had made them—the Hungarian political elite, including genuine democrats—fall in with the Compromise. This was how the thesis could be put forward that the two revolutions involved in and intent on breaking up the Austro-Hungarian Monarchy were to be blamed for tearing apart Hungary. Squaring with the logic of fear, the construct was so complete that facts could be brushed aside—the fact that the scapegoat for Trianon, Mihály Károlyi, had passed power on to the Commune so that it could rectify with arms the expected peace conditions to which he could not agree and that the Commune had fallen primarily because it had tried to fight, while, in contrast, the Entente raised Horthy to power under the condition and in order that the peace treaty would be accepted and signed. The counterrevolutionary regime made up for this grave birth defect by grievance-venting irredentism, tying in very well with the whole construct.

On the social plane, the genteel class, driven now by the fear of proletarian revolution, assimilated further commoner elements into what was now dubbed "the Christian middle class"; though the term sounded more modern, it covered an ever more desperate and open insistence on the immobile and hierarchic mindset of the former gentry class. The intolerability of social petrifaction began to be counterbalanced by the radicalism of *anti*-progressive forces, the fascist squaring of the circle. Many a misunderstanding and a squandering of good intention were rooted in the failure to notice the fundamental immobility of the counterrevolutionary structure. All the reactionary, fascist, and even the few European-minded shades of this counterrevolutionary picture were committed to this essential immobility, the only difference being that some maintained their position consistently while some tried to add new colors by pseudo-reforms or pseudo-revolutions. The political platform of the counterrevolution could not be *developed* in a democratic direction, just as the Compromise system could not, because the essence of both was to rule out change.

It is only knowing this immobility that we can grasp how the Hungarian political elite was capable of upholding the stupefied attitude of the Compromise era toward the nationalities throughout the twenty years of fighting for the revision of Trianon. It was as a consequence of this that when the political scene of the world changed and occasioned reannexations, its first reaction was to grab the opportunity under the guise of obtaining amends for the injustice, but it forgot to ask in the manner that would only have been expected from the champions of justice what the conditions, circumstances, and forces were behind the reannexation and how they related to justice.[17] Second, it indiscriminately accepted the reannexation of all areas that had belonged to historical Hungary, including Muraköz (Međimurje) in Croatia, without concern for the hatred and animosity this engendered in the local population and the neighboring country. Finally, it repeated the same old anomalies, blunders, and brutalities of former Hungarian policy toward the nationalities, only more crudely; on the one hand, it referred to Saint Stephen's concept of the state, which had not been enough even when it had been called Ferenc Deák's Act of Nationalities; on the other, it made gross attempts at Hungarianization and police atrocities that not only did not even invoke Saint Stephen or Deák, but also backfired. The survival of the Werbőczyan, common-noble domineering manner and sense of privilege ensured that there would be enough nobodies with superiority complexes to carry out all this thoughtlessness.

So as counterrevolutionary politics pursued the phantoms of reestablishing historical Hungary and Hungarianizing the peasant crowds of other nationalities, the cause of assimilation came to a serious crisis within Hungarian society. Anti-Semitism had broken out already in the wake of the revolutions of 1918–1919, and now the race-protection explanation that all our miseries were a consequence of the unrealistic shift in the political, social, and intellectual elite of the country due to assimilation caught on, sparing not even the assimilation of Germans. In comparison, the shift in ratios was indeed conspicuous, but in light of the deadlock in which Hungarian social development had been caught, there was no mystery about this. We know that Hungarian society, the vast majority of its peasantry in particular, had lived amid a largely feudal or feudal-like framework. In marked contrast, the detached societies of Germans and Jews in Hungary were by and large free of feudal features and constituted a middle class. The German peasantry and the Jews that lived in their secluded communities continued not to assimilate, like any other nationality, yet found a relatively easy way into the upper echelons of their respective assimilated and urban kind. This move was not unconstrained, but it certainly had the freedom a middle-class society could and a feudal world would not afford. What this meant was that the aspiration of these crowds to reach the upper crust of their assimilated kind was not obstructed by anything but material means, which could be overcome by talent, willpower, or temporary penury; it was certainly not constrained by internal encumbrances and inhibitions.

In marked contrast, the feudal features of Hungarian society put various constraints and inhibitions on the striving to rise, get an education, or be enterprising, and these were only further emphasized by material difficulty. This very simple difference between feudal Hungarian society and middle-class German and Jewish society gave rise to what has been seen as the gaining of ground by Swabians and Jews in business, power, and administration. With our knowledge of this social background, it would be grossly misleading to attribute particular significance to the energies and solidarity of the "ground gainers," and we will hardly get any further by continually measuring the distance or closeness among the Hungarian, German, Jewish, and Slavic selves. The issue is obviously not decided by the degree of differences among the selves. It is a matter of course, that, for instance, the self of a Hungarian gentleman of common noble extraction, taking into consideration the fact that social difference is an important factor in defining self, is closer to that of a Hungarian peasant than to that of a Swabian official or a Jewish tradesman. But this does not in the least change the fact that the Hungarian peasant was administered by a relatively large proportion of German officials with a more or less *different* self identity and his wheat was bought by Jewish tradesmen with a more or less *different* self identity because his *Hungarian* masters with a closer self identity and the society they established were what they were.

All national anxieties that saw the essence of the process as the pushing into the background of the Hungarian race, but failed to radically think through the social meaning of the full liberation of the Hungarian people, inevitably led to having to rejoice over any changes in power and ratios that gave preference to the Hungarian stock over the German or the Jewish. However, as a result of the immobility of Hungarian social development, it was not the Hungarian masses but mostly Hungarian gentlemen who benefited by such changes. Let us for the time being disregard the malicious, German-serving race protection of the counterrevolution and focus on the more consistent and undoubtedly more honest Hungarian race protection that sought to protect the country from both German and Jewish predominance; if we look at the social component and community conditionings in race protection, we will note, behind the not so ever-present peasant romanticism, a "pure-blooded" Hungarian-race version of the Hungarian gentleman retaining the Werbőczyan common-nobility high-handedness and offended superiority complex.

This impasse in the political, social, and national mindset of the counter-revolution undermined the political reasonableness and moral judgment of our elite. Its final consequences came to fruition in the events of 1944; however, as the facts of the preceding period come to light, it becomes glaringly clear that the country's purportedly knowledgeable, cunning, and determined leadership had made its fateful decisions with dumbfounding rashness and blindness. This was how the deception of the counterrevolutionary construction had conjured up the very danger it had been meant to forestall: to ensure territorial change and social immobility, it had maneuvered itself into a war that brought the complete undoing of all territorial change and the collapse of the centuries-old social hierarchy.

REVERSE SELECTION IN A HUNDRED YEARS OF HUNGARIAN PUBLIC LIFE: PHONY REALISTS AND OVERSTRUNG SEERS

After stumbling through the whole series of impasses, beginning with the defeat of its revolutionary freedom fight of 1848–1849 through to the end of World War II, the Hungarian nation had to face reality in the rubble of its state construction, which had been built on fiction, conjecture, claims, and wishful thinking. In the course of these hundred years, it has had to live in the midst of a political and social setup where calling a spade a spade was not only not possible, but also ruled out; things were to be interpreted and explained not in the plain chain of cause and effect but in the name of supposition and expectation beyond; good effort had to be expended on pseudo-problems; actual problems were to be cured by incantation; action was possible and required outside the scope of and without regard for things to be genuinely done; there was no objective measure for the correctness of action, and, in its stead, a system of fears and offenses was used as a moral gauge. All deformations of community life manifest in this period can be traced back to the fundamental spuriousness of the political and social construction.

How was it possible, it may be asked, that the identity of a whole community was changed by the deal a king and the nation had struck in 1867? Quite simply, if a spurious construction, whether in the area of constitutional law, politics, ideology, society, or economy, is for some unfortunate reason built into the structure of a given community, it will start off a reverse selection, as László Németh has rightly pointed out in treating the issue. In the public life of both the Compromise and the counterrevolution, no one could be a minister; a village notary; the chairman of a bank, a trade association, or the academy; or a school inspector who could or would not embrace in a regulation, a disciplinary ruling, or a toast this system of deceptions on which public life had been based. However minor a concession might have been required, it nonetheless started the reverse selection because upright, passionate, and perceptive men would not lend truthful force to lies. In the long run, reverse selection replaced the entire leadership of the community, and its intellectual and moral corruption was its logical conclusion.

Community leadership and governance generally require two things, as does any creative act: practical realism focusing on what can be carried through and a perception recognizing the essentials of the given tasks. When a community is somehow cornered into an impasse, one of its first consequences is that it cannot find realistic and perceptive men to lead it. It will find plenty of realists, who regard practicability and personal ambition above all else, and they will be ready to be "realistic" in the sense that they accept the prevailing construction based on deception as reality. Their realism is thus exhausted in buttressing and upholding a fundamentally mendacious structure and shifting positions under the deceptive conditions. On the other hand, men of perception will seek other forms of expression or withdraw into narrower and smaller communities and become increasingly isolated, sulky, or offended and turn to eccentricity and fierce prophecy; and it will also be only eccentrics and prophets capable of telling the essence.

It is interesting to observe the leaders of the nation and the publicists who formulated the national problematic either as supporters of the Compromise and the counterrevolution or as their opponents. On the one hand, we thus have those siding with the Compromise architect Deák: Ferenc Salamon, the two Andrássys, Albert Apponyi, István Tisza, Sándor Pethő, and Gyula Szekfű, to mention the best—all high-minded men who studied possibilities with due reason, restraint, and practicality, yet whatever theses they put forward on the political situation of Hungarians at the time, they have *nothing meaningful* to say in our day. It is as though they had lived in and spoken to dwellers on the moon when discussing the dynasty, Austria, the Compromise, the nationalities, Hungarianization, revision, Saint Stephen's concept of the Hungarian state, democracy, or land reform with their exemplary moderation and beautiful national spirit. Not because they were conservative and that time surpassed them; a totally old-hat yet truthful and pithy conservatism survives in the way it treats issues, if it does so genuinely. But whatever they said, they based on the belief that the immobile and deceitful political constructions of their times, though indeed capable of asserting themselves for a long time, were identical with political and social reality. No sooner had these constructions collapsed than whatever they had said about them lost its relevance.

On the other side, we have followers of an exiled Kossuth and his fellow internal emigrants: Mihály Táncsics, János Vajda, Lajos Tolnai, Endre Ady, and Dezső Szabó. Now, they were authors whose writings and theses grasped the deception and the insufferableness of the prevailing constructions with desperate passion, still effective poignancy, and an authenticity increasing as time passes; yet they can hardly be envisaged as political leaders deciding priorities and knowing "exigencies." We have named but the very best representatives of either side; and where are all those that swam with the tide—the careerists, the blazoners of platitudes, instigators, jingoists, bamboozlers, cheerless Hungarians, monomaniacs, sectarians, and plotters?!

This twofold reverse selection of community leaders and seers gave rise to and brought to prominence two types of men: the blurry, wishy-washy, paltry type and the dogged-convulsive type. László Németh's attributives for describing the befuddlement of the Hungarian self, *deep* and *thin*, deserve anything but being blamed for murkiness. These images depict genuinely real, not at all hazy, phenomena. We may, nonetheless, *dispute* them, in particular the thesis that the passionate and perceptive seers, including the greatest among them, Ady, manifested the truer, more characteristic and deeper Hungarian self. In order that they be *truthful* Hungarians, they need not also have been *true* Hungarians; they certainly embodied, among the large variety of opportunities worth calling the Hungarian self, not the healthy and complete types that could be proposed as examples or laid down as norms but *one* side of the same befuddlement—indubitably, the more appealing deeper and truer side. The essence of the fact that they and their associates lost the leadership of the country in every field was not that their true Hungarian self came to be a minority but that, generally speaking, all healthy reasonableness, judgment, moral affection, and sense of community came to be a minority in the face of the spurious realism of those making their way and having the doors open up before them.

Now, this has no bearing on assimilation and the ground-gaining of those who were assimilated because, upon entering, they found the fundamental deceptions of Hungarian public life all in place, worked out by true-blooded Hungarians. This phoniness did, however, serve a purpose: it baffled the process of assimilation because an unbroken assimilation depends on the soundness of the forms of the assimilating community. Hungarian forms, at both caste and national levels, had been gradually *warped* from 1867 and hastily from 1919, beginning with the forms of address to the forms of public life; or it had been *pseudo-forms* that had evolved, beginning with Gypsy-music sprees to the Compromise of 1867 itself; and there had been a *cancerous overgrowth of forms*, as in the mawkish coloring of Mezőkövesd folk embroidery or the installment of an Emericana dominus.[18] It was the internal impasses of the assimilating community that was the cause of, the decisive factor in, the maladjustments of assimilation going on at the same time.

In such situations of impasse, amid the extremities of exemplary and guiding minds, the distortions of community forms, the general vagueness of standards, more and more effort is required for maintaining the immediacy of experiencing reality, fearlessly sizing up dangers and troubles, and safeguarding the purity of moral standards and maintaining the sweep of right action. It was independents, radicals, socialists, Communists, rural sociologists, and rebels that sought to find the way out for stranded Hungarian social development, and they did so amid much worse conditions, distractions, and far fewer prospects of success than countries with a more even development.

Various pitfalls endangered these efforts. If uncovering reality and asserting realism were overly cool, rational, or doctrinaire, dogmatic and doctrinaire groups would tend to prevail in the effort and their theses would ineffectively bounce off those emotionally bound to their closed circles of fear and fiction; worse, failing to dissolve them, they would only irritate and thereby reinforce them. On the other hand, when far too responsive to the fears of others, they entered into their minds their false desires, embracing their emotional and conceptual language, and thus the intellectual integrity and the efficacy of their attack were lost. The work they undertook has come to be an abiding value in the development of Hungarian political thought, but the final stimulus had to be given by history, demonstrating to the nation in the unmatched ignominy of the collapse of the counterrevolutionary regime and the bloody ruin of the illusions of revision that its masters were not masters and its ideals were not ideals.

THE PROBLEMS OF OUR DAY

The liberation has radically and finally extricated Hungary from the false constructions in which it had formerly arranged its life. Their collapse has done away with two moments that have encumbered advance for a hundred years—the prolonged survival of the Hungarian feudal social order and the illusion of efforts to maintain the historical borders of the country. The collapse of the power, economic, and psychological structure of the old feudal order has meant an invaluable release for hundreds of thousands and millions of people and their conditions of life. For all the resentment and discontent, this release has been present, though often invisibly, in the sweep and optimism of the reconstruction effort Hungary has seen since the liberation. A community with as bad a conditioning as ours, however, might not necessarily draw the right and productive lessons from the shock of clashing with reality. It is therefore worthwhile to ask whether there are no new lockjaws and impasses deriving from the recent shocks threatening us.

The recent past has meant two major shocks, contradicting each other for various groups of Hungarians. The lessons drawn from them are already well on their way to becoming lockjaws connected to former ones and difficult to allay. One shock, the later one of the two, was that the counterrevolutionary government and the feudal world collapsed as a result of a lost war and in the form of the country becoming a theater of war and being occupied. This shock was not only a matter for the middle class and the intelligentsia but for everyone not outrightly leftist. This enabled the resuscitation of the characteristically middle-class Soviet-Communist-Jewish phantom of the counterrevolution, affording it an even wider mass support. The breakaway and emigration of the right wing of the coalition has reinforced rather than weakened this fear, even though its visible and demonstrative signs have become infrequent.

The whole Compromise-counterrevolutionary mindset has by now been reborn—visibly in emigration and invisibly at home. This new internal and external emigration seems to relate more to the Compromise, in its formally democratic stance, and in the social-political immobility behind it. This is fittingly eked out now and then by the appearance of a legitimist orientation, but practical effectiveness fosters or would foster counterrevolutionary, not only Christian-nationalist, but also fascist trends; and, to make the picture complete, the lack of political power and the conditions of internal and external emigration have oddly added to this reborn Compromise-counterrevolutionary attitude the tragic, cheerless-Hungarian sensibility of Dezső Szabó, an attitude he keenly despised.

It should be noted in passing that the survival of the old world poses a threat not only through its conscious proponents, but also in the ways in which it has conditioned the masses. This threat is first and foremost the hierarchical approach to society, the mania for titles, dominance rather than service in exercising power, and the sense of rank and privilege rather than duty and service in "qualifications" and "posts"; these have so much so permeated our society that they cannot be eliminated by mere political change and replacement; moreover, in many ways, they hinder and compromise the great transformation our society is undergoing.

The other great shock was the one that befell Hungarian leftists in 1944, that the country proved to be so incapable of putting up any resistance; so wanting in community spirit; so narrow-minded, reactionary, and rightist. We saw how precedents can explain this situation, yet we cannot justify or forgive ourselves for this conduct and the general image it created both internally and externally. This fearful lesson has been written into every nerve of Hungarian leftists, and it has only been reinforced by the intermittent reappearances of reaction and fascism. It is to be feared that, as a result, the received opinion on the left will be that the majority of the country is consciously and definitely rightist—in much the same way as, after the Commune, during the twenty-five years of counter-revolutionary government, all Hungarian gentlemen were at heart convinced that the majority of the country was Communist; or even earlier, following the freedom fight, when the dynasty was convinced that the majority were die-hard Kossuthists, while in both cases there was an optical illusion created by the one-sided and misleading interpretation of experiences that had been doubtless fearful and factual.

The same holds for today; it is not true that the majority of the nation wants the rule of the alliance of large estates, big business, and officialdom back; the only way it would is if it were lastingly convinced that the only way it can be freed from its various fears is accepting the rule of these retrograde forces. The greatest threat of this would be if the memory of 1944 were to instill a convulsive fear in Hungarian leftists of spontaneous nationwide mobilization because such a mobilization is the fundamental condition of carrying the liberation process begun in 1945 to its completion in the fields of local government, economy, and culture.

For all successes and results, alarming symptoms are far from wanting. As far as local-government liberation is concerned, the topsy-turvy yet incredibly vigorous local-government life of 1945–1946 has by now been replaced by a rather dampened and top-down-run local-government life, and our state leadership, seeking the ways and means of reinforcing central authority when unable to rely on spontaneous forces, will only have recourse to the historical pattern of *bureaucratic* centralization Keresztes-Fischer left behind.

In the economy, the central authorities of organization, stockpiling, marketing, and credit have been established or restored alongside the land reform, but the bodies of local and spontaneous economic effort have failed to be set up to a matching degree. As result, the central authorities have begun to eerily resemble the cooperative establishments of the prewar era, which had a wonderful ability to combine bureaucratic tardiness indifferent to the people with exploitative wholesale trade likewise indifferent to the people.

Finally, in terms of cultural liberation, we have a promising sign in the increasing network of people's colleges, but a troubling sign is that is not so much a means of radically changing and widening the social background of our educational system but a militant organization rearing a vanguard.

All these shortcomings are obvious and well known; a great deal has been done to remedy them; a lot of good energy is at work on them and in store to help. Yet whenever we ask why the spontaneous forces of the country are not made use of more widely, bravely, and extensively, the answer, reflecting the dark memories of 1944, is that trustworthy men are lacking and spontaneous forces left to themselves could easily backslide. True, the masses have not shown a particular penchant for spontaneous political battle. But mobilization in local government, the economy, and culture advances things even if the participating masses dither about their political and ideological stances. It is only through this that the liberation process begun in 1945 can be carried through to completion. Political liberation can only be completed by an active local-government life stirring to manage public affairs, where people learn by their own experience and not from editorials that public affairs are their own affairs. Economic liberation can be completed only if the land the peasantry acquired and the factory the community took into possession become the immediate economic bases of a peasantry and a labor that are capable of economic orientation and are not exploited by not only proprietors and gendarmes, but also bureaucrats and their agents. The social and cultural liberation of the country can be completed only with an educational system that successfully separates the value systems of the various types of schools from all social rank and sense of privilege and opens up the freedom to choose a career for all between the ages of six and thirty-five.

INDIVIDUAL SELF AND COMMUNITY SELF

We have considered enough facts in Hungarian historical development and the warping of the Hungarian self to be able to raise the issues of the relationship between self and faculties, self and influences, and self and development with general validity. Before going into these questions, we must first clarify how the *individual* and the *community* self relate, concur, and differ.

Up to this point, we have used the same psychological terms for both individual and community phenomena. However, we ought to know and be clear about the nature of this analogy, how far we can go in this direction without straying into any kind of community mysticism. The border is quite definite. Only the individual has a psyche, a consciousness, fears, and acts. The consciousnesses, fears, reactions, and self of a community are comprised of individual faculties, either by simple summation or arranged together in some regular way. Certain sequences of community processes coming into being have a surprising parallel to individual psychological processes. That a man is frightened and does not dare take up a task but starts blustering and becomes pointlessly aggressive in another direction can happen in the very same sequence with communities too. The only thing we must remember is that this happens not because a community has a mind in the same way an individual does and that it happens so not according to the same necessities. Beyond the reactions of individuals, community processes have to add up or be arranged together, implying, first, a far greater number of possibilities and combinations, and, second, a far greater role for deliberateness, intention, community rationalizations, conventions, and objectives. In other words, the same psychological precedents can lead to quite different community processes; for instance, a community or the majority of its members might undergo a shock, yet no interpretation or opinion may occur to or be formulated in the community that gains widespread appeal and is embedded in commonly held notions; thus fright might disappear from community processes without trace. This is why we have insisted on repeatedly taking note of the political and ideological constructions in which the various shocks, requirements, and situations were formulated, interpreted, and became objective.

If we are not watchful about how individual processes add up or are arranged together into community ones, we will inevitably fall into community mysticism when using the imagery of the individual mind. We will not, however, be able to evade this by merely excluding psychological factors or imagery in interpreting community processes. In this case, we will be misled in the opposing direction, regarding the community as utterly differing from the individual. This is community mysticism in the same way as saying that the community is a big individual. A community is not an individual but made up of individuals; it can therefore neither be identical nor absolutely different from individuals.

SELF AND DEVELOPMENT, SELF AND RESPONSIVENESS

In discussing self, we usually mean the sum of nameable and clear characteristics in someone or some people that are defined by the existence, proportion, or combination of certain physical, psychological, temperamental, and talent features and that some mistake, others recognize, and still others point out spot-on as everlasting. Self is both significantly less and more than this. It is significantly less in the sense that it is far less definable, circumscribable, or clear, and it is significantly more in that it is much richer and more liable to change. The physical, mental, temperamental, and talent features, which are the fundamental faculties of an individual or a community, define not what they *will* or *should* be but the many things they *can* be. What an individual *actually* does achieve from these many opportunities is defined not by his originally given faculties but by the social environment, his education, and his personal development, experiences, work, and performance. It is in the course of and through this that the features that make up the *self* of a man or a community are shaped and become definite. Self is therefore, when healthy, not static but continually moving and developing. Thus the healthiness of a self is not in safeguarding certain faculties but in its ability to respond.

If an individual or community comes into conflict with oneself, is lost to himself or itself, this takes place not as though he had lost his catechism with how he ought to be written into it but when, for some reason or other—due to a shock, a loss of courage, or confusion—he loses his healthy responsiveness, his capacity to size up his actual situation and identify and respond with the necessary and possible actions. All the significant symptoms of the befuddlement of the Hungarian self manifest the disorder in response in this sense. The relationship between self and responsiveness is not in finding the right directions for action by a study of the eternal characteristics of our self but vice versa; a healthy responsiveness is what shapes a healthy self in creative action. It goes without saying that the healthiness of response is not in the vehemence, labored effort, and spectacular result of action but in the appropriate choice of duty and undertaking based on the perception of reality, on "seeing things as they themselves are" and then "firmly tending to our business itself," as Bocskai and Zrínyi pithily put it.

This holds doubly true for communities. The essence of a community is not that its members, as it were, wear its common features and characteristics on their foreheads but that they participate in the community as a common undertaking. Instead of dwelling on national characteristics, it is far more important to bring it home to people what the proper perception of reality; breaking out of the vicious circle of helplessness, deception, and fear; and undertaking tasks, joint efforts, and common achievement can do to a community. This is why it is pointless, even pathetic, as it is commonly done, to bewail the various hindrances holding back Hungarian creativity, whining, "What a pity, Hungarians are such a talented, original, and ingenious nation!" Let us come out with it at last that this is meaningless, *simply not true*.

It is only worth discussing and possible to discuss talent, originality, and ingenuity in respect to faculties that are unfolding; anyone can speak of the wonders that could have come of opportunities had they not been choked off, if he wishes, and anyone can believe him, if he wishes, but it will have nothing to do with talent, originality, and ingenuity. There is nothing more barren than decorating ourselves as interesting and behaving like a "damned prince,"[19] which is but a self-exalting excuse for haplessness and a gratuitous remainder of the Hungarian and genteel superiority consciousness gauged for a greater Hungary. It is always a shock for this mentality to have to reckon with the fact that seen from a distance, being Hungarian is no more interesting than being Latvian or Albanian. And there is nothing to be dismayed about in this because if we happened to be Latvian or Albanian, our duty would be to examine reality and go about our business; and if we are capable of doing so, we will be talented and interesting, and our true self will unfold.

Seen in this way, *influence* and *assimilation* will become secondary and merely symptomatic aspects of the confusions of the self. Precisely by responding, acting, and creating, the self also assimilates: foreign influence and people, everything. Assimilation has been apprehended so emotionally and irrationally, there is so much talk of why the foreigner becomes attached to and grows to love this wonderful, exciting, captivating, and charming nation endowed with God knows what other virtues because assimilation took place in a period characterized by the falling apart of community forms. The Hungarian nation therefore assimilated through every kind of decorum it had except one feature, the only true and universal assimilating medium: the sweep of its community life. Assimilation might be tedious and painful, but it is far from being as mysterious and irrational as it is usually pictured in Hungary. Communities with a clear, definite, and well-drawn self profile assimilate not by arousing mysterious resonances in the hearts of the foreigner, whereby he increasingly softens and, finally mellowed, melts into them but by their clearly put and definite customs and rules of pronunciation, greeting, courting, chairing, pursuing amends, holding meetings, and competing, and the foreigner might sometimes be charmed, sometimes thumped on the head, but he will certainly be caught up in the sweep of that community life.

In order to show that seeking national originality and characteristics is neither decisive nor productive, it is worth pointing out that the two nations of Europe with the best-drawn features, the English and the French, shaped their currently known selves by undertaking community enterprises that, to a certain extent, turned against their former selves, their former community orientation. In the case of the English nation, this turning point was taking up the Reformation and the subsequent rise of Puritanism; and in the case of the French, it was the French Revolution and the prior and parallel development of French nationalism. Both enterprises in their given historical contexts meant a major forgoing and remolding of the old, known national characteristics, both post-Reformation England and post-revolutionary France having lost many a hue in the eyes of contemporaries. Nevertheless, both nations became what they now are through these enterprises, both unfolding opportunities that their original, medieval, more colorful but diffusive conditions had not been able to develop. A more recent and similarly major community enterprise is the one taking place in Russia since 1917, which likewise means the elimination of many of the features of the "Russian people's mind"—features formerly regarded as everlasting.

In view of these examples of individual or community development, we might very well feel that beyond the entire development, the changes in self that take shape in the profiles of individuals and communities in the course of a major undertaking, we find a deeper regularity, repetition, self identity, and characteristic features, and those that do not fall into line with them and understand or learn their forms of conduct and requirements will pay a price for it. In such cases, we tend to suppose that the self is more than the mere individual that has developed from a set of faculties, possibilities, and statistical ratios; its is a *regularity* that summarizes, rules, and controls all these. We might have such inklings, but woe be to him who starts to pronounce unambiguously what he has opined to be regularities, formulate them as theses, and prescribe them as rules. We have to treat these as scientists treat God—not that they must not believe in God; they might even use their faith to make a foundation of their scientific approach; but they must certainly not include God in their working hypotheses, in the system of their suppositions, in the justifications of their views of problems; they must not shield themselves with God if they cannot explain something, and they must not invoke God when explaining something in one way or another.

The reference to the regularities or laws of individual or community life is likewise always suspicious when used to justify an act or a failure to act. It is no good hearing when reasons are wanting that this or that political system or arrangement is bad because it clashes with the Hungarian mind or is good because it agrees with it. If it is any good or bad, we should be able to justify it without reference to the Hungarian mind. We can never tell whether the feature that we now consider deep-rooted will not prove to be an obstacle and that, if it is rejected, the self will not unfold deeper, richer, and greater opportunities. It would, of course, be equally a source of trouble if one loses the instinct of constancy and imagines any change possible on rational or dogmatic grounds. The trouble in this case arises not from the clash with the "ancient feature" but from the contrary misperception of *reality*. A healthy sense of reality and a healthy responsiveness will always be able to find the balance between "ancient" and "modern," continuity and innovation, traditionalism and revolution, without recourse to establishing positive regularities.

SELF AND POLITICS

We must therefore make it unmistakably clear that there is no obvious correlation between the attempts to *understand* Hungarian characteristics and the attempts to *renew* the community of Hungarians. We might unearth ever so many Hungarian features without renewing or reinforcing the Hungarian community by upholding or cultivating them. We ought to discover through other means what brings about the renewal of the Hungarian community, and, in doing so, we must assess all phenomena, whether old or new, from the point of view of society and politics, not ethnic character. If it is true that self is primarily manifest in response, the perception of reality, and the undertaking and fulfilling of tasks, then we are justified in saying the quality, the healthiness, and the regeneration of the self is primarily manifest in *politics*. Naturally, we mean by "politics" not the workings of politicians alone but the entire process of fulfilling community tasks.

If, applying all this to our current situation, the only conclusion one draws is that land reform and people's colleges do far more against the Hungarian mind coming into conflict with itself than any musing over the quality of the Hungarian self, he will be right. However, the reassuring statement that we have left the wrong directions of the former era behind does not exempt us from having an open eye for the symptoms of new shocks and impasses we have pointed out above.

1948

THE JEWISH PREDICAMENT IN
POST-1944 HUNGARY

Between 1941 and 1945, over half a million Hungarian Jews perished in labor service, police atrocities, deportations, extermination camps, and during the Arrow-cross reign of terror. No sooner had the first shock passed than anti-Semitism, as witnessed by many a sign, had again cropped up against the survivors and home-comers. Official, semi-official, social, and moral bodies have made various declarations—each essentially putting forward the same two simple theses. The first one holds that the majority of the Hungarian people had not been involved with the crimes committed by the Germans and their hirelings and that the best Hungarians had done all their best to avert them. The second thesis emphasizes that the reappearance of anti-Semitism is to be condemned, and the fight against it should be pursued with every effort.

Should a company of good-willed people come together to say something high-principled, humane, and reassuring, try as they might, they will be able to think up nothing better than the two theses, yet everyone feels that neither of the theses has anything to say, or, to be more exact, both leave something unsaid. All attempts at having it out have ruefully miscarried, prompting open or veiled animosity, which, in turn, has forestalled all serious and sustained debate.

Statements of a certain responsibility and the admission of responsibility by the Hungarian people as a whole for the persecution of the Jews and the killings against them have been rejected both officially and by the public at large on the grounds that it is not right to place ourselves in a worse light than we are. When an unofficial gathering of churchmen went as far as to ask Jews for forgiveness in the name of the Hungarian people and their church, this excessive self-abasement was rejected by a clearly perceptible rumbling murmur of irritation.[1] Officials and the public are observably disheartened by the revelations and detailed descriptions of the horrors, though they do recognize that they cannot quash this natural and human way of trying to come to terms with the terrible experiences. From yet other quarters, there have been statements that emphasize—*against* Jews—that Jews cannot lay an exclusive claim to suffering, or, putting it more graciously, they caution them against losing restraint in demanding reprisals or even call on them to finally forgive and forget the past. On the part of the Jews, these utterances have been received with such vehement fury that they have had to be either revoked or argued away.

Everyone seems to have plotted to make sure nothing substantial is said on the question, only platitudes. True, in itself, ripping up sores will do no good, but glossing over facts and not facing reality are far worse than any ripping of wounds. Let us therefore openly ask whether the two received theses are enough for guidance; is it enough to say that the *majority* of the Hungarian people did not persecute and murder the Jews, and is it enough to condemn, perhaps punish, the *manifestations* of anti-Semitism?

I. OUR RESPONSIBILITY

ANTI-JEWISH LEGISLATION

Let us first sum up what came to pass. After 1919, a fundamentally feudal-conservative regime reigned in Hungary; it was born amid anti-Semitic excesses, founded on the limitation of Jews' entering politics and public office and, simultaneously, on letting them retain their business opportunities, even strengthening their positions through monopoly capitalism. This twofold policy of accepting political anti-Semitism and supporting capitalism largely in the hands of Jews created from the outset a tension wherein the "Jewish question" and its "solution" came to be identified with the elimination of the economic power of Jews and thus became the primary *social* issue of the country. In theory, the conservative-feudal government would have no social issues raised, but when it could no longer prevaricate, it more easily and willingly gave way to bringing up the Jewish issue than the real social concern with all its ramifications. The tension was particularly brought to a head by the Great Depression of the 1930s and even more so by Hitler's rise to power. With this tension in the background, heightened by the neighborhood of a Hitlerite Germany after the Austrian *Anschluss*, the leaders of the country and a nationalist public opinion expected the fulfillment of the territorial claims of the country through a policy that would at least parallel German actions, and they considered going the way of legislation discriminating against Jews.[2] The elements of the establishment with stronger European sensibilities, however, justified this legislation by the necessity of waiting for the outcome of Hitlerism without outright opposition to the Germans and by the assumption that this would be the lesser evil even for the Jews than a direct Arrow-cross rule or an out-and-out defiance of the Nazis. If looked at from the strict point of view of saving Hungarian Jewry, this line of argument *could have* carried weight under certain conditions, as it did from the point of view of the survival of Jewry in Romania, where a policy of this kind spared the majority of Jews the fate they suffered in countries falling fully in line with and countries turning fully against Germany. Yet the only way such a policy could have been justified is if policymakers had been perfectly clear and resolved that *this* was what they wanted; in other words, they went no further than the politically excusable minimum in anti-Jewish legislation, and, simultaneously, they curbed the political advance of extreme rightists through resolute and relentless measures and seized the time-given opportunity to back out of the war.

Alas, nothing happened in this way in Hungary. The fundamental piece of anti-Jewish legislation, the Second Act on Jews, went beyond this minimum on several counts; but it could not become a means of protecting Jews not so much because of its content but because of the circumstances under which the act was passed. It was enacted on the instigation of the extreme right, in the name of competing and bargaining with it, and it was accepted that the act was but a starting point, a beginning. As the legislation was followed not by the complete and severe suppression of the extreme right but by increased public agitation, incitement, and offerings to the Germans by the Arrow-cross and Imrédyite parties, it was only natural that the fundamental anti-Jewish act had to be superseded by newer ones year by year, and these were increasingly based on racism and persecution.

In the meanwhile, the feudal-conservative establishment was relatively successful in ensuring that the anti-Jewish laws would leave Jewish big business more or less untouched and afflict primarily middle-, lower-middle-, and working-class Jews. Whatever social pressure there had been and however perverted it had been in the mood of the masses supporting the legislation, the "question" could continue to be seen as unresolved. The anti-Jewish acts therefore not only did not take the wind out of the sails of the extreme rightists but filled them and did not avert the danger of the bloody persecution of the Jews, but, by being "legal" forms, the acts accustomed Hungarian society to exclude Jews from the shared fortress of human dignity. In the name of competing with the rightists, the anti-Jewish acts were followed by measures that first degraded their human dignity in all walks of life and then, at an ever-increasing pace, deprived them of the means of sheer physical life and personal security.

PERSECUTIONS AND KILLINGS

To begin with, a good number of lower- and high-ranking military leaders started to use and later increasingly used the military administration in the rean-nexed areas to more or less outlaw Jews under their jurisdiction, treating them as they believed a truly nationalist administration should treat them. Soon more and more Jews were drafted for defense labor service, which exposed them to further atrocities, abuse, and maltreatment, and which, with the support of several top officers, came to take the shape of regular exterminations in operational areas. In 1941, shortly after entering the war, the Hungarian authorities deported about twenty thousand Jews to Galicia on the grounds of irregular citizenship; the German military administration took them over and did away with them promptly. After this, further such actions ceased.

Nevertheless, higher- or lower-ranking officials would from time to time set about rounding up, insulting, or clearing away Jews on trains, promenades, or the banks of the Danube in Budapest suburbs. Such actions were stopped again and again but never in a way that would once and for all deter people from engaging in them. Moreover, the peak point of these unaccountable actions, the Újvidék (Novi Sad) bloodbath in January 1942, came after them. Under the guise of a raid on partisans, non-fighting, domestic, regular troops occupied a town and several villages and, encouraged by certain of their higher-ranking commanders, engaged in a massacre not sparing even women and children and in pillage, the majority of the town victims being Jews. This resulted in a newer shock and standstill, though the chief perpetrators could run away to Germany with impunity, and it took another half a year for the competent authorities to as much as believe what had happened.

Nevertheless, from the summer of 1942, during the term of Defense Minister Vilmos Nagybaczoni Nagy, it began to turn out that ravaging troops could be held back—though with difficulty—and that labor service could be managed as a somewhat orderly military service. Though in the meanwhile newer anti-Jewish laws had been enacted on the grounds of satisfying the anti-Semitic mass mood, it seemed that the country could extricate itself from the clasp of the German alliance and that, for all these instances of fiendishness, even the Jews could be spared the fate of those under direct German rule.

On March 19, 1944, however, the Germans started the occupation of Hun-gary; the governor, dithering for three days, gave in and appointed the Sztójay cabinet. The occupiers quickly made their decision on the deportation and extermination of the Hungarian Jews. The occupation complete, the decree that Jews were to wear discriminatory symbols was issued, and then began their herding into ghettoes. The deportations were carried out by the Germans with assistance by Hungarian public-order authorities under Arrow-cross control, the gendarmerie in particular. What this meant in practical terms was that the Germans determined the mode and schedule of the deportations, and the gendarmerie rather ruthlessly gathered together and entrained the Jews; then the Germans took over the trains and drove them out of the country. Unwillingly or willingly, inhumanely or humanely, the Hungarian Army and public administration fulfilled whatever secondary tasks the deportations required: they set up camps, gathered food supplies, issued and reviewed papers, judged exemptions, controlled the trains, etc.

The rallyings themselves, interrogations concerning hidden valuables, and the entrainments took place in appalling circumstances; hosts of pregnant women, women in labor, children, the sickly, and the elderly perished, many in good health going mad. The vast majority of deportees were transported to German extermination camps, into conditions of total disregard for human dignity, unprecedented even if we take ancient and oriental slavery and gladiator games into account. Regardless of age or sex, people were stripped and skinned; selected; quartered in unbelievable conditions without provisions or sanitation; and driven into quarries, overcrowded barracks, days' long marches, field brothels, and medical laboratories experimenting on them—only to end up dying the death usual there: being gassed, burned, shot in the nape, beaten, tortured, overworked, starved, frozen, and medically experimented on.

About seven hundred thousand people were collected together from an enlarged Hungary. The majority died in German extermination camps. About a hundred thousand of those surviving the death camps and who had been interned in milder camps for agricultural labor returned to the country, the rest dispersed in Germany and thence elsewhere.[3]

By the summer of 1944, both the Hungarian authorities and public had acquired a quite clear picture of what was actually going on. Roughly simultaneously, the government received interventions from the Swedish king, the Pope, and Hungarian churches to stop the deportations and Allied statements about their profound abhorrence and grave threats of retribution. It was at this time and in relation to this that the Arrow-cross elements of the Sztójay cabinet were relegated into the background, the Imrédyites having disallied earlier. As a consequence, the deportation of the Budapest Jews did not take place. The Jews living outside the Pest area were driven to a country camp, from where, taken by surprise, Germans deported them.

The next few months were spent with contradictory and ambiguous attempts at finding exemptions for the Jews under various pretexts and pretending anti-Jewish zeal toward the Germans. Then, on October 15, 1944, the governor announced our withdrawal from the war, but without any resistance or command to resist, he handed power over to the Arrow-cross. The suspension of the persecution of the Jews was now followed by actions more chaotic than ever before. The Budapest Jews were herded into a single ghetto, and Arrow-cross commandos patrolled the city, busy with killing off children hidden in children's homes, the sick in hospitals, and randomly picked people from the ghetto. Kept alive to the last, the plans to destroy the ghetto came to naught in the embroilment of the siege and the liberation, which some hundred thousand Jews experienced at home, most of them in Budapest.

The number of perished Jews, including all the deportees and victims of forced-labor battalions and massacres at Újvidék and elsewhere, is above half a million, meaning the full or partial annihilation of Hungarian Jewry in the Hungarian countryside, Subcarpathia, and Transylvania.

HUNGARIAN SOCIETY AND ANTI-JEWISH LEGISLATION

If we want to understand the response of the Hungarian people to these proceedings, we must first distinguish between those many individuals who gave in to the commonly held opinion that the economic containment of the Jews was a central national issue and those many that assisted in the outrage against human dignity and in dragging people off to mass death. Schemes to push Jews to the background in the economy had widespread public appeal at the time. If we ask whether the majority of the Hungarian people were behind this mass mood or not, we will have to be careful not to go into any humbuggery in using expressions such as "the majority of the Hungarian people." The majority of the Hungarian people is made up of the poor peasantry living in a closed rural society that was never for or against any of the issues or conflicts, including anti-Jewish laws, that turned "far-away" city dwellers against one another. If we ignore this passive indifference of the poor peasantry, we will observe that the anti-Jewish laws were, if not supported by a clear majority, not opposed by a greater mass power either. Furthermore, at the time of the 1939 elections, it seemed obviously clear that the support due in Hungary to the most rabble-rousing and dissenting *opposition* party was won by the Arrow-cross and other extreme rightist parties.[4] The only truly organized mass movement in the country, organized labor, was undoubtedly against anti-Jewish legislation. Yet should anyone have wanted to—indeed have been able to—fully mobilize this mass power against these laws, he could have counted only on its most conscious and best-organized core but certainly not any *crowds* such a core could rally.

This mass mood supportive of anti-Jewish legislation was undoubtedly a serious symptom of the impasse of Hungarian political development, of the lack of maturity in the political leadership and the masses, and of the fact that the European concept of political equality and equal human dignity for all men had not taken deep root in Hungary. However, if we take into account the fact that Hungarian political development had been gravely deadlocked in the past hundred years, and in the counterrevolutionary twenty-five in particular, then we should not be surprised at the convincing power and widespread acceptance of the view that the central malaise of Hungarian public and economic life was the conspicuous role of the Jews in the structure of Hungarian capitalism— while this was only an incidental symptom of the fact that the embourgeoisement or middle-class development of the Hungarian masses had been bogged down by a feudal-hierarchical social structure and that there was no direct way of breaking loose from it.

This was how the catchphrase "the Jewish question must be settled somehow" could become such that its point-blank rejection seemed utterly hopeless and the sustained and elaborate refutation of which people would turn a deaf ear to. Quite childishly, the majority understood this "settlement" of the Jewish question as some legislative measures "decreeing" that Jews were to make less and non-Jews more money without any serious change in the social and economic structure. That rousing an anti-Semitic mass mood on the grounds of righting imbalances in income and that discrimination on the grounds of descent enabling this would go over into the persecution and killing of Jews had been a historical experience inscribed on the very nerves of Jews but had had no convincing power in the eyes of others in the 1930s—something indeed at which to be little surprised. It would have been quite unrealistic to imagine that a country—whose leaders had never taken the equality of its own people seriously, whose intelligentsia and middle classes (both Christian and Jewish) had for some hundred years assisted (quite passively) regimes formally basing themselves on the principles of civil equality but being all but earnest about them—would rally major forces against any breach of those principles against the Jews.

In the moral reckoning to be made of the anti-Jewish legislation, there is one even graver item to be considered—the moral decline of society in implementing it. These laws, the state, enabled wide middle- and lower-middle-class or developing lower-middle-class layers to establish new, more advantageous livelihoods with no personal effort, no true and comprehensive social aim or justification, at the expense of others' already established livelihoods. In vain did the entire campaign appear in the guise of social justice: a more even distribution of property; nothing of the sort could arise from it because its essence was to evade genuine social reform, and had social language or demagogy gone beyond the limits, a desultory counterrevolutionary state would immediately have found its fist. The only point of the social phraseology was to assuage the moral qualms of those hesitating—not to mention those many who benefitted by the process only indirectly by the increase of jobs and opportunities—and who did have to directly face those ousted from their livelihoods.

The fundamental deception of the policy was that short of genuine and honest intent at reform, it had recourse to base instincts. It was at this time that many a Hungarian got used to not having to establish a livelihood through his own labors or enterprise but to pick out someone else's business, report him, seek out his grandparents, have him sacked, claim his shop, perhaps get him interned, and take possession of his belongings. These opportunities both brought to light and aggravated the moral degradation of Hungarian society and were an unforgettably dismaying experience not only for Jews, but for any decent Hungarian.

HUNGARIAN SOCIETY AND THE PERSECUTION OF JEWS

With our knowing why the "settlement" of the Jewish problem by way of anti-Jewish legislation could successfully be presented to wide groups of the nation as social reform, it would have been unreasonable to expect the country to have rejected with an overwhelmingly powerful uproar the laws discriminating against Jews, the measures to hold them back in the economy, to curb their participation rates, to redistribute their lands, etc. But it would certainly not have been far-fetched to expect that when all this changed into a blow in the face of human dignity and sheer physical harassment, this same society would shrink back and turn against the action. Certainly there were signs of this; the conduct Hungarian society manifested undoubtedly had its positive sides as well. Multitudes, many who had never before been particularly philo-Semitic, democratic, or antifascist, now began to engage in saving Jews; organizing various actions; running to the authorities; awakening the consciences of officials; mass-producing submissions; hiding people and taking care of children at foreign legations, in monasteries, vestries, labor organizations, private homes, cellars, or village cottages; printing forged papers; and directing people to safer places; sometimes, unexpectedly, help came from the mist of unknowing and oblivion. There must be thousands whose lives were saved by such individual or organized effort.

Yet this was but a drop in the ocean and not so much in an ocean of animosity but, what is worse, of puzzlement, indecision, the fear to help and shunning help. It should not be forgotten that of the two hundred thousand survivors, one hundred thousand went through the siege of Budapest crammed into the ghetto, and they were spared not so much because of those intervening on their behalf, even less because of the goodwill of Hungarian society, but because their executioners had no more time and resolve to destroy them; other surviving Jews came back from the deportations.

It is an illusion to reckon that many of our acquaintances were hidden and saved by the good offices of strangers; those helped were mostly converts, members of various circles, intermarried, or participants in Hungarian professional and intellectual communities or labor organizations; in other words, belonging to closer groups and partaking in the solidarity such belonging implied provided the opportunities and the contacts to help one escape. Those who had no such special relationships yet experienced the goodwill, help, and unselfishness of the average Hungarians they chanced to encounter were no doubt very much a minority. However much help and sympathy they experienced here and there, the persecutees did not and could not feel that the nation, its entire community, took sides with them and had compassion for them. We might relate as many true stories as we want about our heroes of compassion and love, yet no one could seriously claim that Jews as a *whole* have reason to be thankful to Hungarians as a *whole*, that they were *knit together* more than before due to Hungarians' conduct in their persecution—as indeed they were knit together more with the Danish, the Dutch, the Yugoslavs, the French, and even the Italians. This is what counts—the rest is but fairy tales. If a persecutee in Denmark—to bring up the example of a non-belligerent country—ran and sought help at the first door open, the first house in his way, he could expect with a high degree of probability to be offered help; should he not be offered help that went as far as self-sacrifice, he reasonably could count on people identifying with his ordeal; to a lesser degree, he would have to expect to meet with indifference, rejection, or cautious avoidance, and he would have to reckon with the possibility of being given up to his persecutors only as an exceptional misfortune.

In Hungary, in contrast, if he dared knock at the door of unknown people at all, he would with a high degree of probability have to count on indifference, rejection, and avoidance; with less probability, though still realistically, he would have to reckon with being given up, and help would be an unexpected, unhoped-for fortune. These calculations of probability are based on the actual behavior of Hungarians as a whole, as a community, toward the persecuted. Beyond the fact that the majority of the sufferers and the forsaken did not survive, there are more survivors who remember being turned down, forsaken, pursued, and defenseless than those remembering help and compassion. The most heinous experience was not the conduct of the haters of Jews, the openly and simply indifferent, or the cowards. Jews had long known being hated by many throughout the world, including Hungary, and they knew that those in trouble and in need of help experienced indifference, ungratefulness, indolence, and cowardliness.

What is most difficult to forget is not this but the ambiguous perplexity and tone-deaf incomprehension with which decent men who continued to keep in touch with them, who pitied them and would perhaps not refuse them a helping hand, took note of their final defenselessness, huntedness, and agony and the inhumanity, blood-thirstiness, and moral nihilism of their pursuers. What cannot be forgotten is the acquaintance who simply would not believe what Jews had every reason to fear; the person who, having expressed his pity for their trials, expounded to them that he as a Hungarian patriot and a convinced anti-Bolshevik wished German victory; those sympathizers that eked out their pity with bouts of sermonizing: "See, you shouldn't have been like this or that when thriving!" or "See, how pert and pretentious you are even now!"; those who declared they would be willing to help those that "deserved it"; the priest who was glad and obliging to hear of their intention to convert but sharply rebuked them for not learning their catechism properly and for converting without conviction, out of pure "interest"; or the bureaucrat who issued them a certificate but when, upon this they took courage to ask for some alteration in the paper, he indignantly rejected them saying, "See what you are! Out of selfish interest, you've the nerve to goad an impeccable civil servant into an offense." These experiences gave persecuted Jews the unbearable feeling that apart from hatred and cowardliness, all they met with in this country was a wall of obtuseness that could not be torn down.

THE STANDS TAKEN BY THE CIVIL SERVICE AND THE CHURCHES

The organized centers of European sensibility and humanity proved to be insufficient. For all the dead weights burdening the Hungarian situation, they could reasonably have been expected to put up a successful resistance against the trampling under foot of European methods and human dignity. These were the European-minded, cultivated, law-abiding half of the civil service and the

Christian churches. Usually in refutation of point-blank charges of their complicity on the basis of certain vile instances, it is often stated that these distanced
themselves from the persecutions. I do not think it would be reasonable to doubt
that they did distance themselves from the persecutions per se—the trouble was
that they *distanced* themselves far too much from the horrifying facts.

It cannot be called into question that the Hungarian civil service did have a
half that abided by its European standards, the respect of law, professionalism,
and conscience and that this stance stood in marked contrast to the bullying
and dilettante half, which had no concern for human dignity. This better half of
the Hungarian administration and civil service sought to keep the implementation of the anti-Jewish legislation within the framework of law and order and legal security—there was no wiser or more proper course they could have taken.
After a time, notably the German occupation, however, more would have been
needed (e.g., in life-death decisions on citizenship, the implementation of mis-
cegenation laws, etc.); the partial and latter total cessation of political, moral,
and legal legitimacy of the Hungarian state should have been declared and appropriate action taken. Instead, even the more humane part of the civil service
acted in the spirit that it was implementing the legal measures of a legitimate
Hungarian government, and it only led to horrors at the hands of the ruthless
and aggressive enforcement media. Even though reluctantly, leading civil servants, administrators of camps, registration authorities, and officials handling
the matters of the deportations obeyed their superiors and the regulations in the
name of fulfilling duties and without seriously demurring.

There was no sustained or effective boycott of these measures by the Hungarian public administration, a boycott that would have significantly lessened
the risks on individuals, and that would have jeopardized the efforts of those
wanting to carry out the deportations, particularly in the growing disarray of the
war. Not only was there no unified resistance, but even instances of individuals suspending obedience and loyalty were relatively few. The majority of civil
servants, who felt a repugnance for cheating or forging, failed to get it through
their heads that they would have been cheating a murderous and robber state
and assumed that they would maintain their moral purity if they rationally
proved to themselves that forgery were pointless and useless. Few reached the
point of regarding the state as a gang of thugs and its regulations scraps of paper,
thus deeming it a moral imperative to cheat and outwit it and forge papers.
Many got as far as this only belatedly, after the Arrow-cross putsch, but the ir-
resolution of the leadership of the country in announcing the withdrawal from
the war and letting power slip into the hands of Szálasi was enough to confound
a good number of people.

The belief in the legitimacy of the government and a reluctance to face the moral nihilism of Hitlerism debilitated church actions as well. It is not that there is an ecclesiastic anti-Semitism that would not condemn discrimination against Jews within the limits the church set in principle and practice and on which basis churchmen often sermonize to Jews to this day. I am not at all surprised at Jews' dislike of this, yet this is no reason to lump together modern mass-murdering anti-Semitism and ecclesiastic anti-Semitism, a historical precedent of the former, but the two are not to be forthwith identified in terms of either sociology or ethics.

The trouble began at the point when modern mass-murdering anti-Semitism was already being cheerfully drilled into our neighborhoods and the Hungarian churches continued to treat the issue in their customary way. They were delighted to see a conservative Hungarian government in office, emphasizing as it did the European forms and respecting the churches and their interests. It therefore seemed inopportune to sharply address the matter of Hitlerism and the moral nihilism of the racist theory and thereby inconvenience the right-minded government, which had to go somewhat along with Hitlerism for foreign-policy reasons.

The churches voted for the first two anti-Jewish acts on the same grounds as the conservative elements of the establishment with European sensibilities did, the moral reckoning of which we have already made. In several instances, the churches issued statements against the racist theory; the hazy folk-nationalistic metaphysic; and the deification of race, nation, blood, and aggression. The Act on Race Protection occasioned official protestations against the disregard for the concerns of the churches, baptism, etc. The deportations led to a partially successful intervention and protestation against their continuation and the ghettoization of converts. However, not even between the German occupation of the country and the Arrow-cross coup did the churches see any reason to deny due consideration to the Hungarian government that was so respectful of them and to its leaders, whom they knew and were accustomed to, or to identify them, their regulations, and their enforcement organs with the mad, pagan, and criminal Hitlerite state that stood behind and pulled the strings.

This was how, for all the heroism of certain priests, monasteries, and organizations, the churches manifested the same unevenness of conduct as all Hungarian society, ranging from compassionate help through distancing incomprehension to irritated animosity. If it was deemed that a unified stand should be taken in the midst of the extremes, they felt the appropriate path would be to declare their firm, ecclesiological, theological, canon-law position in the face of both the promise-cum-threats of the extreme right and the reproach-cum-expectations of the Jews. The trouble was not that the churches set down their theological positions—what else should they have done?—but that they kept away from the actual political and moral facts and formulated their stances in this way.

Let me illustrate this by just one instance: the position the churches took in respect to baptism. It should be known that, perfectly understandably, irritation had been building up in clergymen for over a hundred years because a considerable proportion of Jews taking up Christianity did so not to join the community sharing the Christian faith and religion but, again perfectly understandably, as a means of abandoning the Jewish religious community and joining a middle-class community unordered by rite. The only problem with this was that the Hungarian churches failed to take notice in the 1940s, but partly not even in 1944, that the issue no longer was their growing reason to be irritated over the increasing number of unconvinced converts but that the motives behind baptism had gradually yet radically changed. With every new anti-Jewish regulation, the earlier or later dates of conversion acquired newer and newer significance and thus provided ways of escape for the various borderline cases, the half-castes, those in mixed marriages, etc. Upon every such enactment, newer and newer crowds converted and stormed church authorities for the administration of Christening, regarded as the token of conversion. Firing up savagely, rightist papers and parties raked the churches over the coals for easily offering baptism and thereby a loophole.

The churches deemed that the most appropriate course to take in the face of rightists paddling about in the murky waters of murderous race theory and Jews seeking "to use the sacrament as a life insurance" was to assume a pure and unquestionable theological position: baptism was a sacrament that was not to be used for other purposes; thus it would be administered after such-and-such amount of monthly catechism classes, and it would also be appropriately and diligently checked whether the convert had indeed converted. That this was officially stated is all right. That this was the more or less general practice until March 1944, the time the country had a more or less consolidated government, was also sort of all right. The trouble was that this practice was continued even after the Germans came in, when Jews dropped to their knees in front of the parish priest to be baptized and not to be asked whether they believed in the Immaculate Conception or predestination.

Thus facing Jews' conviction that baptism was a matter of life or death for them, good-willed churchmen tried to justify their reluctance to administer "light-minded" baptism or forge papers by stating this was mass hysteria in response to various rumors, not a serious way of escape; the right-wing state did not fully recognize baptism, and care should be taken not to devalue baptism in so doing because that would jeopardize the situation of long-time converts without helping the new. This was indeed true in three-quarters of the cases but not for the many borderline cases. It should only have been brought up after recognizing that the new situation had changed the theological problem; as the persecution of Jews had begun to turn cutthroat, the question became whether it was permissible to administer baptism and issue baptismal certificates irrespective of there being or not being enough time for conviction and conversion, only to ward off the direct and actual threat of death hovering over peoples' heads. By this time, this was the question, and I cannot believe that the answer could be doubted. Whether the masses were wrong in assessing the immediacy of the threat and the use of baptism, and whether it would be of no use to them yet put others to peril, was the next question, one to be answered and the appropriate practical guidance elaborated only *after* the first one had been answered. We know very well many asked themselves and answered the question; perhaps even leading figures made principled statements; but no unified, conscious, and definitive position on this was taken by the churches. Under a longer German occupation and Arrow-cross reign, a stance on this and other matters would surely have been taken, but occasion for such an ordeal and moral courage were given to neither the church nor the nation.

THE STANDS TAKEN BY THE INTELLIGENTSIA

In the establishment of a moral reckoning for the nation, the stands taken by the intelligentsia are also crucial to consider. In this respect, however, we cannot limit ourselves to the cause of the Jews and giving them a helping hand; as matters of thought interrelate, we have also to see how Hungarian intellectual life was disposed to fascism and Hitlerism. Apart from a few well-known exceptions, the conduct of the Hungarian intellectuals in this respect did not give reason to be ashamed. The forthright outspokenness of Hungarian scholars, writers, and nobler publicists is well known, and when there was no chance of speaking out, various stands were devised and implicitly taken, and when even this was no longer possible, most writers remained demonstratively silent. Should the counterrevolutionary or shuttlecock policies of the government seek an intellectual rear-guard, they went and listened to the bombast of officials, told them some truths, something general, or kept silent, but they would not give them the service they were after. However, more would have been needed. The avowals of lofty and everlasting ideals should have been cleansed of ambiguities left in them, often purposely. For the avoidance of all doubt, writers should have made it plain that their European sensibilities were not identical with the ruling anti-Bolshevism conceived of in the interest of feudal reaction or that their radicalism was not identical with that of mass-murdering fascism. Having been clear on this, a distinct program for resistance and humanism should have been put forward that would have caught the attention of all good-willed people, youths in particular, wavering over the questions of both Jews and the nation.

Hungarian intellectual life, however, failed to dispel the ambiguities and formulate a joint and unequivocal program for resistance and humanity to make sure that all faults would be incidental and accidental. There were only attempts to take such a stand, and they all proved to be insufficient, feigned, or narrow and were sidetracked in the same way as all Hungarian opposition politics were.

The first and least successful stand was the one official Jewish bodies and left-wing parties took—protestations against the *termination of the civil equality of Jews.* In view of the social tensions and national injuries of the country, a proclamation that claimed civil equality for the Jews without taking a radical stance on the cause of the Hungarian people and masses and that failed to contrast the national grievances that had pushed the Hungarian intelligentsia in the direction of the Germans with a sense of danger to the nation as a whole, not only the Jews, was bound not to find acceptance. Lacking this approach, such statements could not get beyond the language of Millennium liberalism—exhausted as it had been by putting up so easily with the oppression of the masses—and the big-business shedding of tears for Bethlen's consolidation and thus could not dispel the impression that this was a matter of purely Jewish self-defense.

Another stand was assumed by the conservative, European-minded wing of the counterrevolutionary establishment, and it thus had a greater degree of protection and more occasion to be expressed. This stand contrasted the anti-Jewish legislation and persecution with the grave and more acute *German danger* and pilloried the unkemptness, the socialist and revolutionary language, of rightist movements for being related to Bolshevism. This rallied good intellectual powers, yet its fundamental hatred of the crowds and revolutionism; its anti-German stance squinting at legitimism, restoration, and the Saint Stephenesque concept of state; and its jingoism prompted scathing criticism and kept away many good radical Hungarians.

A third stand stressed the necessity of Hungarian survival and confrontation with both the German and the Jewish expansion. Though courageously turning against the Germans and their hirelings, this position assumed the enormous moral risk of providing a pretext to Jew-persecuting rightism and was thus unable to clarify concepts that would have been required for Hungarian resistance against German occupation and Hungarian humanity's holding out against the persecution of Jews in the great trial of 1944.

Bolting away from the ulterior, ultra-conservative, and legitimist agenda of the anti-German position of the establishment, this was the stand many a good Hungarian force rushed to take on. It would be quite unreasonable to lump its earnest national pessimism and romanticism together with the hazy, murderous, and destructive metaphysic of German superiority, but neither should its unrealism and barrenness be ignored because of its earnest romanticism and pessimism. It should well be remembered that Dezső Szabó, the begetter of this type of reasoning, had practically given up on treating the Swabian and the Jewish questions alike as the war broke out and assessed the situation with sometimes astonishing realism, though he was unable to evade the traps of his own particular national-pessimistic and peasant-romantic phraseology.

The socialist leaders of the labor movement took a fourth stand and contrasted the social approach focusing on the Jewish question with the *total elimination of exploitation, the liberation of the Hungarian masses,* and the need for *national* resistance against German fascism in order to achieve this. This was a pure and proper way of broaching the question, but socialism, being cornered and rendered illegal by a counterrevolutionary Hungary, it could hardly count on any response from nationalist forces, whose help would have been required against the expansion of the Germans and the persecution of the Jews. Accordingly, the labor parties relentlessly sought to cooperate with national forces, but the latter were stuck in their divided or confounded state until the last moment.

What would have been needed? Essentially what the labor movement had also said in calling for national resistance, but it should have been stated in a way and from a quarter whereby it could not have been called into doubt that it was stated for and in the name of the nation. What would have been needed, therefore, was a stand taken by representatives of the intelligentsia not ghettoized by either descent or politics that would have, first, clearly and sharply turned against the futility of anti-Jewish legislation and the inhumanity of persecution against the Jews; second, it would have professed the liberty of the Hungarian nation against the German peril, with no legitimist or Saint Stephenesque axe to grind; third, it would have declared the full liberation of the Hungarian people from all—not only Jewish—exploitation but without any class-struggle phraseology; and, finally, it would have offered alliance to all forces wanting this. In other words, the only stand that could have saved the country morally, internally, and internationally would have required the support of a more serious intellectual rear-guard. Naturally, no such stand-taking

could have enjoyed the support or charity of forces and powers that the equivocal, innocuous, and ineffective stands had enjoyed.

In spite of all, taking such a stand did have its encouraging antecedents in
intellectual circles, and there were men who had both the opportunity and fa-
cility to formulate it in a way most appropriate in the circumstances and shape
the foci of association and response. The responsibility for finally not doing so is
to be borne by them, including, among the lesser ones, the author.

THE MORAL BANKRUPTCY OF HUNGARIAN SOCIETY

If, on the basis of the above, we want to summarize the experiences the Jews
went through at the hands of Hungarian society, we cannot but observe that
spitefulness, lack of compassion, obtuseness, and cowardliness stand out among
them most sharply and bitterly. It would be futile to dispute these experiences;
they are perfectly genuine. Yet we know and feel this is not a fundamentally
spiteful, compassionless, or unreasonable nation, and contrary to all appearances, it is not cowardly either. Humanity, compassion, and courage are not individual and self-contained qualities but depend largely on the social environment. It is a romantic notion that the humanity and courage of a nation, society,
or community consist in the number of saints melted in selfless love for others
and of daring heroes undaunted by physical or moral peril. Humanity and courage naturally require personal qualities, but their unfolding hinges on community conditions, whether its functioning authorities are capable of compelling
the visible and invisible organisms of the community to apply the principles of
full-fledged moral integrity; of adding the verve of moral passion to the combativeness of the physically daring; and of bracing up the good-willed unsteady,
shy, or indolent with the approval, support, and solidarity of the community.

This was the very factor that was wanting with us. Moreover, it was precisely
community morals, a healthy community conditioning, that were found lacking.
This process goes back to an earlier period, to the fact that following the suppression of the freedom fight of 1848–1849, the political instincts and sense of danger
of the elite and the intelligentsia of the nation were focused on but one point:
the dread of the dismemberment of historical Hungary. In consequence of this
and the self-perpetuation of the proprietary layers, the spurious and anomalous
political construction of the Compromise came into being, deadlocking and
rendering unproductive the life and activity of the entire nation. These convulsive fears were subsequently reinforced by the revolutions of 1918–1919 and
the Treaty of Trianon, ending up in a final impasse of a grievance-revisionary
and anti-Bolshevik policy. The political class, while retaining its political

bearings, standards, and ability to negotiate—its political routine, in brief—increasingly lost its political conditioning, fundamental to any healthy policy; its ability to immediately respond to dangers, to realistically assess advantages, risks, opportunities, and necessities; and to have a sense of the interests of the community—in a word, its political instincts. More and more convulsive and unrealistic, political obsessions took the place of political instinct—obsessions of restoring and maintaining historical Hungary and the social hierarchy.

The fateful consequences of this came to light in and led to the great political crisis preceding and igniting World War II, and they would then try the political morals and instincts of each European nation. The routine of the Hungarian political leadership glossed over the fateful, gradual decline of political instinct. The way the two Vienna Awards rectifying the Treaty of Trianon were attained—that is, without having to fight a war with the Allies—and then having been embroiled in the war after all and the way the Kállay government gradually distanced itself from the lost cause of the war might have seemed from afar to be the perfect example of political chess. However, from up close, the ostensible successes, as we saw in the moral reckoning of the anti-Jewish legislation, covered up a failure to think matters through and all the temporization, the unstable situation alternating as the experienced or the obsessed gained the upper hand in their unending skirmishes. This was how it could happen that following the successful games of political chess, the most fateful and irresponsible actions could take place totally abruptly; first, the attack against Yugoslavia; then, entering the war; and, finally, after the falling out with Germany and the occupation of the country on March 19, 1944, the collapse of the government and the acquiescence of the governor.

In this respect, grave responsibility inveighs against the policy of the governor and the Kállay government in attempting to back out from behind the Germans without thinking through its consequences and requirements. The extent to which this policy did not know why it acted was laid bare most clearly when it regarded the German occupation as a disaster, a stance that, by all common sense, would have been deemed the success and glory of Kállay's policy, as it offered an excellent opportunity to back out from the war and turn against Germany, carrying along even the majority of a nationalistic public. Instead, the government resigned without a word; the governor appointed the cabinet the Germans demanded; and from then on, the governor and the Germans, the army and the Arrow-cross, who had been lining up against one another only three months earlier, now began to behave as though the all-deciding outcome had been but an incident, the mortal offense merely a misunderstanding, the deadly danger promising cooperation, and the mass killings being prepared a blissful national policy.

This acquiescence brought the political stupefaction and confusion of the political sensibility of the nation to a head; it turned the self-esteem of the army into shambles; it rendered all the concessions, including the anti-Jewish legislation that the Teleki and the Kállay cabinets, trying as they did to keep aloof from the Germans, had made to gain time pointless, making them actually backfire; and, finally, it maintained all Hungarian public life and the entire public administration in the belief of legitimacy, prompting civil servants to assist in all government measures, while, by this time of the war, not only active resistance but simple passive sabotaging could have caused major difficulties for both the occupiers and their puppet government.

Hungary started out with a policy seeking redress for its just, unquestionable national grievances and gradually, without its public noticing the transition, became the last ally of the greatest, maddest, and vilest thug state in the world. In the meanwhile, that the policies of obtaining redress for national injuries and the economic containment of Jews had come to be but adventurism and genocide escaped men with a lack of critical faculty. Major Jewish fortunes were still untouched, and there were still many signs of Jewish affluence while the government had already had several "minor" exterminations of Jews weighing on its conscience, and Jews had been exposed to various insults in the streets and on trains. No one ever pointed out that it was the trickery of a conniving, knife-edge policy that delayed the Hitlerite genocidal apparatus from overrunning the Hungarian island of relative—indeed, relative!—safety.

This was why, when Hungarian state authority acknowledged the German occupation and thus glossed over the actual meaning of the event, many did not realize that power had finally slipped from the hands of the small-minded and reactionary masters, who had nonetheless abided by their own rule and forms, into the hands of veritable madmen and the lowest off-scourings of the nation, and they were unaware of what was to befall the Jews from now on. Everyone saw the sudden increase of insults, but there had been such before, they would think, and *legitimate* state authority would set things right. Thus gradually becoming accustomed, society acknowledged the introduction of the yellow star with no visible resistance—which it had triggered wherever the sensitivity to the breaches of human dignity had remained intact, calling forth manifestations of universal indignation. There was no serious change in mood until the deportations of the countryside Jews began, people seeing its methods with their own eyes. These did shock, abhor, and horrify the majority of Hungarians, but due to the demoralization and loss of courage of society, the sham legitimacy of the situation, this did not lead to any organized and conscious effort at help; whatever help there was was sporadic, and the SS and the gendarmerie did everything they could to deter people from helping.

In vain did it become abundantly clear by the summer of 1944 that it was no longer the economic containment of Jews that was the point, what the real meaning of the "relocation" of Jews was, and that the country had become an ally of mass murderers; dithering, average, and middle-way men continued to fail to respond humanely and courageously partly because of their grave political miseducation and partly because of the disgracefully misleading conduct of the country's leadership. As a result, they believed, for all their horror at the persecution of the Jews, that they had to obey official Hungarian state authority, and, as good Hungarians, they had to want German victory. They tried to make themselves believe that this was but the "degeneration" of an originally good and just intent. If they did pity and help Jews, they did so *in spite of* themselves, with a wavering, divided conscience.

Yet not only did the entire Hungarian society fall prey to moral and visual bafflement, but so too did Hungarian Jewry. We have heard countless stories of hiding and forging papers, but at a close look what was even more dumbfounding was the extent to which the majority of Jews would not have anything to do with going underground or faking papers. Though the actual intent of their persecutors had increasingly dawned on them, they continued to obey the state authority and its organs, to which they had been accustomed in spite of the fact that disobedience was no longer a major risk.

Looking on, Hungarian society observed—with occasional satisfaction!—the obvious defects in the conduct of the persecutees: that instead of a common defense, many of them, often their leaders, sought out dubious ways of exemption, acquiescing in persecution not touching those excepted; that they kept wrangling small-mindedly to the last minute; how they put their helpers at peril with their superfluous requests, etc. If, however, we ask whether these were particularly "Jewish" traits, we will have to note with alarm that this is not the question. Which was the nation that, herd-like, obeyed the obviously destructive intent, that sought, to the last minute, exemption from under the yellow star the Germans had visibly or invisibly pinned on all East European peoples? Which society furnished the examples, in the cellars during the siege of the lack of community sensibility, the unwillingness to help, the selfish abuse of help, or its leaders running away from the duty of taking care of those entrusted to them and trusting them? I am afraid that instead of any "Jewish" qualities, it is the wonders of an assimilating Hungarian society with which we have to reckon. To be more precise, community morals, conventions, and conditionings fell apart in all groups and layers of Hungarian society!

This is the only way to account for the fact that Hungarian society, becoming aware of the mass tortures and murders as it did, if it did not have a sense of its own responsibility, which can be explained away by various causes, lost its *own sense of danger* too. That a German world would treat Hungarians almost in the same way as the Jews was brushed aside with annoyance, as an obvious folly, a childish attempt by Jews sensing their doom to present the danger they faced as a common danger. Yet however unique the hysterical hatred and fear Hitlerism spurred against Jews, it treated, for example, the Poles, particularly their intelligentsia, in much the same way as the Jews. Anyone capable of grasping the mindset of German racism and supremacy and its consequences would easily work out that what was due to Poles would no doubt be due to Hungarians, it being merely a matter of timing.

That this danger could be played down in the eyes of the Hungarian elite and intelligentsia had historical reasons. Since the 1867 Compromise, these groups had been accustomed to having major disputes, constitutional disputes, only with the Austrians, while the Germans had been allies of sorts. Moreover, Hungarians, within their own historical areas, were destined to establish the same role and vocation that the Grossdeutsch worldview accorded Germans throughout the world, and these were also reinforced by the German-Hungarian alliance in the world wars. This was why, on hearing of German claims to power and supremacy over East European peoples, the first thing to occur to certain quarters of the Hungarian elite was not that *we would also be ruled*, but that we also have a claim to leadership and dominion over the nationalities of historical Hungary. This deep-rooted, suicidal attitude "guarded" Hungarians against recognizing their doom in the extermination of the Jews.

THE CASE AGAINST ADMITTING RESPONSIBILITY

We have looked at all the important facts and have attempted to explain some of the graver ones. We have deliberately tried to refrain from immoderate language and not confuse the degrees of moral responsibility. Not that we want to tone down or gloss over issues; rather we want to ensure that should the question of responsibility be brought up, we base ourselves on incontestably valid facts and do not want to receive by way of response the defensive solidarity or counterattack that is a well-known consequence of all unjust and far-fetched generalization. This cautiousness is required because various arguments and counter-arguments are heard should anyone, foreign or Hungarian, Christian or Jewish, draw the conclusion that Hungarian society shares the responsibility for what happened.

The first counter-argument is that we were not the ones who did the extermination of millions of Jew; it was the Germans, and it would be an exaggeration to feel guilty and admit responsibility for their crimes. This is true and not argued. The question might be raised, however, whether we have a share in the responsibility for the *fact* and the *way* the Germans came in. But the question may be turned around; we may grant that there was a positive *chance* of protecting the Jews in the whole anti-Jewish legislation and storm-weathering tactic of the Teleki and Kállay cabinets, and let us lay the responsibility for the March 19 debacle of this policy on the leadership of the country. Let us therefore omit the responsibility of the Germans, as suggested above, and limit responsibility to what remains after them — namely, that the persecution and extermination of Jews was carried out with the conscious assistance of Hungarian civil and military authorities and that Hungarian society, with its various administrative and social bodies, simply *watched* the persecution, deportation, and killing of the Jews.

Another counter-argument often heard is that we ought to speak not of or not only of these, but also of the prisoners of war, wartime suffering, internments, and the abuses of power in the name of democracy; or, "better," it is argued, we should, with a view to all this, not say anything, draw a line, and regard all the suffering of the Jews as evened out by all the suffering of non-Jews for whatever reasons. The question about the mistakes and wrongs committed since the liberation is another issue. In this respect, we must unambiguously lay it down, first, that it is only in connection with prisoners of war, the *unjustly* interned, and the *unlawfully* harassed that we consider this matter at all because, I hope, no one, however compassionate about *all* sufferers, wants to regard the suffering that actual murderers and accomplices undergo when being punished as offsetting the terrible responsibility for the mass murders and monstrosities of 1944. Second, we must also make it unmistakably clear that only a part of these sufferings can be deemed retribution; the rest have no relation to the responsibility for the persecution of the Jews.

Third, it must be pointed out that no war captivity, internment, or police atrocity — all quite different in themselves — can be compared, even if they have had a death toll, to what happened to the Jews. I am not saying this to the mothers, wives, children, and relatives of those who fell victim to any of these because I have no right to rank their mourning and loss and those of Jewish mothers, wives, and children — though we know that, in mourning and loss, the circumstances do matter, and these were undoubtedly more horrific in the case of the Jews. But I am saying it to those who, either as onlookers or detained or harassed innocently, believe they have the right and ability to render a historical reckoning in which the two items set off each other. The imprisonments, privations, and insults on which they base this belong in the group of human sufferings that have, from the beginning of time, always accompanied war, collective detention, and political mass impeachment due to the harshness of historical conditions and the unconscientiousness, ruthlessness, arbitrariness, and corruption of men. We have every reason to fight these, but we should not lose the measure; it would be frivolous or spiteful to match any of them with the mass extermination of Jews.

Throughout not only the Christian era and civilization but in the many centuries of human viciousness, there has always been a limit on cruelty; a certain degree of clemency was to be shown toward the elderly, women, and children, and it was never breached in principle and only seldom in practice. By the intent of racist theory and leaders, however, the mass destruction and killing of Jews were equally directed against the elderly, women, and children as against men. The methods of selection and torturing unto death were such that tens of thousands of survivors lost their sanity in the clinical sense of the word. We have people walking and living in our midst who have had to watch or were capable of watching their naked and skinned mothers and wives being eyed, assaulted, and driven to death; we have parents in our midst who have had to watch or were capable of watching their children being staked, their infants being banged against walls; we have people in our midst who, on the brink of going mad, level the absolutely unfounded accusation against themselves that they let or sent their beloved on the road to death.

In contrast, those whose loved ones have died in shellings, prematurely through disease, or even due to human evil and cruelty, but in nevertheless more customary circumstances of dying, look serene and relieved because they wrestle with an old and familiar friend, abstract and impersonal Death, and not with the images of fury and sadism, artificial, man-made, dense Horror, of which one cannot rid oneself. If anyone has any good or less good reason to brush aside the idea that he might have a share in the responsibility for this yet imagines his own mother, wife, or child in the same situation, he might no longer be in the mood to weigh against these monstrosities so many years of war captivity, hunger-ridden internment, and police atrocity.

Fourth, it must be stated that should we have suffered the same in kind and amount in retribution, it would be reason enough only for not asking for forgiveness, not for evading heart-searching and shirking responsibility.

Another counter-argument often brought up is that the vast majority of Hungarians did not know what was going on in the extermination camps, and if anyone did hear of it, it sounded so improbable that he could not believe it. That one should not believe it on first hearing is only natural. The point, however, is not one's not believing at once or doubting as long as possible but that a man with a sound moral sensibility must be horrified and moved to action the moment the remotest *possibility* that such things could happen occur to him. We, however, started "disbelieving" in the extermination camps when we already knew enough about the deportation trains to believe in their existence; we doubted them not because of our undiminished trust in human decency but to shun our responsibility.

There is also the counter-argument that by overly and continually emphasizing our responsibility, we would afford the opportunity for those, whether at home or abroad, who were or are no better than ourselves to take political or moral advantage of our admission and to add to it political or other consequences or moral disadvantages we do not deserve. It is time, however, to stop enervating the moral fullness of any admission of responsibility by continually furtively squinting at others, wondering how it would affect the Jews, Czechoslovaks, foreign countries, or the world. If we are to take responsibility, let us face it without quibbling; this is the only way we can be a nation that has come of age and mend our morals. In the long run, we can be assured that our esteem in the eyes of the world and our comparison with others will hardly hinge on how much we admit, deny, and explain away but on how serious and resolute we are in establishing our responsibility; only if we do so will we be able to prove ourselves different, more worthy.

It is also usual to extenuate our responsibility by referring to the fact that the centers of action bringing disgrace to our name were the elite, the middle class, and the intelligentsia, while the people—the simple folk, the working class, and the peasantry—kept reprovingly away from it all. A reverse, though less-pronounced, version of this view has gained currency in middle-class and intellectual circles; according to it, it was the European-minded and educated layers that kept away, and it was lackland gentry and working-class boors that took pleasure in baiting and mugging Jews. There is also the view that holds that the Hungarian perpetrators were in fact of German extraction—both the top leadership and the common people.

As far as the elite and intelligentsia are concerned, their responsibility is beyond doubt, if only because they were leaders and intellectuals who were responsible not only for themselves, but for others too, for their influence on others, and for the bad example they set or the good example they failed to furnish. Indeed, on what grounds did they assume leadership if, now, they do not admit the responsibility of political and moral guidance, if, when called to account, they want to be treated as God-fearing, ordinary folk? If, however, our point is that it was the masters who were primarily active in the persecution of the Jews and that the people deliberately kept away from it, we will fall victim to a very dangerous and self-deluding romanticism: that the demise of the world of the masters and the rise of the people to power preclude the possibility of this same people being likewise irresponsible and uncompassionate in a similar situation in the future. Social and political change is not enough to achieve this; it certainly is a precondition of it, but it requires serious growth in political and moral thoughtfulness.

It is of course all the more false to state that the lower classes were the more base and inhumane during the persecution of the Jews. What is true is that it was the *genuinely* refined members of every layer that truly kept away from the horrors, but it is so self-evident that it goes without saying. Saying this with particular emphasis, however, is expressly dangerous; it is a lesson learned long ago that whatever good score refined men in Hungary earn, it is the *masters* who want to benefit by it because they believe that they and refinement are one.

The truth is that if we take a more thorough look at the class distribution of the participants in the anti-Jewish persecutions, we will find among them the serf-driver, peasant-smacker, and tyrannizing, upper-crust representatives of the public administration but also urban civil servants and other members of the middle class, some of whom exemplified a cruelty and thug instinct that even a disillusioned onlooker would never have assumed. The remainder chimed in with the upper- and middle-class standards of European refinement and humanity but was far too passive to significantly alter the moral reckoning of the Hungarian elite.

As far as the people are concerned, the petit bourgeois and semi-proletarian layers who, caught in the impasses of social development, easily responded to fascism, and the totally unscrupulous proletarian scum were likewise represented in appropriate numbers in manhunts and robberies. The remaining class-conscious, organized proletarians displayed a conduct worthy of justification, but, in turn, they were equally members of the proletariat as whole. *Comparatively*, the peasantry kept furthest away from the events; this was partly natural peasant aversion, partly human decency and helpfulness, but it was not a conscious and common moral stand. Finally, as to the role of German blood, many Hungarians of German stock, in undoubtedly greater proportions than average Hungarians, swallowed German racial theory, discovered the German blood in their veins, and felt they should participate in whatever the Germans were involved in; and, were they deterred by any incident, they turned a blind eye to it or deluded themselves and worked themselves into it. All in all, it would be self-delusive fallacy to hold that Hungarian involvement and responsibility was virtually limited to Hungarians of German extraction.

As a last argument against admitting our responsibility it might be brought up that if we have such clear explanations of all the social and political factors, historical shocks, misleading experiences, community impasses, and ill-conditionings that have determined and led the conduct of Hungarian society, why speak of guilt and responsibility when it was the great processes of history that were at work and that should primarily be understood, particularly not overmoralized in the divinity-class terms of guilt and responsibility. This would, however, be an utter misunderstanding of the issue and the nature of guilt and responsibility. A perpetrator's guilt and responsibility are established not by proving that he acted on the basis of *not* his social, community, or educational and personal determinants but, irrespective of these, his free choice to do evil; and, conversely, should he prove that he merely yielded to various determining causes and precedents, he will not be held guilty and responsible. Evil, paltriness, and cowardice consist not in any free and dauntingly devilish choice but in the very fact that we wretchedly, unconsciously, and without free choice do and only do what our social, community, educational and personal characteristics, warped and warping experiences, ingrained biases, meaningless platitudes, and comfortable and foolish formulas dispose us to do. True, there is little point in discussing the *admission* of responsibility in the case of such a man because not even does its meaning reach his consciousness. Yet this does not exempt him from being *held* responsible—in other words, from having to face the consequences of his deeds.

Adulthood and freedom begin when we recognize the paltriness of our actions determined merely by precedents, when we start admitting responsibility, acting freely and responsibly. In Christian terms, sinful man acts in the bondage of original sin, and whatever good he may have done, he was compelled to do it by the law and is therefore worthless; but man, when redeemed and saved, acts by the spirit, freely. In Marxist terms, the actions of man are determined by his class relations; yet if he recognizes them, he will take his stand consciously, and when his class relations put him in the service of the cause of historical development, he will do so consciously; if, however, his class relations turn him against the cause of historical development, he will set himself against his class.

It is in this context that we have to raise the issue of our own, our nation's, and our society's responsibility. If Hungarian society is indeed a serf-minded and herd-wise one that dumps the issues of responsibility on its masters and occupiers, there is no point in raising the question; it will reject it. But I do not believe Hungarian society was or is so deeply lost in this herd-mindedness and in being downtrodden. However much it has not been able to find the real route of its advancement in the past hundred years, it has ceaselessly and consciously been seeking it, with its no lack of great minds taking the lead in the quest. However exasperating it was for us to experience the impasse that Hungarian political and social development slid into in the past century, and particularly in the past decades, and however dire the deadlock in which it was caught during the war, again and again we always expected and hoped that there would be something to set the good in motion, something that would make us feel that not all had been wasted. True, the irresponsibility and the inability of the country to size up the situation and stand its ground in 1944 were beyond our worst expectations. But if we did have more or less reason to expect better, as nations no better than ourselves appear to have put up a better performance and as Hungarians have recently again evinced many a hopeful stirring, then, after all, there is a point in discussing the issues of admitting responsibility and hoping that it will find a response in this country.

We cannot, however, say that taking responsibility *in the name* of the whole nation, society in its entirety, would be straightforward and would surely prompt a response. If this were so straightforward and sure, it would already have happened; we know that attempts at it have miscarried. We have already noted the irritation at a declaration asking Jews for their *forgiveness* in the name of its authors and others. It might be said that asking for forgiveness is perhaps not the right way of putting it because being addressed to the other or others, it carries the danger that the addresser will overdo the humiliation and that the addressee might put on airs of conceit and condescension. A society with a vigorous spirit of admitting responsibility would probably not have found fault with the words or formulas but would have appropriately corrected them and gone on to the essence, establishing, admitting, and bearing the responsibility. This is not what happened with us. The response was a rather irate rejection, and it will be difficult to convince society to give up the arguments or pseudo-arguments it has put forward against admitting responsibility. Now, if anyone wants to say something pithy and true in the name of the Hungarian nation and society, he will undoubtedly face the same annoyed question: Who charged you with that?

The only thing to do in this situation is to establish and admit one's own *personal* share of the responsibility. To state that, for instance, what the author did out of conscience or to help—try to help—when asked was deplorably and pathetically little; what a far cry it was from what should or could have been done; how much it was held back by futile caution and lack of charity; how much it lacked, beyond the effort to make goodwill felt, the pledge for the full care of those that turned to him for help and taking their rescue fully in hand; and that he merely slipped into, rather than consciously went up against, running risks. Everyone should make this reckoning for himself and focus not on his merits or excuses and on how these set off his wrongs or neglects but on what he is *responsible* for, on what he *shares* the responsibility for. In due course, this might lead to a clearer, more courageous, and common national reckoning more ready to face responsibility.

Had we come out with this at the time of the liberation, we could have concluded the matter. We would not have shed light on all the ramifications of the problem but would have said what would have been all too important to have been said after 1944. In the meantime, three years have elapsed, and a new anti-Semitism has cropped up—or the old one has been reborn, and the most common response to any broaching of our responsibility in the mass destruction of Jews is, as mentioned, why we fail to speak of the suffering that non-Jews have had to undergo after that. We cannot therefore avoid discussing the resurgence of anti-Semitism and its causes. Not that, as we have pointed out, the two types of suffering can with any seriousness be matched or placed on an equal footing but because the only way to puncture—at least—a hole in the wall people build around themselves out of suffering, grievance, and a bad conscience is by the force of truth.

II. JEWS AND ANTI-SEMITES

Anti-Semitism resurging in our day, we cannot restrict our analysis to the current situation and events in Hungary. Before that, we will have to examine the origins and causes of anti-Semitism in its full breadth, as well as the social and mental conditions that defined the place of European Jews in the world around them. We have no intention of delving into all the religious, psychological, and economic aspects of anti-Semitism—otherwise we would never reach the end. Our focus is on anti-Semitism as a pathological social phenomenon, particularly the form in which it recently gained political significance in Central Europe. We will therefore only consider the various religious, psychological, and economic factors insofar as they can be reckoned as causes, antecedents, or explanations of the pathological phenomenon.

VIEWS ON JEWRY AND ANTI-SEMITISM

What kind of social entity is European Jewry? For decades, the way this has been put to Hungarian public life was whether it is a race or a denomination.

The wildest anti-Semites and assimilationist Jews agree on putting the question in this way. The anti-Semite is up and proving—it being true, easily—that
the defining significance of Jewish community extends well beyond the area
to which the defining significance of European Christian denominations has
been limited since secularization, and he then draws the conclusion that Jews
are not a denomination but a race. Anti-racists will easily prove, it being true,
that there is no Jewish race; the physical features regarded as typically Jewish
are those of not one but least ten different types, often contradicting each other;
thus the conclusion can be drawn that Jews are not a race but a denomination. The question is therefore put falsely. Zionists, Jews with a national and
political consciousness, hold that Jews are neither a race nor a denomination
but a nation or national minority. But this is true only of politically conscious
Jews; those are genuinely a nation or a national minority. However, not all Jews
belong to a single nation; not all of them share a common national identity, a
common state, or an effort to establish a state. All that the Zionists and others
can say is that they *ought* to share these, that people ought to become conscious
of them. Yet according to all signs, a significant number of Jews do not and will
not take this road. It is thus impossible to grasp in a word, a single formula, the
social situation of Jews, who are in a state of transition in many directions.

In what follows, *Jews* or *Jewry* do not mean and cannot mean the same circle
of people. They mean a range of people at varying boundaries, depending on
the context—those belonging to the ritual community if the ancient community is broached; the followers of the Jewish faith if that is in question; those
with a national context when the Jewish nation or minority is discussed; those
belonging to some sort of Jewish community when the psychological reactions
or conduct of Jews are mentioned; those that their non-Jewish environment
identifies as Jews; and the circle defined as such by persecutors when the persecution of Jews is concerned. I see no point in using any other term than "Jew";
earlier this was avoided, but both Jews and non-Jews use it, and calling them
"Israelites" sounds far too archaic and official, as does "fellow citizens of the
Mosaic faith."

While we have only a handful of opinions on the nature of Jewry to contrast, there is a great variety of explanations about the nature and causes of anti-
Semitism, even when considering only those that claim objective validity and
factual support. According to one of the widespread explanations, anti-Semitism
is rooted in medieval, fanatic *prejudice*, which imputed the crucifixion of Christ
to them and, moreover, leveled various superstitious charges against them. Anti-
Semitism in its current secular form thus essentially descends from this medieval prejudice, and the fight against it would be the same as fighting religious

intolerance, persecution, superstition, and ignorance. This explanation has a good grasp of the starting point but cannot explain how anti-Semitism as a prejudice with religious origins modulated into a prejudice of people for whom religion had no significance in this respect. This explanation has a history-of-ideas quality about it: a prejudice with religious roots takes shape for some reason somewhere, then it begins to live a life of its own, spreads, infests, cuts its religious roots, becomes an independent "ism," and grows in intensity, yet its fundamental cause remains the same as ever.

Historical materialism, however, holds that the causes of anti-Semitism are not ideological but economic and social. Emancipated and increasingly well-to-do, Jews, from the outset, met opposition from anti-emancipationist, feudal quarters and to some extent even from the established middle classes; subsequently, the latter made their deal with them, but the moment that organized labor posed the threat of finally overthrowing feudalism and capital, feudal forces and non-Jewish capital began to fan the anti-Semitism of the ignorant petit bourgeois and scum-proletarian crowds to divert the disposition of the masses and support various pseudo-revolutionary and fascist mass movements. This is how modern anti-Semitism was born, and it will necessarily cease the moment the feudal and capitalist economic order falls and a classless society is seriously set up. This explanation points out relations of indubitable existence and nature, and a society based on an equality of grade and rank will no doubt wither away all movements based on the fundamental difference between men in rank and grade. Yet this view cannot explain why the recalcitrance of certain masses can be turned precisely into anti-Semitism, why it is possible to make multitudes of people believe the obvious folly—one rebuttable with the simplest of facts, contradicting their own experience and interests, yet given credence again and again—that there is a secret agreement between the Jewish industrialist and the Jewish union secretary.

Less portentous than these, a third group of explanations starts out from certain *mental* reactions. One of these attributes anti-Semitism to the *envy* arising due to Jews' growing wealthy, their ability to make money, their talents, and their various successes; or to their being *different* in several respects, a condition that in itself irritates their environment; or to the fact that callous and evil-minded men have a general need to disdain, persecute, and hate others, and, to be able to do so, they choose a group apt for this, separate it, level various unfounded charges against it, and thus gratify their base and aggressive instincts. This certainly is a fundamental factor in the mass hysteria of anti-Semitism, but, yet again, it cannot explain why the same fury is seldom vented at groups that are relatively unprotected or even less protected and also why envy can be successfully "diverted" from moneyed or successful non-Jews to Jews, even *poor* and *unsuccessful* Jews.

Freud's well-known deep-psychology explanation holds that the basis of anti-Semitism is the charge that Jews murdered God but would not admit to it, whereas Christians do and are cleansed from the guilt; at the background of this we have the archetypal guilt of parricide or parricidal desires in archaic communities or childhood.[5] Freud also suggests that certain new, fundamentally pagan tribes abreacted their exasperation at having been forcibly converted to Christianity in the actions against Jews, the predecessors of Christianity. That the definitive starting point of European anti-Semitism is the medieval charge that Jews crucified Christ is perfectly credible, but the idea of anti-Semitism as a retaliation for forced conversion, obviously prompted by the dual hatred of Nazis for Jews and Christians, seems less convincing. However, applying the concepts of psychoanalysis devised for individuals, such as trauma, repression, inhibition, guilt, complex, compensation, abreaction, and release, directly to community phenomena and relations is surely doubtful. Analogies may be extremely productive, but the very decisive factors of concealment and unconsciousness occur in community life quite differently.

According to a simpler psychological explanation, anti-Semitism has the guilt and remorse for the injustices and cruelties committed against Jews at its background. Such moments do have a role in anti-Semitism but only *after* major anti-Jewish persecutions; anyone acquainted with the devilish image anti-Semites have of Jews will know that the suggestion that, deep in their hearts or unconsciously, they feel guilty about the injustices done to Jews among themselves will not hold water.

A less profound yet widespread notion is that *distinctions* among people — any emphasis on, study, or mention of them, *generalizations* about them — from the outset involve the danger of contempt, scorn, and unfounded accusation, and anti-Semitism has its origins in such distinctions and generalizations. Recall, at the time of the first German anti-Jewish acts, the sarcastic witticisms, parodies, and jokes made mostly outside Germany about blonds, the green-eyed, or the knock-kneed being distinguished, herded into ghettoes, and forbidden to be married on the same basis as anyone else. Certainly, such distinctions and generalizations make up the framework, the formulas, and the "logic" of all disdain and persecution. That they have an important role among the *causes* of anti-Semitism and similar phenomena, however, is only convincing for those who have suffered the consequences said to be their "due" on account of such unjust distinctions or untruthful generalizations. Nevertheless, men actually deride and persecute their fellows not because they were not taught not to make distinctions and wrong generalizations; precisely the other way round, they make distinctions and generalization because they want to satisfy the various urges that their grievances and irritating experiences have engendered in them; a man pursuing amends seldom has the opportunity of and is seldom satisfied by avenging himself on his actual injurer; in his stead, he seeks out others on whom he can transfer his passions by way of identification and *generalization*.

In contrast to these explanations of anti-Semitism, which see it is a force directed at Jews from without, we have explanations that see it as a sort of rebound Jews elicit. Among these, I will not consider the theological explanation, my being beyond scholarly deliberation, that the source of all the trouble is that the Jews did not accept Christianity, which had been proclaimed first and foremost among and for them. The only moment that has any validity in this for the social sciences is that had the Jews taken up Christianity at the dawn of the Middle Ages, none of their purportedly racial characteristics would have obstructed the concerns about them becoming void in the course of time. Whether this would have been beneficial or detrimental to them or the world is an alternative put over a millennium after the event—and is therefore unrealistic and unhistorical to ponder.

One such explanation emphasizes a social process picked out from its context, holding that anti-Semitism was a reaction to the rapid and vast expansion in public and economic life of Jews who broke away from their closed religious community, began to assimilate, or were assimilated. The moment that is true in this is that modern anti-Semitism is not a direct, history-of-ideas descendant of medieval, religion-tainted anti-Semitism but that it feeds on modern impulses that indeed relate to the appearance of emancipated Jews coming from their closed religious community into society and the various professions. Jewish expansion, however, does not offer a genuine explanation because modern times have emancipated not only Jews, but also commoners, serfs, laborers, and women, and these emancipations have themselves led to expansions and conflicts—conflicts far more significant from the point of view of social development yet never reaching the destructive and murderous consequences that anti-Semitism has had.

There is also the explanation that, basing itself on problems of *community affiliation*, stresses that one of the main causes of anti-Semitism is the lack of honesty in the assimilationist position of Jews. For all their insistence on merging with the nations around them and claiming indiscriminate equality, they have retained their separate community identity in their conduct, and they have not come out with this essentially self-sufficient national or minority consciousness because otherwise they would not have been able to hold important and advantageous positions in the general public life of the nation concerned. What is certainly true in this is that Jewish assimilation is replete with incongruities; however, this has been resented mostly by intellectuals concerned about community feeling and the ideological, moral, and practical issues of community affiliation, rather than by anti-Semitic masses.

Finally, we have the rather superfluous but widespread explanation that assumes various characteristic *Jewish features*, Jewish virtues or vices, on the basis of historical, sociological, or racial precedents and regards anti-Semitism as a rebound to these. Indeed, the question of the role of Jews in the rise of anti-Semitism, in shedding light on it, has to be raised. It is doubtful, however, whether we will be able to establish any invariable Jewish self that can be put forward in theses and be verified by serious methods, but we can find more or less enduring individual or community forms of conduct that will as a matter of course be counterbalanced by the similar or contrasting forms of conduct by the surrounding non-Jewish environment.

As opposed to these explanations, each based on a single formula and each usually self-seeking about the final result, we will have to set down a schedule in our quest for explanations, ranking the various possible points of view. I believe the correct ranking is the following; first, we have to understand the historical evolution and changes in Jewry as a *community*; the conditions of its combination with other communities, the society around it; the interactions of the resulting form of individual and community conduct; the rebounding effects of all this on individual and mass psychology; and then, finally, we have to place all this in the process of general social development.

JEWS IN MEDIEVAL CHRISTIAN SOCIETY

Some have traced the particular way the Jews have related to their surroundings and their various dispositions back to ancient times, some to their social situation in the Middle Ages, and yet others only to their modern life conditions, defined as they were by capitalism. Going back to ancient times has little social weight because the situation of Jewry has only meant a continuous and examinable relationship from medieval times. It is only worth going back further in time if one wants to dig up not an examinable community relationship but the indeed existing continuity of Jewish religious and metaphysical thought, the Jewish mind, fate, tragedy, calling, sin, or any other eternal Jewish essence. I am aware of attempts that seek to reveal a Jewish mind with a unified substance and a fundamental, continued aspiration (the kingdom of God on earth, etc.) in all manifestations of Jews from the beginning to the present. There are also anti-Semites who trace details of their current image of Jews back to Abraham. Anyone studying the inner world of Jewry will no doubt have to take into account factors going back to ancient times, such as the consciousness of the Chosen People, the flair for moral abstraction and speculation, etc. Nevertheless, I am staunchly convinced that none of these features can be used to explain actual community problems and that the decisive components of the place Jews have in their environment evolved in Europe in medieval times.

The approach that sees anti-Semitism as rooted in the transformations of modern times applies powerful and serious arguments but passes over an important psychological factor: the moral disparagement of Jews, which has had a decisive role in both the mental tribulations of Jews and anti-Semitism and which cannot be explained without unearthing its medieval context.

As difficult as it is to fit Jewry into current European types of community demarcations, so is it straightforward to place the medieval Jewish community. After the fall of their tribal state and their dispersion, Jews became a *ritual community* with national or tribal reminiscences. Ritual communities had a decisive importance in medieval Europe, as they continue to do more or less unchanged in the Middle East from Morocco to India. Throughout the world and in some areas of the Middle East to our day, their determining significance was more powerful than national or racial demarcations, binding and organizing the life, emotions and will, and community solidarity of people far more than the state, which remained but a power structure for a long time. By "ritual" we mean not a confessional or religious denomination in the modern sense but one that defined not only the religious convictions of its members, but also their entire individual and community way of life, social morals, day-to-day customs, and (to use a modern term) their full *ethnicity*.

In the beginning of modern times and in the Middle East only recently, these communities started to lose their significance and give way to national communities in the European sense; these built their structures around the central issue of maintaining or establishing the state and increasingly claimed the community feelings and solidarity of the masses. Ritual communities have had a central role in shaping nations, particularly in the Middle East and the Balkans. Indeed, ritual communities have established states and ritual differences have dismantled them. So it was that churches preserved the national identities of the peoples of the Balkans for a long time and that an Islamic Pakistan ceded from a Hindu India and a Christian Lebanon from an Islamic Syria. So it is that the state identity of many Arab states intertwines with Islamic consciousness and that Jewish-Arab national strife runs parallel to religious difference.

Originally, Jewry was one of these ritual communities of the Middle East and the Middle Ages; it was as such that it lived dispersed from England to Persia, from Morocco to Siberia. As a strange body, it wedged in between the social organizations of the surrounding two great civilizations, Christianity and Islam. What made the situation of Jewry unique in this environment was that it was not a primitive ritual community—as such, it would hardly have survived—but one based on a highly refined, developed religious worldview that both Christianity and Islam recognized as their predecessor and foundation.

At this point, the fate of Jews living in a Christian and an Islam environment split. From its beginning to recent times, Islamic civilization had lived in a fairly simple state and social structure established by warriors and conquerors who, for all their missionary zeal, defined the lives of the ritual communities they ruled through fairly plain and indifferent taxation schemes. The Jews lived the not too pleasant but regular life of closed ritual communities in this environment; they were sometimes oppressed, persecuted, or discriminated against, but usually they had a limited but ordered and human intercourse with the world around them. Being a Jew in the Islamic world was no worse than being a Parsi, a Nestorian, a Copt, or a Greek Orthodox; moreover, there was considerable cultural rapprochement between Jews and Muslims. Anti-Jewish feelings in the European sense are a totally new phenomenon in this area and relate to Jewish immigration and state foundation in Palestine.

MEDIEVAL ANTI-JEWISH PREJUDICE

In contrast, the situation of Jewry in Christendom was considerably graver and more complicated, due partly to the religious notions about Jewry and partly to the particular characteristics of medieval Christian social organization. The summary and simplified thesis that the Savior was "crucified by the Jews" formed part of medieval Christian religious consciousness. This was, it must be understood, what defined the life conditions of Jews and the anti-Semitism surrounding them in medieval Christendom.

We must halt at this point. Nowadays, when it has become burningly important to refute all opinions and views that might support anti-Semitism, it has often been pointed out that the thesis of Jews crucifying Christ is not at all an article of theology. We must first of all lay it down that though we are obviously at the historical root of anti-Semitism when discussing this thesis, it is most unlikely that refuting it is going to have an effect on the endurance or further spread of anti-Semitism. Second, we must emphasize that it is a symptom of deterioration that now, decades after the optimistic period of Jewish emancipation when no one ever gave a thought to theological stances that might govern the predicament of Jews, even non-church publicists find it important and necessary that the churches' position on the crucifixion of Christ be clarified. The churches might be pleased to take this as an occasion to put the issue in its proper theological perspective. However, the theological elucidation of the matter has become opportune not because theological inquiry has come to the fore but because the emancipation of Jews and men in general has proved to be an arduous process in Central Europe, and it has sometimes seemed better to retain and reinforce the meeker methods and narrower, less demanding but more solid guarantees of appreciating human dignity that medieval society had developed through theological categories.

Having made these remarks, we can now state that the thesis that the Jews crucified Christ is, in this form, not an article of theology, while, on the other hand, we have Jesus Christ and all his apostles and disciples as Jews. Beyond the immediate perpetrators, the responsibility lies with everyone as a result of original sin; the theological censure against Jews is not that they crucified Christ but that, though he declared the Gospel primarily to them, they have not recognized him as the Messiah.

This was the way medieval divines and theologically trained social thinkers knew it, and they thus prescribed not censuring or avenging Jews for the death of Christ but missionary zeal toward those of them that could be converted and keeping a distance from, imposing a strict control of, and limiting the social opportunities for and intercourse with those that would not convert. This hindered neither the clergy nor the laity in asserting, at a vulgar, emotional level, the responsibility of Jews in crucifying Jesus Christ. We should not forget the intense medieval passion for detailing the agony of Christ, naturally not concealing the role of the crucifiers. It was inescapable that this story should present Christ and the apostles as persecuted Christians and his crucifiers as Jews, however anachronistic this was and however Jewish they all might have been.

Medieval anti-Semitism as we know it meant that the common aversion to a closed ethnic and ritual community was reinforced by the church with a special religious reason, which was then corroborated and heightened to hysteria by the additional notion that this was a community that had murdered the founder of the Christian religion, the Son of God. And to top it all, the Jews were followers of a religion whose articles of faith, scriptures, and prophets they shared with Christianity. As a result, Jewish religious practice in the Middle Ages elicited notions not of alienation, paganism, or idol worship but downright sacrilege, which together with the charge of crucifixion gave rise to countless hair-raising stories of Jewish religious observance.

Another factor determining the situation of Jews in medieval Christendom was their social organization. Particularly in Western Europe, this was built not on simple power relations but on relationships of rank, service, solidarity, and heritage. These included even the humblest occupations that had little to do with the possessors of power and were predefined and religiously ordained in all their moral and practical aspects. These relationships, along with traditional procedures and existential guarantees, meant, at least where the system functioned appropriately, relatively humane and safe conditions for those within, though it also brought along an overly detailed definition and circumspection of the qualitative differentiation among men and its moral consequences.

This powerful moralization of human relationships made raw power relations more tractable and humanized them at many points, though it also reinforced and stiffened them. This, in turn, entailed, apart from the oppression, added psychological pressure on the lowly and particularly the outsider groups; think of the servility that, so to speak, turned into the blood of European servant groups! Nevertheless, compared to former systems, this one did give something new to everyone. There were only two classes of man, the Fallen Woman and the Jew, that felt the terrifying pressure the system wielded through its disadvantages and moral judgment. Forgoing their class, repentance and conversion were open to them, but retaining their class would be allowed no mitigation, no office, and no blessing; by the practical categories of medieval social morality, a prostitute could hardly be distinguished from a professional cut-throat robber and a Jew from a sacrileger. In practice, however, they could not be continually treated as such, but the possibility was always open that their treatment could be aggravated or deteriorate to this level—all streaks of moral stringency seeking to make their situation unbearable. Hence the fact that the human atmosphere of prostitution has nowhere been as repulsive as in European civilization and that there has been no minority exposed to as much and as enduring a social and psychological pressure as the Jews.

Thus, religious notions and social organization defined the conditions in which European Jewry lived throughout the long centuries of the Middle Ages and much of the modern era, being sometimes even territorially separated and isolated; sometimes afforded free movement; sometimes surrounded by the express spite of authorities and society; sometimes in traditionally regulated and predictable intercourse with non-Jews; sometimes under small-minded, harsh, and discriminatory laws or only a few limitations on taking public office. All these varieties, however, generally remained within the limits of the official positions of the church and the social organizations it sanctified.

There were various mass hysterias, however, always ready to make a rush at the Jews. The official position toward the Jews—that is, the prescription of keeping a distance and moral judgment—was thus eked out by various emotional excesses, mass moods, filthy money scuffles, and power schemes, sometimes erupting in bloody and violent atrocities. The position of the church did not encourage these excesses, but sometimes, in response to mass moods, interests of power, and religious austerity movements, it did take up a harsher line, as in the most outrageous instance, the forced baptism of Spanish Jews—and Muslims— and their expulsion under the pretext that they had retained their religious customs and practices in secret. The governing considerations, however, remained within the limits defined by the application of religious criteria, and no forces appeared that would sever anti-Semitism from its religious roots.

Herein lies the truth of the thesis that modern anti-Semitism "descends" from the medieval prejudice. Though it cannot be traced back to it directly, the medieval prejudice created the starting point and conditions of anti-Semitism in two ways. It was responsible for, first, the marked communal and social demarcation of the Jews, and it was also at this time that the demarcation was formulated beyond its social aspects, in sharp moral judgment too. In other words, it was at this time that the social condition of Jews came to be linked with the possibility and habit of their human and moral disparagement. It was also under this pressure that the forms of conduct the non-Jewish environment identified as characteristically Jewish "features" evolved, and these continued to preserve their role in the rebounds and emotional material of modern anti-Semitism even when the medieval religion-based anti-Jewish prejudice had become much weaker or ceased to prevail.

JEWISH EMANCIPATION

From the beginning of the modern era, the situation of Jews in European civilization started to gradually change. The issues the Reformation raised and the rebounding effects of the religious wars ripened the objectives of religious tolerance and freedom of conscience, which were to have a bearing on the situation of Jews too. The small, close, and personal units and relationships of the Middle Ages, which could only be realized through human qualities strictly circumscribed by upbringing and custom, gave way to larger units, more generally formulated conditions, and more rational methods. In the social and economic order these defined, the Jewish quality could no longer constitute a closed and separate condition with no intercourse with the rest of the world or with one based on conditions not equal. The opportunities of capitalism increasingly opened up for Jews as well. Many have pointed out that Jews can be neither credited nor held accountable for the creation of Western capitalism, yet the advent of capitalism brought about a relatively high degree of Jewish prosperity even in Western Europe, which had a strong non-Jewish bourgeoisie, but it gave them a prominent place in Central and Eastern Europe. The principles of bourgeois social organization reduced the significance of a feudal-aristocratic selection but retained, moreover reinforced, a wealth-based one, a shift that was beneficial for the assimilation of Jews, who, though little influenced by European middle-class development and bourgeois revolution, had lived under similar conditions; lacking a military aristocracy, selection among them was heavily influenced by wealth.

Parallel to this, public thought began to be secularized, breaking loose of religious categories, religion-based prejudices, and church authority and control. Even at the political level, the French Revolution brought about the awareness that the church had lost its social role and birthright social qualities had been eliminated. Social and intellectual life secularized almost through and through; the emancipation of those layers and groups was put on the agenda whose disadvantage had been rooted in the old hierarchical concept of society, the supposition of a qualitative difference among men. Among them, Jews were also emancipated, freed from all discrimination. Secularization began to undermine the Jewish ritual community as well, forcing it to choose between voluntarily maintaining or giving up the closed ritual and ethnic community—the latter option being particularly urged by enlightened intellectual groups, the begetters of the emancipation program. As a consequence, even observant Jews began to lose the traits of ethnicity not expressly required by ritual law. Moreover, a new position also developed, forgoing all the non-worship requirements of ritual law and the various dietary, dress, and procedural rules. The demarcation between Jews and non-Jews became fluid, and thus the more or less forceful, superficial or deep, individual or en masse, assimilation of Jews began. First sporadically, then in increasing numbers, Jews started to fully break away from their community, converting to Christianity or becoming free thinkers and anti-clericals or joining labor parties and unions.

In the meanwhile, the medieval anti-Jewish prejudice ceased to determine the general climate of opinion, yet it continued to influence the views and attitudes of many, conserving the modes of intercourse that had evolved during the seclusion of the Middles Ages. Thus remained the willingness to morally disparage Jews; the sense of non-Jews' superior and the Jews' inferior, disadvantageous condition; the conditioning that it was not customary, necessary, or good to associate with Jews, particularly on an equal footing, and to make friends with or to marry them; the belief that Jewish descent or strain was a handicap, shameful or at least unwanted; and the attitude that there was an alien air about Jews, whereby they simultaneously posed a threat of moral impairment or deception and appeared comical and ridiculous.

On the other hand, for all the fallaways, the successful or less successful assimilation, Jewry remained a clearly discernible community with its own internal life, and it continued to be the permanent and unchanged environment of its members in spite of their casting off the visible features of rite and ethnicity. The non-Jewish and Jewish intellectuals that had initially formulated the program of Jewish emancipation had taken it for granted that the abandonment of the Jewish ritual community would mean melting into the national environment, but the more conservative or identity-conscious part of Jewry would not follow suit and retained its particular sense of community. This communal separation and the less friendly conduct toward Jews undermined the belief in a smooth emancipation and assimilation and ripened the concept of a separate Jewish national identity, the movement for establishing an independent Jewish state, Zionism.

Nevertheless, in the wake of the Jewish emancipation, anti-Jewish prejudice waned, the non-friendly approach to them mellowed, and Jewry as a community shrank throughout Europe, and the process has continued in several countries to our day. From the middle of the nineteenth century, however, attitudes opposing Jewish emancipation and assimilation began to appear sporadically and amorphously at first and then to crystallize into a clearly delineated position, ideology, and movement, *modern anti-Semitism*.

THE RUB OF EXPLAINING ANTI-SEMITISM

Most European countries saw the rise of modern anti-Semitism in the middle of the nineteenth century. Anti-Jewish opinions and moods began to be vented, the fear of being regarded antiquated or reactionary slackened, and an obviously anti-Jewish journalism spread. In tone and language, this anti-Semitism was far from orchestrated. One of its voices clearly arose from the irritation with which the old medieval and clerical view of society, already on the defensive, observed the process of modern social transformation and secularization and the Jews, who partly participated in and benefited by it. It used a sort of conservative, medieval, and clerical phraseology; applied church-ordained distinctions; respected baptism; and was in every respect a descendant of the anti-Semitism of the Middle Ages.

However, a characteristic and an apparently more powerful voice had recourse to neither religious-clerical language nor conservatism, justifying its anti-Jewish stance on grounds that had undoubtedly been brought up in medieval times but always in relation or concomitant to religious charges—Jews gaining ground in the economy, their role in politics and power, and their conduct. There was also a tenor that connected the aristocratic-medieval contempt for Jewish birth with the phraseology of modern nationalism, deeming Jews to be a threat to the nation and race. Not only did this not make use of religious notions, but it also extended its hatred of Jews to Christianity, which was rooted in Judaism and "favored" Jews. These modern, non-religious voices of anti-Semitism were the ones that gained political moment in various European countries and, finally, in the twentieth century, brought about the most monstrous persecution of Jews in history.

How did medieval prejudice and Jew-baiting become modern prejudice and persecution? Any serious attempt at explanation that seeks to put forward more than mere platitudes or imaginative suggestions will have to emphasize two decisive moments: first, the medieval *prejudice*, which, as we have noted above, had been imbued deep in the minds of both Christians and Jews and has lived on in various forms ever since; and second, the *disorders*, various setbacks, standstills, and crises *of modern social development* in the course of which, as we shall see, anti-Semitism, the heightened activity of the social forces with a stake in arresting social development, and the confusion of the political and social orientation of the masses appear simultaneously. Whether the stress is on the prejudice or the social crises, no serious explanation can afford to pass them by. Yet I cannot be satisfied even when joining the two; the whole process seems to be far too simple, the outcome of but human vice and folly, while the no less important question remains unanswered: What makes people believe and accept deceptive statements more easily about Jews than others based on social prejudice—a belief in, for example, witches or anti-landlord or anti-capitalist interests?

Explained by prejudice and social disorder, the anti-Semite, just as the Jew of the anti-Semite, is as dead as a doornail and is but a phantom; this situation might be appealing to the Jews, but it leaves them in total darkness about the *human* conditions of becoming anti-Semitic. Furthermore, it has nothing to say to those among the anti-Semites who have not turned savage and can still be convinced—they will not recognize themselves in the image. It must also be stressed that while conservative anti-Jewish prejudice is embraced by people who have few or only conventional, feudal, or patriarchal contacts with Jews, the modern, emotionally highly charged anti-Semitism is the prejudice of people who have had more or less close business, dependency, or intellectual contacts with them, without being necessarily or exclusively set against them through their economic interests.

There is the rub in the way of explaining anti-Semitism. If anyone knows anti-Semites a little, he will be perfectly aware that they come forward with their anti-Jewish theses, burning with the most earnest passion of personal experience. Without avail would we expound to them that they made them up due to prejudice, interest, or foggy ideology because many signs point in the very opposite direction; it is the emotional intensity of certain experiences that make them believe senseless biases and murky ideologies and regard them as enlightening. Moreover, quarters indifferent or benevolent to Jews have their own, so genuine experiences of Jews that they find anti-Semitism, though they do not share it, perfectly explicable for these experiences or their rebounding effects and think it quite unreasonable when Jews or others begin refuting anti-Semitism by questioning the genuineness of these experiences or by presenting them as general human experiences anyone can have anywhere if he so *wants* to.

On the other hand, if anyone knows Jews a little, he will be perfectly aware that nothing revolts them as deeply and earnestly as the suggestion that they might have a *decisive* role in causing or in representing anti-Semitism. For them, it is such an unquestionable experience that they are the party that suffers more and can justly claim more in the intercourse with their environment that any explanation of anti-Semitism as a "rebound" will seem a ploy easily seen through. The most they will allow is that the conduct of certain individual Jews might give occasion and opportunity to justify already existing aggressive or oppressive intentions that are driven by prejudice, interest, envy, or cloudy mysticism. As a result, Jews and those fighting anti-Semitism are compelled to deny or downplay the role of Jewish-elicited rebound in the coming into existence of anti-Semitism because, should they not do so, they would incite it. However, it is a commonplace Jews and non-Jews likewise know and take into account that the non-Jewish experience of Jews indeed has had a role in bringing about anti-Semitism. The anti-Semitic thesis is not that Jews are among the causes of anti-Semitism but that anti-Jewish urges and actions are *just* and *reasonable* responses to the experiences concerning Jews, and that thesis forgets that, in the face of those experiences, there are the experiences, even prior experiences, Jews have had.

EXCURSION ON COMMUNITY EXPERIENCES AND CHARACTERISTICS

Before unthreading this, we must first clarify what we mean by *experiences*, by Jews *experiencing* their non-Jewish environment and anti-Semites Jews. Philosophy regards, besides thought, experience as the source of acquiring knowledge and holds that the logically self-enclosed, self-propounding, and self-repeating mode of acquiring knowledge through thought must be complemented by the vigorous, intuitive, and testing mode of acquiring knowledge through experience for knowledge to deserve the name of knowledge. In our case, however, this is not an experience of vital relationships but a convulsive and riveted urge- and grievance-ridden experience. This kind of experience has the very opposite effect of common, useful, practical experience because, charged as it is with the sharp intensity of passion, it is fixed on one or one type of element in the infinite variety of experience, and though it is real to the highest degree, it is limited and extremely intense and therefore stands in the way of further experience grasping reality in its fullness.

Such deluding experiences acquire communal or social significance only when incongruous, false, or prejudiced social arrangements—not uncommon—lead people into being repeatedly deluded by such experiences about each other. At the moment, I can think of only a kitchen example, though one that will immediately drive home the entire community predicament. This is the social arrangement of the housewife and her domestic help in middle-class society, during the transition from a feudal hierarchical to a classless society. There is nothing more real than the endless series of experiences of housewives finding that their domestics are slothful, intractable, lacking good will, and untrustworthy. There is nothing more real than the experience of domestics finding that their madams are whimsical, erratic, inhuman, rigid, and straitlaced. For all the *genuineness* of these experiences, neither party is correct because social arrangements juxtapose them in a way that makes them necessarily and typically experience the bad about the other, even though each is the best example of her kind.

Why? Because the conditions of social arrangement that set them against one another are false and incongruent. Their entire relationship is transitory between patriarchal predominance and contractual detachment. As per their interests, they both expect something from the other, which, however, neither can obtain under the given conditions, wanting to secure for themselves the advantages of both a patriarchal and a contractual relationship. As a result, they both encounter, where their interests would want benevolence or compliance, rigid contractual objectivity and, where their interests would require scrupulous contractual fulfillment, the claim for compassionate favor or emotionally charged requests.

Their juxtaposition under false conditions and their mutually resulting *genuine* and *deceptive* experiences of injury do not mean that their injuries are equal. Moreover, the equal reality of their injuries is not going to hinder us in declaring that the truth of domestics is more powerful when *historical justice* is done. This, however, does not alter the recognition that the overall picture of the relation between housewives and domestics should be based not on an anti-master or anti-servant ideology but genuine social experience. By the same token, we have to try and seek those incongruent and deluding conditions of social arrangement under which Jews and non-Jews were juxtaposed and which have made them acquire bad experiences about each other to our day.

Before going into that, we must also clarify the question of community characteristics. Though, as mentioned already, no systematic description of the self, characteristics, or innate faculties of a community or group of people is possible with any serious hope of authenticity, it may nonetheless have features, characteristics, forms of conduct, and conditionings that are peculiar to it, distinguish and identify it in a given environment and period, and elicit simplifying generalizations from its surroundings. A community, group, or several people being in question, a "typical" or "characteristic" feature or conduct always implies merely a statistical proportion. That an Englishman is lean, smokes a pipe, and is self-possessed does not mean that all or the majority of Englishmen are such, only that the number of lean, pipe-smoking, and self-possessed men is greater among them than among others. The same applies to the types of human behavior that might be or are usually associated with Jews; they are not characteristic of all or most Jews; they simply occur more often among them than among others. This is perfectly enough for the surrounding society to regard them as *Jewish* traits. However logically inconsistent they might be, they are not in themselves a source of trouble; man summarizes and generalizes his experiences through them. The trouble comes when emotions appear alongside them, when people start attaching feelings, urges, and consequences to the features they regard as characteristic and distinctive.

THE MUTUAL EXPERIENCES OF JEWS AND NON-JEWS

1. SAGACITY

The experiences of Jews and non-Jews about each other necessarily begin with the *experiences of Jews* because the conditions under which they lived for the thousand years of the Middle Ages were undoubtedly defined by the surrounding non-Jewish society and its political, social, and ideological establishment. What experiences did Jews acquire of the world around them, and how were they conditioned to encounter it?

Their fundamental experience was that, not only because of their ritual and ethnic differences, but also the particular moral disparagement to which they were subject, they were excluded from the common occupations and opportunities of production and livelihood; the vast majority of guilds; allegiance communities; land communities; and the associations of production, welfare, culture, and religion that had a fundamental role in the characteristically European social arrangement. As a result, Jews were forced to linger on the fringes of economic, existential, and human opportunity; the only means of livelihood that were left open to them were those that society abandoned to them, warded off, or did not notice for some reason or other. Had Jewish ethnic separation been the same as that of the Gypsies, they would likewise have become musicians, adobe makers, and soothsayers, as there are analogous Jewish occupations too. Bred in a far more refined ethos, the Jews saw a moral and intellectual challenge in being thrust to the edges of human opportunity. Typically, they developed a permanent readiness, a quick and rational adaptation to circumstances, a keenness amounting to an obligatory sense of social responsibility not to leave out any newly recognized and opened possibility, and a conscious preference for and a familiarity with the rational means of handling opportunities, notably the most rational one: money.

It goes without saying that this sagacity was not a particularly Jewish invention but one of the feasible and widespread means of handling possibilities. In contrast, the traditional and customary mode was for people to base their livelihoods on habitual resources, procedures, and forms and to be generally disinclined to make use of opportunities outside them, should they notice them at all. Reality was naturally between the two extremes, as there can never be a traditionalism lacking reason or a rationalism without the guidance of well-trodden paths. The difference in the two attitudes lies in the ways they near the two extremes or the principles whereby they combine their borderline instances. Particularly in medieval times, human opportunities, livelihoods, and procedures were strictly defined and organized according to custom and tradition; in other words, social arrangements went against rational expedience and the putting to use of strictly personal qualities. In modern times, however, the advent of capitalism and a money economy turned the rational exploitation of opportunities into the social and economic norm. This change took place in the regions of the classical market economy quite apart from Jews, proving that this is not a characteristically Jewish feature, a mark of the Jewish self, but a conditioning that can come about in different social situations.

It ought not to be forgotten that though capitalism is regarded the fundamental principle of social organization in modern times, it became predominant only in America. In Europe, however, large strata—civil servants, medium- and small-scale manufacturers and tradesmen, and smallholder peasants—adapted their production modes and ways of life to capitalism only in acknowledging the conditions, participating in certain business opportunities, and consuming some mass-produced goods, but they retained and developed further their pre-capitalistic forms of human existence. In this situation, the mark of capitalism, which was to regard the rational approach to economic opportunity as "natural," was more beneficial to the Jews, who had already acquired such social conditionings before the advent of capitalism, than to the preceding feudal economic order. This explains the striking speed with which Jews in both Western and Eastern Europe came out from the total seclusion of their Middle Eastern ritual community—as it were, the very heart of medieval times—and picked up the modern, capitalistic methods of thriving, while significant layers, often the majority of European society out of which capitalism had evolved, remained indisposed to the principles of capitalism.

These changes in the structure and development of European society allowed for a wide range of sustenance for Jews, from deprivation at the fringes of opportunity to unmatched affluence. As an example of the lower end of making the best of opportunities others had not noticed and a grotesque, yet more than enlightening gloss on the penury of East European Jews, a Galician Jew comes to mind whose livelihood was to go around annual fairs with his corkscrew in hand and, for a few pennies, open wine bottles for peasants. There are of course the well-known examples at the other end of the spectrum, of rapid fortunes made in financial transactions. Whether it is this or that outcome that is realized is determined by how far the procedures of the surrounding society are defined by tradition; how closed or unmovable they are; or whether they can be broken through or loosened up. In the former example, a society closing up beats back like a stone wall all attempts at rational procedure—with particular acrimony if they are those of Jews. However, if traditional procedures are looser and can be toppled or broken through, a rational mode of proceeding will advance in a society not conditioned for it, yet tolerating it, as though it were a hot knife in butter, and achieve unexpected successes.

It was amid such conditions that Jews and non-Jews acquired their mutual experiences in the area of making use of opportunities. Even not apparently hostile, the surrounding non-Jewish society observes and notes that Jews tend to be more sagacious than others in finding the resources of sustenance; in choosing residence, profession, and lifestyle; in learning languages; in adapting to prosperity or scarcity; and in exploiting dips and booms; and whatever they have deemed best by their sagacity, they carry through and are less likely than others to be concerned about its being customary for either themselves or others. This conduct is so self-evident, natural, and all-governing to Jews that they hardly ever notice that it might strike others as *characteristic* of them individually or as a community. What they themselves are struck by is the conduct of their non-Jewish environment—that it is more likely to behave impractically than they do; more likely to leave possibilities that are opening up unnoticed; to not do what it has come to realize as expedient; to not adapt its lifestyle to the increase or decrease of its means but continue to act as required by its customs, biases, or demands, which outstrip or belittle its actual social condition; it readjusts not on recognition but exigency and makes its greatest efforts not when taking opportunities but when it seeks to secure the lifestyle or living standard to which it is accustomed or insists on.

As indefinite judgments, these can survive for a long time and do not necessarily lead to outbursts of passion and clashes. The non-Jewish environment formulates its fundamental experience with a pinch of appreciation here, a bit of derision there, envy here, express animosity there, saying simply that Jews are resourceful or, less amiably, that they are willing or want to exploit anything or, even less amiably, that they are swindlers and self-seekers. The fundamental experience of Jews, on the other hand, is that their non-Jewish environment is oddly and impractically conservative or, less amiably, helpless or, even less amiably, that it is blatantly foolish.

Most decisively, the individual or common business successes of Jews have been assessed quite divergently and utterly misread. Basing themselves on undoubtedly genuine experience, Jews have tended to think of all their successes as having been achieved in a closed-off and hostile world, under unequal conditions, because finally a greater knowledge and aptitude, a truer cause prevailed—but this holds only to a certain degree. In contrast, the non-Jewish environment, in keeping with its own experiences, has been likely to think that the successes of Jews are always easy gains, based on opportunities and means "decent" people would not use—and this, again, is only partially true. The non-Jewish environment has always been inclined to regard the difference between its procedures and those of the Jews' as its *moral* quality and the Jews' *moral* defect, and the Jews have had a penchant to think of this same difference as their *intellectual* quality and the environment's intellectual defect, while it is neither an intellectual nor a moral quality but a historically evolved conditioning.

2. DISPUTING THE SCALE OF VALUES

The second experience that determined the situation of Jews was that the world surrounding them charged them with various wrongs, passed moral judgment on them, treated them with moral contempt, and exposed them to hysterical outbursts and assaults at times, while it never established the truth of the charges.

The lesson many Jews drew from this fundamental experience was that the moral categories of the surrounding world were essentially flawed, spurious, and unjust, intended solely to cover up morally dubious intentions and dispositions. This resulted in a disillusioned and wary guard against the moral ideals and judgments of their environment, especially those applied to or against them, as well as the conviction that whoever saw through the ruse of these lies had a better judgment; higher moral standards; deeper, experience-hardened persuasions; and was more disillusioned but all the more superior to the world around him. A highly sophisticated Jewish religious ethic provided further ammunition for this suspicion and conviction.

How does this disillusionment and wariness relate to an *objective* reckoning of the social morals of the society surrounding them? The injustice leveled against the Jews by virtue of religious and moral categories from the early Middle Ages belonged among the borderline cases of the functioning or malfunctioning of medieval European social morals; it was not a necessary corollary of the Christian social and moral order, nor was it an *accidental* result of everlasting human folly, hypocrisy, and aggression that warps and abuses all moral systems, but it was an outcome *related* to the discordances and prejudices of medieval morality already mentioned—the excessive elaboration of the qualitative distinctions among men, their being far too closely bound up with the consequences of genuine faith and the unique place Christian religious thought accorded to Jewry.

We must nevertheless be aware that these features of medieval morality did have their historical accomplishments in their time. Linking morality with the *articles of faith* was a far more superior and rational foundation than a morality based on faith in magic power and ritual observance. The detailed elaboration of the moral significance of human qualities did indeed prepare the way for the principle of equal human dignity to overcome the social order based on sheer dominance and human dignity for only freemen.

Whatever *bearing* the medieval scale of social values had on anti-Jewish persecution, it is not enough to be able to determine whether the medieval and early modern European social and moral order was sound or not, effectual or not, worthy of retaining or ripe for casting off. The decay of a social and moral order actually takes place when its core principles and characteristic and typical instances come to manifest its discordances and injustices, and the judgment over them carries weight only if it is born of an internal confrontation with and thorough deliberation on its contradictions, injustices, and consequences and not of experiencing them in borderline cases.

In a moral and social order believed to be functional, congruous, and just for a long time, the world around the Jews therefore had far less reason to regard such opposition and rejection as justified. When facing such a rejection by Jews, its aversion to this critical stance was reinforced by its aversion to the critics themselves. This was how the fundamental now-Jewish experience of Jews evolved that they were by and large inclined to disdain the Christian scale of values, undermine social authority, find and expose base interests and dispositions behind sacrosanct and revered institutions, and have a predilection for the well-known type of humor that renders pathos-filled commonplaces comic by an unexpected, mocking turn of phrase.

Together with the more rational handling of economic opportunity, this perception contributed to the opinion among non-Jews that a large proportion of Jews tended to disregard the rules of everyday morality—that is, put simply, *cheat*—which anti-Jewish prejudice, in turn, would term as follows: Jewish morality sees nothing wrong in deceiving Christians. Hence, where society regarded anti-Jewish prejudice as "official," the use of the word "Christian" in expressions such as "Christian firm," "Christian lodger," and "Christian company," when applied against Jews, denoted "correct" or "trustworthy"—in other words, a social conduct expected of "decent" people.

Reinforced by their mutual experiences, Jews and non-Jews alike have attributed differences in their community conduct to their own moral superiority and the other's moral inferiority. This disdain of the scale of values of the other party then led to the vulgar perception that in the eyes of Jews, Christian social morality served but to cover up aggressive and thieving injustices, while Jewish social morality, in the eyes of Christians, was meant only to justify swindling and cunning. The delusion is mutual: there is nothing superior in being *loyal* to a system of social morality that is advantageous, customary, and emotionally close to us, and, likewise, there is nothing superior in being *critical* of a moral order that is hostile, unusual, and emotionally alien to us.

This aspect of the relationship of Jews and non-Jews had played an important part in the frictions that had sometimes flared up between them in the period of social seclusion, but it came to have an added significance following Jewish emancipation, and it multiplied the occasions when Jews could put across their criticism of the moral system of the world around them. Jewish emancipation itself was carried through by a trend in European social development that had turned against the medieval scale of values. However, irrespective of the Jewish emancipation, the same period saw serious attacks leveled against the centuries-old dominance of Christian ideas of social value. All at once, evidence burgeoned that the social order the Jews had experienced as discordant and unjust was indeed that or had at least become that. Thus the critical attitude of Jews, which had *ensued from their situation*, now became *modern* as well. Jews themselves had hardly brought along with them any of the trammels of the feudal master-serf relationship from their own secluded society, and it had precisely been owing to the fall of the feudal order that they had been emancipated. Moreover, it was those of them who came into closer contact with the surrounding world, emancipated Jews, who severed their traditional links to the greatest extent.

In contrast, however, the European society that surrounded Jews had been steeped in a social view based on the qualitative difference among men, even among the lowest in rank, affecting the inner structures of all layers and occupations and determining social relationships, conditionings, community, and emotional identities. The fall of this approach therefore meant a major shock. Exasperated and desperate, the various structures based on it could or would not acquiesce in their annihilation without putting up stubborn resistance, counterattacks and major hindrances. Thus, as this or that moral structure that Jews had observed with disillusioned criticism for a long while was indeed shaken under the blows of general modern social criticism, the social critical contentions of both Jews and more conservative non-Jews grew more pointed. Jews thus believed they had been proven right in the foresight of their criticism and the sharpness of their moral judgment; moreover, those who had not given up their Jewish identity put this in terms that it was the vocation and role of all of Jewry to bear the banner of reason, progress, modernity, and new values in an intellectually and morally rather slothful and unmoving world. The more conservative quarters of non-Jews or those more confounded by the toppling of the scale of values, however, would not recognize the democratic or progressive spirit of Jews as an example to be followed or a merit; moreover, quite to the contrary, they increasingly held that since Jews had obviously benefitted more or had been less afflicted by the fall of the old world than their non-Jewish counterparts, the changes took place in their interest and at their behest, offering astonishing evidence of their pernicious influence. To prove this, they kept tally of not only Jewish participation in the dissemination of modern social criticism and in social movements, but also on their taking the lead in the commonest matters of fashion, breaking away from old and introducing new vogues, not forgetting their role even though they themselves had given themselves over to what they had initially been averse to.

One of the consequences of Jewish emancipation in the relationship between Jews and non-Jews was that the different attitudes to the scale of values, which had been manifest in the mutual charges of aggression and fraudulence in relation to everyday morals and human intercourse in the secluded worlds of medieval times, now expanded into the more general planes of social criticism and politics as well.

3. GRIEVANCES AND THE PURSUIT OF AMENDS

The third fundamental experience of Jews is all the actual injustices, disadvantages, humiliation, harassment, and monstrous peril they have had to undergo while being forced to the fringes of human opportunity and being morally disparaged. That the actual suffering has hinged on moral disparagement has redoubled the suffering. All those firmly believing that they know all about oppression, humiliation, imperilment, or fear have not the faintest clue about the mental burden of the Jewish predicament: the never-ending defenselessness against the overweening clout of others, their murderous fits of rage, their unrelenting will to harm and belittle them. But even in less severe situations, in simple human and not even unfriendly relationships, it is stupefying how much minor injustice, inequality, and discrimination the surrounding world has forced forbearing Jews to stomach only because they are supposed to be used to worse.

The only possible response to this could be *to seek justice*, as it was the average, representative reaction, which also had its strong tradition in Jewish moral thought. What interests us now is that people are unable to rise above their subjective and egotistic approach to the affairs of the world and their own experience—in other words, the majority of both Jews and non-Jews—so seeking justice, which would have an objective validity, tends to lapse into the *pursuit of amends*, a state of mind fixed on offense, turning it into the sole driving force of conduct, cutting it off from the offenses and justice of others, presenting it as a prerogative and entitlement, and rendering it more important than justice. There is no need to recapitulate here the findings of modern psychology, according to which much of human conduct serves to make up for offenses suffered. Not only do offensive and aggressive behaviors belong here, but so also do all the varieties of pursuing compensation, including the itch to be conspicuous, undue sensitivity, and self-depreciation.

On the other hand, non-Jewish society also knows some degree of injury at the hands of Jews. Even though there was only a limited chance, especially in medieval times, for Jews to inflict harm on members of a far more powerful environment, it was hardly out of the question; in spite of the fact that recurrent charges against Jews smack of exaggeration and horror-story confabulation, it is impossible not to recognize among the ones more believable and palpable the well-known gestures of rational business methods, disillusioned criticism, and the pursuit of amends. The approach to Jews therefore also selects a major or lesser group of people in the non-Jewish environment among whose experience of Jews or "the" Jews the wrongs and injuries suffered at the hands of Jews play an important role.

To be sure, the wrongs Jews and non-Jews suffered do not and cannot be set against each other or regarded as on a par with one another. By objective standards, the injustice Jews have suffered throughout or during certain periods of history is simply incomparable with the various bad experiences or injuries non-Jews have had. However, people hemmed in in a closed system of personal injury will never see the objective quantity and significance of others' injuries or will see them only insofar as those injuries justify, reinforce, disturb or weaken their own. We should also be aware that those wittingly or unwittingly informed by the notion of Jewish inferiority will regard the offenses disdained Jews have committed as multiply humiliating — count them double, as it were — while they regard the wrongs Jews have suffered as not so grave, saying, "They've been used to it." In addition, even people with more goodwill toward them will unknowingly succumb to the suspicion that the miseries of Jews or their laments about them are not quite authentic and somewhat exaggerated.

This bears closely on the fact that Jews and non-Jews have for long not entered into, and still do not enter into, genuinely personal relationships; whatever personal intercourse or friction there is between them, it tends to be between them exclusively as Jews and non-Jews. Their encounters are thus impersonal, inhuman, *dehumanized.* This is why when they do enter into some association, they generally make a reckoning of their liabilities and claims not by virtue of their personal contacts but by their connecting with the other group as a whole, and so they easily find enough injury and grievance to exonerate themselves. As each party expects to receive full performance and personal gratitude from the other, both Jews and non-Jews record masses of "monstrous ingratitude" by the other in times of trouble. The situation is *mutual* in the sense that *pursuing amends* has, in proportion to the varying amount of injuries, become the manner of relating to one another. This was true of the seclusion of the Middle Ages, and though the emancipation of the Jews decreased the quantity of offenses, the mutual bent toward the pursuit of amends has had a far wider currency.

For the Jews, emancipation primarily and naturally meant that they would not be or be far less assaulted with impunity. Yet maltreatment or the chances of maltreatment did not decrease; their sense of security in the face of particularly non-immediate and non-physical harassment did not increase in proportion to the changes in their legal and theoretical status. In the ante-world, they had lived in the smug closeness of a self-contained and autonomous world, exposed to maltreatment only when venturing into the outer world or when being collectively attacked by that world. Now, they had abandoned their decaying old Jewish community and could associate in theory on equal terms and freely with their environment.

Harassment, however, not only failed to cease, but it also became erratic and was not limited in either occasion or motive, as it had been in the period of medieval prejudice. It could be driven by the residues of that prejudice and the willingness to which it led; by the mutual experiences and generalizations discussed above; or by the simple human propensity to attack people against whom one holds a grudge not only in their person, but also in their more conspicuous and general quality—upbraiding a cripple for being a cripple, an old man for being old, a Gypsy for being a Gypsy, a Jew for being a Jew—and adding various epithets as his rage dictates, a stance that is necessarily based on prejudice. The anti-Semite is not necessarily the one who attaches unfriendly adjectives to the word "Jew"; the anti-Semite is the one who uses the word "Jew" itself as a blasphemy. The historical experience of Jews, however, renders it impossible for them to see this distinction; for them, all insults recall the experience of being exposed to the old assaults; their experience tells them that serious harassment and bloody persecution always began with harping on Jews and unfounded generalizations and that these were potential latent humiliation, persecution, killing. However understandable, objectively, this is the same kind of "unfounded generalization" the non-Jewish world makes about the behavior of Jews, usually poisoning even friendly approaches to them.

This is the reason why the majority of Jews tends to regard emancipation as including protection against any unfounded generalizations about them, any unfriendly mention of them, and any belaboring or harping on them. This is why they are disposed to see those guilty of such behavior as accomplices to anti-Jewish persecution and enemies of all emancipation, liberation, and progress; to condemn them and have them condemned as such; and to expect all decent, charitable, and well-meaning people to treat such cases in these terms, and, of course, for themselves to abstain from any such manifestation. This demand is unrealistic and infeasible; these are insults all groups continuously

have to face, and Jews themselves keep committing the sin of unfounded generalizations about the various phenomena of their non-Jewish environment.

The majority of those that demonstrate a well-meaning unconcern or express
friendliness toward Jews fall into belaboring them behind their backs in the
sense that they are aware of their acquaintances' Jewish extraction, discuss it, or
enquire about it; they have more or less justified experiences of Jewry, bear in
mind characteristic Jewish traits, fall into "unjust generalizations," and, when
angered or insulted, they by fits and starts vilify the Jew in their way not only
as a man, but as a Jew. The only principled way to evade this is to be continually loyal to the sensitivity of all absent Jews, bearing in mind that displays of
emotion against or generalizations about them might have more awesome consequences than those about, for instance, the Portuguese, hunchbacks, or old
fogeys. This requires an austere moralist, but austere moralists fall short and
have their lapses too.

Jews sensing or discovering by a slip of the tongue that people making friends
with them desist from belaboring their Jewishness not out of *principle* but out of
tact willy-nilly begin to have the notion that the majority of—God forbid, all—
their environment goes on uninhibitedly about their Jewishness and is therefore
anti-Semitic. Over and above the realistic relation to the *actual* animosity of the
environment, this engenders a more or less make-believe relation to the *supposed* animosity of non-Jews, which, in turn, renders unallayable the tensions
resulting from the offensive and defensive attitudes of pursuing amends.

For the non-Jewish environment, Jewish emancipation meant that a wide
range of opportunities opened up for Jews to take up positions from which they
had been excluded and acquire clout. This increased the chances of maltreatment by Jews in both number and significance because those still living in a
world ranked by human quality would experience certain types of insult that
they had tolerated without a word from those higher in the traditional hierarchy
as an unforgivable offense and unmatched humiliation when committed by
upstart, "lower-ranking," and merely "emancipated" Jews.

All this meant but transitory hitches, short aftereffects of the old situation,
where Jewish emancipation was a *genuine* and *progressive* process. However,
where Jewish emancipation remained superficial and formal, where anti-
Semitism was rife, where it took on political forms as well, and where it was
able to provoke even anti-Jewish persecutions, the vicious circle of assault and
the pursuit of amends was set in motion, with the mental process of emancipation beginning all over again in the wake of the persecutions. What this meant
was that the processes discussed above, what would otherwise have been the

accidental features of transition, acquired a permanence and seemed to be the essential concomitants of the relationship between Jews and non-Jews.

THE JEWISH AND THE ANTI-SEMITIC WORLDVIEWS

We have thus seen the conditions in which Jews and non-Jews acquire their experiences of the other group in sagacity, in relating to the scales of values, and in insult and pursuing amends. False and inhuman social arrangements make both groups often as not encounter the more obscure and morally less committed members of their kind, reinforcing the formulation of their mutual, genuine yet partial experiences as generalizations with diametrically opposed meanings. Considerable quarters of non-Jews characteristically avoid uncustomary social and business opportunities, have an unquestioning belief in the social and moral rules of their own world, and tend to morally depreciate Jews. In their own eyes, these qualities appear to be traditional decency in social procedure, loyalty to social values, and a consciousness of being entitled to judge Jews, while in the eyes of Jews, these qualities are but helplessness, self-righteousness, narrow-mindedness, and an envious and aggressive injustice toward the Jews.

In contrast, prompted by their social and human predicament, Jews handle their social and business opportunities with a rational sagacity, formulate a suspicious and disillusioned social criticism of the moral principles of the society surrounding them, and pursue amends for the wrongs continually suffered. In their own eyes, living as they do in the closed world of their own experience, these can easily be idealized, seen as greater practical wisdom, superior in being morally more exacting, and purely seeking justice, while in the eyes of many a non-Jew, they can easily be presented as greedy profiteering by opportunists, the subversion of sacrosanct values, and vengeance-seeking power lust.

These contrary generalizations had not acquired a separate significance during the seclusion of the Middle Ages, being self-evident parts of the anti-Jewish prejudice of the environment and the inward consciousness of the self-contained Jewish ritual community and tallying with the official and actual relationship between Jews and non-Jews. After the Jewish emancipation, however, these experiences and the generalizations to which they gave rise lost their ideological backing, the old anti-Jewish prejudice becoming antiquated in the eyes of the public. Yet the truth was that mutually negative experiences continued to occur in wide areas and, as mentioned, sometimes were exacerbated and heightened. As a result, there was no longer an official anti-Jewish stance embracing all society, but an unbalanced group, the anti-Semites, stood out from the environment; their experiences of Jews were so sharp and one-sided that the generalizations at which they thereby arrived filled their entire worldview, divesting them of their ability to grasp reality in its fullness.

By "anti-Semites," we should mean not all those who *dislike* Jews, yet not only those inciting against or persecuting them, but all those who have developed and have become addicted to a comprehensive worldview based on the Jews' various dangerous characteristics—greedy and fraudulent profiteering, moral and political destructiveness, vindictiveness, and domineering. In this sense, an anti-Semite might be upright or base, meek or ruthless, innocent or guilty, but he or she has an essentially *warped*, convolutedly fixed view of *but one element of social reality*.

Naturally, that group of Jews for whom the bitterness and injustice of Jewish experience befogged all other experience became even more distinct. This had actually been the attitude of Jews during the medieval seclusion, and how far their proportion among other Jews would decrease with emancipation depended on the concord within the surrounding community and the humanness or inhumanness of the relationship between Jews and non-Jews.

This is why it is so hopeless or preterhuman to try and bring Jews around to grasp the psychological reality of anti-Semitism and the non-Jewish environment to grasp the reality of the Jewish predicament and experience. Jews of a more closed mind will simply not believe that the dispositions of the anti-Semites—regardless of the sinisterness of their prejudices and the mistakenness of their generalizations—are based on genuine experience and feeling; quite to the contrary, they sincerely believe that the anti-Semites when meeting in their secret chambers are perfectly aware of their baseness and injustice. Likewise, the anti-Semites firmly believe that Jews, between themselves and deep in their hearts, admit to the truth of what or most of what anti-Semites say of them.

ANTI-JEWISH PREJUDICE AND EXPERIENCE

The weightiest argument against contrasting the two worldviews in this way is that the two types of experience, *measured objectively*, are *unequal*. On the one hand, there are the experiences of Jews, the reality of which is beyond the shadow of a doubt. On the other hand, there are the so-called experiences of anti-Semites, which prejudice artificially creates or, at least, one-sidedly picks out. It is therefore entirely misleading and even dangerous to discuss the two types of experience in parallel because whoever wishes to can assess the moral equality of the views and the positions to which they lead. This is the opinion that is expressed in the punch line: there is no Jewish question, only anti-

Semitism; anyone broaching the Jewish question wittingly or unwittingly brings grist to the mill of anti-Semitism.

As noted, this is the rub in explaining the entire problematic of the Jewish question and anti-Semitism, to which we have to return, having covered the whole area of the experience concerned. As our starting point, we have to accept that the *final causes* of the inhuman relationship between Jews and non-Jews are finally rooted in the dispositions of the latter and that its *consequences* are disproportionately more grievous on the side of the actions of the latter.

As proved again and again by all detailed investigations, the primary cause of all deterioration in the relationship between Jews and their environment was the medieval, religion-based *prejudice*. This prejudice was what made the environment have a preconceived aversion toward them and an inclination to maltreat them; this prejudice was what established the inhuman or dehumanized conditions and atmosphere—not necessarily ruthless but always devoid of decency—that created the forms of conduct of Jews toward that environment; finally, this prejudice and the sharp demarcation of the Jewish community had a decisive role in the rapid and easy formulation of unabashed and blunt views on the experiences concerning Jews. Yet notwithstanding its influence on assessing experience, *prejudice of itself never brings experience into being*; the prejudice of people who have no experience of encountering Jews, a principled anti-Semitism, may be distasteful or embarrassing, but it will always remain harmless.

Without the prejudice, the forms of conduct that are relatively more characteristic of Jews and that we have discussed above, elicit impressions and appropriate generalizations. These, lacking the prejudice, will be formulated with less bluntness and sense of moral superiority, and they relate not to race or religion but to less definite marks of distinction, such as occupation, place of origin, or residence; nevertheless, their material remains the same. The notion that it is the prejudice that exclusively and arbitrarily brings about or picks out anti-Jewish experience, and that this experience, without the prejudice, has no more independent grounds in the forms of conduct more characteristic of Jews than those of others, has had a decisive role in Jews' lack of awareness of the true image their environment has of them. This is why they attribute great importance to the manner of fighting anti-Semitism that refutes the wildest generalizations and horror stories about them and that, having proved their deceptions, bad faith, and contradictions, believes the statements of anti-Semitism need no further treatment. They are not cognizant of the fact that the experiences of their environment—both anti-Semitic and non-anti-Semitic—are of the *same order*: the *horror images* of the anti-Semites arise from the distorted and perverse assessment of experiences they share with non-anti-Semites. This is why non-Jews tend to find many of the statements of anti-Semitism true or apt, even though they cannot accept them in their entirety. This the Jews find particularly excruciating, sensing in it the anti-Semitism and the anti-Semitism "taint" of their whole non-Jewish environment.

Again, it is undoubtedly true that if we compare the *consequences*, it was anti-Semitism that came to be the cause of events—incomparably more tearful and bloody events—vastly more than Jewish unrealism. This was true of the time before Auschwitz and has been rendered irrefutable in Auschwitz for a long time. Jewish unrealism, however, has had the occasional opportunity to make itself obvious; it is of the same kin in essence and quality alike. Furthermore, we must not forget it is self-deception to notice nothing else in such a warped worldview but the evil and sadism that takes place as its consequence and by reference to it. There are many participants in anti-Semitic actions, the persecution of Jews, as in all persecutions, who are involved not because of the ideology or crowd emotion justifying the persecution but simply because they grasp every opportunity to bait, persecute, rob, and kill. Such action is not accidental to anti-Semitism, yet it stems from a variety of other reasons as well, and the nature of anti-Semitism is often betrayed more by those of its actions that decent, non-sadistic, and non-evil men are not loath to perform.

In a rendering of accounts between Jews and the non-Jewish environment, anti-Jewish prejudice being the *cause* and the *greater quantity of suffering* to which it gave rise, it is the Jews who are the party that has suffered and lost incomparably more and who are justified in their claims. Yet regarding the relation that is to be shaped between Jews and non-Jews after such antecedents, this does not mean that the prejudice of Jews is less of a prejudice, that the warped worldview of Jews is less warped, or that the unrealism of Jews is closer to the truth than that of the anti-Semites. I have probed the experiences of Jews and anti-Semites in parallel not to reduce them to a common denominator, to equalize their score, and to lecture to the parties in turns but to show Jews in particular that it is futile to regard the non-Jewish experience of Jews, however partial and one-sided the reality on which it is based, as a simple horror image born of prejudice and therefore take it for naught. I stress this particularly not because, though the experiences of Jews have been more severe and have a universal scope, the non-Jewish, majority experiences of Jews are more decisive and are the ones that determine the entire situation and all the conditions in the final count. The full truth is that anti-Jewish prejudice and anti-Jewish experience are the joint conditions of modern anti-Semitism, which is inconceivable without either of them.

Nevertheless, even the joint occurrence of these two is not enough for anti-Semitism to turn into a central social issue. It is only natural that both the prejudice and the experience survive after Jewish emancipation. Overnight, emancipation cannot terminate the traditional predicament of the old seclusion, which reinforces or recreates the forms of reciprocal conduct, which, in turn, reestablishes the old predicament. In a healthy environment, this cycle continually abates, and anti-Semitism is increasingly seen as pathological, abnormal. A sound community will not have its members embrace the attitudes of anti-Semitism or the experience of Jewish seclusion. Only a spiritless community that has lost its sense of value lets these become ascendant and allows the problems of its life to be presented as hinging on the conflict of Jews and anti-Semites. Thus, the presence of anti-Jewish prejudice and experience in a society is therefore not enough to give a decisive role to anti-Semitism; this requires a society whose entire social development is confounded and morbid.

ANTI-SEMITISM AND THE DISORDERS OF SOCIAL DEVELOPMENT

The non-Jewish experiences of Jews were not isolated, concurring with the general experience of the social change the modern era had initiated, the collapse and transformation of the medieval social structure based on the qualitative differentiation among men. Observing the relatively higher degree of sagacity among Jews, European, particularly West European, society as a whole gradually changed the traditional and customary ways of handling social opportunities to more practical and rational ones. Finding a disillusioned and suspicious criticism of its scale of values more common among Jews, non-Jewish society saw its scale of values being gradually or radically called into question. Finally, encountering the pursuit of amends for injuries more common among Jews, the non-Jewish environment had to realize that the vast changes in power relations taking place afforded plenty of opportunity for the various manifestations of pursuing amends. That Jews were markedly interested and involved in these processes made anti-Semites of only those who experienced modern economic and social development as a crisis, loss, and confusion; wherever it posed a social problem, anti-Semitism was bound up with these phenomena and signaled some confusion or halt. This would not turn a society with a healthy social development entirely anti-Semitic because it would be obvious to its members that these transformations were driven by forces and interests independent of and greater than the Jews.

This was not the course events took in the countries east of the Rhine with an uneven or arrested social development, where modern capitalism and bourgeois revolution were founded not on the necessities of capitalism's internal development but the economic, political, and intellectual disseminations of established and successful democratic revolutions in Western Europe. Society retained its strongly feudal and aristocratic structure in these countries; its revamping in line with modern capitalism and civil democracy was superficial and formal. After a number of unsuccessful attempts or half-successes, the middle classes lost nerve and gave up the project of breaking up the power of the feudal-aristocratic forces. East of the Rhine, capitalism thus came to be based not on the *collapse*, nor even the weakening, of feudalism but on harnessing its social relations, a situation often resulting in the meanest colonial-style exploitation. In this situation, modern social criticism, which had undermined the feudal-aristocratic authority, conditionings, and beliefs of society but had been unable to overturn them except in Russia, underwent a process in which dogmatism, irrationalism, and the fabrication of false political formulas took the place of action.

All this came to a head in those Central European countries that, apart from being enmeshed in the confusions of the social development mentioned above, drifted also into impasses of national and political development or struggled with the uncertainty of their national existence. In these countries, the national cause came to be related to the policies the various ruling dynasties, aristocracies, and military cliques pursued against one another, and movements that attempted to promote social progress appeared to be in the way of such national struggles. Thus modern national feeling and democracy, which had intertwined during the French Revolution and in all ensuing healthy political movements and countries with a sound development, were set against one another, so a freak was born: feudal-aristocratic, dominance-minded *anti-democratic nationalism*. Central Europe became the hotbed of false political formulas, social and political impasses, and self-contradictory political ideologies replete with horror images—all the more so the more social development was arrested and the greater the confusion and insecurity of national development.

The first among them was Germany. Its democratic movements for national union having miscarried in 1848, it went into pseudo-unification under the Hohenzollerns in 1871. From without, it appeared to be a modern nation-state bursting with national vigor and capable of mobilizing the popular masses. From within, however, it was a huge, helpless mass divided into petty states or aristocratic circles, wholly entangled in a medieval social hierarchy—all putrefying frantically. This contradiction was what fomented the bragging German foreign policy of the turn of the century and unleashed the Great War, only for

Germany to lose it and reap the Treaty of Versailles, which a socially backward and politically immature German populace could not digest.

Another country of this kind was Austria, which had been organized as a modern state in the nineteenth century; its only problem was that none of its constituent members—not even the Austrian Germans—regarded it as their own, each wanting to belong elsewhere. And, unfortunately, also belonging in this group was Hungary, which, after its suppressed attempt at democratic transformation and national independence in 1848–1849, acquiesced in the pseudo-constitutionality and pseudo-independence of the Compromise, fell into a state of aggrievement over the Treaty of Trianon, and sought justice to be able to uphold the illusion of the tenability of a historical Hungary and Hungarian dominance over its national minorities.

Under such circumstances, the relationship and frictions between Jews and non-Jews elicited quite different reactions. A society with a feudal-aristocratic conditioning was scandalized by and unable to digest the rise of a relatively small Jewish layer to the peaks of economic power by way of capitalism. This society was particularly irritated by the fact that an emancipated Jewry had no qualms about taking sides with both the democratic and the socialist branch of modern emancipationist social criticism, annoying not only the upper crust, but also the lower classes, inured as they were to the hierarchical worldview. Finally, there was the stumbling block that the majority of even the wholly assimilated Jews, having different experiences and being interested in ending or alleviating the Jewish predicament, found it difficult to follow the so-called national intelligentsia through the various national hysterias, aggrievements, delusions, and horror images all the way to falling out with democracy.

Though rooted quite differently, these three vexations were precipitated by the same crisis in Central Europe. The shock, fear, and scapegoat-hunting that the chronic crisis of a feudal-aristocratic world—which had been undermined but would not cease to exist—and the unresolved questions of national existence brought about found an almost self-evident common denominator in anti-Semitism for their contradictory ideological stances and social tendencies. For all the individuals and groups—from large-estate owners to petit bourgeois, from officers to history teachers, in whose eyes European social development had lost its authentic meaning and categories due to the impasses of social and national development—the system of anti-democratic and anti-Semitic nationalism appeared to be able to explain all prior problems clearly, place all vexing experiences in a comprehensive scheme, and find all solutions as a matter of course. This was how multitudes gave credit to the obvious nonsense that there was some sort of secret pact between, on the one hand, the Jewish banker, who had made a fortune by sagaciously handling social and economic power yet fully concurred with and was utterly loyal to the feudal-aristocratic establishment, and, on the other hand, the Jewish trade union secretary, who was bent on undermining the authority of the scale of values by a most keen and vehement application of modern social criticism but was simultaneously a die-heard opponent of all aspects of capitalism, and that the aim of this pact was to thwart all national aspirations and thereby raise Jews to power, dominance, and even world dominance.

It is therefore true that beyond the medieval *prejudice* and the vexing *experiences* non-Jews gathered of Jews, a particularly *morbid condition of social development* is required for the Jewish question and anti-Semitism to acquire a central social role. Herein lies the truth of the socialist thesis that the solution of the social question, the establishment of a classless society, will put an end to the Jewish question. However, I believe that Jews and non-Jews will continue to experience friction between one another in such a society for a long time to come; yet I am quite certain that a firm scale of values that consistently puts into practice the equal value of all men, the emancipation of the oppressed, and the genuine freedom of all nations will quash anti-Jewish prejudice and the anti-Jewish interpretation of social crises and make it impossible for the Jewish question and anti-Semitism to acquire a central social role.

FIGHTING ANTI-SEMITISM

Modern anti-Semitism is therefore made up of three components. First, the medieval anti-Jewish prejudice had branded Jews as morally inferior on religious grounds and provided and sometime still provides the framework for modern anti-Semitism, conditioning the aversion and mistrust to them and their moral disparagement. Second, Jews and non-Jews have acquired masses of experience of one another, arming the exhausted and withered framework of the medieval, religion-based prejudice with newer and newer material—as it were, the flesh and blood of anti-Semitism. Third, we have the maladies of modern social development, not letting social processes, movements, and crises run their course and thus making them turn into anti-Semitism. These are what remold the generalizations about Jews into horror images and allow for the Jewish question and anti-Semitism to be central social issues.

In fighting anti-Semitism, we have to take all these three components into account if we do not want to end up shadowboxing. Of the three components, the first and the last, the anti-Jewish prejudice and the disorders of social development, by nature, cannot be fought merely in respect to the Jews. As far as the fight against prejudice goes, knowing the power of the components of anti-Semitism, we ought not to expect it to yield decisive results, and we must direct it at all hatred, persecution, prejudice, superstitious charges, assumptions, and the propagation of any ominous distinctions among men. Likewise, there is no fighting anti-Semitism, deployed as it has been to sidetrack attention from social issues, without tackling the issues in their *entirety*. Any attempt at fighting anti-Semitism without these considerations or in itself will necessarily lead to the plainly unspoken supposition that the hatred of Jews is *more prohibited* than hatred against others and that fighting for their rights is *more progressive* than fighting for that of others. What non-Jews of a more sensitive conscience should consider from this is that, as experience shows, anti-Jewish hatred is more dangerous in its consequences than other hatreds; however, beyond this, the cause of the Jews has no original primacy among the great causes of human dignity and emancipation. The situation in World War II, in which the cause of the Jews became the cause of progressive mankind, was a reaction to the monstrosities of anti-Jewish persecutions in Germany, and due to their termination it has ceased to exist, much disillusionment and soreness arising from its abrupt and unfeeling cessation.

As a result, progressive minds tend to dislike hearing about a *special* fight against anti-Semitism. The relationship between Jews and non-Jews, however, has certain immediate difficulties that cannot be handled pending the end of general and long-term processes, such as the elimination of all prejudice and social problems. Everyone feels it is in the area of direct social experience that the special treatment of the Jewish question, particularly examples of better human conduct, more human rapport, and a certain thaw are needed, and the struggle against prejudice and social progress cannot provide these.

Strictly speaking, the true area of fighting anti-Semitism is social experience. If there is any, fighting is going on in this area only. Yet the individuals or groups engaging in it usually do not bring themselves and others to the awareness that social experience is the hotbed of anti-Semitism, and this is why this is the area where things most easily and most often go awry.

The most common slippage is that anti-Semitism is fought in the way anti-Semitism appears in the experience of *Jews*. Non-Jewish associates involved in the fight usually lack the courage and sharpness to point out how hopeless this is. This is why the representations of anti-Semitism as born of utterly malevolent and unfounded lies and ending up in the persecution of utterly innocent people remain so startlingly and blood-curdlingly without response. Though these took place genuinely and en masse, nothing in them squares with the day-to-day experience of non-Jews. The most terrifying horrors of Hitlerite anti-Jewish persecution and mass murder were needed for this to appear as an actuality in the eyes of larger numbers of non-Jews, leaving their lasting mark only on the consciences of individuals and communities particularly sensitive to matters of human dignity. Generally, however, as the persecutions and killings recede in time, everyday experiences take their place, and these attribute a decisive import to the rebound Jews have elicited among the causes of anti-Semitism. This is why fighting anti-Semitism based on Jewish experience continues to be wholly ineffectual, creating a stir only among Jews, whereby it amounts to but Jews talking among themselves, from which no one is going to benefit.

Fighting anti-Semitism in this manner takes a fatal turn when it moves from the area of influencing the conscience to that of criminal persecution, where the ambiguities of the word "anti-Semite" bring trouble. The anti-Semite inciting a hatred of Jews can and should be punished. However, Jewish experience cannot be the basis of establishing the objective criteria and the perpetration of this crime because it regards all injuries of a piece, whether on this or that side of felony, and it sees all dislike of Jews as anti-Semitism. This is where the deadly attempts at trying to sanction the various manifestations of "harping on the Jews" begin. This might be quite vile and offensive, but whether it is culpable action or not is not to be determined by its hurting someone's feelings. To decide whether an instance of "harping on the Jews" hurts feelings, represents a resolute hatred of Jews, or is the mere generalizations of the environment or the outcome of an occasional squabble, we ought to translate it into, say, Portuguese, and if "harping on the Portuguese" likewise proves to be culpable, then we can be content that we have persecuted an act of punishable anti-Semitism and not bred a new anti-Semite.

It is no less uncouth when, on the other side, well-meaning non-Jews want to "settle" the problem of the Jews or to engage in "honest" rapport with them by taking a non-Jewish experience of them as the fully authentic truth and so lay down moral guidelines on how they should "behave"—that they should be less greedy, conceited, critical, destructive, cynical, sensitive, grudge-bearing, vengeful, etc. so as not to elicit anti-Semitism. Priests in particular tend to believe that they are professionally competent to speak about the sins of others, so the "sin" of the Jews. Such sermonizing will be heard with submission only by Jews prone to self-depreciation; otherwise, it infuriates and deters the rest from learning that Jewish conduct and the reaction to it have a role in anti-Semitism. This sort of advice represents only inimical generalizations and impracticable summons to them, and not even the most fiercely heart-searching Jew will know what to do with them because he experiences the "bad characteristics" of Jews in quite different contexts. Not to mention the fact that this type of advice is usually driven by the characteristic and naive horror image that there is a secret Jewish Sanhedrin where the Jewish chief banker, chief revolutionary, and chief journalist counsel with their long-bearded chief rabbi-chairman and, from time to time, decree how Jews must "behave." As there is none such, the summons, even if addressed to Jews, finds a response only in non-Jewish circles; in other words, it is non-Jews talking among themselves, from which, again, no one is going to benefit.

If all this is blatantly wrong, what can be done at all? As it is experience distorted by anger and misinterpretation on both sides, simple communication and an awakening to consciousness have greater import than any inauthentic sermonizing based on shaky foundations or the making of pacts at all costs. Perhaps we should analyze the issue by defining who can say what for the sake of fighting anti-Semitism.

What might a non-Jew say in this regard to a non-Jew? First and foremost, he must never reinforce with any gesture anyone on his side in the predilection of non-Jewish experience and the distorted abstraction to which it leads but should try and keep himself and others aware of the immediate and concrete sense of all things Jewish and their fundamental oneness with all other things human. Isn't the overrating of an injury fed, he should suggest, by a non-acceptance of the equal humanity of Jews? He should point out the role that the moral sloppiness, self-conceit, and irresponsibility of non-Jews have in the offenses and social anomalies attributed to Jews. Unceasingly and unwarily, he should disclose and repeat all the facts he knows about the innumerable horrors to which Jews have been exposed and speak about all the insults with which the usual moral judgments and moral disparagement top off the physical tormenting and human loss of Jews. He should speak of the responsibility and complicity of the entire non-Jewish community in the suffering of Jews and of the share to which he personally admits in this, without, however, attempting to compel people toward a sense of contrition and responsibility who are not ready to do so.

What might a non-Jew say to a Jew? He might speak of the facts of the non-Jewish experience of Jews without generalizations, interpretations, and moral conclusions—simply of how Jews appear in the non-Jewish world; what that world experiences, finds characteristic, honorable, or insulting about them; and what it cannot understand about them. He should do so without trying to cast the "stark truth" in their teeth or to prescribe in any degree what they should or should not do or how they should behave and without presenting theories of what Jews are like and what the trouble with them might be. He should admit to them the responsibility he feels for the suffering they underwent and undergo;

he should never ask for anything in exchange—particularly not for their forgetting and forgiving their suffering. The most he can ask of them is to not isolate
their cause from the causes of others, their humiliations from all those humiliated, and their seeking of justice from other justice seekers.

What can a Jew say to a non-Jew? He might speak of the reality of the Jewish
experience and its immediate human meaning, and, in spite of all calls to the
contrary, he should speak his mind about the frightful Jewish suffering in the
distant and recent past and about its not having ended in every respect or everywhere. Yet he should not try to make non-Jews accept notions of anti-Semitism
that make Jews out to be exceedingly better and non-Jews exceedingly worse,
and he should in no way enforce any collective guilt against non-Jews because
this repels even those who would of themselves admit their share of that collective responsibility.

Finally, what useful things might a Jew say to another Jew for the sake of
fighting anti-Semitism? The moral and practical lessons of the relationship
between Jews and non-Jews are to be drawn by Jews for themselves. I do not
believe I could add anything fruitful to this. I do suspect, however, that Jewish
self-knowledge is done little service by the kind of thesis the late Károly Pap put
forward—that is, that the Jewish nation is a "suicidal nation"; I believe such
existential formulas do more harm than good because, by arousing a sense of
pseudo-fatefulness, they debilitate a sound sense of reality and a productive
spirit to act, lugging in a formula between man and reality. I should think not
even a Jewish sermonizer can begin with anything other than the beginning
and end of all fruitful moral influence: free yourselves from the prison of subjective experience, and do not confuse the concoctions of your mind with reality. However, it is for Jews themselves to make these theses tangible.

III. JEWISH ASSIMILATION AND IDENTITY

It is now time to address the question of the future of the common fate of Jews
and the Jewish community following such antecedents and in such conditions;
in other words, we have to examine the issues of Jewish assimilation, Jewish minority or national identity, and Zionism. Certain simple theses on these issues
have gained wide currency that, drawing on their partial truths, try to jump to
universally valid generalizations.

VIEWS ON ASSIMILATION

The first of these views is that, medieval prejudice dying out, Jews give up the
most conspicuous elements of their rite, are emancipated, learn the language of

their surrounding nation, take up various occupations, and are immediately integrated into the nation. The socialists believe this will not do of itself, but it will
do when a classless society finally eliminates all the causes that have lead to the
artificial separation and unhealthy occupational and social place of Jews and
that have perverted the rising forces of social transformation into anti-Semitism.
Accordingly, they believe there is no point in dealing with the assimilation into
the upper and middle classes because, on the one hand, it took place in a class
structure that will be liquidated by development, and, on the other, it was not
genuine assimilation, having been based on class interest and snobbery rather
than genuine integration; for the time being, genuine assimilation can take
place only in the forerunner of classless society, the proletariat and its political
movements. In contrast, representatives of the upper and middle classes hold
that assimilation has occurred only in their circles, and there would never have
been any problem with "genteel" Jews had it not been for the uneducated,
filthy, unscrupulous eastern Jews. There is also the view that assimilation is
possible but under the condition that all the aspects of belonging to the Jewish
community are forgone, the precondition of which is baptism. Essentially, this
is the position those churches take that claim a national role in their various
countries and wish to have their say in matters of community assimilation.

At the other extreme of simplification, we have the view highlighting the
impossibility or the almost insurmountable difficulties of assimilation. One of
the arguments brought up on the grounds of not only race, but also society
and social morality is the immutability of Jewish characteristics and their difference from those of the surrounding nations. Another argument refers to the
acuteness of the Jewish sense of identity and solidarity, which is manifest in a
myriad of minor and major instances even after purported assimilation and
which makes a full melting into the environment impossible. Finally, we have
the opinion the Zionists and the various Jewish and non-Jewish ideologues of
nation share that Jewish fate is a definitive momentum that—whether seen as
tragic or simply real, as a mission or a curse, as the consequence of a hostile
environment—no one can shun or avoid, and all attempts at assimilation out of
escape, lack of self-esteem, or pretentiousness are doomed to fail.

THE CRUX OF ASSIMILATION

If we want to find a way through the partial truths of these views, we must first
define what we mean by assimilation. We mean the social process whereby individuals or groups become members of a new community, one to which they did
not heretofore belong; they now melt into, adapt to, and become like it. As everyone has a variety of relationships with several communities at once, ranging

from membership through assimilation to dissimilation, it is best to limit the real crux of assimilation to cases in which individuals or groups leave a community that had a definitive role in establishing their life conditions and cross over into a community with a likewise determining role. Nations, tribes, city-states, religious or ritual communities, orders, and classes are the best-known and most powerfully definitive communities. Among these, it is assimilation into *nations* in the modern sense that is meant, and these are certainly very powerful determining communities. However, we must be aware that along with religion and class, a nation belongs to a *more abstract* types of community, in which membership is not as immediate, embedded in everyday life, or self-evident without inculcation as it is in the case of city-states, tribes, or ritual communities; it implies the sharing of far more complicated, distant, and abstract matters, such as historical consciousness, institutions of political and economic organization, social norms and education, lifestyles, and social morality. Assimilation into such abstract communities, which are beyond immediate social experience, cannot take place exclusively in the abstractions by which the community is represented; it needs — it all the more needs — participation in the real life of the more concrete media of community life, its smaller units.

Though all assimilation implies a process with essentially the same content, we should note the difference between an individual's *personal* and a community's general assimilation. In the case of individual assimilation, stress falls on *leaving* one community, *ending* its defining or binding power, and *joining* something different and new. Unless the community has the forcefulness to bring forth exuberant, sweeping, and rapid assimilation, this process is not at all easy for an individual and takes one or two generations to become complete — hence all the palaver and study of its various problems, difficulties, and pains. In a community's general assimilation, the stress, however, falls not on individuals leaving but on the entire community *dissolving*, gradually losing its defining power and being relegated behind other determiners of community belonging. Yet general assimilation does not or cannot differ essentially from individual assimilation; it is certainly not simpler or easier, as it is made up of masses of individual ones. What perhaps does make it less conspicuous and slower is that those concerned go through it not individually but together with many others. It must nevertheless be a genuine community process as well, taking place in the various smaller units of shared existence; surely it cannot consist only in putting forward various theses or requirements on groups of people belonging here and there, assimilating or being assimilated, or only in classifying or re-naming certain groups according to statistical criteria.

The process of assimilation can be made easy or difficult by various factors, primarily the determining power of the old community, the distance between the old and the new communities, the attractiveness of the new community, its internal order and balance, its conduct toward the assimilated, etc. If we know this, it is obviously clear that it is easier for a Bulgarian to become a Serb than for a Greek to become a Dutchman, and it is easier for a lackland peasant to become a smallholder farmer or a shopkeeper to become a banker than for a peasant boy to become a chief constable or a shopkeeper to become a squire. In this respect, we have to clarify a few points on assimilation.

When we speak of the characteristics, the features, of the assimilated and the assimilators, their changes, and their abandonment or adoption of a community, we usually mean two intertwining yet quite different concepts. On the one hand, we have a group of elemental or fundamental common characteristics that come partly from birth and constitution, partly from ethnicity, and partly from culture and upbringing but are nevertheless or have become *instinctual*. These are what make up the blurry yet distinct profile of a nation or other community, manifest in physical types—not a single type!—of temperament, pace of life, gesture, disposition, humor, musicality, feel for decoration and flavor, invention, and rate of work. Another group of community characteristics has to do with the *forms of community conduct*, such as procedures; idiom; convention; rules of play, honor, and intercourse; unspoken conditions and requirements; and, in the case of more active or combative communities, aims, ideals, and discipline. Naturally, these are related to the more instinctual elements of the national self, but they hardly draw merely on them; in fact, they are determined by upbringing; religious and political systems; schools; historical experience, shocks, and lessons; and social leaders and examples—in other words, by several other factors that reflect the effects of other or universal human types.

The border between these two groups of community characteristics is naturally malleable, but the mass of characteristics that can be and should be assimilated belongs to the latter group. Assimilation does not mean extricating oneself from all typical or observable characteristics or traits, becoming indistinguishable or "pure-blooded"—this has nothing to do with the essence of assimilation; it is perhaps its late or accidental concomitant. Assimilation means living in the actual and vibrant process of the life of a community, knowing, practicing, and accepting its forms of conduct, conventions, and requirements. For all this, one might retain his characteristic nose, cuisine, pace of life, turns of phrase, or alien words; in other words, physical or ethnic features that have little or no significance can remain. Birth or ethnic characteristics seldom appear in the mind of the one wanting to assimilate as hindrances to assimilation, but they often become guises under which animosity and prejudice can limit or obstruct inclusion. The way these become obstacles in the way of assimilation is that the environment, following a clash between community interests and forms of conduct, turns them into some sort of barrier or impediment, such as the color of the skin of the Negro or one's having a Jewish grandmother.

On the part of those assimilating, difficulties arise not so much from birth or ethnicity but from the forms of conduct the community has established for living and working together and handling social opportunity, difficulties we touched on above in discussing the relationship between Jews and their environment and that derive particularly not from birth or race but from social-historical development. This, of course, does not mean that they cannot be the sources of greater friction than birth and ethnic characteristics. These are the forms of social conduct that, when they happen to infringe on those of the environment, can be sources of friction and thereby continually thwart assimilation, without, however, being static features characteristic exclusively of a group and thereby predestining assimilation to failure.

Adopting a new *language* is usually the first among the forms of conduct and basic customs taken up in the course of assimilation to national community. The adoption of language and basic customs, however, will contribute to the assimilation process only if there is greater identity or identification with other aspects of the community life. Nevertheless, assimilation can take place without the adoption of a new language too, especially in communities based on multilingualism.

We have already mentioned the importance of partaking in the *solidarity* of the new community. Again, this is not to be understood in the sense that the essence of assimilation is that from now on, the assimilated will "stick together" with, support, and prefer only the members of the new community and not those of their old one. The issue of solidarity arises not in such abstract contrasts but in quite different, concrete social structures and rather practically. In itself, that assimilated individuals and groups maintain not only a sense of certain separation and belonging together, but also a willingness to support, promote, and financially aid one another, as well as their preference for each other, does not hinder assimilation—as we may observe among the Scotch, the Corsicans, the Székely, and the Jews as well.

It is not this that a partaking in the solidarity of the new community depends on but on whether the assimilated embrace the inner meaning and aims of the procedures, enterprises, struggles, and regulations of the new community's smaller, more real units that they join or whether, having learned them, they see them merely as a means to the ends of their different solidarity—in other words, falsify them. The solidarity, preference, or partisanship of the assimilated turn fateful and detrimental to assimilation not when breaching the limits of objectivity—the majority of people spend their entire lives beyond the limits of objectivity—but when deforming the community structures and twisting the meanings and aims in which they are asserted.

I wish to highlight one of the factors thwarting or easing assimilation that is seldom mentioned in discussions of the community and the mental processes taking place only among the *assimilated*. The most decisive and important factor in assimilation, one that makes it either quite easy or rather difficult, is the inner order or balance of the assimilating community because this is what finally defines the conditions of assimilation. Implicitly or explicitly, each community lays down the conditions of assimilation, which are not always easy to fulfill, and in more closed and narrower communities, these might even be onerous, deliberately making entry difficult; they might make the process of inclusion or exclusion not quite friendly, even ruthless; and the assimilating society might have a wide variety of insults in store for the assimilated who do not greet, emphasize, argue, or manage their business or club affairs in the way they are expected to. Yet in a community with a heedful and balanced inner life, the conditions of assimilation are clear and firm, and once it has admitted a new member, a serious community will protect him. Put simply, a community of consequence *cheats* in nothing, not even in this. In the final count, it is the honest, orderly, and congruous or the deceptive, contradictory, and incongruous life of an assimilating community that determines whether the process of assimilation is straight and clear or crooked and contradictory.

THE INDIVIDUAL WAYS OF JEWISH ASSIMILATION

The assimilation of Jews, whether individual or general, does not and cannot differ from any other assimilation. Both before and after emancipation, the individual assimilation of Jews took place and has been taking place at various junctures through concrete and definite social media, as in all assimilations. Such smaller assimilating media or communities have always been quite varied, including baptism, a joining in Christian religious communities; participation in the communities and circles of European free thinking; membership in professional and labor organizations with intensive inner lives; creative work and participation in the literary, scholarly, and artistic communities of a country; participation in political and social movements and public service; society, school, and country life; intermarriage; friendships; personal relationships; etc. Of all these, baptism, schools, so-called society life (as long as it was and is significant), participation in professional communities (particularly intellectual life), and the labor movement (last in time but with increasing significance) have been the most powerful media of assimilation throughout Europe.

To our day, the assimilation of Jews has continued to be channeled through these media, though, as is widely known, it belongs among the difficult instances of assimilation. Among its impediments, we find the cementing power of the old Jewish community—a heightened religious, national, intellectual, and moral self-consciousness and culture—which kept alive in Jews a sense of superiority and chosenness, couched in various concepts. To a certain extent, the mental burden of their being morally disparaged also encumbered their assimilation, continuing to bear down on those of them who were no longer in the grip of their old community's sense of solidarity and identity—them, sometimes, in particular. This might have ripened the will to assimilate, but it certainly burdened the process of assimilation with the fact that leaving the old community and turning to the new one was driven not only by the attraction of the new but the repulsion of the old community, weighed down as it was by a sense of moral inferiority, disadvantaged birth, and isolation.

In contrast to these difficulties, primarily apparent in the minds of Jews, we see the usually much greater obstacles the environment threw in the way of Jewish assimilation. Whether more or less closed, the surrounding communities were more sequestered to Jews than to others due to the old anti-Jewish prejudice and the existing relationship between Jews and non-Jews.

The difficulties of assimilation on the parts of both Jews and non-Jews stemmed not only from the stances they wittingly or unwittingly took in the matters of assimilation and belonging, but also from the differences in human and community conduct, particularly sagacity, a critique of the scale of values, and gestures toward a pursuit of amends originating in the tension of dominance and subjugation. Even in a friendly atmosphere, these forms of conduct easily and rapidly brought forth a sense of difference and strangeness, and the *familiarity* of the notions of the anti-Jewish prejudice always occasioned turning concrete frictions and differences instantly into *principles* and *generalizations*—much more rapidly than in other cases.

This is the source of all the palaver on the more or less unavoidable *Jewish fate* and the consequential hopelessness of assimilation and the necessity of Jewish self-consciousness. We have dwelled at length on the details of the often tragic process wherein Jewish conditions sustain Jewish forms of conduct, which, in turn, due to the anti-Jewish prejudice, elicit disproportionately detrimental reactions and thereby bring about or have their share in the continuation of the Jewish fate. In adverse social conditions, this becomes a *vicious circle*, which, should we so wish, we might call Jewish fate so long as we attribute to it no meaning of ineluctability either in the mystical or in the social sense. It would be grossly misleading to call a community predicament inherently ineluctable when the prejudice of the environment has such a major part in it, even though we do not accept it to be its sole cause. And it would be outright wickedness to prove the unavoidability of the Jewish fate by the fact that there was a mad political ideology in the twentieth century that dug out the descent of people to their grandmothers and great-grandmothers and that the common suffering, danger to life, and destruction forced onto the people thus herded together was a shared fate. True, those that went through this did become a sort of community, and, as always, due to the persecutions, there were many examples of the indifferent becoming conscious, the midway-assimilated returning, and even the fully assimilated dissimilating. However, this is not an inherent Jewish destiny but a concrete historical tribulation or its effect that other tribulations, communities, or processes can avert or counterbalance.

This is why Zionists and compassionate chiders of Jews go too far in generalizing and drawing consequences, saying, on the grounds of either the persecutions or the hopelessness of assimilation, that the only self-respecting and humanly worthy position to take is the open admission of Jewish national and community identity. Whoever says so does not consider the fact that owning up to Jewish national and community identity is far from a simple and self-evident profession of belonging but the elevation to glory of a historical and morally disparaged predicament shaped under a multitude of stresses and constraints; in other words, it is a passionate and pathos-filled testimony some might be in the mood to make and some not.

Heightened self-consciousness is but one of the more visible and express consequences of the persecutions, and the urge to escape from the community has been equally strengthened. Furthermore, however much injury the environment might have in store for the assimilated, their majority has taken deep root in the environment, but even those whose roots are not as deep have broken away from the Jewish community. It is therefore not true that all the assimilated have to do is discover their never-vanished Jewish identity and their difficulties will be straightened out without more ado. In reality, the way back to the Jewish community for the assimilated, the half-assimilated, or even the dissimilated is just as or more drawn out and wearisome as going on with, completing, or finding another route to assimilation.

JEWS MIDWAY BETWEEN ASSIMILATION AND SELF-CONSCIOUSNESS

Throughout Europe, significant, even disproportionately numerous, quarters of Jewry learned the language of the surrounding society, relinquished the most conspicuous elements of their rite, and took up certain—indeed not all—occupations (mostly in metropolitan commerce) without, however, leaving their former human and social circumstances and joining the life of an actually assimilating community. This was particularly true in Central Europe, where capitalism evolved to greatness without the necessary powerful internal precursors and in a rather colonial manner. The occupations taken up by the Jews, therefore, had had no preexisting assimilating medium, and quite to the contrary, they came into being after and at the price of the dissolution of communities that were primitive in comparison to the new situation. Thus there was a relatively numerous Jewish society that, apart from certain loose business contacts, no personal relations, educational experiences, professional frameworks, or political or community experiences had drawn out of its earlier human, social, and community environment; it continued to live its life in its own original environment without any particular change in the experiences of community that belonged in the great European metropolises.

Internally, Jewry was far from being a unified society; in fact, it was quite divided—into its own aristocrats; nouveaux riches; nameless, well-to-do bourgeois; those living in the depths of everlasting poverty; people of well-established means; shady figures living on the fringes of human and moral opportunity; people with deep roots in their environment; and those emphatically documenting their integration, the assimilated whom both anti-Semites and Zionists derided; in other words, it included all kinds of elements, representing all the extremes in lifestyles, tastes, and moral attitudes. For all its heterogeneity, however, it was far too secluded to be part of the appropriate groups of the societies surrounding it, and it appeared as a unit to the environment. Thus experiential evidence of everything and its contrary could be found in it; it could just as truthfully be said to bring well-being and prosperity to a country as to bleed it dry parasitically. Indeed, it carried many of the economic capacities and skills of capitalism, but, even by European comparison, it included an unrealistically high number of speculative, unnecessary, and over-and-above existences.

The entire mass was held together by a number of major negative features (apart from minor ones), including the fact that it gravitated outside the Jewish condition but did not want to relinquish it fully; that it sought to satisfy itself for its pre-emancipation disadvantages in making money through a reliable business, drudgery, or hand-over-fist, depending on inclination; that it was a follower of liberalism without having a major share in the development toward the rapid or gradual emancipation of the European masses; and that it attached itself to the country in which it lived without participating in its common identity, problems, life, and objectives. The nature, cementing forces, internal standards, talents, virtues, and mistakes of the entire mass assumed a clear shape neither to itself nor to its environment; even in a Central Europe with its many shapeless social formations, it was one of the most amorphous groups, its outlines least defined.

In this respect, the relationship of this transitory group to the evolution of Neolog Judaism is worth mentioning. I have no competence to discuss the significance of this religious movement or the nature of its religious experiences. I am not at all trying to hint that the Neolog movement, due to its inner content, was necessarily a transitory state, a midway condition, because many were absolutely conscious, thoughtful, and deliberate in taking it up—those who saw it not as an easier but as a more settled form of Judaism and those who sought to cultivate the Jewish religious, moral, and intellectual tradition in a way that would let them partake of the entirety of the surrounding European cultural and community life and not have the entirety of Jewry—and certainly not themselves—revert back into a social, political, and militant community with all its passions and vicissitudes. These were possible and pure stands to take but mostly for those who belonged, in some way or another, to the "intellectual elite." For the majority, however, the Neolog movement meant abandoning the conspicuous and distinctive features of belong to Jewry without fully breaking away from the Jewish community. In other words, like baptism, it provided a means of expressing social processes in religious proceedings and categories— baptism for fully renouncing the Jewish community, Neologism for halfway remaining within it.

It would have been difficult to establish of this midway mass whether these were Jews with half-hearted consciousness or citizens of Judaic faith on the way to assimilation, particularly when the situation of Jews did not in the least seem problematic or critical and the question would have little interest. It is nowhere written that if a group of men does not belong to a national community with sharp lines of demarcation and emotional fire, this is a source of trouble in itself. Major parts of the world—the Middle East, for instance—continue to live in a non-national framework, embracing other community identities and taking no particular interest in the state whose power they happen to accept without resistance. But there are groups in West European countries, with a more balanced development as well, whose sense of identity lacks the politicization national identity has, such as the Genevans, the Neuchâtelians, the Wallisians, the inhabitants of the Channel Islands, the Welsh, and the Faeroese, all of whom live at a serene and unsuspecting distance from the respective Swiss, British, or Danish nations of which they are otherwise political members.

However, not even in the calmest periods was the situation of the Jews ever as steady, serene, or unsuspecting as that of those mentioned, and amid the ever sharper conflicts and impasses of the Central European nations, there was little room for such transitoriness; the situation of this layer became more and more critical, and its belonging, affiliating, or being classified somewhere became decisive. For good or ill, people said of this group, the Jews, whatever suited their intentions. The programmatic preachers of assimilation maintained they were a phalanx of invincible patriots, even desisting from complaining of anti-Jewish measures at international fora, particularly Jewish fora. The professors of formal, liberal democracy held them to be a principled and consciously democratic layer with a mission to play the role or a major part of the role of the West European middle classes in a Central Europe where middle-class development had lagged behind. The anti-Semites blazoned that they were a devilish mafia slyly combining Jewish assimilation and solidarity to bleed whichever country they lived in. Finally, the Zionists turned to this mass of Jews that had not forsaken their fathers' faith completely, calling for them to discover the Jewish consciousness dormant in them and take upon themselves the cause of Jewish identity and the establishment of a Jewish state.

In point of fact, this layer of Jewry could neither bear nor accomplish what its devotees or enemies ascribed to it. In the disorganized societies of Central Europe, lacking a shared sense of identity, it lived a life far too isolated to be able to respond to a national sense of community beyond mere flag-waving or affection for the immediate locality. It lacked the self-confidence, self-assurance, and social authority to be able to play the middle-class role in not only the living standard and lifestyle, but social function as well. It was also far too pulverized and featureless to be able put forward any design or program of action, and all the less could it play the devilish double game the anti-Semites pinned on it. Finally, it was far too cautious, respecting of authority, keen on well-being, and sometimes snobbish to sign up for something as pathos-filled as Zionism.

It is in respect to this multitude of midway Jews that the *problem* of assimilation and the Jewish sense of identity arises. The commonplace question of whether assimilation or a particular Jewish national identity is possible at all is foolish and meaningless if it is asked validly in respect to the entirety of Jewry, individually assimilating or self-conscious Jews, because why could either option not be possible? It is a meaningful and sensible question only if asked in respect to this midway mass because it demonstrates the possibilities and the hardly surmountable difficulties of both. All the many pointless arguments brought up against the possibility of assimilation or a sense of Jewish national identity draw their examples from the maladjustments of this amorphous throng, and a large proportion of the verbiage, thought streams, and reasoning about the situation of the Jews is in fact tailored to this group only.

The real problem in respect to this midway mass is whether their collective assimilation was a possibility for them at all; can it be expected that this part of

Jewry, which has learned the language of its environment and abandoned the strictest rites of Judaism, would assimilate in a way that holds them together as a community but limits the significance of this community to cultivating a religious, ancestral, and ritual tradition? There are many instances of this; there were many ritual communities living in utter seclusion throughout Europe, the significance of which was limited to the religious area as a result of the process of secularization. Catholics in Britain and the Netherlands, Protestants in France and Hungary, and Muslims in Yugoslavia turned from almost ethnically closed communities into merely religious or, to a certain extent, lifestyle communities in the last hundred years, almost in front of our very eyes. There is also the case of the ethnically quite different Armenians of Transylvania, whose total seclusion from Hungarians has become limited to only a difference in worship and ecclesiastic structure in the last two hundred years.

To belong to the Israelite faith, however, meant a seclusion more definitive and powerful than any of these even back then; the religious and ethnic features were more closely related and drew a sharper line between insiders and outsiders. Though the social, communal, and ancestral traditions of belonging together have a decisive role in other religious communities as well, in Judaism, due to its very principles and historical content, the proportion of the purely religious and the community-binding elements has shifted so much toward the latter that Israelite religious consciousness can hardly be thought of without Jewish community (ritual community, minority, or national) consciousness. This obviously slows down the process of collective assimilation, making it depend on the clustered or dispersed location of those assimilating; on the social, political, and intellectual currents of both Jewry and its environment; and on various other historical vicissitudes, but it does not render it impossible, as observed in countries or regions with a balanced social development or wherever Jews have had the opportunity of living under firm and peaceable conditions. Yet modern anti-Semitism, persecutions against Jews, and modern Jewish self-consciousness all point to the Jewish community as having an emotionally and communally much more powerful binding force even in the Neolog movement than religious belonging in a secularized century would otherwise engender. The same phenomena, anti-Semitic excesses and persecutions, bring forth the type of the *dissimilated* Jew, the various insults and injuries calling into question and disrupting his more or less successful assimilation but not turning him back to Jewish self-consciousness. This has led to the rather unfortunate situation where lingering between the original community and assimilation—a condition natural to any assimilation—has not only been prolonged but has turned into a rather permanent condition for Jews.

The collective assimilation of Jews therefore cannot be said to have failed everywhere or that it is bound to fail sooner or later, yet its probability has certainly decreased, and the optimism it once had has withered, particularly in Central Europe—whether admitted or not by Jews or non-Jews alike. This throng of midway Jews, we must conclude, experiences no internal or external urge to gradually and hopefully become like its environment while retaining its middle ground. Instead, its experiences prompt it to either assimilate without any respect for the Jewish community or take up and openly profess a Jewish national or minority identity.

It is at this point that we can grasp the full meaning of the dictum that "Jewish assimilation can only be complete through baptism." It should be noted that the "conversion" to non-denominational free thinking or communism indeed amounts to baptism, the stress falling not on a taking up of the new but a forgoing of the old community. Thus the dictum is *untruthful* even in this respect; however, what is true is that remaining within a Jewish religious environment in Central Europe undoubtedly amounts to being exposed to community influences, solidarity needs, and the simultaneous possibility of rejection by a non-Jewish environment that make belonging to Jewry concrete and experiential and belonging to the surrounding nation superficial and fictitious. In this guise, there is a definite difference between being a member of a Jewish community manifest in a religious organization and not having any such membership, only knowing Jewish origin as a fact of descent. Under the long dominance of racial theory, which gave the same footing and treatment to Jews of faith and Jews of origin, we have become accustomed not to appreciate the difference. There might be ever so many Hungarians, Romanians, and whatnot insisting on their Israelite faith, but as far as their descendants are concerned, the bitterness and fury of this region re-begins the struggle for every soul of each generation, confronting each with the alternative: profession of the primacy of the national environment or the Jewish community. This does not mean that midway Jews are going to rapidly separate either way in the near future; the less does it mean that external action, state power, could hasten, compel, or force them to do so. The separation will presumably be gradual, and the features of the midway condition will continue to recur, but they will increasingly cease to be the concomitants of Jewish community existence.

JEWISH IDENTITY

As the possibility and actuality of assimilation cannot be denied, neither can that of Jewish national or minority identity. The Yiddish-speaking eastern Jews and generally most of those that abided by the ritual community thought of their condition in these terms, and, since the advent of modern national organization, they have simply taken the line of being a national minority. Apart from this, the Zionists—much like the Irish, who do not speak their own language but have a separate national identity—are trying to revivify Hebrew, the dead language of the Jews, which has a prospective future in Palestine. Not because a separate language is a necessary condition of national identity and community life but because immigrant Jews speak a wide variety of languages. With regard to Jews speaking the various languages of their environment, however, many factors—indeed often all factors except language—have come together to develop an independent national or minority identity. National motifs have always been intertwined in Jewish religious consciousness, and if they are zealously held on to by some, they can easily become the source of a national consciousness when the religion loses its community-binding power. Furthermore, there are those whose sense of identity with the Jewish community was aroused by the discriminations, insults, and persecutions; from the outset, these have had a share in the rise of Jewish consciousness and Zionism, but the recent Hitlerite horrors have particularly spurred Jewish minds in this direction. It is difficult and perhaps unnecessary to tell whether modern Jewish national or minority consciousness and Zionism would have come into being without anti-Semitism and persecutions, but, I believe, they would have done so because the Jewish community has binding effects—on those that want it to—that will not fade into elements of worship and theology. Whatever role Jewish tradition and suffering have had in shaping Jewish consciousness, Jewish national identity commands a wide following not only in Israel, but elsewhere too. That Jews assume a particular social and occupational role is also not an obstacle in the way of a separate Jewish identity; it might cause difficulties in organizing a full-fledged society and state, but it does not hinder the evolution of a separate Jewish national-minority consciousness.

On this point, I do not see the development toward a classless society having a particular effect on Jewish identity or its making assimilation the only and self-evident route to follow. True, a balanced classless society will not have the symptoms that turned the Jewish question and anti-Semitism into central social issues and will right occupational imbalances too. Such an even social context would undoubtedly be more inviting for assimilation than the deceitfully sharp conflicts of a deadlocked society. As true as it is to say that anti-Semitism is a side effect of social impasse, it would be equally mistaken to declare with the same certainty that Jewish identity is a malaise that a classless society will render pointless and void. The internal balance of a classless society will presumably avoid the dangers of forcing anyone to become Jewish against his will or of anyone being awoken to Jewish consciousness by such persecution, but it will never render a voluntary and spontaneous Jewish identity meaningless and senseless but will allow one to chose between assimilation and Jewish self-consciousness as he desires.

Jewish self-consciousness need not necessarily lead to emigration to Palestine, a Zionist position, or a distant endorsement of the Jewish state. A Jewish minority community can be imagined without a Jewish state, just as the Jewish state does not insist that Jews become national minorities. Nevertheless, the intention to establish a Jewish state has had a central role in shaping Jewish consciousness and orienting the Jewish community toward national organization; without it, Jewish self-consciousness would lack much of its community vigor and pathos. In this respect, the establishment of Israel means a difficult turn; the ideal of an unrealized magnificence has become an unfolding or perishable entity. Jews are *on the way to* obtaining the skills, conditionings, and virtues of establishing a state with all its vicissitudes and the prices it will have to pay, and they have to do so not in a tolerant and benevolent environment, grappling not only with inimical Arabs around, but also with the contrary interests and dispositions of the powers that determine their fate. The public opinion of the world feels a sense of moral debt toward Jews, yet there are enough difficulties and cross-purposes working to sway the same public into believing that the establishment of this state will not bear fruit.

On the part of the Jews themselves, however, there are plenty of obstacles in the way of establishing the state, from their not being accustomed to one another, to the occupational one-sidedness, to the initial puerilities of running a state in the feeling that after all the unbearable monstrosities committed against them, the world has obligations toward them and no claims against them. As a result, the Jewish state will no doubt undergo various crises, which, in turn, will weigh down on the intensity of Jewish consciousness throughout the world. In the long run, however, this will hardly alter the strong likelihood, even the certainty, of the firm establishment of Israel and that the sense of Jewish national identity is going to retain and shape its definite outlines throughout the world.

This will not mean that a Jewry with such a minority consciousness will isolate itself from the public life of its country, as forcibly annexed minorities or those hostile for other reasons tend to do. None the more does it mean that the majority might foist the minority identity onto anyone, oust anyone from their public life, or limit them to minority affairs on those grounds. However, it does mean that the sense of Jewish identity will appear more evenly and openly; it will clearly formulate its interests and claims; allow for and call Jewish causes

Jewish; and express its difference from the assimilated and from those who wish to participate in the life of their country as assimilated. As a result, the environment will also be able to speak more evenly about and discuss matters of the Jewish minority, interests, claims, and self-identity, as opposed to the situation when one, mindful of midway Jews, cannot broach these matters without an anti-Semitic slant or tongue-tied circumspection.

With this clarification, the debate between programmatic-assimilationist and Zionist or minority-identity Jews on the "correctness" of their respective positions—that their choice can succeed only if they drag all the others into their own camp and convince them of their mistake at all costs—seems rather barren. Assimilationists in particular are of the opinion that the assertion of Zionism or Jewish self-consciousness only throws obstacles in the way of assimilation and gives all the more reason for the environment to curtail the opportunities of Jews. This is perfectly amiss. Whatever obstacles *other Jews* have thrown in the way of those wanting to assimilate, whether before or after the rise of Zionism, came not from the manifestations of Jewish self-consciousness but from the throngs of midway Jews deadlocked halfway to assimilation; all forceful arguments brought up against the possibilities and seriousness of assimilation drew their material from this quarter. By compelling this midway throng to take a stand, Zionism and Jewish national consciousness have in no way hindered assimilation, but by clarifying its conditions, they have in actuality furthered it. Pitting the two positions against each other is therefore sterile; their "correctness" can be decided by no reasoned argument because it is a choice made on the grounds of emotional ties, disposition, intention, and actual opportunity.

Some Jews have assimilated or will assimilate; others have professed or will come to professing Jewish national or minority identity; in a calm atmosphere, the former will be the clearer and more straightforward option; in troubling times, the latter; and the midway condition will also have its various manifestations. Sooner or later, however, both Jews and non-Jews will have to realize that neither way can be forced—not even by moral pressure—on anyone as the only alternative.

THE DECEPTION IN THE CONDITIONS OF
JEWISH ASSIMILATION IN HUNGARY

Better than anything else, the history of Jewish assimilation in Hungary illustrates the thesis that whatever difficulties assimilation ran into due to the mental and social conditions of Jewry and the relationship between Jews and their environment, the decisive factor smoothing or standing in the way of assimilation

is the internal order and balance of the *assimilating community*. Particularly in
Central Europe, the disorders of social development, which had an essential
role in the rise of anti-Semitism, disposed the non-Jewish environment to follow
a dishonest and contradictory course with regard to Jewish assimilation. The
final cause of all these incongruities and deceptions was the make-believe democratization, middle-class growth, and liberalization of Central Europe and
the lie that wishy-washy constitutional struggles and institutional reforms in the
wake of the suppressed revolutions addressed these issues as though Central
European social development had set out on the way of European development, while the old social structure, outlook, and practice, based on qualitative differences among men, had been left untouched, the overthrow of which
would have been the sine qua non of any middle class development, democratization, social justice, and, finally, even genuine Jewish emancipation and
assimilation.

However, nowhere else in Central-East Europe was the assimilating community as discordant and the cause of assimilation as replete with deceptions
and contradictions as in Hungary. We would be justified in saying that Hungarian society assimilated under indecent conditions or had offered dishonest
conditions for assimilation from the outset. It deceived itself first, by embed-
ding the entire issue of Jewish assimilation into the great illusion of nineteenth-
century Hungarian politics, the wish-dream of linguistically Hungarianizing
the entire historical Hungary. This shifted the focus of the question from the actual social process of assimilation to a demonstrative renunciation of linguistic
and political separation; this was why assimilation was understood as learning
Hungarian or not even as much, only a declaration of being Hungarian in the
censuses. This is why a millennial Hungarian society overextolled the manifestations of assimilation in this sense, primarily the actual assimilation of urban
Jews and Germans, whereby it cherished its vain hopes of Hungarianizing the
entire land in a matter of decades. However, the linguistic assimilation of the
masses of minority peasants in the areas decisive for upholding the integrity
of historical Hungary continued to be without hope and prospect, while Jewish and German assimilation had no bearing on preserving the borders of the
country.

The exaltation of assimilation impressed upon the urban Germans and Jews,
who were inclined to assimilate anyway, the extraordinary hopes and the notion—inconceivable in the case of serious and balanced communities and assimilation into them—that assimilation was not a process primarily concerning
those being absorbed into the majority but a momentous and praiseworthy act
of moral and national consciousness. This was why the urban Jews and Ger-

mans of Hungary became *programmatically assimilated,* even those of them who had hardly set out on the way to assimilation. This was why, irrespective of its actual social content, assimilation became the only and obligatory program of all religious, social, cultural, and whatever associations—unlike anywhere else. This was why the Grossdeutsch spoke of Hungary as the graveyard of Germans and the Zionists scolded Hungarian Jews for being the most dogged and incurable assimilationists.

However, truth would soon out; the assumptions and conditions of assimilation so conceived proved false, and not only was the country victim to its own self-deception, but so were those inveigled into it, Jews in particular. However widespread their genuine assimilation had been, their majority continued to live in the same largely secluded social environment and the same midway condition as before the fervent exaltations of their having learned Hungarian and made their census declarations. The internal and external inhibitions, difficulties, and prejudices that stood in the way of their assimilation were just as numerous as elsewhere—in fact, more numerous.

As we are aware of this, the various theses on the insufficiencies of Jewish assimilation in Hungary strike us as rather superficial; these include the following: the characteristics of assimilated Jews purportedly differ from those of Hungarians; for all their boisterous denials of a separate Jewish community, they have stood by the solidarity between themselves and their separate sense of interest; and they have, with unique energy, thrown themselves into gaining ground in the economic, political, and cultural life of the country.

As far as adaptation to *national characteristics* is concerned, we have already pointed out that we have to distinguish between, on the one hand, physical, temperamental, and ethnic features that are instinctual and unconscious or have become unconscious and, on the other, the forms of conduct and standards of community life. We have also shown that assimilation has to do with the forms and standards of community conduct, not characteristics that become instinctual. Now, Hungarians have their truly graspable characteristics primarily in the area of instinct and ethnicity, physical type, temperament, pace of life, gesture, and musicality, all of which are, of course, complex and lithely distinct, but they are significantly simpler than, for example, their French or British counterparts. Even the existence of these characteristics is often questioned by stating that Hungarians are said to be a mixed breed; certainly they had lost their distinctness to immediate ethnic experience or the public at the time of the settlement or soon after, and it was only unearthed by scholarship recently. In contrast, ethnic experience and the public are quite aware of types, temperaments, and gestures resulting from the various German, Slavic, and

Jewish assimilations. The "unfounded generalizations" in these are absolutely harmless as long as they have no bearing on social policy.

The trouble is that with regard to community conduct, custom, and discipline, in the area where assimilation actually takes place, Hungarians are one of the most shapeless peoples in Europe, or at least they have lost most of their distinct features in the course of the past century. If they did have social and intellectual forms and standards, those do not seem to have stood their ground against the shocks of modern social transformation, as they did not and were in fact utterly confounded in the last generation. Not because there had been too much assimilation; vice versa, assimilation had been confused, superficial, and contradictory because there had been no community procedure, system of conduct, and assessment to which to assimilate. Hungarian society assimilated by fluff and trappings rather than community, moral, and intellectual conduct and lifestyle. Most of the assimilation that did take place in Hungary meant an adaptation not to the entirety of Hungarians—who did not exist as an entity in this sense—but to their various classes, institutions, groups, movements, and ideals.

One of the gravest symptoms of the confusion has been the fact that—short of any better standard following the collapse of the consciously organized element of the community profile—people attempting to find a cure for the chronic crises, imbalances, and disorientations of society began to seek gauges for assessing assimilation in the instinctual layer of the national self, in the Hungarian temperament, pace of life, musicality, composition, and manner of speaking, and thereby to decide whether a work, a person, or a program was Hungarian or not. This would never improve community life, but those assimilated or wanting to assimilate certainly did get the short end of the stick as they could hardly reproduce such characteristics of temperament and gesture. Their doing so would have been perfectly pointless and not made them any more assimilated, but the skewed exercise did confuse the process of their assimilation and elicited all sorts of skewed gestures from them. In the optimistic period of assimilation, it made those wanting to assimilate try and put on all the trappings of pure-bloodedness—an altogether amusing pursuit. In the defensive, disputed period of assimilation, it educed a state of mind in which the assimilated responded with disproportionate or unexpected irritation to any voicing of national character, mention of "true Hungarians," or even the wearing of a braided jacket, deeming them wicked attempts at discriminating against, insulting, excluding, and persecuting them and childishly believing that they would be better protected against such manifestations if they proved that the Hungarians were a mixed lot from the outset and that there were no genuine Hungarian characteristics anyway. It goes without saying that this elicited no friendlier response from the environment. It was this type of attitude that made a none too tolerant Dezső Szabó scathingly and wittily remark that on account of Jewish sensibility, we will soon be prohibited from distinguishing between Pomeranians and dachshunds and must use the universal concept of "dog" in their stead.

As far as the *solidarity* remaining behind assimilation is concerned, as we have already pointed out, it naturally does exist, but in itself it does not in the least obstruct assimilation. What really counts here is that, the social forms and standards of Hungarian society failing, the various social relations, political programs, struggles, and intellectual stances came to present themselves not merely in their actuality and substance, but by bearing secondary meanings as well that were never made explicit but were understood by all, deforming them in a multitude of ways to be either in the cause of the Jews or in the cause of the dislikers of Jews. In this regard, there is a solidarity at work against that of the Jews—both parties fretting about the other's solidarity being amazingly organized while their own is in shambles in the areas that would particularly need it. In truth, neither is fully in action, but both grab their opportunities wherever they find them.

What is most disconcerting about this is not the ranting about the existence, force, and success of this or that kind solidarity but the fact that the community is so powerless, so fallen apart, that it allows the major concerns of the entire community—national solidarity, universal humanism, traditionalism, and radical change—to depend on the essentially minor issues of what Jews or dislikers of Jews are pleased to hear. A community with a serious inner life will not have any such group handle its major life questions in this manner.

Furthermore, we have to point out that the types of conduct in which, according to the firm conviction of the environment, Jewish solidarity "displays the cloven hoof," "smacks of partisanship," or "evens the score" manifest not the interests or solidarity of Jewry but the natural defense of assimilation and the assimilated and will emerge all the more so if assimilation and the situation of the assimilated are disputed and threatened, if the conditions of assimilation are not clearly laid down, if the security of the assimilated is not guaranteed, and if the anti-Semitism of the environment poses the threat that it will keep the Jewish descent of the assimilated in evidence, question the validity of their assimilation, and relegate them back to the Jewish community in word or deed. Anyone so affected by anti-Semitism will necessarily be "prepossessed," not in the sense of partaking of the community of Jewish interest but in the sense of not being able to afford to be unsuspecting, unconcerned, or undoubting in the given case. We often had to see this when anti-Jewish legislation thrust increasing

groups of the assimilated, half- and quarter-Jews, into the common Jewish suffering and naturally elicited from them the same reactions, the same alarm,
and the same sensibility as from the Jews. Even the non-Hitlerite quarters of
Hungarians were often as blind and inhuman as to identify these as manifestations of "interest" and "partisanship," which had been the consequences of the
predicament brought about by anti-Jewish legislation and persecution, as "blatant" examples of racial *characteristics* and proofs of racial theory.

Finally, as to Jews *gaining ground* in the economic, political, and cultural
life of the country, this is a direct consequence of the impasse in which Hungarian social development had been caught; the Hungarian working classes,
particularly the peasantry, were deadlocked under the wholly feudal-aristocratic
conditions, while the Germans and Jews of Hungary, exempt from any feudal
element in their internal world, constituted a middle class. Within their ranks,
the upward mobility of peasants and laborers was hindered only by the material obstacles the middle class put in their way, while the lower strata of Hungarian society were obstructed in their upward struggle not only by material
disadvantage, but also all the human, social, and mental inhibitions the feudal-
aristocratic structure inured in them. This was the source of what was deemed
to be the difference between German and Jewish expansion, but the sagacity
of the ground-gainers was utterly secondary to the crisis into which Hungarian
society had fallen irrespective of assimilation.

The internal deception of the conditions of Hungarian Jewish assimilation
came to light around the turn of the century. The impasse into which Hungary
had been dragged by the Compromise was exacerbated, and Hungarian liberalism and democracy, resting on the traditions of 1848, lost their vigor after the
disestablishment of the church and Jewish emancipation. As Hungarian society
was increasingly bogged down by the terrifying prospect of historical Hungary's
being dismantled, Jews were more and more left to themselves in their assimilationist and democratic position. The collapse after World War I, the Aster
Revolution, the dictatorship of the proletariat, and the Treaty of Trianon undid
the pact Hungarian national society and Jewish assimilation had concluded under false conditions. The counterrevolutionary regime was established, openly
professing the connection between nationalism, anti-democratism, and anti-
Semitism, on the one hand, and democratism, anti-nationalism, and Jewry on
the other.

It suddenly turned out that Jews who had learned to speak Hungarian and
had declared they were Hungarian in the censuses had no immediate assimilating, inclusive, and protective community around them on which they could
clearly count in spite of the fact the formerly ruling assumptions and conditions

of assimilation had been shaken. Though the official representatives of Jewry based themselves on the old pact, their rank and file, in contrast to their millennial extolment, now experienced outright and ruthless exclusion and ostracism, the social media of assimilation being cut to the bare minimum. Official Jewish organizations and leaders concentrated their efforts on making sure this hardly concealed ousting would not become open and the word "Jew" would not be used officially. The First Act on Jews did.

Just how deceptive and unjust the conditions of assimilation in Hungary had been were evinced by one of the last and most bizarre moments of the Jewish tragedy. At the time of the 1941 census, when Hungarian Jews were not only discriminated against and humiliated, but also exposed to acts of deadly persecution, particularly in the reannexed areas, the Hungarian authorities called on the Jews of Subcarpathia, mostly Yiddish-speaking and with a Jewish identity, to declare themselves as Hungarian-speaking and Hungarian nationals to improve Hungarian rates in the area. In no more than three years' time, the Hungarian authorities, which had little changed in the meantime, handed the same people (including infants), who had been good enough for Hungarians earlier, over to the Hitlerite apparatus of mass murder without resistance.

IV. THE SITUATION TODAY

Having attempted to review the community relations between Jews and non-Jews and the various factors and components of the enmity toward Jewry, we are now in a position to examine the situation that has evolved in Hungary after the liberation. First, we must try and understand what effects persecutions have had on the persecutees themselves and how they find their place in Hungarian society.

JEWISH ASSIMILATION, IDENTITY, AND MISGIVINGS AFTER 1944

The vast majority of the Jews acquired experiences of Hungarian society, the Hungarian nation, and its members that have a crucial bearing on their relationship with this community. Apart from their former or current social and assimilation status, their place in the community is also basically defined by what experiences of belonging or forsakenness they went through during the recent persecutions that have overshadowed all their former memories.

Accordingly, there are a good number of Jews or people with Jewish forbears who are capable of continuing to live in the community of Hungarians without qualms on account of their full assimilation, their active participation in the resistance, their having survived the persecutions fortunately without bodily or mental harm, or simply in spite of their suffering or perhaps because they have attained a peace of mind through their ordeals. From among them, some spent the period of persecutions abroad but did not sever their ties with the country, and the earlier they left, the more impartial their attitude is to their assimilation compared to the excruciation and anxieties borne by the majority of those that remained at home. Nevertheless, many of those who survived here at home were able to reestablish their normal relations with the community without particular difficulty, having been able to give up the anxiety and state of alert after the persecutions ceased. These include the old guard and the new, pure-hearted members of the labor movement, the only one among the major assimilating media to have retained its efficiency and functioning; they are passionately working to build a new society from the great melting pot of social transformation that labor marshals. The number of those whose assimilation has thus remained the same, been restored, or has been completed is more than one would have expected during the persecutions, but according to all signs, they are not the majority.

However, for the majority of Jews, the desolation, ordeals, and losses they went through in the persecutions and deportations have cast doubt on or exhausted the entire meaning of this country being their homeland, and, in severe cases, this feeling might develop into a total estrangement from the nation and its majority. Contrary to the expectations of Zionists and others, this has not engendered a rise in Jewish self-consciousness; instead, it has added further community and emotional strains to existing predicaments. Accordingly, many not only will not affirm Jewish identity and resist Zionist calls and non-Jewish encouragements to do so, but also object to the use of the word "Jew," and should the concept be unavoidable, they prefer "deportee," "forced laborer," or "racial persecutee," etc. In contrast to former times, what is stressed here is not that they wish to avoid being referred to as Jews because, as a result of the Hitlerite genealogizing, even those can privately call themselves Jews or persons of Jewish stock who would have avoided doing so previously; nor has this to do with the assimilationist optimism of the millennium because this quarter of the Jewry will reject with irritation or offhandedly any demand on their belonging to the Hungarian nation and their reckoning with its consequences in the manner that was customary formerly. It is thus not that the one who wants no minority identity will want to be Hungarian and vice versa but that there are tens of thousands of people who like hearing neither of their emphatic belonging to the Hungarian nation because it persecuted them or, to say the least, exposed them to persecution, nor of their belonging to the Jewish nation because it was on this very basis that they were victimized and racked, and their memories tell them that whenever the word "Jew" crops up, it is followed by discrimination against them and persecution.

This group is therefore not the midway or transitory condition between Jewish identity and assimilation but a critical state of community belonging with profound misgivings about both. They no longer see a possibility in the old apolitical relation to the country and the non-Jewish environment and accord all community issues with new significance insofar as they recall the slogans, events, acts, and associations of their persecutions. In other words, their entire anxiety seems to be finding a way out through politicizing and laying down the conditions for their assimilation—namely, a political system that offers them guarantees for the persecutions not to happen again. In this respect, two political systems seem to attract them. The first one is the left-wing labor movement in that it opposed all racial discrimination and national isolation, and the second one is conservative, middle-class liberalism, promising as it does the unconditional security of property. Both, however, lead those who seriously opt for them beyond the Jewish point of view; labor requires an appropriate approval of anti-Semitic but anti-capitalist trends and an indifference to the perils of Jewish property, while in the current Hungarian situation, conservative property-protecting liberalism will willy-nilly link up with counterrevolutionary forces that are simultaneously anti-Semitic as well.

Those unable to become fully reconciled with the country nevertheless seek the solution of their individual and collective problems within Hungary and together with Hungarians; in contrast to them, we also have those who have been finally estranged from the country and its community because of the persecutions. Stalling or retracting assimilation, *dissimilating* in this way, does not necessarily point in one direction. Some have taken up Zionism or have been strengthened in so doing, and there has accordingly been, especially among youths, a major current of emigration to Palestine since 1945. There are many who have come to profess a Jewish national or minority identity yet do not wish to leave and have a clear idea of their relationship with the country. Again, there is a significant number who want to emigrate but not primarily to Palestine, though perhaps via Palestine—it being easier to go there first and then move on to some more peaceable country. Thus, instead of the two unwanted options, they want to choose and assimilate to a third one. They do not want to stay here, they say, because everything recalls the horrors of their ordeal. We suspect that this "everything" means not so much the houses, rooms, cellars, or even the roads or brickworks[6] but the far less forgettable human conduct and animosity of which there are many signs even now.

Most recently, the constraints imposed on capitalist opportunity have heightened this wave of emigration, yet I am convinced that for all the difficulties of readjusting, leaving would never have occurred to the lower-income majority of those concerned had it not been fostered by the awesome memory of their tribulations and a sense of animosity in their environment.

To this day, Hungarian public and political thought has not been clear about the complexities and crises of finding a place in the community after the persecution of the Jews. True, many an authoritative statement has been made, so authoritative as to preclude any further debate in this matter, but they have always emphasized one type of case and one manner of solution.

The official position is that the victims of anti-Jewish persecutions are justified in their misgivings only against the old, reactionary, fascist Hungary, the new Hungary being fundamentally and radically different. Old Hungary has not only the persecution of Jews on its moral slate, but also crimes committed against the entire Hungarian people. Beyond the doing of justice and the making of amends within the bounds of possibility, it is not right and fitting to be too much concerned with the Jewish question, all the more so because the sweep of political and social development is going to establish and restore the conditions of full assimilation. This official position, however, is tailored to the state of mind of those assimilated or rapidly assimilating, but aside from those professing Jewish identity, the bitter experiences of the majority of those concerned are far too personal and extensive to be simply put on the slate of a fallen reactionary and fascist regime. True, social transformation, particularly through education, will have a more powerful assimilating effect in the long run than it can today on those who have been overwhelmed by suffering and loss. However, in foreseeing and tending to a long-term development, we should in no way act as though it has already been completed and not take into account critical situations and their consequences.

In contrast, the Zionists hold that the best—in their eyes the only—solution is to create and openly profess a *Jewish national* or *minority identity*. A democratic Hungary being the assimilator, the government has officially not even considered this as a possible option. Immediately after the liberation, it stoutly disapproved of statements—in no way aggressive—emphasizing Jewish national minority identity and even censured the demonstrativeness in having schoolchildren walk the Budapest streets while singing Hebrew songs. Beyond the principles already mentioned, this definite rejection of Jewish identity was perhaps informed by an attitude far too mindful of possible anti-Jewish sentiments in the public that Jewish national minority organization activity could have a negative impact in the majority of the country, which had been used to expecting Jews to own up to their being Hungarians in every respect even amid the persecutions. As a result, Zionism and Jewish minority identity have been hemmed into the framework of religious organization. Yet for all contrary influences, the community consciousness of Jews remains a far more powerful factor than the cause of religion or religious organization, and its formation and institutionalization, as pointed out, should in no way have a bearing on the possibilities of assimilation; quite to the contrary, it could help define the actual ways of assimilation as opposed to the fictions of general assimilation. Nevertheless, separate Jewish identity will not become the exclusive or majority solution; not only do those assimilated or wanting to assimilate insist on taking their own road, but so do their misgiving and estranged fellows. The memories of the horrors do not necessarily lead to accepting a separate Jewish community; they can lead in other directions as well.

On this score, many might find their own solution in emigration. Nevertheless, we cannot with any degree of objectivity say that emigration will solve their problem. We cannot say so for an *objective* and a *moral* reason. *Objectively*, the opportunity of emigration will probably not be open to all those wanting to leave, and many of them will realize in the crucial moment that this desire is not as strong as they believed it to be. *Morally*, we cannot recommend emigration as a "solution" for those who have profound misgivings about the nation because, since we have every reason to withdraw into ourselves over the monstrous death of half a million Jews, it would be a distasteful joke for us to say that the only "solution" to their problem is to leave because of the mental state their plight has brought us into. History had given us the task of arranging a humane world in this country together with three-quarters of a million Jews; having failed, we ought not to say that we cannot do what we should and could have done together with three-quarters of a million with the remaining two hundred thousand.

We must therefore realize that the problem is not how to choose on the basis of conceptual or theoretical grounds and deductions among the solutions prescribing assimilation, Jewish identity, or the rejection of both. Raising social issues as though they were military objectives is quite dangerous because the "solution" will tend to be worked out in the way wars and battles are. Enough misery has been unleashed on the world by men who believed that solving a problem, which they had themselves turned into an impasse and envenomed, meant establishing conditions by hook or by crook wherein the question would no longer exist. There are problems where it is not finding a "solution" that is the decisive factor but sensing the issues at stake and creating clear conditions and a congenial atmosphere for the various solutions that offer themselves to unfold.

If we rightly sense the crisis in the community conditions of Hungarian Jews, we will probably not only not bustle about advancing a "solution," but will also refrain from exhorting, compelling, calling on, persuading, sermonizing, or enlisting people here or there; we will likely not voice so many catchphrases on the unwavering patriotism of Hungarian Jewry; we will not cite Vörösmarty's dictum, "Here must thou live, and here must die," to those wanting to emigrate; we will address to Jews as a whole fewer calls to appease and integrate; and we will not keep spelling out that democratic transformation has of itself made it pointless to refer to injuries and suffering and keep them in evidence since a reactionary and fascist Hungary inflicted them in the first place. To the contrary, we will apply ourselves to cleansing and humanizing the general and universal conditions, standards, environment, and institutions in which Jews live their individual and community lives, in which their various problems arise and are resolved following *different* directions. Finally, it is no less important that we do not impose any single solution on anyone and not even face anyone with a choice. Every youth or everyone seeking new bearings will have to choose anyway. However, in respect to those that have misgivings about us or are in a midway condition, instead of our raising issues of community belonging and identity, it is far more important to shape the entire atmosphere and the proceedings of the community with greater placidity, compassion, less convulsiveness, and less sharpness and thereby create in them the community and mental conditions of loyalty to the country.

Whether such an atmosphere is actually created or stalled obviously hinges on how it is begun; in our case, it will be the way perpetrators of the persecutions are impeached, the way Jews reintegrate into the life of the country, and the way the rest of the country responds.

NATIONAL RESPONSIBILITY AND THE IMPEACHMENT OF PERPETRATORS

From the outset, the impeachment of anti-Jewish offenses and the indemnification of victims were carried out under conditions not clearly and honestly stated. After the demise of counterrevolutionary Hungary, legal proceedings against perpetrators undoubtedly had to be, in both number and scope, primarily indictments against anti-Jewish crimes; the number of trials against politicians, soldiers, and civil servants who had passed the country into the hands

of Hitlerite rule and committed atrocities against non-Jews were but a fraction
of the court proceedings against those that had murdered, tortured, robbed,
surrendered, and injured Jews. Apart from the disproportion in numbers, the
suffering, injuries, and seeking of redress of the Jews were vastly different in
kind from anything else and did not at all correspond to the impeachment the
Hungarian nation initiated against its leaders who had diverged from the path
of duty.

In the cause of the Jews, the ever-present problem was, apart from the personal perpetrators, the incomparably greater injury to human dignity and that
the *entire, middle-class-led* Hungarian society, which, apart from itself having
been victimized and disabled by fascism, had left Jews to their fate beforehand.
Nevertheless, the cause of the Jews was preferably seldom referred to but was
merged with the general actions to eliminate fascism, as though Jews were only
one type among fascism's many types of victims, as though their suffering were
one among the many equal sufferings.

This was how official public life had intended it, stressing not handling Jews
separately even in the doing of justice. The left wing of the coalition did so because any added emphasis on the Jewish aspect of impeachments would divert
attention from the truly important matters, the campaign against fascism and
the social classes in the way of progress. The right wing of the coalition avoided
any special mention of the Jewish cause because it would have prompted Jews
to lay further claims. To a certain extent, Jews themselves shunned bringing
their own cause to the fore, partly because they themselves disliked hearing
themselves being named, but I doubt whether the majority of Jews would
have assumed, of their own accord, the rather—to use a now obsolete term—
assimilationist position of evading indications of Jewish concerns without public authorities bringing it home to them that if they made express claims to
Jewish redress, they would run into various difficulties and reluctance, but if
they tied in well with the general antifascist language, they would meet with
much less resistance.

This was how those called to represent the nation politically and intellectually failed to address in an authentic and exemplary way the matter of self-
examination, heart-searching, and admission of responsibility by the entire nation for the persecution against the Jews. If any statement to this effect was
made, it was on the transgressions of *others*, or, if it did go beyond this, it failed
to attract a serious response because of the persons making the statement or its
content. Thus nothing has allayed the ceaseless, ever-increasing feeling among
Jews that no one is going to own up to the monstrosities they underwent and
that the whole country, the nation, has tacitly agreed to gloss over and hush

up the matter of responsibility, throwing the blame on a couple of politicians and thugs. It might seem naive of me to attribute so much significance to the national failure to admit responsibility for the persecutions against the Jews and to imagine that words and statements have the ability to mollify such tensions. I know no declaration will bring the dead back to life, make perpetrators walk into prison, and return their pillage of their own accord or the survivors give up their grief and fury. However, general statements of morality, standards, and principle do have a decisive role in the ways people frame their own advised, mindful, and considerate opinions on rulings made by any formal evaluative, review, or impeachment procedure.

This might strike some as rather odd, experiencing as they do that the past three years have been solely about Jews seeking redress, and they do not see anything lacking in this respect. Yet what they find *too much* is closely related to what we have *lacked* above. The success and credibility of any calling to account depends on whether it can find, uphold, and secure the acceptance of demarcations and distinctions that clearly draw the line between punishable crimes and offenses to be sanctioned by lighter procedures; between offenses sanctionable procedurally and conduct that can be disapproved of; and between conduct that can be disapproved of in public and conduct that belongs strictly under the jurisdiction of one's conscience. In Hungary, the nation has both failed to admit responsibility and define the limits of personal redress, as a result of which neither the pursuit of amends nor moral complacency has met with observable limits.

The nature of Jewish injuries, grievances, and pursuit of amends has always been to eke out the objectively graspable offense with the bent of the non-Jewish environment to insult, humiliate, and morally disparage Jews; moreover, many of the wrongs they suffered were particularly sore because of the ideas and experiences with which they were associated. Now, their pursuit of amends and redress—the singularity and incomparability of which the nation has failed to admit—has inundated the entire legal and juridical apparatus of impeachment; it has raised procedures for trying and punishing individual perpetrators or suspects to the level of making amends nationally; and it has so shaped the atmosphere of a calling to account that the victims of the persecutions have added to each borderline and doubtful case all the indifference and spite of which the persons not taken to the dock have reminded them. On the other hand, the failure to admit the responsibility of the nation has led people to construe responsibility in a far too narrow, self-indulgent, and literal way; those that kept away from killing, torturing, giving away, and robbing have begun to feel that they thereby demonstrated their moral eminence and worth and to believe that it is a grave injustice to reproach them for having been wicked, indifferent, or gloating.

Muddying the measures of responsibility and culpability has resulted in a serious and still unresolved tension about bringing perpetrators to account. Apart from pitting the parties against one another, this confusion has undermined the credibility of the judicial system; true, looked at from a distance, its apparatus has sought to maintain a balance between objective truth and the claims of the offended, between efficiency and the quest for justice. While the keenness of the tormented and their pursuit of amends have overwhelmed the judiciary and its regulated procedures of finding evidence, a resentment has developed in its administrators out of either a preexisting or a consequential repugnance to the Jews and the defenses and solidarity of those with a bad conscience. The urges and ploys of charging and defending will soon mount to a level where even the plainest case will become a quandary and the courtrooms will be filled with the confusion of unfounded allegations, biased witnesses, false identifications and non-identifications, suspicious extenuating testimonies, demands for hanging, and the accused being treated as though they were martyrs. Thus the frontlines within the very bosom of the authorities are between those willing to punish even the innocent for the sake of ensuring severe punishment or to leave even perpetrators at large for the sake of ensuring clemency, with borderline cases being decided on the grounds of mere power relations. As a result, the majority of Jews are convinced that the crimes committed against them are punished with deliberate half-heartedness, both the criminal and civil law procedures being bureaucratic, slow, light, sometimes biased, and even outrageously unjust. In contrast, the view that has gained wide currency among non-Jews is that the procedures on charges of fascism have become manhunts and that not even the innocent can feel safe when subjected to them.

The lack of proper measures, limits, and distinctions has led to even graver consequences where adverse existential interests interfered with impeachment or screening procedures. Screening procedures at places of work have acquired rat-race characteristics—the fierce struggle for jobs or positions to which the anti-Jewish legislation had given rise previously. Not a whit do I mistake a procedure excluding certain groups of men from various occupations and livelihoods on the grounds of certain characteristics of birth for one that does the same on the grounds of crimes and inactions committed against the nation and humanity. The less a profession has been under public scrutiny and the more ruthless the one-upmanship has been within its circles, the more warped the impeachment or screening procedure has become in both the indictment and the defense.

The same conflict has surfaced in the daily settling of accounts: the guardians and keepers of Jewish property and belongings have the impression that Jews, immeasurably suspicious, do not hold back from initiating police action, setting aside even trust and friendship and demanding from them valuables or accounts that they could not possibly have kept or maintained under the conditions of war. On the other hand, the victims of the anti-Jewish laws have the feeling that those they had requested to keep their belongings or those that had got hold of their property managed them unconscientiously or thievishly. Naturally, these are mutual experiences—the more genuine, the more one-sided. There were tens of thousands of cases when the belongings deposited were kept in full, but there were likewise hundreds of cases when those unable to render a proper account were left out of harm's way. These are seldom mentioned because people tend to sound off on the wickedness of their fellow men more than their decency.

This is why there has been so much mutual blankness about *gratefulness* and *worthiness*. The majority of Jews are perfectly justified in believing that they have, all in all, nothing to be thankful for from their environment. However, if they apply this community score to those individuals that do deserve gratefulness, this will be yet another unjust generalization—this time on the part of Jews—that contributes to the dehumanization of the relationship between Jews and non-Jews. Non-Jews, on the other hand, tend to measure their acts of decency during the anti-Jewish persecutions not by their inherent worthiness but by the Hungarian average, which was disgracefully low. This is how one's having spoken to Jews has come to be regarded as an act of help deserving gratefulness, one's having left Jews alone as saving their lives, one's having arranged paltry things as taking deadly risks, and one's not having given them away as a brave standing up for them.

We have now to address and evaluate the impeachment procedures taken or attempted against representatives of the intelligentsia. Hungarian intellectual life has been badly in need of an authentic and thorough reckoning of its honors and letdowns, its good works and wrongdoings—one that would clearly distinguish moral and character flaws from differences in ideology and principle. No such assessment by any appropriately authorized and acknowledged forum has been made to any degree of authenticity and acceptability. However, a certain list and a terminology of "writers compromised by fascism" have been promulgated whereby men so dubbed can be discussed, handled, excluded from here or there, not admitted, boycotted, and have legal proceedings taken against them or threatened. The sheer fact that this list has come into being is a glaring example of the decline of our public mind; it has come to include people of all sorts and kinds, from those extolling the German occupation or inciting to racial hatred; men with obsessions; men who participated in manhunts; men overly ambitious; various intermediary figures to men whose character, worth, and conduct are beyond doubt yet who have not taken the position of the non-existence of the Jewish question and have broached the proportions of Jews at various stages—which, true enough, is a dangerous snare, but bringing it up and discussing it with a pure intention and language can be neither prohibited nor morally branded. All these writers are censured in the same tone of voice and faced with the same difficulties, and it has often required major political intervention to avert their being treated in an identical way.

As a most grave consequence, a contrary position has been taken defending all these authors together under the catchphrase "authors pursued and assailed by Jews." In other words, uniform, undistinguishing attacks have a counterproductive effect: instead of reinforcing antifascist struggle, they create a pantheon of national martyrs, making heroes even of undeserving men. This is all the more foolish because the rule that no one can assume the position of judge exclusively, judges themselves being continually examined and subject to judgment, applies to intellectual life more than anywhere else. Nevertheless, I see no justification in being scandalized at those who are driven to such a confusion of moral standards because of their persecutions and suffering and who, on top of it all, have the largely well-founded bitter feeling that the issue of responsibility is being glossed over; we ought to be revolted not at others' lack of temperance but at our own overzealous agreement or morally complacent dumbness.

With solid standards, a balanced intellectual life would surely have shaped if not a regulated procedure, at least a public mentality observing clear limits, which would, first, have created the appropriate means and atmosphere for the common admission of responsibility and, second, cut down to size the various attempts at whitewashing or attacking, meted out the appropriate judgment on acts and failures to act, and protected people from undeserved castigation. This would enable judgments of the following kind: the ideas of X are arguable, but his character is exemplary; the ideas of Y are confused, but his passions are pure; the talents of Z are impeccable, but his morals are foul; A dislikes Jews—when they mingle with masters; B did not behave himself very well but committed no particular crime; C was wicked, deserves some punishment, but should not be silenced; D ought to be imprisoned but should be allowed to write poetry afterward; E's conduct was irreproachable but a little too cautious; F did his utmost best during the persecutions against the Jews, but his die-hard conservatism and feudal outlook prevent him from being an example; G greatly erred but did so out of an ill-conceived social radicalism; H's impeccability had some jockeying to it; J must be not only locked up, but silenced too—Hungarian intellectual life would hardly feel his loss. With nuanced and detailed judgments, a sound intellectual life could outline against whom no further procedures should be initiated; who should not be harmed after suffering certain punishments; who can apply for membership to moral bodies; who requires creative and bread-earning opportunities or membership in work-income and welfare organizations; and some would have to put up with the consequence of having been judged morally inferior and intellectually harmful for good.

The lack of appropriate standards has also thrown off even minor cases, those in particular where people are called to account for "harping on Jews." This is where, with a particularly refined sensibility, distinction should be made between any criminally chargeable propagation of the moral confusion and community danger of anti-Semitic fascism and any generalization, bias, or aversion the environment might have toward the Jews without its becoming objectively punishable. What is punishable is when someone supports and demands the persecution and destruction of Jews, not when he reminds one of a person's Jewishness in an embarrassing way; what is punishable is when someone incites violence against Jews, but not when he damns them out of anger; what is punishable is when someone advertises misleading information on Jews to the effect that they are the cause of all social ills, but not when he remarks upon their role and affluence; what is punishable is when one blazons the morally destructive effect of Jews, but not when he expresses common beliefs in the greater moral uprightness of Christians. Make no mistake; this is not to mean that such manifestations might not be couched in atrociously inhumane and offensive language or might not hide wickedness and that anyone venting such manifestations does not deserve severe reproach, but they might likewise hide lesser evil; however, they certainly do not extend into that area that can be impeached by an authority or that it is wise to do so. It is only natural and understandable that a much-afflicted, long-suffering person immediately associates these manifestations with whatever else he had experienced and takes such blusterers to the police with the fervor of having caught them in the act, but I regard it particularly damaging when authorities make cases out of such. I very much fear that the many terse reasons adduced in sentences for internment and screening-procedure rulings passed on the accused for "voicing fascist slogans" were driven by such motives.

Seeing all these discordances, we should say it is almost a pity that no amends-pursuing turmoil had broken out before any regulated and orderly impeachments; had this happened, on the one hand, the benefits and limits of regulated procedures would be clear for both our entire society and those concerned, and, on the other, much passion would have found an outlet that now finds no other way out but by frequenting trials before the People's Tribunals.

This is how the *official* role of Jews in impeachment procedures has come to be notorious. Many Jews or Jews under the anti-Jewish laws having participated as judges in the investigations and hearings of cases, there is experiential evidence of and widespread appeal to the notion that the essence of impeachment is nothing but retribution, Jews passing judgment over Hungarians as Hungarians had done over Jews. The dangers of this notion have been noticed by many, and it has officially and unofficially been often stated that the screening procedures and the People's Tribunals are meant not to provide an opportunity for Jews to pass sentence over non-Jews but to do justice against wickedness and baseness that injure human dignity and take lives. Accordingly, government authorities have sought to fill these posts with preferably as many non-Jews as possible. However, no one has dared to say that the moment there was a danger that the idea might occur to people that the People's Tribunals and the screenings were but Jews sitting in judgment, what should be said is no longer that *preferably* fewer Jews should participate in the trials but plainly and definitely that *Jews* or persons under the anti-Jewish laws must not participate in any of the special trials for anti-Jewish perpetrators—neither at first nor at a higher instance.

It might be said in response to this that it is fascism itself to distinguish between Hungarians in such a way, there being no Jews, only Hungarians with different religious backgrounds, all equally fit for any job. However, if a middle- or lower-middle-class forced laborer, who had formerly been inactive politically, now comes home only to learn that his family was exterminated and joins the judicial apparatus to interrogate, investigate, and judge, it is but fiction to say that his having been humiliated and having suffered as a Jew does not in the least get in the way of his acting in this capacity and that he is just one of the many Hungarian democrats fighting fascism. I myself have seen several instances of such sublimation of personal motives; indeed, I have been astonished at the large number of persecutees—far larger than I would have expected after the deportations—who passionately sought to and could uphold their objectivity in given impeachment cases, yet I do not know that this attitude is general. Moreover, it is not "careers" that should be closed to Jews, in the way they were under the anti-Jewish legislation, but temporary action, the aim of which is to restore the integrity of the Hungarian nation, insofar as punishment can do so, and to castigate and brand those that injured its honor. It is therefore all important that the moral grounds of such a judgment be indisputable, in no respect questionable or dubitable at any time in the future. After all, the aggrieved party, as the good old rule has it, may not also be the judge, and, in our case, the Jews have the role of the aggrieved party. If the Jews do not demand international court procedures and emphasize their being part of the Hungarian nation, it is only the better non-Jewish part of the Hungarian nation that ought to and can pass judgments with credibility and a serious hope of satisfaction in lawsuits of Jews versus their persecutors.

It would certainly have been better to talk this out calmly three years ago. Many might feel it would have been the duty of some "decent" Jews to bring this up. I think no one has the right to make any such moral claims on Jews or individual Jews; we cannot spare ourselves the embarrassment that, however disagreeable it would have been to say so and thereby elicit irritation, misunderstanding, and accusations from Jews, who are particularly sensitive to anything of the sort, it should have been those that had been *relatively* decent as non-Jews who should have raised this, those who had a degree of moral authority to offer remarks on such matters. It was cowardice and sloth on the part of each one of us not to do so and whine among ourselves about the "lack of restraint" in Jews, when, again, it was the lack of community willpower in the entire nation and ourselves that was the decisive factor. It would have been still easier to say so than carry it through with a partly compromised and befuddled, middle-class-led Hungarian society. To no avail was it repeatedly and loudly emphasized, when the impeachment apparatus was set up and its many posts filled, that one's having been a racial persecutee does not necessarily imply one's being a democrat as well; in the final count, there was always less danger of judges who had been subject to the anti-Jewish laws turning out to have been Arrow-cross henchmen. In practice, therefore, Jewishness and being democratic came to be connected. Yet greater democratic openness and watchfulness could have done a lot of good but would surely have avoided the anti-Semitic mood that has apparently evolved around the impeachment procedures. This problem, however, is not limited to the impeachment of anti-Jewish perpetrators but expands into the entire public life of the new Hungary and requires special discussion.

OLD ANTI-SEMITISM AND NEW ANTI-SEMITES AFTER 1944

At the time of the liberation, anti-Semitism somehow dropped back to point zero. Whoever had had a dislike for Jews did not grow to like them, but the monstrosities that had befallen them dwarfed whatever had been brought up against them, any such word getting stuck in people's throats. Since then, this reticence has utterly vanished. We now have a new, regular anti-Semitism, drawing its references and material from developments since 1945. Ever since its emergence, the cause of this new anti-Semitism has been debated; according to one opinion, it is simply fascism creeping forth again; others hold that the irritation of the elements declassed due to the land reform, B Listing, and other changes has turned against Jews; yet others believe that primarily the former persecutors, but somewhat the whole country, has a bad conscience, and they want to offset this by countercharges against the Jews now. On the other hand, there are friendly or unfriendly remarks about the excesses of the impeachments and inflation profiteering by officials, which are offhandedly rebuffed. The revival of anti-Semitism has also been dubbed neo-anti-Semitism, and others dispute whether such issues should be allowed to be talked about at all and stress that it is the old anti-Semitism, known very well from the mass killings, that has sprung up again and that it is the old anti-Semites plucking up their courage again.

Undoubtedly, old anti-Semites have their share in the rise of this new anti-Semitism. First, there are those whose consciences are burdened by punishable or punished offenses; then there are those who committed nothing culpable, yet a certain meanness, inhumanness, or inaction does weigh down on their consciences enough to make them have a bad feeling when hearing too much about responsibility for the persecution of the Jews, and they offset this bad feeling by taking part in the anti-Jewish mood. Again, there are those that were earnestly sorry for the unwarranted ordeals of the Jews, but as a result of the old social-hierarchy attitude, they had been somewhat satisfied in seeing Jews put in "their proper place," constrained, forced into humility and humiliation, and now they deem it Jewish excess when they do not observe the same fear of death that had been written over their faces when seeking their help earlier. Driven by essentially the same mentality, there is another group of people who truly deplored and even mourned the deathward banishment of the Jews, but they had nonetheless regarded it as a monstrous yet definite solution of the Hungarian Jewish problem or their own particular problem with Jews. They therefore now note with increasing irritation that some of the Jews have returned home and that the majority of the Budapest Jews, who had had the most conspicuous role, have survived—if not many more. Hence, we stumble on people who want to deny the deaths of half a million people because all ten Jewish shopkeepers have returned to their street and two additional ones have come too. Unforgivable for anyone with a sound moral sensibility, so come up jests attempting to frame the death camps and mass killings as cheerier and less harmful.

It would, however, be a grave delusion and a self-deception on the part of Jews to believe that the essence of the new anti-Semitism is only the old anti-Semites throwing of their shyness. No doubt, the nature and basic structure of the new anti-Semitism cannot be different from the old one. This, however, means not that it is the same anti-Semitism certain quarters exercised with increasing monstrosity from the beginning of the 1940s but that it is made up of prejudice, frictions with Jews, and the effects of social problems in the same way as any other anti-Semitism.

As undoubtedly multitudes of people have come to relate to Jews in completely new circumstances since 1944, we can be perfectly sure that the conditions of anti-Semitism have taken shape in some people. There is no *neo-anti-Semitism*, but there are *neo-anti-Semites*. This is obvious in two respects. First, there is an increasing number of people who had emphatically not been anti-Semites before the liberation but have become such, sometimes even professing to be such. Second, the Hungarian peasantry was not anti-Semitic, but there is much more rural anti-Semitism today in Hungary than before. I must stress that by "peasant," I mean working-class smallholder or poor peasants because we know very well that anti-Semitism was not unknown among peasants with large farms and who had an equal rank with the squirearchy, as evidenced by the atrocities in the Hungarian Plains in 1919.

An examination of the social background of the three outbreaks of anti-Jewish passion after 1944 demonstrates that they were not merely about the reappearance of old anti-Semites. In the first peasant action, the role of the nationalist middle class believing the nation to be under Jewish dominion was quite clear. The second was a clearly anti-capitalist proletarian affair, and what made it become a pogrom and be infected by anti-Semitism was not that popular anger turned against two capitalists who happened to be Jews but that the third one, a non-Jew, was allowed to run after a few kicks. The third does not even deserve the name of pogrom because the people whose anger had been aroused by gentlefolk broke the windows of that class of men regardless of their religious affiliation, and it was clear that the radicalized peasant crowd would have no more of gentlemen's leadership or deception.

If it is now asked what conditions and circumstances have made men become anti-Semitic recently, then we first have to mention the post-1945 *losers in the social transformation*—large-estate owners, men and layers that have lost both property and office and who, due to their social status and apart from their inherent birth-conscious sense of superiority, had allowed themselves not to be irritated about Jews (they had been known to be non-dangerous) and have some experience and material on which to ground their identification of democracy, communism, and Jews.

With its shocking experiences, the social transformation may have made anti-Semites of even those whose interests it did not touch or even benefitted them.

With regard to the replacements initiated by the regime change, the old rule holds as ever that people steeped in a feudal-aristocratic outlook will tolerate the leadership, dominance, perhaps even the haughtiness and bullying of classes or persons with a historical authority far more than of those who acquired their power recently, even if they belong among their rank, not to mention if they are different in clearly circumscribable ways.

The frictions involved in the impeachment process have also contributed to the reappearance of anti-Semitism. To no avail has it been stated that only those with a bad conscience have a reason to be afraid of being denounced, indicted, screened, or purged; this will hardly alter the fact that being exposed to denunciation, impeachment, screening, purges, or detrimental adjudication has extended over the entire country. Moreover, taking into account the mental state of Jews after the persecutions and their general mistrust of everyone, we can be sure that these are the very circumstances that create new anti-Semites. The most striking examples of this group are those who had stood up for the persecutees but have now turned against them. On my part, I believe it is unforgivable and shows a lack of sufficient moral sensibility to say, whatever wrongs one may have suffered, "I regret having helped Jews," and I have often experienced that this is said by people who magnify the little or meager help they gave or believe they gave to match the wrong they now suffer. The point is not that the number of such cases or that anti-Semitism is based on them—something rather unlikely—but that such cases are non-negligible factors in *morally* underscoring and reinforcing anti-Semitism with whatever roots.

We could seek out and find other social and individual circumstances that lead to frictions newly reinforcing anti-Semitism. All these have a single common denominator: the obvious change in the power relations of the Jews.

THE JEWS AND POWER RELATIONS

The fall of the counterrevolutionary regime brought about wide-ranging changes in the seats of power; in positions of controlling social, property, and benefit opportunities, which have replaced wealth in many respects; and in all the posts responsible for assessing and selecting people—that is, the distribution of social opportunity. Anti-Semites and Jews in a sensitive humor have produced amazing figures on how far these changes have taken place in the interest of Jews or Jews who had been subject to the anti-Semitic laws. There is no point in trying to shun this question because the country has lost its innocence and unsuspectfulness in this for a long time to come; however alive the bad memories are of examinations of rates by the previous authorities, officials managing affairs continue to calculate numbers off record. We do not have to make any calculations to decide how far these urban-legend statistics reflect reality or not because we can assess the changes without dwelling on any such figures.

Directly after the liberation, parallel to the demise of large-estate owners and the top-brass government officials and business leaders who had been compromised by right-wing politics, the parties of the left-wing opposition and labor rose to power; posts in the public and communized part of the economy were filled by new leaders who had not been compromised by right-wing politics; big business was temporarily restored; and Jews were partially indemnified for their various losses following the elimination of all legal and actual constraints on their economic and social advancement. As a purely transitory phenomenon, there was a short-lived flowering of speculators, black marketeers, or simply people earning a livelihood easily during the inflation. Later, communization cut down big business significantly, increasing the importance of the managers of state-owned companies. On the basis of the known rates of Jews and non-Jews in the various groups concerned, we can be sure that Jews and Jews under the anti-Semitic legislation significantly benefitted by the replacements and the partial restoration of the old conditions. That there has been some sort of common motive behind these changes is disproved by the growing influence of the policy directed against Jewish capitalists and business owners, resulting in a major wave of emigration, which calls into doubt the efficiency of the Jewish power that anti-Semites suppose, and this doubt is not fully counterbalanced by any examination of the rates of the state-owned company managers. The truth is that the entire replacement is based on a partial restoration of the old social and economic structures and positions, on the new socialist distribution of benefits and advantages, and on a temporary boom, and it is quite turbulent. The only common point and denominator it has in regard to Jews is that these partial processes took place at the same time, *after* the persecution of Jews and the fall of their persecutors.

For all the apparent concerns of many, the crux of the problem, regardless of whether the rates are lasting or changing, is not the rates themselves. Let us be clear: so long as all Hungarian people do not have the opportunities for an education, a choice of career, and advancement, even the most radical rearrangements in the distribution of economic, social, and political opportunity cannot get any further than a shifting of the proportions of Hungarian gentlemen, members of the Christian middle class, and those of German or Jewish stock. The road toward middle-class development has been open only to these four groups, and changing their proportions in itself is not going not give us a Hungarian society with a healthier structure, a straighter route toward development, and a calmer state of mind.

Nevertheless, it is worth pointing out that unclarified assessment and selection criteria and unevaluated mass tendencies, attractions, and repulsions do have a bearing on the Jewish and non-Jewish rates. Not that these have resulted in disproportions and not in order that the rates should be "improved" but because false standards of assessment have been provided; it is only after their clarification that the distribution of Hungarian social and political opportunities can be righted. There are two relationships to bear in mind here: first, the one between Jews and anti-fascism and, second, the one between Jews and communism.

The identification of Jews with democracy has always cropped up in countries whose democratic development was uneven and interrupted, where powerful and massive feudal-aristocratic-serf conditionings had to be tackled, and where intense social and emotional ties had to be eliminated in order to develop a social attitude based on the equality of men in value and rank. In such an environment, emancipated Jews, who had no feudal inhibitions to overcome and had largely abandoned their own community ties, found it easier and more self-evident to take sides with democracy than others did. It has always been an illusion to attribute any propaganda or exemplary value to this democratism due to the differences in social background and the isolation of Jews from the rest of society; quite to the contrary, connecting democracy and Jewishness soon became the express program of anti-democratic forces. Related difficulties arose throughout Central Europe, including Hungary, at the turn of the last century, and then the identification of democracy with Jewishness became part of the official propaganda of the counterrevolutionary regime following the defeat at the end of World War I, the Aster Revolution, the dismantling of historical Hungary, and the Commune.

The single most important change brought about by the ascendancy of fascism in this respect was that the simple reactionary misconception of identifying democracy with Jewishness became monstrous political practice. Throughout Europe, the rise of fascism disrupted the institutions and discipline that restrained raw power lust, domineering, human ruthlessness, and selfishness unmoved by aims, ideals, and systems of thought; and, again throughout Europe, it brought to the fore men with a fascist type of morality, brushing off the uncomfortable control of the organizing principles of the objective aims guiding society in order to be able to assert their aggression.

Due to the social forces, passions, and impasses behind fascism and its Central European situation, Hungary was doomed to undergo an anti-Semitic version of fascism; however, without German neighbors and dominance, it could never have produced the known level of anti-Jewish hatred and persecution on its own. This meant that the touchstone of the entire fascist selection became largely its relationship to the Jews or those of Jewish stock, whom the persecutions had forced into an isolation never experienced before. Fascism therefore carried out its political and moral selection exclusively on non-Jewish Hungarian society, and Hungary had not been subject to such dimensions of selection for centuries, including during the war of independence in 1848–1849. In the quite long period between the first anti-Jewish act until the bloody fall of the counterrevolutionary regime, all those not subject to the anti-Jewish legislation faced the greatest possible temptation and opportunity to fall into a power frenzy, to be inhumane and ruthless or ungrateful and wicked, to prevail aggressively and immorally, to acquire power and wealth, and to take pleasure in it all without responsibility. These opportunities not only selected all the wicked and base men from those not subject to the anti-Semitic laws, but also elicited all the wickedness that there had been hidden in average decent men.

And this is the moment that befuddled the moral and leadership selection of Hungarian democratic forces; the fascist selection did not assert itself on Jews and those subject to anti-Jewish legislation, among whom the number of fascist-minded men was the same or insignificantly lower. The moment fascism in Hungary collapsed, the Jewish and non-Jewish parts of society stood face to face with each other, with one part well selected and compromised by fascism and the other with an immense amount of innocent suffering weighing down on them and wholly uncompromised by fascism. To no avail has it been loudly and officially proclaimed that having been subject to the anti-Jewish laws does not make one a democrat; the negative condition of selection, being uncompromised by fascism, was assumed to be given in Jews and was accorded significance in practice—the sufficient number of democrats lacking. Moreover, persons with adequate credibility failed to distinguish, expressly in respect to the Jews, between those who had been involved in the left-wing, antifascist, and labor movement and those who had turned against fascism because of the persecutions not in order to discriminate against the latter but to retain the right of giving an example of and teaching democracy to the former. This distinction wanting, the general uncompromisedness of Jews had two grave consequences: first, the right to teach democracy, sermonize, and demand correction, and, second, that fascist-minded men have come to act in the name of democracy.

Teaching and sermonizing have became particularly dodgy when their representatives pretend to have been the only ones to have seen the real interests of the Hungarian people and clearly recognized the self-deluding and dangerous policy toward the restoration of historical Hungary under fascist dominance and that, as a result of which, they are entitled to rebuke as chauvinists all those who have taken to heart the humiliation of a lost war and the cause of cross-border Hungarians and demand national forwardness and the protection of national interests. Now, the authentic assessment of such issues should certainly be the right of people whose opposition to the various types of fascism and national self-delusion antedates the anti-Jewish persecutions.

The actions of fascist-minded men in the name of democracy have been particularly dangerous in instances of *revolutionary violence*. We should clearly distinguish between revolutionariness and fascist aggression. People with conservative leanings tend to lump them together, thinking of them both as a repudiation of established rights, formal legal procedures, and moderate methods. However, not all determination, unsparingness, and will mean fascism or the like; *principled* determination, unsparingness, and will do not necessarily mean that even when there might be grave concerns about it. The revolutionary and the Fascist can clearly and easily be distinguished; the revolutionary is the one who is ready to put aside forbearance and sensitivity in the interest of and under the strict rule of a *fundamental aim*, while the Fascist is the one who, in order to proceed without forbearance and sensitivity, is ready to enter into the service of any aim or learn any genuine or pseudo-ideology, the aims of which he continually contravenes in following the rules of his savagery. As revolutionariness has come to cover the same ground as communism in our day, we have to broach the problems of identifying communism and Jewishness.

The identification of Jews' power ambitions with communism has been a long-time punch line of the various streaks of European conservatism and fascism. In Hungary, this became a commonplace in the public life of the counter-revolution after the first Commune, so much so that Hungarian middle-class circles have tended to believe that Jewish interests and aims rule both the leadership and the general policies of communism and that it is enough to be well connected with Jews to be able to join up with the Communists. The extent of the confusion of terms is quite clear from a remark I heard recently: "Why all the Communist fuss over N.N.; after all, he has always been a *liberal?*" The wonderfully absurd sentence can only be understood if we are aware that in the Hungarian middle-class manner of speaking, "liberal" means a *philo-Semite* and "Communist," a stakeholder in *Jewish power*. The first step to really shatter this attitude was the unrelenting communization of large-scale industry, which struck down on Jews as well. In a broader perspective, the shaping of the conditions of Jews in Russia is a better example; it clearly demonstrates that without having been "philo-Semitic" in the beginning and becoming "anti-Semitic" later, the development of communism was driven by other forces than its relation to the Jews.

However, it is quite true that Jewish intellectuals and tradesmen found it easier and were quicker to respond to communism, a fact that can quite easily be explained by the different attitude of Jews to feudalism and capitalism and their openness to social criticism. The acceptance of socialism, particularly its Marxist version, implies a readiness to draw the final consequences of the inner logic of capitalism; this is why people steeped in the aristocratic-serf worldview tend to be unable to have a grasp of Marxism. This is how—not through the partisanship between Jewish capitalists and Communists—that capitalism and the communism of Jews relate. This relationship has no masses behind it; it is an elite that is separated from middle-class, democratic Jewish society and finds its place in the huge assimilating melting pot of the labor movement, particularly the revolutionary labor movement. In proportion to the development of the entire society, the conditions of even participation in the socialist movement and its actions will also be created.

In a post-1944 Hungary, the problem is not with old members of the labor movement or those that joined it recently through serious assimilation and selection processes but the masses of new members who joined and are joining as a result of the recent anti-Jewish persecutions. Apart from the mere fact of the persecutions, the massiveness of this movement is related to the special circumstances in Hungary as well. The Europe-wide spread of Hitlerite anti-Jewish persecution was confronted efficiently by two factors: first, militant leftism, primarily communism, and, second, the serious strongholds of the European tradition, churches, conservative bureaucracies, and the middle classes. No doubt, the first group had a greater vitality, while the second commanded major forces not so much for fighting ideological battles but for actually protecting and saving Jewish lives. As pointed out, the occasional efforts of Hungarian conservative forces *as a whole* failed, primarily because the original anti-Semitic infection of the counterrevolutionary establishment undermined their resolution. It was as a consequence of this that the basically apolitical Jewish masses, which had up to then passively followed the conservative-minded liberal-capitalist leadership, now saw only the Communist Party as both morally upright and physically protective in the question of anti-Jewish persecution. This is far from saying that the majority of this mass became Communist, or all the less that it can follow the Communist Party after all the anti-capitalist actions; what it does mean is that a government restoring capitalism in Hungary would lead to counterrevolutionary and anti-Semitic action. No one is entitled to object to this construction of the question, but as a mass phenomenon it does raise some problems.

Some of these problems have been deemed timely and addressed by the labor movement—namely, a large part of this membership follows middle-class conditionings in its lifestyle, ideals, and patterns of thought. I see no need to elaborate on this because the determination and strength with which the party persecutes these middle-class leanings within its framework, excludes them, and curbs the opportunities of trader livelihoods are much harsher than what the outside observer would deem necessary.

A further group of entrants is more difficult to discern, but the problem they pose are quite public and obvious; they are driven into joining the party and going through fire and ice to prove their trustworthiness by the consciousness that Communists are the ones most determined in their attacks and punitive actions against their opponents, primarily the fascists, and the ones who put their followers in strong and efficient positions of power. If need be, this state of mind easily and readily forgoes all its middle-class conditionings and traits.

Two features of this state of mind fall under the scope of moral judgment; the first and quite rare one is the restless pursuit of amends for injuries suffered; the second and more common one is excessive dominance, the love of aggression and power for themselves, that which I called fascist-mindedness above. It is difficult and time-consuming to sift out such tendencies because a stress on omitting harsh methods would jeopardize revolutionarism, and omitting the Jews would not decrease but increase fascist elements.

This has quite a lot to bear on the way party actions go askew here and there or on the popularity of the party. In the light of these, however, can we say that the power structure of Hungarian communism has come to have relations and ties that, taken together, provide opportunities of power for the Jews ? It will strike many as strange, but taking into account all genuine circumstances and development trends, we must say that there is less Jewish power in Hungary now than ever in the modern era and that the entire development of Hungarian society has reached a point where all the problems of Jewish–non-Jewish rates will cease to exist in the foreseeable future.

What would *Jewish power* mean? We must clearly define what we mean by this term if we do not want to fall into the misleading triteness of widespread opinion on this. The personal positions and power opportunities of several or many people can be called their joint power if these personal positions, operational circles, and opportunities are durably coordinated within the structure of society and a shared factor—notably, that these positions happen to be held by Jews—has a fundamental role in leading and regulating this coordination. On this basis, let us be clear: neither Jews as a whole nor Hungarian Jews constitute any single Jewish power because of the multifariousness and disintegration of their varied social statuses, worldview, and national and community belonging. Nor can we say that the expressly religious and other Jewish organizations in Hungary have a significant influence.

The only sense in which we might talk of Jewish power is that there are altogether non-Jewish organizations of power where the Jewishness of persons filling certain positions has a leading and regulating role in their operation and scope. It was in this sense that the Jewish part of Hungarian capitalism constituted Jewish power. It was an organization that branched out into society as a whole through personal contacts, mutual services, and shared enterprises and concerns, the material and personal links of establishing and maintaining existences, and the entire network could be mobilized, deployed, or compelled to make sacrifices for some cause, interest, need, difficulty, grievance, and claim of "the" Jews or certain Jews *as* Jews. Within its broadly and loosely conceived interests, this was an organization that would be willing to promote such causes with its additional weight, and, within the same limits, it was ready to manage these actions and formulate its declarations in a way that would take into account a particular or common Jewish point of view. To a lesser extent, the apparatuses of certain quarters of the press and cultural dissemination and certain left-wing organizations afforded such opportunities as well.

Looked at from up close, these organizations were far from operating in the way the relevant anti-Semitic horror stories would have it, and should any self-conscious Jew have happened to credit these stories and turn to any of these powers, he would have been bitterly disappointed by the non-functioning of "Jewish solidarity" or by the organizations' being influenced by other concerns. He who approached them with more modest claims could experience their being "usable" organizations for Jewish purposes, though without any coherent Jewish design or any profound identity consciousness.

In this sense, there is no established Jewish power currently in Hungary. First and foremost, Jewish livelihoods—without regard for communized big business—have not been able to recuperate from the destruction and disparagement that anti-Jewish persecutions have wreaked upon them, have not been able to reintegrate in economic life to regain their former place in it, and have seen their prospects for this wane as socialist transformation has begun. Moreover, the major organizations that had held individual livelihoods together— those of both capitalism and the labor movement, where Jewish power had truly asserted itself—have, together with their non-Jewish parts, fallen apart, merged, or become wholly dependent.

It is common knowledge that the number of people employed in civil service, communized economic life, and the party organization has increased, but that these livelihoods constitute a power network in the sense that "Jewish capital" had is more than questionable. To no avail are there so many people with Jewish backgrounds in influential positions here and there; it is perfectly uncertain whether these conditions of power influence Jewish concerns, solidarity, or grievances. In respect to many a minor, just, or self-evident claim, Jews, persons who suffered under the persecutions, and Jewish organizations or concerns have had bitter or bitterish experiences with holders of various offices regarded as Jewish who have had little inclination to embrace their causes as Jewish causes in spite of the fact that these claims had neither a positive nor a negative impact on the political line and aims governing state power.

Hence the situation where Christian middle and lower-middle classes are staunchly convinced that Jews in Hungary are having the time of their life and power they never had before and where, for all the circumstances and positions of power and the opportunities of judgment, people sensing the conditions of the Jews as Jews must feel that they are uncertain, fragile, and threatened. From without, this threat is visible only in the manifestations of social forces expecting the victory of counterrevolution and restoration; this is why even non-Communist Jews link this sense of being threatened with the threats of counter-revolutionary restoration. The only real ground for this is that explosion-like anti-Semitic actions would be allowed free rein only in a counterrevolutionary restoration.

The fragility of the Jewish situation, however, exists irrespective of this and goes far deeper. In the past decades, the Jewish predicament has swung between the extremes of counterrevolutionary anti-Semitism and the Jewish security of consolidation, between the anti-Jewish legislation and persecutions and the liberation, undergoing such powerful identifications that the cause of the Jews lost its own right. The almighty Jewish big business and grande bourgeoisie had been able to be but modest ancillaries to the conservative social and political establishment even in a most successful consolidation. Jewish democratism and radicalism, which had identified with various movements in the course of history and had been hemmed together with them in their impasse, have now become dependent on something that will never genuinely identify with them—the revolutionary party of the labor movement. This is a political organization that can least be used seriously and in a larger context for any aim other than what is defined by its internal discipline, rules, and objectives. There might very well be large numbers of people in semi-influential positions of this party who have an acute sense of Jewish identity, solidarity, and suffering that may influence them in the ways they manage affairs, assess people, and judge problems, but these are merely occasional, fragile, and uncertain opportunities.

Only social organizations branching out in the whole breadth of society are suitable for the various relations and networks of social solidarity to settle on. The party of communism has a discipline and internal structure that are intensely and powerfully restrained both upward to the top leadership and downward to the relationship with the masses, and different platforms have no support or counterbalance; they are but accessories to the forces above and below whose position-taking and internal flows determine their survival. There is no possibility for anyone, without jeopardizing his position, to put the party durably, systematically, and institutionally at the service of interests branching out in the full breadth of society. While the openly anti-Semitic counterrevolutionary state power had to pass special legislation to oust Jews from business and state positions, seriously shocking Hungarian life and eliciting grave denunciations of Hungary abroad, if the governing forces of the party come to the conclusion that the future progress of the party requires that a certain number of posts be filled with emphatically non-Jews, they will have no need to pass any legislation and will be capable of so filling these posts without ever uttering the word "Jew."

It goes without saying that those who are of the belief that Jewish power and Communist power are identical, and that the insults they have suffered at the hands of Jews and Communists are the same, will never see why the Communists would want to address the negative consequences of the identification of Jews with Communists. They believe that these negative consequences are fully upon us, and if the Communists do not realize and take steps against them, their only reason for not doing so is that they deem them good and do not wish to do anything about them. However, the timeliness of issues for the Communist Party is determined not by the state of mind of the various social forces, many of which stand opposed to it, but the internal necessities of its development and actions. At this plane, there are two conditions for the Communist Party to address the matter: first, that the identification of Jews with communism becomes a timely threat to the development, unfolding, and success or failure of its actions and thus requires consideration; second, that the new generation of party membership broadening the social background of the party in the wake of the liberation becomes manifest, a change that, in time, will alter the old or more recently acquired structural one-sidednesses we have pointed out above.

Naturally, such events occur not in the way the middles classes tend to imagine—that there is a struggle between the Jewish and the anti-Jewish wings of the party, the latter somewhat sympathizing with nationalist anti-Communists and preparing to make communism somewhat more pleasant. Broadening the social base of the party and the rise of new leaders take place with the common and passionate collaboration of the party leaders of either Jewish or non-Jewish stock, and the new leadership, according to obvious signs, is likewise not going to consider any nationalistic or anti-Semitic expectations. At the lower levels of party leadership and the rank-and-file, dissonant phenomena might come about smacking of anti-Semitism, but, as in other respects, it is inconceivable that the party will be used as a means by forces beyond its ways and aims.

THE WAYS OF SOLUTION

What is to be made of this overall picture of the general persecution of the Jews and their most recent predicament in Hungary? That it constitutes an inhuman and dehumanized relationship between Jews and non-Jews, a vicious cycle of prejudices, fears, community frictions, serious injuries, and persecutions that has several set tracks and patterns in the passions, motions and thoughts of people; and that, even after a period of possible thaw, very little is needed for the dehumanized conditions to be continued, restored, or rebegun.

We have already pointed out that it is hopeless to think up a single "solution," a magic device or spell; what is really required is to slow down the vicious cycle, change the conditions behind it, and humanize the atmosphere around it. In the Hungarian context, it is most important that we first bring about a spirit of admitting the *responsibility* for the *persecutions against the Jews*, shape the public mind so as to take responsibility and guilt very seriously in moral and legal impeachment, yet clearly define its conditions, standards, and limits. Second, we must seriously and simultaneously recognize the reality and possibility of both *assimilation* and a separate Jewish identity in respect to community belonging, establishing clear and benevolent conditions for both and freeing the question of community belonging from all general formulas, compulsions, and demands. Finally, we need to be alert to the recurrence of anti-Semitism, particularly the version that identifies Jews with democracy to make them be hateful through each other, a step, however, that implies an alertness and opposition to the application of selection criteria that might engender such identification. In order to do so, each one of us must, within his or her own circle, confront those who, either as Jews or anti-Semites, hold the misconceived identification of Jews with democracy, however inconvenient and thankless this might be in either direction. This cannot mean demanding a policy expressly revolving around the Jewish question and anti-Semitism or wanting to "improve" rates;

it must be done in the name of a policy that points and steps beyond all the malaises of Hungarian selection, of which the Jewish rates were only an aspect. Striving to establish a classless society, such a policy must focus on the transformation of our entire educational system and on moving the layer of Hungarian society most bogged down in development, the poor peasantry, out of passivity and social exclusion, which are the final and still primary causes of the one-sidednesses of Hungarian selection.

Looking beyond the current Hungarian situation, this agenda may be formulated generally in the following way: what is required is, first, a general struggle pointing beyond the immediate problem of the Jews against prejudices professing any fateful differences in quality among men and for a social order based on the qualitative equality of men; in other words, for a new order and balance in the social environment surrounding Jews, and, second, strictly in Jewish–non-Jewish relations, a rehumanization and revitalization of the ways of intercourse, the gestures and tones of communing, meeting, asking, answering, scolding, explaining, calling to account, and admitting responsibility. Humanizing means not couching issues in general formulas to avoid calling a spade a spade but asserting the human content inherent in Jewish–non-Jewish relations, burdened as they are with prejudice and crude formulas.

V. CONCLUSION

Our train of thought will obviously invite several objections and critical remarks, which is as it should be. Yet in anticipation, I wish to answer certain questions bound to be raised.

The first one is that with the examination of too many moral principles, psychological factors, and individual forms of conduct, this entire argument garnishes the social core of the problem, which boils down to the simple truth that the Jewish question has come to a head due to confusions and difficulties in social development and that as soon as the way of social development clears up and a classless society starts to unfold, the problem will practically cease to exists. On several counts, I have professed the essential and fundamental truth of this thesis. However, the area of hysterias, fascism, anti-Semitism, and their like includes many other moral and psychological problems, without the consideration of which we cannot explain the heightening of conflicts and cannot steel ourselves against surprises.

Another objection that will obviously be raised is that the whole argument becomes unfair precisely because it strives for objectivity; it treats the injuries and experiences of Jews and non-Jews in parallel to such an extent that, even though repeatedly stressing the differences, it creates an atmosphere for the discussion of the issue in which the injuries and negative experiences of the non-Jewish environment seem to equal the terrifying amount of Jewish suffering; and it is particularly dangerous, through an argument claiming objectivity, to foster the idea that Jews have a share in creating anti-Semitism and to analyze the various moods of anti-Semitism, restating many of its theses, because it thereby makes them appear as though they have been accepted. The parallel treatment and the restatement of theses arise not from any wish of mine to justify both sides and to strike a balance between the Jews and anti-Semitism. It comes from the fact that closing the door on social and social-psychological reality cannot be justified in any way or under any pretext, and an argumentation that seeks to influence the moral judgment of people has to attempt to state and assess *all things* related to the reality concerned and to draw the various and opposing people out of the shell they have constructed around themselves out of suffering, grievances, bad conscience, misleading experiences, and a disconnection with reality.

Finally, there will be a third objection saying, in contrast, that this train of thought is far from exceedingly balanced and putting the issues of the enmity between Jews and anti-Semites on an equal footing; it actually treats these all-in-all parallel and essentially complementary matters with the greatest possible one-sidedness and partiality; it severely and copiously censures non-Jews, and with its continuous stress on the responsibility for the persecutions, feeds the Jewish pursuit of amends. However, it does not mention the immoderation of Jews and discusses the effects of Jews' conduct on their environment only wrapped up in cotton wool. This, however, is no mere coincidence. If anyone wants to speak of the reality of the Jewish predicament in a way that Jews will hear, he has to first mellow out of himself all the lesser or greater passions, anger, enmity, or annoyance he has ever had concerning the Jews; second, he has to rid himself of all moral judgment, sermonizing, or drawing of moral conclusions. It is the historical experience of a thousand years that has linked the minutest manifestations of annoyance with the environment with the exposure to the greatest and most unjust injuries, the pettiest moral sermonizing with total moral disparagement, in the minds of Jews. Regardless of this, no expression of moral sentiment or severe judgment has any bearing that does not apply to the speaker as well. So let us leave this to those who can speak in the name and image of Jews.

I have had no reason for any such reserve in respect to my fellow non-Jewish Hungarians because no prejudice, irritation, superiority, coldness, deed, or omission on which I have expended harsh words is such that I have not personally experienced it or for which I am not directly or indirectly responsible. I therefore ask the reader not to stop at what he likes because it has something to say about the other but rather to stop at what bears on him. I also wish that those who cannot come around to sharing the theses of the author accept his *goodwill* as a common point of departure.

1948

APPENDIX:
ADDITIONAL REMARKS TO THE JEWISH PREDICAMENT

With regard to Sebestyén Molnár's critique,[7] I believe I need to try and clarify certain misunderstandings or, where it is not a misunderstanding, highlight the difference between our positions.

ADMITTING RESPONSIBILITY

To dispel doubt, I must emphasize that the guiding thread of my essay is not at all the question of the responsibility of the Hungarian people. This is not the case partly because it would imply holding the Hungarian people responsible and impeaching them. Quite to the contrary, I have refuted the generalizing and abstract formulas without a genuine content of reality that, on the basis of some majority calculations or other, ascribe circumscribable views to the Hungarian people or their various classes and thereby conclude their responsibility or exemption from responsibility. Instead of this, I have argued and still argue for a nationwide awakening of a spirit of admitting responsibility, whereby each member of the Hungarian people and their various classes raise the issue of responsibility in respect to his or her own self. After Sebestyén Molnár's comments, which fall back on the formulas to which I object, let me again, even more emphatically, argue that no bludgeon or responsibility-rejecting formula should be made for individuals through the assessment of the views of the majority of the Hungarian people or their classes. These generalizations are exceedingly bendable and can be grouped arbitrarily, and the results depend wholly on how the representative groups of the major class frameworks are picked out.

So, together with Sebestyén Molnár, we can state that organized labor was against the anti-Jewish persecutions and the poor peasantry kept away from them, and, thus, labor and the peasantry accounting for the majority of the Hungarian people, the majority of the Hungarian people can be said to have been against the persecutions. However, if we start out from the equally true fact that no minor sector of the upper crust, the declassed middle-class layers, the petit bourgeois crowds, and the scum of the proletariat—in other words, the well-known social constituents of fascism—was in favor of the persecutions, we have nothing else to do but interpret the declassed, petit bourgeois, and scum-proletarian layers broadly, an interpretation that will then intersect with wide groups of the peasantry and labor, and we can immediately conclude that the majority of the Hungarian people approved the persecutions. By not *ab ovo* dismissing any single group within the Hungarian people from responsibility, we do not at all diminish the particular responsibility of the leading and ruling layers, a conclusion that derives from the fact that they were the ones, due to their positions, who were ultimately responsible. When we deem the replacement of the ruling circles necessary on grounds of their having totally failed, it would not be a fortunate beginning if we produced formulas for shunning responsibility for the new leading layer.

ASSIMILATION

I have a few points to make with regard to assimilation. For all their convincing and edifying power and interest, the quotes Sebestyén Molnár brings up, I believe, do not illustrate what he means to illustrate with them. When I put particular emphasis on the deceptions in the presuppositions of assimilation in Hungary, I did not mean to say that the en masse assimilation of Jews was smooth and untroubled in other countries. To the contrary, I mentioned the well-known fact, to which Sebestyén Molnár and his quotes also refer, that hopes and expectations attached to massive and common assimilation were seldom fulfilled throughout the world. In most cases it turned out that Jews continued to live within and be exposed to circumstances and injuries that meant the essential continuation of their former predicament. All I stressed concerning the assimilation in Hungary is that the self-deceptions of those believing in straightforward and smooth mass assimilation and of the non-Jewish environment demanding the external displays of assimilation coincided. There might well have been similar phenomena elsewhere, the surrounding environment having a likewise abnormal development apart from its more or less envenomed relations with Jews, yet I do not think there was another country where the assimilation of Jews was deemed such an act of national significance that its external trappings were forced and its jubilation carried to such excesses as in Hungary.

THE CAUSES OF ANTI-SEMITISM AND FIGHTING IT

In view of my concept of the development of the Jewish predicament, the causes of anti-Semitism, and the struggle against it, my critic could not understand how I identify the demand for a spirit of admitting responsibility, for a serious acknowledgment of both assimilation and Jewish identity, and for an alertness to anti-Semitism with the efforts toward a classless society. I must have grouped or stressed my thoughts wrongly if anyone should have concluded from them this certainly incomprehensible idea.

In the evolution of the Jewish predicament and the analysis of the causes of anti-Semitism, I sought to distinguish among the following three factors:

1. The anti-Jewish prejudice of medieval origin, which established the debasement of the human standing of Jews, moreover in a degree beyond common xenophobia and minority oppression;
2. The dehumanization of the relationship between Jews and non-Jews due to the prejudice, as a result of which both groups continually and repeatedly acquire misleading, yet no less genuine and bad, experiences of each other;
3. The disorders and impasses of social development, which seek and find an outlet for explosion in anti-Semitism.

Accordingly, the fight against anti-Semitism has three areas:

1. Fighting the prejudice and superstitious charges, which is a cultural task;
2. Efforts to humanize and mellow the inhuman relationships between Jews and non-Jews, which have to do primarily with statements clarifying concepts and adumbrating issues of morality and conduct;
3. Helping social development to move out of its impasses and deadlocks, which is a matter of social policy.

Whatever I said about the spirit of admitting responsibility and the simultaneous recognition of the possibility of Jewish emancipation and identity, the things Jews and non-Jews should have to say to one other all belong to the second area of action, but the struggle to establish a classless society is naturally not identical with this, belonging in the third group of duties. As most commentators on the issue, Sebestyén Molnár sees serious tasks in the first and third group of activities, in the cultural struggle against prejudice and the social-political struggle for establishing a society without exploitation and class. I myself also hold that both are conditions of improving the Jewish situation and fighting anti-Semitism, but the most important point of the second, analytical part of my essay was to show the difficulties inherent in actual and immediate human relationships in contrast to or besides these well-known explanations and solutions. This is the reason I attempted to anatomize all the misleading, yet no less genuine, immediate experiences in the areas of using social opportunities (sagacity) and relating to social values and the pursuit of amends out of having the upper hand or being suppressed, a point on which Jews and non-Jews continually disagree, bump into, or stumble over when facing each other's sensibilities or actual activities.

THE INHUMANITY OF THE RELATIONSHIP
BETWEEN JEWS AND NON-JEWS

I wish to dwell on these concrete relationships to avoid any illusion that they are but details of personal and contingent relations and individual moral conduct, which cannot be included in the scope of generally valid knowledge and assistance. First of all, I must highlight that the vast majority of human relationships is based not on individual and singular conduct but established forms of human conduct; they follow well-trodden routes and simplified patterns. In itself, there is no problem with this; humankind saves oceans of energy in doing so, though there are many dangers of their becoming petrified in social formalism and immobility. It is, however, hopeless to generally fight forms; all we can do is seek better, more real, flexible, and just forms and try to improve existing ones. What makes the relationship between Jews and non-Jews so particularly vexing is that the patterns and types of concrete and mutual conduct are exceedingly *inhuman* and *dehumanized*. I wish now to highlight this with a few examples.

What kinds of conduct would be humane toward a minority by the majority surrounding it? Roughly three quite simple ones. First, a conduct that *receives the minority without reserve*, regarding minority status merely as a sort of curiosity rather than a fundamental community condition; this implies a friendly emotional attitude to the group as a whole. Second, a conduct that reckons with the differing features of the minority, regarding them as having a bearing on community life, yet is fair and expects to maintain equal opportunities in both theory and practice. Third, a *separating* conduct that consciously treats the minority as a different community, a stance that usually goes hand in hand with a dislike or emotional reserve toward the minority. This latter kind of conduct cannot be just in the case of Jews, and it can at times be dangerous to them, yet it is a possible one.

In contrast to these, what kinds of inhuman conduct has the majority displayed toward the Jews? The first one is that of the anti-Semite, who burns with a hatred for them and preserves horror experiences and entertains horror stories about them; the second is that of the one who consciously maintains a difference in rank with and a distance from Jews; the third is that of the one who has intercourse with Jews yet upholds the difference in rank and fraternizes with them but in a condescending way; finally, there is the conduct of the prescriptionary philo-Semite. The last needs some elaboration, elucidation why I regard it among the inhuman forms of conduct. Obviously, I mean by it not people who like Jews but those who not only sympathize with and have an understanding for the state of mind and historical experience of Jews, but also identify with the often unrealistic worldview a significant number of them embrace in response to them. The prescriptionary philo-Semite's manner is counterproductive because it helps Jews sustain this unrealistic worldview and deludes them that they can have intercourse with the world surrounding them while they commune with people that do not bring them into contact with the reality of that surrounding world, covering up the distance that separates them from it. (On this head, there is a rather poignant remark to be made in the Hungarian context. It is by now common knowledge and openly discussed that it has been a fateful aspect of Hungarian political development that leftism and its various historical manifestations were identified with the Jews—naturally with the active approval and assistance of anti-progressive forces. True, various numbers of Jews or people with a Jewish background might have had a share in this, but this is unlikely to have had as decisive a role as the prescriptionary philo-Semite attitude, which assisted in formulating matters of progress in the way they appeared primarily to Jews. It thereby made the psychological impression on those wanting to or close to joining leftist organizations that by joining they would share the Jewish predicament.)

Conversely, what kind of conduct by a minority toward the majority would be humane? Roughly, there are likewise three types. First, we have those fully assimilated to the majority; second, there are those that practice assimilation in several respects yet retain their separate, self-conscious community; and, third, there is the isolated minority who lives a life closed to the majority. What actual forms of relationship have Jews developed toward their environment? Most usually have formed none of those mentioned; instead the following forms of conduct have dominated: first, the Jew who preserves the memories of injuries and persecutions at the hands of the majority and is mistrustful and offensively secludes himself; second, the Jew who does not emphasize the seclusion for practical or political purposes but has a view to it in every situation; third, the assimilationist conduct that overemphasizes assimilation; fourth, the conduct of full assimilation to the environment but without an ability to relieve oneself of the mental burden of Jewishness or Jewish origin.

On both sides, these forms of conduct are wholly inhuman and dehumanizing because they are based on horror images or injuries suffered, an unfounded sense of rank and superiority, or an unjustified sense of inferiority. These are not necessary parts of minority experience as such, and though there are many examples of similar forms of conduct and relation in other areas of social life, these have nevertheless burdened the Jews far more than any other social group. In actual situations, these forms of conduct assert themselves with extraordinary force, and even the most idiosyncratic, personal, and moral conduct can slip into any of them. The fateful effect of these is that they elicit or create the appropriate opposite dehumanizing form of conduct in the other party even when one had not been inclined to it beforehand. For all the discussion it has prompted, the difficulty in assimilation is not in one's becoming like one's environment—it not being any more difficult than in other cases—but in shedding inhuman forms of relationship and conduct.

This is why the often-mentioned notion that "there is no Jewish question, only anti-Semitism" should be received with due reserve. The way we are meant to understand this is that the problems and dangers of the Jewish predicament exclusively stem from the conduct and stances of the environment. What is certainly true in this is that the prejudice and the social disorder that turn the Jewish question into a central social issue come from the environment. It is also undoubtedly true that the various forms of inhuman and dehumanizing relationships and conduct have been established in response to anti-Semitic religious prejudice and social disorders. Once they come into being, however, they become mutual and perpetuate themselves with extraordinary pertinacity; they will not cease to exist of themselves even after improvements in social and cultural development; they will survive them, and they will keep their poisonous material while prejudices wane and social development starts to turn virulent again as the conditions of the environment change for the worse much later.

Uncovering and fighting this is far more difficult and far less resolvable by simple and rough formulas than the cultural struggle against prejudices and the political struggle against social disorders, which, difficult as they might be, are tasks that can be grasped and defined. This is why I cannot agree with Sebestyén Molnár, who holds that the fight against anti-Semitism should focus exclusively on the cultural fight against prejudice and on the political struggle against disorders in social development. Without underestimating and giving up on a cultural and political struggle, I continue to believe that a specific struggle has to be undertaken to mellow the inhuman forms of conduct between Jews and non-Jews, and the only way to do this is to shape human, honest, and realistic forms and patterns of conduct; clarify concepts; and set forth principles of conduct and morality.

DECLARATION (1956)

Hungarians,

Prime Minister Imre Nagy went to the Soviet Embassy for talks early this morning and has not been able to return. Apart from Zoltán Tildy in the Parliament Building, only Ministers of State István B. Szabó and István Bibó were able to attend the meeting of the Council of Ministers convened this morning. When Soviet troops surrounded the Parliament Building, Minister of State Zoltán Tildy reached an agreement with them to avoid bloodshed, whereby they would occupy the building while civilians could leave unharmed. In keeping with the agreement, he left. Representing the sole legitimate Hungarian Government, I, the undersigned, Minister of State István Bibó, was the only one to remain in the Parliament Building.

Under these circumstances, I make the following declaration:

Hungary has no intention of following an anti-Soviet policy; moreover, it wants to live fully in the community of East European peoples who want to organize themselves in the name of a free, just, and exploitationless society. Before all the world, I reject the slander that our glorious revolution was marred by fascistic and anti-Semitic excesses. Irrespective of class or denomination, the entire Hungarian people took part in the struggle, and it was astonishing and uplifting to see the humane and wise conduct, the ability to distinguish, of the people who had risen up, turning only against foreign oppressors and their henchmen. The Government would have been forthrightly able handle the few instances of street justice and the appearance of unarmed arch-conservative forces. The statement that a vast army had to be called in or called back to put this down lacks all seriousness and is cynical. Quite to the contrary, the presence of that army is the main source of anxiety and unrest.

I hereby call on the Hungarian people not to regard the invading army and the puppet government it might set up as a legitimate authority and to deploy the weapon of passive resistance against it—save the public supplies and utilities of Budapest. I am not in a position to command armed resistance; I joined the Cabinet a day ago, I have not received any information on the military situation, and it would be irresponsible of me to dispose of the dear blood of Hungarian youths. Hungary has paid with enough lives to show its insistence on freedom and justice to the world. It is now the turn of the great powers of the world to show the authority of the principles laid down in the UN Charter and the power of the freedom-loving people of the world. I call for a wise decision from the great powers and the UN in the interest of my nation.

I hereby also state that the only legitimate representative of Hungary abroad and the only legitimate head of its foreign representations is Minister of State Anna Kéthly.

Done in the Parliament Building on November 4, 1956.

István Bibó
Minister of State

MEMORANDUM:
HUNGARY, A SCANDAL AND A HOPE OF THE WORLD

Hungary has become the scandal of the entire world.

The scandal, first, of the Western world, which has been beating the drum for over a decade to say that the East European countries did not choose the one-party government system to which they were introduced with the assistance of the Soviet Union, and, for more than a decade, the West has been arousing hopes in the peoples of the region that they can in some way or another have the form of government they choose. It has not promised to start a nuclear war for their sake, and it has not called on them to senselessly take up arms. But these encouragements have included the statement that should the political situation of the world and substantial action by the people so allow, the Western world would bring all its economic, political, and moral influence to bear to put the case of these peoples on the agenda and bring about a solution satisfying to them. The Hungarian Revolution has established all the conditions and rights for an international deal of this kind. In hindsight, it has become fashionable in both right-and left-wing circles to regret the rash momentum of the revolution, its going beyond, for example, the Polish movement. Such regrets have little substance, primarily because the Hungarian and the Polish cases are interrelated: it was the shock over the Hungarian case that enabled the Poles to halt where they halted. Second, it was not the rashness of the Hungarian Revolution that caused its momentum but the obduracy of the state leadership and the bloodbath by the armed forces, and, in spite of its unpreparedness, its lack of organization, and its being a response to monstrous carnage, it was strikingly humane and moderate. If it has subsequently been declared hopeless, it was made so not by its rashness but by its having been forsaken. There might yet be greater uprisings in Eastern Europe, with more weapons, fighters, and heavier

357

losses, but there is little likelihood of a country establishing such immaculate legal, political, and moral rights for being put on the agenda of world politics; it overturned the hated, oppressive, and bureaucratic dictatorship, and it lawfully brought to power a convinced Communist, who, reckoning with the political and moral discredit of the Communist Party in Hungary, accepted multiparty parliamentary democracy and declared that the country wanted to exist outside military blocs. What more is needed if this was not enough to force the world powers to convene a conference and, giving satisfactory guarantees to the Soviet Union, negotiate the independence and freedom of Hungary?

Instead, what we have is dramatic debates over the Hungarian situation in the General Assembly of the United Nations, adopting solemn and ineffectual resolutions—to the unfathomable detriment of the UN. As everyone knows, the UN as a means of peace is worth, by the will of its founders, as much as the force and intentions its great-power parties have; without this, UN negotiations cannot but be spectacular disputes and resolutions. In such cases, what fails is not the UN but the political and moral responsibility of the great powers. In the course of the past 150 years, the past 50 in particular, after miserable letdowns, backslidings, and two world conflagrations, a recognition has slowly been brought home to the more advanced quarters of the world that the only possible policy is a principled and moral policy, which is simultaneously the only fruitful realpolitik. The most severe consequence of the crushing of the Hungarian Revolution for the West is that its decade-long policy and propaganda of invoking principles and moral values has come to a point where not only have its reasonableness and prospects been questioned by many but also its honesty.

Third, Hungary has become the thundering scandal of the Communist camp. Since 1953, the most important and not altogether unsuccessful efforts of the Soviet leadership and Communist thinkers have been to mop up so-called Stalinism. It would be more precise to call it Stalinist political practice because it constituted no new ideology that could be pieced together from Stalin's writings on theory and economics, nor was it simple tactical or technical mistakes and errors; it was a coherent ruthless system applied indiscriminately and unscrupulously. The idea that there is no absolute moral measure of human action had already cropped up in Lenin and even Marx; however, they both assumed that interest relations rightly conceived—that is, objectively conceived—served as the norm. For Stalin, however, the interests of the working class and building a Communist society were simplified to a sheer power struggle, and the latter reduced to the will of the leadership or the leader. Changing according to tactical considerations, these acts of will were subject to all kinds of error and impulse yet claimed to be the moral standard and the objective necessity. Thus what Marx had conceived of as a brief phase and Lenin as a longer interval—the dictatorship of the proletariat—instead of gradually making a place for more democratic methods became a permanent form of government by simply declaring itself the highest form of democracy for a long time to come. Now this, as the ancient rule of tyranny has it, confounded the normal functioning of the very interest relations that were meant to be the norms of proper individual and community action. The machinery of terror meant to crack down on "the enemy" followed its own internal laws, creating rather than "eliminating" enemies, and spread fear and animosity from the actual enemy to the entire population. The same apparatus came in handy in breaking the internal opposition of the party and doing away with more popular rivals, but it undermined its internal democracy and Communist integrity. Economic planning became subject to arbitrary will and made it impossible for production to be regulated by the real, collective, and individual interests of society, crippling production and destroying the work ethic. The same mindset shaped the relationship between the Soviet Union as the leading Communist state and the Communist parties, later countries, eroding international Communist solidarity and bringing forth, as a backlash, so-called national communism, the enforcing of normal and realistic national interest relations in the face of external interference.

For all these weighty repercussions, the Communist-ruled countries and the Communists of the rest of the world were loyal to the Soviet Union as the first and most powerful Communist state, and even non-Communist socialists were interested in and respected the Soviet enterprise. After Stalin's death, his successors began a widespread abatement of Stalinist political practice; thwarted attempts to establish a new personal power; at the Twentieth Party Congress, broke with certain Stalinist theses as a matter of principle; and subjected the person of Stalin to criticism and thus aroused the hope among Communists that there were forces in communism, primarily the Soviet Communist Party, that were capable of returning to the proper road to socialism.

What happened to Hungary on November 4 and after has dashed these hopes, perhaps unredressably. We cannot tell what caused the Soviet decision—a realpolitik assessment of the situation in the wake of the Suez attack or bafflement over the Hungarian events. What is certain, however, is that as realpolitik, it has been proved wrong and as amazement, it was excessive: the free development of the Hungarian situation would soon have demonstrated that it would not only not have been perilous to the cause of socialism, but would also have had a productive effect on it. Explain it away as one might in reprieve, saying that the Hungarian Revolution was, became, or could have become a counterrevolution, its most striking surprise was that the turn that had been supposed by everyone to be counterrevolutionary and restorationist was, in fact, not at all that. All the forces—the youths, workers, and soldiers—who sided with the revolution and took up arms were not only socialists, but also raised as Marxist-Leninists, even if their worldview had come to a crisis. If, as freedom was unleashed, conservative restorationist forces showed up (hardly any fascists!), this was terrifying only for those who had got used to believing that proscribing something meant that it had ceased to exist, and so if anything was able to show itself and speak up, it was thus terrifying.

By the time the Soviets interfered, the situation had begun to be consolidated, popular verdicts had ceased, resolute and authoritative voices had defended socialist accomplishments, and a government of national unity had been set up that had no reason to move to the right or to be overzealously rightist. Whoever has had any contact with the resistance after the crushing of the revolution has had to sense, even if he does not want to admit it, that it was the beginning of a most thrilling experiment in socialism that the Soviet tanks blasted out and replaced by something that resembles anything but a future-building society. Prior to this, all future-oriented programs had had to face the possessors of power and wealth and the administration and police at their service, building on youths, workers, and creative intellectuals and seeing their conviction and keenness as proofs of their commitment to the future. The current Hungarian regime bases itself on a bureaucracy that knows it is in the minority, has lost its security, and is fighting manically for its positions, and on the police forces, and it regards youths, workers, and creative intellectuals as its chief enemies.

History knows many regimes that fought against writers, workers, and schoolchildren, but none have achieved their goals; more important, none of them have ever called themselves revolutionary or socialist. These are the features the new Hungarian Communist Party has come to bear; no Communist Party in the world is like it, but any can become so if it does not take care. As yet, all Communist parties have been made up as follows: a core of passionate, single-minded, self-sacrificing, and unflagging men were surrounded by a less intelligible but highly disciplined group whose members were masters of unscrupulously deploying the harshest means of rising to power and holding on to it; these were followed by enthusiastic masses, mostly workers, who eagerly did the work of organization and spreading the idea; finally, following takeover, came the outer circle of opportunists and bureaucrats, for whom the party meant a way of getting on and securing their well-being. The focus of the Hungarian Communist Party has shifted totally to the last group. The top leadership has shrunk to a very limited group, announcing its actions either in a desperately convoluted style or in cynical openness. Flustered, the technicians of power around the leadership opt occasionally for brutality and occasionally for concession, both ineffective and both dangerous. For them, enthusiastic crowds, worker masses in particular, have ceased to exist. Only the outer circle is intact, made up of the police forces and bureaucrats afraid of losing their jobs.

No Communist party has ever existed with such a low rate of worker membership. Communist parties elsewhere have also had problems of bureaucracies gaining the upper hand over their worker rank and file, but, as a specter, the end point of this development arose out of the ashes and flames of the downtrodden Hungarian Revolution: a party made up of a bureaucracy and the police as against workers as such. The country itself, which could only experience its atomization in the face of the organization of power, now unforgettably saw the perfect isolation of the police forces, propped up only by foreign support. This has been all too exasperating for those who take the ideals of communism more seriously, who regard communism as more important than people of a certain opinion being in sheer power. All the Communist parties of the world have gone out of their way to find their own particular socialist paths while holding onto the ideology of Marxism-Leninism regarded as victorious. The people's democracies dither between uneasily apportioning concessions and intractably not yielding in Stalinist orthodox fashion. Upholding the Hungarian regime at all costs is as bad an example for them as surrendering it would have been, a step the Soviet Union was not prepared to take with them in mind as well. The associations of sympathizers brought together with so much labor in the non-Communist world show the symptoms of grave damage, even collapse—peace, women's, and youth organizations, which embodied a great deal of enthusiasm, commanded a great following among workers, intellectuals, and youths, and on which communism could always count. In a word, the Hungarian action of the Soviet Union, which had been meant to avoid surrendering a position, has only dealt a blow to the position of communism.

Fourth, Hungary has become the scandal of all honest *"third-way"* forces and ideas too. Alongside a number of responsible Asian countries, as well as socialist and Social Democratic parties all round the world, India professes that a world divided into capitalism and socialism is struggling with phantoms and pseudo-problems. These phantoms revolve around the shared bias of both orthodox capitalists and orthodox Communists that socialism—that is, a society without exploitation—cannot be established without the long-term rejection of the Western techniques of freedom. In contrast, the "third way," the only actually possible way, holds that the aim of creating a society without exploitation is but a station in the universal development of mankind toward freedom and

that fighting exploitation cannot mean or tolerate the rejection of the established forms of political and public freedom. The entire edifice of freedom—
which is built on the separation of powers, multiparty free elections, liberties
(the freedom of the press and expression in particular), the independence of
the courts, and the rule of law and which has made the Western world, for all
its faults, so humane and tolerable—is not a "bourgeois" superstructure but
plainly an objective technique, the most developed and still unsurpassed technique of freedom, the superiority of which can just as well be acknowledged as
a Western-made fountain pen or Morgan's theory of heredity without endanger-
ing the cause of socialism.

If anywhere ever, this "third way" was what wanted to come to life creatively
in the Hungarian Revolution. The active forces involved in the revolution had
no intention of undoing any of the genuine achievements of socialism and had
all the power to stall any such attempt. They simply could no longer stand the
techniques of oppression and resulting aggression and lies swamping all areas
of life and turned to those techniques that provided institutionalized safeguards
against them.

The questions of how and in what manner to achieve the safeguards were
not clarified in the first moments of the revolution, but its tendencies were
quite clear to discern, and after its suppression, the public developed a rather
unequivocal notion of how to link the upholding of socialism with the Western techniques of freedom, a system limited to parties accepting the common
base of socialism. The Workers' Councils meant a new technique reinforcing
democracy and socialism. If so much sacrifice, good effort, and clear determination were not enough for this Hungarian experiment to come to life; if
the Soviet Union found it worthwhile to use all its military might to force this
country, which had been lost to single-party rule and Soviet military presence,
back to the road it had left; and if the ensuing Indian mediation had to fail, we
have to face the terrifying conclusion that *no "third way"* is possible; not only
is the polarization of the great powers inevitable, but so is the breakup into two
camps of the moral consciousness of the world.

And this is the point where Hungary has become the fourth and greatest
scandal of the world, the scandal of world peace, for in the current state of affairs, the Hungarian cause has come to question the possibility of world peace
and conjures up a frightful parallel: it will be the penultimate scene before the
outbreak of World War III, as the forsaking of Czechoslovakia had been before
World War II. Nothing demonstrates this more than that significant quarters of
the Western world drew the conclusion from the Hungarian case that Stalinism
had been revived, that it had never really ceased to exist, and that this was the

only possible and natural form of communism, while the Communist world drew the same conclusion only reversing the signs: Stalin had indeed been right, and the Communist camp could only be held together with his methods. At the level of international affairs, Stalinist political practice meant wrecking and internally falsifying the popular front policy and the international cooperation grounded in it.

The popular front policy was the recognition that in the face of fascism, the cult of sheer and brutal power, there was a moral and military community between the socialist objective of an exploitation-free society and the Western position of insisting on the achievements of political freedom. Seeing it as mere tactics for dividing the "monopoly capitalist" enemy, which they thought was united, Stalin and his associates subscribed to this policy by simultaneously killing it. They believed it was permissible to corrupt popular front partners by any means and, when opportunity presented itself, liquidate them in Central-East Europe at least. This has prevented popular front policy, the cooperation of the powers defeating fascism, on a worldwide scale. Again, this proved that an ethic of sheer power and will was impossible to humanly live with, and at the level of international affairs, this meant the unavoidability of war.

Different political, social, and economic systems can coexist peacefully but not if they do not share a belief in certain moral principles. True, Stalin, in contrast to Hitler, had, by all signs, no intention of getting entangled in a world war, but his policies rendered him and his opponents mutually unable to reckon realistically with the other's motives and intentions. So opposed, the parties have occasionally taken each other's lies at face value and occasionally not believed each other even when they spoke the truth, and, not supposing any moral motive in the other, they have regarded each other either as unreasonably cowardly or as unreasonably aggressive. Sooner or later this is bound to lead to a situation where, by the mutual and total misunderstanding of the parties, the world slips into a world war, even a nuclear war, however afraid of it both parties are. Not that the Hungarian case will necessarily cause a world conflagration (though East European countries do have the distressing privilege of world wars breaking out around them). But if the Hungarian case is truly unredressable, it follows that there are innate reasons for the great powers of the world not to speak a common language and have no understanding for one another, and the mere rational recognition that nuclear war is madness and suicidal will not provide enough protection against it. Is the situation truly so exasperating? Is there no way out from the dead end Hungary and the world have gotten into?

No doubt this is where the current state of affairs points. Yet in the final count, apart from actualities, all historical situations have potentials as well, the realization of which depends on effort and good will. Taking them also into account, we will note that the potentials of the Hungarian case and the world situation are now far more hopeful than at any time in the previous decade.

Hungary thus also means hope for the Western world for several reasons. the policy that has been nourishing hopes in the internal opposition circles and among émigrés from Eastern Europe has often been seized with doubt as to what kind of government these countries would establish after the fall of the one-party system. It was common knowledge that social and national oppression and feudal rule had burgeoned in a variety of forms before World War II in the region and that émigrés had been driven West partly by the collapse of their outdated ways of life and partly by their desire for liberty. It has been a common thesis among Western politicians and thinkers that the genuine and proper functioning of the Western institutions of freedom has no prospect of success anyway beyond a line to the south and east; we must take cognizance of the fact that these countries, from Central Europe to East Asia, from the Iberian Peninsula to South America, have lived and will live under milder or stricter forms of tyranny. There was only one difference: left-wing well-wishers recommended Communist one-party systems, and right-wing well-wishers, conservative police states. This disillusioned view amounts to holding the entire liberation policy as no more than cynical power politics, though it has also been prompted by the loss of hope in the night terrors that war tensions will not cease in the foreseeable future.

Thus, first, the movements in Hungary, Poland, and other Communist countries have most amply demonstrated that there is a genuine and active demand for the reality of freedom and its most developed techniques. Precisely for never having been satisfied, this demand has come to be manifest in a freshness of conviction and passion that significantly surpass the conviction of the Western world, which has grown accustomed to its achievements. These movements have proved that the demand for change is not limited to the victims of the one-party regime; it indeed came forth most fervently from those the single-party system brought up, its youths; there need be no worry that they would lead to the restoration of outdated social and political forms. This conclusion should not be limited to Eastern Europe or drawn with regard primarily to Poland, Czechoslovakia, and Hungary on the grounds that they are countries that have always belonged to Western Christendom. The principle to be drawn is that it should never be supposed of a people, whether they be Malayans or Germans, that a desire for freedom is wanting in them. Economists have already become aware that the destitution of one people is contagious and threatening to the well-being of others; this is a lesson to be learned at the level of politics too. The

Hungarian Revolution and the popular movements of Eastern Europe mean that the Western world can and should follow a policy line that is neither aggressive nor informed by power considerations but is more active and enterprising and aims not to impose its economic and social system on others but step by step seeks to win East European countries and finally the Soviet Union over to the Western techniques of freedom and the shared political morality in which it is grounded.

Second, odd as it may sound, the Hungarian Revolution is a hope for *world communism* too, even though in the wake of the Hungarian events, the inimical view has been more staunch than ever in the past forty years in denying its ideals and seeing in it no more than a fascist-like will to power. A deeper examination of the Hungarian and Polish events clearly shows that the decisive factor in them was the fact that intellectuals and Communist youths came to be at profound odds with the liberating ambitions of communism and the demoralizing and corrupting effects of the indiscriminate use of the means for realizing those ambitions. This pure fact means a fundamental difference as compared to fascism, where no such crisis could ever have developed because its ideal was a crude and naked wielding of power, and thus the ideals and means did not diverge.

The contradictions that led Communists into conflict with themselves in the Hungarian and Polish movements were manifest in three demands; first, there arose a demand for a government that particularly respected the consensual autonomy of the immediate communities and organizations of the people in the face of a centralized, omnipotent, and arbitrary state; second, there arose a demand for speaking intellectual and public truth in the face of the communication and teaching of a reality arbitrarily distorted for the purposes of power; and third, there arose a demand for direct and institutionalized concern in economic activity—that is, economic self-government—in the face of an economic policy that had eliminated economic exploitation but put off raising living standards under the guise of building socialism. Now, these demands are more poignant formulations of themes that were the focus of the thaw that started in 1953: the observance of legality, the restoration of party democracy, freedom of criticism, efforts to disclose facts truthfully (especially about the West), the raising of living standards, and a decentralization of the economy.

We cannot tell whether straight and gradual development in this direction is assured or not, but it is certain that these needs have surfaced in a form unknown to us yet with such force that they were immediately put on the agenda in a shaky situation after the death of Stalin. This is why, for all our concerns for the future, we still have reason to regard 1953 as a decisive turning point, for those leaders who wanted no new Stalin came through, while the one wanting to be the new Stalin fell. This is why the process culminating in the Twentieth Congress should not be regarded as mere tactics; it indeed was part of the cause of the Hungarian and Polish developments, which brought forth so much significant moral and intellectual value. This is not meant to reinforce the moral capital of the Soviet leadership with the moral capital of the Hungarian Revolution that it crushed but to recognize that we have a single and coherent process taking place, and it is in this light that we should grasp and judge the contradictions of the Soviet leadership. It is equally senseless to regard Soviet leaders as fundamentally well-intentioned but pathologically distrustful men, as Roosevelt did, or to see them as fundamentally malevolent but capable of satanically feigning good will, as many have imagined and continue to imagine. The point is that this state leadership is hindered by weighty historical and ideological precursors from allowing for moral concerns in politics, from supposing that their opponents' policies might have moral motives that they ought to grasp, and that they are perturbed by the question of what means they are to use in leading the ideology and world empire entrusted to them toward a more promising and stable future. They sense that rational self-interest and justice would require their making concessions and going along the way of the thaw— that is, the very opposite of what Stalinism means in every respect—but they perceive Western capitalism as being most malevolently ready to strike down the moment it sees the slightest weakness. They sense that closing the valves internally is going to lead to a boiler explosion, but then suddenly opening the floodgates would destroy the dam; hence their alternation between concession and clamping down.

Taking all these into consideration, it would be more reasonable to think of the intervention in Hungarian today, a time of demonstrative attempts to restore Stalinism, not as the rebirth of Stalinism but as a flinching back on a road that must be gone along sooner or later.

Needless to say, there is no point in regretting the excessive momentum of the Hungarian Revolution, which, in effect, halted the entire Soviet thawing process. The same lesson is to be drawn from the Hungarian Revolution whether victorious or crushed: the issues of the policy of thawing, political and economic self-government, legality, public truthfulness, a reduction of bureaucracy, and the raising of living standards are all interdependent; it is impossible to resolve the more convenient ones and put off the ones more dangerous, and it is likewise impossible to carry out a policy of thawing within the Soviet Union but not in the people's democracies. The price of the energy and value wasted by the attempts at government against the will of the people will have to be paid, in the final count, by the Hungarian and Soviet people, and that price will be freedom and living standards, and this is what aggravates the very situation the intervention was meant to avert. Hope is therefore in the very fact that the issues of the whole complex are inseparably interconnected and interdependent; this is why it is possible and to be expected, though not inevitable, that development will return to the point from which it deviated by the fateful decision of the Soviets to intervene.

This is why the Hungarian Revolution means hope for the forces of the "third way." In our time, the central issue of the various quarters of the world is how to make use of the opportunities of freedom. The Western world possesses the most developed techniques of freedom, parliamentary democracy based on popular representation and liberties, and it more or less respects the universal ethics that are the grounds for the institutions of freedom and the condition of their functioning. It furthermore possesses an economic system called capitalism, the most important constituent elements of which are free enterprise, the acceptance of making profit as a regulatory principle, and individualistic private law. In spite of the fact that many have considered it dead for over a century, this system has provided striking proof of its resilience and ability to perform; true, it has changed a great deal from its original structure. However, for all the mending done on it, it is still unable to do away with the sense of moral insufficiency that it elicits in many. What is scandalous in it is not free enterprise—this is a genuine achievement of human liberty—but that its institutions perpetuate the property stock of society; not only do they open the way to the type of amassing of wealth that had been known for long centuries before free enterprise and the rule of law were established, but they also lead to aggression disguised in legal forms, an abuse of state power, the expropriation of public and community property, state concessions, corruption, and political intrigue. The forces of free society and peaceful social reform are so powerful in the West, however, that, though slowly and gradually, without radical dispossession, these antediluvian social forms of mammoth property, particularly its regeneration, are driven back. In other words, the poor of the West slowly but surely become richer, while the rich, poorer. However, the simple introduction of the techniques of the rule of law and free enterprise among other peoples of the world—the semi-colonial countries of Latin America and prewar Eastern Europe, colonies and former colonies—has meant and continues to mean that the great masses of simple folks, primarily peasants, not trained in the ways of these liberties, become prey to the aggressive and corrupt generation of such great property. The institutions of free enterprise, the rule of law, and (if it exists) representative democracy easily become the puppet shows of estate owners, financiers, and corrupt politicians. A process of the poor becoming poorer and the rich becoming richer ensues, and there is no chance of its turning around within a reasonable time.

In contrast, we have the Communist solution, which, taking possession of all political power, radically appropriates all mammoth property, but small property as well, and, annulling the techniques of freedom dubbed "bourgeois" and practically all forms of free enterprise, brings about the wholesale bureaucratization of social and economic life. That this is the only and exclusive way possible is justified by the fate of semi-colonies, colonies, and the countries of Eastern Europe and Asia before the Communist takeover. In truth, however, the bureaucratization of economic life equally hinders a rise in the living standards of the people. The entire semi-colonial world and former and current colonies are tossed about between these two insufficient solutions. Countries, like India, that seriously strive to surpass this alternative are far from being beyond the threat of this polarization. Nowhere has the almost egg-of-Columbus solution become historical fact, the proposal by radical East European peasant movements that large estates and big businesses be radically appropriated, while the political techniques of freedom and properly regulated free enterprise be bravely introduced or reinforced. And now in the Hungarian case, this solution, which has never had the opportunity of being realized between the two bad alternatives with a greater historical force, appears as the only way out because appropriation of big property carried out by the effective, though not exclusive, intervention of the Communists has become such a definitive historical fact in a decade, the undoing of which no one could reasonably consider, as least of all the active participants of the revolution did. On the other hand, the full and complete loss of credibility of the Hungarian Communist Party makes one-party rule, even in its mellower form, impossible in Hungary in the long run and calls for the introduction of the techniques of a multiparty and rule-of-law system as the only way out, naturally within the limits of upholding socialist achievement.

A multiparty system so constrained would elicit mistrust from both sides at first. The Western, "bourgeois" observer would say that if parties against socialism are barred from running, it is not freedom. However, all historical democracies began by a preliminary agreement on the shared fundamental principles of the majority, and those questioning these principles had no right to establish political parties. Dutch, English, American, and French parliamentary freedom started out by more or less banishing the followers of absolute monarchy from the parliamentary arena and applied even excessive, rather unjust, personal constraints as well. Yet genuine freedom could unfold because the obligatory platform was broad enough to include the vast majority of society. The same would hold in a Hungarian multiparty system constrained by the recognition of socialist achievements as a basis. On the other side, the acknowledgment of a multiparty system would mean the forsaking of the Leninist heritage for the Communists, the understanding that their party, the sole trustee of truth, would be downgraded to the same rank as any bourgeois or semi-bourgeois interest group. The fact is, however, that without several parties, running, "free" elections would be but puppetry because there would be no opportunity for drawing up lists of nominees or, at least, the mention of a prior agreement on those "to be deleted" as opposed to the official list; if we allowed for such organizational activity, we would come to parties, whatever we call them. Where the Communist Party retained its authority and there were no serious parties aside from it, multi-list elections could be held not only by way of allowing old or new parties to run, but also by the Communist Party dividing into several lists on the basis of the trends within the shared platform that, lacking better and principled criteria, we usually identify with leaders.

No elimination of exploitation is realistically possible without the genuine functioning of the institutions of freedom. However, the thesis holds the other way around as well: no institution of freedom is realistic without radical land redistribution, the appropriation of mammoth property, and a legal system efficiently safeguarding against exploitation. A third-way experiment, whatever prospects it is deemed to have, would therefore be most instructive for the West; the Communist world; and the semi-, current, and former colonial countries.

This is why the Hungarian case means hope for world peace too. The crux of world peace is the tension between the Western world and the Soviet Union and the system of power positions the two sides have set up and insist on upholding in their fear of each other. For now, the Soviet Union shrinks back from giving up positions because it believes that the governments of the people's democracies left alone would not be able to cope with their profound unpopularity resulting from ten years of Stalinist political practice, and leaving one to its fate would trigger a chain reaction in the others. How utterly strained the situation is is epitomized by the divided countries, particularly Germany, which is untenable per se, but there is no prospect for concessions on either side.

What hope can the Hungarian case have in such a grave impasse? It is that, in this series of interrelated deadlocks, it is the one case where concession and compromise are the nearest at hand. Nearest because, first, since the October events, holding onto Hungary's position, aside from immediate military and prestige concerns, has become more a burden than an advantage, and retaining the Communist government of Hungary has become just as worrisome as its abandonment would be for the rest of the Communist countries. Second, there is an opportunity of concession and compromise because there are no serious forces in Hungary, as opposed to Germany, that could bring about a capitalist restoration in the event that the present government is given up; moreover, the likelihood is that Hungary would remain in the group of socialist countries, a position that could even be guaranteed by prior agreement. Finally, concession and compromise are possible because Hungary has a political stand that is capable of commanding a national following; supports freedom and socialism; opposes all restoration; is intent on eliminating the overblown bureaucracy humanely, gradually, and with no persecution; and is not anti-Soviet, and not only has it not the slightest intention of turning the country into an anti-Soviet base, but it also has a profound inner understanding of the problems and concerns of the Soviet leadership.

This opportunity of compromise means that under joint guarantees by both the Western world and the Soviet Union, Hungary could establish a social and political system that neither of them are particularly keen on but which means the only way out. If they have the courage to agree on this experiment, it will soon turn out that not only is it not a threat, but that it is also instructive for other pending issues, that it will bring to light such as yet unknown opportunities of rapprochement that now, strained as relations are, remain unused or unnoticed. The conditions that evolved in the Polish case, where West and East outdid each other in their concern for the success of the Polish elections, could be repeated with a broader base in Hungary, proving that the success of balanced solutions is in the interest of both parties. Such an atmosphere would certainly ease the crisis of confidence, which has been the greatest obstacle in the way of resolving other major issues—the nuclear experiments and nuclear armament and disarmament.

The issue arises, however, that though the conditions of concession and compromise are given in the Hungarian case, they would, in the final count, mean that the Soviet Union would be giving up a military position, and no one can reasonably expect the Soviet Union to do so without obtaining serious offsets. We have already pointed out that giving up Hungary, under guarantees given at international, political, and internal social-policy levels that the country would not become an anti-Soviet base would in itself be more of an advantage than a drawback for the Soviet Union. We must, however, raise this issue on a military plane; with some resourcefulness, an appropriate offset can surely be found. Obviously not in Germany, where it is usually sought because it is far greater a military position and difficulty than the Hungarian cause could bear if it were tied up with it. One might come up with the fleeting idea that the offset area could be the region of Denmark, Norway, or Iceland. With a view to laying the foundations of peace in Europe, there would be much point in having the same number of northern and Danube basin countries simultaneously ceding both military blocs. The northern countries could retain the capitalist and Hungary the socialist system.

All in all, this is what makes Hungary both a scandal and hope of the world; hope, however, means no historical necessity; it is an opportunity that can be grasped or bungled. The question therefore is what is to be done by the various power factors and leaders of the world to put an end to the scandal in the Hungarian case and to bring to fruition the hope inherent in it. I believe these duties are as follows:

1. It is the duty of the Western world, in spite of all frustrations, to keep the Hungarian case on the agenda, the reassuring resolution of which is the precondition of resuming an East-West dialogue.
2. It is the duty of the followers of socialism in both the Soviet Union and elsewhere to always bear in mind that the future of socialism and the Soviet Union depends on the elimination of Stalinist political practice, and Hungary has become a touchstone of whether this is possible or not.
3. It is the duty of the forces of the "third way" to be aware of the fact that it is not only their weight and say in international affairs that hinges on their ability to mediate and their success in so doing, whether the current polarization intensifies or abates, but also their very existence.
4. Finally, it is the duty of the Hungarian people, who now bear both all the glory and the brunt of the historical role, to reject all cooperation with whatever is falsehood and aggression even at the cost of reducing their living to mere vegetation. It is not their duty to start a new uprising and provoke new retaliations. But it is their duty to hold onto the flag of their revolution in the face of slander, forgetting, and weariness—it is the flag of a freer mankind.

THE MEANING OF EUROPEAN
SOCIAL DEVELOPMENT

AN IDEA OF THE COMMON DEVELOPMENT OF MANKIND

Politics is the one area of human life that has resisted scientific inquiry. To be more precise, it has been the subject of earlier, primitive forms of science, even providing opportunities for science to take its first steps—to record and sort experiences and thereby arrive at intuitive notions of order or principle in it. It has nevertheless lacked the certitude that makes a body of knowledge become science: assurance gained through experimentation. Clearly formulating a question, an experiment that can be repeated under the same conditions, is what proves or disproves an intuition. In politics, however, experiments take the form of revolutions, wars, reforms, administrative overhauls, constitution-making, and mass movements, which are indeed impossible to emulate accurately, and it is here that all attempts at making politics a science have foundered. Political schemes claiming to be scientific are but experience-based generalizations verified or refuted by their proponents or opponents, who have any number of historical examples to invoke. To this day, such schemes or political concepts have derived their convincing power solely from the mass of historical examples referred to and are a far cry from science in the modern sense of the word.

Schemes of world history—that it is a series of class struggles, acts of divine economy, or a process of accumulating material goods—cannot be proved or disproved as such; examples of each and their exact opposite—that, for instance, history is a series of class compromises—can be brought up endlessly. Therefore, the way such issues are settled is that when a student of politics thinks up a comprehensive explanation of government, his next step is not to justify it in as many scholarly debates as possible but to present it with as much convincing

372

force as to bring a greater or lesser part of humankind around to start experimenting on its basis. He is like a physicist who has an ingenious idea, but it is far too expensive to work out experimentally, so he has to reason moneyed men into funding his experiments. A student of politics has to persuade whole nations or social groups to work out his principles through transforming their very lives, and it is through this working out that his initial concepts move toward being verified, though they never reach the level of verification that the natural or even the social sciences require.

There is thus no greater danger in politics, in political theory and practice, than when such a scheme or concept is declared scientific and its followers are thereby deluded into a certainty this area does not allow. Anyone fostering such misleading certainty will necessarily live in falsehood. No political practitioner or theorist can avoid recourse to intuitive, evocative, and artistic means in his political actions. As a matter of course, this is not to say that all such actions necessarily issue from a state of emotional excess. For all its artistic, evocative, and intuitive means, politics can and should be very serene, reasonable, circumspect, and tactful, but it certainly must be aware that whatever experiment it tries to induce humankind to make may take its toll of hundreds and thousands of human lives, and it therefore can never reach the accuracy of the natural sciences. Putting the lives of people to the stake, as political experiments inevitably do, they must be undertaken with a keen sense of responsibility. Nothing jeopardizes this heightened mindfulness more than the childish and smug certainty of a man or a group that believes he or it possesses a scientifically accurate political program—a kind of ultimate key—for the happiness of mankind and applies it without restraint or doubt.

In passing, let me remark that what I have said in the foregoing about politics holds true also for a much-disputed and rather elusive manifestation of human life: religion. There, again, what we have is someone summarizing and ordering the experience of humankind, formulating a concept; then, if he has a degree of personal magnetism, he can induce people to try out his concept. Accordingly, to put it rather simply, he might proclaim that the essence of human life is active love, as Jesus did, or that it is resigned desirelessness, as the Buddha did. However, while a city might suffice for a political experiment, a so-to-speak religious experiment will need whole cultures and many centuries to demonstrate what will become of mankind if it wishes to settle its ultimate questions on the grounds of this or that concept. This is not to say that that cognition employs different methods in the natural sciences and in other delicate areas. It is essentially the same process everywhere: gaining and ordering experience, an intuitive grasp and formulation of a comprehensive concept, and, finally, its experimental demonstration or refutation. The difference is that in politics, and even more so in religion, an experiment takes centuries and requires great numbers of people, involving risks and human suffering, and it ought never to be started rashly, cynically, self-righteously, or conceitedly.

In what follows, I wish to outline a similar concept, an idea of the common development of mankind, its possibilities, and its meaningful and favorable aims—fully aware that it can make no claim to full certainty or scientific accuracy.

THE LOST STATE

A concept of human community or polity usually starts out from the observation that the condition of various major or minor groups of mankind is not healthy, balanced, ordered, or promising and that it needs to be put right. So the concept points out the direction of development that would be advantageous. This often goes hand in hand with a characteristically ulterior idea that either humankind or some of its groups once enjoyed a more hopeful and fitting condition that has been lost for some reason or other and now needs to be restored. Broadly speaking, this is the concept behind Rousseau's State of Nature and the Marxist primitive community—both reenacting in a worldly context the tripartite process of innocence, fall, and delivery. Such a starting point seems to me to be more than doubtful. A state of absolutely paradisal innocence, taken even in social terms, as a past condition of peaceful human coexistence has no foundation. Anthropology has found peoples living very amicably, but it has never brought to light any evidence of absolute goodness and innocence among the primitives. Nonetheless, a scheme that holds that something in the community life of mankind and its relation to the world was disrupted and undone in not only the recent past, when doubly felt, but also long before, and now calls for redress and that not only points to the future, but also seeks to draw lessons from the past, necessarily implying that the past was more balanced, has a lure difficult to withstand. I shall now attempt to delve into the meaning of this once balanced and now lost state.

MORTAL FEAR

I wish to take as my starting point the existentialist thesis that man is the only being aware of his death. The appearance of consciousness is probably responsible for both the many imbalances and wonderful opportunities in man. I want to switch back to the very archaic moment that it dawned on man that he would die and thus made him be conscious of his own existence in a way that no other living being is capable of as far as we know. Recall that he ate from the fruit of the Tree of Knowledge.

That man is cognizant of his mortality is the source of an entirely new mental malady, one likely to be the root and final cause of both polity and religion: the consciousness of fear. All living beings have fear when confronting actual danger—it being also a mechanism helping them hold out in danger; but he who is aware of his ensuing death reaches the point of being afraid of his own thoughts. He creates fear in his mind, and thus fear becomes a thing in itself in his life. It is in the wake of this that he recognizes external dangers: perils to his life, natural forces, accidents, and catastrophes; however, man living in a community soon acquires a new, highly significant experience: that the source of his most intensive fears is another man. He can be the cause of my greatest fears. Small wonder that man, when representing dreadful natural forces, also personifies them. In the course of natural and social development, quite soon I believe, he reaches a stage when the majority, even the vast majority, of dangers he faces come from the other man. If, in the face of all deadly perils I face and the fears by which I am tormented, I want to feel that I am powerful and strong, the first opportunity that I seem to have is to subject my fellow men to my will, while it is the coercion exercised on me by another that is capable of arousing fear in me. And it is in opposition to this that the need to be immune, to be free from the control and fear of the other, emerges in me.

Let me anticipate my ensuing train of thought by immediately stating that the most important recognition behind it is that to gain power by coercing the other and to overcome fear by subjugating him is false. I am deceived if I want to rid myself of fear by increasing my power, my domination, and my sense of control. The way to shake off fear is precisely to be, and to put my fellow men, under no oppressive constraint.

In most of its history, humankind has not been able to break free of the vicious circle of fear, coercion, and submission. The way societies of any complexity started out was that large concentrations of power—tyrannies—evolved, and then the chief endeavor was to sacralize them, provide them with religious sanction—a step that need not mean religion per se; a religious ideology of sorts would do; nevertheless, the essence was to derive their power from superior forces in order to humanize them, to induce restraint in the powerful and acquiescence in the subjugated and thereby provide the polity with some order. It is crucial to recognize that this is not the way to break out of the fearful vicious circle of power because concentrations of power are bound to provoke individual or mass hysterias, tyrannical rages, dynastic struggles, and violence of all kinds. That there might be a way out has seldom been perceived in the history of mankind.

THE GRECO-ROMAN AND THE CHINESE EXPERIMENTS

The idea that freedom and the rule of a composed, fearless reason can be established was conceived in but two cultures—the Greco-Roman and the Chinese. It was in these two that political ideology and practice attempted to transcend, as Guglielmo Ferrero put it, the history of mankind as a tedious alternation of tyrannies and sought to durably and institutionally humanize and moralize power, to subject it to the control of freedom, and to finally eliminate it. The originality of the Greek experiment is that the Greeks were the first to recognize that constitutions could be made, man-made, but they also devoted their public life and even freedom to experiments in all conceivable constitutional makeups—affording ample opportunity for Aristotle to give a uniquely systematic overview of the kinds of constitutions men can forge. He also penned the highly significant insight that given a constitution, people are ruled not by people but by law. In and of itself, the Greek experiment would have remained incomplete or would only have proved that constitutions based on great freedom are not distinctly durable. However, the Greek experiment was actually rounded off by the Roman one, which, apart from likewise trying out several constitutions, proved the contrary: it created a durable legitimacy, one that had no match either in the constitutional arrangements or the monarchies or dynasties of ancient times. The legitimacy of Rome spanned roughly the period between the sixth century BC and the third century AD, its fundamental institution, the Senate, incorporating elements of monarchy, democracy, and aristocracy. The Roman experiment came to ruin in the third century, when a characteristic institution of Mideastern sacred kingdoms, the emperor god, seemed to overwhelm and bury the Greco-Roman experiment in freedom and organized constitutionalism, leaving nothing of it but the chaos and disarray brought about by Roman emperors lacking sufficient sacred grounding and unable to withstand mass movements. It was at this moment that Christianity stepped in—launching the processes of modern history.

The Chinese experiment had quite different roots. There we see a stern sacred empire, but an ethical system designed for state organization, Confucianism, came to be the ruling ideology, and it turned the state, from fathers through provincial governors right up to the emperor, into a hierarchical order of obligations and exercises of duty, and, by the very marked emphasis on obligation and its inculcation in society, it managed to establish a relatively highly moralized, rationalized, and humanized governance. Without distinguishing the cause from the effect prematurely, we might observe an interesting relationship here between the relative rationalization of polity and the level of mysticism in religious outlook. Both the Greco-Roman and the Chinese experiments took place in circumstances on which the oppressive power of mysticism and sacredness did not heavily weigh down, allowing a rationalized, obligation-based, moral interpretation of the sacred kingdom in China and the overthrow of sacred monarchy and experimentation with other forms of constitution in its stead in the Greek and Roman world. We could make the point that the more a society is subject to tyranny, the more it engenders mystical religious systems bafflingly impervious to reason and inquiry, and, vice versa, the more rational and free social organization is, the more demand there is for religion to be perspicuous and intelligible, to be an area of life open to reason.

A RATHER UPSETTING FEATURE OF HUMAN LIFE

Let me now enlarge further on my train of thought on man's becoming aware of his fearful condition exposing him to danger and death and his reaching the point where he seems to have reason to fear not so much the external dangers to his life but his fellow men, the human world. Becoming aware of his own death, he is filled with a fear he can overcome only by—no means of staving off death being available—surrogates that give him the illusion of triumph over death. The first of these is the power of life and death over another man and the life-and-death struggle between them for that power. Any victory in this struggle seems to be a victory over death, though it only steps up the race with death—a rather upsetting feature of human life.

On this view, it is a particularly false interpretation of nature to regard the life-and-death struggle among animal species as an example for and justification of human life and society. The struggle for survival among animals cannot be brought into parallel with the destruction man wreaks on his own kind—a feature almost unique to the human race. Indeed, animals rarely engage in life-and-death combat with members of their own species, usually only in relation to reproduction and extreme danger to their kind. But even the struggle among the species that prey on one another is not nearly as keen as many would have it. Those analogizing the devastation men do to one another to the destructive activity of animals and nature take most of their examples from predators. True, predators corner their victims, who desperately fight for their lives unto the last. Preying, however, is not the only type of natural interaction; it is not rare, but it cannot be taken to be representative either. It is an extreme manifestation of the symbiosis that generally exists among the species of the natural world. Moreover, this symbiosis has some highly reassuring and tremendously meek examples. The way autumn leaves become the humus of the coming year or a whale swallows millions of protozoa in a mouthful of water hardly suggests a struggle for survival but rather a mutual interdependence, and surely it cannot serve to justify the carnage men are willing to do to one another.

For all its instances of life-and-death struggle, nature exhibits a far greater proportion of solidarity and interdependence and the notion that it is only exceptionally in the interest of a species to annihilate another of their kind. To the contrary, it is in the interest of, so to speak, all species of nature that all facets of life be more extensive, abundant, and powerful. This broad solidarity of the natural world is of course not in the least mawkish; it does not tally with the concept of human love, but it is nonetheless akin. The warmth of organic life seeks the warmth of other organic lives throughout the breadth and depth of nature, and in this regard, the activity with which the organic world cuddles together and the activity with which it might destroy the other by gobbling it up seem to be related. The crux of the matter is that annihilation for its own sake is alien to nature; it is the privilege of man.

The life-and-death struggle among men is therefore not a law of nature but the result of a process of deformation. This process was begun by man's rise to consciousness, his becoming aware that he happens to belong to a species marked by individuals whose lives are limited in time, and who, in comparison with the physical force of the surrounding nature, are rather weak; only to come to life, they need nine months; to reach average capacity, they need a further twenty years, while a mere few seconds are enough for their obliteration. In contrast to other species, all this dawns on man, triggering a process in his mind that leads him to feel that his power and strength are enhanced and that he is exalted as he slaughters another man.

This is a way of rephrasing in a modern idiom and with, I believe, a valid meaning the mythic idea that man ate from the fruit of the Tree of Knowledge and fell. Indeed, all religions, all ethical views of the world, speak of what man should do in his individual life, how he should conceive of his life to free himself from the consequences of this fall. All theories of state, all genuinely high-minded politics, speak of what human communities and the community of mankind have to do to free themselves of the consequences of these fears.

THE RISE OF CHRISTIANITY

We can now pick up the thread of our discussion on the Roman Empire, which, after legitimately functioning continuously without major interruption for seven or eight centuries, succumbed to what classical Roman mentality had passionately abhorred: oriental despotism. Deploying the means of Asiatic tyranny, Diocletian in the third century and Constantine in the fourth attempted to reorganize and stabilize the empire, whose republican and rational institutions had fallen into anarchy. This seemed to put an end to the great Greco-Roman experiment in the pragmatic, open-minded, and valid organization of human community. However, it was only the eastern, Byzantine part of the Empire that set about organizing itself along oriental-despotic and bureaucratic lines; the western part sank into anarchy. And it was in this very anarchy that productive forces sprang up, enabling the resumption of the Greco-Roman tradition and the initiation of an experiment in humane and rational social organization even more significant than its predecessors. More conspicuous than these, the organizing forces of tribal kingships spread throughout a disarrayed western Roman Empire. These, however, provided merely an external framework; the real fermenting factor that began to exert its influence, blend with the Roman tradition, and inaugurate a new culture was Christianity.

At the turn of the century, it was habitual to represent the rise of the new religion in the ancient world—Anatole France was the grand master of this—as the unwashed and fierce prophets of a sect encroaching upon the world of wise, skeptical, disenchanted Greco-Roman gentlemen, who regularly took steam baths and had every reason to loathe the rancor. There is an element of truth in this: conjure up the image of the Alexandrian "Christian" mob dragging in the dust the lynched body of the extremely beautiful, brilliant, and erudite young woman philosopher Hypatia—by no means a bright point in the history of Christianity. In its entirety, however, the contrast is false. On the one hand, the Greco-Roman world had been far more laden with misery, fear, superstition, witchcraft, and so on than a modern-day freethinker imagining himself in the place of a Roman or Greek would have believed. On the other hand, irrespective of the issue of tyranny, Christianity did have its radiantly truthful and close-to-life characteristics. This requires that we treat the personality of Christ because taking up and entering into this religion has from the outset to our own day meant a personal encounter with his figure, so poignantly described in the Gospels.

CHRIST

No doubt Christ arose from a minor Jewish sect preaching asceticism and the imminent end of the world; we would be justified in calling it a sect hostile to life. However, some of his most important traits, without his ever calling into doubt the basic teachings of his sect about the coming of Judgment Day or the vanity of worldly life—his intimate closeness to life, his profound understanding of the simplest things, and his tenderness toward his fellow men—pointed, in both time and space, far beyond the limits of the sect of which he was obviously a devoted member. Furthermore, he uttered some extraordinarily significant, almost unforgettably plain, sentences on the power of meekness; the futility of anger; and the inherent relatedness of wrath, the life-and-death struggle, and killing, and not only did he utter sentences, but he also made exemplary gestures—likewise unmatched in their kind. He had an extraordinary gift of using word and gesture to calm people incited to hate, strike, judge, scold, or vent other wretched forms of fear and open their eyes to the futility of their intentions or conduct. Sayings like "He who is without sin among you, let him throw a stone at her first" (Jn 8:7) and "Render therefore unto Caesar the things which be Caesar's, and unto God the things which be God's" (Lk 22:25) hit right in the middle of fear, hatred, and truculence—so to speak, the essence of the fall of man. Furthermore, he was also able to speak about faith, which, for him, had nothing to do with believing in any theology or doctrine. Faith, in the way he talked about it, was a childlike trust in the capacities of the human soul and an ability to arouse them.

More than any others, his perceptions on the power of meekness stand out, and gross misunderstandings abound about these. The advice on "Whosoever shall smite thee on thy right cheek, turn to him the other also" (Mt 5:39) is not in the least an indication of haplessness; on the contrary, it is one of the disarming gestures that make senseless aggression become aware of its own irrationality. There is an interesting point here, a mere hypothesis: we have reason to infer that Jesus personally experienced the power of meekness, having, by nature, been prone to passions, outbursts, and even aggression, but having recognized the power of meekness, he did not become miserable; instead, through it, he achieved greater things than he could have through combativeness. His beating the temple traders (Mk 11:15), his cursing the fig tree (Mt 21:19), and other rash reactions of his suggest that in speaking of the power of meekness and the need to withstand evil, he offered for all mankind the lesson of the futility of the peevishness he had overcome in himself. Now, this conduct has extraordinary consequences on the mode of organizing human community in spite of the fact that the environment from which Christ had come had had no intention of perfecting it, wanting but to exhibit the futility of all human endeavor to itself and the world.

THE CHURCH

The gospel of Christ was then turned into a world religion by his crucifixion, the interpretation the apostle Paul gave it, and his propagation of the faith throughout the Roman Empire. Though this is quite different material from the actual message of Christ as we know it in its most salient form in the Sermon on the Mount (Mt 5–7), it would be unfair to charge Paul with distorting or totally changing it. What he added was certainly distinctive, but it was also an organic continuation of Christ's gospel, starting out as it did from the crucifixion, which had been the consummation of Christ's gestures to illustrate the convincing power of patience. Paul was the one who connected Christ's death on the cross as an act of redemption with Adam's fall; he was the one who established the theology of Christ's divinity and humanity, which was later to develop into endless, sometimes abstruse though not wholly insignificant, debates; Paul was the one who dissociated faith from its simple and close-to-life concept that Christ had preached and diverted it in a more speculative and impenetrable direction, difficult as it is to regard as beneficial; however, he did have portentous things to say about the relationship between moral action and law. If we acknowledge that Christ's elevation to divinity was unavoidable given the state of mind of the disciples and the cultural environment, we must concede that Paul managed to formulate the divinity of Christ in a way that took account of his full human identity without impairing it, a concept, it should be remembered, that was to prevail without yielding a whit of Christ's humanity in the ensuing debates over the Trinity. This would prove vital in the future; it meant that the fundamental experience of those encountering the Christian religion was that God knew our tribulations and that, in order to break away from our burdened human condition, we needed to connect with a human personality of the same fabric as our own.

The most repulsive traits of Christianity, which developed as it came to be institutionalized in the church in a few centuries, are its animosity to life and bent for doctrinal intolerance, but the close-to-life, liberating, and inherently tolerant tone of Christ's personal message has always rung clear. (Let me remark parenthetically that it has always seemed to me to be vastly ludicrous that there are people who, even having read the synoptic gospels, can entertain the notion that Christ never lived and was mere fiction. So round and weighty a character emerges from these writings that if anyone were to have intended him as a literary character, he would have been the greatest founder of a religion.)

AUGUSTINE

Whatever bearing the Christian message had on the good organization of human community, little of it was converted into reality in the areas of eastern Christendom, where sacred-monarchy-turned-oriental-despotism determined social structures. The grounds for such conversion was the anarchy in the western Roman Empire, where a still living Roman social tradition and the new social impulses of Christianity together initiated an experiment in rational, humanizing, and moralizing social organization. The old Roman insistence on rational social organization and the new Christian insistence on a life without fear, hatred, and violence were first blended in the work of Saint Augustine, particularly in *The City of God*, his greatest book. One might justly have reservations about Augustine's theological positions, but they need not concern us now. What matters for us now is what he has to say about the City of God; though maintaining the utter inferiority and futility of this world as compared to the divine one, he holds up its standard to judge worldly things in a way that wonderfully leads out of the fundamentally other-worldly orientation of Christianity to allow for a possibility of approximating this world to the heavenly one. In other words, something can be done to improve this vale of tears in the spirit of Roman practicality. This is the gist of his prescriptions telling the good king or the good master what to do if he does not want his kingship to be mere plunder, his masterhood, sheer tyranny, and carnage.

In the eyes of a social reformer in our own day, these might seem but outrageous palliations to slaves and subjects wanting to revolt, attempts to make them acquiesce to tyranny and believe they have good kings and masters. However, these are to be measured not against modern standards but the actual situation of slaves and subjects having little hope of a successful revolt. Augustine therefore addressed not potential insurrectionists to soothe them but masters and rulers, to instill in them a higher sense of morality. From this moment on, all teachers of Western Europe drew their categories from the works of Saint Augustine, whether they read them or not. They applied them against Germanic and other tribal rulers, who swarmed all over the Roman Empire and who, being at a much lower level of sacred monarchy than their oriental counterparts, were culturally less assured of being capable of governing a more complicated world. In this environment of incapacity, the priestly, Augustine-reared intelligentsia became factors in social organization by tutoring and administering for these rulers and, if need be, rebuking them from the pulpit. As monarchs tamed down, partaking of power marred the clergy; all in all, however, this meant that power was so steeped in morality even in medieval but certainly in modern times that it surpassed all other experiments in moralizing the exercise of power. When censuring the European exercise of power for its atrocities, we tend to forget that we do so because we have become accustomed to relatively high moral standards in that exercise and indeed to conceiving that high moral standards can be applied to power at all, an issue that would simply not surface in the Middle East.

CHRISTIAN SOCIAL ORGANIZATION

After several centuries of groundwork, the experiment in social organization by the Christian clergy culminated around the time of the Cluniac Reforms in the ninth and tenth centuries in what we now term rather perfunctorily medieval Christian feudalism. It should be borne in mind that this was a unique experiment, and it is misleading to lump it together with the forms of feudal organization available throughout the world and thus to believe that it is a necessary stage in human social development. Social development has no necessary stages and occurs whenever there is a meaningful aim to pursue. No natural law prescribes that we must develop from slavery to feudalism, from feudalism to capitalism. There are attempts at meaningful social development, like the Chinese experiment, which, in its earlier form, has by all accounts come to an end and given way to Western inspiration, and like the Greco-Roman-medieval-European experiment with its many jerks and jolts. It is therefore justified to speak of social development and occasionally revolution only where such experiments do occur. In contrast, it would hardly be fair to speak of any revolution in the Middle East or India, apparently areas of invariable tyranny, where popular movements have led to, at most, palace revolutions and alternating reigns of good and bad kings. In China, however, it would be legitimate to speak of the kind of revolution that calls a ruler to account for not meeting the standards of the proper exercise of power and that begins with a demand for social reform, as the great Chinese peasant revolts did, often paralleling their European counterparts. Likewise, we encounter revolutions in Europe in which an ideologically more or less trained clerical intelligentsia had a leading role through repeatedly formulating the requirements of the proper exercise of power. Far from being necessary, development is the collective effort of some cultures and not others and may even fail. We are not in the comfortable position of either being able to establish, as a kind of natural law, the rule of the right and wrong development of society or being discharged by any such natural law from the responsibility of leading the great activity of organizing human polity in the wrong direction, a dead end, or, most recently, the total annihilation of mankind.

CHRISTIAN FEUDALISM

Medieval Christian feudalism should be assessed bearing this in mind—as a unique enterprise, not the European manifestation of a universal scheme. To understand its complexities, we first need to dwell on its generally known schemes. Its customary, earlier concept saw it as primarily relations of allegiance connecting the lower levels of society with its upper echelons in a hierarchical order, and the power of allegiance was what held the social pyramid together. Feudalism in this sense appeared in vastly different cultures and periods and continues to appear even in our day. A feudal relationship thus binds together a core made up of a warlord or tribal king and his armed escort, and being that allegiance is upheld even in the most barbarian conditions, a common war effort, it is permeated by several strongly moral factors. If such a warlord is capable of conquering larger territories, the core organization is multiplied. Members of his escort become liege lords or castle lords and themselves acquire armed escorts; if their territory expands, these lords in turn also surround themselves with servants, fighters, and squires, and thus a pyramid-like structure comes into being, held together by a more or less strong, obviously allegiance-based relation, though somewhat loose at the top. Not a characteristically European phenomenon, it was brought to Europe by less organized medieval tribal kingships from the Germanic woods and the eastern steppes, and it can be found in the Arab world, parts of India, Japan, and so on.

According to the other, classical Marxist concept, feudalism is a characteristic form of exploitation, where those subdued are not in their full physical being enslaved to and the possessions of others but, enjoying a minimum of personal freedom, live in a strongly personal system of bondage, submission, and service, briefly called serfdom, which, in this view, is the most characteristic institution of feudalism. Without the feudal armed allegiance of the former concept, serfdom likewise appears throughout world history, returns in refeudalizing tendencies, but, interestingly disregarding all schemes, also occurred in the social organization of ancient Egypt and Babylon in periods well before classical slavery. In the long history of China, it was always more characteristic than slavery, which was only known in its domestic forms.[1]

SOCIETY-ORGANIZING CLERGY

Thus, going back to the German woods and East European plains, European feudalism was marked by the hierarchical order of allegiance among members of the armed aristocracy and reaching down below them, as well as by serfdom, the foundations of which had already been laid in the late Roman period and found in its areas by the newcomers. However, apart from these, it was also characterized by a genuinely unique feature: the social organizing role of the clergy—a role that is perhaps unmatched in all of world history. Priests performed similar functions in all other cultures, but these were limited to sacralizing the ruler, elevating him to divine rank. Priestly bodies in the courts of rulers—as in theocracies like that of ancient Egypt—could acquire significant political influence,

but this was focused merely on the hubs of power, did not diffuse throughout society, and had no social organizing role. It was in the anarchy in the wake of the
decline of the Roman Empire that the clergy and the parallel monastic orders
assumed a role in social organization. We noted above that the tribal kingdoms
founded on the ruins of the Roman Empire had to organize themselves in a far
more advanced society, whose complexities surpassed their capacities, and were
thus forced to accept the assistance of the clergy and monastic orders, which
somehow or other represented their superior knowledge, expertise, and customs. It was no coincidence that this social organizing role of the clergy was far
more conspicuous north of the Alps and the areas of Italy exposed to migration.
In southern Europe, Italy and Spain, several elements of the lay intelligentsia
remained in place as the organizers of civic life. The Roman civitates retained
their notaries and civil scribes in an almost unbroken continuity, surviving even
in the Middles Ages, and thus had many similarities with the Byzantine world,
where the clergy formed closed groups and lived secluded from the world, ex-
erting its influence usually only at the tops of hubs of power and leaving the
organization of society to civil intellectuals and imperial and local bureaucrats.
Apart from certain areas of Italy and Spain as mentioned, however, there was
virtually no civil intelligentsia in the anarchy following the Roman Empire in
Western Europe, and the clergy gradually slid into the administrative-clerical
role at the side of unknowing Germanic kings, a role that would otherwise have
been played by lay intellectuals.

In an old issue of his magazine *Tanú* (Witness), the writer László Németh
quotes from the letter of a Roman intellectual putting up with all the vicissitudes of the great migration to his friend living in the safe haven of the eastern
part of the empire: "Here I am writing, as the bellowing of drunk Burgundians
penetrates from the outside; they come to hail me six times every morning as
though I were their grandfather."[2] We ought to picture the Roman Empire falling under barbarian rule not through the image of magnificent and superior
Germanic conquerors but that of grotesque and perplexed red-bearded kings
and warriors, either barbarously aggressive or comically respectful.

This was the atmosphere in which barbarian rulers, baffled by the, for them,
incomprehensible tasks of governance, sought advice from Roman civil intellectuals increasingly difficult to come by or from the considerably less learned
priests and monks coming in their stead but who still knew a lot more than
any Germanic tribesman did. It was out of compassion for this environment
profoundly at a loss that West European monastic orders—almost in spite of
themselves and in stark contrast to their secluded counterparts in eastern Christendom, which were focusing on sanctity, exercises of love, and mysticism or

eremitism—began to spread methods of agricultural production, set up hospitals and provide medical care, and establish homes for the poor and needy. This is why this clergy was given extraordinary respect and, though diminished in numbers, still is, still not regarded as a wholly useless, parasitical mass, a situation that is diametrically opposed to the one in Southern and Byzantine Europe, where the priesthood sometimes fulfills a function similar to that of magic and is revered accordingly; however, in the day-to-day life of society, this reverence is rather fickle and can drop very low. In a Western Europe organized by priests and friars, the clergy never declined to such an extent and continues to function in the areas from the north of Spain and Italy, including the British Isles and Scandinavia and, in the east, Poland, the Baltic region, Hungary, and western Yugoslavia. Having inherited something of the matter-of-factness, the administrative and legal pragmatism of the Roman mind, and the rudiments of Augustine's vision of state and society, this clergy sought to reinterpret and extol the various situations of dominion occurring in society as functions, duties, and Christian obligations. This was what made European Christian feudalism far more than a close bond of allegiance among warlords and their armed subordinates and considerably more than a simple one-sided relationship of subjugation between landlords and their serfs.

FREEDOMS, PRIVILEGES, PATENTS

After the Cluniac Reforms, as the keeping of written records spread, this society-organizing clergy increasingly inclined toward structuring society through privileges and patents and sought to steep all varieties of social relation in a sense of vocation and mutuality. Thus, it framed the ideals of the Good King, the Good Liege, the Good Knight, the Good Citizen, and the Good Tiller, and, though allotting to each a quite different share of labor and leisure, it tried to base their relationships on mutuality so that all the parties would give and take and even the lowliest would have a measure of human self-esteem. The entire structure was held together by the Christian image of the world to come and the model of conduct Christian redemption delineated, which granted everyone the possibility of final ascent; even those lowest in degree were able to finally surpass the mightiest, who in turn could incur eternal damnation—just as anyone else could.

On this view of the world, the clergy was occasionally able to fill even those on high with the fear of damnation and haul them over the coals for their iniquities; it is grossly mistaken and a cynicism projected back in time to belittle this and not see its significance in social organization. Not only did this ethos justify established power relations and the outrageous differences in social opportunities, but it also enabled the leveling of criticism—to use a word anticipating future outcomes, revolutionary criticism—at potentates. If the situation of the king was an obligation he had to fulfill, as was that of the liege, the landlord, or the knight, then, by implication, so too was criticism of the king, the liege, the landlord, or the knight who did not live up to his vocation. It was from this outlook of Christian feudalism that the revolutions of the early Middle Ages grew.[3] Though in a slow, gradually evolving process (a rather long one, lasting as it did until the end of the eighteenth century), it finally did come to light that the king, though mostly the liege and the landlord, met a social need they themselves had created with their lack of restraint: robber barons brought about the anarchy in which it was reasonable for a poor man to put himself under the protection of one robber baron against another. The moment these forms of organization reached a level of consolidation where the robber barons no longer engaged in direct fighting and the king took over the task of maintaining the peace of the land, it became questionable against whom the landlord was providing protection and how far this was actual performance in contrast to the very tangible performance his serfs delivered. The charge grew more pointed as money payments and luxury increased and the same landlords tried to extort further dues from their serfs. This was the background of the great peasant revolts of the Middle Ages, sharply expressed in the famous English couplet of 1381: "When Adam delved and Eve spun, who was then a gentleman?" It was Christian feudalism that engrafted the possibility of such criticism into the minds of people, serfs, petty intellectuals, and petty clerics; the conception of the roles of king, knight, and serf as functions in the spirit of St. Augustine provided grounds for the social criticism of the king, knight, and serf who did not fulfill their functions.

Cities and citizens had a special place in medieval Christian feudalism. In the nobility, the clergy faced a group that had brought along its traits of pugnaciousness, bellicosity, barbarism, self-conceit, extravaganza, and ostentation from the pre-Christian warlike world and had to tame these traits with the help of various Christian categories, turning them into virtues, such as knightly honor, but the guise could never fully hide the barbarian underside. Likewise, it had to provide Christian sanction to the paganism of the peasantry resulting from its closeness to nature. It was in respect to towns and citizens that the clergy could embark on social organization as it wished, deploying its most ancient Christian heritage. It is not the Mediterranean and North European seaside towns I have in mind, where the citizens quickly flourished through commerce and set the tone, but the inland towns that provided crafts and commercial services for not particularly large agricultural regions. It was in these smaller towns, where, under the eyes of the clergy, a limited and sometimes small-minded world of industrious and permanently working men came into being, that the ideal of creative craftsmanship and a sentient conduct contrasted with the essentially idle, pugnacious, and flaunting lifestyle of the nobility and thus fomented attitudes that would later do away with the social function of the aristocracy. It was in towns that the clergy could genuinely play its role of social organizing through written records, and it was again in towns that, on the model of guilds, a new layer of non-priestly and non-clerical lay intelligentsia came into being consisting of scribes and university teachers.

Another hub of priest-led social organization and the use of written records was of course the royal court. Though itself rooted in the bellicose and flaunting world of the rest of the nobility, it gradually assimilated, through the Augustinian culture of the clergy, something of the public attitude of the Greek and Roman organization of polity, the concept of rule that transcended personal power and manifested itself in laws. This was what the court clergy salvaged and eked out with Augustine's theory of state and so turned the royal court into another center of using records. Furthermore, many European courts found good allies in the citizens fulfilling their functions, the king and the citizens joined forces against an aristocracy lacking significant functions to perform.

Parallel to the many and increasingly institutionalized forms of subjugation, this kind of social organization also offered a whole array of freedoms, privileges, the rights of estates, and the assemblies of estates, which gradually established many, not quite modern but certainly constitutional, institutions throughout Europe. In the framework of the estates assemblies, a further, genuinely novel institution, representation, came into being precisely to facilitate feudal relationships. Not knowing about this, Rome had not been able to genuinely extend citizenship throughout its empire; the Roman citizen had to turn up at the forum and cast his vote, and he obviously could not have done so had he happened to live in the eastern or western part of the empire. However, medieval feudalism, particularly the fact that the liege represented his vassals, established the constitutional means by which one person represented others at political assemblies. In the beginning, the liege himself represented his men, but later independent forms of representation became widespread, so much so that by the apogee of the Middle Ages all Europe enjoyed a variegated and complicated, yet constitutional, system of freedoms. Little does this resemble our modern concepts of constitution; it applied no set of unified categories but endowed various people with an amazing variety of freedoms, patents, and privileges, based as they were on the widespread use of records.

COMBINATION IN REVOLT

It was this Medieval feudalism that had to face a whole series of major crises in the transition to the modern age. The social and economic causes that brought about its flowering and final demise are well known. From the ninth and tenth centuries, the European clergy had started a massive campaign against castle lords and the private wars of the feudal nobility. When this by and large achieved success, a period of relative calm began, in the shades of which townsfolk could enrich themselves, providing for both moderate living conditions and the wonderful flowering of cathedrals, their affluence coming somewhat later. In this situation, various fermentative factors came into play.

The nobility thus began to lose its social functions, but it concurrently increased its demands, provoking bloody revolts by townsmen and peasants. Though it then tried to strengthen its positions also by adding substance to its functions, its falling into the background was inevitable. In this situation, the king could usually assert his power and reinforce his functions. These struggles took place in at least three different types of combinations, also warning us not to interpret medieval social conflicts as simply between the oppressors and the oppressed. In the first type of combination, peasants, sometimes joining forces with townsfolk, attacked all feudal responsibilities, all those who were idle parasites in contrast to their industrious and productive way of life. These attacks were mostly countered by an alliance between king and nobility and put down without delay. However, the suppression of revolts could only temporarily limit economic growth and the improvement of the life conditions of the peasantry and townsfolk.

The second type of combination occurred when an increasingly powerful monarch, through the offices of the clergy, struck an alliance with the cities to counter a truculent nobility. In the long run, this process, primarily in France, led to the complete defeat of the nobility, taming it into court, but it was also counterproductive in that it opened the way to royal absolutism, which dispensed with the articulate estate constitution, disrupted the rich texture of social organization of medieval times, atomized society, and fashioned itself into a single, one-sided hub of power—albeit one that never reached total tyranny, not even under Louis XIV.

The third type of combination took place when the increasingly moneyed citizenry and a nobility taking sides with them countered royal authority. By this time, the citizenry, to a certain extent all society, commoners, had usually grown into the constitutional rights the nobility had wrested from the monarch. This was the process that took place in Britain and the Netherlands; in the long run, this proved to be the most healthy and productive, as it did away with one-sided hubs of power and fostered the claims to freedom in the whole of society.

THE DUTCH EXAMPLE

Apart from the early but isolated success of the Swiss revolution, Holland represented the first breakthrough in this type of social transformation. The significance of the Netherlands cannot be overemphasized in this respect: from the sixteenth and seventeenth centuries, the Dutch shaped a society endowed with a degree of freedom that had no match in Europe for long a time. Dutch society provided a way of escape for the social reformer sects that had been banished from a Germany arresting the Reformation and that, via Britain, could take root in North America. The example of the Dutch inspired the English revolution, the American war of independence, and other free societies undergoing middle-class development or embourgeoisement.

These revolutions primarily did away with royal authority or rendered it purely symbolic and offered the aristocracy a way of survival in a society whose center of gravity had already shifted to the citizenry. Like their earlier Swiss counterpart, both the Dutch and the English revolutions organically developed from medieval constitutional traditions. The Dutch revolution was carried through in the face of the monarch by the estates, citizens, and nobles alike; the English revolution was fought by Parliament, a body medieval in its roots; and even the revolution that would be the model for all modern revolutions to come and that would sever all its ties with the past began with the convening of the Estates-General.

THE UNMATCHED SUCCESS AND FAILURE
OF THE FRENCH REVOLUTION

Starting a new chapter in the history of revolutions and revolutionism, the French Revolution can be regarded as a monumental attempt by the wealthiest and most developed country in Western Europe, which had nevertheless been hobbled by the fetters of absolutism, to match the immense progress the Protestant countries of Northern Europe and America had achieved in terms of freedom. In continental Europe, the great medieval experiments in constitutionalism had fallen short; in particular, the attempts at conciliar reform in the fifteenth century had failed, leaving absolute power to the papacy. As rebounding effects, Protestant Northern Europe was effectually cut off from the continent, and the rest, including significant parts of Protestant Germany, was subjugated to absolute rule. Absolute monarchy did not crush the German aristocracy; it in fact conserved Europe's "most successful" aristocratic structure in the form of the Holy Roman Empire. For all its welfare measures, European absolutism meant such a bureaucratically regulated, centralized state that the average individual national, let alone a peasant, had no or few rights and freedoms left.

This was the situation the French Revolution tried to overcome. To say that it was a bourgeoisie-inspired revolution and that its ideology was formulated to voice only bourgeois interests is very dubious wisdom. Certainly no revolution can succeed without the support of powerful social forces, but the social-criticism type of revolution characteristic of Europe—which calls the groups assuming positions of power in the social structure to account for their deeds and, having established their non-fulfillment of the function, sets the aim of overthrowing them—is far more than ideological design by a given social group. This requires a socially critical intelligentsia, which descends from medieval clerics, has grown weary of and thrown off the religious element of the struggles for reformation of the early modern era, and couches the obsolescence of royal and aristocratic privilege in terms of social criticism. To say, as has often been said, that the French bourgeoisie was particularly shrewd in formulating such an efficient ideology is totally amiss and naive, almost utterly inverting the sequence of events. The French bourgeoisie had been very much accustomed to tying up with royalty. It is no wonder that the eighteenth-century French bourgeois found it laughable that there was no king in Venice. Indeed, the French bourgeoisie little imagined a world without a king and would have been all too happy to be able to join forces with the king to abolish the privileges that the entirely parasitic aristocracy enjoyed and that, being economically certainly the equal of the aristocracy, it justly resented. But it would have gone no further than that, as it hastened to carry through such a settlement after the revolution.

Starting out with a fundamental program for social organization, the French Revolution went far beyond the ideological needs of the bourgeoisie; it was the result of an exceptional moment in history, the sudden collapse of the putrefied *ancien régime* and the gap it left behind, when only an aggressive and ideologically motivated intelligentsia was capable of envisaging a program at all. Though the French bourgeoisie seized the opportunities opened up by this gap, it, being far less ready to undertake social duties than its English or Dutch counterparts, hardly deserves the name and rank of ideology maker. All revolutionary changes have their inspirers and beneficiaries. The beneficiary of the French Revolution was the layer that was in the best position to fill in the power gap left by the fall of the monarchy and the aristocracy: the moneyed bourgeoisie, which was more a beneficiary than an inspirer. In other revolutions, the beneficiary might be a bureaucracy, but again only a beneficiary, not an originator. In all transformations, there are groups that hustle forward to be beneficiaries, but it is a grave mistake to regard them as the chief causes in retrospect. The French Revolution would hardly have been what it was without its intellectual ideology, which was not formulated by the bourgeoisie and which went far beyond what the most audacious bourgeois would have envisioned in the second half of the eighteenth century.

THE TERROR

At this point, we need to discuss the question of revolution and revolutionary violence. All social organization, but one that has had such lofty moral and humane aims as the European one has always had, necessarily seeks to decrease violence and the fear of violence. This had been the aim of the Christian feudal state organization, as it was the aim of the early modern revolutions preceding the French one; they all resorted to violence, not in the name of a cult of violence but rather to restore the peace an aggressive, ruthless, and troublemaking ruler had breached. The reigns of both Philip II in the Netherlands and Charles I in England were like this, and neither revolution engendered any belief in the productivity of revolutionary violence for its own sake; this would have been far from their ideologies. The French Revolution was what hatched such a notion. Why?

The French Revolution was both the most successful and the most unsuccessful revolution in European history. It was the most successful because it achieved a rational remolding of society to an extent no revolution had ever achieved before, and it was unsuccessful because it aroused a fear from which the Western world has never been able to recover. What is it that justifies revolutionary violence? If we consider the fact that all fear derives from the fear-ridden, malformed mental state of man, we must necessarily reject all notions that violence as such has a liberating and creative effect and that no social progress is possible without some form of violence. All productive social organizations are based on the recognition that there are no insurmountable differences of interest among people, only fears—perhaps intractable fears rooted in hard-set social circumstances, but nevertheless rooted not in genuine clashes of interest but in clashes of interest arising from rigid social situations. Revolutionary violence is thus useful and productive only insofar as it enables the quick dissolution or destruction of rigid power circumstances. The role of revolutionary violence is thus to demonstrate through the force of a few violent gestures that an ostensibly invincible, fearful, mighty, and authoritative hub of power that has no function any longer is in fact functionless and powerless; such a role thus inspires great mental and actual liberation and creativity in the subjugated.

The moment revolutionary violence puts the victors in the mood to increase the violence and set aims that can be realized through continued violence against not only the mighty but society as a whole, it prepares not revolution but tyranny and fosters not creativity but boundless terror. Overnight, the revolution brought it home to French society that neither the monarchy nor the aristocracy could stand up against its uprising and that aristocratic privilege and certain historical deadweights could be shaken off at once. However, as the cautious bourgeoisie, which had never really dominated the revolution, passed the reins to a rationalist, society-organizing intelligentsia driven by ideological motives, the terrifying temptation emerged that unleashed violence need not be ended and achievements beyond those readily attainable, as the limitation of royal power and the abolition of aristocratic privileges had been, could be pursued. Due to its anti-clericalism, provoked by a church ossified in its counter-reformation posture, this enlightened intelligentsia set out to eliminate the ecclesiastic hold over the minds of men. However modern and timely it might have deemed this aim to be, it ran into a resistance far more fearful and powerful than it had ever expected; its struggle turned out to be not against a fictitious power that could be overthrown by, as it were, a flick of a finger but an endless and desperate strife that would estrange the better part of the nation from the revolutionary cause, and this strife would lose touch with the genuine and concrete interests of social reform and would never lead to the undoing or remolding of the religious ties of the people.

As a matter of fact, it had been on this issue, this rather knotty issue, that the monarchy and an otherwise hapless king had become invincibly or at least irrevocably obstinate, resisting and turning against the revolution. He had defied the National Constituent Assembly over the issue of a civil constitution for the clergy. This was what prompted him to attempt flight and Central European powers to intervene and what ultimately brought about revolutionary terror, the final fall of the monarchy, and a perpetuation of violence in comparison to which the absolutism of Louis XIV seemed timid. Whatever vast torrents of ink were consumed for its justification, the Terror was a cul-de-sac, the failure of the revolution. It is an untruth that revolution requires terror; it only needs terror when it sets aims that are beyond what can be achieved by reasonable means. It was because of the Terror that the revolution, which had at first met with widespread sympathy, aroused widespread dread and hatred throughout Europe.

It was the Terror that gave rise to two wholly unproductive types of man whose attitudes have held sway over European thought ever since: the professional reactionary and the professional revolutionary. A genuine politician, statesman, or social reformer can uphold tradition, remold society, or perhaps take revolutionary steps as actual conditions require and by definition be neither a reactionary nor a revolutionary. It was the French Revolution that chose these two utterly sterile species: one that convulsively guards everything and one that convulsively attacks everything. Neither attitude is constructive; their opposition is always related to some unshakable fiction; and they both engender an abrupt growth in social violence when the only raison d'être of any social reform, whether revolutionary or not, is to decrease the fear, violence, and hatred built up in society. The reactionary and the revolutionary constantly indulge in laying bare sinister conspiracies when actually the vast majority of social problems stem not in creepy plots but in stiffened interest relations and when these would need dissolving rather than alarm bells ringing. In power, both the reactionary and the revolutionary continue to scent out conspiracies, sometimes going as far as to trump up plots only to bear down on the alleged perpetrators amid great clamor.

THE SOCIAL ROLE OF VIOLENCE

At this point, we need to discuss the social role and possible use of violence in general, revolution being only a sub-issue of this. We have already pointed out that the violence among men has nothing to do with any natural law because mutual destruction and aggression is not nearly as general and voluminous in the world of animals as the special examples of predators would seem to suggest, and a mutual interest in life is far more significant than mutual antagonism. Moreover, the manifestations of aggression among animals usually brought up as examples occur almost exclusively among species or in borderline cases. The notion that life-and-death struggle is a kind of primeval natural law is wholly mistaken and only covers up the fact that the violence and mortal struggle among men are driven by and are the manifestations of the fear complex that is a distorting side effect of man's advance to a higher level, his achieving consciousness and becoming aware of his death. This recognition makes it clear that virtually all religions and state organizations attempt to dissolve the throes of fear, hatred, and aggression that the consciousness of death infuses in man by organizing his inner being and his external relations respectively. European history is thus part of, call it, the Christian experiment at this. The Christian answer to violence, fear, and hatred is to focus on active love, the force capable of dissolving all human fits and quell and wipe out all aggression in the parables and exemplary gestures of Christ. We must emphasize again that the Christian prescriptions concerning violence—for example, "If someone throws a stone at you, throw bread back at him"[4] or "All they that take the sword shall perish by the sword" (Mt 26:52), etc.—preach no helplessness and encourage no passive conduct. Passivity is contrary to the personality of Christ as we know him; by all accounts, he was exceedingly active. No, the emphasis is on the fact that all aggression stems from some convulsive state and that to counter any gesture of violence there is always a gesture of love that is more powerful and is capable of disarming all gestures of aggression. The saying "If someone throws a stone at you, throw bread back at him" means not that we inanely tolerate aggression against us or that we oafishly seek the graces of our enemies but that we find the gesture that will awaken shame in the stone thrower and make him realize the futility of his conduct.

All the dismissals of this Christian prescription that say we are thus meant to bear the executioner's and henchmen's attacks and threats against our loved ones and not take our swords to protect them are grossly mistaken. It only means that insofar as I am capable of upholding active love, compassion, and sympathy to the very last, there is always a gesture against the vilest henchman—whether it pertains to his child, his mother, or any other mental background depends on the situation—that can hold back his hand lifted to strike and awaken him to the vainness of his act. It should be added that the more terrifying and abstract the perpetrator of violence—for example, a war or an apparatus—is, the less hope there is that such a gesture may stand a chance. The point, however, is that there is a disarming gesture for every aggression, and this is what we ought to seek. If we cannot find it, all we can do is protect those entrusted to us with all our might and, as a worse option, with violence, but force is always the worse option. Any use of just force must be undertaken in a mental state of not self-jubilation but deep shame, and afterward it should always be remembered that we did hold out, but we were unable to find the real act, the disarming gesture of love, and thus we failed. It is only with such shame that the necessary gestures of violence can be accepted—by no means glorifying or celebrating it or propagating its necessity.

It is in this light that we should answer the seemingly quite different, but fundamentally related, questions concerning war, revolution, and the parental slap. All three are perfectly analogous and show that such acts can overcome a convulsive, foolish situation of power or violence and have a genuinely liberating effect. In given circumstances, all three can be useful and justified but only, as noted, as necessary evils, as solutions instead of which no better ones could be found.

Is it thus permitted to beat a child? It is better not to beat him and find gestures that alleviate his fits and lead him toward disciplined human life. Should he be uncontrollable or unable to contain himself and should he turn against social conduct, it is no doubt better to give him a clout on the back of his head in time than not do anything. It is also better to rise up against an insufferable tyranny than not do anything about it. This does provide a relative justification of war, revolution, and parental slaps; however, it must be stressed that these are not absolute goods; they are never final and necessary; though helpful or useful, they are far from the best possible actions in a given situation. Here again, we have the examples of Christ: Christ beat the traders out of the temple with a whip, but, I am inclined to think in line with the above, he must have been ashamed of himself and pondered how he should have made them sneak out of the temple in shame.

THE REACTIONARY AND THE REVOLUTIONARY

Let us now return to my main train of thought, the assessment of the French Revolution and its consequences. As mentioned, the unmatched success and failure of the French Revolution, its degeneration into a reign of terror, gave rise to two kinds of man. One, the revolutionary, the ardent believer in revolution, tried to justify the most unproductive period of the French Revolution, the Terror, by a whole array of external security and internal political reasons, in spite of the fact that it was but a mass hysteria that did not defend the revolution against precisely those it was meant to defend it against; it discredited the revolution throughout the world and killed off its outstanding corps so that only cynics and those capable of anything survived. The revolutionary is the type of man who studies and devises the methods of making and perpetuating revolution; he dedicates his whole life to preparing for it in spite of the fact that the best revolutionaries have always been those who set out on this road in response to the exigencies of the moment.

The other, equally unproductive type is the reactionary, who, starting out from the shock of the French Terror, convulsively opposes any revolutionary step; he therefore attacks all manifestations of revolutionary conduct, even reform and critical outlook, and ingrains a defensive conduct in the various power institutions, thus discrediting their very values as well. The danger of this reactionary conduct is particularly significant in the bourgeois world, call it the capitalist world, which upholds the achievements or some of the achievements of the bourgeois revolution and where a convulsive fear of revolution discredits the great historical values of civil democracy.

THE RISE OF SOCIALISM

This atmosphere of the cultic reverence and the sacred horror of the French Revolution in the hundred years of its aftermath particularly encumbered the next step in European social development, the conception of socialism. Essentially, socialism is but the logical conclusion of the bourgeois revolution. The bourgeois revolution can be said to be the ascendance of the creative and dexterous type of man over the ostentatious, aggressive, and aristocratic type. In its own time, the feudal, aristocratic order of Europe had been a manifestation of the great violence-taming social organization of Christianity, albeit a far-reaching compromise with the belligerent, pugnacious, and barbarous aristocracy that established and ran European states. Insofar as the peace-organizing duty made advances, the lack of function of this barbarous aristocracy was brought out into the open, and though by the eighteenth century the aristocracy did achieve a high degree of refinement—its members became unmatched patrons of the arts enabling great periods of cultural thriving-its privileges were hardly in proportion to their social performance. The beneficiaries of a social system cannot be justified solely on grounds of their patronage of the arts; what counts is their performance in social organization. By the end of the eighteenth century, it became obviously clear that the achievements of the aristocracy did not in the least square with their rights; it had transferred the duties of social organization into the hands of a bureaucratic intelligentsia to such an extent that it necessarily provoked the rise of this intelligentsia and the production-organizing bourgeoisie against it.

THE SOCIALIST REVOLUTION

In this sense, the bourgeois revolution is a logical conclusion of feudalism, the system of medieval feudal liberties. This continuity was most apparent in England, the Netherlands, and some of the northern countries, but in spite of its many interruptions it can be observed in France as well. However, there is a closer link between the bourgeois and the socialist revolutions as far as their tasks are concerned than there is between themselves and the violence-reducing social organization of Christian feudalism. What socialism essentially says is that as the social function of birthright had outlived its time and was therefore to be abolished, as it was in the bourgeois revolution, so the function of property by birth was becoming outlived, and the full victory of the creative and dexterous mode of life required that not only lord-lieutenancies and thrones but also factories be barred from what could be inherited and only actual creative performance be rewarded.

This being its essential meaning, socialism is thus the second stage of a single process. However, at the time when socialism was first conceived, the French Revolution, unable to fulfill its role, ran into the crisis of its interpretation, and restoration began to ravage. Revolutionaries and reactionaries stood pitted against one another, and thus the formulation of the program of socialism focused on revolution; instead of an outline of desired social conditions, the ineluctable necessity and all-renovating grandeur of revolution was advocated, claims that, it goes without saying, are falsities. Revolution cannot be desired, though it might need to be undertaken in given circumstances, but to concoct an ideology that certain changes are possible only by way of revolution is utterly mistaken; without the romantic cult of revolution, no man in his right mind would ever have hatched it. In connection to socialism, the often-repeated catchphrase that no ruling class has ever forgone its power is sheer bombast, like its sister sentence—history is but a series of class struggles—and it is just as worthless as its contrary. Sooner or later, all ruling classes lose their self-confidence and cannot help giving up their positions. History has scores of examples of ruling classes relinquishing their power because they lost faith in themselves or simply wanted to extricate themselves from the difficulties of ruling, from the late Roman aristocracy to the aristocracy of the British Empire. This voluntary surrender leads to compromises, the partial and temporary retention of positions, and the prolongation of transition; the great, exhilarating revolutionary experience of the dramatic fall of the powers that be is thus missing, and its postulation at all costs is neither necessary nor productive.

Nevertheless, the necessity of socialism was thus formulated as the necessity of a newer revolution following the bourgeois revolution—oddly soon, especially in comparison with the long periods between revolutionary changes in the relevant Marxist scheme. If slavery and feudalism were systems spanning many centuries and if capitalism is equal to them as a possible social order, what makes it obsolete and obliged to give way to socialism in a matter of but a few decades? The reason is that capitalism was by no means carefully thought through, and it is not nearly as full a social system as Christian medieval feudalism was; it is merely a transition on the way from the aristocratic bondage of feudalism to complete liberation, a condition where the oppressive domination of rank by birth has been shaken off but that of property by birth has not yet;

however, these constitute not two revolutions but are parts of one only. Consequently, if looked at more thoroughly, it turns out that a socialist revolution is next to impossible in the countries where bourgeois revolutions were carried through because the first revolution released minds from the oppressive psychological weight of domination by birth and there was a chance of bringing about the second transformation in a prolonged yet peaceful manner. In contrast, however, in the countries where there has been a socialist revolution, what we see on careful examination is that the two revolutions nearly coincide, only a few months separating them in Russia. So in this case, we have not two revolutions but only one with two stages. In the first stage, the rather weak and inefficient bourgeoisie steps into the power vacuum but cannot really manage, so in the second stage, the trained and prepared revolutionaries of the socialist revolution set up a permanent dictatorship. In actual fact, in neither case did the necessary revolution take place in full, only in part, but that with added burdens.

SOCIALISM AND FASCISM

The nineteenth-century followers of French democratic revolution, from Garibaldi to Petőfi, though going out of their way to justify the Terror, made no haste to emulate it and merely believed in freedom, its institutions, and humankind; however, the nineteenth-century proponents of socialist revolution took it as a matter of principle that not only was revolution necessary and all-healingly great, but that the perpetuation of revolutionary terror was also necessary to achieve aims that pointed beyond the productive reforms momentary violence could attain, reforms derived from their ideological attitudes, not genuine social needs. The cult of violence of revolution for its own sake came to a head at the end of the nineteenth and the beginning of the twentieth centuries. By this time, all the forces that democratic revolution had unsettled or destabilized and that were intent on defending themselves and striking back rallied together. The bourgeois revolution shattered the positions of primarily the aristocracy, which did not disappear completely but was significantly weakened; then the petite bourgeoisie, the majority of which was pushed to the background by big business; then the salaried bureaucracy, which felt shortchanged by the bourgeois economy; and then the many layers of the peasantry too, uncertain as they were in adapting to or protecting themselves against capitalistic forms.

In contrast to the proletariat, which undertook total opposition in its depravity, these intermediary groups chose not revolution but an ideology of turning toward the past, of making a cult of the past, which, however, took over the cult of unlimited violence from revolution, and it was essentially these social factors that brought about what we now call fascism. We cannot now digress on the particular national quandaries that contributed to fascism, but the point here is that fascism was one of the most terrifying offshoots of the failure of the French Revolution; almost an equally fierce offshoot was what we may term Stalinism, which, like the French Jacobins, applied terror against not only the ardent opponents of the revolution and representatives of the *ancien régime*, but also recalcitrant or rival groups within its corps. These offshoots thus unleashed an unending fury of violence on their own societies, dangerously compromising the very cause of the revolution and putting politics in the hands of clever administrators, ruthless schemers, and cynical survivors of terror, as their French predecessors had been.

Though World War II wiped out the most extreme forms of fascism, the world continues to be trapped in the gruesome, artificial, and forced opposition that the interpretation of the French Revolution and, now we can add, the Russian Revolution have engendered, that of the two types of man, the revolutionary and the reactionary, as well as their deformations, the Stalinist and the fascist or (to use a more timely name) the McCarthyist. These types, in a manner of speaking, live off one another; they have an intense need of each other; they justify all their foul deeds with the other, would be in grave trouble without the other, and, from time to time, plot and themselves make up the other to rationalize their conduct.

SOCIAL DEVELOPMENT TODAY

Where does the front of necessary social development stretch in modern-day Europe? First of all, we have capitalism as it is, where power is in the hands of the grande bourgeoisie, which, like the aristocracy formerly, no longer provides social performance alone but together with an intelligentsia that has intertwined with it though is quite different from it, and we also have a very large class of people who have tremendous financial opportunities and little matching sense of personal responsibility. Lacking social function, they could be done away with just as much as the aristocracy had been formerly. What is it that obstructs this kind of radical turn?

There are many obstructions. The most important one is that this would take place in a society that is beyond the great bourgeois revolution and has its established institutions of freedom. It is thus in the possession of all the means of initiating gradual change—though, in comparison with the task, far too slow change—and it therefore cannot produce a stratum and force that would carry through such a revolution. Furthermore, as Herbert Marcuse has pointed out, in the shadow of this shrewd capitalism, even organized labor has come to have a share of power, albeit a second-class share, and has ceased to be an absolutely revolutionary layer. There is thus no realistic prospect for a genuine revolution. So starting out from the dogma that revolution there must necessarily be, Marcuse is forced to enlist as agents of revolution marginal elements outside the fundamental, productive apparatus of society—university youths, racially oppressed groups, the various layers driven to the peripheries of society—but he fails to explain how these groups would be able to carry out a revolution entailing the takeover of power. He is unable to draw the quite self-evident conclusion that the positive and productive social criticism these groups level can lead to the desired changes because the ruling grande bourgeoisie has at any rate been lacking in self-confidence and, out of an abject horror of a socialist revolution for the past fifty years, has been forced to, on the one hand, attempt self-justification, to apply knowledgeable welfare policies and power-sharing tactics, and, on the other, disseminate a technocratic ideology that treats it as one with the technocratic intelligentsia. However, a bourgeoisie based on inherited wealth can hardly be identified with a technocratic intelligentsia, and for all its efforts at so ranging itself, it remains a mere drag on that intelligentsia.

Forged in centuries of Christian social organization and human formation, West European capitalism is certainly a far more moralized institution than one to be insensitive to criticism shaking its confidence as soon as its critics cease from aimlessly frightening it with a revolution they can never make good. Socialists, especially Marxists, shoot themselves in the foot by not only insisting on revolution but also focusing on economic factors, providing an opportunity to measure the value of a social system by economic well-being. In this race, capitalism, to say the least, has proved to be competitive, sometimes far more competitive, while it is nowhere written that the goodness of a society is determined by the quantity of goods it produces and the rapid growth of welfare it spurs. Growth in welfare can be the source of as much trouble as benefit. What is decisive is the internal balance a society generates, its relative increasing non-violence, and the justice it dispenses to the satisfaction of society as a whole. This is the measure of a good social order, not the level of growth in productivity. The crisis of capitalism lies in the fact that in spite of the vast growth of productivity and the extension of its benefits to the working class, it engenders discontent due to the social injustice it creates by, on the one hand, providing extraordinary advantages to a large number of people who, however, perform no matching social function, and, on the other, keeping large numbers of people in conditions of depravity. Neither the revolutionary manifestations of the young intelligentsia nor the desperate actions of marginalized groups can overthrow this established social order, but if these were coupled with constructive social criticism, they would be able to shake the confidence of the layers in possession, who are headless, disintegrating, and have no real hub of power. I purposely do not use the term "ruling classes" because the essence of democratic revolution is the wide-ranging distribution of power, and a social criticism always scenting ruling classes and assuming that they have an esprit de corps and an ability to take concerted action they are far from actually having is but the anachronistic projection of the monarchic ruler onto modern conditions. There is no ruling center or layer that could be regarded as disposing of society—hence the use of such grotesque terms as ruling circles. What is meant by these "circles"? Is it salons, clubs, or the boards of stock companies that rule? It is a very complex system of balances that results in the totality of the wielding of power in a country where the civil democratic institutions of freedom are in place, and this can be engaged at several points, its internal confidence shaken and disrupted, and an alliance can be struck with elements of it.

THE HOPELESS PHRASEOLOGY OF REVOLUTION

What this requires is to radically give up the hopeless phraseology of revolution and come to the awareness that revolution can be very useful in given contexts and quite ineffectual in others. Rephrasings, such as that revolution can be achieved peacefully, by parliamentary means, are pointless because I either turn the word "revolution" into a figure of speech or I accomplish some sort of power takeover through parliament and then take up a violence I had formerly concealed, a maneuver that would easily be seen through, triggering the old abject horror and leading to the victory of reaction, as so many times in history. If a change achieved through the exercise of freedom and parliamentary means is called a revolution, it would be an extension of its meaning for the sake of upholding revolutionary romanticism, and it would amount to not calling a spade a spade—that is, social reform or gradual transformation, both anathemas to revolution. Naturally, it would be justified to anathematize these categories if somebody were trying to resolve everything by reform, peacefully and at all costs, even though it would be quicker, more expedient, and beneficial via revolution. The other extreme, when someone is adamant on revolution even when it has no hope of success, is the same narrow-mindedness. I must add that in the countries of Latin America, for instance, where actual ruling classes, steeling themselves against conscience, wield their power brutally and fiercely, the classic conditions of classic revolution are given, revolution is justified, and its successes can even be observed. Nevertheless, it is extraordinarily important that this classic revolution maintain democratic institutions and that it never turn into the rule of a minority by force, oppressing the majority and instilling abject horror in its opponents, a process that, in the long run, plays into the hands of reaction again. Plainly said, the classical democratic forms of revolution should be retained wherever the conditions of revolution are present. No wonder that it is classical democratic revolutions—the great early, Bastille-destroying period of the French Revolution and the Hungarian uprising of 1848, with their claims to universal human values, non-class-struggle aims, and intellectual agents— that are more attractive in the eyes of youths even in our day, when, according to the ideological blueprint, they are obsolete forms of revolution and are inferior to socialist revolution; nevertheless, they are more appropriate as examples than the revolutions prepared and run in accordance with the alleged science of revolution.

POPULAR FRONT EXPERIMENTS

Socialist revolutions, starting with their precursor, the Russian October Revolution, have again and again been forced by social realities to join forces with all democratic forces, including civil democratic forces claiming full human rights and freedoms, to promote a so-called popular front policy; however, the dogmatic position that the dictatorship of the proletariat is the only true socialist program has repeatedly impelled the agents of socialist revolutions to handle popular front policy as a mere tactic and back out of it as soon as opportune. In other words, the history of socialist revolutions is essentially the launch and arrest of experiments in the popular front; and this course would right itself if it were at long last recognized that the popular front was not merely an experiment in tactics but the only possible and productive way of social reform in a Europe where there is no practical possibility of a revolution by desperate masses. An attempt to return to such an experiment was crushed in both the Hungarian Revolution of 1956 and the Czechoslovak transformation of 1968, and it was the danger of reaction and capitalist restoration that was brought up to justify such a move. In all likelihood, however, the elimination of large estates and big business had initiated changes no change of regime could ever undo, and no serious danger of reaction or attempts at restoration occurred in either of these countries. There might have been various signs of extremism, but a reactionary or restorationist setup would have stood little chance of reestablishing itself. In contrast, however, the one-party system that was established and the non-application of, even contempt for, the Western techniques of freedoms and rights not only deprive the citizens of these countries, including the Soviet Union, of these techniques, which, though dubbed bourgeois, actually promote freedom in any social system, but also hinder the worldwide dissemination of socialism.

The universal Western technique of freedoms and rights—the combination of the parliamentary and multiparty system, the freedom of the press, fair trials, independent courts, and judicial protection against public administration— though branded bourgeois, is one of the greatest, most enduring, and successful achievements of Western social organization, and together with its distant Christian roots, it is the only realistic and stable crystallization of the Christian program of non-violence. To label this as a specialty of capitalism and the bourgeoisie amounts to justifying the forbidding cult of violence that came down to us from the French Revolution in order to rationalize political and power structures whose sustenance requires a sometimes loose, sometimes intensified, but perpetual use of violence—violence beyond the amount a civil democracy requires. If the ruling elites of socialist countries had the daring to take the step that seems all too risky today—to jump headlong into Western-type freedoms and rights—they would probably be surprised to see that after an initial wavering, the achievements of socialism would not be seriously endangered but that, in contrast, an unprecedented amount of creative energy would be released, and the socialist countries would have a redoubled effect on the Western world enmeshed in moral and political crises.

THE REMEDY FOR BUREAUCRATIZATION AND RIGIDITY

All that is needed is that we do away with the one-party bureaucracy, perhaps through the partial dissolution of state bureaucracy, and that we recognize that modern society, which has thrown off the deadweight of hereditary aristocracy, has partly thrown off and wishes to throw off the deadweight of the also hereditary-like moneyed aristocracy and does not want or need to be governed by another aristocracy or ruling class, based on another kind of selection, because the reduction and elimination of violence means the reduction and elimination of power. Modern society needs but a freely moving elite based on performance and no aristocracy, no ruling class, nor any other group claiming power over it ex officio. On the other hand, the criticism Chinese Communists and the most extremist Western student movements level against Soviet-style bureaucratic revolution is that it is a *"medicina peius morbo,"* a remedy that worsens the malady, for these movements do not step out of the vicious circle of the revolutionary cult of violence, merely replacing bureaucratized violence with anarchic violence. In the end, such a violent regime would end up either in bureaucratization and rigidity or in some retrograde rebounding. A social reform that seeks not realization but perpetual reform and revolution and that has no vision of a balanced system is squaring the circle. The only remedy for bureaucratization and rigidity in an established system is the reduction of violence and the brave augmentation of freedom. It is only the institutionalized forms of freedom, which are, however, imbued by the vivid spirit of freedom, that can provide genuine, vigorous, and constantly operating means of resistance against (to use a fashionable term) the establishment, the bureaucratic and oppressive factors in social and political circumstances.

THE EUROPEAN SYSTEM OF FREEDOMS

At this point I wish to enlarge upon the European system of freedoms, which was molded jointly by English political practice and the ideological program of the French Revolution. The core of this system is made up of the following: a separation of powers; a representative parliament convened through general elections; an executive body responsible to parliament, or delegated and recallable by the people, or serving limited terms; a judiciary independent of executive power and whose scope covers the acts of the executive; a free press, the freedom of expression, and the right of assembly for the control of all these institutions; and wide-ranging local government—all of which create an interdependent chain, none of the links of which can be removed without impairing the whole. Rooted far back in history and reaching hopefully far into the future, this system cannot be limited to such transitory phenomena as capitalism, plutocracy, or bourgeois ideology. It is the most uncontested, durable, authentic, humane, and least dangerous of the achievements of Western civilization, which, though anticlerical in its final form, originates in the social organization Christianity launched in Western Europe. To be more precise, it goes back to Greco-Roman political practice, which Christianity-inspired social organization developed further. It is perhaps the only seriously successful realization of the Christian moral program preaching non-violence.

History knows no other system that has freed all political and social life from the terror of the violence of rulers and others to such a degree that it has enabled incumbents to hand over their power to those momentarily better suited without having to face violent death or the gallows and that has made it possible for the people to oust politicians they dislike in the decisive moment. It goes without saying that this system of freedoms and democracy does not mean that the people act directly through the political institutions. Power continues to be exercised by a minority, though not an irreplaceable one, and this is the great achievement. Democracy based on freedoms and rights does not stop a minority from craftily carrying through things the people never set as aims, but it is certainly apt for stopping the possessors of power to act in a way diametrically opposed to the will of the people.

THE REFORMATION

On a religious plane, the Reformation meant the rescinding of the compromise that early Christianity had made with paganism in respect to various institutions and rites, taking over and absorbing such elements of it as the veneration of the Virgin Mary and the saints, as well as the greater or lesser distortions of rituals into magic exercises, etc. It also meant opposition to deformations resulting from the fact that the papacy had become a hub of power within the Roman Catholic Church. It also rejected the more or less magic-mystic interpretation of virginity. The more Christianity and its social organization imbued society, the more these factors inherited or ostensibly inherited from paganism seemed uncalled for onuses. This resistance was more marked in North European countries, where, as a result of deep groundwork by Christian clerical and monastic social organization, people tended to take Christianity more seriously than in Mediterranean countries, which accustomed themselves to easier forms of Christianity. The schism that this brought about had quite negative effects in many ways.

First, it shriveled the wonderful structure of medieval universal Christianity; second, it did away with or deprived universal credence from the moral and ideological teaching authority of the papacy, which, having had its seeds or germs, would have been fit for far greater achievement; and third, German reformation willy-nilly reinforced princely absolutism. On the other hand, for all their ill side effects, Puritanism and Pietism in Protestant countries had a fundamentally positive role in taking morality more seriously than before, even in deadly earnest. Another positive effect was what occurred, oddly enough, only in England and the Netherlands: the development toward modern freedom was founded directly on medieval institutions of freedom. It should be noted, however, that the late-modern rationalist concept that the Reformation particularly advocated political freedom holds neither for Lutheranism nor Calvinism — only for some of the free sects. Their real influence was in developing a morally more exacting type of man who would later have greater claims on political freedom as well. The most dire consequence of the schism was that in areas that remained Catholic, the papacy became petrified in its partly worldly, partly moral, power structure, building on the means of moral coercion rather than of internal moral organization; moreover, the establishment of papal absolutism indirectly assisted in creating princely absolutism and eradicating almost all Christian-inspired constitutional institutions in Catholic countries.

As a result, the freedom movements starting out in England and Holland upheld their organic relation to the medieval institutions of liberty, while the development toward freedom in Catholic countries, France in particular, meant a radical break with the past and anti-clericalism, the adverse effects of which have already been broached.

EXPLOITATION

Exploitation is treated as an absolute phenomenon in the Marxist scheme: it appears in primitive form in the beginning and disappears in the highly developed society at the end, and it has three forms in between. But in reality it should be conceived of as far more relative and dynamic. It must first be stated that, in the same way as in the case of revolution, we can speak of a development from exploitation and an exploitative society to a non-exploitative system only when there are serious social endeavors to decrease violence and injustice, with the appropriate ideology and institutions. As I have pointed out, such an enterprise was undertaken by the Greco-Roman and the Chinese civilizations. If there is no such comprehensive social effort, there can be no development from exploitation toward non-exploitation, only a revivification of its forms; exploitation is as self-evident as the superiority of those ruling. It is usual to speak, and worth speaking, of exploitation in condemnatory terms only where there is a collective attempt at moving toward freedom and justice. In this sense, the question of whether a society is exploitative or not is determined not by property—private, slave-owning, or serf-bonding ownership—but by how far a society, given its beliefs and structures, provides for mutuality in the services rendered by men to one another.

In a society that professes the belief that men's status at birth is passed on by heredity, as did all slave and feudal societies, there is little point in discussing the exploitative nature of power by heredity. Though the danger of exploitation is of course present, it is within the terms of this belief that we have to ask whether the prevailing social order prescribes reciprocal services for the practitioners of power or not; whether masters have obligations that somehow square with the obligations of those subdued or not; so long as the masters proportionally fulfill their obligations to the subdued, that society is not exploitative within the terms of its beliefs. It becomes exploitative when the masters cease to perform their functions or the functions of the masters become useless due to social development. But the danger of functions turning useless is not limited to known systems of exploitation; any future or utopian system, where, for example, the means of production are publicly owned, can become exploitative if its leaders become its beneficiaries without fulfilling their functions. Plainly put, as long as the landlord performs his duties vis-à-vis the serf, he is the one who provides the serf protection for safe work. So long as the capitalist plays an active social organizing role, he is the one who gives work to the laborer. So long as a party bureaucracy delivers an active and positive leadership, it sustains a non-exploitative modern socialist society. However, if the landlord becomes functionless, he turns into a sluggard for whom the serf provides. Likewise the capitalist, instead of whom a much wider group of people organizes the economy due to the expansion of capitalist development, and he thus lives off labor. And losing its positive role in social organization, a single-party bureaucracy can similarly grow to be a parasitic class.

Exploitation is therefore relative and is to be judged within the context of the given organizational forms of a society. We must be particularly aware of this because the Marxist scheme has inculcated unwarranted expectations in us and deluded us into believing that public ownership will immediately do away with exploitation. Far from it! Public ownership will end exploitation if a clean-handed and morally responsible bureaucracy administers for the good of all. If it proves to be a mere beneficiary and an abusive element, then the shocking and distressing recognition comes that socialism can equally be exploitative. The manager of a factory who overworks his staff only to earn personal distinction or promotion is just as exploitative as a capitalist who pockets the surplus value. The concept of exploitation should thus not be used in the narrow sense because if the catastrophic disillusionment crops up that even socialism can be exploitative, it will open the way to the blandest cynicism. But we have no reason to be cynical and suppose that all systems are oppressive and exploitative; a society based on freedom and free from exploitation is certainly possible, but what it primarily requires is a continuous operation of the institutions of freedom, one that is more robust than ever before, because the lack of institutions of freedom is the hotbed of economic exploitation.

It is in this light that nationalization, often deemed a great socialist achievement and rightly criticized even by some Marxists, should be judged. Whether carried out by socialists or non-socialists, nationalization is no achievement if it leads to a greater concentration of power. Generally, the state is the classical hub of power concentration, capable of exploitation more dreadful than that by any private ownership, while it is doomed to wither away in an unspecified, distant future according to the Marxist scheme. It is fundamentally absurd to assume that state ownership can be a wonderful, anti-exploitative and freedom-enhancing achievement—as it was equally absurd to state that the nationalization of schools freed schools from the tyranny of the clergy when it would actually have been the autonomy of schools, the self-government of the teaching community and students, that could withstand any tyranny, whether that of the church or the state. How could such an oddity occur that nationalization, whether of the economy or another area, could appear as an achievement of liberty?

This required a unique European antecedent: a duty-minded, highly moralized, highly loyal and conscientious European administration and bureaucracy, which was again one of the significant, though often danger-laden, consequences of the gradual imbuing of European state organization with a sense of morality and obligation, which paralleled the development of the institutions of freedom. It was only the European and the Chinese civilizations that knew a relatively decent and trustworthy civil service, institutionally driven by and selected on ethical principles. Marx had no respect for this apparatus and did not realize that it was indeed its very existence that could suggest the idea that something could be put in straighter, fairer, less corrupt, and freer terms through nationalization—that is, subjection to a state bureaucracy—than formerly. In countries, mostly the third world, where no such morally reared bureaucracy exists, nationalization is horror itself and probably only breeds further corruption.

PROPERTY

I broach this issue because a conceptual confusion needs to be dispelled. Ownership is the main point of contention in the struggle between socialism and capitalism and thus hatches misconceptions. On the one hand, the advocates of property stress that it enhances a man's status as a personality and his personal freedom, as the *Rerum Novarum* encyclical also points out. The extent to which this holds and does not hold becomes clear as soon as we distinguish between genuine property, which establishes a direct relationship between a man and the object that increases his freedom—be it a spit of land he tills, a house in which he dwells, or a tool or a workshop he uses—and property that, by its sheer size, cannot be spanned by the activity of a single man. In the latter case, property is not a relationship between a man and an object but a power relationship between one and others, where the owner, by way of the object called his property, makes use of the services of the others with no or little reciprocity. It is absurd to speak of the status- and freedom-enhancing nature of property in the case of mammoth estates and enterprises that endow their owners with unlimited power over thousands. Herein lies the deception of the advocates of property. Not making this distinction leads us similarly astray because if we said that we could counterbalance the monstrosities of property only by general collective ownership, we would remain under the magic spell of property, large-scale property to be more precise, which puts people at the disposal of those in control, whether they are called mammoth owners, magnates, tycoons, or some sort of stewards.

The problem of property should therefore be solved not by nationalization or even collectivization but by its partition and humanization. This has nothing to do with its incorporation into a single bureaucracy; the point is its distribution, either in the form of effective division or a sharing in its disposal, which amounts to the economic application of workers' self-government. We have again stumbled into the institutions of freedom, the fact that mammoth property embodied in either a person or a centralized state bureaucracy is an enemy to freedom. The need that nationalization is meant to satisfy should be met not in terms of state power concentration but a common concern for the management of the property. The point is not that institutions of public concern, such as railways, roads, postal services, and schools, should not be at the disposal of private persons but that they serve the public interest and that, for this purpose, they ought to be put under the control of not the possessors of state power but public and not private interest.

More often than not, that the state represents public interest is a fiction; it can only occur where state bureaucracy is relatively decent and uncorrupt, and even so, the possessors of power at the tops of state hierarchies do not necessarily represent the public interest, or they do so only insofar as they depend on the public. It is therefore a significant development that certain fortunate countries enjoying a state of freedom from strife, such as Sweden, have endowed their public agencies with increasing professional autonomy capable of protecting their disciplinary interests against both private interest running riot and state interference justified merely by political externalities or considerations of power.

CLASS

A similarly absolute concept is that of class. When Marxism sets the aim of overthrowing class power, it actually follows the great pattern of the French Revolution, that of toppling absolute monarchy and the court aristocracy surrounding it. It does not recognize that the leading capitalist class is a multi-headed stratum, disunited by its divergent interests and conflicts, but in order to dramatize the deposition, it represents it as a single, aggregate ruling will. In its actual operation, however, capitalism is divided into various, contrasting streaks, interested or not interested in the military industry, interested in or rejecting state intervention, and interested in quality labor or mass labor reduced to poverty. The solidarity of which it is sometimes capable is largely in response to the challenge of socialism; capitalists hold together and organize themselves against the threats and dread of socialism. The moment the transition to socialism takes on a human shape and becomes less laden with dramatic overturnings and ejections, nothing is more straightforward than making use of various elements of capitalism, divergent as it is in its interests, clearly distinguishing between a capitalism of (for example) military and heavy industry, which would necessarily be the target of social reform, public control, and appropriation, and a capitalism that could be given a wide scope in order that its resourcefulness and organizing abilities be put to use; the moment a tactful state has recourse to these divergent interests, the purportedly keen and ever-prevailing class solidarity of capitalism falls apart.

The only reason for postulating this solidarity is to magnify the future fall of capitalism, to satisfy an emotional need, the emotional need created by the great example of the French Revolution, the changes in power through fire and flames and burning palaces. Useful as this might be in suggesting the possibility of redress to people, it has actually only delayed and not assisted the social reforms or revolutions that were necessary. For all its scientific guise, Marxism outlines a quite unrealistic picture of the ruling class. It depicts it, on the one hand, as unbelievably foolish in order to assure us that it is going to thoughtlessly go along to its inevitable doom and, on the other, as extraordinarily shrewd and cunning in order to blame it for any future blunders than can be attributed to it in most far-fetched ways. Having no scientific grounds, this depiction of both foolish and sharp only satisfies an emotional need—that I be assured my opponent is doomed to failure and that I can hate him or it unreservedly and justifiably. So there was a heavy penalty to be paid for this unrealistic over-and underestimation: this very description prompted capitalism to be exceedingly shrewd in defending itself and putting organized labor on its side as a second-class stakeholder and to be smart enough not to run blindly toward its doom as it should have done according to official doctrine.

It was this emotional need that was satisfied by various sententious theses that no ruling class had ever given up its position of its own accord, theses that any number of examples could equally prove or disprove, or by Lenin's dictum that it would be beneficial to strike a deal with capitalists and pay them

off, although fortunately he stated this would not be a possibility; even drawing the despicable picture of a peaceful transition was to be ruled out because
capitalists were as they were. The truth is that no winding-up agreement can be
reached with capitalists because they have no single head. Nevertheless, there
are many possibilities of partially and gradually eliminating capitalists—exactly
in proportion to the vigorous functioning of the institutions of liberty—and
thus serious mass demands can be met. The Marxist-Leninist form of socialism, however, played into the hands of the capitalists by turning the majority of
society, due to its claims to small-scale ownership and freedom, into an interest-
sharing partner of capitalist freedom rather than its exact opposite, the turning of small-scale owners into interest-sharing partners of labor and the poor
peasantry. This need has sometimes raised the banner of the popular front, but
as soon as opportune, the banner was thrown away and the allies were pushed
aside—and they could be happy if they got off with a mere pushing aside; and
then came the exclusive power claim of the ideologically closed group, a step
that necessarily entailed the perpetuation of violence, which in turn obstructed
the functioning of the institutions of liberty and questioned the cooperation of
the majority of the people.

A HOPEFUL VISION OF THE FUTURE

Let us now turn back to our main argument that a political program of socialist reform can be advanced through the perpetuation of neither bureaucratic
power nor energetic revolutionary action. The question to be discussed is not
whether it is a bureaucratically institutionalized socialist power, a socialist establishment, that is to be created or a society artificially held in a state of permanent revolution; indeed, no word or argument should be wasted on what the
correct path to change is, what the technique of takeover is, how a revolutionary
party is to be organized, how its remaining in power is to be ensured, and how
the revolutionary party is to be perpetuated. These are pointless debates because
there is no—not only scientific, but even obvious—answer to them at all. Due
to the intuitive and artistic element in politics, the appropriate answers are to
be found from case to case, depending on the given circumstances. The most
morbid aspect of the current debates over socialism is that endless and sterile
arguments on socialist tactics have entirely suppressed the shaping of an encouraging vision of post-reform society. Once, socialism regarded its most important duty as the drawing of a colorful picture, a picture that might have been
naive and utopian, but it was based on genuine social criticism and promised
the elimination of real injustices. When implemented, this picture proved to be

naive and utopian; we now know many things cannot be done in the way they were: the family cannot be done away with, as nineteenth-century socialists had imagined; the nation cannot simply be abolished, as many had believed; but this does not necessarily mean that no realistic and hopeful vision of the future can be presented to the people. Disillusionment can be felt in the countries where socialism has been implemented or came to rule, and the loss of bearings in the socialist revolution in capitalist countries can be partly attributed to the lack of certitude in the vision of a future society. No one is concerned about this; instead, people engage in sterile disputes about the path leading to it, essentially seeking the best technique of violence, while it should finally be understood that there is no better technique of violence. It is only the best method of decreasing violence that is worth discussing.

If we want to gather the elements of a proper and agreeable vision of a future society, we need to consider the following. Any hopeful vision of the future must be based on a vigorous functioning of the classical institutions of liberty—in other words, popular representation; national and popular self-government; an executive power under some form of control; the independence of the courts; judicial control over administration; the freedom of expression, the press, thought, and assembly; and, last but not least, the separation of powers. The classical, French, pre-revolutionary formulation of the separation of powers primarily meant a contrast between the executive and legislative branches—that is, king and the people—with judicial independence as the third element. This will not do today, although it should not be brushed aside but supplemented. As with the independence of the judiciary, the independence of the functions of teaching, scholarship, and mass culture should also be developed; granted a more robust self-government, the courts and educational and scholarly institutions alone will provide an objective and professional management of science, central as it is to modern social development. Conditioned for military and foreign policy, state power is utterly incapable of such even today. Economic activity will likewise have to have a separate self-government, from the top national-level industrial, agricultural, and other production and service apparatuses down to those in which workers and employees are directly involved. It is equally absurd that labor has but an employee status vis-à-vis the centralized bureaucracy of socialism and that in capitalism it has no responsibility in overall production as it is debarred from management, though it does enjoy limited rights in sharing central power. Quite to the contrary, in the vision of a future society, the self-government of people directly involved in work must vividly function in a pyramid-like structure in order that the worker can again assume responsibility for his labor, that irresponsible strikes and the irresponsible repression of strikes will be out of the question, or that they will be regulated procedures.

No doubt the alienation of work from its objective is in many ways related to technology and thus can hardly be prevented. It is precisely because we are beyond the point where the worker shapes and enjoys the end product of work, because he no longer finds satisfaction in it, that it should be counterbalanced by self-government. We should also be aware that the Marxist and Leninist notion that socialism will need an unspeakably simple administration, consisting of but registries and lists any cook can fathom, is a lost cause. To the contrary, future society will obviously require a vastly complicated, computerized administration, and the liberation of the average man from under the power and the tendency toward anarchy, which is not quite alien from Marxism either, will not be realized by a return to some sort of primitivism, a reduction of human life to simple forms anyone can grasp—an outcome that can surely be excluded. The way power is going to become an-archic, free from dominance, dissolved, is that everyone will want and effect that all functions heretofore known as power wielding are turned into services in both their organizational and moral content and that all society is remolded into a system of mutual services where everyone assumes the roles of both the person serving behind the counter and the client being served and, at the top of the organization, no relation between the possessor of power or ruler and the person petitioning in front of him comes about. This is a possible social organization—an-archic, free from dominance—that does not reduce society to primitivism but takes the growing integration and complexity of society into account. This primarily requires change in the moral content of exercising power but in such a way that every act of moral deliberation has its defense and support in appropriate organizational forms, as no state organization is capable of being moralized by the mere proclamation of moral maxims.

A society so organized will evidently have to do away with all unaccountable mammoth property concentrated in the hands of a few persons; indeed, it will have to do away with all conditions of power and privilege devoid of function— the ownership of factories, banks, and industrial plants can be allowed to pass into the hands of neither infants nor adults, in the same way as the inheritance of kingdoms and aristocratic conditions was questioned. In this respect, we may calmly go along with the original appropriating aims of socialism. It must, however, be borne in mind that the significance of the functions of the intelligentsia has greatly increased in modern societies; to a certain extent, all society is undergoing the process of intellectualization, and thus especially creative intellectuals should have great freedom of disposal; a genuine inventor should have almost the same right of disposal that a capitalist owner of a factory has today, though it should also be integrated into the self-governing management—that is, his successor should not be his children but his colleagues, including all the workers.

The appropriation of capitalist property should be carried out in accordance with the given political situation either as a dramatic act of revolution or as the implementation of a deliberate and systematic long-term plan; in the latter case, the capitalists should be clearly informed of both the final result and the forms and possibilities of the transition, including the appropriate augmentation of worker self-government. The phenomena of mammoth property, unrestricted large-scale disposal, should certainly be limited primarily by the institutions of liberty, the means of self-government applied at a variety of levels. In this respect, capitalism and communism share the fault of the cult of mammoth property, private or public.

In respect to the intellectualization of society, it should be noted that it is all too easy to conceive of and arrange that the transformation in which the ostentatious feudal lord is replaced by the merchant and industrial bourgeois, who in turn are supplanted by the creative and organizing intellectual, involves the latter becoming a ruling stratum. It is particularly tempting for the organizing intelligentsia, having often played second fiddle to the feudal lord and the moneyed bourgeois and now having left them behind, to regard its role as rule. In contrast to the intelligentsia formulating political and moral ideologies, the organizing intelligentsia often appears to regard the inept interference of the masses, referenda, parliamentarism, democratic forms, autonomy, and workers' self-government as mere interference in its highly professional activity. Again, this is a danger that is a threat in both capitalism and communism, the economic technocrats of capitalism and the functionaries of the single party in communism—that is, the professionals of political organization—being the carriers of this danger. It must therefore be stressed that high-level professionalism and widespread democratism are equally important requirements for modern social organization. Neither should be forgone, and no intellectual administration should be established without matching widespread self-government under either social system.

Finally, the misery of marginalized groups—racial minorities, the lonely, and people in areas on the peripheries of production—should be given heightened attention. It is the responsibility of society as a whole that these people also enjoy their share of the social goods, an aim that might be particularly difficult to achieve due to cultural differences. It is again the common sin of capitalism and communism that these people are abandoned, the layers immediately

involved in the productive process being favored and the dangers and significance of marginalized groups being played down at least within each of their
worlds. Care for them or enabling their particular ways of life must be included
among the responsibilities of the social whole.

DIGRESSION ON THE REVOLT AGAINST DECLASSING

We have noted one of the decisive factors behind fascism — the fact that classes
not wholly dispossessed revolted against being declassed. This was how fascism
drove together a decadent aristocracy, the part of the bourgeoisie existentially
threatened by liberty movements, a declassé petite bourgeoisie, and elements
of the bureaucracy and peasantry; and this was why it left out labor, which had
been excluded from early capitalist and bourgeois transformation and thus had
no original condition to which to be reinstated, so its program was to establish
something new. This was the root cause of the hatred fascism displayed toward
socialism. Aristocratic groups hated socialism because it would carry their degradation at the hands of the bourgeoisie even further, to complete equality; the
hatred of the petit bourgeois was fueled by the fact that socialism reduced them
to the level of the proletariat, trying to prove to them that they were likewise
proletarians and oppressed, while, being only half-declassed, they would not
admit this.

The other necessary factor behind fascism was anti-Semitism, which appeared in all regions where fascist social tendencies encountered larger groups
of Jews. Their hatred was directed against Jews who were winners rather than
losers of the bourgeois transformation and who had often climbed high up the
social ladder — unforgivable for those forced down. This was what gave rise to
the notion, which all sane observers regarded absurd but which seemed logical
and enlightening to fascists, that evil Jews were the begetters of both capitalist
ploys, which had deprived them of their status, and socialism, which sought to
continue their dispossession to total elimination.

DIGRESSION ON BEING BOTH A LIBERAL AND A SOCIALIST

We have noted how gravely difficult Marxism has rendered the clear and unbroken formulation of the idea of freedom by rejecting, together with capitalism,
the bourgeois concept of liberty, depicting the bourgeois libertarian tradition as
a mere function of capitalism, or if it did not wholly repudiate it, it downgraded
it to the extent that it created a breach between the phraseology of socialism and
liberalism in the ensuing century and a half. This led to a grotesque situation.

Both liberalism and socialism aim at realizing a libertarian program in a given social situation: the former seeks to undo birthright privileges, while the latter, the privileges of property, which in turn also become birthright privileges. By making two phases of social development out of capitalism and socialism (the folly of which can be observed in that the capitalist phase can shrink to a few months, socialism directly defeating socialism), Marxism pitted liberalism and socialism against each other, a step that so burdened them with features having little to do with their essence, the libertarian program, that no one taking the libertarian program seriously today can confess to being a socialist or a liberal without carefully worded riders. But if he formulates these riders properly, he will have to concede to being both a liberal and a socialist. He cannot call himself a liberal if by "liberalism" he means the accumulation of wealth and capital, the one-man rule of capital, the principle of the absolute exclusiveness of the capital owner over employees or if he seeks to provide the same protection to mammoth property, which is actually not property but a condition of power, and to direct personal, productive, or non-productive property necessary for personal fulfillment. Thus he must reject the liberal cult of mammoth property insofar as he wants to define himself as liberal within the libertarian program. And under the socialist program, he has to reject collectivism at all costs, dictatorship, the one-party system, and the glorification of the vanguard of society, which is but a new aristocracy; having rejected all these, he can call himself a socialist in the name of the full libertarian program against wealth, capital, and capitalist ownership, and then he can safely call himself both a liberal and a socialist.

DIGRESSION ON A NON-FORBIDDING SOCIALIST APPROPRIATION

Marxism anticipated as sharp a revolutionary change in the transition to socialism as the overthrow of feudalism had been and thus elicited forces of resistance that capitalism had never inherently had. Small wonder that Marx was born and gained his experiences in Germany, where the capitalist bourgeois transformation had gone through many holdups and was heavily burdened by feudal traits. It was in those circumstances that Marx could depict capitalism as a monster capable of an overpowering effort and undaunted will, brushing aside all democratic aspirations—a depiction that certainly did in a way invoke these fearful features from capitalism. This was how capitalism necessarily became the begetter of fascism in the Marxist outlook, although it actually begets fascism only if there is enough feudal resolve and savagery behind it. In countries where bourgeois transformation was fairly complete, where the institutions of liberty had been operational and proficient and had been experienced by society as a whole, fascism, for all its attempts, could not achieve a takeover. Even where external forces helped fascist-like regimes to power, as in France under German occupation, these were fundamentally weak and were blown away by the first wind after their external support had collapsed. Likewise, no fascism came of de Gaulle's ascendance to power, though it had been driven by several similar motives.

The point now is how to find a formulation of a socialist program in a way that will not provoke capitalism to a self-defensive hardening and the savagery of a cornered wolf. If we want to find the possibilities of this, we have to realize that capitalism and its leading strata, quite to the contrary of the relevant Marxist legend, have been one of the least compact; least united; least, so to speak, class-conscious dominant groups in all history; and little is needed to give up the solidarity among its members and settle for conditions they might find bearable, though not supportive of full-fledged capitalism. A socialist program, therefore, if it wants to avoid turning capitalism into a monstrosity and avoid its rebounding effects of fascism or reaction, will first of all have to precisely and clearly define its framework of appropriation. Appropriation will be necessary in two areas, the first one being the large, formerly feudal estates that capitalism went on to sustain. These estates were themselves rooted in illegal appropriation, one element of which consisted in the riddance of public functions attached to land ownership. These estates had once been endowed together with public duties, such as border protection and state administration; however, these became inheritable in accordance with the mindset of the time, and the inheritors threw off the public functions and kept the land as private property, a move that was a form of payment for the performance of public duties in a primitive economy. The other element of the illegal appropriation was against the peasants, who had been placed under the estates on account of taxation but without losing their property rights. Landlords turned the taxation into feudal services. Socialist transformation will have to appropriate this kind of large estate and should make it clear that this is its intention. Naturally, this does not entail revolutionary intimidation or the dramatic imagery of palaces burning, but it has to be clearly stated.

The other area where appropriation is required is the sector of capitalism, heavy industry in particular, that provides extraordinary power to influence, out of mere private interest, even the state, its military, and other policies. It is thus mines, banks, and heavy industry, on the one hand, and large estates, on the other, that need to be nationalized. Though not comparable in weight of property, the vast majority of this class is comprised of petty capitalists, almost

artisans, retail traders, and owners of light industry plants; a level-headed socialist program would be well advised to not appropriate their property at all or to
prolong it for several generations, outlining a long-term program for labor growing into ownership. The moment capitalists encounter such a program, they
will immediately recognize the opportunities of profiting by it and will fall in
with it without resisting desperately.

A separate issue arises from the fact that capitalism and large-estate ownership overlap, as do heavy and light industry; should a certain degree of capitalism be sustained, appropriation would be unjust against those capitalists who
happened to invest in land; this problem has to be and can be resolved through
a property tax, providing reparations to them at the expense not of workers or
peasants but the remaining capitalists.

This is not an easy project but one that can be implemented and would
have a future, all the more so because revolutionary socialism has apparently
run into a dead end in a number of capitalist countries. The latest concession
Marxism-Leninism has made, declaring that socialist transformation can take
place within a parliamentary framework, does not mean that it has given up its
unequivocally threatening attitude to the whole class of capitalists, and it has
thus exposed the extraordinarily promising and hopeful experiments, such as
the Chilean one, to reactionary coups d'état. Recall the theory of the prominent
writer on war, Liddel Hart; according to it, a direct, aggressive attack hardens
the resistance of the enemy, multiplies its lines, and boosts its morale to desperation. The secret of the great military victories lies in an indirect approach—
outflanking, encircling, cutting off, etc. The same military wisdom holds for socialist strategy; it is much more important to get around and divide the enemy,
to create situations where its resistance becomes senseless, than to proclaim
direct war against it, a tactic that not only multiplies its physical and material
force, but also musters its moral power and starts a counter-offensive that can
shatter the confidence of socialism worldwide.

In areas where appropriation does not take place immediately, it would be
highly important to find new legal and organizational forms to replace the fundamental institution of capitalist organization, the share company, which sub-
jugates all production to finance capital. The basic legal meaning of property
is that any yield that accrues in relation to an object and that is not taken by
somebody under some entitlement is due to the owner. If we extend this to the
share company, we realize the falsity of the institution because the position of
the owner is that of the collectivity of shareholders. They are owners who can
give notice to the manager, lay off all the workers, and sell out the plant. The
falsity lies in the fact that the buyers of shares have no intention of obtaining

property; all they want is to contribute money to make money. Their proper and natural position would therefore be that of the creditor. A form of share company should be found where the shareholder is in the position not of owner but creditor; he is naturally entitled to a profit to the degree of a fair interest rate, but it cannot be that all returns that are not taken as wages or other entitlements are due to the shareholders, resulting in exorbitant dividends that, if called interest, would be regarded usury by all.

Where a gradual transition to socialism is projected, a form of share company should be established in which the position of owner is assumed by all the collectivity of workers. It will therefore not be the shareholders who will pay the employees, from the managing director to the last laborer, and take all the profits, but it will be the collectivity of employees who pay the creditors embodied as shareholders and take the remaining yield. This is not an easy matter, as profits do not always accrue. In order to assume the position of owner vis-à-vis the industrial plant and, if necessary, undertake the risk of loss or a decreasing income, a change of mindset is required in the workers, and it will be a serious, though unavoidable, educational challenge. By simply putting all capitalist property in the hands of the state, the worker is not going to become an owner, and his conduct will not be able to be that of a proprietor; it is only through workers' self-government and property, established through several generations, that labor can develop a proprietary conduct in respect to plant, equipment, factory, and the means of production.

DIGRESSION ON CLASS WAR TO THE DEATH

The picture Marxism draws of the ruling classes—that they will not give up their positions without fighting a war to the death—and that this is why revolution will have to be a war to the death, though it claims to be scientific, is mere romanticism, and if there is any credibility to this image, it suggests not the hell-bent capitalist but the hell-bent aristocrat and projects him into a social law. Again, it is not a mere coincidence that this theory of the ruling classes was concocted in a semi-feudal Germany. But before going into this, we must be clear: the theory that no ruling class will forgo its position without fighting to the last extremity is simply not true historically. The truth is that beginning with the Roman aristocracy, which gave up its position with no ado out of simple enervation, degeneration, and the lack of a moral basis, to the astonishingly quick decay of the aristocracies of Asia and Africa in our day, the only aristocracy not to yield with ease is the one that has particularly strong moral supports.

Now, it should be known that the European aristocracy, though being the main obstacle in the way of the modern libertarian movement, was a particularly moralized social stratum that had acquired its sense of duty in the course of medieval Christian development and training by priests, and it did whatever it did with a stronger sense of vocation than any of its counterparts. Though stories can be related endlessly on its frivolity, recklessness, cruelty, and hedonism, the European aristocracy always turned out a superior elite that fulfilled significant duties of governance with a refined moral sensibility, believed it was indispensable in so acting for centuries, and was so accepted by its environment. For the last time in the eighteenth century, this aristocracy proved to be a magnificent rearguard of the cultural flowering, even though it had members such as the archbishop Colloredo-Waldsee of Salzburg, who had Mozart thrown down his staircase.

It was the moral rearguard of this aristocracy and its first bridler, monarchy, that managed to put up a Europe-wide resistance lasting a century and a half (and still not fully ceased) in order to restore the power it had unexpectedly lost during the French Revolution. In several places it was successful and thus provoked further revolutions. What did it need in order to do so? How can a declining aristocracy fight a war to the death? Only if society is full of simpler men who are loyal to the aristocracy and monarchy unto death; it is only with such a rearguard that it can wage a war to the last extreme and sometimes even achieve restoration. Without a moral rearguard embodied in the loyalty of men, the moment the aristocracy and monarchy fall from power, they cease to exist with no hope of restoration. This is why, in the third world, in Islam, where aristocracies have been overthrown, restorative tendencies do not seem to occur (I am not talking of East Asia, where we do encounter very strong aristocracies), and nowhere are they as fierce as the European monarchies and aristocracies, who waged resistance for over a century in the wake of the French Revolution, who managed to regenerate their systems, and who are still capable of stoutly fighting in the rear.

This amounts to no glorification or cult of the aristocracy because it does not change the fact that the libertarian program of modern social development, the program of equal human dignity, cannot recognize aristocracy based on birthright and privilege; at most it can acknowledge surplus opportunities based on performance, which is under constant democratic control, and this system has no room for either birthright monarchy or birthright aristocracy. However, if a movement wants to establish a fighting tactic against an enemy, it has to know its enemy, not fabricate horror stories about it, and face its resources, and its moral resources ought not to be neglected.

DIGRESSION ON THE TYRANNY OF THE INTELLIGENTSIA

Not anticipated by Marx, the danger of the tyranny of the intelligentsia requires a sustained and special exposition. We note the well-known theory that capitalist rule has now been replaced by managerial rule and that all libertarian programs are but idle talk; what counts is a change in power: instead of capitalists, managers crack the whip now. It is not without reason that the author of this concept, James Burnham, is one of the staunchest representatives of the dominance approach to society and is in this respect no way inferior to Marx or Lenin. There is a repeated illusion involved. The European feudal social program, an essentially priestly-aristocratic outlook, once had a concept of what made a good aristocrat, how he should look after the people with whom he was entrusted. Then came the actual aristocrat, and he tried as much as he could to convert this obligation into dominance and shrug off the obligation element, a factor that is the kernel of the birth of the secular estate. The next was the libertarian project of the bourgeois revolutions of Europe, declaring that birthright privileges should be replaced by a society of men equal in rank. It later turned out that the primary beneficiary of this was the moneyed bourgeoisie, the stratum most irritated by aristocratic privilege because it was closest to being equal to aristocrats, but privilege stood in its way. This was what gave birth to the distorted view Marxism and Leninism advertised, stating that it was this moneyed bourgeoisie that had its intellectual agents formulate its libertarian program; as Lenin himself said, the bourgeoisie was particularly endowed with genius to be able to turn out such an excellent ideology. Naught did it turn out, not an ideology! Benefiting from a change in power relations, the bourgeoisie merely stepped into the shoes of spirited, genuinely libertarian and egalitarian ideologues and then pooh-poohed them. It took advantage of and profited by the revolution it had not in the least moved.

The same process took place after the socialist revolution. Presenting itself as the fulfillment of the libertarian project, it provoked a takeover, and then the beneficiary of the change, the functionary aristocracy, the intelligentsia, rose to ascendancy. And thus with hindsight, the irate enemies of socialism could righteously say that the whole affair was but the skulduggery of a minority that had hatched the socialist ideology only to establish its power. This is just as much untrue as it is to say that the bourgeois libertarian ideology had been devised by its beneficiary, the bourgeoisie. The same type of men—makers of ideology, creative organizers and social reformers—forged the libertarian ideology for both the French and the socialist revolutions. And the changes incepted are always exposed to the danger that a minority group, steeped in a dominance approach, believes it is privileged to rule.

As the capitalist has lost his function in both the socialist transformation and where capitalism is retained, we note a parallel process: the ascendancy or, as the case may be, tyranny of the intelligentsia is realized by technocrats in the West and single-party bureaucrats in the East, and such ascendancy is the current danger of our social development. This is difficult to assess clearly because capitalism is still extant, tolerated by the technocratic layer involved in establishing an intellectual tyranny, as the grande bourgeoisie tolerated and mixed with an aristocracy much weakened in power and even assisted in salvaging it. It is this falsity against which the libertarians of our day, students primarily, have rebelled because, as Herbert Marcuse has pointed out, labor has come to be involved in this rule, as a kind of a second-class vehicle of it, no longer being a revolutionary layer as it had been at the time of its utter deprivation. It is little wonder that these Western student movements are senseless, confused, and impractical to the point of being wholly frivolous, while their Eastern counterparts are quite sober and realistic and have a concrete libertarian project. The reason is that in the West, the institutions of freedom are in place without major want, so the students cannot be passionate about their libertarian program; they are only forcing an open gate. They do sense the falsity of the situation—that many drones feed on society and that the rule of technocrats humiliates the individual, as does any rule, turning men into manipulated crowds—but they do not recognize the enemy. They fight the established order, the establishment, the powers that be, but there cannot be a social reform against any establishment. It is not against established institutions of social reform, legal institutions, regulations, coercive rules, even prohibitions, that struggles should be waged but against the coming into being of hubs of power. In other words, it should not be forgotten that the final aim of any social reform, whether European or extending further afield, is a society of mutual services, where there is no technocrat or technical ruler, no vanguard, no oligarchic social group claiming ascendancy, only mutual services and the services the social organizer provides; however extensive and significant these might be, they carry no greater moral weight than those provided by so-called everyday men, nor do they confer different human rank: the technocrat or the functionary cannot claim that he is a special human type, just as the aristocrats were denied this ranking. The student movements in the socialist countries have a particularly powerful claim to freedom, a human and moral depth, and a concrete program because the technical operation of the institutions of freedom is extremely rugged in these countries; they thus have realistic demands: actual institutions of freedom, a separation of powers, judicial independence, free elections, and freedom of the press. In the West, however, students fight in a vacuum, protesting against any institution.

DIGRESSION ON MASS POLITICAL HYSTERIAS

It could be that the newer and newer encroachments of power are a necessary consequence of history, against which it is futile to struggle; the change from the rule of aristocratic tribal chiefs to the dominance of the intelligentsia has to be tolerated; there is no way around it. But there must be! The task is not to change those in power but to terminate the phenomenon of ruling. Ever since the emergence of modern libertarian programs, humankind has become exceedingly sensitive to the falsification of ideas. As a result, in countries where a program of liberty, equality, and brotherhood has been seriously drawn up, has been taken up by major movements, and has also allowed for beneficiaries and encroachments of power, particularly dangerous mass political hysterias have erupted, people being drawn to the ideology of violence out of desperation. History knows no such desperate movements in areas where no significant attempt has been made toward the moralization of power—the human propensity to hysteria being manifest in religious-sectarian currents in these areas. That carrying out the social-liberty program and dashing its hopes give rise to fearful, hysterical, furious, frenzied mass movements ready to destroy everything precisely shows that from the moment the libertarian project was seriously worked out, humankind could no longer stop short of organizational forms and moral conditions that enabled the realization of the project without power encroachment. If it cannot carry this through, humankind will sooner or later go mad; it can even now destroy itself.

Indeed, the extraordinary savagery of Marxism, its cult of violence, is itself one of these hysterical developments. It came into being in response to the disillusionment caused by the usurpation of the libertarian ideals of the French Revolution, and this was what led to its adumbrating the theories of the dominance of economic factors and the dependence of morals on them, the program of a social life-and-death struggle. Implemented Marxism, however, can provoke the same kind of hysterical movements against itself because ever since the movements for moralizing power have been able to topple governments and bring about mass effects in Europe and throughout the world, the thwarting of expectations has had particularly dangerous and dire consequences. Taking principles in earnest is no longer a mere moral requirement; it is actually a matter of life insurance for the incumbents. This is not dogmatism at all; it means that the fundamental libertarian program is being taken seriously, that there has been actual institutional progress toward a society where dominance is replaced by mutual services; lacking dominance, it is, in a sense, an-archy. This is not to say that there is no administrative apparatus; it is in fact becoming very complicated and ramified; even power-enforcement organizations of some sort will continue to exist for a long time, but the point is they will not be the fundamental institutions of society. One of the several reasons why Marxism-Leninism is not a modern ideology is that it accords central significance to power-enforcement organizations, to the coercive power of the state; it multiplies the significance of the state and paints such an unlikely picture of the desirable an-archy that it makes its realization seem utterly lacking in seriousness.

DIGRESSION ON DEMOCRACY ANCIENT AND MODERN

It should be emphasized that there is a fundamental difference between ancient and modern democracy. Though Aristotle had already made the important distinction that it was not people but laws that ruled the polity, his basic categorization was that monarchy was the rule of one, aristocracy was the rule of some, and democracy was the rule of many. In ancient times, democracy was certainly the rule of the many, but it was also a very fragile and dangerous form. True, it gave rise to some glorious periods, but it was brittle; exposed to demagogues; and hatched a type of person that lived off politics, the parasite of public life; thus it was taken as self-evident from ancient to modern times, even up to the French Revolution, that monarchy with aristocracy was a better form and that democracy would fail if not intertwined with elements of aristocracy or monarchy. This had been the Aristotelian and Ciceronian ideal of state that the Roman Empire sought to establish under Augustus, mixing elements of democracy, aristocracy, and monarchy. This truth has been upheld to our own day in every form of state: the monarchic element is the rule of one man; aristocratic, the rule of a group; and democratic, the control of the whole community. The novelty of modern democracy is not the direct rule of the many but that it seeks to do away with the concept of dominance, to terminate the phenomenon of ruling as such. The moral requirement of modern democracy is equal human dignity to all; what this means is that in accordance with the libertarian program, all men have the right to express that they are not satisfied with the minority that leads and governs them and to participate in its replacement. This is quite different from ancient democracy in the sense of the rule of the many, and it was just to say at the time that democracy was a fragile and not ideal form of state; however, modern, moralized democracy, which seeks to establish not the rule of the many but to terminate dominance as such, has proved to be a better state form than any so far.

DIGRESSION ON "THE WILLIAM"

I have already pointed out that it was only England and the Netherlands that organically developed their modern structures from their medieval institutions of liberty. This lent an evenness to their development and a depth to their institutions of liberty that other countries have not been able to match, though some northern countries have developed similarly. In order to pinpoint how medieval freedoms connect to modern freedoms and where they diverge—medieval freedoms prompting modern freedoms in some places and aristocratic and anti-libertarian privileges in others—I wish to delve into the Dutch national anthem, "The William," which is extraordinarily interesting and, at first sight, exceedingly unintelligible.

What has it to say? It is the leader of the Dutch war of independence, William of Orange, speaking in the first person. He first states his titles and declares his program. The text is as follows: "William of Nassau, scion / Of an old German line, / I dedicate undying / Faith to this land of mine. / A prince of Orange, / I am undaunted, ever free, / To the king of Spain I've granted / A lifelong loyalty. / I've ever tried to live in / The fear of God's command / and therefore I've been driven / From people, home, and land, / But God, I trust, will rate me / His willing instrument / And one day reinstate me / Into my government."

The first stanza seems to be the most incomprehensible. A certain William of Nassau pronounces that he has German blood in his veins, that he possesses a French principality called Orange, and that he has been loyal to the king of Spain all his life. Then he goes on to say that he is faithful to a land the text does not even bother to mention. We, of course, know that it is neither Germany nor France, neither Orange nor Spain. What is the point of listing these titles? Each sentence has its particular significance, and the particular meanings are related to the whole of the libertarian program, the whole system of medieval liberties. "William of Nassau, scion / Of an old German line" means that as a prince of Nassau, he is a member of the German estates. As he writes in a concrete letter of his, "We in Germany are not used to the oppression the Spanish king exercises in the Netherlands." What is this German liberty? It is the fact that the central authority of the king could not subdue the princes and that they enjoyed a princely freedom unmatched in Europe. In the course of history, their feudal princely liberty later proved to be more than harmful because it had originally been particularly limited: all but seven princes had the right to elect the Holy

Roman emperor, three hundred other princes had some rights, and their subjects were deprived of virtually all rights. But for William the right to resist the German emperor, Charles V in particular, meant a program for the Dutch in holding out against him; William, who had been brought up in German liberty, organized the resistance not of the princes but of all the estates—the people, as we would say today. In other words, the hierarchy of freedoms of medieval times was a homogenous system: a regional prince could vindicate the same right for himself in the face of the king. A certain sense of liberty inspired him, and he could transpose it to the freedom fight of the estates of another country. This is the import of William of Nassau being a "scion of an old German line"; as a German prince, he was indeed a subject of the German emperor but one who enjoyed certain rights, and he wanted to make good these rights elsewhere as well, though they were not granted there.

Let us now skip "I dedicate undying / Faith to this land of mine" and discuss the third dictum: "A prince of Orange, / I am undaunted, ever free." Now, William of Nassau had inherited Orange as a child from a cousin who had fallen in battle, and Orange was interesting because it lay on the banks of the Rhône River and had evolved in the neighborhood of certain papal estates, on the border between the Holy Roman Empire and the French kingdom. As a result, the princes of Orange, on the grounds of certain treaties and documents, claimed Orange was an independent principality and sovereign as a result of a balancing game between the two powers. In other words, it was not subject to either the French king or the German emperor. This is what William of Orange meant by stating, "A prince of Orange, / I am undaunted, ever free." As a German prince, I am a subject, a free subject, of the German emperor, but as a prince of Orange, I am equal to these emperors and kings.

This is a very significant moment. A popular uprising would find no meaning in an idea of liberty reduced to a king or ruler, but this case had the very practical significance that William of Orange issued letters of marque for the fleet of the Dutch uprising, the Dutch Sea Beggars, which, in today's terms, pirated Spanish ships. In other words, the Beggars, thanks to the offices of William, Prince of Orange, were a fleet equal in rank with the Spanish one and vindicated the appropriate rights for themselves. It goes without saying this fleet was based not only on the support of William, but also on the extraordinary shipping skills and economic power of the Dutch. Nevertheless, the legal fulfillment of this shipping force was provided by the fact that William of Nassau regarded himself as a sovereign prince of Orange.

Finally, the last lines of the stanza: "To the king of Spain I've granted / A lifelong loyalty." William was a sovereign ruler in Orange and a free vassal in the Holy Roman Empire, but he also had large estates in the Low Countries, and this was how he could put himself at the head of the Dutch uprising; however, on the basis of these lands, he was neither a vassal prince nor a sovereign ruler but a subject of the Spanish king; as such, he declares he never intended to overthrow the king's rule; he has always based himself on law; he sought to make good the rights of the Dutch estates against the Spanish monarch. Now, the Dutch estates, most of whom had undergone embourgeoisement and lived in corporate cities, practically meant all the people. It is in this context that William makes his second, for us more intelligible, statement: "I've ever tried to live in / The fear of God's command." With this, he refers to the most pressing and straining libertarian issue of medieval times—religious freedom, the right not to be subject to any king in matters of conscience; however, the second part of William's statement is again a wholly medieval concept: "and therefore I've been driven / From people, home, and land, / But God, I trust, will rate me / His willing instrument / And one day reinstate me / Into my government." The king rules; he rules over the Dutch territories and the Low Countries, but he was obliged to share his power with the estates, as a consequence of which he had to install leaders of the local aristocracy as regents, William of Orange having become the leader of the Dutch uprising because of his being the regent of Holland. He had the right to govern the Low Countries and claim that the Spanish king install local nobles, not foreigners, in office.

This is the point where the medieval hierarchically articulated concept of freedom in all its variegation stands out: the very concept of freedom that had led William of Nassau as prince to extend the many freedoms of medieval German feudal princes to the estates of the Netherlands and assert them in the face of the Spanish king was to pave the way to princely absolutism in the Germany of the eighteenth and nineteenth centuries, which would sell hundreds of its subjects as soldiers in America; and the same William of Nassau, whose cousin was a despotic king in Nassau, won the freedom of the Dutch nation in the face of the Spanish king and established the most and earliest liberal state in Europe.

It is with this in mind that we should assess the kind of medieval liberty instrument that the Hungarian Golden Bull of 1222 was. We would be justified neither in magnifying its value by arguing that it established modern democratic freedoms, nor in belittling it by saying that it merely provided for the liberty of the lords. The liberty of the lords is a type of freedom, and the Middle Ages knew but this type of hierarchically articulated freedom; however, at best, it could induce the liberty of all. In this respect it is worth drawing a, for us, painful analogy between William of Orange and Ferenc II Rákóczi (1676–1735). Prince Rákóczi represented his rank in the same tripartite fashion, stressing, for us incomprehensibly, that he was a prince of the Holy Roman Empire; that, for us understandably, he was the prince of Transylvania, who had the rank of an independent ruler in the concert of European powers; and that his position against the king was absolutely lawful: he as a Hungarian landlord was entitled to resist in the name of the Hungarian estates. He was less fortunate than his Dutch counterpart, but he too demonstrated that the utterly feudal sense of liberty of a feudal lord, given an appropriate environment, moral rearguard, and mass support, could become the driving force of a libertarian movement that involved even the peasantry, as Rákóczi's movement did.

DIGRESSION ON WORKERS' SELF-GOVERNMENT

The most common method of refuting workers' self-government has been to point out that this form of organization has never stood the test. It is interesting that the very same argument is brought up against it by both the most passionate capitalist opponents of socialism and the adherents of Marxism-Leninism—in fact, any form of centralized socialism. To disprove this, let me present a historical analogy. In a 1777 letter, Maria Theresa wrote to her son, Emperor Joseph II: "I cannot resign myself to your espousal of religious freedom; in my experience, the countries that have gone the way of religious freedom, for instance, England and the Netherlands, have never been able to extricate themselves from permanent disorder." In other words, religious freedom, two centuries after its proclamation, still very much seemed to imply chaos, uncertainty, and confusion, compared to the neat, stable tranquillity of absolute monarchies with their single religion.

Maria Theresa called her son's attention to all the turmoil and calamity that befell the countries trying religious freedom and could fairly point to the peace and calm in her lands. Thus, even in the second half of the eighteenth century, two hundred years after the declaration and even the experimental working out of religious freedom, it was still the climate of opinion that religious and other freedoms, the democratic modes of organization, were a worse option, inevitably leading to chaos and imbalance. It was only the most delicate and far-sighted minds that had the courage to argue that it was not only the better option, but also the only possible one worthy of man.

It is much the same with regard to workers' self-government. It has purportedly always miscarried. But under what conditions? It certainly did miscarry in the shadow of a prevailing capitalism, as it did in the shadow of a centralized state set on grabbing all power and bent against it. However, if we study the existential and human issues of labor, we are bound to realize that workers' self-government is not only a better option, but the only possible one, the feasibility of which can be measured only if it is unconditionally supported by a well-meaning government and social environment. Not even Yugoslavia can be regarded as an example because for all its experiments in workers' self-government (upon which both external observers and internal experimenters came to the conclusion that it was not practicable or not easily practicable), it is a one-party state, *ab ovo* opposing the spirit and organizational mode of workers' self-government, and accordingly it put it under several constraints.

Recently, a new counter-argument has cropped up: as a result of modern industrial development, labor as a characteristic productive class is going to vanish or shrink in number, and it will be next to impossible to place future, massively automated factories, run by a handful of managers and operators, under workers' self-government. The thesis, however, that workers' self-government is not only necessary, but also the best possible option has much deeper foundations. To grasp this we must first realize that one of the oddest and most adverse side effects of European intellectual development has been the exclusion of labor, the doers of productive work, from the ownership of the means of that production and gradually even the meaning and joy of work itself. This was why the historian István Hajnal once felicitously remarked that the intelligentsia, by raising work to a scientific level, sapped labor of the meaning of work, the worker by and large becoming incapable of seeing the intricacies and meaning of his work and of delighting in creative exercise, especially in contrast to the former craftsman, who had carried out the entire process of work from design to finished product.

Today's intellectual division of labor has work pre-designed to the extent that the worker is reduced virtually to the rank of an automaton. Scores of literary works, including Chaplin's famous *Modern Times*, have been devoted to the depiction of the hideousness with which the worker is expected to participate, body and soul, in a wholly mechanical process of production as a mechanical part, virtually a machine, a situation that is of course both debasing and impossible. Today, with the advances in automation, we face the prospect that all mechanical work processes will be carried out by clever machinery, relieving man of this burden. The point here is that this is not merely a technical or scientific, but a fundamentally moral requirement as well. It was once declared that no man was to be the possession of another, then that no man was to be a mere means in the hands of another, and then that no man was to be the hired manpower machinery of another, so now it should be pronounced with profound moral censure that no man should be put to mechanizable work, that it is immoral to force anyone to do such labor. That is, automation, wherever it is possible and regardless of the cost, should be carried out so that no person is employed in the purely mechanical phases of work.

This may have odd consequences; it has, for instance, been recognized that administrative labor is more germane to automation than physical labor. The obvious implication is that the work of an unduly uppity bank or office clerk is in fact inferior to physical labor. The work of tens of thousands of administrators is likely to be automated in the future, while the skillful loading of a hay cart, a wagon, or a ship will continue to be entrusted to adroit men; in other words peasants, loaders, and porters often perform more original tasks than do many so-called intellectual workers. In our transition to intellectual society, an obviously distorted scale of values deems purely mechanical desk work intellectual labor and accords it with unfounded social prestige, while it denigrates physical work, especially that done in grimy conditions. A scale of values will have to contrast purely mechanical labor and original, creative intellectual work.

As far the other objection is concerned—that labor as a social class is going to disappear or at least significantly shrink—it is quite obvious that labor employed directly in production and the peasantry are going to decrease in number, while the services sector will grow. Those working in services do not perform directly productive work; nevertheless they work and continue to be laborers, and the majority of society will be justified in claiming some sort of proprietorship in or control over the management of the services organizations. In proportion to the lack of fulfillment in work, the sense that one is not in charge of his work from its beginning to its completion and that it is not his own creation, sharing in work management and ownership should be increased in proportion to this alienation, to counter it, to make up for it, whereby the worker will again become concerned in the whole process of work.

Neither does the objection hold against the grounds on which those involved in less creative work would have the right to control more creative work. The question is of the same order as the objection to democracy—that is, on what basis can the half-informed majority endowed with mediocre intellectual abilities control the few dozen distinguished men genuinely capable of running the administration of a country? However, neither democracy nor workers' self-government, both expressing the very same requirement, have anything to do with saying that the individual voter or worker is cleverer than the learned and gifted minister or the highly trained manager; each merely states that the individual has an inalienable right to have a say in his working conditions, to fulfill his duties under the leadership of men he trusts.

The expression of this trust needs to be institutionalized because if it is not, people will be at the mercy of others, a situation that includes not only exploitation, not only being at the mercy of others' physical power, but also at the mercy of others' intellectual power—a sin against the Trinity, to use a Christian moral term. It is not the meaning of democracy or workers' self-administration to have unskilled crowds make decisions requiring high-level expertise; their essence is that a man can work and live his community life under conditions set by leaders in whom he has confidence. It is an old wives' tale that the average man cannot stand the leadership of outstanding men; in fact, he very much desires to have exceptional men above him. The complaint that average men deride prominent men is usually heard from the mouths of members of the elite or, in other words, oligarchies that have lost or are not fulfilling their functions, and it is in experiencing the rebounding effects of their loss of function that they start moaning about the senseless crowds scorning them for belonging to the elite. Senseless crowds do want to be able to look up to eminent persons but have no wish to have to look up to people without justified reasons—reasons of birth, ideology, the authority of a not really creative intelligentsia or peremptory order.

Genuine labor power can be conceived of only if workers' self-government is taken seriously. The situation of workers becomes particularly preposterous, as we experience in our very environment, when labor power is established by a one-party system; parallel to this, as a requirement of the development toward intellectual society, it is possible to maintain labor power only by having workers or their sons take up key professional positions. This is right and proper in a transitory situation, when, for instance, large estates and big businesses are partially or fully appropriated or collapse and a good many talented men, who were forced into the lot of labor and peasanthood by a class system, now break out and assume leading positions. This was the case in Hungary in 1945; scores of genuinely talented organizers and leaders emerged from the working classes. Sadly, this positive tendency of finding the best men turned into the selection of the most docile ones; nevertheless, this was but a side effect of the process of the occupation of intellectual positions through the placement of worker cadres and education. The next step in the process would be significant; however, there has been no concern for those who remain workers and peasants, that they do so with an enhanced sense of dignity, confidence, and courage. In fact, the opposite evaluation has evolved. People who, in spite of all favors and advantages, have not been able to elevate themselves into leading-cadre positions or to pass the admission examinations for intellectual posts have come to be judged as second-rate men. It has come to be regarded as natural that if one is not admitted to university, he should be admitted to college; if not college, to a polytechnic; if not to a polytechnic, he is worthy of being but an unskilled hand. In other words, the average worker becomes an apt-for-nothing-special leftover type of man whose opportunities and rights of human dignity are seriously breached in a society increasingly accepting intellectual values.

Being a worker today therefore implies a much greater sense of inferiority than it did before; a worker in the period of capitalism could feel that he was an agent and carrier of the future and that his oppression, deprivation, and being forced to take up mean work were a result of injustice; if the same person were a worker under today's socialism, it would have been better if his parents had not had the care to put him through school because with the general acceptance of the intellectual scale of values, he would be regarded an unskilled laborer only because he had failed all possible examinations and had not even dared take them. Again, social judgment has to be updated in this respect as well. A scale of values is needed that will appreciate both those that seek to meet the requirements of an intellectual society—a more or less restless and snobbish society that has little room for contemplation, introspection, closeness to nature, or worthwhile human amusement—and those that have the same valuable human demands but seek to achieve them not through restless work pursuits but by undertaking relatively simple occupations and spare-time entertainments such as sports, stamp collecting, private studies or amateur research, travel, contemplation, a love of nature, hiking, etc.

Equal opportunities should also be available in training for higher intellectual professions and skilled jobs so that those choosing the latter will not be only the washouts of higher-level examinations but the genuinely interested. The current situation is hopelessly distorted because, thanks to decades of brainwashing, the only way we can imagine labor power is that working-class men or their sons occupy intellectual-type positions of power and not that their masses have full-fledged human status, one in which they certainly do not feel as their having fallen behind others. However odd, the fact is that a dictatorship of the intelligentsia develops under existing socialism the same way as in the world technocracy, and this is the case even though men with a working-class background exercise their intellectual dictatorial power, as what matters is not working-class origin but that an intellectual function wields a dictatorial or oppressive superiority over non-intellectuals.

I must also add that workers' self-government obviously does not imply that in the era of automation, large-scale national projects are to be subject to the self-administration or private property of merely those few who happen to be working them. Obviously, the right of intervention by national organizations in charge of such grand investments will have to be worked out in ways not prejudicing workers' self-government. Nevertheless, workers' self-government is fully possible in the area covered by conventional notions of property—that is, where investment needs do not extend beyond the financial and proprietary capacities of those actually working them.

DIGRESSION ON THE LEGAL CONCEPT OF PROPERTY

In connection to the above, it is quite obvious that in either a gradual or a radical transition to socialism, we should abolish the so-called fetishization of private property in a way that does not destroy the aspects of property that bear human status and freedom. As is well known, the often-quoted papal encyclicals justify private property by emphatically relating it to free human dignity; they would be right in so doing had they distinguished between property needed for the fulfillment of human status and property that expands beyond the immediate activity and fulfillment of a person, beyond his home, his workshop, the piece of land he tills himself, and provides him power above others. Obviously, no one needs a large estate or a factory for the fulfillment of his status as a person; only outstanding inventors would be justified in claiming whole factories for themselves and only for the period of invention, certainly not for the sixteenth generation. Property in the case of large estates or factories means the right to the disposal of the means of production, ultimately people. An owner like this could hardly even budge without disposing of other people; as a result, what is at stake is not property but power over others, quite a different concept that not only does not develop human status, but also impairs it. The moment the papal encyclicals make this distinction and draw the necessary conclusions, whatever they have to say on property developing a person's status will be true. Nevertheless, as no one person should be granted the unlimited property of a large estate or a factory, providing him power over others, so no major establishment should be subject to the exclusive self-government of a handful of workers running it with automated machinery. To put it simply, it is the correspondence between the means of production and the person concerned that is justly called property and deserves to be protected.

It would seem to me to be particularly useful in the formation of legal concepts to limit the concept of property to the area where its object and the human activity it concerns concur; whenever the object of property extends far beyond the capacity of the man disposing of it, it should be called right of disposal. This would make the misrepresentations that the entire ideology of unlimited property enables glaringly clear and show what a false ideology of freedom so-called Western liberalism attaches to it. Let us take an example that can be conceived of even in the midst of civil law institutions going back to ancient

Roman law: imagine a property object, a piece of land, owned by somebody. As a result of the owner's premature death, his infant child inherits it. In the child's stead, his guardian has the right of disposal and decides to lease it; then the lessee goes on to sub-lease it; again, the sub-lessee has his land farmed under a métayage system. Here we see a man actually tilling the land and a babe lying in swaddling clothes with no relation to farming. What is the meaning of saying that the baby is the owner of the land? What it means is that though the sharecropper tills the land, the sub-lessee can prevent him from so doing if and when certain conditions are repudiated, but the lessee can also get rid of the sub-lessee; the guardian can oust the lessee when the term expires; and then, in turn, the guardian is discharged of his duties when the child comes of age. Thus the land falls back to the child, the various rights of disposal being unwrapped to the remaining right of disposal, the property right of the child somewhere at the end, and if all those wedged in between are paid their due, what the child receives is the leftover.

By analogy, this holds for what we said about share companies, where the question is who the owner is. If the shareholder is regarded as the owner, he receives whatever is left over after paying all the dues of the workers, managers, and administrators of the company. But if the construction is modified so that the owner should be not the shareholder but the worker, then the latter pays all the dues of the casual workers, the creditors taking an equitable interest, as do the state investments and contributions; all the remainder, the profit, goes to him. Seen this way, the proprietorship of the shareholder is none other than that of the creditor taking a usurious interest. This is how the concept of property ought to be reassessed: not anathematizing it but maximizing all its papal and liberal praises with the condition that protection and sanctity are due only to decent property and not fictitious mock property that merely disguises a situation of power, abuse, and helplessness.

DIGRESSION TOWARD A CRITIQUE OF MARXISM

In conclusion, we need to plunge into criticizing Marxism. I wish to focus on two of its central tenets; putting them in the appropriate light might bring us closer to the core of the entire problem. The first tenet is that the teachings of Marxism are scientific or scientifically proven. The second is that society and social action are fundamentally driven by interest, economic interest in particular; all else is but a superstructure based on this foundation; not only culture, but, more important, even what we call morals and ethics are determined by economic interest.

As far as the scientific nature of Marxism is concerned, we have already pointed out that the process of human cognition, the central issue of science, is essentially unified. Whether it is natural or social science, the acquisition of political knowledge or religious experience, the process is the same. First, we gather experiences; then intuit general theses; then put them to the test of experiments; and finally, based on the resulting full or partial proof or disproof, we arrive at a more complete formulation of scientific truth, all phases of which are open to further comprehension and corrective theses. Like earlier civil democracy, Marxism is essentially a program for social reform and is part of the process of acquiring knowledge: we first gather experiences on the unsatisfactory nature of the existing old social order, instinctively formulate this experience, then try and have it accepted by the masses and perhaps also by active state apparatuses. The practice they then establish is going to partly prove and partly disprove the thesis, and history will have the final say on the proportion of the two. In this sense, the historical process Marxism launched is a process of acquiring knowledge and establishing laws, just like science; however, what Marxism calls science is not science but mere suggestion, indeed an exceedingly intuitive formulation of the general interpretation of a variety of social experiences, and it is the proving or disproving role of subsequent political practice that is going to turn that intuition into valid knowledge. It is therefore wholly mistaken to put Marxist theses on an equal footing with scientifically verified ones; Marxist theses are but maxims whose amenability to verification lies merely in dispute and reference to examples; the true verification of Marxism is its acceptance by the masses and the social practice it founded, the proving or disproving effect of the social reform to which it led.

Marxism and Leninism are thus verified not in books but in the practice of state organizations they set up, a practice that now has a history going back several generations and that calls for debate. A train of thought the prematurely deceased Hungarian sociologist Béla Reitzer put forward is quite instructive: discussing the argumentation of a Marxist educator, he pointed out the almost childishly transparent debating technique of Marxists and Leninists, by which they contrast the actual anomalies, abuses, faults, and contradictions of the world of their opponents with ideal Marxist requirements. In other words, they set their ideal, imaginary, good Marxist and Communist world against an actual bad and non-Marxist world in practice. Using such tactics, anyone can win a debate—and his opponent can likewise: counter all the anomalies, contradictions, and abuses of the fifty years of existence of Marxist-Leninist states with the abstract requirements of liberal democracy. Obviously, the comparison can be validly made only under equal conditions, either comparing facts with facts or requirements with requirements, but facts disadvantageous to our opponents cannot be set against our superior requirements.

It goes without saying that a major social reform program cannot be denounced on the basis of the major or lesser errors of its first years. This is the point where the decisive question that distinguishes social reform programs from scientific verification comes into play—the factor of time. The demonstration of the rightness or wrongness of a major social reform program needs at least two or three generations. For the sake of comparison, we may add that a short-term political reform needs ten to twenty years and an economic reform project five to ten years, while a series of scientific experiments requires a period between a couple of weeks and a year; to top this all, the experiment working out of a religious truth, a truth worth giving one's life for, the lives of millions for, a truth that makes their lives meaningful, requires several centuries. It is thus the difference in time that distinguishes religious, social-reform, and political cognition from scientific cognition, the latter being capable of limiting its scope to the critical issue, whereby a question raised can be given a lucid answer. Such clear delimitation is far less possible in political and social-reform propositions, not to mention religious ones. Hence the far more long-winded debates over the truth or untruth of a religion or social reform and the need to be extraordinarily careful to keep clear of judging things we dislike by their partial failures and of pronouncing the things we like on the basis of ideal requirements, programs, or constitutional texts. It is grossly mistaken, for example, to compare data on actual mass poverty in capitalism with the constitutional requirement of a socialist country that each of its citizens is entitled to work and vacation; facts should be measured against facts, requirements against requirements.

If, in this respect, we raise the question of why it was important for Marxism to represent its social-reform program—a mere proposal to improve society, the final verification of which could only be its implementation—as a complete, self-contained, and verified scientific result, we first have to take note of the magical authority a reference to the sciences, particularly the natural sciences, acquired, given that the sciences had made staggering advances in the eighteenth and nineteenth centuries. The longer a proposal takes to verify, the more difficult it is to convince people to undertake the tedious task of implementing it. The more difficult it is to convince them, the more accidental factors are needed to win them over to embark on an enterprise lasting several decades or centuries. This is why the founders of religion, apart from revealing the truths they have wanted men to follow—such as active love, desirelessness, the upright observance of tradition and rules, the fulfillment of obligations, or the seeking of joys—have for hundreds of centuries had to deliver, in order to bring people closer to their fundamental theses, a whole gamut of extras—in a manner of speaking, scams: wonderful healings, miracles, and prophesies—the success of which had no actual bearing on their basic message. The irritation of Jesus with foolish people craving signs was a significant mark of his greatness, though he too produced such signs in spite of his repeated emphasis on their secondary nature. This was why the fate of Mani, the hapless founder of a religion, could hardly have befallen Jesus; the Persian prophet was summoned to heal the ill son of his king, but God so willed that the poor lad die, and the wrathful king had Mani put to death. Of course, Jesus would also have been powerless in the face of a ruthless king, but he certainly would have had the opportunity and would not have failed to say how vain and childish it would be to make the credit of his truth dependent on his ability to heal the king's son. Scores of miracles—falls into trances, murky words uttered in a frenzy, epileptic fits—provided many religious founders the accessory manifestations that helped them convince people to plunge into the great moral undertaking that the acceptance of the fundamental truths of a significant religion means.

Likewise, in the case of political enterprises, which last considerably less long but are long-haul all the same, it has been the demagoguery and rhetoric of politicians, their successful forecasts, and their knowing the ins and outs of given situations that have given credit to their ability to carry out significant social-reform programs, the validity and appropriateness of which have had nothing to do with the eloquence or efficiency of the politicians' language, their luck in foretelling outcomes, or their making masterly strokes in knotty situations. These are secondary to major political reforms but are unfortunately necessary for bringing the masses around to lending their well-being, their lives, and their futures to an experiment in which a politician beckons them to partake.

From religion all the way to chemistry, the process of human cognition is thus fundamentally unified. However, there is a significant difference between knowledge that can be proved or disproved in limited experiments, which take a short while in comparison to a human life, and truths that can be proved or disproved in periods outlasting a lifespan—that is, where undertaking the experiment requires a whole array of additional performances—not to mention the fact that such an experiment cannot be conducted in a way that limits it to the essential problem; history is bound to enmesh it in scores of accidental and irrelevant factors. If we ask with this in mind why it was so important for Marxism to present its reform program as full-fledged science, we have to say that it had the same function as rhetoric in political life or miraculous healings in founding religions. In a world where miraculous healings give credit to the founder of religion, they have to be delivered, even though they are not the point; in a world where science has the greatest authority, the scientific quality of a social-reform project needs to be underscored in order to get it accepted, even though it is not science. With a tinge of sarcasm, we can say that a social-reform program calling itself science is a nineteenth- and twentieth-century means of mass propaganda equivalent to the miracles of religious founders because everyone is meant to be bewildered by it and everyone is meant to bow down before it.

The essential content of Marxism is its reform program, not its claim to science. The truth of the reform program is to be proved or disproved by ongoing but mostly future events. What is essential to this reform program is the critique it levels against the former social setup, the moral indignation at its defects, which are irremediable by the old means; and the moral indignation with which it points out all phenomena of exploitation. Camus was perfectly right in seeing Marx's greatest significance not in the general scientific nature of this or that thesis of his but in the moral pathos with which he unmasks injustice, hypocrisy, lying, and the deception and exploitation of the masses. Herein lies the great oddity of Marxism: it does not openly profess its moral pathos but seeks to divest it of its moral nature; it presents it as something secondary, stating that all moral stands hinge on relations of interest, and it is bent on demonstrating that interests are the heart of the matter. Let me anticipate that this approach is guided primarily by propaganda and rallying motives. If I were to say that I am morally indignant about this or that issue, that I want to redress it, and I call all concerned against it, I would be inviting them to a fearful venture. However, if I say that I possess a scientific means that will guarantee our victory, blight all the moral counter-arguments of the enemy by decrying all moral counter-arguments, I will predestine us to the position of progress, and the enemy will be doomed to fall. This is sheer propaganda, extremely useful in undergirding the zeal and certainty of socialist warriors indoctrinated by Marxism-Leninism, but its reduction of morality to secondary rank is extremely cumbersome, instigating, as we can well observe, a peculiar nihilism.

We observed above that in the entire history of social development only those movements can be called progressive that have reduced the fear caused by men in one another, the means of which are the humanization, rationalization, and moralization of social techniques. This development, with its Greco-Roman foundations, was uniquely spurred by medieval Christianity and then, cutting its Christian ecclesiastic bonds, unfolded in European libertarian movements with even greater sway. One of the most significant and logical outcomes of this process is what we now call socialism. This is what the next steps in making social techniques be more human, decent, and moral would mean. In its stead, rather than fulfilling all these preliminary steps, Marxism has declared all steps taken in this direction invalid and all moral effort beside the point because of its being dependent on class interest and that the steps must therefore be started all over again, restated in the interest of the proletariat, the vehicle of the future. Now, this has meant a monstrous destruction of all achieved results and has had a debilitating effect on actual social techniques. We have an over two-thousand-year-old effort behind us of putting the state at the service of the community, the collectivity, honesty and goodness, the function of decreasing violence, and now Marxism comes and tells us that the state, having been used for dishonest class purposes for hundreds of centuries, must be regarded as an institution of violence, and as its moral aims have often been abused by our enemies, we should not be gulled and most cynically take advantage of it. However, the truth is that the moralization of the function and operation of the state had already made major advances in the Christian Middle Ages and particularly in the modern era, the period of the democratic state, and that the moralized state engendered and developed a numerous and significant social stratum that is particularly close to the practice of the functions of an honest state, far closer than to any class interest. Now, instead of buttressing these agents of the functions of the honest state, we instill this ideology in them, lest they should forget that they are agents of an institution of violence and should behave themselves accordingly. This has led to the debasement of the humane and moral practice of the state even though it is or is believed to act in the name of significant social-reform objectives.

To bring up another example: the independence of the courts is the result of several centuries of European development. We have hardly rooted out prejudice from the hearts of men, nor can we ever, but with independent courts, we have made major steps in that direction. Now comes Marxism and pronounces that the courts have never been independent, and we should not even try to maintain them so but treat them as sharp weapons in the class war. There is no better way of doing in the function of administering justice than treating it as a sharp weapon because courts are by definition a means of social equalization. Small wonder that it was in the hotbed of Marxism-Leninism that horrors of jurisprudence we would have thought long dead were reborn—purportedly in the service of the most modern ideology. It is the distorted vision we already pointed out in referring to Béla Reitzer that is behind this: I refute my opponent's position on the grounds of his abuses but measure my own according to my ideals. As the capitalists could make good use of a state born of the phraseology of liberal democracy, so (I can imagine Lenin so believing) it was these capitalists that concocted the French Revolution and its whole ideology to protect their own very best interests. On this same basis, we could very well state that Marxism-Leninism and socialism were root and branch concocted by a functionary stratum to enforce its interests, a stratum that, as we now see, is a beneficiary—a not particularly useful, nay, a particularly harmful beneficiary—of this ideology.

This is not to say that this layer concocted socialism in its own interest. For that matter, interest is not a stable category on which social interpretation could be based. It is far too broad for any social explanation; things depend not on the economic or non-economic nature of interest but on a more or less superior conception of interest. The interest of the saint is redemption, the interest of the ambitious is glory, and economic interest has nothing to say in this respect. The question is how clever a man or a social group is in grasping his or its best interest. The cleverer they are, the greater the likelihood that their interest will not diverge much from the common social interest. Thus, we will never arrive at a valid social explanation if our starting point is the sharpest opposition between the most foolish grasps of interest.

Hence the loss of the normal human faculty of tracing things to their own causes in a man with an average Marxist education; it was drummed into his head always to look for some economic cause, so if the cause is most patently different, he will come up with some interest in oil or something else with which he can explain all things under the sun. Indeed, he explains naught; he merely applies the same scheme to everything, sparing himself the effort of further thought. What lies behind the reasoning of Marxism, which represents itself as science and as the unmasking of cynical class interests, is a profoundly passionate conduct.

Moltke was reported to have said to a young soldier that if he wanted to read good books on military strategy, he should read the ancient authors because they never lost their faculty of tracing things back to their own reasons. Contemporary European public thought seems to be in great want of this faculty. It is not only Marxism that is to be blamed; with its ideological explanations of the world, Christianity has probably done much harm to the human capacity of attributing simple things to their own causes and not squeezing them at all costs into some special scheme, whether redemption or divine providence, whether class interest or a class society.

NOTES

INTRODUCTION

1. Cf. Mommsen 1978; Nipperdey 1983; Gall 1990; Sheehan 1993, 1999; Langewiesche 2000.
2. BIM 2, 97–106.
3. Brown, Scheflin, and Hammond 1998; Felman 2002; Sarat, Davidovitch, and Albertstein 2007; Campbell et al. 2011; Breakwell 1986; Erickson 1994; Young 1995; Caruth 1996; Kolk, McFarlane, and Weisaeth 2006; Danieli 1998; LaCapra 1998; Leys 2000; Herman 2003; Alexander, Eyerman, Giesen, Smelser, and Stompka 2004; Wilson 2005; Kirmayer, Lemelson, and Barad 2007.
4. Schivelbusch 2003.
5. Breakwell 1986; Erickson 1994; Young 1995; Caruth 1996; Zerubavel 1996; Brown, Scheflin, and Hammond 1998; Danieli 1998; Felman 2002; Herman 2003; Hartog 2003; Shivelbusch 2003; Alexander, Eyerman, Giesen, Smelser, and Stompka, 2004; Wilson 2006; Kolk, McFarlane, and Weisaeth 2006; Kirmayer, Lemelson, and Barad 2007; Sarat, Davidovitch, and Albertstein 2007; Campbell et al. 2011; Thum 2011; Davis 2012; Dénes 2012b, 2012c; León 2012.
6. BIM 12, 11–18; G. Kovács 2004, 19–23.
7. Kenedi 1991; G. Kovács 2004, 19–23, 154–157.
8. BIM 12, 11–22; G. Kovács 2004, 19–23; Romsics 2005, 104–149, esp. 141–149; Bárdi, Fedinec, and Szarka 2008, 14–59.
9. BIM 5, 166–192; Romsics 2005, 112–149.
10. Romsics 2005, 235–270; Romsics 2006, 13–93.
11. BIM 2, 29–311.
12. BIM 5, 47–134.
13. MTAKK, Ms 5111/3; G. Kovács 2004, 30–40; G. Kovács 2012.
14. Bibó 1976.
15. The populist writers sought to eliminate the large-estate system, implement social reform and political democracy, and ensure Hungarian independence. Their first

political organization was the March Front, founded in 1937–1938; the second was the National Peasant Party, which operated between 1944 and 1949 and as the Petőfi Party in 1956 and of which Bibó was a member.

16. Dezső Szabó (1879 [Kolozsvár]–1945 [Budapest]), a writer and an influential ideologue of national radicalism.
17. BIM 7, 11–29, 49–176, 180–194, 207–293, 300–400.
18. Trencsényi 2011a, 36–85, 298–346; Trencsényi 2011b.
19. Jászi 1971; Szabad 1967, 1977; R. Várkonyi 1973; Varga 1982, 1993; Hroch 1985; C. Kecskeméti 1989; Bérenger and Kecskeméti 2005; Miskolczy 2006, 2012; Szabó 2006; Trencsényi 2007; K. Kecskeméti 2008; Dénes 2009.
20. I have used the typology of political languages József Takáts elaborated (2007, 14–21). Jászi 1971; Varga 1982, 1993; Hroch 1985; C. Kecskeméti 1989; Bérenger and Kecskeméti 2005; Miskolczy 2006, 2012; Szabó 2006; Trencsényi 2007; K. Kecskeméti 2008; Dénes 2009.
21. Szabó 1989, 2003, 2006; Trencsényi 2008; Dénes 2009, 2012c.
22. Dénes 2011, 64–122; Trencsényi 2011a, 346–465; Trencsényi 2011b.
23. László Németh (1901 [Nagybánya]–1975 [Budapest]), novelist, thinker, polyhistor.
24. BIM 7, 60–67.
25. BIM 7, 11–29.
26. BIM 7, 68–73.
27. BIM 2, 29–311; BIM 5, 47–134; BIM 7, 103–176.
28. BIM 7, 120–176.
29. Dénes 2011, 137–261; Trencsényi 2011a, 450–465; Trencsényi 2011b.
30. Dénes 2011, 82–122; Trencsényi 2011a, 346–449; Trencsényi 2011b.
31. Komoróczy 2012, 2:377–437, 505–622; Komoróczy 2013, 971–1149.
32. Braham 1981; Komoróczy 2012, 2:505–866, 881–885; Komoróczy 2013, 971–1149, 1149–1286.
33. BIM 12, 18, 68–69.
34. BIM 8, 9–20; BIM 12, 58–59, 121–138; Balog 2004, 191–206; G. Kovács 2004, 193–215.
35. BIM 8, 21–31; BIM 12, 21–28, 40–41, 49.
36. BIM 11, 57–69.
37. BIM 11, 73–87. Cf. Lochak 1989, 1994, 1996, 2006; Paksy 2011, 52–82. I am grateful to Péter Cserne (University of Hull, School of Law), who provided me the data on the Duverger affair. The Duverger affair was a legal and philosophical dispute on the "neutrality" of the legal order and the conduct of civil servants in Vichy's France, which in fact was collaborationist.
38. BIM 11, 91–118.
39. György 2011, 44.
40. From the letter of ministerial counselor Béla Szathmáry, head of the Presidential Department, to István Bibó, dated November 20, 1944 (40039/1944. Magyar Királyi Igazságügyminisztérium. Elnöki Osztály, MTAKK. Ms 5109/69, 1–2); also in BIM 11, 93.
41. Letter of appeals court judge Endre Kőházi to István Bibó, dated November 23, 1944 (40528. 1944. I.M.E. MTAKK, Ms 5109/70, 1–2); also in BIM 11, 94.
42. BIM 8, 39–220. Cf. Balog 2004, 190–270.

43. BIM 8, 39–220, 221–229; BIM 11, 315–326, 374–375; BIM 12, 123–138; Balog 2004, 190–270. Cf. E. Kovács and Vajda 2002. Béla Dénes (1904 [Budapest]–1959 [Tel Aviv]), writer, physician, Zionist politician, and press officer of the embassy of Israel that was being established, responded warmly to the study in his letter dated January 14, 1949 (MTAKK, Ms 5117/146,1); also in BIM 11, 317–318. In the letter, he also mentioned that he was working on founding a Hungarian-Israeli cultural association and would count on István Bibó. Accused in a show trial known as the Zionist case, Dénes was arrested and imprisoned in 1949. Freed in 1954, he emigrated to Israel in 1957, where he published his memoirs: B. Dénes 2002.

44. BIM 8, 230–315. Cf. Balog 2012.

45. Romsics 2005, 285–296.

46. BIM 3, 20–79.

47. BIM 5, 13–44; BIM 12, 79–123, 138–152; G. Kovács 2004, 242–246.

48. Kenedi 1991, 445–446; G. Kovács, 2004, 242–246.

49. BIM 1, 307–332.

50. BIM 10, 441, 444, 445. Iván Balog found and published the notes taken down by István Szentpéteri (1926–2002), a student of István Bibó and professor of law at Szeged University.

51. BIM 12, 155–156.

52. BIM 11, 151–194.

53. Kenedi 1991, 447; G. Kovács 2004, 242–246.

54. BIM 9, 128–129.

55. BIM 4, 7.

56. BIM 4, 7–21. Cf. BIM 12, 196–216, 238–240.

57. BIM 12, 216–238; G. Kovács 2004, 319–327; I. Bibó Jr. 2012.

58. BIM 4, 36–37.

59. BIM 4, 38–39. Cf. I. Bibó Jr. 2012, 125–128; Kenedi 1993, 1996.

60. BIM 4, 40–46.

61. BIM 4, 73–95; BIM 12, 216–238.

62. BIM 12, 238–283; G. Kovács 2004, 342–354.

63. BIM 9, 157–448; BIM 12, 278–283; G. Kovács 2004, 389–472; Balog 2010, 10–12.

64. BIM 1, 285–332; BIM 2, 29–311; BIM 6, 33–145; BIM 9, 9–299; BIM 10, 264–381, 431–479; BIM 11, 24–33, 44–48. Cf. Bibó 1976, 9–103, esp. 35–52. See also Ferrero 1941, 1961, 1972.

65. BIM 2, 29–311; BIM 9, 9–299, 380–448.

66. BIM 2, 29–311; BIM 9, 9–299, 380–448.

67. Bibó 1976, 35. Cf. Balog 2004, 14–88, 89–189, 190–270; G. Kovács, 1999; G. Kovács 2004, 354–388; G. Kovács 2012.

68. Bibó 1976, 35–52.

69. Réz 1991.

70. Dénes 1999, 2011, 2012a; Balog 2004, 2010; G. Kovács 2004; Trencsényi 2007, 2011a, 2011b, 2012; Perecz 2008.

71. Bibó 1976.

72. Berki 1992.

73. Bibó 1991a.
74. Cf., among others, Bibó 1946–47, 1986, 1990, 1991b, 1992, 1993, 1994, 1997, 2004, 2010; Finkielkraut 1987, 1999; Laignel-Lavastine 2005; Camallonga 2012; Davis 2012; Dénes 2012b, 2012c; León 2012.
75. Berki 1992, 513; emphasis in original.
76. Róbert Nándor Berki (1936 [Budapest]–1991 [Hull]), professor of political science and director of the Institute of European and Dutch Studies, University of Hull.

ON THE BALANCE OF POWER AND PEACE IN EUROPE

The original Hungarian title of this work is "Az európai egyensúlyról és békéről. Béke-csinálók könyve." Written between 1942 and 1944, it was intended by Bibó as a handbook for the peacemakers after the war, though it never got to the Paris Peace Conference, and except for a part of it published as "The Miseries of East European Small States," the next chapter in this volume, it was never published in his lifetime. Book I discusses the causes of World War II, and Book II goes into the details of elaborating a lasting peace—this is not included in this volume.

1. This study was written in 1942, as a polemic against both the Vansittartist position on the inherent bent of the Germans toward aggression and against those who explained all German distortions by social reasons and believed in the ability to redress them through mere social reform. Since this writing, no chance of finalizing the text in the hope of publication has arisen. *I. B.* (1973).
2. These terms, the use of which is not unified even in individual psychology, cannot be applied to the phenomena of community psychology without reserve, and as yet we are far from a precise knowledge of where it is and where it is not expedient to use them. The fact that the meaning of these terms in individual psychology varies, however, not only renders the description of analogous community-psychological phenomena more difficult, but also affords some degree of freedom in the use of analogous terms. [Bibó's own note.]
3. "The German nature will cure the entire world."
4. The section referred to is not included in this edition.
5. This translation does not include the entire work; see unnumbered note above.

THE MISERIES OF EAST EUROPEAN SMALL STATES

The original Hungarian title of this work is "A kelet-európai kisállamok nyomorúsága."
1. Properly, Ruthenians or Rusyns, a Slavic group that had lived in Hungary. Bibó's use of "Russian" here is either a typo or a tactful deference to Soviet-Russian nationalist claims.

THE PEACE AND HUNGARIAN DEMOCRACY

The original Hungarian title of this work is "A békeszerződés és a magyar demokrácia."
1. After Hungary reoccupied its former territories in Yugoslavia, the invading troops—without warrant—massacred about 3,000 civilians (a third of them Jews) while hunt-

ing partisans in January 1942. The atrocities were stopped, and after parliamentary intervention, the perpetrators were tried and sentenced, though they fled to Germany. When the Yugoslav partisans took the area back in October 1944, they massacred about 20,000 Hungarians. Why Bibó, in discussing the problem (see p. 236), did not mention the Yugoslav atrocities—to keep the peace at home, the goodwill of the Yugoslav government at the Paris Peace Conference, or because he did not know—cannot now be ascertained. The Yugoslav authorities never acknowledged the killings. In 2013, however, the Serbian Parliament issued a declaration condemning the crime.

THE WARPED HUNGARIAN SELF

The original Hungarian title of this work is "Eltorzult magyar alkat, zsákutcás magyar történelem."

1. See László Németh, *Kisebbségben* (Being the Minority) (Kecskemét, 1939). Németh wrote his book-length essay on assimilation and dissimilation in response to Gyula Szekfű's call on leading Hungarian intellectuals to contribute to a volume on Hungarian characterology entitled *Mi a magyar?* (What Is the Hungarian?) (Budapest, 1939). Finally, Németh's study was not published in the volume.
2. See Sándor Karácsony, *A magyar észjárás és közoktatásügyünk reformja* (The Hungarian Turn of Mind and the Reform of Public Education) (Budapest, 1939).
3. This "common nobility" (a literal translation of the Hungarian *köznemes*), which was marked by small holdings (largely equal to peasant holdings) and noble privilege—i.e., political rights—came to be known as "gentry" in the nineteenth century, spelled *dzsentri*, being an English loan word; note the difference between the use of the same word in the English context ("people of gentle birth and breeding, class immediately below the nobility") and the Hungarian one ("people with noble background but unpropertied and declassified").
4. Fleeing the battle, King Louis drowned in a river, and the Hungarian crown was claimed by Ferdinand I of Habsburg.
5. See Németh, *Kisebbségben*, pp. 8–11.
6. The revolutionary April Articles of 1848 terminated serfdom in Hungary, the Socage Letters-Patent of 1853 reinforcing emancipation and carrying it further.
7. See Németh, *Kisebbségben*, pp. 38–42.
8. Having demanded the acknowledgment of the April Articles of 1848 and rejected the October Diploma, the Hungarian Parliament was adjourned by Franz Joseph.
9. See Németh, *Kisebbségben*, pp. 42–44.
10. The Second Italian War of Independence (1859) and the Austro-Prussian War of 1866.
11. Count Friedrich Ferdinand Beust (1809–1886), the foreign minister, in particular—a liberal and staunch Grossdeutscher.
12. In fact, the Letters-Patent of February, which disregarded Hungary's historical rights and independence.
13. Kossuth's famous open, so-called "Cassandra Letter," to Deák, written from exile in Paris on May 22, 1867, calling on him not to enter into the Compromise because he saw in it "the death of the nation."
14. These included rule by military tribunals and the suspension of all political bodies.

15. So called because the prime minister, Count Géza Fejérvary, had been the commander of the infantry.

16. See Németh, *Kisebbségben*, p. 42.

17. Pace Bibó and his truth, Prime Minister Pál Teleki committed suicide for precisely this reason (April 3, 1941).

18. A patron of the Association of Catholic University Students, disbanded in 1946. N.B.: by 1949, all self-governing, non-Communist-run societies and associations were banned in Hungary.

19. Reference to a folk tale in which a prince is damned by his father to live in the skin of a little yellow snake.

THE JEWISH PREDICAMENT IN POST-1944 HUNGARY

The original Hungarian title of this work is "Zsidókérdés Magyarországon 1944 után." This was the last lengthier study Bibó could publish in Hungarian in his lifetime. Indeed, the journal *Válasz* (Answer), where it appeared, would be quashed by the Communists in a few months' time, as would the journal *Huszadik Század* (Twentieth Century), where Bibó published his response (appended in the text) to a piece of Marxist criticism. Bibó's essay on the Jewish question was one of the last of its kind to address any burning issue in non-Marxist terms for almost half a century.

1. A national meeting of the Reformed Awakening (c. Evangelical) Movement held in Nyíregyháza on August 14–17, 1946, published a proclamation stating: "Under the burden of responsibility and making amends, together with our people, for the crimes and neglect committed against Jewry, feeling the terrible pain surviving Jews carry for the cruel deportation and horrendous extermination of their beloved, though belated but in the presence of God, we ask the Hungarian Jewry for forgiveness" (Országos Református Szabad Tanács, Budapest, 1946, p. 73).

2. The First Act on Jews (XV/1938) was passed in 1938, the Second (IV/1939) in 1939, and the Third (XV/1941) in 1941.

3. More precisely, a total of 618,007 Jews were deported from the enlarged area of Hungary, and 440,000 of them died in the extermination camps. By the end of 1945, 116,500 had returned to Hungary. See Randolph Braham, *The Politics of Genocide* (New York, 1981), vol. 2, pp. 1143–1144.

4. The extreme rightist alliance won 19.2 percent, the Social Democrats 2 percent, and the Smallholders 6 percent of the votes.

5. See Sigmund Freud, *Moses and Monotheism* (London: Hogarth, 1939), p. 213.

6. Usually, Jews were herded into brick-factory yards before deportation.

7. Sebestyén Molnár [penname of Sándor Millok], "Zsidókérdés Magyarországon 1944 után," in *Huszadik Század*, vol. 37, no. 1 (February–March 1949), pp. 40–47. Millok was a leading Social Democrat, a Holocaust survivor, and a convinced Marxist but opposed the merger with the Communist Party and was thus excluded from it in 1948. He withdrew from politics.

DECLARATION (1956)

The original Hungarian title of this work is "Nyilatkozat (1956)."

MEMORANDUM

The original Hungarian title of this work is "Emlékirat. Magyarország helyzete és a világhelyzet."

THE MEANING OF EUROPEAN SOCIAL DEVELOPMENT

The original Hungarian title of this work is "Az európai társadalomfejlődés értelme."

1. There is no ground for regarding feudalism as the necessary stage following slavery. The economic organization of society takes on freer forms even in the most primitive and archaic conditions, and only under exceptional circumstances does it become based on slavery, which usually remains within the limits of domestic service and becomes pervasive in extraordinary situations—e.g., it is the constant warfare a world empire wages against the surrounding areas culturally inferior to it that provides opportunity for a fresh supply of slaves in unusually large numbers. It was the same factor that had revived it in sub-Saharan Africa until recently, but slave labor also occurred in the quite different economic circumstances of German concentration camps. At the same time, serfdom can also surface in quite different social contexts, whenever anarchy dishevels bureaucratically set and arranged forms and forces people into more or less equal relations of mutual service. [Bibó's own note.]

2. The reference is to Sidonius Appollinaris (433–479?); the quote is loose; cf. László Németh, "Róma utódai," *Tanú*, nos. 5–6 (1936).

3. The term "revolutions of the early Middle Ages" was used by Péter Váczy in his history of the Middle Ages (*A középkor története*), volume 2 of the four-volume world history edited by Bálint Hóman, Gyula Szekfű, and Károly Kerényi (*Egyetemes történet*; Budapest: Révai Testvérek, 1936).

4. This is a Hungarian proverb often attributed to Christ.

BIBLIOGRAPHY

Alexander, J., R. Eyerman, B. Giesen, N. Smelser, and P. Stompka. 2004. *Cultural Trauma and Collective Memory*. Berkeley: University of California Press.

Amselek, Paul, ed., 1994. *Théorie du droit et science*. Paris: Presses Universitaires de France.

Balog, Iván, 2004. *Politikai hisztériák Közép-és Kelet-Európában: Bibó István fasizmusról, nacionalizmusról, antiszemitizmusról*. Budapest: Argumentum Kiadó and Bibó István Szellemi Műhely.

Balog, Iván, 2010. *Bibó István recepciója: Politikai átértelmezések*. Budapest: Argumentum Kiadó and Bibó István Szellemi Műhely.

Balog, Iván, 2012. "Bibó és a zsidókérdés." In Dénes 2012a, 213–230.

Bárdi, Nándor, Csilla Fedinec, and László Szarka, eds. 2008. *Kisebbségi magyar közösségek a 20. században*. Budapest: Gondolat and MTA Kisebbségkutató Intézet.

Bérenger, Jean, and Charles Kecskeméti. 2005. *Parlement et vie parlementaire en Hongrie, 1608–1918*. Paris: Honoré Champion Éditeur.

Berki, Róbert Nándor. 1992. "The Realism of Moralism: The Political Philosophy of István Bibó." *History of Political Thought* 13, no. 3:513–534.

Berlin, Isaiah. 1980. *Concepts and Categories: Philosophical Essays*. Oxford: Oxford University Press.

Berlin, Isaiah. 1981. *Against the Current: Essays in the History of Ideas*. Oxford: Oxford University Press.

Berlin, Isaiah. 1991. *The Crooked Timber of Humanity: Chapters in the History of Ideas*. New York: Alfred A. Knopf.

Berlin, Isaiah. 1996. *The Sense of Reality: Studies in Ideas and Their History*. London: Chatto and Windus.

Berlin, Isaiah. 1999. *The Roots of Romanticism*. London: Chatto and Windus.

Berlin, Isaiah. 2002. *The Power of Ideas*. Princeton, NJ: Princeton University Press.

Berlin, Isaiah, 2006. *Political Ideas in the Romantic Age: Their Rise and Influence on Modern Thought*. London: Chatto and Windus.

Bibó, István. 1946–47. "La crisi della democrazia in Ungheria." *Rivista di Studi Politici Internazionali* 13, nos. 3–4 (July 1946), and 14, nos. 1–4 (October 1947): 476–499. Translation, foreword, and notes by Paolo Sanctarcangeli.

Bibó, István. 1976. *The Paralysis of International Institutions and the Remedies: A Study of Self-Determination, Concord among the Major Powers, and Political Arbitration*. Hassocks, Sussex: Harvester Press.

Bibó, István. 1986. *Misère des petits états d'Europe de l'Est*. Translated from the Hungarian by György Kassai. Paris: L'Harmattan.

Bibó, István. 1990. *Zur Judenfrage: Am Beispiel Ungarns nach 1944*. Translated from the Hungarian by Béla Rásky. Frankfurt am Main: Verlag Neue Kritik.

Bibó, István. 1991a. *Democracy, Revolution, Self-Determination: Selected Writings*. Edited by Károly Nagy; translated by András Boros-Kazai. Highland Lakes, NJ: Atlantic Research and Publications. Distributed by Columbia University Press.

Bibó, István. 1991b. *Die deutsche Hysterie: Ursachen und Geschichte*. Translated from the Hungarian by Hans-Henning Paetzke, with an epilogue by György Dalos. Frankfurt am Main and Leipzig: Insel Verlag.

Bibó, István. 1992. *Die Misere der osteuropäische Kleinstaaterei*. Translated from the Hungarian by Béla Rásky. Frankfurt am Main: Verlag Neue Kritik.

Bibó, István. 1993. *Misère des petits états d'Europe de l'Est*. Translated from the Hungarian by György Kassai. Paris: Albin Michel.

Bibó, István. 1994. *Miseria dei piccoli stati dell'Europa orientale*. Edited by Federigo Argentieri. Translated from the Hungarian by Armando Nuzzo. Bologna: Società Editrice Il Mulino.

Bibó, István. 1997. *Isteria tedesca, paura francese, insicurezza italiana: Psicologia di tre nazioni da Napoleone a Hitler*. Edited by Federigo Argentieri. Translated from the Hungarian by Melinda Mihályi. Bologna: Società Editrice Il Mulino.

Bibó, István. 2004. *Il problema storico dell'indipendenza ungherese*. Edited by Federigo Argentieri and Stefano Bottoni. Translated from the Hungarian by Federigo Argentieri, Stefano Bottoni, and Gigliola Spadoni. Venice: Marsilio.

Bibó, István. 2010. *Nędza Małych Państw Wschodnioeuroppejskich*. Translated, edited, and with a foreword by Jerzy Snopek. N. p.: Alkano.

Bibó, István, Jr. 2012. "A század legizgalmasabb szocialista kísérlete: Bibó István és 1956." In Dénes 2012, 115–146.

BIM 1–12. 2011–2012. *Bibó István munkái: Centenáriumi sorozat*, 12 volumes. Budapest: Argumentum Kiadó and Bibó István Szellemi Műhely

BIM 1. *Az államhatalmak elválasztása*. Budapest: Argumentum Kiadó and Bibó István Szellemi Műhely,.

BIM 2. *Politikai hisztériák*. Budapest: Argumentum Kiadó and Bibó István Szellemi Műhely.

BIM 3. *A magyar demokrácia válsága*. Budapest: Argumentum Kiadó and Bibó István Szellemi Műhely.

BIM 4. *1956*. Budapest: Argumentum Kiadó and Bibó István Szellemi Műhely.

BIM 5. *A kelet-európai kisállamok nyomorúsága*. Budapest: Argumentum Kiadó and Bibó István Szellemi Műhely.

BIM 6. *A nemzetközi államközösség bénultsága és annak orvosságai: Önrendelkezés, nagyhatalmi egyetértés, politikai döntőbíráskodás*. Budapest: Argumentum Kiadó and Bibó István Szellemi Műhely.

BIM 7. *Eltorzult magyar alkat, zsákutcás magyar történelem*. Budapest: Argumentum Kiadó and Bibó István Szellemi Műhely.

BIM 8. *Zsidókérdés*. Budapest: Argumentum Kiadó and Bibó István Szellemi Műhely.

BIM 9. *Az európai politikai fejlődés értelme*. Budapest: Argumentum Kiadó and Bibó István Szellemi Műhely.

BIM 10. *A jogfilozófiától a politikáig*. Budapest: Argumentum Kiadó and Bibó István Szellemi Műhely.

BIM 11. *A demokratikus közösségi értékelés és magatartás mintái*. Budapest: Argumentum Kiadó and Bibó István Szellemi Műhely.

BIM 12. *Visszaemlékezések*. Budapest: Argumentum Kiadó and Bibó István Szellemi Műhely.

Braham, Randolph L. 1981. *The Politics of Genocide: The Holocaust in Hungary*, 2 volumes. New York: Columbia University Press.

Breakwell, G. M. 1986. *Coping with Threatened Identities*. London: Meuthen.

Brown, D. P., A. W. Scheflin, and D. C. Hammond. 1998. *Memory, Trauma Treatment, and the Law*. New York: W. W. Norton.

Camallonga, Salvador Orti. 2012. "A 'European Memory of the Jewish Extermination'? Spain as a Methodological Challenge." *European Review* 20, no. 4:475–491. https://www.journals.cambridge.org/erw.

Campbell, Kirsten, et al. 2011. *Testifying to Trauma: The Codification of Atrocity in Humanitarian Law*. Oxford: Routledge.

Caruth, Cathy. 1996. *Unclaimed Experience: Trauma, Narrative, Memory*. Baltimore, MD: Johns Hopkins University Press.

Conrad, C., and S. Conrad. 2002. *Die Nation Schreiben: Geschichtswissenschaft im internationalen Vergleich*. Göttingen: Van den Hoeck and Ruprecht.

Danieli, Yael. 1998. *International Handbook of Multigenerational Legacies of Trauma*. New York: Kluwer Academic.

Davis, John A. 2012. "How Many Italies? Reconciliation, the Risorgimento and Italy's North South Divide." *European Review* 20, no. 4:505–513. https://www.journals.cambridge.org/erw.

Dénes, Béla. 2002. *Ávósvilág Magyarországon: Egy cionista orvos emlékiratai*. Budapest: Kiadó nélkül.

Dénes, Iván Zoltán, ed. 1993. *A hatalom humanizálása: Tanulmányok Bibó István életművéről*. Pécs: Tanulmány.

Dénes, Iván Zoltán. 1999. *Eltorzult magyar alkat: Bibó István vitája Németh Lászlóval és Szekfű Gyulával*. Budapest: Osiris.

Dénes, Iván Zoltán, ed. 2006. *Liberty and the Search for Identity: Liberal Nationalisms and the Legacy of Empires*. Budapest and New York: Central European University Press.

Dénes, Iván Zoltán, ed. 2008a. *Liberalizmus és nemzettudat: Dialógus Szabó Miklós gondolataival*. Budapest: Argumentum Kiadó and Bibó István Szellemi Műhely. Eszmetörténeti Könyvtár 8.

Dénes, Iván Zoltán. 2008b. "Personal Liberty and Political Freedom: Four Interpretations." *European Journal of Political Theory* 7, no. 1:81–98.

Dénes, Iván Zoltán. 2009. *Conservative Ideology in the Making*. Budapest and New York: Central European University Press.

Dénes, Iván Zoltán. 2010. "Liberty versus Common Good." *European Review* 18, no. 1:S89–S98. https://www.journals.cambridge.org/erw.

Dénes, Iván Zoltán. 2011. *Az "illúzió" realitása: Kollektív identitásprogramok*. Budapest: Argumentum Kiadó and Bibó István Szellemi Műhely. Eszmetörténetikönyvtár, 16.

Dénes, Iván Zoltán, ed. 2012a. *Bibó 100: Recepciók, értelmezések, alkalmazási kísérletek*. Budapest: Argumentum Kiadó and Bibó István Szellemi Műhely. Eszmetörténeti Könyvtár 17.

Dénes, Iván Zoltán. 2012b. "Overcoming European Civil War: The Patterns of Consolidation in Divided Societies, 2010–1800." *European Review*, 20, no. 4:455–474. https://www.journals.cambridge.org/erw.

Dénes, Iván Zoltán. 2012c. "Adopting the European Model versus National Egoism: The Task of Surpassing Political Hysteria." *European Review*, 20, no. 4:514–525. https://www.journals.cambridge.org/erw.

Erickson, K. 1994. *A New Species of Trouble: Explorations in Disaster, Trauma, and Community*. New York: W. W. Norton.

Felman, Shosana. 2002. *The Juridical Unconscious: Trials and Traumas in the Twentieth Century*. Cambridge, MA: Harvard University Press.

Ferrero, Guglielmo. 1941 (1940). *The Reconstruction of Europe: Talleyrand and the Congress of Vienna, 1814–1815*. New York: Putnams.

Ferrero, Guglielmo. 1961 (1936). *The Gamble: Bonaparte in Italy 1796–1797*. New York: Walker.

Ferrero, Guglielmo. 1972 (1942). *The Principles of Power: The Great Political Crises of History*. New York: Arno Press.

Finkielkraut, Alain. 1987. *La défaite de la pensée, essai*. Paris: Gallimard.

Finkielkraut, Alain. 1999. *L'ingratitude: Conversation sur notre temps avec Antoine Robitaille*. Paris: Gallimard.

Gall, Lothar. 1990. *Bismarck, the White Revolutionary*. London: Unwin Hyman.

György, Péter. 2011. *Apám helyett*. Budapest: Magvető.

Hartog, F. 2003. *Des régimes d'historicité: Présentisme et experiénces du temps*. Paris: Éditions du Seuil.

Hayward, J. 2007. *Fragmented France: Two Centuries of Disputed Identity*. Oxford: Oxford University Press.

Herman, S. Judith. 2003. *Trauma and Recovery*. New York: Basic Books.

Hroch, Miroslav. 1985. *Social Preconditions of National Revival in Europe: A Comparative Analysis of the Social Composition of Patriotic Groups among the Smaller European Nations*. Cambridge: Cambridge University Press.

http://cliftonchadwick.wordpress.com/2010/05/17/baltazar-garzon-crusading-spanish-judge-suspended-finally.

http://www.baltictimes.com/news/articles/17774.

Jahanbegloo, Ramin. 1991. *Recollections of a Historian of Ideas: Conversations with Isaiah Berlin*. New York: Charles Scribner's Sons.

Janowski, Maciej. 2004. *Polish Liberal Thought before 1918*. Central European University Press, Budapest-New York.

Janowski, Maciej. 2006. "Marginal or Central? The Place of the Liberal Tradition in Nineteenth-Century Polish History." In Dénes 2006, 239–272.

Jászi, Oscar. 1971 (1929). *The Dissolution of the Habsburg Monarchy*. Chicago: University of Chicago Press.

Jedlicki, Jerzy. 1999. *A Suburb of Europe: Nineteenth-Century Polish Approaches to Western Civilization*. Budapest and New York: Central European University Press.

Kecskeméti, Charles. 1989. *La Hongrie et le réformisme liberal: Problèmes politiques et sociaux 1790–1848*. Rome: Il Centro de Ricerca.

Kecskeméti, Károly. 2008. *Magyar liberalizmus 1790–1848*. Budapest: Argumentum Kiadó and Bibó István Szellemi Műhely. Eszmetörténeti Könyvtár 10.

Kenedi, János. 1991. "Bibó István életrajzi adatai." In *Réz Pál, szerk, 1991 (1980)*, 2: 440–449.

Kenedi, János. 1993. "Bibó szocializmus-felfogása kihallgatótisztjei előtt." In Dénes 1993, 269–283.

Kenedi, János, editor, annotator, and writer of introduction. 1996. *A fogoly Bibó István vallomásai az 1956-os forradalomról*. Budapest: 1956-os Intézet.

Kirmayer, Laurence J., Robert Lemelson, and Mark Barad, eds., 2007. *Understanding Trauma: Integrating Biological, Clinical and Cultural Perspectives*. Cambridge University Press, Cambridge.

Kis János. 2003. *Constitutional Democracy*. Budapest and New York: Central European University Press.

Kis János. 2007. "Az összetorlódott idő." *Élet és Irodalom*, December 21.

Kis János, 2008. *Politics as a Moral Problem*. Budapest and New York: Central European University Press.

Kolk, B. A., A. C. McFarlane, and L. Weisaeth. 2006. *Traumatic Stress: The Effects of Overwhelming Experience on Mind, Body, and Society*. New York: Guilford Press.

Komoróczy, Géza. 2012. *A zsidók története Magyarországon*, 2 volumes. Pozsony: Kalligram.

Komoróczy, Géza. 2013. *"Nekem itt zsidónak kell lenni": Források és dokumentumok (965–2012). A zsidók története Magyarországon I-II.kötetéhez. Szöveggyűjtemény*. Pozsony: Kalligram. Hungaria Judaica, 28.

Kovács, Éva, and Júlia Vajda. 2002. *Mutatkozás: Zsidó identitás történetek*. Budapest: Múlt és Jövő.

Kovács, Gábor. 1999. "Can Power Be Humanized? The Notions of Elite and Legitimation in István Bibó's Political Philosophy." *Studies in East European Thought* 51, 307–327.

Kovács, Gábor. 2004. *Az európai egyensúlytól a kölcsönös szolgáltatások társadalmáig: Bibó István, a politikai gondolkodó*. Budapest: Argumentum Kiadó and Bibó István Szellemi Műhely. Eszmetörténeti Könyvtár 3.

Kovács, Gábor. 2012. "Az elitektől a reális utópiáig: Bibó István politikaelméleti koncepciója." In Dénes 2012a, 263–294.

LaCapra, D. 1998. *History and Memory after Auschwitz*. Ithaca, NY: Cornell University Press.

Laignel-Lavastine, Alexandra. 2005. *Esprits d'Europe: Autour de Czeslaw Milosz, Jan Patocka, István Bibó*. Paris: Calmann-Lévy.

Langewiesche, Dieter. 2000. *Liberalism in Germany*. Princeton, NJ: Princeton University Press.

León, Pablo Sánchez. 2012. "Overcoming the Violent Past in Spain, 1939–2009." *European Review* 20, no. 4:492–504. https://www.journals.cambridge.org/erw.

Leopold, Lajos. 1917. *Elmélet nélkül*. Budapest: Benkő Gyula Könyvkereskedése.

Leys, Ruth. 2000. *Trauma: A Genealogy*. Chicago: University of Chicago Press.

Lochak, Danièle. 1989. "La doctrine sous Vichy ou les mésaventures du positivisme." In Danièle Lochak et al., *Les usages sociaux du droit*, 252–285. Paris: Presses Universitaires de France.

Lochak, Danièle. 1994. "Une néutralité impossible." In Amselek 1994, 293–309.

Lochak, Danièle. 1996. "Écrire, se taire. . . . Réflexions sur l'attitude de la doctrine française" in "Le droit antisemite de Vichy." *Le genre humaine*, Summer–Autumn 1996: 433–462.

Lochak, Danièle. 2006. "Entre l'éthique du savant et les convictions du citoyen: Juriste face à ses dilemmes." In *L'architecture du droit: Mélanges en l'honneur de Michel Troper*, ed. Denys de Béchillon et al., 639–649. Paris: Economica.

Miskolczy, Ambrus. 2006. *A modern magyar demokratikus kultúra "eredeti jellegzetességeiről"* 1790–1849. Budapest: Napvilág Kiadó.

Miskolczy, Ambrus. 2012. *Milyen nemzetet az emberiségnek? Kazinczytól Kossuthig— Széphalomtól Turinig*. Budapest: Gondolat Kiadó.

Mommsen, Wolfgang. 1978. "Der deutsche Liberalismus zwischen 'Klassenloser Bürgengesellschaft' und 'Organisiertem Kapitalismus.' Zu einigen Liberalismusinterpretatione." *Geschichte und Gesellschaft* 1.

MTAKK. *Magyar Tudományos Akadémia Könyvtára, Kézirattár*.

Nipperdey, Thomas. 1983. *Deutsche Geschichte 1800–1866: Bürgerwelt und starker Staat*. Munich: Thomas Beck C. H.

Paksy, Máté. 2011. "Hart 'visszatérő kérdései' és a francia jogbölcseleti hagyomány." Doctoral dissertation, Pázmány Péter Katolikus Egyetem Jog-és Államtudományi Iskola, Budapest. https://jak.ppke.hu/uploads/articles/12332/file/Paksy%20Máté%20PhD.pdf.

Perecz, László. 2008. *Nemzet, filozófia, "nemzeti filozófia."* Budapest: Argumentum Kiadó and Bibó István Szellemi Műhely.

R. Várkonyi, Ágnes. 1973. *A pozitivista történetszemlélet a magyar történetírásban*, 2 volumes. Budapest: Akadémiai Kiadó. Tudománytörténeti tanulmányok 6.

Rawls, John. 1971. *A Theory of Justice*. Cambridge, MA: Belknap Press.

Rawls, John. 1993. *Political Liberalism*. New York: Columbia University Press.

Rawls, John. 1999. *The Law of Peoples with "The Idea of Public Reason Revisited."* Cambridge, MA: Harvard University Press.

Réz, Pál, ed. 1991 (1980). *Bibó-emlékkönyv*, 2 volumes. Budapest: Századvég, and Bern: Európai Protestáns Magyar Szabadegyetem.

Romsics, Ignác. 2005. *Magyarország története a XX. században*; third, corrected edition. Budapest: Osiris. Osiris tankönyvek.

Romsics, Ignác. 2006. *Az 1947-es párizsi békeszerződés*. Budapest: Osiris.

Rosanvallon, P. 2004. *Le modèle politique français: La société civile contre le jacobinisme de 1789 à nos jours*. Paris: Éditions du Seuil.

Sarat, A. N., N. Davidovitch, and M. Albertstein. 2007. *Trauma and Memory: Reading, Healing, and Making Law*. Stanford, CA: Stanford University Press.

Schivelbusch, Wolfgang. 2003. *The Culture of Defeat: On National Trauma, Mourning and Recovery*. New York: Henry Holt. Picador, Metropolitan Books.

Sheehan, James J. 1993. *German History, 1770–1866*. Oxford: Clarendon Press.

Sheehan, James J. 1999. *German Liberalism in the Nineteenth Century*. New York: Humanity Books.

Szabad, György. 1967. *Forradalom és kiegyezés válaszútján (1860–61)*. Akadémiai Kiadó, Budapest.

Szabad, György. 1977. *Hungarian Political Trends between the Revolution and the Compromise (1849–1867)*. Budapest: Akadémiai Kiadó.

Szabó, Miklós. 1989. *Politikai kultúra Magyarországon, 1896–1986: Válogatott tanulmányok*. *Budapest*: Medvetánc.

Szabó, Miklós. 2003. *Az újkonzervativizmus és a jobboldali radikalizmus története (1867–1918)*. *Budapest*: Új Mandátum.

Szabó, Miklós. 2006. "The Liberalism of the Hungarian Nobility, 1825–1910." In Dénes 2006, 197–237.

Szabó, Zoltán. 2011. *Nyugati vártán: Esszék és publicisztikai írások*, 2 volumes. Budapest: Osiris Kiadó and Európai Protestáns Magyar Szabadegyetem. 1:274–302.

Takáts, József. 2007. *Modern magyar politikai eszmetörténet*. Budapest: Osiris. Osiris tankönyvek.

Thum, Gregor. 2011. *Uprooted: How Breslau Became Wroclaw during the Century of Expulsions*. Wroclaw: Via Nova.

Trencsényi, Balázs. 2007. *A politika nyelvei: Eszmetörténeti tanulmányok*. Budapest: Argumentum Kiadó and Bibó István Szellemi Műhely. Eszmetörténeti Könyvtár 6.

Trencsényi, Balázs. 2008. "Jön a tatár!" A nemzeti antiliberalizmusok kihívása Kelet-Közép-Európában. In Dénes 2008, 241–269.

Trencsényi, Balázs, 2011a. *A nép lelke: Nemzetkarakterológiai viták Kelet-Európában*. Budapest: Argumentum Kiadó and Bibó István Szellemi Műhely. Eszmetörténeti Könyvtár 14.

Trencsényi, Balázs, 2011b. *The Politics of National Character: A Study in Interwar East European Thought*. Oxford: Routledge.

Trencsényi, Balázs. 2012. "A kelet-európai agrárpopulizmus, mint értelmezési keret." In Dénes 2012a, 295–327.

Varga, János. 1982. *Helyét kereső Magyarország: Politikai eszmék és koncepciók az 1840-es évek elején*. Budapest: Akadémiai Kiadó.

Varga, János. 1993. *A Hungarian Quo Vadis: Political Ideas and Conceptions in the early 1840s. Budapest*: Akadémiai Kiadó.

Wilson, K. M., ed. 1996. *Forging the Collective Memory: Government and International Historians through Two World Wars*. Providence, RI, and Oxford: Berghahn Books.

Wilson, P. 2006. *The Posttraumatic Self: Restoring Meaning and Wholeness to Personality*. New York: Routledge.

Young, Allan. 1995. *Harmony of Illusions: Inventing Post-Traumatic Stress Disorder*. Princeton, NJ: Princeton University Press.

Zerubavel, Yael, 1996. *Recovered Roots: Making Israeli Collective Memory*. Princeton University Press, Princeton NJ.

INDEX

Page ranges in boldface indicate the complete work.

Marxism (*continued*)
socialism, 416–17; national idea denied,
150–51; as political hysteria, 424–25; primitive
community concept, 374; on revolutions, 105,
417, 420, 424–25; vs. Stalinism, 358–59; on the
state as institution of violence, 440. *See also*
communism; Marx, Karl; Marxism-Leninism;
socialism
Marxism-Leninism: on administration, 414;
and the bourgeoisie, 422; and capitalism,
411–12, 419; and dictatorship, 358–59; and
the Hungarian Revolution of 1956, 360; as
hysterical movement, 424–25; and multi-party
systems, 368–69, 419; regarded as victorious,
361; world's reaction to violence of revolution, 16–17. *See also* Bolshevik Revolution;
communism; Leninism; Marxism; socialism;
Soviet Union
Masaryk, Tomáš Garrigue, 155
materialism, national, 155
"Meaning of European Social Development,
The" (Bibó), 4, 16–17, 372–441
meekness, 377–78, 380
"Memorandum: Hungary, a Scandal and a
Hope of the World" (Bibó), 4, 18, 357–71
Menon, Kumara Padmanabha Sivasankara, 18
Metternich, Prince Klemens Wenzel von, 178,
203, 205, 210
middle class: the bourgeois revolution, 391,
393, 397–99 (*see also* French Revolution);
capitalism and, 400; in Central-East Europe,
147–48, 292; fascism and the bourgeoisie, 416;
in Hungary, 9, 203, 213–15, 217–20, 225, 235,
239–40, 256–57, 349; and national consciousness, 132–33; and nationalism, 34, 133
militarism, 42, 67–69, 73, 88, 92–93, 153
minorities, 157–60, 196, 352–53, 415–16. *See also*
ethnic groups; Jews; language
"Miseries of East European Small States, The"
(Bibó), 7, 130–80
Molnár, Sebestyén (Sándor Millok), 349–51,
354, 448(n7)
Moltke, Helmuth von, 441
monarchy: Austro-Hungarian Monarchy, 75–76
(*see also* Austria-Hungary; Habsburg dynasty);
Christianity and the spiritualization of,
31–33, 62, 375, 382, 386–87; decline of, 32–33,
44; democracy and, 425; fall of, in 1918, 84;
feudalism and, 384; French vs. German monarchies, 50–51; historical role and function,
61–63, 382, 384; Hungary and constitutional
monarchy, 211–12; and international relations
and peacemaking, 36, 86; and the nation as

political framework, 52; "phony monarch"
figure, 33, 63, 74–75; resistance to revolution,
421. *See also* aristocracy; feudalism; Habsburg
dynasty; Hohenzollern dynasty; *and specific
countries, empires, and rulers*
mortal fear, 374–76, 377. *See also* fear
multiparty system, 368–69, 419
Munich Agreement, 30, 49, 112–13, 123–24, 143.
See also Austria; Czech lands
Mussolini, Benito, 128

Nagy, Imre, *vii*, 17, 18, 355
Nagy, Vilmos Nagybaczoni, 236
Napoleon Bonaparte: German states invaded,
53–54, 56, 87; as phony monarch, 33, 63,
74; Poland invaded, 139; as revolutionary
dictator, 49; state-making by, 59, 65. *See also*
Napoleonic wars
Napoleonic wars: Austria and, 70; effect of on
peacemaking, 175–76; and the French birthrate, 118; Germany and, 53–54, 56, 64–65, 87,
109; Italy and, 125–26; Napoleonic state-
making, 56, 59, 65; nature of war changed by,
175; and Poland, 139; Spain invaded, 49, 56
Napoleon III (Louis Bonaparte), 87
nation(s): Austria as nation-state, 100, 102–3;
birth of European nations, 51–53, 130–33;
border fluctuations, 130–32, 137 (*see also* borders); Central-East European existential anxieties, 149–51; moralized state, 440; national
consciousness, 150–51; national vs. community identity, 307; as political concept, 136;
rulers' power, 152–53; self-determination of
(*see* self-determination, principle of); territorial status of Central-East Europe jumbled by
creation of, 30–31; territoriocentric concept
of, 159–60; vision for the future, 413. *See also*
nationalism; *and specific nations*
national characterology, 10–12
nationalism: anti-democratic nationalism, 79,
151–54, 292–94; and anti-Semitism, 273; birth
of German nationalism, 54–56; dangers of,
20; democracy and, 34, 54–55, 133, 148, 151–52
(*see also* democracy); democratic nationalism
and international relations, 36–38, 86–88; fascism and, 107–9; French Revolution and the
birth of modern nationalism, 33–36, 54, 130,
132–33, 134; Jewish national consciousness,
311–13 (*see also* Jews: Jewish identity; Zionism
and Zionists); linguistic nationalism, 135–37,
153–54, 166; not a self-reliant ideology, 19;
politicization of culture, 153–54
nationalization, 408–10, 418–19